Praise for *Ancient Mediterranean Civilizations*

Ancient Mediterranean Civilizations is the best text available. It is eminently readable with enough detail to vivify events and enough interpretation to help students see events as part of a larger framework.

—STEPHEN RUZICKA
University of North Carolina, Greensboro

Ancient Mediterranean Civilizations offers a refreshing and engaging approach to studying Ancient History. It is well designed for a semester-long ancient history course like those taught at many major institutions. It offers a fresh but easily accessible perspective that I imagine many students will enjoy.

—EDWARD WATTS
Indiana University

Ancient Mediterranean Civilizations is a welcome addition to the texts available for Ancient World courses. It is clearly written, up to date, well organized, and handsomely illustrated. Students should find it stimulating.

—JONATHAN ZOPHY
University of Houston, Clear Lake

ANCIENT MEDITERRANEAN CIVILIZATIONS

FROM PREHISTORY TO 640 CE

Ralph W. Mathisen

UNIVERSITY OF ILLINOIS AT URBANA-CHAMPAIGN

NEW YORK   OXFORD
OXFORD UNIVERSITY PRESS

Oxford University Press, Inc., publishes works that further Oxford University's
objective of excellence in research, scholarship, and education.

Oxford New York
Auckland Cape Town Dar es Salaam Hong Kong Karachi
Kuala Lumpur Madrid Melbourne Mexico City Nairobi
New Delhi Shanghai Taipei Toronto

With offices in
Argentina Austria Brazil Chile Czech Republic France Greece
Guatemala Hungary Italy Japan Poland Portugal Singapore
South Korea Switzerland Thailand Turkey Ukraine Vietnam

For titles covered by Section 112 of the U.S. Higher Education
Opportunity Act, please visit www.oup.com/us/he for the latest
information about pricing and alternate formats.

Published by Oxford University Press, Inc.
198 Madison Avenue, New York, New York, 10016
http://www.oup.com

Library of Congress Cataloging-in-Publication Data

Mathisen, Ralph W., 1947–
 Ancient Mediterranean civilizations: from prehistory to 640 CE
Ralph W. Mathisen
  p. cm.
 Includes bibliographical references.
 ISBN 978-0-19-537838-2
  1. Mediterranean Region—Civilization—Textbooks. 2. Mediterranean
Region—Antiquities—Textbooks. 3. Mediterranean Region—History—
To 476—Textbooks. 4. Mediterranean Region—History—476–1517—
Textbooks. I. Title
DE86.M37 2012
937—dc22   2010051385

Printing number: 9 8 7 6 5 4 3 2 1

Printed in the United States of America
on acid-free paper

CONTENTS

SPECIAL FEATURES *vii*
PREFACE *viii*
NOTE ON SPELLING AND PRONUNCIATION *xiv*
ABOUT THE AUTHOR *xvi*

PRELUDE TO HISTORY

CHAPTER 1 The Origins of History: Civilization Before
Civilization (2,000,000–3000 BCE) *1*

PART I THE CRADLE OF CIVILIZATION

CHAPTER 2 Mesopotamia and the Bronze Age
(6000–1200 BCE) *31*

CHAPTER 3 Egypt and the Bronze Age
(5000–1200 BCE) *65*

CHAPTER 4 Coastal Civilizations of the Eastern
Mediterranean (2500–800 BCE) *97*

CHAPTER 5 Iron Age Empires: Assyria, Babylonia, and
Persia (850–500 BCE) *124*

PART II THE GLORY THAT WAS GREECE

CHAPTER 6 Greece in the Dark and Archaic Ages
(1100–500 BCE) *153*

CHAPTER 7   Sparta, Athens, and the Classical Age
(500–387 BCE) *180*

CHAPTER 8   Alexander the Great and the Hellenistic Age
(387–31 BCE) *221*

PART III   **THE GRANDEUR THAT WAS ROME**

CHAPTER 9   The Rise of Rome and the Roman Republic
(753–121 BCE) *265*

CHAPTER 10   The Decline of the Republic and the
Founding of the Principate (149–21 BCE) *303*

CHAPTER 11   The Roman Peace (27 BCE–192 CE) *333*

PART IV   **THE WORLD OF LATE ANTIQUITY**

CHAPTER 12   Crisis and Recovery: The Formation of the
Late Roman Empire (192–337) *373*

CHAPTER 13   The Christian Empire and the Late Roman
World (337–476) *397*

CHAPTER 14   The End of Antiquity (476–640) *429*

GLOSSARY *G-1*
ILLUSTRATION CREDITS *C-1*
INDEX *I-1*

COLOR PLATE SECTION FOLLOWS PAGE *240*

SPECIAL FEATURES

A Picture Is Worth a Thousand Words

The Venus of Laussel 8
The Victory Stele of Naram-Sin 55
Narmer Unites Egypt (ca. 3000 BCE) 76
The Mycenaean "Warrior Vase" 107
The Behistun Inscription 145
Greek Hoplites on the March 172
The Athenian Tribute Lists 205
Ptolemy II and Arsinoë II 242
The Servian Wall 285
Caesarion and Cleopatra 328
The Gemma Augustea 344
The Arch of Constantine 392
A Late Roman Governor Hears a Case 409
The Court of Justinian and Theodora 444

Historical Controversy

The Origin of Noah's Flood 10
The Chronology of the Bronze Age 46
The Date of the Biblical Exodus 119
"Black Athena" 167
The Nature of Athenian Democracy 193
The Personality of Alexander 230
The Dark Side of Romanization 357
Constantine's Christianity 395
The Barbarian Settlement 426

In Their Own Words

The Mystery of the Vinča Signs 23
The Code of Hammurabi 60
The Autobiography of Weni 84
Ramses III Defeats the Sea Peoples 110
Two Accounts of the Siege of Jerusalem 130
The Education of a Tyrant 175
The Education of Spartan Women 184
The Periplus of the Red Sea 248

The Decree of the Senate on the Bacchus Worshippers 300
Sulla's March on Rome 314
Aelius Aristides, "Praise of Rome" 354
Diocletian's "Edict on Maximum Prices" 388
Claudius Postumus Dardanus and the Retreat to the Countryside 412
The Conversion of Clovis 439

The History Laboratory

Otzi the "Ice Man" 26
The Role of Climate and Ecology in History 36
Deciphering the Rosetta Stone 73
Volcanos and the Fall of Civilizations 104
Setting the Value of the Coins 147
Using Dialect Patterns to Reconstruct the Dark Ages 155
The Construction of a Greek Trireme 198
The Antikythera Device 260
Reconstructing Early Rome 272
Caesar's Siege of Alesia 320
Reconstructing the Deeds of the Deified Augustus 342
The Debasement of the Silver Coinage 378
The Creation of the Christian Biblical Canon 420
Ethnicity versus History versus Culture 433

Mysteries of History

King Scorpion 71
The Ten Lost Tribes of Israel 134
The Origin of the Etruscans 270
Cleopatra, the Legend and the Reality 324
The Destruction of the Library in Alexandria 454

PREFACE

For a long time it has been my goal to write a textbook that incorporated not only my own ideas and philosophy about what the most significant developments and historical processes in ancient history were and what they can teach us but also the results of my interactions with students during some thirty-five years (and counting) of teaching ancient history at all periods and levels at the University of Wisconsin, the University of South Carolina, and the Chicago and Urbana-Champaign campuses of the University of Illinois. Over the years I have taught, by my rough estimate, more than ten thousand students, and their responses to how I developed the material have significantly informed my presentation of the material in *Ancient Mediterranean Civilizations*.

This textbook is much more than how I personally view ancient history, although that of course is a large part of it. It also reflects what moves our students and what works for them. Students like to see how history works, that is, what kinds of factors bring to pass the events we study—not only global considerations such as social and economic factors, religious movements, and, yes, even wars and battles, but also, in particular, the considerations that connect individual people to what happened in history. Students also like to see continuity, that is, how one period in history leads into and is influenced by what went before it. They like connectivity, to learn how similar sets of circumstances in different places at different times produced similar results. And they are fascinated by stories that help to contextualize and bring to life both individual events and the grand historical processes that lie behind them.

Ancient Mediterranean Civilizations attempts to meet these needs in several ways. It emphasizes (1) evolution and continuity, depicting history as a cumulative process; (2) connections, looking at recurrent themes to show how similar phenomena occur in different places at different times; (3) causality, depicting how historical events happen for a reason; and (4) cultural diffusion and cultural diversity. And it should be stressed that I distinguish between "culture," the attributes of any human society, and "civilization," a specialized subset of culture that meets certain fundamental criteria, such as the use of agriculture, writing, metal technology, urbanism, social differentiation, and specialization of labor. Civilization is not treated defensively, nor is it assumed that cultures that do not qualify as civilizations are somehow "worse" than civilizations. This text also integrates material culture directly into an understanding of how history is reconstructed and goes beyond, "Here's a pot. Isn't it pretty." And it shows how the study of ancient history can serve as a laboratory for the study of modern sensitive issues, such as tolerance and intolerance and attitudes toward race, ethnicity, gender issues and roles, slavery, religion, and imperialism. *Ancient Mediterranean Civilizations* thus does not shy away from the discussion of potentially sensitive issues, such as, for example, ancient popular perceptions of Christianity and the pagan backgrounds of Christianity.

Several features of *Ancient Mediterranean Civilizations* set it apart from similar texts. For one thing, it covers in depth the full range of the human past, from the Stone Age until the very end of antiquity in the seventh century CE. The entire first chapter is devoted to the concept of "civilization before civilization," a period during which very complex cultures developed that did not happen to meet all of the artificial criteria used by modern historians to define "civilization." Nevertheless, for some five thousand years—a period equal in length to the period during which "civilizations" have existed—sophisticated societies that manifested to a greater or lesser degree nearly all the attributes of civilization existed in Europe and the Near East. All of this demonstrates that the rise of civilization around 3000 BCE was not a sudden phenomenon determined by a set of unique circumstances but the natural consequence of thousands of years of human development.

The final chapter, on the other hand, continues after the point at which most traditional texts leave off, bringing antiquity to its logical conclusion at the end of Late Antiquity in the mid-seventh century CE. Doing so not only brings the narrative full circle with a return to the Near East, where civilization had originally developed, but also depicts the disintegration of the unified culture that had gradually developed during the preceding millennia. The disintegration resulting from the barbarian occupation of the western Roman Empire on the one hand and the rise of Islam and the early Muslim conquests in the Near East, North Africa, and Spain on the other collectively created the "three worlds of the Middle Ages" that eventually would manifest distinguishing elements that continue to characterize the modern world.

The volume also breaks with convention in other regards. The Minoan and Mycenaean civilizations of Crete and Greece, for example, are discussed in the context of other Bronze Age civilizations rather than being held in reserve and lumped in with later Greek civilization. This, I believe, highlights the role of the early Greeks in their largely Near Eastern context rather than creating a Greek ghetto that implicitly suggests that the Greeks were somehow different from, and superior to, the peoples of the Near East. And elsewhere, there is a focus more on connections than on discontinuities, and what usually are treated as lines of demarcation are seen here as linked, bridge periods. Thus the fourth chapter bridges the gap between the Bronze and Iron Ages and helps to correct the common presumption that Mesopotamia and Egypt were the only centers of Bronze Age civilization by giving full billing to cultures that arose outside the major river valleys. It discusses bit players of the Bronze Age who anticipated future religious developments (the Hebrews), mainstream lifestyles, uses of technology, and forms of economic activity, commerce in particular.

In a like manner, Chapter 10 covers the fall of the Roman Republic and the creation of the Roman Empire in the same chapter. Even though the political creation of Augustus' Principate marks the logical conclusion to the political developments of the late Roman Republic, other texts create a break here and talk about the creation of the Principate in a separate chapter on the Roman Empire. But this text puts Octavian's political solution to the political problems of the Republic in the same chapter as the fall of the Republic and not only highlights the degree of continuity of Octavian's political actions with what had gone before but also eliminates the awkward necessity of recapitulating in the next chapter. Students thus can see this crucial transition as it happened, comprehensively, and not artificially broken up into two chunks. In this model, the subsequent Roman Empire chapters then can concentrate on the future of Roman society, culture, and politics rather than having to backtrack to the Republican past.

Likewise, Chapter 12 not only discusses the Imperial Crisis but also smoothly segues into the reign of Diocletian, showing clearly how and why one followed on the other. And by covering this crucial period all in the same chapter, the volume implicitly deals with the transition between classical antiquity and Late Antiquity and with the fuzzy question of just when Late Antiquity started: All of the suggested starting points are included in one chapter, and students will be able to see many of the elements that distinguish the two periods from each other.

Other features of *Ancient Mediterranean Civilizations* are intended to bring the ancient history textbook into the modern world. For one thing, the teaching of introductory history has increasingly become a lowest-common-denominator situation. More and more courses, even upper-level ones, have fewer bona fide prerequisites as departments fight to keep their enrollment levels up. Western civilization textbooks have responded to this development by providing textbooks with pedagogical aids that go far beyond the de rigueur source quotations and maps and are intended to help guide students who have not been exposed to premodern history. Ancient history textbooks, however, have been behind the curve in this regard, perhaps on the assumption that an ancient history survey course attracts more motivated students who don't need to be babied or patronized with high-schoolish pedagogical features. Whereas the first part of this reasoning is, on balance, correct, I don't agree with the second, for the kind of students who will be taking a survey of ancient history will have the same kinds of academic backgrounds as students taking western civilization and will have many of the same kinds of pedagogical experiences, needs, and expectations. Yes, they will, on balance, be more engaged and more motivated, for if they were not such, they would be taking western civilization. But this does not mean that they will be any better prepared academically and any less receptive to pedagogy that western civ students might just ignore.

In addition, just like western civ students, ancient history students have grown up in a multimedia world and will find a traditional "block-text" book just as boring and uninviting as anyone else does. Ancient history students like to have their attention drawn to the equivalent of different hypertext links, to different manifestations of the information they're studying. This textbook, therefore, includes pedagogical features that will not only guide students to a better understanding of the material but also satisfy their innate desire to experience the kind of exposure to material that they are used to receiving electronically. Collectively, the features are designed to show how students can interpret historical evidence, both written and material, to form a reasoned analysis of what happened in history and what it meant.

Thus, even though this text still is organized around a central narrative designed to show how history works, the volume also has a number of features intended to catch the attention of students who spend much of their time surfing web pages. For example, each chapter includes four boxed features that can stand on their own and thus be useful either for classroom discussions or out-of-class assignments, including: (1) "A Picture Is Worth a Thousand Words," in which a material artifact, such as a building, fresco, pot, statue, and so on, is discussed in detail, in the context of the chapter themes, to show how nonliterary material can shed light on an ancient cultures; (2) "In Their Own Words," an extended quotation from a literary or epigraphical text that illustrates the chapter's main themes and demonstrates how different kinds of written documents can teach history; (3) "History Laboratory," which shows how scientific methods, theoretical models, and quantification can be used to understand ancient history on the one hand and debunk pseudoscience and modern popularizers on the other; and (4) either "Mysteries of History," dealing with an unknown aspect of the past, or "Historical Controversy," dealing with divergent modern models or interpretations of an ancient phenomenon.

In addition, smaller boxed features provide added learning opportunities when appropriate, including "Learning from History," which demonstrates what history teaches us about themes and issues of broad significance that also have an impact in the modern day, such as those relating to race, ethnicity, gender, slavery, religion, and so on, as well as "The Legacy of Antiquity," which considers how what happened in history continues to affect the modern day; "Historical Causality," which focuses on the factors that make history happen; "Thought Question," which challenges students to put to use what they have learned; "Cross-Cultural Connections," which looks at similarities between different cultures in different places at different periods; and "Alternative History," discussion points revolving around questions of how historical processes or events might have turned out differently.

Finally, interspersed throughout the pages of the book are marginal "stickies" that draw attention to modern analogies to or survivals of ancient phenomena and indicate to students that the present can still be related to the past. And throughout the text, important terms, events, and concepts are highlighted in bold to draw students' attention to them, help students study for exams, and indicate that these items will be found in the Glossary, which provides brief descriptions and a guide to pronunciation. The volume also is heavily illustrated. Whereas two commonly assigned ancient history textbooks have forty and sixty-five maps and illustrations, this volume has well over two hundred. The robust visual quality of this text will help make ancient history more up close and personal for modern students. I feel that it is important for students to be able to associate the visual with the verbal not only because these are cultures that, outside of Hollywood portrayals, students are essentially unfamiliar with but also because in this multimedia age students' first encounters with new material are often through highly illustrated web pages.

And finally, a word on the title. The word "Mediterranean" is not intended to suggest that all of the civilizations discussed were located directly on the Mediterranean Sea, as were those of Egypt, Greece, and Rome, but rather that they all, in some sense, looked toward the Mediterranean or were closely connected to civilizations located directly on the Mediterranean. Thus, the primary external associations, say, of the Near Eastern civilizations of Mesopotamia or the the Celtic cultures of northern Gaul, were with cultures located in the area of the Mediterranean. In this way, the Mediterranean Sea served as a unifying element, as a facilitator rather than as a gatekeeper, with regard to forms of cultural interaction, and rightly can be viewed as a focal point of what long has been known as "western civilization."

The results of my personal study of ancient history have appeared in many different venues, including ten monographs and edited volumes, more than one hundred scholarly articles, and even the introductory chapters of a western civilization textbook, published by the old Houghton Mifflin Press in 2008, that incorporated abridged and heavily edited versions of my ancient history lecture notes. *Ancient Mediterranean Civilizations* had its genesis as a result of a meeting with Robert Miller, executive editor and classics editor, of Oxford University Press in November of 2007, who responded much more favorably and enthusiastically than I ever could have expected when I suggested to him that a new ancient history textbook might be in order. And the rest, as they say, is history. The project moved quickly along as I updated and expanded decades of lecture notes into a coherent and comprehensive whole. In 2009, Robert passed the classics editor torch to Charles Cavaliere, who with tremendous enthusiasm has shepherded this volume to completion. At the same time, the work was greatly facilitated by the dedicated assistance of several Oxford staff persons, including Christina Mancuso, Kristin Maffei, and Lauren Aylward. In addition, I also would like to thank the many colleagues who at one point or another refereed some or all of the chapters, including Ann Delehanty (Reed College), Diana McDonald (Boston College), Mark Munn (Pennsylvania State University), William M. Owens (The Ohio State University), Gail W. Pieper (Benedictine University), Jana S. Pisani (Ferris State University), Stephen Ruzicka (University of North Carolina, Greensboro), Edward Watts (Indiana University), Ronald J. Weber (University of Texas at El Paso), Jonathan Zophy (University of Houston, Clear Lake), and several anonymous reviewers. Their careful readings and trenchant comments not only opened my eyes to a much wider range of interpretations and source material, and thus made this a much better volume, but also saved me from a multitude of egregious and embarrassing errors.

NOTE ON SPELLING
AND PRONUNCIATION

Because ancient names and words were written in languages other than English, they can be converted into English using many different methods. The spellings used here are widely used spellings, but readers should be aware that other publications sometimes will use spellings that are different from the ones used here.

In addition, a few general guidelines can make it easier to approximate the pronunciation of many ancient words.

(1) In ancient words, adjacent vowels that in English would form diphthongs often are pronounced separately. For example:

Cuneiform =	coo nay′ ih form	not	coo nay′ form
Gudea =	Goo day′ ah	not	Goo′ dee
Aryans =	Air′ ee ans	not	Ar′ yans
Ea =	Eh′ ah	not	Ee

(2) Likewise, in diaeresis, the second of two adjoining vowels is printed with an umlaut and is pronounced separately, for example:

Pasiphaë =	Pa si′ phah ee
Taÿgetus =	Tah ih′ jih tus
Tanaïs =	Tah na ees′

(3) Foreign words and names do not have silent e's at the end, for example:

Cyrene =	Si ree′ nee	not	Si rene′
Thales =	Thay′ lees	not	Thayles

(4) Some letters of modern languages are printed with diacritical marks, for example:

ç =	"ch" as in "church," e.g., Çatal
č =	"ch" as in "chocolate," e.g., Vinča

š =   "sh" as in "shock," e.g., Šuplja
ü =   "oo" as in "food," e.g., Hüyük

(5) Pronunciation of vowels in Greek words (printed in italics in the text):

a =   "ah" as in "shah"
ē =   "a" as in "cake"
ō =   "o" as in "vote"
y =   "oo" as in "room"

(6) Pronunciation of Latin words:

(1) Every vowel or diphthong represents a separate syllable, e.g.,

proles =   pro′ lace   not   proles

(2a) In words that have not been anglicized, there are no silent vowels, and words are divided into syllables following a vowel and/or preceding a consonant, e.g.,

familia =   fa mee′ lee ah   not   fa mil′ ee ah
Trasimene =   Tra si mee′ nee   not   Tras ih mene′

(2b) But some Latin words have been made into English words and thus are pronounced in English, for example, "Caesar" is pronounced "See′ zer" in English not "Kai′ sar" (as it would be in Latin).

ABOUT THE AUTHOR

Ralph W. Mathisen has appointments in history, classics, and medieval studies at the University of Illinois at Urbana-Champaign. His research interests include ecclesiastical history, barbarian studies, late Latin literature, prosopography, and the society, culture, and religion of Late Antiquity. He has authored, coauthored, or edited ten books, including *Making Europe: People, Politics, and Culture* (coauthor) (Houghton Mifflin 2008); *People, Personal Expression, and Social Relations in Late Antiquity*, 2 vols. (University of Michigan Press 2003); *Society and Culture in Late Antique Gaul: Revisiting the Sources* (Ashgate 2001) (with D. R. Shanzer); *Law, Society, and Authority in Late Antiquity* (Oxford University Press 2001); and *Ruricius of Limoges and Friends: A Collection of Letters from Visigothic Aquitania* (Liverpool University Press 1999). He currently is working on books on "How the Barbarians Saved Civilization"; on the late Roman comedy "The Querolus"; and on the life and letters of Desiderius of Cahors. He has published more than sixty scholarly articles. He is director of the Biographical Database for Late Antiquity Project and a fellow of the American Numismatic Society. He has degrees in astronomy and physics (B.S., University of Wisconsin, 1969), mechanical engineering (M.S., Rensselaer Polytechnic Institute, 1972), classical languages (M.A., University of Wisconsin, 1973), and ancient history (Ph.D., University of Wisconsin, 1979).

CHAPTER 1

THE ORIGINS OF HISTORY

Civilization Before Civilization
(2,000,000–3000 BCE)

The entire extent of the human past covers over a million years. But when we speak of "history" and of "civilization," the time frame dwindles to merely the previous five thousand years. For nearly the entire human past, therefore, people lived a wandering, hand-to-mouth existence that focused on merely surviving. Not until about 3000 BCE, in the river valleys of Egypt, Mesopotamia (Iraq), India and Pakistan, and China, did complex urbanized cultures based on the extensive exploitation of agriculture arise. Two of these cultures, the Egyptian and Mesopotamian, began a train of "western" cultural development that would lead to Greece, to Rome, and thence to the modern day. The story of the human cultural developments leading up to the creation of civilization will cover thousands of years in just a few pages. We will see the transition from hunting-and-gathering cultures to societies that lived in permanent settlements, controlled their own food supply, and communicated over long distances.

LAYING THE GROUNDWORK

Before beginning the study of **history**, it is necessary to understand some fundamental concepts. Perhaps the most basic one involves just what "history" is. The entire human past can be divided into two periods: "history" and "prehistory." History did not begin until peoples began to keep records using a written language. This happened at different times in different parts of the world. It happened for the first time, in restricted areas of Egypt, Mesopotamia, India and Pakistan, and China, about the year 3000 BCE. Only over time did the knowledge of writing spread to larger and larger regions. Because this book is primarily concerned with peoples who kept written records, the areas of the world being discussed start out being fairly restricted but then expand as time moves on.

The invention of writing is very closely tied to the concept of **"civilization,"** because one of the things that defines a civilization is the ability to keep records using some kind of system of writing. In addition, when we speak of "western" civilization, we need to be aware of geography. In this case, we are speaking of the cultures of all the peoples who lived in the area of the **Mediterranean Sea**. These included not just the cultures of western Europe—which arrived on the scene rather late in history—but, and in particular, the cultures of western Asia, Egypt, and North Africa.

Another important concept is the use of dating. Even though many students heartily dislike learning dates, **chronology** and the ways that human cultures develop over the course of time are crucial for an understanding of history. Modern conventions use a dating system that is divided into two great periods: the two-thousand-plus years of the "current/common era" (CE) and the thousands of years "before the current/common era" (BCE). These dating conventions replace the older system of "BC" ("before Christ") and "AD" (*anno domini* = "In the year of our Lord"), which many now feel has an exceptionally religious basis. Fortunately for historians, however, the dates themselves remain the same.

It is important to remember that "AD" appears before a date, e.g., "AD 1950," whereas "BC," "BCE," and "CE" all appear after the date, e.g., "1950 CE."

Finally, historians always have to keep in mind where their evidence comes from and how they interpret it. There are two categories of evidence. First of all, of course, there is written evidence, which occurs in many forms, ranging from literature to business inventories to graffiti. But equally important is the evidence of **material culture**, which is recovered by means of archaeological excavations. Both kinds of evidence require interpretations by specialists—historians and archaeologists—before their significance can even begin to be understood. On the one hand, written evidence always reflects the history, culture, religious views, and so on of the people who wrote it. When a historian reports what an ancient document—such as the Bible—contains, that means not that the historian endorses or believes what the source says but that it must first be cited before it can be discussed and understood in its own context. And, on the other hand, material artifacts are open to a multitude of interpretations that are all too often influenced by **presentism**, the assumption that people who lived thousands of years ago must have behaved in much the same way as modern people. Historians therefore rarely are in complete agreement about how the evidence is to be interpreted. There always is room for reconsideration of what we thought we already knew, which is one of the things that makes history such an exciting and intellectually stimulating field of study.

An Acheulean hand axe from Kent in England. This style of hand axe was the standard human tool for well over a million years.

THE PALAEOLITHIC AGE (2,000,000–10,000 BCE)

The first and longest period of human existence, roughly 99 percent of it, is commonly known as the **Palaeolithic Age**, a term introduced in 1865, based on Greek words meaning "Old Stone," by John Lubbock in the book *Pre-Historic Times*. Lubbock also introduced the common tripartite division of the Stone Age into the Old Stone Age, Middle Stone (or Mesolithic) Age, and New Stone (or Neolithic) Age. The Old Stone Age is likewise divided into three periods, the Lower, Middle, and Upper Palaeolithic. The name Stone Age is derived from the most durable material used to manufacture tools during the period. Of course, other materials, such as wood and animal soft tissue, also were used to make tools and clothing, but these do not survive. Well before the end of the Old Stone Age, about 10,000 BCE, completely modern humans had evolved.

Stone Age Tool Making

The first stone tools, if they even can be called that, were naturally occurring rocks and pebbles that were used to pound and beat things. Eventually, near the end of the geological period called the Pliocene Epoch around 2,500,000 BCE, ancestors of humans in eastern Africa known as "**homo habilis**" ("skillful human") learned to chip flakes off nodules of stone such as flint. Doing so created simple choppers and scrapers with sharp edges, often called pebble or Oldowan tools (after the Olduvai Gorge in Africa), that were used for butchering scavenged animal carcasses.

During the geological **Pleistocene Epoch** (2,500,000–10,000 BCE), when the Earth experienced a series of Ice Ages, the ancestors of modern humans evolved both biologically and technologically. Between one and two million years ago, a human population known as "**homo erectus**" ("upright human") learned the use of fire and developed distinctive oval and pear-shaped biface (worked on two sides) stone hand axes in the Acheulean style (named from Saint-Acheul in

TABLE 1.1 CHRONOLOGY OF THE STONE AGE

Geological Epoch	Date (BCE)	Stone Age Period	Date (BCE)
Pliocene	5,000,000–2,500,000		
Pleistocene	2,500,000–10,000	Palaeolithic Age	2,000,000–10,000
		Lower Palaeolithic	2,000,000–180,000
		Middle Palaeolithic	180,000–25,000
		Upper Palaeolithic	25,000–10,000
Holocene	10,000–present	Mesolithic Age	10,000–8000
		Neolithic Age	8000–3000
		Chalcolithic Age	5500–3000

France, where early examples were discovered). Made with points and cutting edges from a central core, these sophisticated tools allowed homo erectus to hunt large game animals in Africa, Asia, and Europe. The Acheulean hand axe was the most important tool used by humans for the majority of the human past, from as early as 1,800,000 BCE to about 100,000 BCE. Meanwhile, the next development in human evolution began about 400,000 years ago with the appearance of "**homo sapiens**" ("thinking human").

The Middle Palaeolithic Period, from roughly 180,000 to 35,000 BCE, saw the appearance circa 150,000 BCE of the human subspecies known as the **Neanderthals**, named after the Neandertal Valley in Germany, where specimens were found in 1856. The Neanderthals manufactured more finely worked hand axes and complex **flaked-stone** implements in the Mousterian style (from Le Moustier, site of a southwestern French rock shelter) using the Levallois technique, in which long, thin flakes were struck from a prepared core. The flakes then were refined into specialized tools such as scrapers, awls, knives, and projectile points. These improved tool kits allowed humans to become less dependent on scavenging and more effective hunters of large game such as antelopes, horses, deer, and bison.

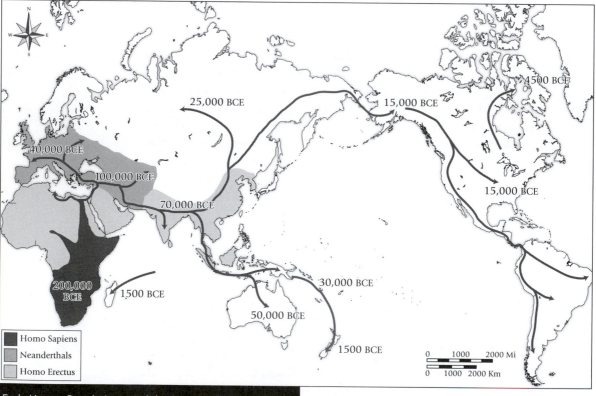

Early Human Populations, and the Spread of Homo Sapiens

About 100,000 BCE, fully modern humans, known technically as "**homo sapiens sapiens**" ("thinking, thinking human"), appeared in Africa and began to spread throughout the world, where they encountered the descendents of human populations who had left Africa hundreds of thousands of years earlier. By a not yet understood process, which may have involved factors ranging from better adaptability to violence, all these other human subspecies then gradually disappeared.

The third and final period of the Old Stone Age was the Upper Palaeolithic Period, from circa 35,000 to 10,000 BCE. During this period, homo sapiens sapiens spread into Europe and into the Americas not only via the Bering Straits land bridge and but also possibly via ice floes from Europe. Upper Palaeolithic populations known as the **Cro Magnon** peoples (from a rock shelter at Crô-Magnon in southwestern France), a general term referring to the earliest modern peoples of Europe circa 45,000 to 8,000 BCE, bore DNA (deoxyribonucleic acid, a substance found in the nucleus of cells that preserves genetic information and transmits it from one generation to the next) well within the range of modern human DNA. New technological developments gave people the opportunity to exploit the natural food-producing environment more effectively. More complex forms of stone tool making developed, utilizing narrow blades struck with a punch from a single flint core and including tools such as awls, burins, and finely made "leaf points." Tiny, finely crafted sharp-edged flint slivers known as **microliths** were made into light projectiles and barbed arrowheads. At the same time, other kinds of materials were increasingly used in tool making, such as ivory, antler, and bone. But human societies still were dependent on nature for the provision of most of their food supplies.

The rapid evolution of stone tool technology was reflected in successions of European cultures, all named after the sites in France where their artifacts were found: the Aurignacian or Perigordian, 35,000–20,000 BCE, with more sophisticated blade and bone technology; the Solutrean, in southwestern Europe 19,000–15,000 BCE, with an advanced flint industry using pressure flaking rather than flint knapping (chipping) and characterized by its bifacial leaf point, and Magdalenian, 16,000–9,500 BCE, high point of a bone tool industry used to manufacture harpoon points and needles.

Palaeolithic Society and Economy

In Old Stone Age societies, the provision of adequate supplies of food always was a primary concern. Initially, all human societies made use of a "**hunting and gathering**" kind of economy. People had to go wherever they could find food. Most food consisted of fruits, vegetables, roots, and leaves gathered from naturally occurring plants. This diet was supplemented, whenever possible, by animal products acquired by hunting, fishing, or scavenging. Organ meats, such as kidneys and livers, were particular favorites. People survived by

TABLE 1.2   REPRESENTATIVE TOOL-MAKING CULTURES

Culture Type	Date (BCE)	Human Population	Characteristic
Oldowan	2,500,000–1,500,000	Homo habilis	Pebble tools
Acheulean	1,800,000–100,000	Homo erectus	Symmetrical axes
Mousterian	300,000–30,000	Neanderthal	Levallois flakes
Aurignacian	35,000–20,000	Homo sapiens sapiens	Blade/bone industry
Soloutrean	19,000–15,000	Homo sapiens sapiens	Bifacial leaf point
Magdalenian	16,000–8000	Homo sapiens sapiens	Bone tool industry

their wits and by carefully observing their surroundings and taking note of patterns. They quickly learned that some areas produced more food products than others. Nut and berry-carrying bushes and trees grew in known places. Migrating animals and birds traveled by certain routes at known times. Fish congregated in observed areas of lakes and streams. But no matter how successful human groups were in seeking out food, they continued to live a very hand-to-mouth, "feast-or-famine" existence. When food was plentiful, as after a successful hunt, people would gorge themselves; at other times they would be close to starvation. Their food supply was controlled by nature, and they had to travel with the seasons and follow the animals. Altered animal migration tracks or a period of drought could easily lead to starvation.

The mobile lifestyle also meant the need to travel light. Containers were made from leather and wickerwork, and there was little accumulation of property. The landscape was unable to support large populations. Traditions developed that only the strong should survive. Infants who appeared to be sickly or deformed were exposed to die. If the population grew larger than the food supply could support, groups of young "volunteers" would be expected to depart from the group and seek a new livelihood somewhere else. Conflict could arise between groups of humans over control of areas where the hunting or food gathering was good.

For shelter, during the early Palaeolithic people used both caves and open-air campsites with windbreaks; subsequently, people made greater use of caves and rock shelters, which offered protection from the weather, security from wild animals, and good gathering places. If no caves were available, huts could be built using materials as diverse as tree branches held down by stones, or mammoth tusks. Toward the end of the Old Stone Age, roofed timber huts with packed clay and stone walls were being built in central Europe.

The rigorous nature of life during the Old Stone Age also conditioned gender roles. Males generally hunted and engaged in activities that took them far afield from wherever they were residing, whereas women gathered plant foodstuffs and occupied themselves with infant and child care. In addition, the manufacture and sharpening of stone tools—something that would be necessary during hunting expeditions—was mainly a male activity, whereas women primarily performed tasks at home, such as scraping and curing hides and food preparation and preservation.

Intellectual Development

Over time, humans began to conceive of some kind of relationship between themselves and powers greater than they. As early as 300,000 years ago, formal burial practices emerged, with designated areas ("cemeteries") being developed for the interment of the dead. One Neanderthal burial even was accompanied by flowers. The earliest representations of the human form, in the shape of crude female figurines, appeared at the same time. Human thought became more sophisticated, and early forms of religion developed. Even very early human populations had ideas about forces and powers greater than themselves. Religion begins with a belief in a supernatural power that oversees the world and somehow controls all the important aspects of life (food production, fertility, natural phenomena) and death. The way in which this power is conceptualized and manifested varies: It can appear as undefined forces, concrete divinities, ghosts, or demons. In addition, these supernatural powers were almost always thought to be sensitive and responsive to human desires expressed through ritual or prayer. Even very early human societies demonstrate through their remains a belief in the existence of supernatural powers.

Beginning ca. 30,000 BCE, development of modern concepts of art among the Cro Magnon and other peoples were reflected in the creation of painting and sculpture. Rock paintings of animals, often deep in caves in Spain and southern France, were created from ocher (iron oxide), manganese oxide, hematite, and charcoal pigments that were blown or spit onto the rock. The designs suggest the performance of religious rituals involving hunting magic. Some animals in the paintings are transfixed by spears so as to make their magical point even more clear. A French painting, called "the Little Sorcerer," depicts a man—perhaps some kind of **shaman** (a holy man able to communicate with the spirits)—with a bearded face, a bison's horns, and a horse's tail. A painting from Spain, probably representing a fertility ritual, shows nine women dressed in knee-length skirts dancing about a small naked man. Even more elaborate female statuettes called "Venuses," originating in Russia and with grossly exaggerated hips and breasts, suggest a belief in supernatural powers related to female fertility. In general, the power to beget life was mystically attributed to women in the artwork long before any male role was acknowledged.

The meaning of the so-called "Little Sorcerer" drawing from a cave at Trois-Frères in France has engendered much debate. It is not even clear whether the figure is meant to be seen standing or crawling in a hunting position.

A PICTURE IS WORTH A THOUSAND WORDS

THE VENUS OF LAUSSEL

The so-called "Venus of Laussel," a seventeen-inch high, twenty-thousand-year-old limestone relief from the Dordogne region of southwestern France, shows a large-breasted, broad-hipped woman holding a buffalo horn incised with thirteen lines, which it has been suggested represent the thirteen menstrual cycles per year. Figurines such as these indicate not only a belief in divine powers that could be controlled, but also an increasing awareness of biological processes related to reproduction. As such, they can be considered to be not only religious but also scientific in nature. And it also might be noted that in most ancient societies, concepts of female attractiveness revolved around a full-bodied rather than a slim figure.

Burial ceremonies likewise became more elaborate. Bodies were accompanied by **red ochre** (a red mineral powder perhaps representing blood and intended to make corpses look more lifelike), clothing, shells, beads, tools, and burnt parts of slaughtered animals, items that the deceased could use in the afterlife. Skulls were sometimes used for sacramental purposes, including being made into drinking cups. And entire bodies sometimes were wedged into place with stone or even tied up, perhaps to prevent the deceased from returning to haunt the living.

It has been said that the primary concerns of Stone Age societies were food production, reproduction, and simply staying alive. Until people could be more confident that these needs would be met, they would continue to concentrate their efforts there and simply not have the time or motivation to seek out a better quality of life and standard of living.

Climate and the Mesolithic Age

The development of human technological change was influenced by variations in the climate as the Earth went through several glacial and interglacial periods. The end of the last Ice Age, about 10,000 BCE, marked the end of the Pleistocene and beginning of the **Holocene Epoch**, the current period of geological history. Great changes occurred in human lifestyles, perhaps in part the result of the warming climate that brought the melting of the northern glaciers, a rise in sea levels, and the flooding of coastal plains (and the submersion of any human settlements there) that had provided a major food source for human populations. It also brought the end of the Old Stone Age and the beginning of a brief period known as the **Mesolithic** (Middle Stone) **Age** or "Epipalaeolithic" ("Peripheral Stone") Period (ca. 10,000–8000 BCE), a transitional period characterized by technological advances based on Old Stone Age technology and by the exploitation of new sources of foodstuffs.

The beginning of the new period was marked by a major change in the supply of foodstuffs known as the Holocene Extinction Event, which had begun during the late Pleistocene Epoch, during which large numbers of plants, animals, amphibians, reptiles, and arthropods became extinct, most notably large mammals known as megafauna, including the wooly mammoth and cave bear in Europe; the dwarf elephants of Cyprus and Sicily; the horse, camel, mastodon and mammoth, and saber-toothed tiger in North America. Explanations for these extinctions include glacial retreat, overhunting by humans, and asteroid impact. Whatever the reason for them, human populations were forced to adapt to the changed circumstances.

Societies and economies based on the hunting of megafauna needed to find new sources of food. Previously glaciated northern areas gave rise to large forests and accompanying wildlife. Some groups of people developed a more **sedentary** style of hunting and gathering, specializing in particular kinds of local plant and animal foodstuffs more characteristic of temperate climates. Some, for example, hunted red deer and boars in the forests. Near oceans, lakes, and rivers, others turned to fishing, and some of these specialized even further, focusing on eels, cod, or shellfish. Fishing weirs were constructed by building stone or brush fences in tidal estuaries: When the tide receded, the fish were trapped behind the weir. In the summer, inland camps were established to exploit naturally growing crops, ranging from acorns to strawberries, as well as wild animals. In northern Europe, fur-bearing animals such as marten, wolf, squirrel, and otter were hunted for garments. The village of Lepenski Vir on the Danube River in eastern Serbia, for example, dating to between 7000 and 5500 BCE and with more than one hundred private and public buildings, had a seminomadic population with an economy based on fishing.

The Mesolithic Period also saw the intense development of microliths that were used to create composite tools by gluing them with resin into wooden

THE ORIGIN OF NOAH'S FLOOD

One of the best-known stories of Jewish, Christian, and Islamic scripture is that of Noah, who was said to have been advised by God to build a great wooden ark and load it with his family, animals, and birds. Subsequently, a rain of forty days and nights created such a flood that all mankind was destroyed. Only Noah and his passengers survived. According to biblical reckoning, the flood occurred roughly around 2300 BCE. In the modern day, controversy has raged regarding just how historical the flood was and just how literally this account is to be taken. Some would see it as purely metaphorical, whereas others have attempted to identify the flood with some historical Near Eastern flood on not such a grand scale. In the nineteenth century, it became clear that stories of a great flood in the distant past also appeared in the literature of other Near Eastern peoples. The *Epic of Gilgamesh,* for example, a Mesopotamian story whose earliest surviving copies date to about 2100 BCE, tells how King Gilgamesh met an immortal man, Utnapishtim, who had been warned by a friendly god to build an ark to save himself, his family, and his cattle from a great flood that the other gods intended to use to destroy humanity. And in Greek mythology, Deucalion and Pyrrha were warned by Prometheus, the son of the god Zeus, to build an ark because Zeus intended to destroy humanity. In this account, the flood lasted only nine days.

One interpretation of these stories is that they represent folk memories of the many disastrous floods known to have stricken the early cities of the lower Tigris and Euphrates rivers. But a more recent theory proposes a different hypothesis. The last major melting of glaciers beginning about 10,000 BCE caused sea levels to rise precipitously. As the Mediterranean Sea rose, about 5000 BCE it began to spill over the Bosporus in northwestern Anatolia into the lowlands surrounding a freshwater lake on the site of the Black Sea. The water level rose nearly a foot a day, eventually rising more than five hundred feet and inundating vast amounts of land, including any areas of human settlement. Perhaps a memory of this cataclysmic flood is what lies behind the Near Eastern flood stories. And a 1999 archaeological expedition did appear to find an ancient underwater shoreline that become inundated about 5000 BCE. Proponents of this theory also suggest that refugees from the flood contributed to the spread of agriculture in the Balkans at just this time, when many extra mouths would have to have been fed.

But clear confirmation of any of the flood hypotheses has not yet been forthcoming. Beginning in the nineteenth century, searches for Noah's Ark at various sites, such as Mt. Ararat in Anatolia, all have produced negative results. Likewise, attempts to find remains of human occupation below the surface of the Black Sea also have been unsuccessful. Until such time as archaeological excavations come up with hard evidence of a Neolithic or Chalcolithic flood of massive proportions, speculation about the nature of "Noah's Flood" will continue to be made without much hard evidence.

or bone handles to make knives and other tools for hunting and fishing. The bow and arrow were used, and tiny barbed microliths were bound to wooden shafts to create arrows, permitting more efficient hunting. Bone was worked into fishhooks, barbed harpoons, and pins. The bodies of the dead often were decorated with necklaces, pendants, breast ornaments, and headdresses of shell and bone. And the Mesolithic Period also probably saw the domestication of the dog, the first animal to be introduced to human society.

THE NEOLITHIC WORLD (8000–5500 BCE)

The culmination of the Stone Age came with the **Neolithic**, or "New Stone," Age, lasting from ca. 8000 to 3000 BCE, during which stone-tool technology reached at the same time its most complex development and a dead end. In the first phase of the Neolithic Age, stone tools were exploited to their maximum advantage. The Neolithic Age also brought massive changes in food-producing technology that on the one hand gave people greater control over their food supply but on the other made them more dependent on artificial means of food production.

The "Neolithic Revolution"

The Neolithic Age, which began in the Near East about 8000 BCE, marked the final development of stone-based technology. Finely crafted stone and bone tools filled every kind of need. Ground and polished stone tools were used to make axes and adzes and other tools for grinding, chopping, and cutting. Weaving and pottery were introduced.

Most significantly, the Neolithic Age brought two revolutions in food production techniques: the domestication of animals and the domestication of plants. Technological advances had brought a higher standard of living that also resulted in population growth. Greater control over the food supply was crucial. Animals such as sheep, pigs, and cattle were domesticated and were kept in flocks and herds. Control over domestic animals gave people a dependable supply of milk products, clothing, and meat, although it usually was only in times of famine, for ceremonial purposes, or when an animal unexpectedly died that the animals—which also served as a form of wealth—were actually eaten.

This new lifestyle is called **pastoralism** because the people who adopted it, known as pastoralists, were constantly wandering about in search of new pastures. The diet they received from their animals was supplemented by vegetable products they gathered in the course of their travels. Pastoralists still were subject to the unpredictable climatic changes. Prolonged periods of drought could have disastrous consequences. And their mobile existence inhibited the accumulation of large amounts of property. Nevertheless, the pastoral lifestyle offered much greater security than the old hunting-and-gathering economy, and it quickly spread over nearly all the inhabited world.

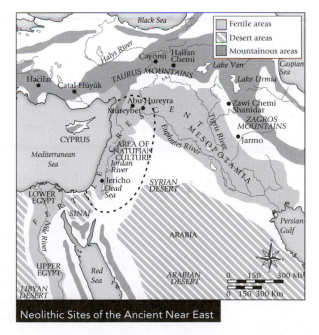

Neolithic Sites of the Ancient Near East

Even more revolutionary was the domestication of certain kinds of grains, which may have occurred first in the Near East. Indeed, one of the mysteries of history is how, when, and where people first settled down to cultivating crops on a permanent basis. For millennia, hunter-gatherers would have observed that naturally sown seeds yielded a greatly multiplied harvest in the fall. Since before 10,000 BCE, hunter-gatherers around the world experimented with cultivating locally growing grains, such as rye in Syria and rice in China. One of the earliest hunter-gathering peoples known to have cultivated grain is the **Natufians**, who lived in Syria and Palestine during the late Palaeolithic and early Mesolithic Periods, between 10,500 and 8000 BCE. The Natufians had an economy based largely on the hunting of gazelles in grasslands that also contained several cereal crops that the Natufians harvested. In order to exploit these food resources, they established permanent villages with populations of about 150 persons. Semiunderground houses had stone foundations and superstructures of brush and central fire pits. One Natufian village, for example, was Jericho, established just before 9000 BCE in Palestine near the Jordan River. By the end of the Natufian Period, Jericho's population was growing and harvesting its own grain on a regular basis. Razor-sharp microliths were used to create composite sickles for harvesting grains, and ground-stone mortars were used to grind the grain.

Similar experimentation went on at Zawi Chemi Shanidar in northern Iraq, where between 10,000 and 9000 BCE a semipermanent settlement was composed of round thirteen-foot-diameter huts, with storage pits on the floor. The inhabitants used **obsidian** tools, had rudimentary grain mills for grinding wild or domestic grains, and raised sheep for both food and wool. A third site that documents the transition from foraging to permanent agriculture is Abu Hureyra in northern Syria, where settlers lived in two phases. During the first, about 9500 to 8500 BCE, hunter-gatherers pursued wild gazelles and harvested wild einkorn wheat and emmer wheat (both tough-husked varieties that grow in poor soil), rye, and lentils. By ca. 9000 BCE they seem actually to have domesticated some of them. From about 8500 to 5000 BC, inhabitants of a much larger settlement cultivated domesticated oats, barley, emmer wheat, and lentils. Before they could be consumed, the grains had to be dehusked with a mortar and pestle and then ground. Inhabitants lived in mud-brick houses. During the eighth millenium (a thousand-year period) BCE both weaving and pottery appeared. The repetitious grinding of grain was a most labor-intensive activity, and the constant kneeling at stone grindstones, called querns, caused deformations in the toes of women—who did the grinding kneeling with their toes bent forward—as well as chronic knee, hip, and back injuries.

It still is unclear how and why agriculture developed. Some historians speculate that the incentive for growing one's own grain was provided by a period of cold and drought known as the Younger Dryas, from about 11,000 to 9500 BCE, during which the wild grains on which the Natufians, for example, had come to depend could no longer grow on their own and needed human cultivation. But a problem with this hypothesis is that observed developments of agriculture do not always match up with the dating of the Younger Dryas, which in some cases came before and in some cases came later. On the other hand, evidence also now increasingly suggests that sedentarism occurred before the large-scale exploitation of agriculture and was, in fact, one of the causes rather than effects of agriculture. The exhaustion of local resources of naturally occurring foodstuffs may have forced people to plant crops—a process they already understood but had not yet exploited—as an alternative to migration.

It took some time before agriculture became established on a large scale, perhaps because Mesolithic cultures were so well adapted to the food production opportunities of their particular economic niches; indeed, in some places, as at 'Ain Ghazal in Jordan, people even abandoned farming to return to pastoralism. Regardless of the reasons for its adoption, by not long after 8000 BCE many populations in the area of the Near East known as the **Fertile Crescent**, which runs from Egypt up through the **Levant** (the eastern Mediterranean coastal area) and then around into **Mesopotamia** (modern Iraq), had adopted village life and were cultivating grain crops, such as wheat, barley, and emmer, on a large and regular basis. Other crops, such as peas, beans, and figs, also were grown. The lack of weed seeds found on archaeological sites demonstrates the care that early farmers took in their cultivation. Domestic animals also were kept, but they only supplemented the grain-based diet and did not require changes of residence. The number and size of agricultural settlements increased dramatically. In southwestern **Anatolia** (modern Turkey), for example, the village Hacilar developed between 8000 and 7000 BCE, consisting of small rectangular houses built on stone foundations with mud-brick exterior and smooth-plastered interior walls. The inhabitants cultivated barley and emmer wheat, and there were storage pits, querns for grinding grain set into floors, and hearths for baking. Obsidian tools also were used. Another permanent agricultural village, dating to about 7000 BCE, was Jarmo in northern Iraq, with twenty houses with sun-dried mud walls set atop stone foundations that housed about 150 people. Along with emmer wheat and barley, residents also grew legumes such as peas and lentils. Domestic goats and pigs also were kept. Tools included obsidian cutting tools, ground stone containers, and scratch plows made of sticks with fire-hardened points.

The knowledge of agriculture also appeared in Africa, India, and China, where as early as 9000 BCE rice was being cultivated, although it did not become the diet staple until about 5000 BCE. Meanwhile, in Central and South America, the cultivation of squash began as early as 10,000 BCE, and corn and bean production began about five thousand years later. Over the millennia, knowledge of agriculture spread into most areas of the world where there was

> **HISTORICAL CAUSALITY**
>
> The adoption of either pastoralism or agriculture gave people dramatic new ways of gaining control over their food supplies. To what extent do you think that the decision to adopt either of these lifestyles would have been made for the same or different reasons?

sufficient rainfall and where soils could be tilled with simple wooden **ards**, or scratch plows, that could be pulled by either humans or animals, such as oxen. A continuing debate among historians is the means by which, during the seventh millenium BCE, agriculture spread into the southern Balkans, reaching northern Europe about a thousand years later, with some arguing that it was done by groups of migrants, some of whom might have been invaders, and others supposing that it occurred largely by diffusion. Given the hundreds or even thousands of years involved, the diffusion hypothesis would seem to be both more realistic and less dramatic.

The Consequences of Agriculture

Although the **Neolithic Revolution** did not occur quickly and some societies got along quite well without it, where it did occur it created the most significant economic watershed human society has ever seen, for once societies had become dependent on agriculture, there was no turning back: No other form of economy could support the much larger populations that naturally followed. There were several effects of dietary change. Preagricultural societies had a varied and less predictable diet, but after the introduction of agriculture, even though, at least initially, agricultural diets continued to be supplemented by hunting and gathering, diet was limited to a more restricted package of domesticated animals, grains, and other plants. The shift to a diet more heavy in carbohydrates had physical consequences, such as increased tooth decay. In addition, increased population density would have led to poor sanitation conditions and increased prevalence of disease, as well as greater sensitivity to climatic variations, such as droughts or floods, which could result in food shortages, which in turn could have much more disastrous consequences on agricultural as opposed to hunting-gathering societies.

Whereas the Old Stone Age had seen fairly standardized cultural assemblages throughout the world, with the use of roughly the same kinds of stone tool kits and methods over large geographical areas, the Mesolithic and Neolithic Periods brought increasing particularizations of culture, with unique cultures developing in discrete geographical areas based on the climate and natural resources of that particular region. Permanent Neolithic villages, based on sedentary lifestyles, agricultural economies, and larger populations, created new kinds of economic and social models for human societies. As populations became not only more sedentary but also more prosperous as a consequence of the creation and storage of food surpluses, people developed needs for economic goods that they either no longer could obtain on their own or that increased wealth and status made increasingly desirable. This brought an increase in trade in both essential and luxury items. The most extensively traded items included obsidian, a volcanic glass that could be used to create especially sharp points and edges and that was in heavy demand by most

Neolithic societies. Obsidian from the island of Melos in the Aegean Sea, for example, was widely traded throughout the Near East. Also traded were salt, used as a condiment and for meat preservation, and ochre, which was used for religious ritual purposes.

The domestication of the ox, the donkey, and the camel made it easier to transport goods over long distances, although difficulties in harnessing the horse long delayed its effective use. And the dugout and birchbark canoe demonstrated the potential of water transport. Regional trading zones extended over hundreds of miles, and extraregional trade routes went even farther. Baltic **amber**, for example, circulated in north central Europe (although, contrary to some modern assumptions, not far beyond). Obsidian from central Anatolia made its way south and east to the Levant and Mesopotamia, as well as further west into Anatolia. Salt from sources in central Anatolia and the Dead Sea in Palestine circulated for hundreds of miles around. In the central Mediterranean, Sicily also was a node of trading in the fourth millennium BCE. Sicilian flint and ochre went to the island of Malta. Obsidian from the Lipari Islands off the Sicilian coast made its way to Italy, Dalmatia, and southern France. In addition, as early as the fifth millenium BCE there is thought to have been a long-distance trade in the shell of the **spondylus**, a form of mussel, which was crafted into personal ornaments such as bracelets, pendants, and belt buckles.

A mining industry, derived from late Palaeolithic predecessors, exploited several kinds of minerals, but in particular ochre, flint, and obsidian, whose geochemical signatures dispersed material from the same site to be traced over long distances. An artificial cave called the "Lion Cave" in Swaziland in southern Africa, for example, was used to mine hematite (a source of red ochre) as early as forty-three thousand years ago, and an ochre mine in Hungary operated as much asthirty thousand years ago. Two quarries in northern Italy were the source of ceremonial stone axe heads made from jadeite and other stones that circulated throughout Europe beginning before 5000 BCE. Flint mining was carried out in chalk-rich regions running in a band extending from Britain through France and Belgium, and thence east to Poland. Flint miners showed a good practical knowledge of geology and engineering, knowing where to find flint-bearing strata by sinking shafts into the ground and by digging drainage holes to keep water from filling the mines. Neolithic miners worked flint out of the surrounding chalk with picks made of antlers. Excavated flint was shaped into rough blanks that then were shipped elsewhere for manufacture into stone tools. At Grime's Grave in eastern England, for example, a large late Neolithic flint-mining industry existed ca. 2100–1800 BCE. Flint quarried in France south of Tours has been found as far away as the Netherlands. At Spiennes in Belgium, mining works extended forty feet into the ground. Distinctive chocolate-colored flint from tenth-millenium BCE mines in central Poland was circulated for hundreds of miles. More exotic minerals also were mined, such

A map of Çatal Hüyük dating to ca. 6000 BCE, the earliest attested map in the world, shows a village of many houses sitting at the base of the double peaks of the Hasan Dag volcano, which seems to be erupting and may represent an eruption geologically dated to ca. 7500 BCE.

as variscite, a green mineral used to make jewelry, which was mined at Gavà in Spain, ca. 4000 BCE.

An early Neolithic village that took advantage of its access to sought-after trade goods was **Çatal Hüyük**, a thirty-acre site in southern Anatolia inhabited from 7400 to 6000 BCE. The five thousand or more inhabitants grew emmer wheat, barley, peas, and lentils and kept sheep and goats. The entire occupied space appears to have been devoted to private dwellings, and there is no evidence for communal buildings or public space. Windowless mud-brick houses occupied by individual families had their own food storage pits, obsidian stores, hearths, ovens, and work areas. There is no evidence of central storage spaces. Bodies of the dead were buried under platforms in the main living quarters, and the plastered walls sometimes were decorated with paintings. Every so often, houses were renovated by demolishing an old house and building a new one on the ruins. The fact that all the houses were more or less of the same size has led to suggestions that Çatal Hüyük had an egalitarian society. Çatal Hüyük is one of the first villages to show evidence of fortification. There were no streets; the houses often were just inches apart and had entry holes in the ceilings reached by ladders. The blank outer walls thus would have provided a defensive barrier.

It has been hypothesized that one reason the inhabitants needed fortification was to protect their commercial interests. The inhabitants of Çatal Hüyük engaged in several kinds of commercial activities. Exports included obsidian from the neighboring Hasan Dag volcano and salt from the neighboring salt lake of Tuz Gölü. Raw obsidian also was used to manufacture tools. The ability to identify obsidian originating in Çatal Hüyük has led to the detailed re-creation of trade routes running west into Anatolia and south down the Mediterranean coast. The inhabitants also manufactured pottery figurines and pots and worked copper items, such as polished mirrors. Its residents thus benefited from an extensive trading network that resulted in the circulation of trade goods throughout the Neolithic Near East.

Another village that took early advantage of the new Neolithic lifestyle was Jericho between 8350 and 7370 BCE. Jericho's more than two thousand residents

lived in round mud-brick houses and
grew barley, emmer wheat, and pulses
(such as kidney beans and chickpeas).
The city fortifications, the first known
example of monumental stone architecture in the world, protected some ten
acres and included a stone wall ten feet
thick and thirteen feet tall that ran just
outside a thirty-foot-tall stone tower. In
spite of its size, there is no indication of
a street system. After being unoccupied
for about 150 years, a second phase of
occupation, from 7220 to 5850 BCE,
was represented by rectilinear mud-
brick houses set on stone foundations.
These were organized around a central
clay-floored patio and consisted of several rooms with reddish pink terrazzo

A stone tower dating to ca. 8000 BCE set just inside the wall at Jericho,
is thirty feet tall and twenty-eight feet in diameter with an enclosed
stairway, a sign of the times, when villagers felt the need to construct
protective fortifications.

floors covered by reed mats. The largest room, about 20 by 12 feet, would have
been the primary living quarters, and the smaller rooms would have been used
for storage. No pottery was used, although several large plaster statues survive.
As at Çatal Hüyük, the dead were buried under the floors, but the grander houses
also suggest social stratification based on wealth.

Because the wall seems initially to have been erected before the extensive cultivation of plants began, it has been suggested that it was meant to protect trade
goods and only later was used to protect surplus food supplies. The residents
of Jericho exported salt and **bitumen,** a tarlike form of petroleum also called
pitch or asphalt, from the area of the Dead Sea. Bitumen was used as mortar
in building construction, as a waterproofing material for boats and containers,
as an adhesive for jewelry and pottery making, as a disinfectant or insecticide,
and as an embalming agent. Its flammable nature is consistent with the report
in the biblical book of Genesis that the cities of Sodom and Gomorrah, which
God destroyed with fire, were located in a valley "full of bitumen pits." Imports
into Jericho included obsidian, turquoise, and cowrie shells from Syria, the Sinai
Peninsula, and the Mediterranean for the manufacture of tools and ornaments.

*The Dead Sea was called
Lake Asphalites by the
Greeks because of the
lumps of bitumen that
washed ashore; this is
origin of the word asphalt.*

Social, Political, and Religious Institutions

Larger populations and permanent settlements brought with them the need to
have more sophisticated means of social and political organization. On a micro
level, the individual family unit seems to have attained greater importance.
Evidence suggests that certain religious rituals (such as burials) and the storage
and perhaps even the ownership of property, such as foodstuffs, devolved out
of the hands of the group as a whole and into the control of individual families.

In some places, single-family dwellings became more common, as opposed to communal private and public spaces.

At the macro level, on the other hand, methods for organizing large numbers of people for political, military, economic, and religious purposes also developed. It remains unclear exactly how Neolithic societies were governed. One school of thought argues that Neolithic societies were egalitarian, with property held in common and little sense of a need for the accumulation of wealth, and no evidence explicitly suggests that Neolithic societies functioned under any dominating class or individual. But other evidence for a growing differentiation in the size of residences suggests not only economic differentiation but also the development of a political hierarchy in which persons with greater political authority enjoyed a more grand existence.

Inextricably intertwined with concepts of social organization is the role of religion, for it is clear that at this period the organized performance of religious rituals could bring together large numbers of people. Neolithic societies clearly had some concept of life after death, as burials often were accompanied by grave goods ranging from personal ornaments, such as beads, pendants, bracelets, necklaces, and earrings, to foodstuffs. Some societies also seem to have practiced forms of ancestor worship that often involved the removal of the skulls of the deceased. In Natufian society, for example, skulls were decorated with shell beads, and at Jericho and Çatal Hüyük, skulls were covered in clay and painted with ochre. At Jericho, facial features were reconstructed from plaster and shells used to represent eyes, and in a burial at Çatal Hüyük a decorated skull was reinterred snuggled up to a later corpse.

Formal "mother goddess" cults arose. A "female principal" was based on the earth as the provider of crops and herds, whereas maleness was identified with the sky as the source of life-giving rain. The fertilizing aspect of maleness made its way into ritual with the appearance of phallic imagery. These two principles may have manifested themselves in forms of animal worship at Çatal Hüyük, for example, with use of feline and bull symbolism; a figure of woman sitting on a throne flanked by two lionesses is especially striking. The great prevalence of female **cult objects** in early Neolithic societies has led some to argue that Palaeolithic and Neolithic Europe was initially inhabited by peaceful peoples living in **matriarchal societies** characterized by mother-goddess worship.

Another form of social and political organization involved warfare. The need to protect local resources, commercial products, and agricultural produce led to the construction of defensive edifices at other places than Jericho and attest not only to a perceived need for defense against potential attackers but also the existence of sophisticated organizational and leadership skills. Toward the end of the Neolithic Period, in the fourth millenium BCE, fortifications of various sorts came to characterize Neolithic sites throughout the Old World, perhaps as a result of increasing conflicts over resources

THE LEGACY OF ANTIQUITY

The development of the Neolithic Age that had the greatest impact on the modern day was the introduction of agriculture. In what ways does agriculture continue to play an important role in modern society and the modern economy?

resulting from population increases. One northern European site was six acres in size and was protected by a two-thousand-yard ditch and timber palisade.

Fortifications were needed for protection against hostile forces, which must have had their own form of leadership and organization. These forces wielded an increasing array of weapons of war, including not only hunting tools, such as the sling and the bow and arrow, but also bashing tools, such as the mace, more specifically designed for use in human conflicts. The first clear evidence of warfare comes from an Egyptian site designated as "Cemetery 117," located on the Nile just on the Nubian side of the Egyptian border and dated to circa 11,740 BCE. Some twenty-five of the fifty-nine persons interred there—including men, women, and children—died of violent wounds, many being found with stone projectile points embedded in their heads and abdomens. Several were shot multiple times, some apparently execution-style in the neck. A Neolithic site in England also came under attack—hundreds of flint arrowheads were found in the entrances—and was burned and abandoned. Some have connected a rise in violence at this time to food shortages caused by the Younger Dryas drought.

THE CHALCOLITHIC PERIOD (5500–3000 BCE)

Technologically, the Neolithic Age was a dead end. Even when pressed to their limits by Neolithic peoples, stone tools were limited with regard to durability and functionality. The introduction of metal tools, even if initially very imperfect ones, meant that the days of the stone tool were numbered. The Late Neolithic Period brought several significant technological developments, including the widespread use of pottery by ca. 5500 BCE and the increasing use of metal implements, giving rise to the final period of the Stone Age, the "**Chalcolithic**," or "Copper-Stone," **Age**, also known simply as the "Copper Age." It once was thought that the use of copper began much earlier in the Near East than in Europe, but this now seems not to have been nearly so much the case. The Chalcolithic Age brought innovations ranging from pottery and weaving to fermenting and distilling. By the end of the Chalcolithic phase of the New Stone Age, human societies in the Near East had become sufficiently complex that they qualified to be what historians call civilizations.

Technological Innovations

The Chalcolithic Period brought technological changes that included not only an increase in the production and distribution of implements fashioned from smelted and native copper, but also, and even more significantly, by the widespread use of pottery. The origin of pottery, which seems to have occurred in the Near East, is something of a mystery. Experiments were undertaken to find more effective kinds of containers better than bitumen-sealed baskets. At Jericho, for example, coarse vessels made of fired lime plaster were used. The first attested use of sophisticated fired pottery is by the Yarmukian Culture of Israel ca. 5600–5000 BCE, where it appears as a fully developed technology. The sudden appearance of ceramic technology at different places in the Levant at the same time suggests that the technology was imported, probably from the north, and was not a local development. From the very beginning, coarser and finer wares were manufactured side by side. Some vessels were crude and lumpy, utilitarian, and probably made in village homes or by part-time potters, but others were clearly made by professionals: finely fashioned, polished, and decorated with red or yellow painted stripes, sometimes in a large, wide herringbone design. Other methods of decoration included applying red slips to entire vessels and incising decorations into the surface. Pottery initially was fired in pits, but the use of pottery kilns soon developed.

Different regions developed their own idiosyncratic styles, and aspects of pottery manufacture, such as shape, quality, and modes of decoration, are relatively reliable indicators of the chronological and cultural source of a piece of pottery. Indeed, chronologies based on pottery have become one of the primary means of dating ancient cultures. Virtually indestructible pottery pieces and sherds are the most ubiquitous artifact found on archaeological sites, and many archaeologists have spent their careers drawing up pottery taxonomies that allow pottery sherds found at different sites but representing the same cultural traditions to be dated with a reasonable degree of accuracy. A number of scientific methods for classifying and dating pottery also have developed. Trace element analysis, mostly by neutron activation, allows the sources of clay to be accurately identified; thermoluminescence, which involves the release of electrons trapped in higher energy levels by the firing process, provides an estimate of the date of firing; and traces of iron in the clay record the exact state of Earth's magnetic field at the moment of firing.

Earlier in the Stone Age, clothing had been made from animal skins held together by animal sinews and bone and antler pins. During the Chalcolithic Period, the large-scale spinning and weaving of sophisticated textiles emerged as another major activity. Instead of twisting animal or plant fibers into thread by hand, as occasionally had been done in the Old Stone Age, thread was pulled from the raw material and twisted onto a stick called a spindle attached to a rotating spindle whorl, a round perforated ceramic or stone piece that was used as a flywheel. The thread then was turned into fabric by one of two methods. In knitting, a continuous length of thread was repeatedly looped back on itself. In weaving, lengths of thread of equal length were interleaved in a criss-cross pattern on a loom, on which tension was kept on one set of threads, the warp threads, by loom weights. Thus archaeological sites that yield spindle whorls and loom weights must have been producing fabrics. Woven wool from Çatal Hüyük occurs as early as 5800 BCE, and the weaving of linen, using fibers from the flax plant, is attested ca. 5000 BC in Egypt and may have been done as early as ca. 7000 BCE in upper Mesopotamia. The improvements in weaving technology also brought the emergence of a dyeing industry for the production of many varieties of colored textiles.

Economic changes also resulted from new developments in tool-making technology. Stone-tool manufacture had peaked in the Neolithic Period with the introduction of polished stone technology. But the next change utilized entirely different raw materials—metals. For millennia, no doubt, people had been attracted by brightly colored stones and metal nuggets. Some metals, such as gold, occurred in a natural state and could be easily worked into beads and jewelry. Native copper, too, sometimes was found and beaten into jewelry in the early Neolithic Period and earlier. But other metals, such as silver and iron, only rarely occurred naturally. In addition, the attractive green and blue colors of copper ores such as malachite and azurite gave away their location. At some point, quite possibly by chance, it was discovered that these copper ores, heated to about 1400 degrees Fahrenheit, well below the actual melting point of copper, could be smelted to produce "sponge copper" that then could be beaten and hammered into pure copper. These temperatures already were accessible by 5000 BCE in pottery kilns, meaning that copper metallurgy by that time was within the reach of Neolithic societies. In addition, at a temperature of about 1980 degrees Fahrenheit, which could be reached in furnaces by the use of blowpipes to increase the oxygen supply, molten copper could be cast into any shape.

Copper ore, therefore, was mined as early as 5000 BCE in the Balkans using the same techniques that had been used for mining flint. Miners heated ore-bearing veins in hillsides with fires and then threw cold water on them, which caused them to crack sufficiently to be broken out by antler picks and stone mauls. Some veins were followed up to 60 feet into a hillside. The first items manufactured from copper seem to have been beads and other items of jewelry; only later were weapons and tools, such as axes and daggers, made, but even these might have been primarily ceremonial, for copper was so soft that stone tools and weapons would have continued to be more effective.

Social and Economic Developments

A necessary consequence of increasing technological development was greater specialization of labor, as these new technologies called for the development of specially trained personnel. At the same time, increases in wealth brought about by agricultural economies, accumulations of trade goods, and control over sources of metal and other products resulted in an increased need for social organization, aimed not only at defending what one had but also at taking what someone else had. In central Europe, between 5500 and 4500 BCE, representatives of the **Linear Pottery Culture**, whose pottery consisted of handleless cups, bowls, vases, and jugs, built villages composed of narrow windowless "long houses" made of timber, the largest freestanding structures in the world as of that time, about sixty feet long and twenty feet wide and housing twenty to thirty people. The far end was used for grain storage, the middle for eating and sleeping, and the end near the door for working, suggesting an egalitarian society based on families. Villages were defended by large concentric circular ditches and sometimes contained large burial mounds, indicating that some means of labor organization was in place. The need for such defenses is confirmed by evidence of Chalcolithic massacres at sites on the Rhine and in southern Germany and Austria dating to ca. 5000 BCE, where bodies with arrow wounds and skull trauma were found at the bottom of defensive ditches and in mass graves. This evidence for warfare and conflict contradicts models of Chalcolithic society involving peaceful coexistence.

The **Vinča Culture** of the lower Danube in the central Balkans, which followed on the Lepenski Vir Culture and flourished between the sixth and third millennia, provides a good example of a European Chalcolithic culture. The population kept domestic cattle, along with goats, sheep, and pigs, and cultivated einkorn and emmer wheat and barley. People lived in villages, usually located next to rivers, characterized by houses with several rooms built of mud-covered wood. Streets ran between the houses. People slept on woolen mats and furs and made clothing of wool, flax, and leather. Utensils and other objects were fashioned out of bones, horns, and stone. In addition, copper ore was mined in eastern Serbia and smelted using sophisticated furnaces as early as 5500 BCE to produce ornamental items such as bracelets and beads. Copper ore mined at Rudna Glavna in eastern Serbia is dated to 4500–3500 BCE based on Vinča pottery found in the shafts; cinnabar (a mercury compound used for coating ceramics) was mined at Šuplja Stena, twelve miles away. Imported items included salt, obsidian from the upper Tisza valley, and spondylus shells from the Aegean Sea. Ceramics of a high artistic and technological level were produced. Clay figurines depict women wearing jewelry and dressed in miniskirts and short tops. Some pots and other ceramic objects bear signs, known as Vinča signs, that some scholars suppose to be a form of protowriting (see "Mystery of the Vinča Signs"). Evidence for increasing social differentiation is seen in the evolution of housing styles from approximately equal-sized single-roomed family dwellings to the inclusion of some larger multiroomed buildings of more than five hundred square feet, with furniture such as benches and tables built into the walls.

The largest Balkan villages of this time exceeded in size even those of contemporary western Asia and Egypt. Some communities accumulated amounts of wealth worth both protecting and fighting for. The people of Varna (4600–4200), a Neolithic settlement on the Black Sea coast of Bulgaria, represented by nearly three hundred burials, exported salt from the Provadiya rock salt mine and copper items manufactured from ore mined in the Sredna Gora Mountains

THE MYSTERY OF THE VINČA SIGNS

Hundreds of objects from more than fifty sites representing the "Vinča Culture" (5500–3500 BCE) of the central Balkans bear combinations of scratched lines known as the "Vinča signs" (also known as "Old European Linear" or even "Old European Script"). A total of more than two hundred different signs have been found incised on pottery, spindle whorls and loom weights, figurines, and small tablets. The signs appear either singly or in groups of as many as eight to ten. Initially thought to have been influenced by Sumerian writing from Mesopotamia, it soon became clear that the Vinča signs predated Sumerian writing by thousands of years.

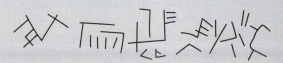

Examples of some of the more than two hundred attested Vinča signs.

One widely used set of signs was used almost exclusively on pottery. They often appear singly and may have been used to indicate the owner or maker of the pot, a hypothesis supported by the observation that many of these signs are unique, including complex pictograms such as stylized animal or human figures. The fact that there were so many different signs, however, would seem to disprove the suggestion that the signs indicate the contents of the pot. Some signs that appear on pot bases, such as a series of lines, dots, or chevrons, could represent numbers.

Figurines and tablets, on the other hand, often carry just two signs, and groups of multiple signs usually are found on spindle whorls and loom weights, in spite of the need to squeeze them into the small space available. Some signs occur only in sign clusters and never independently, suggesting the existence of a rudimentary syntax of sign usage. In addition, a third set of signs was used in all venues, either singly or in groups.

Because there are no actual texts written using the Vinča signs, they clearly do not represent a fully developed writing system. But the repetitious nature of some of them, coupled with the consistent ways in which they are used (such as the different sign sets) and their use over long periods of time and in many different places, makes it clear that the Vinča signs are more than merely decorative and must have had some kind of meaning associated with them that was shared by many communities over time and distance. And the reason for the development of these symbols quite possibly is to be sought in the increasing sophistication of the Neolithic economy, which made the development of some kind of record keeping increasingly necessary.

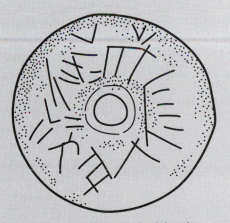

Vinča signs on a spindle whorl dated to ca. 5000–4500 BCE.

to the west. Gold was panned from rivers in the Carpathian and Sredna Gora mountains and used to manufacture the thousands of gold ornaments, ranging from beads to animal figures, unearthed at Varna and other central Balkan sites. Spondylus shells were imported from the Mediterranean.

At the end of the fourth millennium (ca. 3000 BCE) a new form of burial, under large mounds of earth called kurgans, became common across the northern part of southeastern Europe from the Lower Danube to the Carpathian Basin. These burials have earlier parallels in the east, in Moldova and the Ukraine, and some scholars have associated them with the first arrivals of Indo-European speakers in Europe.

Megalithic Europe

Southern, western, and northern Europe exhibited their own shared charactistic cultural traits during the Neolithic Period between 4500 and 1500 BCE. In particular, these areas were the homes of Neolithic societies that produced large stone monuments known as **megaliths** (from Greek for "big stone"). Megaliths occured in several types. Menhirs were standing stones, sometimes set up in rows, as at Carnac in Brittany, where some three thousand menhirs were erected ca. 3300 BCE, and sometimes organized in circles, as at Stonehenge in southern Britain, where ca. 2500 BCE lintels were placed atop menhirs weighing up to fifty tons to create simple archways. The standing stones sometimes had astronomical significance, being aligned, for example, with the summer and winter solstices. These alignments could have been used to mark the agricultural calendar and might also have provided the opportunity for religious festivals. Other megalithic constructions served as burial sites. A dolmen was a chamber made from three upright orthostats (standing stones) and a capstone that were covered with earth; in "passage graves," the chamber was accessed by a long straight passageway; and in "gallery graves," the passage and chamber were combined to form rectangular barrows. The great effort expended on the construction of megalithic tombs attests to the great ritual significance attached to the burial of particular individuals.

The erection of huge megaliths also exemplifies the Late Neolithic ability to organize society and mobilize large numbers of individuals, although it remains unclear just who was responsible for doing so. Some of the menhirs at Stonehenge, for example, were transported from 250 miles away. The extent of the **Megalithic Culture** indicates the existence of a common culture and shared values that extended throughout much of Europe. The international nature of megalithic society is exemplified, for example, by the grave near Stonehenge, dated to ca. 2500 BCE, of a middle-aged man known as "the Amesbury archer," whose tooth enamel identified him as a native of the Swiss-German Alps (roughly the same area, coincidentally, from which Otzi the "Ice Man" came at a rather earlier date). The foreigner was buried with stone, copper, and gold artifacts. The international aspect of the Megalithic Culture also is demonstrated in the use of artistic motifs carved into the

The construction of Stonehenge, a megalithic site in England, would have required the sophisticated organization of massive amounts of labor.

monuments, most extensively spirals but also lozenges, zig-zags, and "cup-and-ring" marks. These symbols appear consistently throughout western Europe and attest to the existence of some sort of commonly understood symbolic, ritual iconography.

The Neolithic Period lasted for five thousand years, a length of time equal to our entire civilized history from 3000 BCE to the present. During this period, humans experienced a great deal of social, political, religious, cultural, and technical evolution. The Neolithic Period in Europe, western Asia, and northern Africa was a world in its own right, complete with settled lifestyles, human control over food supplies, and long-distance communications. Towns of several thousands of persons arose. Pottery, weaving, metallurgy, methods of food preparation and preservation, painting, and other art forms all became common. Trade routes that extended throughout the European, western Asian, and North African worlds resulted in the exchange of goods, including obsidian, copper, and seashells. Social organization capable of mobilizing large numbers of persons for the creation of great stone monuments developed. Sophisticated religious concepts, including concepts of life after death, developed. As of the Late Neolithic Period, Europe was the primary center of social and technological development, and by the Chalcolithic Period, nearly all the trappings of what we call "civilization" already existed in many places. In fact, a modern person transported in time back to a thriving Neolithic town would believe him or herself to have arrived in a place not much different from some places in the modern world.

> **THOUGHT QUESTION**
>
> According to most modern definitions, a society must make use of writing to qualify as a "civilization." Do you think that the complex Neolithic, Chalcolithic, and Megalithic societies discussed here qualify as "civilizations" even though they did not have writing?

OTZI THE "ICE MAN"

In 1991, two hikers in a glacier in the Ötztal Alps on the Austria-Italy border came upon a mummified body protruding from the ice. Thought to be a modern corpse, the body was removed with a jackhammer while tourists made off with some of the clothing and tools associated with it. Only after the body had been scientifically analyzed was it discovered that the body dated to the fourth millenium BCE. A dispute over ownership was resolved when the discovery point was established to be just over one hundred yards inside Italy. Since that time, Otzi, as the "Ice Man" was nicknamed after the location at which he was found, has been housed in Bolzano, Italy, and has been examined extensively by scientific means. A wealth of information has been gleaned about what his life during the Late Neolithic Period was like.

Otzi was about five feet five inches tall and weighed about 110 pounds. Tooth enamel analysis shows that he grew up about thirty miles south of where he was found. His last meal consisted of venison and bread made from einkorn wheat.

He wore a cloak made of woven grass; a coat, leggings, and a loincloth, all made of leather strips; wide waterproof shoes made of bearskin and deer hide good for hiking on snow; a bearskin cap; and a belt with a pouch holding a scraper, drill, and awl (the ancient equivalent of a Swiss army knife). Otzi also carried a fire-making kit consisting of flint and pyrite for making sparks and several kinds of dried fungus for tinder. For hunting and protection, Otzi carried

A reconstructed image of Otzi depicts him dressed and equipped as he was at the time of his death.

LOOKING AHEAD

No matter how complex Late Neolithic cultures became, they still do not qualify as civilizations, for they lacked one of the most important criteria that define a civilization and also history: writing. For the purposes of this volume, the first experiments in civilization would occur in the river valleys of Mesopotamia and Egypt, and as the centuries and millennia progressed, greater and greater numbers of the peoples of the western Asian, Mediterranean, and European worlds would adopt civilized lifestyles, creating a culture that would extend from Nubia to the Rhine and from Scotland to India.

Otzi's copper axe fit neatly into a haft, here reconstructed, made of tough yew wood.

a flint knife with an ash handle and an unfinished yew longbow, accompanied by a quiver holding fourteen arrows, two of which were tipped with flint points. He also carried a valuable copper axe, and analysis of his hair shows a high level of copper and arsenic (which was alloyed with copper to make bronze), suggesting he might have been involved in metalwork. But analysis of his pelvis and leg bones indicates a lot of walking over steep terrain, which suggests life as a shepherd. Otzi also had no less than fifty-seven tattoos made from soot centered on his left knee, right ankle, and spine, which could be from a form of acupuncture given that X rays indicate arthritis in these joints.

A number of theories have been advanced about how Otzi died, ranging from being caught in a storm to being a victim of ritual human sacrifice. But scientific investigation revealed an arrow point in his shoulder, and it therefore was suggested that he bled to death. Additional investigation, however, demonstrated not only that the arrow's shaft had been removed but also that Otzi had suffered trauma to his head, wrists, and chest, suggesting a fall, if not something more dramatic, such as being bludgeoned to death. Equally imaginative is the suggestion, based on Otzi's possession of a copper axe, that he was part of a raiding party that came to a bad end. And even more so is the discovery of genetic indicators of reduced fertility, leading to hypotheses that he might have been ostracized by his own people (although this seems unlikely given that, historically, women have almost always borne the blame for infertility). Be that as it may, there is no doubt that study of Otzi will continue, as will the number of theories about how he lived and died.

FURTHER READING

Bailey, Douglass W. *Balkan Prehistory: Exclusion, Incorporation and Identity.* London: Routledge, 2000.

Bar-Yosef, Ofer, and Francois R. Valla, eds. *The Natufian Culture in the Levant.* Ann Arbor: University of Michigan Press, 1992.

Barber, Elisabeth J. W. *Prehistoric Textiles: The Development of Cloth in the Neolithic and Bronze Ages with Special Reference to the Aegean.* Princeton, NJ: Princeton University Press, 1991.

Barnett, William, and John Hoopes, eds. *The Emergence of Pottery.* Washington, DC: Smithsonian Institution Press, 1995.

Bonsall, Clive, ed. *The Mesolithic in Europe: Papers Presented at the Third International Symposium, Edinburgh, 1985.* Edinburgh, UK: John Donald, 1989.

Burgess, Colin, et al. *Enclosures and Defences in the Neolithic of Western Europe*, 2 pts. Oxford: Oxford University Press, 1988.

Cappers, R. T. J., and S. Bottema, eds. *Dawn of Farming in the Near East.* Berlin: Ex Oriente, 2002.

Curtis, Gregory. *The Cave Painters: Probing the Mysteries of the World's First Artists.* New York: Knopf, 2006.

Drews, Robert. *The Coming of the Greeks: Indo-European Conquests in the Aegean and the Near East.* Princeton, NJ: Princeton University Press, 1989.

Gimbutas, Marija. *The Goddesses and Gods of Old Europe, 6500–3500 BC: Myths and Cult Images*, 2nd ed. Berkeley: University of California Press, 1996.

Hodder, Ian. *The Leopard's Tale: Revealing the Mysteries of Çatalhöyük.* London and New York: Thames & Hudson, 2006.

Price, T. Douglas, ed. *Europe's First Farmers.* Cambridge: Cambridge University Press, 2000.

Simmons, Alan H. *The Neolithic Revolution in the Near East: Transforming the Human Landscape.* Tucson: University of Arizona Press, 2007.

Srejovic, Dragoslav. *Europe's First Monumental Sculpture: New Discoveries at Lepenski Vir.* New York: Stein and Day, 1972.

Stanford, Dennis, and Bruce Bradley, "The North Atlantic Ice-Edge Corridor: A Possible Palaeolithic Route to the New World." *World Archaeology* 36, no. 4 (2004): 459–78.

Winn, S. *Pre-writing signs in Southeastern Europe: The Sign System of the Vinca Culture ca 4000 BC.* Calgary, Alberta, Canada: Western, 1981.

Whittle, A. W. R. *Europe in the Neolithic: The Creation of New Worlds.* Cambridge: Cambridge University Press, 1996.

THE CRADLE OF CIVILIZATION

CHAPTER 2

MESOPOTAMIA AND THE BRONZE AGE
(6000–1200 BCE)

By the sixth millennium BCE, a high level of social, political, and technological culture based on an agricultural economy already existed in many places in Europe, western Asia, and North Africa. An agricultural economy permitted people to live in permanent villages and towns constructed from mud brick, stone, timber, and other materials. The amount of food produced could be expanded by bringing additional land under cultivation, and agricultural foodstuffs could be stored to provide a dependable food supply. Larger populations and the ability to remain in one place encouraged specialization of labor, with different people serving as potters, carpenters, basket makers, traders, and shepherds, not to mention fighters to protect the food surpluses and luxury items stored in the villages.

But, as in the case of the culture of the Old Stone Age, the economic and technological developments of the Neolithic and Chalcolithic periods eventually expanded to the point where there was no further room to expand based on contemporary social and technological levels of development. All of the geographical regions and economic niches suitable for this kind of society became occupied, even relatively marginal areas with little rainfall. Thus, if different kinds of societies and economies were going to develop, it probably would happen somewhere else. And this is exactly what happened. The next significant social, economic, and cultural developments occurred in large Near Eastern river valleys, in Mesopotamia (modern Iraq, eastern Syria, and eastern Turkey) and Egypt, where huge tracts of rich alluvial soil were available for cultivation in the deltas at the mouths of the rivers. The problem that initially kept this soil from being exploited, however, was that these areas were very marshy, were subject to severe flooding from upstream, and had very little rainfall. Thus, before the soil could be cultivated, the marshes had to be drained, flood control systems had to be created, and elaborate irrigation systems had to be established. These endeavors required the organization and

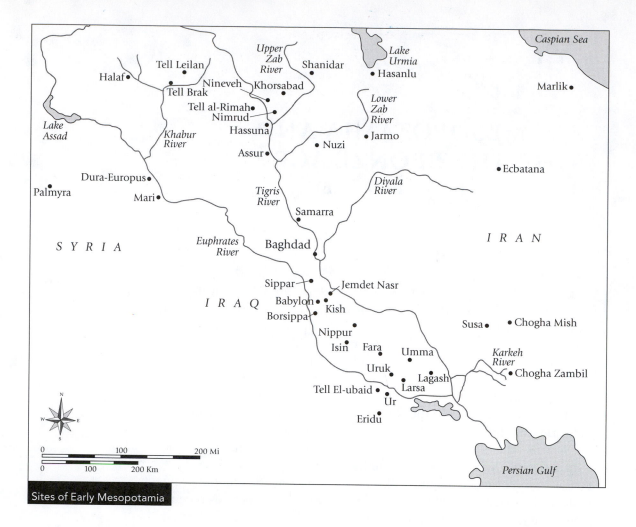

Sites of Early Mesopotamia

mobilization of huge amounts of human labor (much more, for example, than used to build Stonehenge), something not available to most Neolithic and Chalcolithic societies.

THE ORIGINS OF MESOPOTAMIAN CIVILIZATION (6000–3000 BCE)

Beginning around 6000 BCE, a series of agriculturally based cultures arose in Mesopotamia, first in the upper river valleys and then in the lower. Over the course of the next 3,000 years, cultural evolution occurred based on the special geographical conditions of these areas. By approximately 3000 BCE a particular kind of culture known as "civilization" had developed, first manifested by a people now known as the Sumerians.

The Settlement of Mesopotamia

As they initially arose, the agricultural cultures of Mesopotamia, primarily in upper Mesopotamia, developed along the same lines as Neolithic and Chalcolithic cultures in other areas of the Near Eastern and Mediterranean worlds. Toward the end of the seventh millennium BCE, for example, the first attested farming communities in upper Mesopotamia were established on the upper **Tigris River** in the neighborhood of Hassuna, which gave its name to the **Hassuna Culture** (ca. 6000–5250 BCE). The presence of sickles, grain storage bins, ovens, and grinding stones indicates a settled agricultural lifestyle in a region with very little annual rainfall. Villages of several hundred people contained adobe (a mixture of clay and straw) houses built around a central courtyard. The Hassuna people produced a distinctive pottery, with reddish linear designs painted on a light background, that replaced the coarser earlier ceramics.

In order to cope with as little as ten inches of rainfall per year and lacking the resources to undertake massive irrigation, the people used an agricultural technique now called dryland farming, which involves practices such as "fallow rotation," in which one crop takes two seasons to grow; contour plowing to reduce water runoff; and leaving crop residue or laying out straw to retain water. Lower yielding but drought- and heat-resistant crop varieties were planted, and dry farmers had to be prepared to endure one or more years of crop failure. The expansion of agriculture into these kinds of marginal areas indicates the pressure that there must have been to find land, any land, that was suitable for farming.

Another site, Tel Halaf, on a tributary of the **Euphrates River** in far upper Mesopotamia, gave its name to the Halaf Culture (ca. 6100–5400 BCE), which overlapped the end of the Hassuna Culture. The Halaf Culture is best known for its pottery, known as Halaf ware, a hard-glazed polychrome (multicolored) pottery fired at a high temperature bearing mostly geometric designs. Seal stamps pressed into wet clay may have served to identify private property. A number of theories have been proposed, ranging from gifts for elite persons to use as trade goods, for why this fine pottery developed at a time when perfectly serviceable locally made painted pots already were widely available. Public buildings consisted of circular chambers know as *tholoi* that were approached through long rectangular entrance halls. Circular houses were built of mud brick or mud-plastered reeds. Lacking the resources to develop irrigation, the people of Tel Halaf likewise used dryland farming to grow emmer wheat, barley, and flax.

Beginning circa 6000 BCE, the culture of Mesopotamia began to differentiate itself from other Neolithic and Chalcolithic cultures as major settlements, representing new cultures, moved further downriver. A large site developed at Samarra, on the Tigris River just north of modern Baghdad,

A typical example of Ubaid geometric pottery dated to the late fifth millennium BCE.

giving rise to the **Samarra Culture** (ca. 6000–4800 BCE). Evidence of irrigation suggests how the large population was put to work, and the characteristic pottery, with geometric designs and stylized birds and animals against a dark background, was widely traded and became a standardized pottery style throughout Mesopotamia. Samarran architecture is noteworthy for the introduction of loaf-shaped rectangular mud bricks, approximately 60 cm. long and 15 cm. wide and made from molds, which permitted the construction of more homogeneous buildings. Some Samarran towns also were protected by defensive walls, indicating that there were threats from somewhere.

It also should be noted that for this period of history, any speculation about ethnicity has to be based on the material culture left behind, and it often has been suggested that people who shared the same kinds of material culture also shared the same ethnic identity. But this need not be the case. Evidence from later periods of history demonstrates that it is quite possible for people from different ethnic backgrounds to adopt elements of the same culture. Therefore, when speaking of cultures in the preliterate period of the human past, we always must bear in mind that people sharing the same culture need not necessarily have shared the same history, had the same ethnic identity, or spoken the same language. And with that in mind, it is certainly impossible to identify any of these peoples as the direct biological ancestors of any of the modern-day people who happen to live in the same place.

The Ubaid Culture

The earliest attested settlement of the alluvial plain of lower Mesopotamia was discovered at the site of al-Ubaid, which gives its name to the **Ubaid Culture** (ca.5400–4000 BCE). The same culture was identified at the ancient city of Eridu, whose great antiquity was attested in later Sumerian legends, in which Adapa, the mythological first man (parallel to Adam of the biblical book of Genesis), and the first Sumerian kings came from Eridu. The Ubaid Culture, which initially was derived from the Samarra Culture to the northwest, was represented by large villages with rectangular multiroom mud-brick houses. Ubaid pottery included greenish-colored fine ware with geometric designs in brown or black paint. Because of the lack of stone, tools such as sickles often were made of fired clay. There was less than five inches of rain per year, and what there was fell mostly during the winter; the hot summer sun left the soil completely dry, and large-scale agriculture based on rainfall was impossible. Farming was initially aided by water drawn from the high water table, but this could not be a large-scale solution.

Burial evidence, with richer deposits in some graves, suggests that there was increasing social differentiation, which also is suggested by the appearance of forms of wealth that included jewelry made from precious stones such as lapis lazuli. It is unclear, however, whether the elite were political chieftains, a priestly class, successful farmers, heads of families, or something else. These elites must have been involved in the supplying and coordinating of the labor needed for the first irrigation projects—extensive networks of irrigation ditches—in lower Mesopotamia, initially attested ca. 4700 BCE, with canals running several miles to the Euphrates River. Flood control was effected with dikes and dams creating artificial ponds for water storage.

The rich delta soil was so productive that a population explosion resulted, and the latter part of the fifth millennium BCE brought intensifying urbanization. Eridu, for example, had about four thousand inhabitants. Between 4500 and 4000 BCE, the Ubaid Culture spread peacefully into northern Mesopotamia, where it replaced the Samarra and Halaf Cultures. In lower Mesopotamia, the Ubaid Culture is represented at a number of urban sites, all of which were located on the rivers and near the Persian Gulf coast.

Changes in the courses of the rivers and the receding coastline have put Sumerian sites far from the water in the modern day.

The Ubaid period also provides the first examples of large public temples. As early as the middle of the fifth millennium, Eridu had a central shrine, built of mud brick with a plastered floor and probably plastered and painted walls. Subsequently, the shrine was enlarged multiple times by building larger temples on top of the earlier ones, often with tripartite (three-roomed) plans. By the end of the Ubaid period, the temple measured forty by seventy-five feet. In the main room was an altar for offerings, but the image of the god probably was kept in a sacred recess and brought out only for special rituals. Numerous offerings of fish are consistent with the attested devotion of Eridu to Enki, the water god.

The great antiquity of the Eridu temple has led to suggestions that it might have been the original "Tower of Babel" of Jewish and Christian scripture.

Finally, it also must be noted that large-scale urbanization had some inherent problems. For one thing, extreme emphasis on grain production could lead to unbalanced diets. In addition, large populations living in close proximity without adequate means of waste disposal brought increased susceptibility to communicable diseases such as tuberculosis, smallpox, malaria, and plague. Communities with food surpluses were liable to be raided by pastoralists short of food. Farmers also destroyed the environment. On land that had been deforested for agriculture, the soil could be blown away. And fertilization with human and animal waste, watering with brackish irrigation water from storage ponds, and the rise of a saline water table contributed to the gradual **salinization** of the soil as the water evaporated and left salts behind, resulting in decreased crop yields. In lower Mesopotamia, the encroachment of sand dunes also could make agriculture more difficult. But it is clear that Mesopotamian civilization developed in spite of these difficulties as the resourceful population learned to deal with them.

The American "dust bowl" of the 1930s demonstrated how unprotected, overfarmed soil could just be blown away.

THE ROLE OF CLIMATE AND ECOLOGY IN HISTORY

A popular activity of historians and nonhistorians alike long has been to try to associate historical developments with changes in the climate and ecology of different regions. Historical models known as "climate determinism" and "ecological theory" attempt to relate historical developments to changes in the natural environment, which have been seen as influencing both the rise and fall of civilizations. In Mesopotamia, for example, it has been suggested that cool and dry conditions led to the beginning of civilization ca. 3000 BCE and that a hot and dry period around 500 BCE led to the decline of Mesopotamian civilization. In between, various other ecological conditions, such as deforestation, soil exhaustion, overpopulation, and even man-made climate change, have been adduced to explain nearly every major social, economic, and political change.

But complex models that hypothesize long-term and far-reaching effects of climate and ecology on history have problems. One is that, so far, no one quite agrees as to just when the cooler, warmer, drier, or more humid periods were. One model has the Sahara as drying out in the fourth millenium BCE and leading to an influx of population into the Nile River valley, whereas another has the Sahara as being "much more humid" at the same time. Another problem is misconceptions about the results of climate change on certain kinds of economies. For example, it has been suggested that lessened rainfall brought an economic decline in lower Mesopotamia because this area was "particularly vulnerable to lower rainfall amounts"; but given that all of the crops were irrigated, the economy in fact would have been quite insensitive to the amount of rainfall, which never was sufficient for extensive farming in the first place. In a like manner, overgrazing and deforestation are blamed for the decline of societies that already had altered their economies to cope with just these issues—for example, by planting salt-tolerant barley instead of wheat when the soil became salinated.

Another problem is that these theories often are proposed by persons with excellent credentials in other fields of study but who are not specialists in antiquity. As a consequence, they tend to underrate the degree to which ancient societies were able to deal with problems confronting them or to determine their own destinies. For example, nonspecialists make the mistake of assuming that climate variations caused civilization to appear quite suddenly around 3000 BCE, when in reality all of the important components under discussion—that is, irrigation and food production methods—had been in place for over a thousand years. It was the development of other factors not so clearly related to climate, such as writing, metallurgy, and potter's wheels, that resulted in these cultures being defined in the modern day as "civilizations." In addition, the peoples of antiquity were quite capable of recovering from disasters and of responding to changes in very imaginative ways. Thus it will be seen, for example, that the movement of the centers of culture and civilization increasingly toward the west was part of a long process of human economic and social development, not simply the result of a a hot and dry period around 500 BCE, as climate determinists contend.

Which is not to say, of course, that nature had no effect on human societies. Long-term droughts certainly could cause people to migrate, seeking new food sources. Some kinds of short-term variations in the natural environment, such as failures of the Nile River to flood, had clear consequences for agricultural productivity. And it may well be that increasing pressure on resources in Mesopotamia did lead to a consolidation of urban areas into larger centers and an increase in warfare, in a manner analogous to what would happen in the early Archaic Age of ancient Greece. But it is dangerous to be too prescriptive in assigning a particular historical event to climatic or ecological changes; climate change did not lead to the creation of intensive irrigation systems, much less to "civilization." And, in general, it also is always dangerous to argue "post hoc propter hoc," that is, that just because something happened after something else, it must have happened because of that something else.

The Uruk Period

The next period of early Mesopotamian cultural development, characterized by the city of **Uruk** (also known as Erech in the Bible or Warka in Arabic), lasted from 4000 to 2900 BCE and brought further social, administrative, and technological developments meant to meet the changing needs of the expanding cities. Cities centered on large temples grew to over ten thousand inhabitants. They had centralized administrations—perhaps overseen by a **priest-king** who combined the duties of king and chief priest—that included both men and women and used legions of specialized workers. Long-distance trade extended the economic reach of the lower Mesopotamian cities to as far away as Anatolia and Iran; trade in Uruk, for example, was facilitated by a system of canals penetrating right into the city.

The increasing concentration of population, specialization of labor, and wealth in the river valleys during the Uruk Period brought further economic and technological developments. By ca. 3500 BCE, a precursor of writing appeared, consisting of **pictograms**—pictures of the actual objects being referred to—scratched on a clay surface with a pointed reed stylus. At the same time, cylinder seals with designs incised on them were rolled over wet clay to indicate ownership of property.

The "Uruk vase," made from alabaster, just over three feet tall and dated to just before 3000 BCE, was found in the temple of Inanna in Uruk and is one of the earliest surviving narrative sculptures, that is, one that tells a story. The bottom register shows a procession of animals above fields of grain and reeds alongside the river, the second shows naked men carrying bowls of sacrificial offerings, and the top shows the offerings being presented to the goddess Inanna. The vase was looted from the Iraq National Museum during the U.S. invasion in 2003 and returned the next year.

Uruk seems to have exercised a sort of political hegemony over many of the cities of lower Mesopotamia. Perhaps as a sign of the city's authority, a massive raised platform known as a **ziggurat** and topped by a temple in honor of the creator god An was repeatedly expanded in seven phases of construction, culminating around 3000 BCE with a sixty-foot-long tripartite temple, covered in brilliant gypsum plaster, known as the "White House" that rose seventy feet off the ground and could be seen from miles away across the flat plain. The city also was graced by four temples of the fertility goddess Inanna/Ishtar. By 2900 BCE, Uruk had as many as fifty thousand inhabitants and was the largest city in the world.

It also was around this time that the potter's wheel appeared in Mesopotamia. In the past, pots had been made by laboriously piling up coils of clay, beating the coils flat, and then shaping the stationary pot by hand, a process that

TABLE 2.1   CHRONOLOGICAL OVERVIEW OF BRONZE AGE MESOPOTAMIA

Designation	Location	Date (BCE)
Hassuna Culture	Upper Tigris River	6000–5250
Halaf Culture	Upper Euphrates River	6100–4500
Samarra Culture	Middle Tigris River	6000–4800
Ubaid Culture	Lower Euphrates	5400–4000
Uruk Culture	Lower Euphrates	4000–2900

not only was very time-consuming but also resulted in irregularities of shape no matter how careful the potter was. With wheel-thrown pottery, the rough portion of clay sat in the middle of a very heavy horizontal clay disk that spun on a bearing and continued to rotate under its own inertia. The clay was shaped, both inside and outside, as the wheel spun. The wheel not only allowed ceramic vessels to be created much more quickly but, in the manner of a lathe, also permitted surface irregularities to be smoothed out, resulting in much more regularly shaped products. The potter's wheel thus became one of the first attested mechanical labor-saving devices. And the concepts implicit in the potter's wheel led to an even more important technological revolution: wheeled vehicles.

In addition, by means that still are unclear, metal smiths discovered that copper combined with small amounts of certain other elements created an alloy, **bronze**, that not only had a melting point—around 1922° F—less than that of copper but also was much harder and could be used for tools or, more commonly, weapons. The first form of bronze, made from about 95% copper and 5% arsenic—the ore for which is fairly common in the Near East—appeared about 3500 BCE. Subsequently, however, because of nerve damage caused by overexposure to arsenic, smiths turned to manufacturing bronze from about 90% copper and 10% tin, which created a stronger alloy that was easier to cast. Tin, however, was much less common in the Near East and had to be imported from mining sites not only in southern Anatolia, where hundreds of thousands of tons of tin-smelting slag have been found, but also from as far away as the British Isles. By about 2500 BCE, the copper-tin combination had become the norm.

The effects of arsenic poisoning may explain why Hephaestus, the Greek god of smiths, was lame.

Bronze Age Civilization

Around 3000 BCE, the sum total of the cultural, social, economic, religious, and technological developments that had occurred during the Neolithic and Chalcolithic periods led to a new form of culture called "**civilization**." Historians define an Old World civilization as a society that manifests certain characteristics. Its economy must be based on agriculture. It must exhibit specialization of labor and social differentiation. It must have cities that are used as administrative and, usually, population centers. It must have a well-developed technology, usually based on the use of metal. And it must have a system of writing used for record keeping. As of 3000 BCE, civilizations meeting these criteria developed in four areas of the world: Mesopotamia, Egypt, India, and China. This book is primarily concerned with Mesopotamia and Egypt, and this chapter focuses on Mesopotamia.

With the exception of metal technology, New World civilizations, such as the Mayan civilization, exhibited the same traits as Old World ones.

Because of the importance of metal technology as a determinant of civilization and because bronze was the metal most commonly used for items such as weapons and jewelry, this first phase of civilization is called the "**Bronze Age.**" But the Bronze Age also is defined by other characteristics. The most representative Bronze Age cultures were based on extensive exploitation of agriculture. They had large populations. And they were located in rich river valleys—the Tigris and Euphrates rivers in Mesopotamia, the Nile River in Egypt, the Indus River in India, and the Yellow (Huang He) River in China. This means that during the Bronze Age, only a very small part of the Earth as a whole was the home to civilizations. This was the case not only because these regions had the richest soil and easiest access to water but also because bronze was too expensive to use for agricultural implements, and intensive agriculture required soils that could be tilled by a simple wooden ard, or scratch plow.

Civilized institutions were not limited only to the river valleys, for over the course of the centuries many of the practices that arose in the river valleys were assimilated by peoples hundreds and thousands of miles away. Nor were peoples who did not live in the "civilized" areas necessarily less culturally sophisticated than the river valley people. Civilized institutions arose as a result of the need to have them. Writing, for example, developed only when administrative and economic demands created a compelling need for massive record keeping. In addition, at the same time that new concepts were spreading outward from the civilized regions, other ideas from agricultural and pastoral peoples living outside the civilized areas were flowing into the river valleys. The result was the gradual creation of a global culture that continues to bring people together in the modern day.

THE RISE OF SUMERIAN CIVILIZATION

Mesopotamian civilization began in **Sumer** (or Sumeria), the rich agricultural land of the lower Tigris and Euphrates river valleys, roughly from just south of Baghdad to the Persian Gulf, which then, moreover, was over a hundred miles further upstream. The name Sumerians, however, was a name used by later inhabitants of the region; the people who lived there at the time referred to themselves simply as "the black-headed people." Sumerian civilization was based on large independent cities heavily focused on agriculture. Life in Sumerian cities revolved around religion; the gods were believed to be the actual rulers of the cities, and by far the largest building was a huge step pyramid known as a ziggurat.

The Origin of the Sumerians

One of the unsolved mysteries surrounding the development of Sumerian civilization is just who the Sumerians were and where they came from. Neither historical records nor myths and legends help to answer this question. On the one hand, the indigenous languages of Mesopotamia were **Semitic** languages used by persons who might originally have emigrated from Arabia and who lived both as pastoralists in the desert fringes of Mesopotamia and as farmers in the river valleys, especially upriver from Sumer, as at Kish. But the Sumerian language is otherwise unknown and bears no linguistic connection to the Semitic languages, which could suggest that the original Sumerians came from somewhere else and overlaid themselves on the existing populations. If so, this did not occur before non-Sumerian words dealing with issues such as specialized occupations (such as *carpenter* or *priest*), agriculture (such as *furrow* or *plow*), and metal use (such as *coppersmith*) already had appeared and been absorbed into Sumerian.

But the linguistic diversity also could be explained by early archaeological remains hinting that, rather than being a single people who occupied lower Mesopotamia, the Sumerians actually were an amalgamation of three different groups of peoples: immigrants from upstream Mesopotamia, who brought with them agricultural experience; pastoralists with herds of sheep and goats from the desert fringe; and hunter-fishers from the Arabian coast, who were the original inhabitants of the region. In addition, the clear cultural continuity of Sumerian culture with practices that had evolved in lower Mesopotamia over the previous three thousand years also suggests that Sumerian culture was an indigenous development.

The Sumerian Mindset

Even though the Bronze Age civilizations in different parts of the world had the same general characteristics, they also had many individual differences as a result of varying geographical conditions and philosophical outlooks. Thus, in order to understand the mentality of not only the Sumerians but also all Mesopotamians, it is necessary to understand their geographical surroundings. Mesopotamia was a wide, flat plain with no natural defenses; to the east was the Persian Gulf, to the north lay the Zagros Mountains of western Iran, and to the south and west was the Syrian-Arabian desert, an area that received enough rainfall to be able to support pastoralist populations. Life in Sumer revolved around the Tigris and Euphrates rivers, both of which run southeast from eastern Anatolia to the Persian Gulf. The Tigris, whose name has been traced to a Persian word meaning "like an arrow," flows quickly through deep banks, and the upper reaches are not navigable. The Euphrates, on the other hand, whose name may come from a word meaning "fruitful," has lower, wider banks, flows more slowly, and can be navigated far upriver. The name Mesopotamia thus unsurprisingly came from Greek words meaning "between the rivers."

Although lower Mesopotamia itself received very little rainfall, the upper reaches of the rivers were subject to very heavy rain, which could pour down the rivers and flood the cities downstream without any warning; a Mesopotamian curse called for "flood waters surging down on an enemy land." In addition, Mesopotamians never knew when they would be raided by mountain dwellers from the north or desert peoples from the south. As a result, life in Mesopotamia was insecure and full of uncertainties, and the Sumerians adopted a primarily pessimistic outlook on life. For example, an account known as "The Lament for Nippur" moaned, "For how long would Enlil neglect the Land? Tears, lamentation, depression and despair! How long would his heart not be placated? Why were those who once played the drums spending their time in bitter lamenting? They were bewailing the hardship that beset them."

Sumerian pessimism was reflected in their views of their gods, whom they believed were not particularly concerned with people. The Sumerians had little confidence that the gods, who after all were the ones who brought so many insecurities on them, were going to be effective managers, impose order on the world, or look out for their interests. The Sumerians thus attempted to organize their world to make it as secure as possible. They even attempted to impose their own system of control on the gods. For example, in order to ensure that the gods were always looking over them, individual Sumerians placed small votive statues of themselves in the temples. The Sumerians attempted

Placing an expensive stone votive statue that represented oneself in a god's temple ensured that the god would be looking after one. Men with shaved heads were priests, whereas those with beards were administrators and soldiers. The wide-eyed expression is typical of those who were in the presence of a god.

to get some idea of what the gods were thinking by using **divination**, the mystical interpretation of phenomena ranging from dreams to animal entrails to wisps of smoke. And the Sumerians also attempted to compel the gods to do their bidding by using magical charms, for example, to try to cure illness.

In addition, the most important gods in the Sumerian **pantheon** (from the Greek for "all the gods") were assigned numbers that were proportional to their relative status. An, the father of the gods, was the god of the universe. His symbol was a star. An lived out among the stars and was generally unconcerned with what happened on earth. He was assigned the number 60, the fundamental basis of the Sumerian **hexagesimal** ("relating to the number 60") number **system**. An established **Enlil** and Enki as rulers of earth. Enlil, god of the air, was a sky and storm god who controlled lightning and thunder. He was considered by the Sumerians to be the most important god to be directly concerned with the earth and was assigned the number 50. Enki, the water god, was given the number 40. Nanna, the moon god, was number 30, and **Utu**, the sun god, got the number 20. Inanna, the goddess of fertility, received the number 15 and was second only to Enlil in popularity. The consorts (spouses) of the primary gods also were assigned numbers— for example, Ki, consort of An, was 55; Ninlil, consort of Enlil, was 45; and Ninmah, consort of Enki, was 35.

The Sumerians' negativity also was reflected in their views of the afterlife. If life in this world brought misery, the life after death was even worse. Only gods had a pleasurable immortality; anything deceased humans could expect was very unpalatable. The "Land of No Return," as the underworld was called, was ruled by the goddess Ereshkigal and her partner Nergal, the god of war. The dead were buried with grave offerings, but these were seized by demons. Those admitted to the underworld wore feathers, ate clay and dust, and spent eternity weeping over their fate. The Sumerians also believed that one's ghost remained with one's bones after death. It thus was possible to gain vengeance on enemies after death by disrespecting their bones and hence bringing pain to their ghosts. In either regard, the most that one could expect after death was only to be a pale shadow of one's former self.

HISTORICAL CAUSALITY

In what way did their geographical circumstances result in the development of a pessimistic mindset by the Sumerians?

Sumerians dreamed of being able to escape being sent to the underworld by finding immortality. The most famous Sumerian legend told of how, after the death of his friend Enkidu, Gilgamesh, the king of Uruk, tried to escape death by finding the tree of life, whose magic fruit kept one eternally young. Gilgamesh eventually did find the fruit, only to have a serpent steal it. Another legend related that the wisdom of the first man Adapa was so great that the god An offered him bread and water of life so that he could become a god. Concerned about the gods' unpredictability, Adapa declined the offer, and he and the rest of humanity thus were forever denied immortality.

Sumerian Civilization

The beginning of Sumerian civilization coincides with the **Early Dynastic Period**, beginning ca. 2900 BCE, about the time when nonlegendary dynasties of Sumerian kings begin to be recorded. Sumer was home to some twenty principal cities, including Eridu, Ur, Uruk, Larsa, Lagash, Sharuppak, Sippar, Umma, Isin, Nippur, and Kish, most of whose origins went back to the Ubaid period. By then, all of the available land near the river was taken, and city borders were marked by boundary stones and canals. The cultivated, irrigated land of the Sumerian cities was adjoined by unirrigated grazing land known as "Edin." Each Sumerian city was believed to be under the protection of one of the many Sumerian gods: for example, **Enlil** looked over Nippur, Enki over Uruk, Nanna over **Ur**, and Ningirsu over Lagash. The principal cities could measure around seven hundred square miles, with populations of over fifty thousand persons. Although the cities all shared the same culture, they rarely were united politically, and, in fact, political disunity came to be one of the defining characteristics throughout Mesopotamian history, resulting in yet one more uncertainty in Mesopotamian life. Any Mesopotamian rulers who tried to unify Mesopotamia faced a daunting task.

It has been suggested that Sumerian Edin, uncultivated land, was the origin of the biblical concept of the Garden of Eden.

Our knowledge of Sumerian civilization comes from archaeological remains and written records. The Sumerian writing system, known as **cuneiform**, evolved out of the earlier pictograms. From about 2900 BCE, many pictograms began

The word cuneiform comes from the Latin word cuneus, or "wedge."

to lose their original function, and the signs were reduced to about 1,500 ideograms, signs representing a thought or a word, such as a star representing "the sky." The system became increasingly phonetic as each sign came to represent just the sound of the object. By about 2600 BCE, the number of symbols had been reduced to a syllabary of about six hundred symbols that represented not only syllables, such as *ba-, be-, bi-, bo-*, and so on, but also consonants and other sound combinations, including a good deal of duplication of signs representing the same sounds and meanings. At the same time, the mechanics of writing were simplified with the introduction of a wedge-shaped **stylus** that was pushed into the wet clay instead of making scratch marks. Only then did cuneiform come into widespread use and become applied to a multitude of purposes. The lack of an earlier writing system, therefore, means that the earlier period is largely lost in myths and legends retold at a much later date.

	3000 BCE I	2800 BCE II	2500 BCE III	1800 BCE IV	600 BCE V	
1						ar
2						ki
3						la
4						tal
5						kur
6						gene
7						tag
8						ka
9						sinda

This chart of the evolution of cuneiform shows the transformation of early pictograms, such as a sign for a head or a star, to a sound, such as "tag" or "ar."

The Sumerians had very little literature in the modern sense. Nearly all Sumerian written documents were commercial, such as inventories, accounts, or receipts, reflecting the compulsive Mesopotamian desire to keep lists of things. The clay tablets, generally sun-dried and stored on flammable wooden shelves, usually were not intended to be permanent. Most of the surviving tablets were inadvertently baked when a city was burned, either by an accidental fire or by military action, and left to be recovered by modern archaeological excavations or illegal looting.

Paradoxically, it was the destruction of a Mesopotamian city that led to the preservation of its records.

Sumerian Mythology

The Sumerians developed a mythology that explained how the gods had created the universe, natural processes, and humans. According to a sketchily preserved tradition, the world and universe originated from a chaotic ocean of Apsu, sweet water. Apsu created Nammu, the goddess of the salt sea, who created An, the god of the heavens, and Ki, the earth. From the union of An and Ki came Enlil, who became god of the air. Enlil also usurped the position of his father as master of the world, and from the union of Enlil and his mother Ki came the water god Enki. In a like manner the other gods came into being. Then, because the gods were lazy, Enki created people from Apsu mixed with clay to do the gods' work. After drinking beer at a feast, Enki and his wife Ninmah had a contest to see whether each of them could find a purpose for an imperfect human made by the other. Thus, when Ninmah created a blind man, Enki made him a musician. But when Enki created a creature with impaired vision, bowels, heart, lungs, nerves, and limbs, Ninmah had to confess that she could find no purpose for it, and later generations of humans thus were condemned to misery.

The Sumerians also had some surprisingly perceptive ideas about the origins of civilization. According to Sumerian legend, Eridu, the earliest attested Sumerian city, had been founded by Enki, who also was the god of civilization, demonstrating the realization of the importance that control of a good water supply played in the creation of a civilized society. In a revealing story, Inanna, the fertility goddess, desired to bring civilization to her own favored city of Uruk by any means possible, saying, "I shall direct my steps to Enki, to the Abzu [Enki's watery temple], to Eridu, and I myself shall speak coaxingly to him." Enki, thinking to seduce her, "made her feel as if she was in her girlfriend's house" and engaged her in a drinking contest with beer and wine. But it was Enki who became drunk, and he presented Inanna with a multitude of "divine decrees" encompassing all the elements of civilization. For example, "Holy Inanna received the craft of the carpenter, the craft of the coppersmith, the craft of the scribe, the craft of the smith, the craft of the leather-worker, the craft of the fuller, the craft of the builder, the craft of the reed-worker." Other gifts included sedentary living, the office of priest, the royal throne, judging, decision making, the plundering of cities, sexual intercourse, kissing, prostitution, grandiloquent speech, musical instruments, and the art of song. After sobering up and learning what he had done, Enki attempted to recover his treasures. but Inanna was protected by her messenger Ninshubur, who fended off various giants, sea monsters, and monstrous fish until Inanna returned to Uruk and the divine decrees were read out.

HISTORICAL SUMER (3000–2300 BCE)

Accounts of the earliest history of Sumer are shrouded in myth and legend and reveal some of the general attitudes of the Sumerians toward the world around them and the outlines of how Sumerian culture evolved. Only in the middle of the third century BCE do written records documenting more specific aspects of Sumerian culture, such as political and economic accounts, begin to appear. These permit us to acquire a much more exact idea of the nature of Sumerian civilization.

The Sumerian King List

Although the Sumerians had no written history in a modern sense, they and later Mesopotamians were compulsive list makers. The Sumerians' own version of their early history thus is best represented in a document known as the **Sumerian King List**, which contains a sequence of cities whose kings reigned supreme in Sumer going back to the establishment of the first Sumerian cities and occasionally includes brief descriptions of events. Like many such documents compiled in antiquity, the earlier sections are full of folktales, including life spans of several thousand years and direct contact with the gods. The King List also mistakenly has one city succeeding another in ruling all of Sumer when it is clear from other documents that there were, in fact, multiple kings in different cities ruling at the same time. Nevertheless, the King List does preserve what the Sumerians thought about their ancient history, and the later sections do give an increasingly accurate account of who was ruling where for how long. As the list evolved, it was used to legitimatize the authority of contemporary kings, who would be grafted on to the end of the list with the implicit claim that a new king was part of a tradition of rule going back thousands of years.

The King List opens with the words "After the kingship descended from heaven, the kingship was in Eridu" and then begins with two kings of Eridu who ruled for 64,800 years, followed by three kings, including "Damuzid the shepherd" of Bad-tibiria, later a town of only minor importance, who governed for 36,000 years. These reigns are absurdly long, but the evidence of the list should not be completely rejected. Not only are the places mentioned in fact some of the most ancient places in Sumer, but also, if one were going to invent such a list, there would be no point in including an insignificant town like Bad-tibiria. Moreover, the inclusion of many undistinguished persons as kings, such as the shepherds Etana and Lugalbanda, Meche the smith, and Mamagal the boatman, likewise suggests that the list does reflect genuine folk traditions. The King's List then cites an event that the Sumerians clearly saw as one of the defining moments of their past: "Then the flood swept over."

The flood separates the clearly legendary material, with twenty-thousand-year life spans, from increasingly historical material. It also served as a backdrop for other Sumerian legends. In one, a huge flood was sent by the god Enlil to destroy humanity, but the water god Enki advised one man, Utnapishtim, to build a great ark and fill it with animals. Utnapishtim survived the flood and then became immortal. As noted in the previous chapter, stories of a prehistoric flood were a common motif in ancient myths and legends; it may be that a genuine local flood lay behind this version, such as one that might have been responsible for an eleven-foot layer of silt found at Ur separating the period before 3000 BCE from the later period.

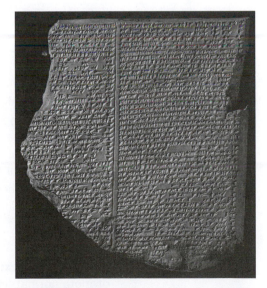

The most famous cuneiform tablet, found in the Assyrian palace at Nineveh, tells the story of how Utnapishtim built an ark in order to escape the flood sent by the god Enlil to destroy humanity.

THE CHRONOLOGY OF THE BRONZE AGE

In the nineteenth century, standard chronologies of the ancient world were created that put events in Mesopotamia, Egypt, and the Bible into the same integrated chronology. The conventional way of creating such chronologies is to begin with dates that are beyond dispute, such as some of the dates from Assyrian history, and then work backward by comparing events reported from different areas. The further back one goes, the greater the chance of systematic errors creeping in. Over the past century, there has been an increasing tendency to create ever "shorter" chronologies with increasing realizations that the earlier versions systematically dated events too early. Thus the early-twentieth-century "long" chronology dated the reign of Hammurabi to 1848–1806 BCE; the "middle" chronology, which until recently was standard and still is found in most of the literature, placed it at 1792–1750 BCE; the new "short" or "low" chronology, used here, dates it to 1728–1686 BCE; and the even newer "ultra-low" chronology dates it to 1696–1654 BCE.

The older chronologies had only written records to go on, but this could result in errors, as when reigns of rulers that overlapped were treated as if they had occurred in sequence (as in the Sumerian King List), where mistaken connections between two sources (such as Biblical and Egyptian accounts) were made, or where the sources give different, confusing, or no lengths for a reign. More modern methods of establishing chronologies also can make use of scientific methods, such as carbon-14 dating, which measures the decay rate of a radioactive isotope that is absorbed by all living things but stops being absorbed when they die. But, along with a sizable margin of error, scientific methods also can give erroneous results, as when measurements of the age of wood from the pyramids suggested a much earlier date for the pyramids because the wood already was hundreds of years old when it was put into the pyramids.

The result of the adoption of the "short chronology" means that the dates given in all works published before about 2000 need to be recalibrated and demonstrates the fallacy of placing too much emphasis on exact dates, which no doubt will be revised once again at some future point, as our knowledge of Near Eastern history becomes even more refined with further research.

After the flood, twenty-three kings of **Kish** are listed, ruling a total of 24,510 years, followed by twelve kings of Uruk, ruling for 2,310 years. These numbers are still absurd at an average of just over 1,000 years each but heading in the right direction, and they are not much different from some of the long life spans of the descendents of Adam in the early sections of the biblical book of Genesis. In addition, two of these kings of Kish are the first kings in the King List to be named in other sources, also suggesting that the list is becoming more historical.

Urban Development

It was only the next dynasty, from the city of Ur, that boasted kings with reigns of more normal length, the last two ruling twenty-five and thirty-six years, respectively. And the reigns of the remaining kings also look realistic. These kings thus bring us into the realm not only of biological possibility but also of historical reality, for Mesannepada, the founder of the First Dynasty of Ur in the King List, is historically attested in contemporary documents as ruling around 2600 BCE, by which time Ur had become one of the most important Sumerian cities and exercised authority over much of Sumer. It was not until ca. 2600 BCE, therefore, that Sumerian political record keeping became sufficiently accurate to represent reasonably well what was going on in the real world.

Whereas up through the Uruk period the Sumerian cities seem to have lived mostly in peace, by 2600 BCE, serious conflicts among Sumerian cities had broken out as expanding populations brought increasing pressure on cities to expand their economic productivity. Once all the land within irrigation distance of the rivers had been occupied, the only way to expand was to take land or water rights from someone else. This led to conflicts between cities, resulting in yet one more uncertainty in life. One indication of a growing need for security seems to have been a trend for smaller cities to consolidate into larger ones around 3000 BCE, a practice that might be reflected in Uruk's having two primary deities, An and Inanna, rather than just one. In addition, one sees not only the rise of a new social class of professional soldiers but also the construction of increasingly massive defensive walls. King **Gilgamesh**, for example, is said to have built the walls around Uruk just before 2600 BCE. Subsequently, various cities attempted to lay claim to a greater level of hegemony in Sumeria; one means of doing so was to secure the support of Enlil, who was believed to control life on earth, by gaining control over Nippur, Enlil's sacred city.

Sumerian Religion, Government, and Economy

Sumerian life revolved around religion, which provided the patterns for living one's life. Most of the gods were thought to be **anthropomorphic** and to behave very much like people, except, of course, that they were immortal and had supernatural powers. The center of worship was a ziggurat intended to house the city's primary god. By now, ziggurats had evolved from the simple platform of the Uruk Period to massive step pyramids, as much as 150 feet on a side and more than 100 feet high, built with an exterior of fired bricks bound together by bitumen or mortar over a mud-brick core and with as many as seven levels. Although none has survived, a temple—the actual home of the god—probably stood on top. Only the priests were permitted entry to the upper levels of the ziggurat. The ziggurat was the most important architectural monument of the city and was visible from anywhere in the city territory. It would have looked like a staircase rising to heaven. Smaller temples of other gods also were scattered about the cities.

Although the god was the true ruler of the city, the god was never there to do the actual work, so each city was ruled by a representative of the god, who at first probably was a priest who also served as king. But the growing need for effective military leaders tended to reduce the role of priests, who usually did not make very good generals, as rulers. The king was assisted by a Council of Elders who provided

A reconstruction of a Sumerian ziggurat depicts worshippers proceeding up to the second level, as high as they were allowed to go; only the priests could ascend to the temple at the top.

advice and consent. At the dawn of Sumerian history, moreover, women played a significant role in government, which could explain why the god of the moon, a body generally associated with women, had a higher rank than the sun god. And the King List cites as ruler of Kish, just before 2600 BCE, a woman named Azag-bau, said to have been a tavern-keeper, making her the first attested woman to rule in her own name. Other early evidence for powerful women comes from around the same time, when Pu-abi of Ur, a queen or priestess, was buried in an elaborate tomb containing not only grave goods made of gold, silver, and lapis lazuli but also the bodies of eighteen companions, an apparent form of human sacrifice so she could be accompanied in the afterlife. This practice, however, soon died out. And any role of women as rulers soon was taken over by men.

Kings came in different forms, and a king could be known as an en, ensi, or lugal. The significance of these different terms is unclear; it has been suggested that they were just different terms used in different cities, or that the en or ensi was a form of priest-king, or that the lugal was either a king of multiple cities or a military general who had risen to be king. The king was responsible for overseeing foreign policy, including defense, and coordinating city administration, such as mobilizing the labor necessary to ensure that the irrigation and flood control systems operated properly—no easy task, given that changes in the course of a river could make a whole irrigation system useless and even necessitate moving the location of a city. But the king could not do this work alone. A class of **nobles** served as generals and administrators and controlled large tracts of land. And a class of priests, with the same social rank as the nobles, oversaw the temples and the landed properties of the gods.

The government largely controlled economic activity, and economic transactions

TABLE 2.2 MESOPOTAMIAN WEIGHT SYSTEM

Talent	60 minas	3600 shekels	62 lb.
Mina	1 mina	60 shekels	1.03 lb.
Shekel	1/60 mina	1 shekel	¼ oz.

took place using bartar, that is, by exchanging goods and services, for coinage did not yet exist. Commodities, including gold and silver, were traded by weight using a system in which a **talent** (about sixty-seven pounds, although this varied from city to city) was subdivided into sixty minas, and a **mina** was subdivided into sixty **shekels** (about one-quarter ounce each). The government collected taxes in labor and in produce. Landowners, for example, paid a percentage of their crops, which then could be expended on the production and distribution of other goods and services necessary for the smooth operation of city services. Centralized warehouses stored items ranging from grain and fruits to pottery and weapons. These resources were used to pay the salaries of government employees, such as palace bureaucrats, soldiers, craftspersons, fishermen, and shepherds. A government worker's typical annual salary was thirty bushels of barley and four shekels of silver. Less privileged people were drafted to work on public works projects, such as temple building and digging and cleaning irrigation ditches. Sumerian government also was very bureaucratic and kept detailed records of every distribution of rations, tax payment, and bit of labor that was done.

The lack of any local resources besides water, dirt, and vegetation created a great demand for raw materials acquired through trade. Although there was some private enterprise, this could be very risky, and most foreign trade by both land and sea was centralized and regimented under government supervision. Sumerian cities exported grain, dyed and bleached woolen cloth, and engraved gems (processes invented by the Sumerians), cooking oil, and worked metal items such as weapons; they imported both raw materials and luxury goods. From the mountains to the north and west came copper, tin, and timber. As early as the fourth millenium BCE, Sumerian merchants traded with the land of Dilmun, which may have been located in Arabia near modern Oman, where they obtained copper. Others sailed further to trade with the Bronze Age Harappa civilization of India, obtaining gemstones and spices.

The Sumerian People

Kings, priests, and nobles formed a very small privileged group at the peak of the social pyramid. Other social classes filled out the Sumerian social order. The next rung of privilege was occupied by soldiers and a multitude of palace bureaucrats. Both groups were largely parasites on the economy, because they were a great expense but rarely made any contribution to the local economy except on the rare occasions that soldiers brought in some war booty.

Artisans and specialized laborers, including such people as potters, metal-workers, scribes, and merchants, stood next in the social hierarchy and made up a sort of middle class. But the vast majority of the population was occupied in farming. Some independent peasants worked their own land, but most agricultural workers were sharecroppers on thirty-acre or smaller plots belonging to the nobles or priests. They paid rents of up to one-third of their produce and thus received but a scant livelihood. Those with the least privilege were the slaves. Slaves included war captives, condemned criminals, persons who been sold into slavery to pay debts, and those who had been born as slaves. There were not many slaves—there simply was not much place in the economy for them—but nearly all of them were native Sumerians and thus had a well-defined place in the community. There was no stigma attached to slavery—slaves were viewed as unfortunates down on their luck and often were freed after several years of service.

Another underprivileged class in Sumer, as in all ancient societies, was women. Women's lives revolved around family and marriage, and the life trajectory of a woman was expected to be from daughter to wife and then perhaps to widow. The law generally favored men. An infertile woman could be divorced, and a destitute husband could sell his wife and children into slavery to repay debts, albeit with the expectation that he would redeem them if his luck changed. Women whose families could not find husbands for them or whose fathers could not support them could be left to work in one of the temples, some, apparently, as sacred prostitutes in the temple of the fertility goddess Inanna. But women did have rights. Women also could engage in business in their own names, and in default of a husband or grown son, the wife controlled the family property. A Sumerian wife also controlled the **dowry** her father had provided to support her and her children and had equal authority with her husband over their children. The children themselves, however, had no legal rights and could be disowned by their parents at any time.

There were occasional attempts to improve the rights of the less privileged, as happened in Lagash in the twenty-fifth century BCE after the priests levied excessive taxes on weddings and funerals. King Urukagina, acting in the name of the city's guardian god Ningirsu, fired corrupt officials, forbade nobles to force lower ranking persons to sell anything against their will, and "solemnly promised Ningirsu that he would never subjugate the orphan and the widow to the powerful."

Sumerian Lifestyles

Most Sumerians lived a simple life. Country houses were constructed from bundles of reeds plastered with adobe on the outside. Floors were made of beaten earth, and farm animals lived with the family. City houses of just a few hundred square feet were made of sun-dried mud bricks and were crammed together on narrow streets, some only four feet wide, to gain maximum benefit from the protected space within the city walls. Thick walls and a lack of windows helped keep them cool but also made them stuffy. A flat roof was used for cooking and sleeping. When fifty thousand or more persons were packed into the city, and even more in times of trouble, a Sumerian city could well be described as an "anthill society."

For the average Sumerian, everyday household items included much pottery, which was used for storing food and water, for cooking, and as tableware. Baskets and other storage items were made of leather or woven from reeds. Wooden furniture was minimal, consisting perhaps of stools, bed frames, and storage chests. Metal items, such as jewelry, small tools, and knives, were very expensive. Hearths and fireplaces were used for cooking and baking purposes, meaning that there was a constant danger of fire. Food consisted primarily of grain products, onions, lettuce, lentils, fish, and beer. A rudimentary drainage system conducted waste to the river, but the smell still would have been overpowering to a modern nose. The usual garment was a woolen rectangular piece of cloth; women draped it from the left shoulder and men wrapped around it their waists. Sumerians wore caps for protection from the sun and sandals on their feet. Women adorned themselves with necklaces, ear and finger rings, bracelets, and anklets. And for entertainment, Sumerians played board games that are viewed as the ancestors of backgammon and enjoyed singing accompanied on the lyre, a handheld harp.

> **MAKING CONNECTIONS**
>
> Compare the diets of pastoralists and river valley farmers. Which kind of economy do you think brought the most healthy diet?

THE SEMITIC PEOPLES AND THE FIRST NEAR EASTERN EMPIRES (2300–1200 BCE)

In the semi-arid regions of northern Arabia and Syria to the south and east of Sumer lived groups of pastoralists who spoke **dialects** of the Semitic family of languages and therefore are known as the **Semitic peoples**. They had no political unity, but they had a long history of contact with the settled, agricultural peoples of the river valleys. Indeed, many of the original settlers of the Sumerian cities probably were Semitic speaking. The Semitic peoples who remained pastoralists were aware, of course, that the riverine peoples grew and stored large surplus food supplies, and in times of need the pastoralists could gain access to these foodstuffs by two means: trading or raiding. In good times, in exchange for payments of meat, wool, and milk products, pastoralists were allowed to pasture their herds on grain stubble after the summer harvest. But in times of drought, pastoralists would attempt to pasture in the grain fields, or even to seize the grain.

In addition, in the years after 3000 BCE, the Semitic people known as the **Akkadians** moved into the river valley themselves, just upstream from the Sumerians, adopted Sumerian culture, and gave their name to Akkad, the region surrounding modern Baghdad. They assimilated much of the culture of the Sumerians and created their own agricultural civilization. But they retained, for example, the names of their gods, which were equated with

TABLE 2.3   SEMITIC EQUIVALENTS OF SUMERIAN GODS

Sumerian Version	Semitic Version
An	Anu
Enlil	Marduk
Enki	Ea
Nanna	Sin
Utu	Shamash
Inanna	Ishtar

A bust from Nineveh with the hair bound up for combat often is identified as Sargon, although this is by no means certain. The semiprecious stones used for the eyes were pried out when the tomb was looted in antiquity.

Sumerian gods; thus Sumerian An was Semitic Anu, Enki was Ea, Utu was Shamash, Nanna was Sin, and Inanna was **Ishtar**. As the centuries wore on, other Semitic peoples likewise would make their way into the river valleys, either peacefully or by force, and adopt the civilized style of life.

Sargon and the Akkadian Empire

Around the year 2270 BCE the ruler of the Akkadians, a very able individual named Sharru-Kin ("the True King"), or **Sargon** (2270–2215 BCE), embarked on a career of empire building. According to a story attributed to Sargon himself, as an infant he was cast adrift in the Euphrates River by his mother, possibly because he was of illegitimate birth. After being rescued and raised by a gardener, he became the "cup bearer" (a greatly trusted and influential official who protected the king from poison) of the king of Kish. To enhance his status, Sargon claimed to be the lover of the goddess Ishtar. He managed to seize power and went on to defeat Ur, Uruk, and the other Sumerian cities. At the sacred city of Nippur he was declared King of Sumer and Akkad. He also claimed to have conquered territory reaching to the Mediterranean Sea and Anatolia in the west, into **Elam** in southwestern Iran to the east, into Gutium in the Zagros Mountains to the north, and far down the Arabian coast in the south. He thus is considered to have established the first Near Eastern **empire**, a term used to describe a state that incorporates several nations and peoples under a single government.

Sargon had no previous models for how to run an empire, so he had to play it by ear. In many regards, he simply used what was already there. The Sumerian writing system was adopted but in an evolved form, with a greater use of signs representing syllables. He established his capital at Agade on the Euphrates, just upstream from Sumer. Even though he favored his own goddess, Ishtar, he showed respect for the Sumerians by taking the title "The Great Ensi of Enlil."

But in other regards, Sargon ruled with an iron fist. Rather than delegating his authority, he kept personal control of all levels of government. He humiliated defeated rulers, turning former city kings into mere local governors; he forced the Sumerian cities to tear down their walls; and he scattered Akkadian officials throughout the empire. Sargon even named his daughter Enheduanna as priestess of the temple of Nanna at Ur. She wrote several surviving poems in the Sumerian

language and is the earliest known author of anything written in cuneiform
and the first to write in the first person.

In several ways, Sargon attempted to unify the empire. There was a regular messenger service, and a calendar based on naming years after important
events became standard. In addition, the size of the empire created a much-
improved economy of scale. The gathering of produce in the form of taxes could
be centralized, and food shortages in one part of the empire could be compensated for by surpluses in other parts. In addition, the territorial expansion gave
the Akkadians access to raw materials beyond the borders of Mesopotamia
proper that in the past the Sumerians could gain only by trade, thus creating a more internally homogeneous economy. In reality, however, although
Sargon claimed to rule all of this territory directly, his empire may have been
more a loose collection of **vassals**, that is, peoples and rulers who acknowledged Sargon's authority but who also were ready to revolt at the first sign of
weakness.

After Sargon's death, his two sons (2215–2291 BCE) had trouble holding
the empire together. Subject cities and peoples revolted, and both sons were
assassinated. His daughter Enheduanna was expelled by King Lugal-Ane of
Uruk, who revolted against the Akkadians and destroyed Uruk's famous temple of Ishtar. In a poem called "Praise of Ishtar," Enheduanna called on Inanna/
Ishtar to avenge her, presenting Ishtar as a fearsome goddess who would bring
destruction on Lugal-Ane: "The radiant en-priestess of Nanna am I. My Queen,
beloved of An, may your heart be calmed for me. That you are as high as heaven

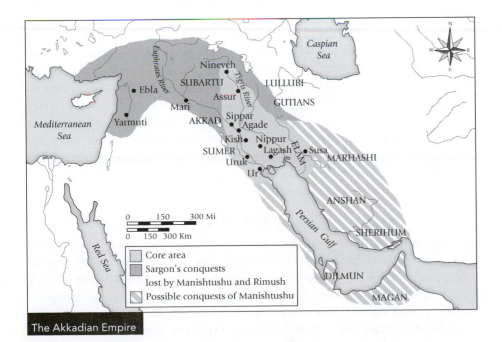

The Akkadian Empire

shall be known! That you are as wide as the earth shall be known! That you annihilate rebelling territories shall be known! That you roar against the enemy lands shall be known! That you crush their leaders shall be known! That you devour corpses like a predator shall be known! That your glance is terrible shall be known! My Queen, beloved of An, I will announce all of your wrath! I have heaped the coals, prepared the purification rites. My Queen, draped in enchantment, to you, Inanna, be glory!"

Sargon's grandson **Naram-Sin** ("Beloved of Sin") (2190–2154 BCE) had better luck. He put down the revolts in Sumer and restored Enheduanna to her office. The Sumerians later believed that Enheduanna's prayers to Ishtar had been so successful that her poem became a standard text in Sumerian schools, with hundreds of surviving copies. Naram-Sin assembled an army supposedly numbering 360,000 men, many of whom were farmers who needed work in the winter, and expanded the frontiers of the empire, conquering and destroying the powerful trading city of **Ebla** in Syria and campaigning against the Lullubi, a people of the Zagros Mountains. In an attempt to give himself more authority, Naram-Sin gave himself the grandiose title King of the Four Quarters of the Universe, that is, king of the world. Naram-Sin's megalomania even led him to portray himself as a god in his own right, but after he destroyed the temple of Enlil at the holy city of Nippur, it was believed that he and Akkad were cursed by the Sumerian gods.

After the reign of Naram-Sin's son Shar-Kalli-Sharri (2153–2129 BCE), who even more grandiosely called himself "King of All Kings," the Akkadian Empire went into its final decline when confronted by Sumerian revolts and raids by the **Gutians** from the Zagros Mountains to the north. The Sumerian King List lamented, "Then who was king? Irgigi was king, Imi was king, Nanûm was king, Ilulu was king, and the four of them ruled for only three years. Then Akkad was defeated. Then the reign of Akkad was abolished and the kingship was taken to Uruk. Then the reign of Uruk was abolished and the kingship was taken to the land of Gutium." In 2115 the capital Agade was destroyed by the Gutians so thoroughly that it never has been found, and the curse against Naram-Sin was fulfilled. It has been suggested that a dry period resulting in lowered river levels and an encroachment of neighboring pastoralists into the river valley areas also contributed to a decline of the Akkadian Empire. The most lasting legacy of the Akkadian Empire was the establishment of the Akkadian language as an common language that was used throughout the Near East.

Sumer Strikes Back

Mesopotamia then returned to its usual condition of political disunity. The Gutians attempted to establish rule over Mesopotamia but were ill equipped to do so, and their poor management of the irrigation system led to widespread famine. The Sumerian cities reasserted their independence. Gudea (2080–2060 BCE), a king of Lagash, gained control of seventeen other cities and skirmished with the kingdom of Elam to the east.

THE VICTORY STELE OF NARAM-SIN

On this victory stele, more than six feet tall and erected to commemorate a victory over the northern Lullubi people, the Akkadian king Naram-Sin, carrying a bow, an arrow, and an axe, assaults the enemy's strongholds in the Zagros Mountains. He is followed by standard bearers (as seen also on the Narmer palette from Egypt) and soldiers carrying bows and axes. It is the first known Mesopotamian attempt to depict natural geography and shows pig-tailed Lullubi soldiers being killed and routed; one, with a spear in his throat, kneels before Naram-Sin, and behind him one of the Lullubi, perhaps King Satuni, begs for mercy. Naram-Sin's much larger size demonstrates how much more important and powerful he is, and his horned helmet indicates that he was claiming to be divine himself. As he climbs higher, he approaches the heavenly sun and stars above him. The fragmentary inscription, in which Naram-Sin's name is preceded by a sign reserved for gods, reads, "Satuni, king of the highlanders, assembled for battle. Naram-Sin defeated them and heaped up a burial mound over them and dedicated this to the god." The stele was found in Susa in Elam, where it had been carried off by the Elamites after a raid into Mesopotamia in the twelfth century BCE; it now is in the Louvre Museum in Paris.

He was not a native of Lagash but had married the previous king's daughter, and he needed to gain support and establish legitimacy. To achieve the former, he canceled outstanding debts—always popular with everyone except the moneylenders—and allowed women to own family land in their own names. And as for the latter, in an age of increasing personalization of the rule, Gudea circulated a multitude of statues of himself, the first attested use of a form of mass media to gain religious and political authority.

Subsequently, the **Third Dynasty of Ur**, founded by Ur-Nammu (2112–2095), reasserted the authority of Ur by gaining control over Uruk, Lagash, Kish, and other Sumerian cities. Ur-Nammu took the title King of Sumer and Akkad and attempted to consolidate his control by issuing a law code that was distributed throughout the kingdom. The code was not a legal reform but merely preserved in written form what must have been the prevailing practices. The surviving thirty-two laws dealt with issues such as crimes against the public good, marriage, the treatment of slaves, personal injury, courtroom testimony, and farming. Murder and robbery, serious crimes, were punished by death, but personal injuries were compensated by monetery payments—for example, one-half mina (about half a pound) of silver for putting out an eye, two-thirds of a mina for severing a nose, and one mina for "smashing the limb of another man with a club." A man accused of sorcery was subjected to the "river ordeal" (apparently being thrown into the river) to ascertain guilt or innocence; good swimmers probably stood to benefit here.

The code also clarified the legal position of women. On broken marriage engagements, it stated, "If a prospective son-in-law enters the house of his prospective father-in-law, but his father-in-law later gives his daughter to another man, the father-in-law shall return to the rejected son-in-law twofold the amount of bridal presents he had brought." About adultery, it said, "If a man accused the wife of a man of adultery, and the river ordeal proved her innocent, then the man who had accused her must pay one-third of a mina of silver." And regarding divorce, it decreed, "If a man divorces his first-time wife, he shall pay her one mina of silver. If it is a former widow whom he divorces, he shall pay her half a mina of silver. If the man had slept with the widow without there having been any marriage contract, he need not pay any silver." And insolent female slaves were punished by having their mouths scoured with a quart of salt.

After Ur-Nammu was killed in battle against the Gutians, he was succeeded by his son Shulgi, who expanded on the cult of personality by claiming extraordinary powers, such as being able to run the one hundred miles from Ur to Nippur, and by proclaiming himself a god. During his reign the surviving Great Ziggurat was built, 150 feet high in at least three stories and 210 feet on a side, and Ur became the largest city in the world, with a population estimated at sixty-five thousand. But Mesopotamia then was faced by new rounds of invasions. Ur was destroyed by the Elamites around 2000 BCE, and even more serious invasions came from Semitic peoples in the west. Sumer soon lost its independence completely. The Sumerian language went out of use except in schools and temples, where it survived until as late as the first century CE.

The Old Babylonian Empire

Beginning around 2000 BCE another group of Semitic peoples, collectively known as the **Amorites** ("westerners"), entered Mesopotamia from the west. Included among them were the **Assyrians**, who settled in the upper Tigris River valley, and the **Babylonians**, who occupied Akkad in the middle section of Mesopotamia. The Assyrians would not rise to prominence for several centuries, so the Babylonians are discussed first.

Like earlier pastoralist peoples who moved into Mesopotamia, the Babylonians assimilated much of earlier Sumerian culture, using cuneiform to write their language. The Babylonians also adopted most of the Sumerian deities, although they did retain their own supreme god, the storm god **Marduk**. In order to enhance Marduk's status in the sacred hierarchy, the Babylonians composed a poem known as the "Enuma Elish" ("When on high"), a modified version of the Sumerian creation myth that made Marduk the most powerful god on earth. In this account, the world was created when the goddess Tiamat, the salty sea, was mingled with Apsu, sweet water. In the process of mingling, they engendered the gods. But because the young gods created a great racket, Apsu planned to kill them, only to be killed himself by Enki. Enraged, Tiamat bore many monsters to take revenge on her children, but, led by Enki's son Marduk, the younger gods killed Tiamat, and Marduk created the universe by splitting her body, half of it becoming heaven and the other half earth, with the Tigris and Euphrates flowing out of her pierced eyes. Marduk then assigned the gods their duties and created humans. In this version, the Sumerian god of the heavens An had a fairly minor role, and Enlil was simply replaced by Marduk.

The modern division of the hour into sixty minutes and the minute into sixty seconds is an artifact of the Babylonian system of timekeeping.

The Old Babylonians were especially noted for their study of mathematics and astronomy. Mathematical calculations were based on the number sixty rather than, as in the modern decimal system, on the number ten. In addition, the year was divided into 360 days (6 times 60), the day was divided into six parts, and the hour into sixty parts. Using this rather cumbersome system, Babylonian mathematicians dealt with complex concepts such as square roots and algebraic unknowns (called "false values"). For a zero, the Babylonians substituted a blank space. Babylonian mathematics had practical applications, such as calculating compound interest or estimating how much building material was needed for a ziggurat.

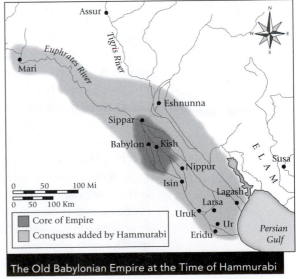

The Old Babylonian Empire at the Time of Hammurabi

TABLE 2.4 BABYLONIAN DAYS OF THE WEEK

Babylonian Day	Planetary Body	Modern Day
Shamash	Sun	Sunday
Sin	Moon	Monday
Nergal	Mars	Tuesday
Nabû	Mercury	Wednesday
Marduk	Jupiter	Thursday
Ishtar	Venus	Friday
Ninurta	Saturn	Saturday

Most of the Mari tablets, which were discovered in the 1930s, still have not been studied.

Babylonian astronomy initially was based on recording observational data, such as changes in the amount of daylight during the year, the dates and times of eclipses, and the movements of the sun, moon, and planets. When enough observations had been made, it became possible to predict future occurrences, for example, of eclipses. The Babylonians also introduced the idea of creating constellation images, based on mythology, from groups of stars and conceived the idea of naming the days of the week after the planets, which were identified with certain of the gods. At the same time, it was believed that the positions of astronomical bodies had a direct effect on what happened on Earth, giving rise to the science of astrology.

The Babylonians established a city at **Babylon**, initially a fairly unimportant place, which became the home to the Babylonian kings. The greatest Babylonian ruler was **Hammurabi** (1728–1686 BCE). By using a shrewd mixture of military force and diplomacy, Hammurabi expanded his authority. In 1694 BCE, for example, he destroyed the ancient city of Mari, whose archives of more than twenty thousand tablets were baked and preserved. Hammurabi was able to unify Mesopotamia under his control, thus creating the second Near Eastern empire. In later history, Akkad and Sumer would be known collectively as **Babylonia**.

Hammurabi was faced with the same problem as Sargon: how to unify the disparate and contentious peoples of his empire. To enhance his status, he, too, took the title King of the Four Quarters of the Universe. He also undertook to introduce institutions that would give unity to the peoples of his empire. For example, Hammurabi mandated the use of standardized measures, such as the kush, or cubit (about 21 inches), for length; the sar, or "garden-plot" (about 350 square feet) for area; and standardized weights, based on the talent, mina, and shekel, in the markets under his control. But, like Sargon, he maintained personal control of the empire and did not create a new imperial bureaucracy, preferring rather to rule using existing local administrations.

Hammurabi is best known for his code of laws, ostensibly received from the sun god Shamash, that placed all the inhabitants of his empire under a single legal system. Like the Sumerian Code of Ur-Nammu, the **Code of Hammurabi** was a compilation of existing laws and custom relating to civil and criminal procedures. It therefore reflected accepted practices that the greatest number of people would agree were right and just. Perhaps because of its imperial nature, it assumed a greater role of the government in enforcement. With regard to criminal law, the penalties were much harsher than in the Sumerian laws, suggesting that they also were intended to have a deterrent role, no surprise in a society that had neither a police force nor a prison system. In addition, its only interest was in retribution for criminal acts, not whether something happened intentionally, involuntarily, or through negligence. Some kinds of crimes—such as rape, kidnaping, robbery, breaking and entering, stealing temple property, stealing slaves or harboring escaped slaves, receiving stolen property, making false accusations, and shoddy construction—were punished by death in an unspecified manner. In other cases, particularly horrific forms of execution were mandated. Male and female lovers who had their spouses killed were impaled, and a man convicted of incest with his mother was burned alive. Likewise, those caught looting a burning house were thrown into the same fire and burned alive. A common punishment was to be thrown into the river, as happened to women who abandoned husbands without cause and women who were accused of adultery. In these cases, being thrown in bound was tantamount to a death sentence, but being thrown in unbound could be used to prove one's innocence if one could make it to shore.

The lack of any system of incarceration meant that most punishments were immediately enforced. Many involved some kind of physical mutilation. Having one's hands cut off was the penalty for physicians who botched operations, for fieldhands who stole grain, and for sons who struck their fathers. Men found guilty of incest with their daughters were simply exiled. A man who slandered a woman was punished by having his forehead scarred. There also was a great deal of concern with various kinds of sexual crimes. A couple caught in adultery were bound and thrown into the river, as was a man guilty of raping his son's wife. Other penalties involved a monetary fine.

Many laws dealt with civil cases. Some concerned business and property. A good number had to do with agriculture, such as one stating that someone whose dam broke and caused flooding was sold as a slave to pay for the damages. The Code established the prices for certain kinds of manufactured items and the wages for laborers such as sailors, barbers, physicians, homebuilders, and farm workers, not to mention the rental rates for various kinds of draft animals. The code also specified means for settling disputes over contracts and business transactions. For example, one law stated, "If a female tavern-keeper does not accept grain according to gross weight in payment of drink, and the price of the drink is less than that of the grain that was offered, she shall be thrown into the water." If a written contract had not been drawn up—which the Code repeatedly recommended as the sensible thing to do—the only recourse was to swear oaths in the presence of a god.

There also were many marital laws. Several concerned the disposition of marital property, the disposition of dowries in cases of divorce, and the division of estates among heirs, a situation complicated when there were children by multiple wives or maidservants. Men were permitted a second wife if the first was childless or became disabled. Men without children could divorce their wives by

> **LEGACY OF ANTIQUITY**
>
> Ur-Nammu and Hammurabi published written law codes that were intended to unify the different peoples under their rule. In what ways do modern laws attempt to control or unify peoples from different cultural backgrounds?

THE CODE OF HAMMURABI

The surviving copy of the Code of Hammurabi, inscribed on a seven-foot-plus basalt stele, depicts Hammurabi receiving the code from the seated sun god Shamash. Unlike Naram-Sin, Hammurabi did not claim to be a god himself and ruled only as a representative of the gods. Like the stele of Naram-Sin, the Code of Hammurabi was carried off as plunder to Susa in Elam in the twelfth century BCE and now is in the Louvre Museum in Paris. The Code demonstrates the importance of the written word for the spread, standardization, and preservation of information. It begins with a lengthy preamble in which Hammurabi declares the support of the gods, and then continues with about 285 laws. It concludes with a statement of what Hammurabi hoped to accomplish by issuing it. Cited here are some of the laws dealing with marriage and the family, some of which could be quite complex, attesting to the importance of these concerns in Mesopotamian society.

> [Preamble]
> Anu and Bel called by name me, Hammurabi, the exalted prince, who feared God, to bring about the rule of righteousness in the land, to destroy the wicked and the evil-doers; so that the strong should not harm the weak; so that I should rule over the black-headed people like Shamash, and enlighten the land, to further the well-being of mankind . . . When Marduk sent me to rule over men, to give the protection of right to the land, I did right and righteousness and brought about the well-being of the oppressed.
>
> [Laws]
> [128] If a man take a woman to wife, but have no intercourse with her, this woman is no wife to him.

simply returning their dowries or paying a set price in gold. A man who wished to separate from a wife who had borne him children was compelled to support her until the children were raised. Only then could she marry someone else. Women could sue for divorce on the grounds of neglect or abandonment, and if they won their case they would recover their dowries. Otherwise, if a woman desired a divorce, her husband could either release her or force her to remain as a servant in his house after he remarried.

[129] If a man's wife be surprised with another man, both shall be tied and thrown into the water, but the husband may pardon his wife and the king his slaves.

[131] If a man bring a charge against one's wife, but she is not surprised with another man, she must take an oath and then may return to her house.

[137] If a man wish to separate from a woman who has borne him children, or from his wife who has borne him children: then he shall give that wife her dowry, and a part of the use of field, garden, and property, so that she can rear her children. When she has brought up her children, a portion of all that is given to the children, equal as that of one son, shall be given to her. She may then marry the man of her heart.

[141] If a man's wife, who lives in his house, wishes to leave it, plunges into debt, tries to ruin her house, neglects her husband, and is judicially convicted: if her husband offer her release, she may go on her way, and he gives her nothing as a gift of release. If her husband does not wish to release her, and if he take another wife, she shall remain as servant in her husband's house.

[145] If a man take a wife, and she bear him no children, and he intend to take another wife: if he take this second wife, and bring her into the house, this second wife shall not be allowed equality with his wife.

[153] If the wife of one man on account of another man has their mates murdered, both of them shall be impaled.

[154] If a man be guilty of incest with his daughter, he shall be driven from the city.

[155] If a man betroth a girl to his son, and his son have intercourse with her, but he (the father) afterward defile her, and be surprised, then he shall be bound and cast into the water (drowned).

[157] If any one be guilty of incest with his mother after his father, both shall be burned.

[167] If a man marry a wife and she bear him children: if this wife die and he then take another wife and she bear him children: if then the father die, the sons must not partition the estate according to the mothers, they shall divide the dowries of their mothers only in this way; the paternal estate they shall divide equally with one another.

[Conclusion]

My words are well considered; there is no wisdom like mine. By the command of Shamash, the great judge of heaven and earth, let righteousness go forth in the land: by the order of Marduk, my lord, let no destruction befall my monument. In E-Sagil, which I love, let my name be ever repeated; let the oppressed, who have a case at law, come and stand before this my image as king of righteousness; let him read the inscription, and understand my precious words: the inscription will explain his case to him; he will find out what is just, and his heart will be glad, so that he will say: "Hammurabi is a ruler, who is as a father to his subjects, who holds the words of Marduk in reverence, who has achieved conquest for Marduk over the north and south, who rejoices the heart of Marduk, his lord, who has bestowed benefits for ever and ever on his subjects, and has established order in the land.

As in all ancient cultures, Babylonian society was highly stratified. Hammurabi's Code recognized three social classes: nobles, free persons, and slaves. The distinctions among the classes were often made clear in the code. In many cases, the punishment for various crimes was dependent on one's social status. For example, a free person who struck a noble received sixty lashes from an ox-whip, but if he struck someone of equal rank, he just paid a fine. If a slave struck a free person, his ear was cut off. A noble who was convicted of breaking a bone or putting out an eye of another noble was subject to the "law of retalia-tion" and suffered the same injury. If he inflicted such harm on a freed person, the penalty was a fine of one mina of gold, and for a slave it was half of the slave's value. It would appear, therefore, that for nobles it was felt that honor was of prime importance, whereas for non-nobles it was the cash that counted. On the other hand, nobles were expected to pay more for medical services. The expected fee for curing the tumor of a noble was ten shekels of silver; for a free person it was five, and for a slave three.

Slavery was an integral part of Mesopotamian society, but this also was a society in which the legal difference between a free person and a slave was not always very great. For example, if an ox gored a free person to death, the penalty was one-half a mina of silver, whereas for a slave it was one-third of a mina, nearly the same. In many cases, slaves were local people who had fallen into debt and had had to sell their families or even themselves into slavery, but in these cases the law granted leniency, for another law stated, "If any one fail to meet a claim for debt, and sell himself, his wife, his son, and daughter for money or give them away to forced labor: they shall work for three years in the house of the man who bought them, or the proprietor, and in the fourth year they shall be set free." Slaves were members of society with acknowledged legal rights. Slaves were allowed to marry free women, with the children being free.

In other regards, there also was an interest in treating fairly those who had encountered misfortunes. Judges who rendered bad decisions were fired, and victims of crimes were reimbursed by the community. Merchants who ran-somed indigent prisoners-of-war held in other cities were to be repaid by the temple or the palace, and prisoners-of-war who escaped were permitted to reclaim property that had been sold or seized in their absence. Female children whom a father was unable or unwilling to support could be devoted to temples to serve either as temple virgins or temple prostitutes but retained a claim on the paternal property. Because there were no prisons, in the case of crimes mer-iting imprisonment, such as nonpayment of a debt, the plaintiff was in charge of imprisoning the defaulter; if a free man died in prison, the jailer was killed; if a slave, a fine in gold was levied.

The Indo-European Peoples

In spite of Hammurabi's attempts to unify the diverse peoples in his empire, it began to disintegrate soon after his death, and Mesopotamia soon returned to its natural state of disunity. His son Samsu-Iluna (1686–1678) was confronted not only by rebellious cities but also by representatives of a new group of invaders, the **Indo-European peoples**, whose homeland lay in the steppe lands of south-ern Russia. The Indo-Europeans, like the Semitic peoples, consisted of groups of pastoralist peoples who spoke dialects of the same basic language. The Indo-European family of languages was the ancestor of modern languages such as Sanskrit, Persian, Greek, and Latin. Every so often, groups of Indo-Europeans would head off seeking new homes. Around 2000 BCE there was a mass movement of Indo-European peoples, perhaps caused by a combination of over-population and food shortages. One group, the **Hittites,** made their way into Anatolia, where they established a kingdom known as the "land of the Hatti," after the people who had previously resided there. The Hittites established what may be the first constitutional monarchy, in which the activities of the king were overseen by a high court known as the Pankus. Another group began to move south into the Balkans. And a third, the **Aryans**, entered modern-day Iran; around 1500 BCE a group of Aryans invaded India, destroying the Indian Bronze Age civilization.

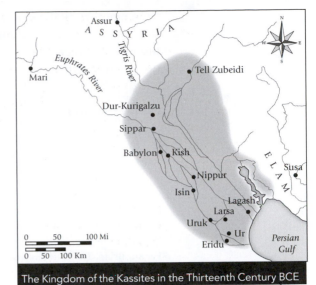

The Kingdom of the Kassites in the Thirteenth Century BCE

Various Indo-Eurpoean peoples made their presence felt in Mesopotamia. During the reign of Samsu-Iluna, the **Kassites**, who had assimilated Indo-European culture if they were not themselves a subgroup of the Aryans, launched raids into Mesopotamia from western Iran. In 1595 BCE, the Hittites made a massive raid into Babylonia and carried off the statue of Marduk from Babylon. Another people with Indo-European connections, the Hurrians, moved from the Caucasus Mountains between the Black and Caspian seas into upper Mesopotamia, introducing the use of the war chariot—hitherto, chariots had been used for troop transport rather than fighting. Around 1500 BCE the Hurrians established the kingdom of Mitanni on the upper Euphrates.

Meanwhile, the Kassites, using a new military technology that utilized the horse and chariot, had begun establishing their own principalities in Mesopotamia. The Kassite king, Agum III, even recovered the statue of Marduk from the Hittites. By about 1400 BCE, Kassite kings gained control over much of Mesopotamia and created a kingdom they called Karduniash. Kassite kings such as Burnaburiash II (1360–1333 BCE) corresponded with the pharaohs of Egypt. Always a minority, the Kassites imposed themselves as civil and military administrators. But they also assimilated Mesopotamian culture, including religion, dress, and language, so thoroughly that nearly the only aspect of their original culture that they preserved, at least for a time, was their names. The new Kassite capital city at Dur Kurigalzu, on the Tigris west of Baghdad, had a ziggurat and temples of Sumerian gods. The Kassites continued to rule middle and lower Mesopotamia until the end of the Bronze Age, ca. 1200 BCE.

LOOKING AHEAD

The Bronze Age civilization of Mesopotamia was not the only river valley civilization to arise at this time in the ancient Near East. Indeed, at exactly the same time, another civilization was developing in the Nile River valley of Egypt, a civilization that was similar to that of Mesopotamia in its general outlines but was also very different in the way that it responded to its own particular geographical circumstances.

FURTHER READING

Ascalone, Enrico. *Mesopotamia: Assyrians, Sumerians, Babylonians.* Dictionaries of Civilizations 1. Berkeley: University of California Press, 2007.

Bottéro, Jean, André Finet, Bertrand Lafont, George Roux, *Everyday Life in Ancient Mesopotamia.* Baltimore: Johns Hopkins University Press, 2001.

Charvát, Petr, *Zainab Bahrani, Marc Van de Mieroop, Mesopotamia Before History.* London: Routledge, 2002.

Crawford, Harriet E.W. Sumer and the Sumerians. Cambridge: Cambridge University Press, 2004.

Fagan, Brian. *The Long Summer: How Climate Changed Civilisation.* London: Granta Books, 2004.

Kramer, S. M. *The Sumerians, Their History, Culture, and Character.* Chicago: University of Chicago Press, 1963.

Leick, Gwendolyn. *Mesopotamia: The Invention of the City.* London: Allen Lane, 2001; Penguin, 2002.

Matthews, Roger. *The Archaeology of Mesopotamia: Theories and Approaches.* London: Routledge, 2003.

Newgrosh, Bernard. *Chronology at the Crossroads: The Late Bronze Age in Western Asia.* Leicester: Troubador, 2007.

Nissen, Hans J. *The Early History of the Ancient Near East, 9000–2000* B.C. Chicago: University of Chicago Press, 1990.

Roux, Georges. *Ancient Iraq.* London: Allen and Urwin, 1964.

Van de Mieroop, Marc. *A History of the Ancient Near East ca. 3000—323 BC.* Oxford: Wiley-Blackwell, 2006.

CHAPTER 3

EGYPT AND THE BRONZE AGE
(5000–1200 BCE)

As had occurred in Mesopotamia, a Bronze Age civilization likewise arose in the Nile River Valley, similar in its broad outlines to the Mesopotamian one but very different in its specific manifestations. As in Mesopotamia, the manner in which civilization developed in Egypt and the role that people played in it were heavily influenced by geography, although the geographical characteristics of Egypt and Mesopotamia were very different. In particular, Egypt's geographical isolation created political unity, as opposed to the characteristic disunity of Mesopotamia. Being for the most part unaffected by either internal disruption or outside invasion, Egyptian history passed relatively smoothly through three periods, the Old, Middle, and New Kingdoms, each with its own particular characteristics.

BEFORE THE PHARAOHS (5000–3000 BCE)

As in Mesopotamia, Egyptian civilization was the result of a long process of evolution from the cultures of the Neolithic and Chalcolithic ages, although in Egypt the lead-up to civilization took only about half as long as it had in Mesopotamia. Likewise, geography played a significant role in how Egyptian culture and civilization initially developed. Gradually, Egypt became increasingly politically unified as regional rulers gained greater authority. By 3000 BCE, Egypt had become unified under a single, all-powerful ruler.

Geography and Culture

Egyptian civilization, too, arose in the context of a major river valley. But that was about as far as the similarities with Mesopotamia went. In Egypt, life revolved around the river even more than it did in Mesopotamia. The flooding of the **Nile River** was quite predictable and very different from the irregular, often catastrophic Mesopotamian floods. The summer monsoon rains in central Africa poured into the Nile, which overflowed its banks in mid-August. The water gradually receded during the fall, leaving behind a layer of fertile soil. Egypt was easily the richest agricultural land in the Mediterranean world, yielding up to three crops a year. Life in Egypt was based on the repeating Nile cycle, resulting in the three four-month-long Egyptian seasons: "Iinundation" (flood), "Going forth" (planting), and "Deficiency" (low water and harvest). In order to forecast the seasons, the Egyptians created a calendar based on the moon, with twelve months of thirty days each. Five days were added at the end of each year to make a 365-day year that serves as the basis of the modern calendar.

The Nile Valley was divided into two sections. **Lower Egypt** consisted only of the Nile delta, and **Upper Egypt** extended all the way to **Nubia**, the region south of Egypt that controlled access to the products of central Africa. Eventually Egypt was further divided into about forty-two smaller districts called **nomes**, twenty-two in Upper Egypt and twenty in Lower Egypt. Egypt was bounded to the east and west by the increasingly inhospitable Sahara Desert, which eventually harbored very little human habitation. In many places, the desert cliffs directly overhung the cultivated fields. Ancient Egypt, therefore, was a strip of agricultural territory six hundred miles long but only four to twenty miles wide. People never were far from the river, which served as the primary transportation route up and down the river valley. Journeys were made by boat, and there was no need in early Egypt for roads or for wheeled vehicles and horses to pull them.

If Mesopotamia was characterized by cultural change resulting from constant contacts with foreign peoples, Egypt was generally isolated from foreign contact and was marked by cultural continuity. The only easy means of access into Egypt were via the Nile River either in the north or the south. As long as these approaches were protected, Egypt was safe from invasion and even to some degree from outside influence. The predictable replenishment of the soil, coupled with the lack of fear of floods or invasions, gave the Egyptians a completely different outlook on life from the Mesopotamians. The Egyptians were supremely optimistic, convinced that they were the best people, with the best life, on Earth. In fact, they thought that foreigners were somehow not quite human.

The Origin of the Egyptians

A century ago it was thought that Egyptian history began with dynasties of **pharaohs**—as the Egyptian rulers came to be known, from a word meaning "Great House"—in the early third millenium BCE, but it now is recognized that predynastic Egypt had a long history extending millenia into the past. During the late Palaeolithic Period, until about 5500 BCE, the Nile Valley was exploited for hunting gazelles, giraffes, wild cattle, ducks, and geese; for fishing,

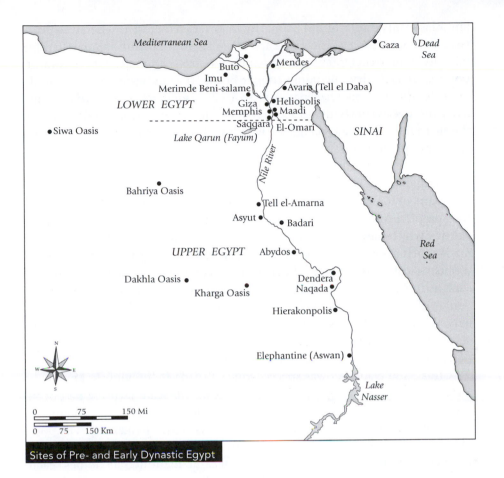

Sites of Pre- and Early Dynastic Egypt

especially for Nile perch and catfish; and for gathering wild grains such as millet. In the Nile Valley, therefore, agriculture commenced a bit later than it did in Mesopotamia, in part because the Sahara region received enough rainfall to be able to support a pastoral lifestyle. But as of about 5500 BCE, the Sahara began to dry out as a consequence of changing weather patterns. As the grassland disappeared, both animals and people were forced out in search of new food sources. Many of the people settled in the Nile River Valley and found it advantageous to adopt an agricultural lifestyle.

An older view that Egyptian civilization was imported by eastern invaders from Mesopotamia now has been abandoned for a model that sees it as an indigenous development.

By about 5000 BCE, a sophisticated Chalcolithic culture, first located at al-Badari in Upper Egypt and known as the Badarian Culture (ca. 4500–3800 BCE), had arisen. Cattle, goats, pigs, and sheep had been domesticated, and antelopes, gazelles, giraffes, and elephants continued to be hunted. People living in small villages pursued an agricultural economy, perhaps the first in Egypt, cultivating barley, wheat, and lentils. The culture is characterized by a distinctive pottery, made without a potter's wheel, with reddish brown bodies

HISTORICAL CAUSALITY

How was the role of geography similar and different in the development of the civilizations of Egypt and Mesopotamia?

and black rims that is found primarily in desert cemeteries, where the dead were laid out on mats. The existence of social stratification is suggested by persons with richer grave goods—such as cosmetic materials, decorated pottery, and jewelry, including copper beads, that indicated a belief in an afterlife—being buried in separate sections of a cemetery. At this time, moreover, the river valley culture was not yet differentiated from the culture of the surrounding semi-arid regions, which still were able to support a considerable population.

The succeeding culture, dating from ca. 4500 to 3500 BCE and also from Upper Egypt, now is called the Naqada I Culture after a modern town on the west bank of the Nile (it previously was known as the Amratian Culture, after the site of el-Amreh near Abydos). Along with adopting much of Badarian culture, which they first overlapped and then supplanted, the Naqada I people made much use of copper and highly worked flint. Society became even more differentiated, as reflected in the inclusion in graves not only of grave goods such as food, weapons, jewelry, and decorated pottery but also of miniature figures of women and slaves, made from ivory and clay. These could suggest a belief in an afterlife in which all of the deceased's needs, including servants, continued to be met. Carved stone ceremonial maceheads indicated particular prestige.

Circa 3500 Naqada I was succeeded by Naqada II (previously known as Gerzean, after the village of Gerzeh). By now, full-scale farming had been mastered, with dams, dikes, and canals used to store water and conduct it to larger areas of farmland in what is known as "basin irrigation." The population increased in much the same way that it did in Mesopotamia, and villages grew into towns and cities that became identified as nomes, each of which was represented by a symbol, usually an animal totem. Different cities expressed their local identity by their preference for certain of the Egyptian gods.

An obsession with status and prestige is a characteristic of most societies, up to and including the modern day.

Society became further differentiated as a result of an increasing obsession with status; the rich were buried in tombs lined in mud brick and including elaborate grave goods, such as ivory, lapis lazuli, and the first gold ornaments attested in Egypt. The elite individuals represented in these burials would have been local princes or kings and would have controlled sufficient local resources to be able to build and furnish increasingly elaborate tombs. An elaborated belief in some form of afterlife is suggested by the burial with the dead of grave goods such as food, clothing, jewelry, crockery, and even small clay servants, all intended for use in the next world. Long-distance trade routes, controlled by the rulers of the cities of Upper Egypt, where all traffic was funneled along the Nile, brought in prestige goods from Mesopotamia and Palestine to the north and sub-Saharan Africa to the south, where Egyptian rulers expanded their authority. By this time, moreover, the river valley cultures increasingly dominated the surrounding desert cultures.

Meanwhile, in Lower Egypt to the north, the earliest known settlement of the Nile Delta was found at Merimde Beni-salame, a Neolithic agricultural village dating to about 4800–4250 BCE, contemporary with the Badarian culture to the south. It consisted of reed huts laid out on winding streets. Emmer wheat was cultivated, and there also were domesticated cattle, sheep, and pigs. Hunting and fishing provided an appreciable part of the diet. A distinctive herringbone pottery style was used, and flax was spun for cloth. The bodies of adults were buried in the settlement without any grave goods.

Currently, no early delta sites are dated between the end of the **Merimde Culture** and ca. 3800, when the **Maadi Culture**, named after modern Maadi and lasting until ca. 3200, appears in the western delta, roughly contemporaneous with the Naqada II period in Upper Egypt. Although there was a copper industry, the Maadian culture was not as complex as the Naqada culture. Oval huts with grain storage pits indicate a permanent sedentary lifestyle. For the first time, cemeteries outside the settlement area were used with grave goods, suggesting a belief in an afterlife. At this period, moreover, life in Lower Egypt seems to have been rather more egalitarian than in Upper Egypt. The houses were better built than those at Merimde, but grave goods and architecture do not suggest any social stratification, and there was little specialization of labor. The presence of artifacts from outside the area does, however, indicate an increasing involvement in trade.

During this period, all of the arable land near the Nile had been occupied by permanent settlers. There was no more room for new settlers, a problem exacerbated by an influx of desert dwellers as the Sahara continued to dry out; by 3000 BCE it had reached the current state of hyperaridity. Thus the possibility of hostile action arose. The village at Maadi, for example, was protected by a ditch and wooden palisade, and scattered human bones and layers of ashes, coupled with the lack of many items of any value, suggest that on at least one occasion the village was captured and sacked and testify to the insecurities that could arise once one had anything worth stealing.

TABLE 3.1   CULTURES OF PREDYNASTIC EGYPT (ALL DATES BCE)

Upper Egypt		Lower Egypt	
Badarian	5000–3800	Merimde	4800–4250
Naqada I/Amratian	4500–3500	-----------	-----------
Naqada II/Gerzean	3500–3200	Maadi	3800–3200
Naqada III	3200–3000	Naqada III	3200–3000

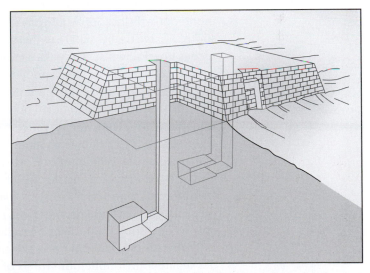

Reconstruction of an Egyptian mastaba. The actual tomb chamber was underground and not part of the mud brick superstructure.

The Naqada III Period

As of 3200 BCE, the beginning of the Naqada III period (3200–3000 BCE), the graves of rulers in Upper Egypt are marked by very rich grave goods and indicate a status- and prestige-based society in which the ruler was markedly supreme. The mortuary practices of elites and rulers throughout Egypt developed a form of burial architecture known as the **mastaba**, from an Arabic word meaning "bench." Above ground, a mastaba consisted of a mud-brick boxlike rectangular enclosure as much as thirty feet high with sloping sides and a flat top that contained a small space for leaving offerings. Inside there was one stone- or brick-lined room for leaving offerings and another containing a statue of the deceased. The actual burial chamber was cut into rock beneath the sunken room and was accessed by a narrow shaft that was filled with rubble to protect the burial. Sliding and false doors also were used to inhibit tomb robbers.

Egyptian sites can be known by ancient Egyptian, ancient Greek, and modern names. Here, the Egyptian and Greek (in parentheses) versions usually are given.

During this period, Egypt became increasingly unified. Two kingdoms developed in Upper and Lower Egypt; the ruler of Upper Egypt wore the Hedjet, a tall white crown, and the ruler of Lower Egypt wore the Deshret, a broad red wicker crown bearing the curly proboscis of a honeybee. The most important centers in Lower Egypt were Per-Wadjet (Buto), represented by the cobra goddess Wadjet, and Zau (Saïs), devoted to the water, war, and weaving goddess Neith. Upper Egypt had three influential centers. The name of Nubt (modern Naqada), meant "city of gold," probably reflecting the exploitation of nearby gold deposits. The god of Nubt was Set, a storm, and the rulers of the city controlled much of the surrounding territory. Elite burials reflected wealth compounded by commerce. Further south on the Nile was Nekhen (Hierakonpolis), which had as its totem the falcon god known as **Horus**. Its more southerly location would have given the city control over commerce to the south. A large timber palace with a mud-brick gateway and a series of recessed niches now known as the "palace facade" style apparently was the residence of a king; a circular stone area represents the first known stone temple precinct in Egypt. The elites developed their own private cemetery of elaborate burials.

This (Abydos), located north of Naqada, worshiped the local cemetery god Khentiamentiu. Here, the so-called tomb U-j, from ca. 3150 BCE, consists of eight mud-brick chambers containing many objects of foreign origin and an ivory scepter, the symbol of rule. Also included were bone labels with the earliest attested Egyptian writing, which also was used in serekhs, a method for writing royal names consisting of a stylized palace facade containing simple symbols, such as animals, representing the ruler's name. Some of these symbols were absorbed into later hieroglyphs, but others went out of use. These early records provide some very sketchy evidence for the existence and activities of late-fourth-millenium rulers of Egypt.

Archaeological evidence shows that Nekhen (Hierakonpolis) and This (Abydos) became the main competitors for power in Upper Egypt. Initially,

KING SCORPION

The Scorpion King uses a hoe either to open an irrigation ditch or plow a furrow.

The history of the rulers of Egypt prior to the definitive unification under Narmer ca. 3000 BCE is shrouded in mystery. According to the Royal Annals, some twenty-five kings, many identified with animals, ruled before the official First Dynasty. A few of these predynastic kings, such as Crocodile, Iry-Hor, Ka, and Scorpion, are independently attested. Although the Royal Annals have these kings ruling in sequence, many of those that actually existed probably ruled different bits of Egypt concurrently.

The best evidence for "King Scorpion" comes from a ceremonial mace head found in 1898 in a temple in Nekhen (Hierakonpolis) and now in the British Museum in London. It depicts a man wearing the tall crown of Upper Egypt whose towering stature indicates his great status with respect to other people. In front of his face are a rosette, which may have indicated royalty, and a scorpion that, based on other analogies, represented the hieroglyphic version of his name; but because these never became standard hieroglyphic symbols, it is impossible to know what sounds the signs represented, and the king is known simply as "King Scorpion." He holds a hoe that could signify either plowing a furrow or, more likely, opening an irrigation ditch. Elsewhere on the mace head, the depictions of dead lapwings—wading birds— hanging from standards, perhaps meaning defeated cities of Lower Egypt, and nine bows, a symbol used later to indicate enemies of Egypt, are interpreted as references to warfare in which King Scorpion was victorious. A whole raft of theories have been proposed to try to work King Scorpion into what else is known of predynastic history, including (1) an identification of Scorpion with Narmer under a different name (pharaohs had several different names), (2) an identification with Narmer's predecessor Ka, again using a different version of the name, (3) that King Scorpion did not come from Nekhen (Hierakonpolis) but from This (Abydos) (even though no tomb of his has been found there), (4) or even that this King Scorpion is just a reference to an earlier King Scorpion and did not exist at all. But it seems most likely that King Scorpion was one of many powerful rulers of different regions of Egypt, some of whom even may have momentarily gained some degree of control over most or all of Egypt just prior to the final, definitive unification of 3000 BCE.

the rulers of Nekhen, such as **King Scorpion**, controlled much of Upper Egypt. Their authority extended all the way into Lower Nubia, where an incense burner portrays **Horus** and a ruler in the crown of Upper Egypt. Meanwhile, the rulers of This (Abydos) may have extended their authority over the less politically sophisticated Nile Delta area and even have become rulers of a partially united Egypt. The rulers of these cities are known collectively as "Dynasty

Zero" because they ruled before the time when Egypt is believed to have been united under a single ruler. Most of them are known very poorly. Their written Horus names, consisting of a falcon standing on a serekh, appear on pottery and rock carvings and are very difficult to interpret because of continuing difficulties in deciphering early Egyptian writing.

THE EARLY DYNASTIC PERIOD (3000–2700 BCE)

By the end of the Naqada III period, the drying out of the climate was complete, leading to the final desertification of the lands surrounding the Nile and making the population of Egypt completely dependent on extensive exploitation of agriculture that could be accomplished only by the mobilization of large numbers of people for labor in agriculture and water control. This made some form of centralized control even more necessary and no doubt played a role in the appearance, toward the end of the fourth century BCE, of a unified Egypt ruled by a pharaoh who not only received authority from the gods but also was perceived as a god himself. The process by which unification occurred is poorly known, although there is evidence for at least some military action. And the historian's task is made a bit easier by the increasing use of writing.

The unification of Egypt occurred at the same time as the beginning of Egyptian civilization, as defined in the first chapter. Historians organize the long history of ancient Egyptian civilization by two different methods. One divides ancient Egyptian history up into three main periods, the Old Kingdom (2700–2200 BCE), the Middle Kingdom (2050–1730 BCE), and the New Kingdom (1570–1070 BCE). A preliminary, formative period, the Early Dynastic Period (3000–2700 BCE), preceded the Old Kingdom. Each of these periods had certain unique identifying characteristics that distinguished it from other periods. The three main periods are separated by two Intermediate Periods during which Egyptian unity disintegrated. A much more detailed chronological organization, which was used in antiquity, is based on **dynasties**, or families, of Egyptian pharaohs, running from the First Dynasty in the early third millenium BCE to the Thirty-first Dynasty in the fourth century BCE.

Egyptian Record Keeping

As in Mesopotamia, the first few centuries of Egyptian civilization are shrouded in mystery. Writing was still in a developmental stage and was little used for what we would consider to be historical record keeping. Early documents recorded the deeds of pharaohs or the receipts and expenditures of royal and temple property. Egyptian writing, known as **hieroglyphs**, developed quite differently from Mesopotamian writing and always retained its ideograms, with some seven hundred symbols used to represent different words, thoughts, or meanings. In order to represent difficult words, such as foreign names, consonant values (without vowels) were assigned to twenty-four of

THE HISTORY LABORATORY

DECIPHERING THE ROSETTA STONE

The last attested use of Egyptian hieroglyphic script occurred during the Roman Empire in the fourth century CE. Subsequently, even though many monumental hieroglyphic stone inscriptions were visible, no one could translate them. Attempts to decipher hieroglyphs by Arab scholars began as early as the ninth century CE. European scholars did the same beginning in the fifteenth century, but with no success. The key to the decipherment was an inscription discovered in 1799 at Rashid (Rosetta in French) in Egypt during Napoleon's Egyptian invasion. This **Rosetta Stone** had what looked like the same text written in three different languages: Egyptian hieroglyphs, Egyptian **demotic** (a simplified hieratic script that also was untranslated), and Greek, which any educated person could read: it was a document written in 196 BCE under the Macedonian king Ptolemy V of Egypt restoring tax exemptions to Egyptian priests. Ptolemy claimed to be the most recent in the long line of pharaohs, describing himself as "King like the Sun, the Great King of the Upper and Lower Lands," which explains why the document also was written in hieroglyphs.

But how the Egyptian scripts were to be understood remained a mystery until the 1820s, when the secret of hieroglyphs was finally cracked by the French scholar Jacques-François Champollion, who wrote, "It is a complex system, writing figurative, symbolic, and phonetic all at once, in the same text, the same phrase, I would almost say in the same word." The key to breaking the code lay in the recognition that some of the demotic symbols were preserved

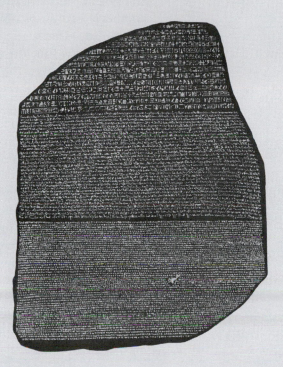

in the contemporary Coptic language and that the king's name, Ptolemy, in the Greek text matched the hieroglyphs in the cartouches in the Egyptian text. The knowledge gained from understanding some of the hieroglyphs then was used to translate the rest of them. The stone itself was captured from the French by the British in 1801 and now is in the British Museum in London.

the hieroglyphic symbols. For example, a falcon symbol also represented the consonant "M." In this way, Egyptian writing incorporated the concept of an alphabet, but it was never anything more than a last resort. Other signs represented combinations of two or three sounds. True hieroglyphs were used only for large ceremonial inscriptions written on stone monuments. A cursive form of hieroglyphs called hieratic was used for writing with pen and ink on papyrus or on the walls of tombs.

Papyrus was made from a type of bulrush that grew along the Nile. The outer skin of the hollow papyrus stem was peeled off and the inner pith was split, flattened, and cut into strips up to fifteen inches long. The strips were laid side by side vertically, slightly overlapping, creating an uneven side, with another layer of strips laid horizontally, edge to edge on top, creating a smooth side. The two layers were moistened, pounded together, and then dried under pressure in the sun. The gum released by the fibers helped to fuse the strips into a uniform sheet. The sheets were rubbed with pumice dust and trimmed. A standard papyrus sheet thus was usually around ten inches square. A papyrus scroll was made by gluing many papyrus sheets together, with the smooth layers on the same side, to create rolls up to thirty-five feet long. Writing usually was done only on the smooth side.

Like the Mesopotamians, the Egyptians preserved lists of their rulers, often for the purpose of demonstrating the legitimacy and antiquity of a contemporary ruler. Thus selective lists of a particular ruler's predecessors— omitting recent adversaries or earlier rulers from rival cities—were painted on the walls of temples or inscribed on stone. The earliest preserved list, known as the Royal Annals and preserved in stone fragments at Palermo in Sicily and elsewhere, lists pharaohs from the First to the middle of the Fifth Dynasty. This list, like the Sumerian King List, begins with thousands of years of legendary pharaohs. It then has **Menes** unifying Egypt and continues up to pharaoh Neferirkare (ca. 2475–2455 BCE). It includes year-by-year accounts of information such as the height of the Nile floods, religious festivals, buildings, taxes collected, and wars. Later lists were painted on the walls of temples and consisted of single names, without other information. The Royal List **of Abydos**, for example, dates to the reign of Seti I (1291–1278 BCE) and lists seventy-six of his ancestor pharaohs. Other such lists, not nearly so well preserved, also survive.

In addition to these "official" lists, composite lists presumably making use of them also were compiled at later times. The most significant of these, the Turin Papyrus, dates to the reign of Ramses II (1279–1212 BCE) or later. It has been pieced together from 160 tiny papyrus fragments from a document originally about five feet long; the beginning and end are lost. Beginning with gods who supposedly first ruled Egypt, it lists the names of pharaohs, beginning with Menes, organized into groups based on what city they lived in, with the length of the reign either in years or in years, months, and days. Then, in the third century BCE, the Egyptian priest Manetho composed a "History of Egypt" that organized the pharaohs into "**dynasties**," groups of pharaohs that seemed connected to each other. The organizational structure and sequence of rulers provided by these lists, coupled with correlated dated evidence from the civilizations of Mesopotamia, permits a detailed chronological framework of Egyptian history to be created.

In this section of the Royal List of Abydos, in the temple of pharaoh Seti I (1291–1278 BCE), Seti and his son, later pharaoh Ramses II (1279–1212 BCE), worship their ancestors whose names are listed before them.

The Unification of Egypt

Ultimately, probably just before 3000 BCE, the rulers of This (Abydos) triumphed over other local Egyptian rulers and united Egypt under a pharaoh who established the First Dynasty. Political unity then became the standard condition of ancient Egypt. In contemporary documents and king lists, this ruler's name is represented by the hieroglyphic symbols catfish and wedge, whose later phonetic values have been interpreted as "Narmer." A problem with this interpretation, however, is that later king lists are unanimous in calling the first pharaoh not Narmer but Menes. Although many complicated solutions have been proposed to explain the discrepancy, such as a suggestion that Menes is to be identified with Aha, the second ruler of the First Dynasty, the simplest explanation is based on the fact that pharaohs had up to five different names. Along with the aforementioned Horus name, a Two Ladies name began with a vulture and cobra representing the goddesses of Upper and Lower Egypt, Nekhbet of Nekhen (Hierakonpolis) and Wadjet of Per-Wadjet (Buto); and a Horus of Gold name began with the Horus falcon above the sign for gold. Two additional names, the Throne Name, preceded by signs meaning "Lord of the Two Lands," and the Son of Ra name, the name given at birth and preceded

NARMER UNITES EGYPT (ca. 3000 BCE)

by the symbols for a duck (meaning "son") and the sun, each were placed in a rectangular enclosure known as a **cartouche.** The Son of Ra name is the one preferred by modern historians. Given that Narmer was a Horus Name and Menes (or Min) was a Son of Ra name, it is quite likely that Narmer and Menes are, in fact, the same person.

Although some have suggested that the unification was carried out largely peacefully, it is clear that at least some military action was involved: the so-called "Libyan palette," for example, depicts attacks on fortified cities, and the famous "Narmer palette" shows King Narmer bashing an enemy, large numbers of defeated enemies, and an attack on a city. The normal condition of Egypt now was to be united under a single ruler, in stark contrast to the customary disunity of Mesopotamia. Once Egypt had been unified, continued unity became a royal idealogy: unity was good, disunity was bad—a concept contrary

The two-sided Narmer palette, found in the temple of Horus in Nekhen (Hierakonpolis) and originally used for mixing cosmetics, is thought to depict the unification of Upper and Lower Egypt by **Narmer**, the founder, ca. 3000 BCE, of the First Dynasty. Although it contains some very rudimentary writing, most of its importance comes from interpreting its iconography.

Atop both sides, between heads of the cow goddess Bat, is a serekh bearing the symbols for catfish and wedge, representing the sounds "n" and "r," which are interpreted as "Narmer." On the front, the same signs reappear in the upper left in front of a standing ruler wearing the broad crown of Lower Egypt and holding the mace and flail, traditional symbols of the pharaoh's authority. The ruler's status also is indicated by his much larger size. Behind him stands his sandal bearer, possibly his son, marked by a rosette probably representing, as on the King Scorpion mace, a sign of royalty. In front of him is a much smaller man, perhaps a general, with the name "Tshet" accompanied by four even smaller men carrying standards consisting of an animal skin, a dog, and two falcons. To their right are ten headless corpses with symbols for a ship, a falcon, and a harpoon above them, possibly signs of defeated cities. Below them, two men hold on leashes two serpopards, mythical lions with snakelike necks; it was in the space between the necks that the cosmetics were mixed. Below this a bull, probably representing the king, batters down a city wall while trampling yet another defeated enemy.

The back of the palette shows the king, in the tall crown of Upper Egypt, using a ceremonial mace to bash the head of a defeated enemy, probably an enemy king. To the right, the Horus falcon of Upper Egypt tramples the papyrus plants of Lower Egypt and hooks a captured enemy emerging from them. The six stalks may represent hieroglyphs for six thousand captives. Below are two sprawled enemies accompanied by symbols that may represent defeated cities.

The depictions of Narmer as ruler of both Upper and Lower Egypt, coupled with First Dynasty king lists that show Narmer as the first pharaoh, not to mention the consideration that Narmer not only was buried at This (Abydos) but also was commemorated at Nekhen (Hierakonpolis) (King Scorpion, for example, was commemorated only at Hierakonpolis), make it clear that as far as the early Egyptians were concerned, Egypt had been united by Narmer. Later Egyptian pharaohs wore the Pschent, a double crown that united the crowns of Upper and Lower Egypt and bore a cobra (the uraeus) and a vulture, and Horus became the god that personified the pharaoh.

to Mesopotamian idealogies that focused on the centrality of individual cities. Unity coupled with a degree of geographical isolation meant that Egyptian civilization could develop in peaceful conditions during which cities did not even have defensive walls.

Egyptian Civilization

Although civilization is deemed to have begun in Egypt about 3000 BCE, it took a while, as in Mesopotamia, for writing to develop to the point at which historical records of use to the modern historian were being created. Little, therefore, is known of the first two Egyptian dynasties (ca. 2920–2649 BCE) beyond the names of the pharaohs and a few stray pieces of information, such as Manetho's report that Menes "was snatched and killed by a hippopotamus." Even after the unification, Nekhen (Hierakonpolis) retained an important place in the kingdom, and the rulers of the First Dynasty from This (Abydos) left funeral dedications at both cities. Traditionally, Menes established a new capital city for a united Egypt at Ineb-Hedj (**Memphis**), "the City of the White Walls," just south of where Upper and Lower Egypt met, which became the new center of government. The city god of Memphis, **Ptah**, was seen as the god who created the world simply by speaking. In fact, the word "Egypt" comes from the Greek mispronunciation of the Egyptian word "Het-Ka-Ptah," or "House of the spirit of Ptah," a reference to Memphis. The Egyptians called their land *Kemet*, "the black land," an allusion to the rich alluvial soil repeatedly deposited by the Nile. During the Second Dynasty, Ra (or Re), a god of the noonday sun worshipped just across the river from Memphis at Om (**Heliopolis**), became the most important god of Egypt.

It also has been suggested that the term "black land" referred not to the soil but to a Black African population that originally settled Egypt, but given that the Egyptian term Kemet *customarily was contrasted with Deshret, the "red land" of the desert, this is unlikely.*

During this period all of the basic elements of Egyptian culture, religion, and government developed. Rather than being merely representatives of the gods, as in Mesopotamia, Egyptian rulers were full-fledged gods in their own right. They also shared identity with the most important gods of the Egyptian pantheon. For example, the pharaohs identified themselves with Ra by making his name part of their own and by styling themselves the "Son of Ra." They also shared identity with Ptah and Horus. This kind of mixing and matching of gods sometimes troubles people in the modern day, who like to have everything in its place. In that way, we are like the Mesopotamians. But the Egyptians had no problems with seeing their gods, and pharaohs, functioning in different modes at different times. The pharaoh's family consisted of a chief wife, who, because he was a god, often was also his sister; several other wives and **concubines**; and his children, one of whom would succeed him as pharaoh. This usually would be a son, even though was no constitutional bar to having a woman pharaoh, as occasionally did happen.

The entire machinery of the state revolved around the pharaoh. He owned all of the land and all that it produced. The Egyptian system of dating was based on the regnal (ruling) years of the pharaoh; thus an event might be dated "Fifth regnal year, third month of Deficiency, day six, under the Splendor of Pharaoh so-and-so." But the pharaoh could not administer all of Egypt by himself. He needed assistance. As a result, a complex administrative bureaucracy arose. The pharaoh was assisted by a **vizier**, known as the "Superintendent of All the Works of the Pharaoh," a kind of chief executive officer who oversaw the administrative details. Produce was stored in a central granary at Memphis and redistributed to those who worked the land and carried out other functions at court. Records were kept of the rise and fall of the Nile, allowing future flooding to be predicted. The centralized Egyptian bureaucracy thus was quite different from the fragmented administrations into which Mesopotamia was divided.

Subordinate to the vizier were the governors of Upper and Lower Egypt, and the nomes were administered by nobles called **nomarchs**. Ranking below them was a growing bureaucracy that included persons ranging from the "Overseer of the Two Granaries," in charge of keeping track of grain storage and distribution, to priests, scribes, canal diggers, and tomb diggers. Other skilled workers including potters, carpenters, metalworkers, sculptors, painters, weavers, dancers, musicians, and embalmers. In a society in which advancement was based on the goodwill of the pharaoh, there were many opportunities for social advancement, as seen, for example, in the fourth-dynasty case of a certain Metjen who rose from scribe to nomarch, or the later example of Weni, who durng the Sixth Dynasty began his career as keeper of a storehouse and rose to be Governor of Upper Egypt.

But the mass of the population consisted of peasant farmers who worked the rich land. They lived in small permanent houses on the higher ground bordering the flood plain and commuted to work in the fields. Unlike Mesopotamia, there was little private landholding, and most of the people worked land that belonged to the pharaoh either directly or indirectly, being overseen by nobles or priests in the name of the pharaoh. Unlike in Mesopotamia, few native Egyptians were enslaved, the exception being a small number enslaved as penalties for crimes. Most slaves came from foreign lands, either through purchase or from occasional raids into the Sinai or Nubia. In general, Egyptians lived in secure and blissful ignorance of the rest of the world. There were no walled cities and no standing armies or professional soldiers: armies were recruited on an as-needed basis from among the general population, and Egyptian military policy was to overwhelm any enemies by sheer weight of numbers.

Unlike the Mesopotamians, the Egyptians did believe that there was a divine order to things and that there was justice in the world. The Egyptians had faith that the gods, led by the pharaoh, had their best interests at heart and would take good care of them. They believed that just as everything had gone well in the past, things would continue to go well in the future. Upholding Egyptian optimism was their belief in the concept of **Ma'at**, the divinely mandated order, stability, and justice that governed all activities involving both people and the gods. Even the pharaoh was bound by Ma'at to rule equitably and efficiently and could be trusted not to exceed the bounds of his authority. As a result of their confidence in the gods and in the pharaoh, the Egyptians felt no compulsion to impose order on the universe: it was already there. They felt no need to issue law codes because everyone already knew what the laws were. The Egyptians were so supremely confident of the superiority of their ways that they believed they were the only real people in the world; views of other peoples were based on difference, not similarity, as seen in the Great Hymn to Aton of the fourteenth century BCE, which stated, "You place every man in his place. Tongues are separated in speech, skins are made different, for you make foreign lands different." For the Egyptians, contamination by foreign cultures was something to be avoided as much as possible.

The Egyptians' confidence in themselves, their rulers, and their gods resulted in a great degree of conservatism in Egyptian culture. Things did not change very quickly, if at all. Egyptian artistic styles, for example, which depicted stiff formalized figures shown in frontal or profile perspectives, remained unchanged for thousands of years. The cumbersome hieroglyphic writing system likewise remained in use throughout Egyptian history, long after other, much more effective systems of writing had been developed by foreign peoples. For the Egyptians, the preservation, and eternity, of their ancient culture validated them in their certainty that their way was the best.

THE OLD KINGDOM (2700–2200 BCE)

It is only with the Third Dynasty, beginning around 2700 BCE, that Egypt manifests a fully developed civilization, including large stone architecture, complex government and administration, and a sophisticated literature. This period, from 2700 to 2200 BCE, is known as the **Old Kingdom**. Its primary characteristics are the all-powerful position of the pharaoh and the initial construction of huge monuments known as **pyramids**.

The Age of the Pyramids

For much of the Old Kingdom the pharaohs not only were thought of as gods but also had the absolute authority of gods. This meant, among other things,

> **CROSS-CULTURAL CONNECTIONS**
>
> In what ways did the pyramids constructed in Mesopotamia and Egypt have similar and different construction methods and functions?

that they had the power to mobilize the entire population of Egypt to do whatever they wished. Along with putting the people to work in agriculture, the pharaohs of the first two dynasties soon also used their labor to construct elaborate brick mastabas. These tombs were intended to protect the mortal remains of a pharaoh, who, after all, was a god and therefore immortal. Dead pharaohs were accompanied by grave goods that would permit them to enjoy in the afterlife the same kind of life they had had while they were alive. Only the pharaoh had a full-scale afterlife; others could only hope to share it by being buried nearby. The very earliest pharaohs were accompanied in death by their servants, who either committed suicide or were sacrificed and buried in pits that surrounded the pharaoh's mastaba. Soon, however, dead retainers were replaced in the tombs by **ushabtis**, clay figures of servants who would care for the deceased in the afterlife.

Around the beginning of the **Third Dynasty** (ca. 2688 BCE), pharaohs began experimenting with different building techniques. The Royal Annals record that the last pharaoh of the Second Dynasty or the first of the Third built the first stone building in Egypt. This has been identified as a large enclosure, not studied until the 1990s, at **Saqqara**, just north of Memphis. It was made of layers of roughly cut limestone blocks and could have been an attempt to build a stone mastaba or other funerary structure.

The step pyramid complex of Djoser includes not just the pyramid itself but a maze of underground chambers and tunnels, an enclosure wall, and several pavilions, chapels, and temples associated with the cult of the dead pharaoh.

Much more significant innovations occurred during the reign of **Djoser** (2668–2649 BCE), the second pharaoh of the Third Dynasty. For one thing, the royal burial ground was moved from Abydos to Saqqara. Djoser's able vizier Imhotep designed a new kind of tomb by stacking up on top of each other six mastabas, now constructed from small stone blocks shaped like the mud bricks used in the mastabas. The result was the first large stone structure ever built, a step pyramid two hundred feet tall and about four hundred feet square, which was completed around 2650 BCE. It contained not only Djoser's mortal remains but also items from the times of nearly every earlier pharaoh and a large collection of early cursive ink writing. It also demonstrated a new ability of the pharaoh to mobilize huge amounts of labor.

The **Fourth Dynasty**, beginning about 2600 BCE, marked the golden age of pyramid Building. Pharaohs experimented with different forms of the pyramid tomb. The small stone bricks were replaced by large stone blocks. Sneferu (Soris) (2613–2589 BCE), the founder of the Fourth Dynasty, built no less than three pyramids. The first began as a seven-step pyramid but later had limestone facing added to smooth the sides into a true pyramid shape. In addition, the actual burial chamber now was within, not under, the pyramid. The so-called "Bent Pyramid," the largest pyramid to that time, began with a very steep fifty-five-degree angle of incline that then was lessened to forty-three degrees when it became apparent that the pyramid probably would collapse with such steep sides. Sneferu's last pyramid, the "Red Pyramid," is much simpler, having benefited from previous experimentation. It also appears to have fewer passages built into it, but it may be rather that the design was so sophisticated that Sneferu's remains—which never have been found—still lie concealed within secret passages and chambers. Sneferu' reign also is the best known reign of the early pharaohs. The Palermo Stone describes several foreign military expeditions, such as a campaign in Nubia that resulted in the capture of seven thousand slaves and two hundred thousand head of cattle. Henceforward, Egypt would maintain close social, political, and economic connections with Nubia, and Nubians, sometimes identifiable in the art by their darker skin pigmentation, became well integrated into Egyptian society. And to the north, the Palermo Stone records quarrying expeditions to the turquoise mines of the Sinai and eighty thousand measures of myrrh, used in the embalming process, imported from Punt on the coast of modern Somalia.

Three successive pharaohs, Khufu (Cheops) (c.2585–2566), Khafre (Rekhaf) (c.2558–2532), and Menkaure (Mycerinus) (c.2532–2514), then built gigantic pyramids. The largest of them, that of Khufu, took twenty-three years to build and is known now as the **Great Pyramid**. It was 781 feet at the base, 481 feet tall, and contained 2.3 million stone blocks ranging from two to fifteen tons each. The pharaoh's burial chamber was hidden deep inside the pyramid, protected by massive stone blocks and, it was hoped, safe from grave robbers. The pharaoh was accompanied not only by all the goods and materials he would need in the afterlife but also by **Pyramid Texts**, magical spells that were written on the walls to ensure that the pharaoh's transition to the afterlife would go smoothly. The pharaohs' pyramids also were accompanied by smaller pyramids that held the remains of other members of the royal family.

The pyramids later were considered to be the most monumental of the **Seven Wonders of the World**. Even in the modern day, there are those who believe that people could not possibly have constructed such marvels and that the Egyptians must have had the help of alien gods from outer space. But there is nothing really high-tech about the pyramids. All one needed to build one was lots of stone, lots of labor, and lots of time. These three pharaohs had all three. Nor should we credit the Hollywood version of pyramids being constructed by oppressed slave gangs—far from it. Work on a pyramid was viewed as a way of worshipping the pharaoh. Indeed, in many ways the work was an all-expenses-paid summer vacation, which carried with it tax exemptions for the work that was done. Once the crops had been planted or when the Nile flooded, tens or hundreds of thousands of Egyptians traveled up or down river for work on the new pyramid. There, they were fed and housed at the pharaoh's expense while they undertook the laborious and monotonous job of dragging limestone blocks, ferried in during the flood season, up earthen ramps to be stacked at the top of the pyramid. When the pyramid was complete, the ramps would be removed and the sides smoothed and covered with casing stones of polished white limestone—most of which, however, have fallen away.

Each pharaoh would have been able to calculate how long it would take to build his pyramid. Work would have commenced as soon as he took office. Little time would be spent finishing an uncompleted pyramid of a predecessor. As a result, pharaohs did everything that they could to make sure that the work proceeded as quickly as possible. Pharaohs gave tax breaks and other special privileges to nomarchs who fulfilled their material, supply, and labor quotas. Nobles and temples, and the priests who oversaw them, were granted their own estates, thus gaining direct ownership of land that in the past, at least in theory, had belonged to the pharaoh. The aforementioned Metjen, for example, received 200 *stat* of land (about 133 acres) for his service as nomarch. Granting these privileges aided individual pharaohs in the short term but made fewer resources available to their successors. The pharaohs also were dependent on the nomarch for other services as well, such as the provision of peasants for occasional military service. The nobles began to get inflated ideas of their own importance. Nomarchs asked that their sons be allowed to succeed them. In return for good behavior, the pharaohs acceded. As a result of their growing sense of self-esteem, nobles' challenges to the pharaoh's authority arose in the nomes.

> In the twelfth century CE, the Sultan of Egypt attempted to destroy the great pyramids but found it an impossible task.

The First Intermediate Period

The consequences of the development of nobles' self-consciousness can be starkly seen in the archaeological remains. On the one hand, the pyramids became smaller and smaller. And on the other, nobles began to locate their tombs not next to the pharaoh's pyramid but in their own nomes. They even put the pyramid texts in their own tombs, a sure sign that they now believed that they had a good afterlife in their own right and no longer needed to share in the pharaoh's. As the pharaoh's authority declined, powerful nobles moved in to take advantage of his weakness. The pharaoh Pepi II (2278–2184 BCE), the longest attested reigning monarch in history, had no sons despite his ninety-plus years of rule. His failure to produce many offspring, as well as his loss of authority, may have been related to his sexual preferences; it was rumored that he had a homosexual relationship with his general Sisene, and the Egyptians, who valued a pharaoh's bull-like heterosexual attributes, would have found this difficult to accept.

The last pharaoh of the Sixth Dynasty was said to be Nitocris (ca. 2180–2175), the first woman to rule Egypt. She was described as "the noblest and most beautiful woman of her time with blonde hair and a fair complexion" and was believed to have committed suicide because of the troubled times, which might have been worsened by a reduction of the annual floods. After her death, the nobles revolted, and Egypt lost its hard-won unity and stability.

THE AUTOBIOGRAPHY OF WENI

An example of the interaction between nobles and pharaohs is provided by the career of Weni, who served three different pharaohs of the Sixth Dynasty, Teti, Pepi I, and Merenra, approximately 2315–2270 BCE. His autobiography was ostentatiously recorded in fifty-one columns of hieroglyphs placed in his own tomb. Weni repeatedly refers to the great favor the pharaoh showed him. As a general, Weni campaigned against "sand dwellers" perhaps as far away as Palestine. As governor of Upper Egypt, he was able to repay the pharaoh for all the favor shown to him by providing materials for the pharaoh's pyramid. At the same time that Weni dutifully repeated the conventional praises of the pharaoh, he still felt self-confident enough to construct an elaborate tomb in which he glorified himself as much as glorified the pharaoh. Weni's account demonstrates that by this time, Egypt had a fully developed literature written by sophisticated, self-conscious authors.

The Governor of Upper Egypt, honored by Osiris, Weni says:

I was a youth under the majesty of Pharaoh Teti, my office being that of custodian of the storehouse, when I became inspector of the palace. When I was overseer of the robing-room under the majesty of Pharaoh Pepi, his majesty gave me the rank of companion and inspector of priests of his pyramid town. When I begged of the majesty of my lord that there be brought for me a sarcophagus of white stone from Tura, his majesty had a royal seal-bearer bring me this sarcophagus from Tura. While I was senior warden of Nekhen, his majesty made me a sole companion and overseer of the royal tenants. When there was a secret charge in the royal harem against Queen Weret-yamtes, his majesty made me go in to hear it alone. Never before had one like me heard a secret of the pharaoh's harem; but his majesty made me hear it, because I was worthy in his majesty's heart beyond any official of his, beyond any noble of his, beyond any servant of his.

When his majesty took action against the Asiatic Sand-dwellers, his majesty made an army of many tens of thousands from all of Upper Egypt, from Lower Egypt, and from Irtjet-Nubians, Medja-Nubians, Yam-Nubians, Wawat-Nubians, Kaau-Nubians; and from Tiemeh-land. His majesty sent me at the head of this army. This army returned in safety. It had

A period of disruption known as the First Intermediate Period (2200–2050 BCE) followed. Nobles contended with each other for power, and four different dynasties from Memphis and Henen-Nesut (Herakleopolis) in Lower Egypt tried to claim Egypt. Other competitors for power arose in Zawty (Lycopolis, modern Asyut) in Lower Egypt and Waset (Thebes) in Upper Egypt. The lack of a centralized administration meant that large-scale irrigation disintegrated. Famine stalked the land. It seemed to many that the world was turned upside down. The once-godlike pharaoh now seemed to be just another man trying to deal with his problems. One of the literary works composed during this period, known as "The Prophecy of Neferti," is set in the good times of the pharaoh Sneferu, who is asked by the prophet Neferti whether he would prefer to hear about the past or the future. Sneferu chooses the future, and Neferti tells of a ravaged the Sand-dwellers' land. It had flattened the Sand-dwellers' land. It had sacked its strongholds. It had cut down its figs, its vines. It had slain its troops by many ten thousands. It had carried off many as captives. His majesty praised me for it beyond anything. His majesty sent me to lead this army five times, to attack the land of the Sand-dwellers as often as they rebelled, with these troops. I acted so that his majesty praised me for it beyond anything.

When I was chamberlain of the palace and sandal-bearer, Pharaoh Merenra, my lord who lives forever, made me Governor of Upper Egypt because I was worthy in his majesty's heart, because I was rooted in his majesty's heart, because his majesty's heart was filled with me. I did a perfect job in Upper Egypt. Never before had the like been done in this Upper Egypt. I acted throughout so that his majesty praised me for it. His majesty sent me to Ibhat to bring the sarcophagus "Chest of the Living," together with its lid, and the costly august capstone for the pyramid "Merenra-Appears-in-Splendor." His majesty sent me to Yebu to bring a granite false door and its libation stone and granite lintels and to bring granite portals and libation stones for the upper chamber of the pyramid

"Merenra-Appears-in-Splendor." I traveled north to the pyramid "Merenra-Appears-in-Splendor" in six barges and three towboats in a single expedition. Thus everything his majesty commanded was done entirely as his majesty commanded. His majesty sent me to Hatnub to bring a great altar of alabaster. After it was quarried at Hatnub, I had it go downstream in this barge I had built for it, a barge of acacia wood of sixty cubits in length and thirty cubits in width. Assembled in seventeen days, in the third month of summer, when there was no water on the sandbanks, it landed at the pyramid "Merenra-Appears-in-Splendor" in safety. His majesty sent me to dig five canals in Upper Egypt, and to build three barges and four towboats of acacia wood of Wawat. I did it all in one year. Floated, they were loaded with very large granite blocks for the pyramid "Merenra-Appears-in-Splendor." As pharaoh Merenra who lives forever is august, exalted, and mighty more than any god, so everything came about in accordance with the ordinance commanded by his ka. I was one beloved of his father, praised by his mother, gracious to his brothers, the true Governor of Upper Egypt, honored by Osiris, Weni.

time—the time of the work's author—when Egypt would be in disarray and the usual rules would no longer apply:

> Lo, the great no longer rule the land,
> What was made has been unmade,
> The land is quite perished, no remnant is left,
> Dry is the river of Egypt,
> One crosses the water on foot;
> Foes have risen in the east,
> Asiatics have come down to Egypt.
> What should not be has come to pass.
> All happiness has vanished;

> The land is ruined, its fate decreed,
> Deprived of produce, lacking in crops,
> The land is shrunk—its rulers are many,
> It is bare—its taxes are great;
> Ra will withdraw from mankind:
> The beggar will gain riches,
> The slaves will be exalted.

All of the benefits of a unified country and a shared cultural vision had been lost. The Egyptians were bewildered about how to react or what to do, for their secure and sheltered world had been turned upside down.

THE MIDDLE KINGDOM (2050–1786 BC)

Not until 2050 BCE was the nomarch Montuhotep II (2060–2010 BCE) of Thebes, a member of the Eleventh Dynasty, finally able to reunify Egypt, commencing the period now known as the **Middle Kingdom** (2050–1786 BCE).

Like the Old Kingdom, the Middle Kingdom had its own particular identifying characteristics, such as weaker pharaohs and an expansion of the opportunity to have an afterlife.

THE LEGACY OF ANTIQUITY

How have ideas about, concepts of, and the significance of preservation of the mortal remains of the dead changed between ancient Egypt and the present?

Gods and Pharaohs of the Middle Kingdom

In general, the pharaohs of the Middle Kingdom were in a weaker position than those of the Old Kingdom. Even though the pharaoh still was looked on as a living god, his authority was threatened on the one hand by contentious nobles and on the other by a priestly class that controlled more and more of Egypt's resources. In spite of these difficulties, pharaohs of the Middle Kingdom did their best to promote prosperity. For example, Senusret III (Sesostris) (1878–1841 BCE) expanded south of the second cataract of the Nile into Nubia. As in the Old Kingdom, the army was composed of native troop levies plus foreign mercenaries, often recruited in Nubia. His son Amenemhat III (1841–1796 BCE) expanded agricultural operations in the Fayum, a large oasis area west of the Nile, in an attempt to raise enough food for the expanding population. And also as in the Old Kingdom, the pharaohs continued to be buried in pyramids, albeit much smaller ones. And rather than being built of solid stone, pyramids now had a stone framework filled with mud brick and rubble and covered with a limestone outer facing. The result was that most Middle Kingdom pyramids eventually disintegrated and now are just piles of debris.

In addition, as a symbol of the change of rule, the chief god of Thebes, Amon, whose name means "hidden" and who often was represented as a bull, became the primary god of Egypt. But so as not to abandon the old god Ra completely, by a process known as "syncretism," whereby the attributes of different gods were merged together, Ra often was grafted onto Amon, resulting in a composite chief god Amon-Ra.

Mythology and Religion

By the Middle Kingdom, the afterlife that once had been available only to the pharaoh had become open to everyone. In order to understand the expanded significance of the afterlife, one must understand a bit about Egyptian views of religion. The Egyptians had several different ideas about the origin of the gods and the world. In the most widespread version, the world emerged from a chaotic ocean called Nun. There then arose "the Great Ennead," a family of nine main gods. The first to come out of chaos was the creator god Atum, a bisexual god also known as the "Great He-She." Atum created the world and, by masturbating, gave birth to Shu, god of the air, and Tefnut, goddess of the rain. Shu and Tefnut produced Nut, the goddess of the heavens, and Geb, the god of the earth. Nut and Geb in turn produced the brothers **Osiris** and Set and the sisters **Isis** and Nephthys. Isis and Osiris brought civilization to Egypt and were the last gods to rule Egypt before the pharaohs. Set, jealous of Osiris' success, captured him and suffocated him in a great coffin. Isis found the body, was impregnated by his corpse, and gave birth to Horus. Set then chopped Osiris into pieces, which he scattered all around Egypt. Isis and Nephthys gathered the pieces and put him back together. Isis breathed life back into him, and he settled in the underworld, where he became judge of the dead. Horus then overcame Set and became the defender of the dead when they were judged. And, in general, Horus stood for those who lived according to the dictates of Ma'at, whereas Set symbolized people who lived without justice and order.

If Osiris could survive happily after death in the underworld, then, the Egyptians believed, so could they. They supposed, in essence, that they could enjoy in the afterlife all of the best things that they had enjoyed in this world. This was not just true of spiritual things but of material things as well. But in order to continue to enjoy material pleasures in the afterlife, it was crucial that one's physical body be preserved after death. As a result, the process of **mummification**, originally a natural process resulting from the desiccation of burials in the desert sands, became much more sophisticated. In its most elaborate form, mummification preserved a body after death by bathing it in a bath of natron, a salt solution that removed moisture. All the internal organs except the heart were mummified separately. The brain was pulled and sucked out through the nose and discarded. Thus the actual mummy consisted of just the skin, bones, and muscle. The process could take up to seventy days to complete. The corpse then was wrapped with linen bandages before being placed into an elaborately carved coffin.

The Egyptians believed that they had no less than three different souls that had to be cared for after death. The ka was a spiritual double that continued to

In the nineteenth century, mummies, which had no export category, were exported from Egypt as "salted fish," perhaps in recognition of the saltiness of the mummification process.

live after death. It remained with the body and needed food and drink. The ba represented one's unique personality and vitality. It could leave the body after death and represent the body outside the tomb, but it had to rejoin the body at night. It continued to enjoy bodily pleasures, such as food, drink, and sex. Finally, the akh represented an eternal soul that was created after death. It left the tomb and lived with the gods, either in the underworld or in the heavens. The transition from life to death to the afterlife was a process full of anxiety. Those who were found wanting during the judgment by Osiris would be devoured by a being that was part crocodile, part hippopotamus, and part lion and known as the "eater of the dead." But the Egyptians did everything to ensure that a wonderful afterlife was available to all. A collection of spells known as the **"Book of the Dead"** was wrapped around the mummy and provided the answers to the questions that the deceased would be asked by Osiris. And when one's heart was weighed in the balance against Ma'at to see whether the deceased had led a just life, the jackal god Anubis saw to it that no one's heart was found wanting. Thus, even in death, Egyptian optimism prevailed, with the presumption that everyone deserved immortality.

Pharaohs, too, participated in the afterlife of dead Egyptians. When pharaohs died, they became Osiris. In this way, one's judge on earth continued to be one's judge after death. Pharaohs also became Horus and continued to be one's defender in death just as he had been in life.

In this two-part scene from the "Book of the Dead," a deceased person on the left has his heart weighed in the scales against Ma'at to see whether he lived a just life. In the center, the jackal god Anubis keeps his hand on the weighing bar to ensure that the deceased passes the test, and Thoth, here portrayed with the head of an ibis, records the judgment. On the right, Anubis introduces the deceased, who has in fact passed the test, to Osiris, who wears the white crown of Upper Egypt, holds the staff and flail, symbol of the pharaoh's authority, and is accompanied by Ma'at.

Egyptian Lifestyles

During the Middle Kingdom, the good life was open to a much broader segment of the population. Men and women had equal status, as demonstrated by their portrayal in equal sizes in the artwork. Both sexes could own and dispose of property, pursue legal cases, hold government positions, serve in temples, practice skilled professions, and marry and divorce as they saw fit. In general, women had equality with men when it came to careers, owning property, and pursuing court cases.

Egyptian marriage contracts were similar to modern prenuptial agreements.

Egyptians treasured their family life and were not reluctant to show it. Egyptian art depicts the affection parents felt for their children or between husbands and wives. An Egyptian proverb advised parents to treat their children equally, saying, "Do not prefer one of your children above the others; you never know which one of them will be kind to you." Thus male and female children inherited the family property equally. Even though marriages of young persons usually were arranged by their families, young people fell in love and even wrote love letters and poems. One young woman wrote about a young man, "I love to go and bathe before you. I allow you to see my beauty in a dress of the finest linen, drenched with fragrant unguent." Egyptians usually married in their teens, and marriages often had contracts that specified the rights of the husband and wife to their own possessions, the size of the allowance that the wife would receive, and how the property would be divided in a divorce. In the marriage ceremony, the bride simply moved her possessions to the house of her husband. Either party could initiate a divorce, and divorced wives received continued support from their ex-husbands.

Egyptian homes were made of adobe brick, and a room on the upper story with an open wall could be used for sleeping on hot nights. Doors and windows were covered with mats to keep out insects, and sewage and garbage were dumped directly into the river. Furniture was simple, consisting of stools, sleeping mats, and jars for storing food and personal items. The diet consisted mainly of bread, accompanied by fruit, fish, and beer made from barley. Clothing was made from linen. As work clothes, men wore loincloths and women short skirts. On special occasions, women wore dresses held up by straps and men wore kilts. Both men and women wore jewelry, including earrings, rings, beaded necklaces, bracelets, and

The tomb of the palace servant Sennedjem and his wife Lyneferti, dating to the late fourteenth century BCE, shows the two engaged in a number of domestic activities. Here, in the underworld, Sennedjem guides an ard, or scratch plow, pulled by a pair of oxen, while Lyneferti sows seeds behind him.

anklets, made from gold, copper, and semiprecious stones. The use of cosmetics, such as red cheek and lipgloss and black and green eye shadow, also was very prevalent.

The Second Intermediate Period

The Middle Kingdom pharaohs eventually were confronted not only by internal opposition but also by foreign encroachment. Border control in the north began to break down, and desert pastoralists made their way into the delta area. It may have been at this time that some **Hebrews**, a Semitic people of Palestine, began to drift into Egypt. The Twelfth Dynasty ended with another woman pharaoh, Sobeknefru (1789–1786), and the next dynasty consisted of sixty short-lived pharaohs. Once again, Egypt entered a period of disunity, known as the Second Intermediate Period (1786–1575 BCE). About 1730 BCE disaster truly struck when Egypt suffered the first successful foreign invasion in its history. A little known Semitic people from the Levant known as the **Hyksos** (a word perhaps meaning "shepherd kings") attacked. They utilized the latest military technology, including updated bronze weapons, the composite bow (made by gluing horn to the wood to give it greater strength), and the horse and chariot, suggesting a possible tie to the Hurrians. The Egyptian kingdom, with no standing army and unwalled cities, was unable to resist. But fortunately for the Egyptians, there were not many Hyksos. They could not occupy all of Egypt. They became pharaohs at Avaris in the eastern delta but left the rest of Egypt in the hands of native Egyptian vassal rulers, who were left alone so long as they paid their taxes and acknowledged Hyksos authority. Four different dynasties, two Hyksos and two Egyptian, ruled at the same time.

It has been suggested, with very little authority, that the Hyksos were in fact Hebrews.

For the Egyptians, accustomed to considering themselves the best people in the world, the conquest by the Hyksos brought tremendous culture shock, and subsequent Egyptian propaganda portrayed the Hyksos as godless and brutal. The truth, however, seems to have been rather different. The Hyksos enthusiastically adopted Egyptian culture, being particularly devoted to the god Set. They even sponsored the preservation of documents dating to the beginning of the Old Kingdom that otherwise would have been lost. Their biggest crime, however, was in being foreigners, something that the Egyptians could not tolerate.

The Egyptians learned quickly. They adopted the same military technology as the Hyksos. They developed their own professional soldiers and mastered the use of the bow and chariot. In 1534 BCE, led by Ahmose I (1550–1525 BCE) of Thebes, the founder of the Eighteenth Dynasty, they counterattacked. The Hyksos were expelled from Egypt and pursued up the coast of Palestine, where they were destroyed in detail. It took Ahmose three years to defeat the other local Egyptian rulers and to reunify Egypt under a single rule. The Egyptians then destroyed nearly every indication that the Hyksos had ever been in Egypt. But the Egyptians could not undo what had been done. Egypt had been forcefully exposed to the wider world, and the Egyptians realized that henceforth they could ignore what went on beyond their frontiers only at their peril. The Egyptians were left determined never to let another foreign invader attack Egypt.

THE NEW KINGDOM (1534–1070 BC)

This second reunification of Egypt marked the beginning of the **New Kingdom** (1534–1070 BCE), which, like the Old and Middle Kingdoms, had its own identifying characteristics. In particular, the New Kingdom was characterized by strong pharaohs, still headquartered at Thebes; a standing army; and the rise of an Egyptian Empire.

The Pharaohs and the Egyptian Empire

Support from the army now gave the pharaohs the means to reassert their dominance over unruly nobles and priests. The pharaoh therefore assumed

The Egyptian Empire at Its Height

the role of military leader. In Egyptian art, the pharaoh was now customarily depicted as shooting a bow from a war chariot, a forceful reminder to all of the source of his authority. Soldiers were recruited from among the aristocrats and free men. The pharaoh supported them and often provided them with land on retirement, thus gaining their unswerving loyalty. At the same time, the pharaoh's chief wife was promoted to the rank of "god's wife." As a result, the royal family was able to regain much of the authority and status that it had lost during the Middle Kingdom.

The first task of the pharaohs of the New Kingdom was to use the army to ensure the security of Egypt. This meant not only defending Egypt's frontiers but also establishing a military presence beyond the frontiers. Pharaoh Thutmose I (1506–1493) campaigned south into Nubia and north to the Euphrates River, thus impressing Egypt's neighbors with his military might.

Thutmose's ambitious daughter **Hatshepsut** (1479–1458) had herself crowned pharaoh. To enhance her status, she claimed that she was the daughter not of Thutmose but of the god Amon himself. In order to play down her female sex, she wore male royal clothing and a false royal beard and even masculinized her name to "Hatshepsu." As commander-in-chief of the army,

Egyptian expansion into Nubia in the south was even more extensive than that into Palestine. A painting from the tomb of the noble Huy in Thebes shows Hequanefer and other Nubian chiefs submitting and bringing tribute to the pharaoh Tutankhamon.

she led an attack into Nubia, but her primary military contribution lay in the construction of border fortifications. She also built a huge terraced mortuary temple in honor of Amon, for in the New Kingdom, pharaohs no longer built pyramids. Their building activities were focused on building temples, which often advertised their military achievements, and for nearly five hundred years most of them were buried in elaborate underground stone tombs in the cliffs west of Thebes, an area now called the Valley of the Kings. Two obelisks, tall granite pillars inscribed with hieroglyphs, in the temple built at Karnak by Hatshepsut in honor of Amon, preserve her own words regarding her achievement: "I have done this with a loving heart for my father Amon, I did not forget whatever he had ordained, now, my heart turns to and fro, in thinking what will the people say, they who will see my monument in after years, and shall speak of what I have done. I swear, as I am loved of Ra, as I wear the white crown, as I appear in the red crown, as I rule this land like the son of Isis, so as regards these two great obelisks, in order that my name may endure in this temple."

But it was Hatshepsut's son Thutmose III (1458–1425) who expanded Egypt's power to an even higher level. In the course of seventeen campaigns, he created an **Egyptian Empire** by laying claim to territory in Palestine and Syria. In 1457, for example, he defeated a coalition of Canaanite kings at the Battle of Megiddo, which is seen as the first battle in history for which we have a full account thanks to detailed records kept by the scribe Tjaneni. By getting behind and outflanking the Canaanites, Thutmose won a complete victory.

Instead of annexing the northern conquests and making them part of Egypt, Thutmose followed the Hyksos model of making defeated rulers into vassals and allowing them to stay in power so long as they remained loyal, paid their taxes, and sent hostages to Egypt as guarantors of their good behavior. Conquests southward on the Nile in Nubia, on the other hand, being closer to Egypt geographically and culturally, were directly annexed and administered by an official called "the King's son of Kush" (as Nubia also was known).

Every year or so, Thutmose and his successors would assemble the Egyptian army and march north to make the rounds of the northern parts of the Empire and remind Egyptian vassals, who were often ready to revolt at a moment's notice, of his irresistible power. Doing so reinforced the pharaoh's position as military commander and renewed the army's loyalty to him. And, back in Egypt, two viziers, stationed at Memphis in the north and Thebes in the south, looked after local administration.

The Reforms of Akhenaton

The Egyptian Empire remained stable for about one hundred years, until Amenhotep IV (1351–1334 BCE) ascended the throne. Amenhotep long had been a worshipper of the relatively minor sun god **Aton**, who was represented artistically not as a person or animal, but as a simple sun disk, whose descending rays terminated with hands. It soon became clear that Amenhotep's devotion to Aton went far beyond mere personal preference. He was determined to make Aton the single most important god in Egypt and to create a form of monotheism (worship of one god only) known as **henotheism**, which acknowledges the existence of other gods but focuses on one god in particular. He changed his name to **Akhenaton**, meaning "Glory of Aton." He prohibited the worship of other gods and decreed that only the royal family could engage in the worship of Aton. He established a new capital city at Akhetaton ("the Horizon of Aton"), modern Tel el-Amarna. He often is portrayed in artwork soaking up the rays of Aton along with his wife, Nefertiti, who participated fully in the religious reforms and may even have shared power with Akhenaton, as suggested by the fact that she and Akhenaton are portrayed the same size in the artwork. On one relief, Nefertiti is even depicted smiting the head of a female captive with a mace, a function traditionally reserved for male pharaohs.

Akhenaton's reforms did not go down well with the Egyptian population. The priests of other gods faced the loss of their positions and livelihoods. The

Hatshepsut, wearing the full regalia of a pharaoh, including the ceremonial beard, and displaying only token female breasts, presents offerings to her father, the god Amon.

In this relief, Akhenaton, on the left, and Nefertiti play with their daughters as they bask in the rays of the sun god Aton, demonstrating Akhenaton's devotion to his family. It has been suggested that Akhenaton's physical appearance resulted from Marfan's syndrome, a genetic condition that also afflicted Abraham Lincoln.

general population faced the loss of their afterlife if they were prevented from worshipping Osiris. Unrest grew. The army was compelled to remain in Egypt to maintain order. Without the regular presence of the Egyptian army, the Egyptian Empire began to slip away. To make matters worse, a revived Hittite Empire, with its capital city at Hattusas in east central Anatolia, was expanding to the south under King Suppililiuma (1344–1322), who, after defeating the powerful kingdom of Mitanni in upper Mesopotamia, was eager to take advantage of Egyptian weakness. After their appeals for help to Akhenaton were ignored, many of the Egyptian vassals in Syria and even Palestine either revolted or were annexed by the Hittites. The Hittites, who had a formidable army of chariots, also were experimenting with a new secret weapon, a technological advance that permitted them to smelt iron ore and to create iron tools and weapons, although it is unclear whether these were of sufficient quality or manufactured in great enough quantities to have any military value.

Akhenaton finally lost the support of the army, which no longer had faith in him as an effective ruler, much less as an effective general. We do not know what happened to Akhenaton. He simply disappeared from history, to be followed by several short-lived boy pharaohs. One of them, Tut-ankh-aton (1333–1324 BCE), soon changed his name to **Tut-ankh-amon**, a sure sign of the return to favor of the old god Amon and the suppression of Aton. Akhenaton's name and that of his god were erased from the monuments. When Tut-ankh-amon died he was buried so quickly and secretly that his tomb was the only pharaoh's tomb not to be looted in antiquity, and it was not finally discovered until 1922, when the boy king gained the name of "King Tut." Soon after, a general, Hor-em-hab (1319–1292 BCE), became pharaoh, suggesting that the army finally had taken matters into its own hands.

An American tour of Tut-ankh-amon artifacts in the late 1970s attracted eight million visitors and even led to a dance called "the Tut."

The Recovery of Egypt

Hor-em-hab named another general, Ramses I (1292–1290), as his successor, thus beginning the Nineteenth Dynasty. There was a lot of recovery work to be done. Ramses and his successors, most of whom also were named Ramses, struggled to restore the Egyptian Empire. After his father,

Seti I, had recovered part of the empire, **Ramses II** (1279–1212 BCE), the greatest warrior pharaoh, repeatedly skirmished with the Hittites. At the **Battle of Kadesh** in 1274 BCE, Ramses faced the Hittite king Muwatalli II in what probably was the greatest chariot battle of all time, with as many as six thousand chariots engaged. The battle began badly for Egypt, with Ramses being caught in a Hittite ambush that virtually destroyed an Egyptian chariot division. After barely being able to fight his way clear, Ramses heroically led a counterattack that drove the Hittites back into Kadesh. But being unable to besiege the city, Ramses was forced to withdraw. Both sides declared victory, and the campaigning con-

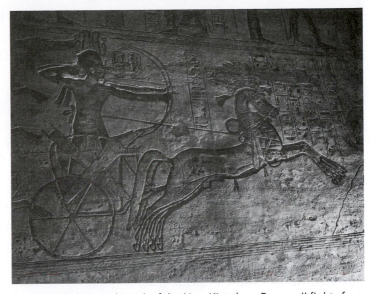

As a typical warrior pharaoh of the New Kingdom, Ramses II fights from his chariot at the Battle of Kadesh in 1274 in this painted relief from Abu Simbel.

tinued. Finally, in 1258 BCE Ramses and the Hittite king Hattusilis III (1267–1237 BCE) agreed to make peace. Their treaty, in both Egyptian and Hittite versions, is the earliest international treaty to survive from antiquity. The versions are essentially the same except that each side claimed that the other side had first sued for peace. The two powers established the boundary between them; promised not to attack each other; entered into a mutual defense alliance, including assistance in civil wars; agreed to return refugees and fugitives (the first attested extradition agreement); and permitted free trade across the border. To seal the bargain, Ramses married Maathorneferure, the daughter of Hattusilis.

With the end of hostilities against the Hittites, Ramses spent much of the rest of his reign engaged in massive building projects. He not only constructed large numbers of temples in his own name, such as the Ramesseum, his mortuary temple, in Thebes and rock-carved temples at Abu Simbel deep in Upper Egypt, but he also erased the names of his predecessors from their monuments and replaced them with his own. He also constructed a new capital city in the delta called Pi-Ramses.

By the time of Ramses II's death in 1213 BCE at the age of over ninety years, great change was in the wind. The New Kingdom would continue until 1070 BCE, and Egypt would have occasional bursts of energy, but the Bronze Age was drawing to a close, and new peoples representing new cultural, political, religious, and economic developments soon would appear.

The "Ramses" brand of condoms, discontinued in 2005, honored Ramses II's fathering of 160 children.

LOOKING AHEAD

Most surveys of the Bronze Age focus on the great river valley civilizations of Mesopotamia and Egypt, where the extensive exploitation of agriculture was the primary economic focus. But outside of the river valleys, people who did not have access to the rich alluvial soils and easily available water supply looked to other methods, and especially to commerce, as a means of expanding their economies. These peoples would establish an economic pattern that would provide a model for moving from the Bronze Age into the Iron Age, an age of smaller cities located outside of the river valleys, whose economies were much more heavily based on commerce.

FURTHER READING

Aldred, Cyril. *Egyptian Art in the Days of the Pharaohs 3100 B.C.–320 B.C.* New York: Oxford University Press, 1980.

Andreu, Guillemette. *Egypt in the Age of the Pyramids.* Ithaca, NY: Cornell University Press, 1997.

Andrews, Carol. *The British Museum Book of the Rosetta Stone.* New York: Dorsett Press, 1981.

Bard, A. Kathryn. *An Introduction to the Archaeology of Ancient Egypt.* Malden, MA: Blackwell, 2008.

Grajetzki, W. *The Middle Kingdom of Ancient Egypt: History, Archaeology and Society.* London: Duckworth, 2006.

Pinch, Geraldine. *Egyptian Mythology: A Guide to the Gods, Goddesses, and Traditions of Ancient Egypt.* Oxford: Oxford University Press, 2004.

Redford, Donald B. *From Slave to Pharaoh: The Black Experience of Ancient Egypt.* Baltimore: Johns Hopkins University Press, 2004.

Reeves, Nicholas. *Akhenaten: Egypt's False Prophet.* London: Thames and Hudson, 2001.

Tyldesley, Joyce. *Ramesses: Egypt's Greatest Pharaoh.* London: Viking/Penguin: 2000.

Shaw, Ian, ed. *The Oxford History of Ancient Egypt.* Oxford: Oxford University Press, 2000.

Silverman, David P., and David O'Connor, *Ancient Egyptian Kingship.* Leiden, Netherlands: Brill, 1995.

Wilkinson, Toby A. H. *Early Dynastic Egypt,* 2nd ed. London: Routledge, 2001.

CHAPTER 4

COASTAL CIVILIZATIONS OF THE EASTERN MEDITERRANEAN
(2500–800 BCE)

The Bronze Age quite correctly is viewed as the great age of river valley civilizations. But we ought not to think that there was nothing going on outside the river valleys at the same time. In an unobtrusive way, other peoples were pursuing other ways of life and finding niches of opportunity. These bit players of the Bronze Age, inhabiting the Levant, the island of Crete, and mainland Greece, anticipated future mainstream lifestyles, uses of technology, and forms of economic activity that bridged the gap between the Bronze and Iron Ages and facilitated the spread of civilization out of the river valleys to encompass much larger regions and numbers of people. These cultures also help to correct the common presumption that Mesopotamia and Egypt were the only centers of Bronze Age civilization and demonstrate that by the early Iron Age the river valley cultures of the Bronze Age had run their course.

EARLY CIVILIZATIONS OF THE LEVANT (2500–1500 BCE)

The major Bronze Age civilizations of Mesopotamia and Egypt were based on the massive exploitation of agriculture. They did, of course, make use of trade, especially as a means of gaining access to raw materials, ranging from tin to gemstones, that were not available in the river valleys, but the fundamental basis of their economy was agriculture. Trade was an extra, and it was pursued for the benefit of a minority of the population. There were other Bronze Age peoples, however, who did not have the blessing of being located in a fertile river valley. In order to expand their economies, they found niches of opportunity by turning to trade, and in the process of doing so they created sophisticated, albeit less well-known, civilizations in their own right.

Ebla

The earlier belief that major Near Eastern civilizations were limited to the river valleys was given the lie in 1968 when an Italian archaeologists excavated **Ebla**, a Syrian city mentioned in Egyptian and Akkadian documents but whose location had hitherto been unknown. Its location was given away by its being located on a **tell**, an artificial mound created by centuries of human habitation on the same spot. Excavations revealed that as early as 2500 BCE Ebla had been a Bronze Age commercial center, with walls enclosing an area of about 125 acres and housing some thirty thousand persons.

Some eighteen thousand cuneiform tablets were discovered, written in languages including Sumerian, Akkadian, Assyrian, Hittite, and a previously unknown western Semitic language, the language of the Eblaites themselves. Ebla thus was a cultural crossroads, a place where Semitic, Sumerian, and western peoples interacted. Because some of the tablets were glossaries that gave equivalent word meanings in different languages, such as Sumerian—a very useful tool for merchants who had to deal with many different peoples—the language of Ebla was deciphered relatively easily and tells us much about the people living there.

City government seems to have been run by an aristocracy of merchants who chose kings with fixed terms of office. The territory controlled by Ebla extended from southern Anatolia in the north to the upper Euphrates River and was in a position to oversee trade west into the Mediterranean, north to Anatolia, south to Egypt, and east to Mesopotamia. Trading in products such as textiles, fine inlaid wooden furniture, timber ("the cedars of Lebanon"), silver, copper, and beer, the city's signature product, the city reaped yearly profits of approximately one thousand pounds of silver and twelve pounds of gold. In regard to religion, the people worshipped gods ranging from the western Semitic Ba'al to the Mesopotamian Ishtar. They also used names such as Ab-ra-mu (Abraham), Da-u-dum (David), and U-ru-sa-li-ma (Jerusalem). This is not to say, of course, that these are the same names that appear in Jewish and Christian scripture, but they do attest to the currency of these names at a very early period.

Ebla also had great pretensions, going so far as to claim that Sargon of Akkad was its vassal. But when Ebla's diplomatic and military initiatives, including the destruction of its Mesopotamian rival, the city of Mari, began to interfere in the Akkadian sphere of influence, that was too much. In about

A tablet from Ebla detailing arms shipments ca. 2300 BCE; it has been suggested that Ebla's military aggression led to its destruction by the Akkadians.

2250 BCE Ebla was captured and burned by the Akkadian king Naram-Sin. As a consequence, the tablets in the palace archives were baked and preserved. The city was rebuilt, but never regained its stature.

Coastal Commerce

The eastern coast of the Mediterranean remained a center of commercial activity, where merchants and traders found niches of opportunity. As of 1500 BCE, trading cities such as Sidon, Tyre, Byblos, and Ugarit developed in Kinahu (biblical **Canaan**), as the lands bordering the eastern Mediterranean coast were called. Although they preferred being independent, they often were dominated by imperialist states such as Egypt or the Hittites. A significant innovation at **Ugarit** was the invention of a writing system, based on Egyptian characters and written on clay tablets, that used thirty symbols to represent individual consonants. The invention of this vastly simplified proto-alphabet meant that writing, rather than being the monopoly of scribes and priests, became much more available to the general population, and in particular to merchants.

> **CROSS-CULTURAL CONNECTION**
>
> What kinds of advantages might there have been for peoples who adopted the use of the alphabet as opposed to Mesopotamian cuneiform or Egyptian hieroglyphics?

The proto-alphabet of Ugarit was the first writing system to have the letters in roughly the same order as our modern alphabet.

AEGEAN CIVILIZATIONS (3000–1100 BCE)

The early Bronze Age also brought civilization based on trade westward into the Mediterranean region, first on the island of Crete and then in mainland Greece, where access to seaborne trade routes and specialized trade goods resulted in Bronze Age civilizations occupying additional economic niches.

The Minoan Civilization of Crete

A spectacular example of a Bronze Age civilization based on commerce rather than on agriculture arose on Crete, in the heart of the Mediterranean Sea south of Greece. It now is known as the **Minoan civilization**, named after the legendary King Minos of Crete. As early as 3000 BCE, a culture centered on coastal urban centers had developed. By 2000 BCE, several palace complexes had developed near the coast, as at Knossos in the north and Phaistos in the south. The Minoan palaces were built in the "agglutinative style": roughly equal-sized rooms were placed around a central plaza, and the palace could be expanded simply by adding rooms on the periphery. Rather than being centers of population, the palaces were centers of administration, manufacture, storage, and distribution. They also were unwalled, a sign that they were not threatened by attack either from each other or from outside. The population, therefore, was free to live either near the palace or in the countryside. Minoan houses were very much like ours, with doors, windows, and indoor plumbing. Nor is there any evidence that all of Crete was united into a single country: the several palace complexes were all roughly equal in size, and there were no roads

A fascination with Greek legends of King Minos influenced Sir Arthur Evans to begin excavations in Crete in 1900.

Minoan and Mycenaean Sites The Minoan and Mycenaean cultures of Crete and Greece took civilization out of the Near East and into the Mediterranean Sea and Europe.

connecting them. Each of the cities, rather, seems to have functioned as an independent unit.

Because Crete did not have large river valleys to exploit for large-scale grain production, people had to look for other sources of economic opportunity. For example, the sunny climate and hilly terrain were ideal for cultivating olive trees. Like the Canaanites, the Minoans looked to commerce as a way to expand their economic base. They imported amber from the Baltic and metal from Italy and the Aegean islands, and they crafted trade goods including stoneware, fine pottery, carved gemstones, and elaborate metal jewelry. Olive oil also was exported. Being unable to trade by land, they constructed ships that carried their goods to Greece, Anatolia, Palestine, and Egypt. Egyptian wall paintings, for example, portray a people from "the islands in the great green sea" called the Keftiu, who generally are identified as Minoan traders. Merchant ships were propelled by sails, and oar-driven warships protected the Minoan trading fleet. To expand their commercial interests, the Minoans founded **trading colonies** on islands in the Aegean Sea, such as Thera, and on the Anatolian coast. From about 2000 to 1400 BCE, the Minoans enjoyed a virtual monopoly on Mediterranean trade.

Like the Egyptians and Mesopotamians, the Minoans also developed a writing system. Their documents were similar to the Mesopotamian ones in that they were written on clay with a sharp-pointed stylus. But the characters were very different from cuneiform and represent another Bronze Age writing system. The earlier form of Minoan writing, **Linear A**, is still undeciphered, but the purpose of the documents is clear. Most consist of lists of words followed by numbers and clearly represent accounts and inventories.

Minoan civilization also was different from Near Eastern civilizations in other ways. Minoan religion, for example, was much more low key. The Minoans had no powerful anthropomorphic gods worshiped in ostentatious temples. In fact, we do not know the name of a single Minoan deity. Nor is there much evidence for a class of priests. Minoan religion was personal in nature and was carried out in small shrines and caves in the countryside, for many of the gods and goddesses were nature deities. Minoan worshippers deposited what archaeologists call **cult objects** in their shrines. One of the most common is a small golden double axe called a *labrys* by the later Greeks. Its function is unknown, except that it was used by Minoans to demonstrate their devotion to their gods. Another common object is a statue of a goddess wearing a flounced open-breasted dress and holding two snakes in her raised hands. Depictions of Minoan religious practices suggest that Minoan worshippers dressed up like the deity they were worshipping and then worked themselves into a religious ecstasy that culminated with a vision of the god. Both men and women appear to have had an equal role in religious ceremonies.

The Minoan "Lady of the Wild Things" exemplifies Minoan nature worship.

The Minoans seem to have had a nonviolent nature. Like their religion, their artwork centered on nature. Typical pottery motifs include geometric designs, leaves and other vegetation, or animals, such as bulls and octopuses. Only rarely were human figures depicted in the artwork. In a famous funeral scene, men and women are shown bearing offerings, including a boat and a bull, to some god. Some Minoan paintings also depict apparent sporting events. Boxers appear in several scenes. But the most famous of all Minoan physical activities is what has been called "bull leaping." Time-lapse portrayals show a long-horned bull charging a young person who grabs the horns, flips over the back of the bull, and lands with arms outstretched—much like a modern gymnast—behind the bull.

It seems clear what is happening in this portrayal of ca. 1500 BCE of "bull leaping" from Knossos: a participant flips over the back of a charging bull. But what it means is unclear: a religious ritual? A sport? No one knows. The importance of bulls in Minoan religion also may be reflected in the Greek legend of the Minotaur.

The Minoans also were unassuming with regard to government. There were no all-powerful kings who self-consciously erected monuments detailing their great deeds. In fact, it is difficult to find any depictions of rulers in Minoan artwork. Nor were there any grand audience halls in the palace complexes. The "throne room" at Knossos, as it is called, is actually a quite modest chamber with an unpretentious stone chair that may have been the chair of a local administrator.

This image of low-key nature worshippers is rather contrary to the picture of the Minoans that one gains from later Greek legends. According to later Greek historians, Minos, the powerful and tyrannical king of Crete, created a powerful **thalassocracy**, or sea power. The legend related that after Minos' wife Pasiphaë mated with a bull and produced the **Minotaur**, a bull-headed man who feasted on human flesh, the Greek inventor Daedalus trapped the Minotaur in an elaborate maze in the palace basement called the labyrinth. Eventually the Minotaur was slain by the Athenian hero Theseus. Extravagant as they may seem, these legends preserve various grains of truth, such as the Minoan dependency on sea power and the association of the word *labyrinth* with the ancient word *labrys*, a possible connection to the ritualistic double axes.

Archaeological excavations show that around 1400 BCE several Minoan cities were destroyed. Some of them were subsequently rebuilt, others were not. Several theories have been proposed about what happened to the Minoans.

One of them, often seen in the popular media, is that the Minoan civilization was destroyed by a cataclysmic volcanic explosion of the island of **Thera** (modern Santorini), which created huge tsunamis and ash falls that devastated Crete. More recent study, however, suggests not only that the eruption—which did in fact destroy a Minoan colony on Thera—had little effect on Crete but also that it happened 200 years too early.

The Mycenaean Civilization of Greece

The real cause of the decline of the Minoan culture is to be found in a more mundane cause: the destruction caused by hostile invaders. For as of about 1400 BCE the Minoan Linear A script was replaced by a variant form known as **Linear B**, which used the same symbols to write what was clearly a different language. These tablets often were found in locations that had suffered destruction around 1400 BCE, and Linear B also was used on tablets found at sites on the Greek mainland. Linear B was deciphered in 1953 and, to the amazement of all, was identified as an early form of Greek. The appearance of Linear B tablets on Crete after 1400 BCE suggests that it was invading Greeks who destroyed the Minoan civilization and then reoccupied some Cretan cities themselves.

The Linear B tablets demonstrated that Greek civilization began far back in the Bronze Age, much earlier than once had been thought. The Greeks who destroyed the Minoan civilization were the descendents of the Indo-European invaders who had moved into the Balkans as of around 2000 BCE. They are known as the Mycenaeans, and the Mycenaean civilization is named after the Bronze Age city of **Mycenae** in central Greece. After interacting with Minoan traders and assimilating much Minoan culture, the Mycenaeans created the first European civilization by 1600 BCE.

Excavations at Mycenae, begun in 1876 by the wealthy German businessman Heinrich Schliemann, who already had excavated the city of Troy, demonstrated the historical background of Greek legends.

The Mycenaeans and the Minoans had much in common. For example, Greece, like Crete, did not have any big river valleys. But its sunny dry climate and hilly geography were ideal for the cultivation of specialized crops such as grapes and olives. The Mycenaeans mimicked Minoan methods of pottery manufacture. They copied Minoan artistic styles and used many of the same geometric, vegetal, and animal motifs, such as octopuses and bulls. They even copied aspects of Minoan religion, although with some alterations: Mycenaean representations of the Minoan snake goddess do not feature snakes.

The Mycenaeans also copied Minoan administrative and economic practices and built their own palaces, adorned with stone sculpture and painted frescoes, at places such as Pylos in the west, Mycenae and Tiryns in central Greece, and Athens in the east. As on Crete, there was no unified Mycenaean state, for later Greek legends tell of independent cities. The Mycenaean palaces were centers for the accumulation, storage, and distribution of resources. Manufacturing activities, such as weaving and the creation of gold ornaments,

VOLCANOS AND THE FALL OF CIVILIZATIONS

The effect of volcanic eruptions on the development of human society long has had a hold on the popular imagination. Past volcanic eruptions even have been blamed for nearly wiping out the human race. One eruption whose effects continue to be debated is that of the island of Thera—modern Santorini—in

likewise were controlled from the palace. As their economy became more complex, the Mycenaeans developed a need for a writing system and adapted the Minoan Linear A characters to suit their own needs. They assigned about thirty of the characters a syllable value and were thus able to accommodate it, sometimes rather clumsily, to their Greek language. For example, the Greek *basileus*, "king," was represented by the syllables *pa-si-re-u*. Eventually, the Mycenaeans developed an extraordinarily obsessive bureaucratic accounting system in which the total resources of the city, and every bit of palace income and expenditure, were painstakingly catalogued every year.

But in other ways the Mycenaeans and Minoans were very different. Mycenaean cities were built on defendable hills, near to but not on the coast.

the southern Aegean Sea, which created a huge crater and buried the Minoan colony there under volcanic ash. Excavations of the Minoan town found no bodies—the inhabitants apparently had warning and fled—but did turn up marvelously preserved wall paintings, such as this scene of the Minoan trading fleet departing from a river with several mouths—probably the Nile—and sailing to Thera, where the inhabitants would have had no idea of the cataclysm to come.

In the early twentieth century, excavations at Knossos revealed clear evidence of destruction, and it was suggested that the eruption created huge deposits of volcanic ash that overwhelmed the Minoan civilization of Crete, only sixty miles away. But this theory failed when only a fraction of an inch of ash could be found. In addition, it was clear that the Minoan cities continued for at least some fifty years after ca. 1500 BCE, when it was estimated the eruption had occurred. Nevertheless, a hypothesis that a civilization had been destroyed by a volcanic eruption was too attractive to pass up, and many respected historians, archaeologists, and commentators continued to propose ingenious theories to make a connection. One hypothesis was that there were in fact two eruptions, the second of which destroyed Knossos and other cities. But after the decipherment of Linear B, it became clear that the destruction in Knossos was caused not by a volcanic eruption but by a violent occupation by Mycenaean Greeks.

Recent years have seen more sophisticated and ingenious attempts to find evidence for the effects of the volcano. Studies of Cretan mud cores, for example, suggest a tsunami of up to forty feet high; this would have flooded some lowlands, but there is no evidence for any destruction of cities. Other theories have envisioned a form of global cooling caused by large amounts of sulfur dioxide emitted into the atmosphere—but this theory would have had worldwide effects, and not have been limited just to the Minoans. The volcano hypothesis received another blow in 1987 when ice cores from Greenland redated the eruption to 1645 BCE, a date more recently confirmed by an analysis of tree rings dating it to 1627/1600 BCE, both dates a good two centuries before the decline of the Minoan civilization. This redating left commentators scrambling to come with new theories trying to connect the eruption to the decline, such as that the explosion eventually caused the Minoans to lose faith in their gods. The explosion even has been connected to the Atlantis myth.

One problem with all of these theories is not only that they begin with the assumption that the eruption must have had a disastrous effect on Minoan civilization and then proceed to find it, but also that they continue to persist with a model even after it has been shown to be wrong. And the lesson here is that historians should be guided first by their evidence, not by their models and theories. Sometimes an eruption is just an eruption.

They also were surrounded by massive walls constructed from huge, roughly hewn blocks, a style of architecture called **"Cyclopean"** because the later Greeks believed that the walls must have been built by the Cyclops, mythical one-eyed giants. Their fortifications demonstrate that the Mycenaeans were much more concerned about security than the Minoans. Indeed, unlike Minoan culture, Mycenaean culture was full of violence and warfare, and Mycenaean art portrays decidedly unpeaceful activities, such as hunting and military actions. Boars, bulls, and lions were the favorite prey of Mycenaean hunters. Both men and women are depicted driving chariots. And men's tombs are full of the implements of war, including daggers, swords, armor, and ceremonial headwear made of boars' tusks.

This Mycenaean jug may have held wine or olive oil. The graceful painted Linear B inscription, reading in part *ka-ku-jo-wa-to-ri,* may indicate the jug's owner and place of origin.

Another thing that the Mycenaeans learned from the Minoans was the pursuit of trade as an effective method of economic development and acquiring wealth. They took to the sea and competed in the same markets as the Minoans, where they put their warlike ways to good use. As already seen, by 1400 BCE, the Mycenaeans had invaded Crete and destroyed many of the Minoan palace complexes. Some they rebuilt and occupied, although not, it would seem, as part of an early Greek empire but as additional independent Mycenaean trading centers. The Mycenaeans also established trading colonies of their own in Anatolia and Syria and on eastern Mediterranean islands such as Cyprus. For the next two hundred years, the Mycenaeans monopolized trade in the Mediterranean, and their income made them phenomenally wealthy.

The role of violence in Mycenaean culture suggests that the Mycenaeans retained kings as war leaders, a hypothesis consistent with the portrayal of Mycenaean kings in Greek legends such as the *Iliad* and the *Odyssey.* The high status of Mycenaean kings also is demonstrated by their burial in massive forty-foot-tall stone-lined underground "beehive" tombs filled with gold ornaments, including massive golden death masks, which suggest a cult of personality focused on the king.

Reconstruction of a Mycenaean palace, modeled on the Minoan palace at Knossos.

A PICTURE IS WORTH A THOUSAND WORDS

THE MYCENAEAN "WARRIOR VASE"

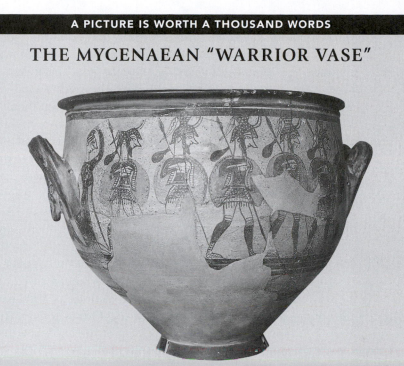

The military nature of Mycenaean society is demonstrated by strongly fortified cities, the use of weapons as grave goods, and even the glorification of warfare in the poems of the later Greek poet Homer. This crater (a vase used for mixing wine and water), found at Mycenae and dated to ca. 1200 BCE, depicts what must have been a common sight in the Mycenaean world: a heavily armed Mycenaean body of troops heading off to war. The soldiers are armed as typical Greek "hoplites," as Greek soldiers were known, carrying spears and shields and protected by shields, helmets, greaves (shin guards), and body armor. In addition, the woman left behind who is waving goodbye, probably a mother or wife, adds a poignant domestic touch to this otherwise militaristic scene. The Mycenaean ability to seize control of the seaborne trade routes that once had belonged to the Minoans must be attributed to one primary factor: Mycenaean military superiority. The military idealogy seen in Mycenaean art is something completely lacking in Minoan art.

The End of the Bronze Age

The Bronze Age ended with a bang. By 1200 BCE, change was in the wind. It had been some time since there had been any major new technological, economic, or cultural developments in the river valleys of Mesopotamia and Egypt. Innovations had occurred outside the river valleys, in the Levant, Crete, and Greece. The end of the Bronze Age was marked by a period of disruption characterized by massive movements of peoples who appear in the Egyptian records as the "**Sea Peoples.**" It is unclear what set these movements under way, but they may have begun with another southward migration of Indo-Europeans from the steppes of central Asia. Mediterranean peoples also joined in these movements, which were cited in contemporary documents and recalled in later legends.

One recollection of disruption can be found in the famous Greek legend of the Mycenaean war against **Troy**, a wealthy and powerful trading city of northwest Anatolia. Centuries later, the Greek epic poem the *Iliad*, written by Homer, reported how King Agamemnon of Mycenae led a Greek fleet of one thousand ships (each carrying about fifty men) against Troy. After a ten-year siege, the city was captured, sacked, and burned. In modern times, it was thought that the Trojan War was just a legend and that a city of such importance could not have existed then. But in the late nineteenth century Troy was discovered and excavated and turned out to be much as the legend had described. Moreover, the legendary date for the fall of Troy, 1184 BCE, is remarkably consistent with the activities of the Sea Peoples just after 1200 BCE. So is the appearance in the Egyptian lists of Sea Peoples of the "Danuna" and "Akawasha," whose names are strikingly similar to the "Danaans" and "Achaeans," as the Homeric Greeks were called. It is very possible, therefore, that bands of Mycenaeans accompanied the southward movement of the Sea Peoples and that Troy was the first city to suffer.

Nearly every part of the eastern Mediterranean faced attack by groups of Sea Peoples, who formed different coalitions as circumstances dictated. Surviving correspondence among the local kings tells of the great concern that their movements aroused. The king of the Hittites wrote to the king of Ugarit warning about "the Shikala who live on boats." The Shikala would be the Shekelesh, who appear in the Egyptian list of Sea Peoples. Hammurabi, the last king of Ugarit, reported the appearance of enemy ships to the king of Cyprus, who replied, "If this is true, then make yourself very strong. Where are your infantry and chariots stationed? Aren't they with you? Be on the

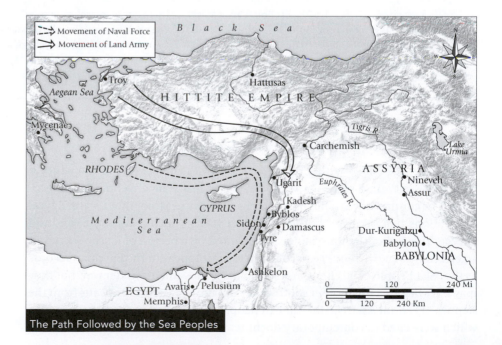

The Path Followed by the Sea Peoples

lookout for the enemy." Hammurabi's answer depicts dire developments: "Enemy ships have come and set my ships ablaze, and have done wicked things to the country. All my troops are in Hittite territory and all my ships are off fighting the Luki. They have not yet returned and the country lies undefended. Seven enemy ships have landed and done much damage to us. If there are other enemy ships, let me know. I want to be kept informed!" But all for nought. The Hittite Empire was destroyed, and Ugarit was sacked and burned.

The Sea Peoples then advanced on Egypt, the most fertile agricultural land in the Mediterranean. Scenes from the funerary temple of Pharaoh Ramses III (1182–1151) at Medinet Habu show the Sea Peoples not only arriving by sea but also moving on land in oxcarts with women, children, and their possessions. In 1174 BCE they attacked the Nile River delta, where they were resoundingly defeated by the Egyptian army and navy led by Ramses III. The Sea Peoples who escaped then scattered, creating more havoc throughout the Mediterranean. The Peleset, for example, settled in Palestine, where they became the biblical Philistines and gave their name to the country. Following this final burst of energy, Egypt then sank into obscurity. Eight more pharaohs named Ramses ruled until 1070 BCE, the traditional end of the New Kingdom. Subsequently, Egyptian unity again fragmented during the Third Intermediate Period (1070–664 BCE), and Egypt increasingly came under the influence of foreign peoples. The high priests of Amon at Thebes in Upper Egypt competed for authority with a new dynasty from Lower Egypt, which in turn was overthrown by Libyan mercenaries who established their own dynasty. By the eighth century BCE, Egypt had fragmented into no less than eleven independent city-states.

Back in Europe, disruption continued. As a result of the disruption in the eastern Mediterranean, the Mycenaean trading economy collapsed. Around 1100 BCE, the **Dorians,** another Indo-European people, perhaps taking advantage of the Mycenaean decline, migrated from northern to southern Greece. Reports from the archive of Pylos on the western Greek coast tell of an approaching threat. One speaks of the "watchers on the coasts" and reports that hundreds of rowers had been assigned to warships. Another relates, "The enemy grabbed all the priests from everywhere and without reason murdered them secretly by drowning. I am told that the northern strangers continued their attack, terrorizing and plundering." But, again, all for nought. Pylos was sacked and burned. Gradually all of the other Mycenaean centers, except for the citadel of Athens, fell. And in Mesopotamia, additional disorder occurred at roughly the same time. In the 1220s BCE, the Kassites were defeated by the Assyrian king Tukulti-Ninurta I (1243–1207), and Babylon was sacked; after a brief recovery, the Kassite kingdom was definitively destroyed around 1155 BCE by the Elamites of Iran. The Bronze Age thus ended in chaos throughout the ancient world.

ALTERNATIVE HISTORY

What kind of effects on western civilization might there have been if the Sea Peoples had been successful in their attack on Egypt?

IN THEIR OWN WORDS

RAMSES III DEFEATS THE SEA PEOPLES

The Egyptian account of the battle against the Sea Peoples in 1174 BCE is the longest known hieroglyphic inscription and demonstrates the importance the Egyptians attached to their heroic resistance. The accompanying artwork shows the Egyptians, led by a larger-than-life Ramses III, showering the Sea Peoples with arrows and then leading off multitudes of prisoners into captivity.

[Summary]

Year 8 under the majesty of Ramses III. The foreign countries made a conspiracy in their islands. No land could stand before their arms: Hatti [the Hittite homeland], Kode [Cilicia], Carchemish [a city on the upper Euphrates], Arzawa [western Anatolia], and Alashiya [Cyprus], all were cut off at one time. A camp was set up in one place in Amor [Syria]. They desolated its people, and its land was like that which has never come into being. They were coming forward toward Egypt while the flame was prepared before them. Their confederation was the Peleset, Tjeker, Shekelesh, Danuna, and Weshesh, lands united. They laid their hands upon the lands as far as the circuit of the earth, their hearts confident and trusting: "Our plans will succeed!" Now the heart of this god, the Lord of the Gods [the Pharaoh], was prepared and ready to ensnare them like birds.

[Statement of Ramses]

I organized my frontier in Djahi [Syria-Palestine] and prepared before them princes, commanders of garrisons, and maryanu [Asiatic warriors]. I have the river mouths prepared like a strong wall with warships, galleys, and coasters, fully equipped; for they were manned completely from bow to stern with valiant warriors carrying their weapons. The troops consisted of every picked man of Egypt. They were like lions roaring upon the mountaintops. The chariotry consisted of runners, of picked men, of every good and capable chariot-warrior. I was the valiant Montu [a war god] standing fast at their head. Those who reached my frontier, their seed is not; their heart and their soul are finished forever and ever. Those who came forward together on the sea, the full flame was in front of them at the river mouths, while a stockade of lances surrounded them on the shore. They were dragged in, enclosed, and prostrated on the beach, killed and made into heaps from tail to head. Their ships and their goods were as if fallen into the water. I have made the lands turn back from even mentioning Egypt; for when they pronounce my name in their land, then they are burned up. Since I sat upon the throne of Har-akhti [a manifestation of Ra], and since the Great-of-Magic [the serpent symbol of kingship] was fixed upon my head like Ra, I have not allowed foreign countries to behold the frontier of Egypt and to boast to the Nine Bows [traditional Egyptian enemies]. I have taken away their land, their frontiers being added to mine.

THE IRON AGE IN THE EASTERN MEDITERRANEAN (1200–800 BCE)

In the Near East, the Bronze Age was succeeded by the **Iron Age** around 1200 BCE, bringing new patterns of civilization that first made their mark on the eastern coast of the Mediterranean Sea. There, peoples who had lived on the fringes of the civilizations of Mesopotamia and Egypt achieved an expanded degree of self-expression. As with the Bronze Age, the Iron Age is defined by many other factors besides just the use of iron, including a shift from large

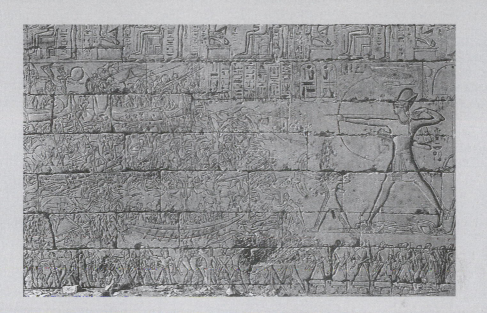

Their princes and their tribes-people are mine with praise.

[Summary]

The northern countries quivered in their bodies. They cut off their own land and were coming, their soul finished. They were teher-warriors [chariot borne spearmen] on land; another group was on the sea. Those who came on land were overthrown and killed. Amon-Ra was after them, destroying them. Those who entered the river mouths were like birds ensnared in the net. Their leaders were carried off and slain. They were cast down and pinioned. They penetrated the channels of the river mouths. Their nostrils have ceased to function. His majesty has gone forth like a whirlwind against them, fighting on the battlefield like a runner. The dread and terror of him have entered into their bodies. They are capsized and overwhelmed where they are. There, the heart of any whom he may have wished is pierced; and the fugitive is become one fallen into the water. His majesty is like an enraged lion, attacking his assailant with his arms: plundering on his right hand and powerful on his left hand, like Set destroying the Serpent Evil of Character. It is Amon-Ra who for him has overthrown every land under his feet.

cities in river valleys focusing on agriculture to smaller cities out of the river valleys concentrating much more heavily on commerce.

Iron and the Iron Age

The initial use of **iron** actually occurred in the Bronze Age, but, like bronze, it was a luxury item. In the nineteenth century BCE, for example, Assyrian merchants gave iron a value of forty times its weight in silver. The pharaoh Tut-ankh-amon was buried with an iron dagger, with a hilt and sheath of gold

HISTORICAL CAUSALITY

What factors led some societies to use trade to expand their economies? Why were some societies better equipped than others to pursue a trading economy? Discuss the pluses and minuses of agriculture versus trade as a means of creating a productive economy.

decorated with rock crystal. The most common source of metallic iron was meteorites, but in this form it was extremely rare. Otherwise, iron occurred not in metallic form, like copper and tin, but in intractable ores chemically combined with elements such as sulfur and oxygen. The ore had to be smelted for the iron to be released. This was not easy. The relatively low melting point of bronze, around 1922 degrees Fahrenheit, made it easy to work with in pottery kilns. But the smelting of iron ore required a temperature of 2800 degrees Fahrenheit. Yet, if the technology for smelting iron were available, a huge, inexpensive metal supply would become available, for iron is very common, comprising 5 percent of the Earth's crust, whereas copper and tin are only trace elements.

Early iron production often is associated with the Hittites, who sometimes are said to have used it as a "secret weapon." But they, in fact, produced only small quantities of iron daggers and swords before their empire collapsed at the end of the Bronze Age. Not until then did the knowledge of iron smelting become widespread enough for iron to come into common use in western Asia. One can only speculate as to whether the movements of peoples at the end of the Bronze Age were a factor in the spread of this specialized knowledge. By 1100 BCE, knowledge of iron working had diffused into southwestern Europe, and it reached Britain by about 700 BCE. River valley civilizations, however, lagged behind; not until the seventh century BCE did iron become widely used in Egypt.

The beginning of the Iron Age can be defined as the time when iron-working technology became sufficiently widespread and economical for commonplace, utilitarian items to be manufactured. Once this had happened, the transition from bronze to iron as the metal of choice for many items occurred quickly. Metal became available to a much larger segment of the population, rather than just to elites, and could be used for everyday objects such as household utensils and tools. Farming implements in particular, such as plows, now could be made from iron rather than wood. As a result large areas, such as the Rhine and Danube river valleys whose tough soils hitherto had been difficult to work with scratch plows, were opened up to agriculture and thus to the spread of more complex cultures.

A misconception about iron is that it replaced bronze for weapons right from the beginning of the Iron Age. This was not the case. Early cast iron was soft, brittle, and did not retain a sharp edge. Bronze thus at first remained the most suitable metal for weapons, and it took a while for the development of a technology that could manufacture iron weapons of sufficiently good quality. It did not matter if a plow or axe broke because the iron shattered, but weapons had to be more reliable. Over time, methods for creating effective iron weapons were developed, such as hammering, carburizing (alloying iron with about 1 percent carbon), quenching (immersing heated iron suddenly in water), and tempering (reheating quenched iron and allowing it to cool slowly).

In addition, the characteristics that define the Iron Age go far beyond the use of iron. The civilizations that characterized the Bronze Age had been based on the extensive exploitation of agriculture in river valleys, but, lacking natural resources, they long since had exhausted their possibilities for further technological and economic expansion. By the beginning of the Iron Age, the centers of cultural and economic development had moved out of the river valleys, and, in general, they tended to move toward the west, first to the Levant, then to the Balkans, and finally to western Europe. Because cultures located outside the fertile river valleys could not seek economic expansion in agriculture, they found an alternative form of economic development in manufacturing and trade. Along with the luxury items that had been traded in the Bronze Age, Iron Age merchants also exploited trade in less expensive bulk materials, such as mass-produced pottery, textiles, and agricultural produce. For these societies, trade was not just an adjunct to agriculture but the primary means of economic expansion. At the same time, there also was an increasing interest in the accumulation of wealth, often acquired through commerce.

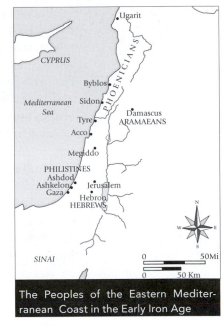

The Peoples of the Eastern Mediterranean Coast in the Early Iron Age

During the early Iron Age, previously marginalized peoples took advantage of the collapse of Bronze Age powers in Egypt, Anatolia, and Mesopotamia to expand their own influence. This was a period of small, fortified cities located either on higher ground for security or near seacoasts for access to water transportation. The first cultures to provide examples of the characteristic traits of Iron Age civilization are found in the Levant, on the eastern Mediterranean coast. There, four different peoples, the Phoenicians, Aramaeans, Philistines, and Hebrews, recovered quickly from the disruptions at the end of the Bronze Age and responded to the changed times in somewhat different ways.

The Phoenicians

Many seacoast cities of Phoenicia (modern-day Lebanon), as the northern coast of Canaan came to be called after 1200 BCE, found new life after the attacks of the Sea Peoples. Because the forested and hilly coastland was unsuitable for massive agriculture, the **Phoenicians**, another Semitic people, expanded their economies through commerce. Cities such as Byblos, Sidon, and Tyre picked up where Ugarit had left off and became major trading cities. Phoenician cities were independent **city-states** governed by a king advised by a council of nobles. The cities reinvigorated a trading economy based on seaborne commerce. The Phoenicians used nautical technology borrowed from the Sea Peoples to construct ships with keels rather than flat bottoms, which permitted ships to sail across or even a bit against the wind, that were capable of lengthy voyages.

The city of Byblos exported so much Egyptian papyrus that it gave its name to the Greek word for book, "biblion," and hence our word Bible.

Phoenician merchants were recognized far and wide. The Bible, for example, described the people of **Tyre** as those "whose merchants are princes, whose traders are honored in the world." The Phoenicians imported luxury items, including gemstones, ivory, and peacocks, from Africa and India; papyrus from Egypt; spices such as myrrh, frankincense, and incense from Arabia; and metals including gold, silver, tin, and copper from Britain, Spain, Africa, and Cyprus. These materials were either reexported as part of a carrying trade or used to create locally manufactured luxury items. Phoenician glassblowing, including the creation of transparent glass, was a tradition that lasted well into the Roman period. Luxury furniture was made from local cedar and hardwood forests. Other exports included locally produced products such as timber, salted fish, and wine. But the best known Phoenician product was a purple dye that came from the murex, a local shellfish. It was used to create the "Tyrian purple" textiles that often were thought suitable only for royalty. Indeed, the very name *Phoenicia* came to mean "purple" in Greek.

Needing an effective way to keep commercial records, the Phoenicians created a true **alphabet**, modeled on the proto-alphabet of Ugarit, with twenty-two letters, beginning with aleph, beth, and gimel. The Phoenician alphabet, technically called an *abjad* because it lacked vowels, subsequently was borrowed by the Greeks, for whom the first three letters became alpha, beta, and gamma, whence it traveled to the Etruscans, the Romans, and then to us.

The Phoenicians sailed the Mediterranean and beyond. Like all ancient sailors, they hugged the coast and put in to shore at the approach of bad weather. Simple navigation was done by the sun, the stars, and dead reckoning, that is, by informed guesswork. Merchant ships were propelled by the wind rather than by oarsmen; oarsmen were expensive, but the wind was free. Because ancient sailing vessels were unable to tack effectively, a merchantman might be forced to remain in port for days or weeks waiting for a favorable wind. Along with its merchant marine, Phoenician cities maintained navies to protect their trade. Warships were propelled by oars because they had to be maneuverable and not dependent on the wind. Like the Minoans and Mycenaeans, the Phoenicians established colonies to further their commercial interests. **Carthage,** founded in 814 BCE on the coast of modern Tunisia in North Africa, later became a commercial and military power. And Cadiz, on the Atlantic coast of Spain just outside the Straits of Gibraltar, was a port for ships that traded up the Atlantic coast to Britain.

Modern theories that Phoenician sailors reached India, Brazil, or Australia cannot be confirmed.

The Phoenicians worshiped a triad (group of three) of gods. **El**, a word that meant simply "god," was described as the "father of the gods" and "the creator of the creators." The son of El was the storm god **Ba'al,** who eventually eclipsed El just as Enlil had overshadowed An in Mesopotamia. Ba'al appeared in many forms; in Tyre, for example, he was Melqart. The primary female deity was Astarte (Ashtoret in the Bible, Ishtar in Babylon, Aphrodite in Greece), who represented fertility, sexuality, and war. A surviving cult statue of Astarte has holes in her breasts that were blocked with wax, which was subtly melted during a religious rite, allowing milk (stored in her hollow head) to flow from her breasts. The concept of a divine triad was reflected in the architecture of Phoenician temples, which had three chambers. Initially, Phoenician worship included human sacrifice, which persisted in Carthage even after it had been abandoned back in Phoenicia.

A representation of a Phoenician war galley from Nineveh, ca. 700 BCE, now in the British Museum. With rows of shields, multiple banks of oars, a bronze ram, and an armed body of marines, a Phoenician galley would have been a fearsome sight to any pirate.

The Phoenicians, like the Egyptians, believed in an afterlife and preserved their dead in elaborate tombs, although Phoenician mummies did not long survive in the damp coastal climate. One king had the following words inscribed on his coffin: "I, Tabnit, priest of Astarte, king of Sidon, am lying here. Whoever might find this coffin, do not disturb me, for such a thing would be an abomination to Astarte. If you do disturb me, may you have no descendents among the living and no rest among the dead." Tabnit's tomb lay undisturbed until it was discovered in the 1800s.

The Aramaeans and Philistines

If the Phoenicians controlled the sea trade, the **Aramaeans** were heavily engaged in trade by land. They were a Semitic people who had emerged from the northern fringe of Arabia during the movements of peoples just before 1200 BCE. They defeated the local Assyrians and Kassites on the inland side of Phoenicia and established their own city kingdoms, such as the great caravan city of Damascus. Their merchants transported goods south to Egypt and Arabia, north to Anatolia and central Asia, and east to India. As a consequence of the presence of Aramaean merchants throughout the Near East, the Aramaean language became a lingua franca that allowed travelers to communicate when they were away from home. It even replaced Akkadian as the language of international diplomacy.

On the seacoast south of the Phoenicians lived the Indo-European **Philistines**, descended from the warlike Peleset, one of the Sea Peoples, who had settled there just after 1200 BCE. They established five independent city-states (Ashkelon, Ashdod, Ekron, Gath, and Gaza) that were allied for mutual defense and ruled by leaders known as *seranim*. Unlike the Phoenicians and Aramaeans, the Philistines left no written records of their own, so they are known mainly from the scripture of their Hebrew enemies, in which they appear as threatening warriors with iron weapons who were always eager to take advantage of weaker peoples who lived around them. Their use of iron

As a consequence of their bad reputation in the Bible, the Philistines' name survives as a modern word signifying a materialistic person lacking in culture.

is confirmed by archaeological remains, such as a furnace for making iron swords. In spite of their military reputation, the Philistines were primarily farmers. They lacked good seaports and thus never became sailors, although in spite of this they became wealthy by taxing the sea and land traffic passing north and south between Phoenicia and Egypt. They adopted the worship of the Canaanite god Dagon, a fertility deity who supported the Philistines in war. And like the Phoenicians, they also worshipped Astarte, who in their pantheon was Dagon's consort. Larger Philistine buildings, such as temples, were constructed using multiple roof timbers supported by columns at the point where they joined.

THE HEBREWS (2000–900 BCE)

Of all the peoples of the Levant at this time, it was the **Hebrews,** who eventually settled just inland from the Philistines, who had the greatest impact on history. The Hebrews developed a very personal relationship with their god that made their religion unique among the religions of the pre-Christian period. For one thing, they came to preserve their beliefs in a standardized written form, making it resistant to change over the centuries. The Hebrew **Bible** described the Hebrew peoples' history and relations with their god, and it was this book, more than anything, that gave the Hebrews their sense of identity.

The Bible is treated here like any other historical source, without any preconceptions about its historical accuracy.

The Origin of the Hebrews

Early Hebrew history is known primarily from the Bible, although more and more archaeological material also is becoming available. The study of Hebrew history is not without its controversies, which often result from a conflict between literal interpretations of scripture and archaeological evidence. The Hebrews traced their ancestry back as early as 2000 BCE to Semitic pastoralists who lived on the arid edges of the Mesopotamian river valley. They lived in tents, kept sheep and cattle, and traveled in search of pastures. Even though they rejected urban life (they attributed the first city to the fratricide Cain), the ancestors of the Hebrews picked up many elements of Mesopotamian culture, including legal concepts, the word *Edin* (a flat plain), accounts of a great flood, reports of ziggurats ("the tower of Babel"), and stories of heroes cast adrift as infants.

The first period of Hebrew history is the **Age of the Patriarchs**, when bands of wandering Hebrews, consisting of an extended family group and its dependents, were led by an elderly male **patriarch**. Women had an inferior status in this male-dominated society. Property was controlled by men, who could have both wives and concubines. Wives could be put aside for any number of reasons, including being infertile, or second wives could be taken to provide children. Around 1800 BCE the patriarch **Abraham**, who was looked on as the ancestor of the Hebrew people, led his family group from "Ur of the Chaldeans," usually identified as the Sumerian city of Ur, to Harran in western Mesopotamia. During this period, the Hebrews began to form a unique personal relationship with their god, who then was known as El, the same name as the principal Phoenician god. The Hebrews believed that God made a pact with Abraham known as a **covenant**, a word used to describe a contract between superior and subordinate parties in which each has fixed responsibilities. In this case, Abraham promised to accept El as the god of his people, and God promised that Abraham's descendents would become his "chosen people" and would inherit the promised land of Canaan. As a sign of their commitment to the covenant, Hebrew men were circumcised. Even though these early Hebrews did not deny the existence of other gods, they now were moving toward **monotheism**, the belief that there was only one, single god.

The Hebrews never settled down, although occasionally they remained somewhere long enough to harvest a crop of grain. According to the Bible, the descendents of the twelve sons of Abraham's grandson, the patriarch Jacob (also known as Israel), created twelve disunited tribes. To escape a famine, Jacob's son Joseph and his family moved to northern Egypt, perhaps around 1700 BCE, when Egypt's northern frontiers were open to intrusions during the Hyksos period. After the expulsion of the Hyksos, the Hebrews are portrayed in the Bible as agricultural workers or slaves employed on building projects. Their sojourn in Egypt thus transformed them from wandering pastoralists into settled farmers and artisans. In addition, as of the thirteenth century BCE, one finds generic, often derogatory, references in Near Eastern documents to people called the Ha-bi-ru, or "the dusty ones." They appear as slaves, laborers, bandits, and mercenaries: Egyptian records, for example, speak of "the Ha-bi-ru who drag stone for the great building of Ramses II." This generic name eventually was applied to the Hebrews alone.

The word tribe here reflects the Roman usage of a subdivision of a larger group of people.

There is no evidence that the monotheistic views of Egyptian Hebrews influenced Akhenaton's religious reform, or that Akhenaton's form of monotheism influenced the Hebrews.

Creating an Identity

One of the greatest Hebrew leaders was **Moses**, who, according to biblical tradition, had been cast adrift in the Nile by his mother because the pharaoh had ordered Hebrew male children to be killed. After being rescued by an Egyptian princess, he was raised in the pharaoh's household. This account is consistent with the name Moses being of Egyptian origin, as seen, for example, in the name of the pharaoh Thutmose. After killing an Egyptian whom he saw beating a Hebrew, the Bible continues, Moses took refuge in the Sinai Desert with the Midianites, a Semitic people. While there, according to tradition, he encountered the Hebrew god, in the form of a burning bush, who revealed his name as "YHWH" (or **Yahweh**, the Christian Jehovah, a word meaning "The Name of Names"). Yahweh ordered Moses to return to Egypt and lead the Hebrews to freedom. Following several confrontations with the pharaoh, Moses successfully guided several thousand Hebrews across a water-covered area—suggested identifications range from a branch of the Red Sea to a more northern swampy area—and into the Sinai Desert in a migration known as the **Exodus**, one of the greatest events in Hebrew history.

The Exodus was one of the very few occasions in history when a persecuted minority succeeded in escaping from its oppressors, and it was taken as a sign that Yahweh had performed his part in the covenant. These Hebrews became the kernel of the people who now were called "the children of Israel," that is, the descendents of Jacob/Israel. During their time in the Sinai, the Hebrews finalized their covenant with God, who again promised to make the Hebrews his chosen people and to lead them into the Promised Land. For their part, the Hebrews agreed to obey Yahweh's laws and to worship no other god but Yahweh. But the Hebrews still acknowledged the existence of other gods as seen in the commandment, "You shall have no other gods before me." The real ruler of the Hebrews was Yahweh, just as Mesopotamian gods were the true rulers of Mesopotamian cities. But, unlike Mesopotamian gods, Yahweh was a real presence. He communicated his will directly through chosen spokespersons of any social class or gender. Hebrew leaders such as Moses could converse and even negotiate with Yahweh. Leadership thus was a consequence of direct contact with Yahweh.

It was their following of the behavioral guidelines established by Yahweh as much as their worship of a single god that unified the Hebrew people, gave them an identity, and kept them separate from other peoples. The most important of God's rules were the Ten Commandments that God had given to Moses, but over the course of the centuries many other regulations were established in the **Torah** (the first five books of the Hebrew Bible) and elsewhere that governed the Hebrews' interactions with each other and with outsiders. But maintaining unswerving loyalty to Yahweh was not easy. The Bible reports many occasions on which Hebrews worshipped other gods, the worst possible offense against Yahweh.

In Judaism, overt obedience to the law was the most important element, whereas in modern Christianity, faith and belief in Christian doctrine are.

The Hebrew regulations were often more specific than the laws issued by the Mesopotamians, because they dealt with not only criminal and civil law but also the most intimate aspects of personal conduct, such as who could marry whom. They emphasized personal morality, ethical behavior, and social justice. As in Mesopotamia, the punishment for serious offenses was usually death. For personal injuries, Hebrew law mandated the same "eye for an eye" penalty found in the Code of Hammurabi. As elsewhere, women were disadvantaged and were prohibited from owning or selling property or initiating lawsuits or divorces. And although women initially were able to participate in some religious rituals, over time they also lost this right.

THE DATE OF THE BIBLICAL EXODUS

A great deal of controversy surrounds the historical accuracy of the Bible, most of whose accounts cannot be corroborated by any other source. Whereas some historians, the "traditionalists," accept most of biblical scripture as historical, others, the "minimalists," treat the Bible as a legendary source and look for a kernel of truth in the midst of "historicized fiction." The date of the Exodus is one of the thorniest controversies of biblical studies, for here the Bible contradicts itself. On the one hand, the biblical book of Kings states that Solomon's temple, constructed around the year 966 BCE, was built in the 480th year after the Exodus. This would date the Exodus to around 1446 BCE, at the same time as the creation

Atop the Merneptah stele, Merneptah worships Amon-Ra, who is identified by his twin crowns.

of the Egyptian Empire. In this historical context, one might wonder whether what the Hebrews recorded as a heroic Exodus was in fact an expulsion of undesirable foreigners by chauvinistic pharaohs who already had expelled the Hyksos.

The book of Exodus, on the other hand, states that the Hebrews left "from the city of Ramses," and the references to massive building projects suggest Ramses II (1279–1212 BCE). This is consistent with the earliest nonbiblical evidence for the Hebrew kingdom, a black granite stele erected at Thebes in the mortuary temple of the pharaoh Merneptah (1212–1202 BCE) and now in the Cairo Museum. It primarily commemorated victories in 1208 BCE over the Libyans and their Sea People allies. Its final lines refer to a military campaign regarding which Merneptah stated, "Plundered is Canaan; Carried off is Ashkelon; seized upon is Gezer; Yanoam (a city in Palestine) is made as that which does not exist; Isiral [Israel] is laid waste, barren of seed." The stele thus indicates that the Hebrews already were known as "Israel." Moreover, at this time, Israel apparently was an insignificant place, being named after three Canaanite cities that Merneptah also had defeated. Nor did the Egyptians know exactly how to classify Israel—an uninformed reader probably would presume that "Isiral" was just another Canaanite city, as opposed to a people or nation. A date in the thirteenth century BCE also is suggested by archaeological finds showing destruction that has been attributed to military campaigns during the initial Hebrew occupation of Palestine. This evidence would put the Exodus around 1270 BCE and the settlement in Canaan forty years later, leaving plenty of time for the Hebrews to have begun to create an incipient state that was laid waste by Merneptah a few decades later. There seems to be no easy or convincing way to resolve the inconsistencies about the date of the Exodus, although as things stand, the later date is generally thought to fit the evidence rather better.

The Promised Land

After forty years in the desert, the Hebrews finally emerged into Canaan. A long period of disruption then ensued as, initially led by Joshua, they began to carve out their own nation, often in the uplands. Canaanite populations sometimes were massacred in order to protect Hebrew culture from foreign influence. The Hebrew migration thus provides another example of the disruptive population movements that occurred at the beginning of the Iron Age. The Hebrew tribes had no political unity, although they did have some religious unity based on a shrine at Shiloh where the Ark of the Covenant preserved the original Ten Commandments.

The most important Hebrew leaders after the Exodus were **judges**, who, under the authority of Yahweh, appeared in times of trouble and led short-lived coalitions of tribes against hostile peoples. The unsettled nature of the times gave women opportunities to hold significant leadership positions, as occurred around 1150 BCE when the judge Deborah raised an army against the Canaanites. More commonly, however, the Hebrews' disunity made them easy prey for their enemies, and in particular for the Philistines, who lived on the coastal plain to the west. One Hebrew who resisted the Philistines was the warrior Samson, who killed many Philistines and served as judge for twenty years. Samson's downfall, it was said, came at the hands of the bewitching Philistine woman Delilah, who had been offered several thousand pieces of silver by the Philistine lords to betray him. He was captured, blinded, and enslaved. During a festival of Dagon, Samson was mocked at the god's temple. Being familiar with Philistine construction methods, he used his great strength to dislodge the support pillars and bring down the roof, causing great destruction.

Meanwhile, things continued to go badly for the Hebrews. Around 1050 BCE the Philistines captured the Ark of the Covenant and forbade the Hebrews to use iron. In despair, the Hebrew people asked the prophet Samuel, "make us a king to judge us like all the nations." After winning a victory over a neighboring people around 1050 BCE, the judge Saul (ca. 1050–1010 BCE) was duly declared king, thus creating the Hebrew kingdom and bringing Hebrew political development more into line with that of neighboring peoples. An ensuing confrontation with the Philistines then was decided by single combat, in which the Hebrew hero **David** defeated the Philistine Goliath.

The Hebrew Kingdom

The great age of the Hebrew kingdom came under the next two kings. David (1010–970 BCE) captured from the Canaanites the heavily fortified city of **Jerusalem**, which became the Hebrew capital city. He also expanded the kingdom to include Canaan all the way to the coast.

Under David's son **Solomon** (970–930 BCE), the Hebrew state completed its transformation from loosely organized groups of pastoralists united by a shared religion to an urbanized and politically centralized nation. The Hebrew kingdom now stretched from the Sinai Peninsula to the Euphrates River and controlled the trade routes running between the Mediterranean and Red seas, and thence to India. Caravans traveling through were taxed, and commerce brought profits on goods such as gold, silver, ivory, and exotic animals. From Arabia, for example, came gold and incense, as well as the frankincense and myrrh needed for Hebrew religious rituals. Tribute and gifts from foreign rulers also flowed in. For example, the queen of **Sheba**, an Arabian kingdom on the Red Sea, brought camels, spices, gold,

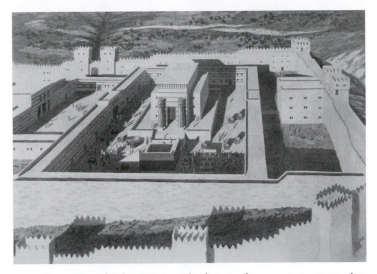

A reconstruction of Solomon's temple shows a three-part structure, similar to the style of Phoenician temples.

and gems. And a mutually beneficial agreement with king Hiram of Tyre gave Solomon access to the Mediterranean Sea and Hiram access to the Red Sea. Solomon used Phoenician expertise to construct fleets of trading ships for use on the Red Sea, and he and the Phoenicians engaged in joint trading expeditions. The Hebrew kingdom became so wealthy that the Bible could declare, "Solomon made gold and silver as plentiful as stones in Jerusalem," and "King Solomon exceeded all the kings of the earth for riches."

It thus appeared that the Hebrew kingdom had become a full-fledged participant in the life of the early Iron Age. Solomon himself became another high-profile Near Eastern ruler. He controlled an army of over ten thousand cavalry and one thousand chariots. And his personal influence became such that he was thought fit to marry a daughter of the Egyptian pharaoh, the only one of his seven hundred wives and three hundred concubines cited in the Bible to be mentioned (although not named) as an individual, attesting to the great significance attributed to this alliance.

Solomon unified the Hebrew kingdom even further by building a **temple** in Jerusalem to contain the Ark of the Covenant and serve as the center of Hebrew cult practices. The temple was designed by architects from Tyre and built at exorbitant cost, using 70,000 haulers, 80,000 quarryers, and 3,300 foremen and taking seven years to build. Solomon also acquired a reputation for great wisdom in his judicious handling of disputes and lawsuits. But Hebrew kings, like all Near Eastern monarchs, also could behave tyrannically, as when David connived to take Bathsheba from her husband Uriah the Hittite, a foreign **mercenary** in Israel's army, by sending him to the front line of battle, where he soon was killed.

Hebrew prophets provided models for later Christian holy men who spoke out against the actions of emperors and kings.

After Solomon's death around 930 BCE, unrest over high taxes split the kingdom in half. In the south, the tribes of Judah and Benjamin became the **Kingdom of Judah**, with its capital at Jerusalem, whose inhabitants now became known as the **Jews**. The other ten tribes became the northern **Kingdom of Israel**, with its capital at Samaria, and came to be known as **Samaritans**. Having lost their unity, the Hebrews also lost their short-lived political and economic significance and again fell prey to more powerful neighbors. This also was the great age of Hebrew **prophets**, popular figures who were directed by Yahweh to speak out against the worship of foreign gods even if it meant criticizing the policies of Hebrew kings.

The northern kingdom of Israel continued to develop as a typical Iron Age state, with trade and cultural exchanges with foreign peoples, especially the Phoenicians, from whom some northern Hebrews adopted the worship of the god Ba'al, who was portrayed in the Bible as Yahweh's primary competitor. One king of Israel, Ahab (ca. 869–850 BCE), married a Phoenician princess named Jezebel, who later came to symbolize the wicked seductress. After Ahab built a temple of Ba'al for her, they were punished by Yahweh. Ahab bled to death in battle, and Jezebel was cast from a building by **eunuchs**, castrated males who often served in ancient Near Eastern palaces, and eaten by dogs.

The city of Megiddo, the site of several ancient battles, gave its name to "Armageddon," the great battle that Christian scripture states will take place at the end of time.

Meanwhile, the more conservative and rather more isolated kingdom of Judah was less affected by foreign influences. Ca. 925 BCE, it survived an attack on Jerusalem by the Egyptian pharaoh Shoshenq (biblical Shisak) (945–922 BCE) that resulted in the capture of other cities such as Megiddo. The kings of Judah consolidated the status of the temple in Jerusalem as the religious center of Judaism. At this time, Hebrew oral traditions about their relations with Yahweh and their history as a people began to be written down using the Phoenician alphabet. A move toward stricter monotheism also occurred, as seen, for example, in the book of Deuteronomy, in which Yahweh says, "I am Yahweh, and there is none else. Besides me there is no god."

LOOKING AHEAD

The period when small kingdoms and city-states could participate fully and freely in the economic and political life of the Iron Age ended with the rise of Iron Age empires that were even larger and more powerful than their Bronze Age counterparts. Like the small cities, these empires likewise had significant commercial interests and created concentrations of wealth that in the past had been undreamed of.

FURTHER READING

Baikie, James. *The Sea-Kings of Crete.* London: Adam and Charles Black, 1913.
Dickinson, O. T. P. K. *The Origins of Mycenaean Civilization.* Göteborg, Sweden: Åströms, 1977.

Bernal, M. *Black Athena: The Afroasiatic Roots of Classical Civilization.* Vols. 1, 2. New Brunswick, NJ: Rutgers University Press, 1987, reprinted 1991).

Callender, Gae. *The Minoans and the Mycenaeans: Aegean Society in the Bronze Age.* Oxford: Oxford University Press, 1999.

Chadwick, J. *The Decipherment of Linear B,* 2nd ed. Chicago: University of Chicago Press, 1990.

Crowley, J. L. *The Aegean and the East.* Jonsered, Sweden: Åströms, 1989.

Ehrlich, C. S. *The Philistines in Transition: A History from ca. 1000–730 BCE.* (Leiden, The Netherlands: Brill, 1996.

Finkelstein, Israel, and Amihai Mazer. *The Quest for the Historical Israel: Debating Archaeology and the History of Early Israel.* Atlanta, GA: Society for Biblical Literature, 2007.

Gesell, G. C. *Town, Palace, and House Cult in Minoan Crete.* Göteborg, Sweden: Åströms, 1985.

Lipínski, Edward. *The Aramaeans: Their Ancient History, Culture, Religion.* (Leuven, Belgium: Peeters, 2000.

Marinatos, Nanno. *Minoan Religion: Ritual, Image, and Symbol.* Columbia, SC: University of South Carolina Press, 1993.

Markoe, Glenn. *Phoenicians.* Berkeley: University of California Press, 2001.

Palmer, Leonard R. *Mycenaeans and Minoans,* 2nd ed. New York: Knopf, 1965.

Sandars, N. K. *The Sea Peoples: Warriors of the Ancient Mediterranean 1250–1150 BC.* London: Thames & Hudson, 1985.

Shanks, Edward. *Ancient Israel: From Abraham to the Roman Destruction of the Temple.* London: British Archaeological Society, 1999.

Wardle, K.A., and Wardle, Diana. *Cities of Legend: The Mycenaean World.* Bristol, UK: Bristol Classical Press, 2000.

CHAPTER 5

IRON AGE EMPIRES

Assyria, Babylonia, and Persia
(850–500 BCE)

Just as in the Bronze Age, empires also developed in the Iron Age as one people or nation imposed its authority on another. But whereas the Bronze Age empires had been fairly short term and unstable, lacking in cohesiveness, the Iron Age empires showed an increasing ability to control larger and larger amounts of territory and to gain economic advantages from it. The Assyrians created an empire based on military might and economic exploitation that eventually included both the Mesopotamian and Egyptian river valleys. But the Assyrians were unable to win the goodwill of their conquered peoples, and their empire eventually fell to revolt. Several successors to the Assyrians practiced empire building on a smaller scale, but it was the Persians who ultimately created the greatest and most successful Near Eastern empire by developing a system that benefited not only themselves but also their conquered peoples.

THE ASSYRIAN EMPIRE (850–605 BCE)

The age of small states that characterized the beginning of the Iron Age ended when some powerful peoples of western Asia began to create new and larger empires. The first of these was the Assyrians, a people who for centuries had been victimized by their more powerful neighbors. During its long history, the Assyrian kingdom experienced several cycles of prosperity interspersed with periods of weakness. When the Assyrians finally got the upper hand, they missed no opportunity to let their subjects know who was in charge.

The Rise of Assyria

The **Assyrians**, named after their war god Assur, were an Amorite people who settled in the upper Tigris River valley around 2000 BCE. In language, culture, and religion, they were very similar to the Babylonians, who had settled in central Mesopotamia at the same time. Unfortunately for the Assyrians, their

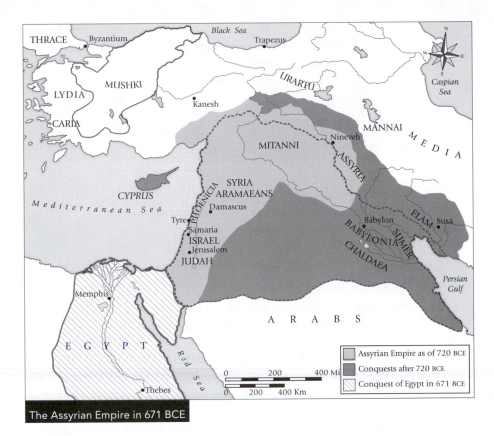

THRACE
Byzantium
Black Sea
Trapezus
MUSHKI
LYDIA
Kanesh
CARIA
URARTU
MITANNI
Nineveh
ASSYRIA
MANNAI
M E D I A
Caspian Sea
CYPRUS
PHOENICIA
SYRIA
ARAMAEANS
Damascus
Tyre
Samaria
ISRAEL
Jerusalem
JUDAH
Mediterranean Sea
Babylon
Susa
ELAM
BABYLONIA
SUMER
CHALDAEA
Persian Gulf
A R A B S
Memphis
E G Y P T
Red Sea
Thebes

Assyrian Empire as of 720 BCE
Conquests after 720 BCE
Conquest of Egypt in 671 BCE

0   200   400 Mi
0   200   400 Km

The Assyrian Empire in 671 BCE

territory not only had no natural defenses but also was situated squarely on the travel routes used by both traders and invaders going to and fro across upper Mesopotamia. For much of their history, therefore, the Assyrians were exposed to attack from surrounding peoples: southwest lay the Aramaeans; the kingdom of Mitanni was to the west; the mountains to the northeast were inhabited first by peoples such as the Gutians and Lullubi, and later by the kingdom of Urartu; in the east, the Elamites of western Iran continued to meddle in Mesopotamia; and downriver to the southeast lay the ambitious empire builders of Mesopotamia. The Assyrians thus were engaged in a constant struggle for survival. People living under such conditions will either come under foreign domination or develop a very effective army. Thus it was with the Assyrians. They suffered many ups and downs, but throughout it all they remained a united kingdom bent on survival. For many centuries, the Assyrians competed with other Mesopotamian powers for influence. Gradually they built the most effective military machine that the Near East had yet known. The Assyrians also were confronted by economic challenges. The soil of the upper Tigris valley was not nearly as rich as that downstream. The Assyrians therefore took advantage of their easy access to trade routes and became another Bronze Age people to take an early interest in trade as a means of supplementing their

TABLE 5.1 SOME ASSYRIAN KINGS

FIRST STRONG PERIOD

Puzur-Assur I (ca. 1970–1960)

Shamsi-Adad I (ca. 1809–1781)

SECOND STRONG PERIOD

Assur-Ubalit I (1353–1318)

Shalmaneser I (1265–1235)

Tikulti-Ninurta I (1243–1207)

Tiglath-Pileser I (1115–1076)

THIRD STRONG PERIOD

Adad-Nirari II (912–891)

Tikulti-Ninurta II (891–884)

Assur-Nasir-Pal II (884–859)

Shalmaneser III (858–824)

Shamsi-Adad V (823–811)

Sammuramat (ca. 810)

Assur-Nirari V (754–745)

Tiglath-Pilezer III (745–727)

Sargon II (721–705)

Sennacherib (704–681)

Esarhaddon (681–668)

Assurbanipal (668–627)

economy. In addition, Assyrian kings led raids into neighboring lands in search not of additional territory but of loot.

The first Assyrian kingdom (ca.2000–1750 BCE), with its capital at **Assur**, traditionally was established by Puzur-Assur I just after 2000 BCE. In the late twentieth century BCE, King Ilushuma made the first Assyrian mark on history by undertaking a raid for loot south into Mesopotamia that he claimed reached Babylon and Ur. Around 1950 BCE, Assyrian merchants established a trading colony at Kanesh (modern Kültepe) in the middle of Anatolia. Assyrian merchants, under the protection of the local king, traded luxury items, spices, and woven cloth for locally produced wool and tin. Under Shamsi-Adad I (ca. 1809–1781 BCE), the Assyrians raided into Lebanon and even occupied the kingdom of Mari, which controlled trade between Mesopotamia and Anatolia, giving the Assyrians control of upper Mesopotamia. But after his death, his short-lived empire crumbled, and Assyria came under the domination first of Hammurabi of Babylon and then of the kingdom of Mitanni.

The second Assyrian dominant period (ca. 1350–1200 BCE) began when King Assur-Ubalit I (1353–1318 BCE) defeated the kingdom of Mitanni. Subsequently, King Shalmaneser I (1265–1235 BCE) built a new capital city at Kalhu (modern Nimrud) and not only claimed to have defeated the rising power of **Urartu** to the north but also implemented various methods of demoralizing defeated enemies, ranging from the blinding of 14,400 captives to the **deportation** of defeated enemies to faraway lands. Tikulti-Ninurta I (1243–1207 BCE) defeated the Hittites and captured Babylon from the Kassites. But then, in the chaos marking the end of the Bronze Age and the beginning of the Iron Age, the Assyrian kingdom experienced economic distress and again went into a period of decline. Once again, Assyria was threatened by potential enemies such as the Aramaeans to the southwest; the Mushki, or Phrygians, of central Anatolia to the northwest; and Babylon to the southeast. Tiglath-Pileser I (1115–1076 BCE) momentarily stemmed the tide by defeating a massive invasion of Mushki, attacking the Aramaeans twenty-eight times, capturing Babylon, and advancing far into Urartu, a good source of iron and copper. But he was murdered, and Assyria again sank into decline. Nevertheless, against all odds Assyria remained a united kingdom and resisted the fragmentation that usually had led to the permanent decline of other Mesopotamian powers.

As of about 900 BCE, a third period of Assyrian dominance (ca. 900–612 BCE) began. The Assyrians now possessed the world's most advanced army and the first military machine based on iron-weapon-making technology. Indeed, nearly 150 tons of iron bars, perhaps a strategic reserve, were found in one Assyrian palace. In the eighth century BCE, the army numbered about 150,000 men. Like the later army of the Roman Republic, the Assyrian army

Assyrian archers assisted by a battering ram attack a city as dead defenders fall to the ground, from the palace at Nimrud, ca. 728 BCE.

initially was recruited from peasant farmers, who became available in the summer after their crops had been planted. Unlike previous Mesopotamian armies, which were raised only irregularly, the Assyrian army was called up almost every year and became very experienced. The backbone of the Assyrian army continued to be the infantry, but the Assyrians also assimilated the military tactics of the steppe **nomads** to the north. Horses were imported from the area of Lake Van to the north, and warriors mounted on horseback superseded chariots. Cavalrymen had no stirrups or saddles but merely held a set of reins while sitting on a blanket. Lances were ineffective—if they were used, cavalrymen would slide off the back of the horse—but short spears and swords were used for jabbing and hacking. Mounted archers served as mobile shock troops. Specialist corps also included engineers expert in **siege warfare** utilizing battering rams, sappers who tunneled under walls and caused them to collapse, scaling ladders, and movable towers. Against the Assyrians, therefore, strong walls were no longer an effective defense.

The Assyrian recovery and expansion began under Adad-Nirari II (912–891 BCE), under whom defeated states were made into Assyrian vassals. Under Tikulti-Ninurta II (891–884 BCE), Assyrian territorial gains were consolidated by establishing garrisons on hills and trade routes and by changing vassal territories into provinces administered directly by Assyrians. His son Assur-Nasir-Pal II (884–859 BCE) granted land to colonists who settled in adjoining occupied territories.

King Shalmaneser III (858–824 BCE) undertook no less than thirty-one campaigns and claimed to have defeated the Aramaeans, the Babylonians, the kingdom of Urartu, and the Medes, an Indo-European people of northwestern Iran. A victory stele erected after a war against the Aramaeans bragged, "To

The Assyrian Black Obelisk shows Jehu, king of Israel, pledging loyalty to Shalmaneser III. The accompanying legend reads, "Tribute of Jehu, son of Omri. I received from him: silver, gold, a golden bowl, a golden beaker, golden goblets, pitchers of gold, lead, staves for the hand of the king, javelins."

offer battle they marched against me. Biridi of Damascus sent 1,200 chariots, 1,200 horsemen, and 20,000 men. Ahab of Israel sent 10,000 men. With the noble might granted by the lord Assur I fought with them. I slew 14,000 of their soldiers. I desolated and destroyed the city, I burnt it." Afterward, Shalmaneser made Jehu, king of Israel, into an Assyrian vassal. But the most colorful Assyrian ruler of this period was Queen Sammuramat (811–808 BCE), the wife of King Shamsi-Adad V (822–811 BCE), who ruled the empire for three years or more as regent for her young son Adad-Nirari III (810–783 BCE).

She became known in legend as **Semiramis** and was said to have been the daughter of the fertility goddess Astarte from the Philistine city of Ashkelon. In legend, she was said to have reigned over forty years and fought many wars, even attacking India. Her fame as a builder led many Near Eastern monuments to be credited to her.

The greatest of the Assyrian kings was **Tiglath-Pilezer III** (745–727 BCE), also known as Pul in the Bible, who was said to have begun life as a gardener, become a soldier, and made king by the army on account of his great military ability. It was he who made the territorial acquisitions that created the true **Assyrian Empire**. In short order Tiglath-Pilezer expanded the empire to the west. Phoenicia and northern Syria were annexed in 742, and Damascus fell the following year, giving the Assyrians free access to the ports of the Mediterranean Sea and the timber of Phoenicia. In the process, thirty thousand Syrians were deported to the Zagros Mountains in the north. In 734 he seized Babylonia, where a Semitic people called the **Chaldeans** recently had settled. Israel became an Assyrian vassal, and Tiglath also claimed to have annexed the Mighty Mada, the Assyrian name for the Medes.

Expansion continued under **Sargon II** (721–705 BCE), who conquered the northern Hebrew kingdom of Israel and its capital Samaria in 721 BCE. Much of the Hebrew population was deported to Iran. Soon afterward, the Assyrians gained control of the entire eastern Mediterranean coast by annexing the five Philistine cities. In order to avoid being attacked, Hezekiah, king of the southern Hebrew kingdom of Judah, became an Assyrian vassal. In 714, Sargon launched a massive invasion of Urartu, sacking the capital city and acquiring one ton of gold and five of silver. Soon afterward, Mita, king

Mita, king of the Mushki, appears in Greek mythology as king Midas, whose touch turned everything to gold, no doubt an allusion to the gold-bearing streams of western Anatolia.

of the Mushki, submitted. But in 705, Sargon was killed in a battle against the Cimmerians (the biblical Gomer), an Indo-European people who had been expelled from southern Russia by the **Scythians** (a generic term for steppe nomads) and the first Indo-Europeans to reach Mesopotamia directly from central Asia.

In 703 BCE, Sargon's son **Sennacherib** (704–681 BCE) brutally suppressed a Babylonian revolt by deporting 208,000 people to Assyria; Sennacherib's son Assur-Nadin-Shumi was made king of Babylon. Two years later the Assyrians attacked Judah, where King Hezekiah had rebelled and made an alliance with Egypt, now ruled by the Twenty-Fifth Dynasty, also known as the **Nubian** (or Kushite) **Dynasty** (760–656 BCE). In preparation for a siege, Hezekiah gave Jerusalem a dependable water supply by building a 1,750-foot- long tunnel, which still survives, to wells outside the walls. But when the Egyptians failed to come to his rescue, Hezekiah paid

The Assyrian king Sargon II depicted as a lamasu, or winged bull, in a relief from his palace at Khorsabad, demonstrates the association of Near Eastern rulers with the power, and virility, of bulls.

Sennacherib off and once again became an Assyrian vassal. Meanwhile, in 694 BCE the Elamites launched a surprise attack on Babylonia, capturing the city and carrying off Sennacherib's son. Sennacherib responded in 689 BCE by recapturing the city and destroying it so thoroughly that it was unoccupied for some years.

In 681 Sennacherib was assassinated by his sons, one of whom, Esarhaddon (681–668), became king after defeating his other brothers and executing their sons. An attack on northern Assyria by the Scythians was defeated in 676; to ensure future peace, Esarhaddon married one of his daughters to a Scythian prince and hired Scythian mercenaries. The land of the Medes was penetrated as far as modern Tehran. In 671, Esarhaddon attacked the Nubian Dynasty of Egypt, which had been attempting to interfere in eastern Mediterranean territories claimed by Assyria. He seized Lower Egypt and declared himself king of not only Upper and Lower Egypt but also Nubia, even though the Nubian pharaoh had not been defeated. But he lacked the troop strength to occupy the entire country and therefore, like the Hyksos, imposed tribute appointed native administrators, such as Necho in the nome of Saïs. This marked the first time that the Mesopotamian and Nile river valleys were controlled by the same power. Yet, even though the empire now appeared to have achieved its greatest success, there were signs of trouble on the horizon. The Medes of Iran and Chaldeans of Babylonia continued to chafe under Assyrian rule. And the Scythians were very unpredictable.

TWO ACCOUNTS OF THE SIEGE OF JERUSALEM

In 701 BCE, the Assyrian king Sennacherib attacked the southern Hebrew kingdom of Judah. It is our good fortune to possess accounts of the attack written from the perspective of both sides. The Prism of Sennacherib, a six-sided baked-clay stele fifteen inches tall, found in Nineveh and now at the Oriental Institute in Chicago, preserves Sennacherib's official account of his attack on Hezekiah, king of Judah:

> As for Hezekiah the Judahite, who did not submit to my yoke, I besieged and took forty-six

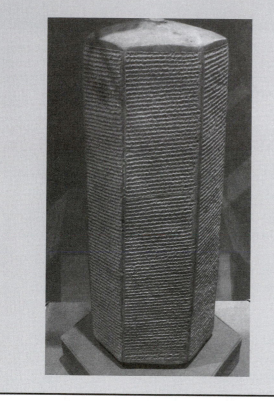

of his strong, walled cities, as well as the small towns in their area, which were without number, by leveling with battering-rams, by bringing up siege-engines, by attacking and storming on foot, and by mines, tunnels, and breeches, I brought away from them and counted as spoil 200,150 people, great and small, male and female, horses, mules, asses, camels, cattle and sheep without number, Hezekiah himself, like a caged bird I shut up in Jerusalem, his royal city. I threw up earthworks against him. Anyone coming out of the city-gate I turned back to his misery. His cities, which I had despoiled, I cut off from his land and gave to Mitinti, king of Ashdod, Padi, king of Ekron, and Silli-bêl, king of Gaza [all Philistine cities]. The terrifying splendor of my majesty overcame Hezekiah, and the Arabs and the mercenary troops that he had brought in to strengthen Jerusalem, his royal city, deserted him. In addition to thirty talents of gold and eight hundred talents of silver, he brought after me to Nineveh gems, antimony, jewels, large carnelians, ivory-inlaid couches, ivory-inlaid chairs, elephant hides, elephant tusks, ebony, boxwood, all kinds of valuable treasures, as well as his daughters, his harem, his male and female musicians, which he had brought to Nineveh, my royal city. To pay tribute and to accept servitude, he dispatched his messengers.

Meanwhile, Hebrew scripture, in 2 Kings 18–19, gives a detailed account of Assyrian negotiations prior to the attack on Jerusalem, and a rather different account of how the siege turned out:

"How Not to Run an Empire"

The Assyrians went to war for two reasons: defense and economic expansion. For defensive reasons, peoples who previously had attacked the Assyrians, such as the Babylonians and Arameans, were defeated and neutralized. Much

In the fourteenth year of King Hezekiah's reign, Sennacherib king of Assyria attacked all the fortified cities of Judah and captured them. So Hezekiah king of Judah sent this message to the king of Assyria at Lachish: "I have done wrong. Withdraw from me, and I will pay whatever you demand of me." The king of Assyria exacted from Hezekiah king of Judah three hundred talents of silver and thirty talents of gold. So Hezekiah gave him all the silver that was found in the temple of the Lord and in the treasuries of the royal palace. At this time Hezekiah king of Judah stripped off the gold with which he had covered the doors and doorposts of the temple of the Lord, and gave it to the king of Assyria. The king of Assyria sent his supreme commander, his chief officer and his field commander with a large army, from Lachish to King Hezekiah at Jerusalem. The field commander said, "Tell Hezekiah, this is what the great king, the king of Assyria, says: On what are you basing this confidence of yours? On whom are you depending, that you rebel against me? Look now, you are depending on Egypt, that splintered reed of a staff, which pierces a man's hand and wounds him if he leans on it." Then the commander called out in Hebrew, "This is what the king of Assyria says: Make peace with me and come out to me. Then every one of you will eat from his own vine and fig tree and drink water from his own cistern, until I come and take you to a land like your own, a land of grain and new wine, a land of bread and vineyards, a land of olive trees and honey. Choose life and not death! Do not listen to Hezekiah, for he is misleading you when he says, 'The Lord will deliver us.' Has the god of any nation ever delivered his land from the hand of the king of Assyria? Have they rescued Samaria from my hand? How then can the Lord deliver Jerusalem from my hand?" Now Sennacherib received a report that Tirhakah, the Kushite king of Egypt [Taharqa, who actually was the son of the pharaoh Sebitku], was marching out to fight against him. So he again sent messengers to Hezekiah with this word: "Say to Hezekiah king of Judah: Do not let the god you depend on deceive you when he says, 'Jerusalem will not be handed over to the king of Assyria.' Surely you have heard what the kings of Assyria have done to all the countries, destroying them completely." Hezekiah received the letter from the messengers and read it. And Hezekiah prayed to the Lord, "It is true, O Lord, that the Assyrian kings have laid waste these nations and their lands. Now, O Lord our God, deliver us from his hand." Then Isaiah son of Amoz [a Hebrew prophet] sent a message to Hezekiah, "Therefore this is what the Lord says concerning the king of Assyria: 'He will not enter this city, or shoot an arrow here. He will not build a siege ramp against it.'" That night, the angel of the Lord went out and put to death a hundred and eighty-five thousand men in the Assyrian camp. When the people got up the next morning, there were all the dead bodies! So Sennacherib king of Assyria broke camp and withdrew. He returned to Nineveh and stayed there.

The Hebrew account actually contains two variant versions of the story; in one, consistent with the Assyrian account even to the amount of gold tribute paid, Hezekiah simply paid off Sennacherib, but in the other, awkwardly tacked on to the first, the Assyrians were compelled to depart by the actions of Yahweh.

as they had done for Egypt, conquered territories also created a defensive buffer zone between Assyria and potential enemies. In addition, the empire was a moneymaking enterprise, and no opportunity for economic gain was overlooked. The Assyrians, of course, had had a long interest in using commerce to

In a relief from the Assyrian palace at Nineveh, Assyrian soldiers impale Hebrew captives during the siege of Lachish in 701 BCE.

expand their economy, and warfare was viewed as a means of bringing in income. This was done in several ways. Regular tribute was assessed on defeated peoples, and additional contributions also were extorted from them. In addition, raids for plunder were made beyond the frontiers. In general, the Assyrians were unconcerned with the economic well-being of the conquered peoples and had no intention of incorporating them into Assyrian society or giving them a share in the benefits of empire. They just drained off as much wealth as they could and offered nothing in return. This shortsighted policy resulted in ceaseless unrest and revolt in the subject territories.

Assyria virtually collected enemies, having antagonized at one time or another all the neighboring peoples and nations. The records of the Assyrian kings are peppered with so many accounts of revolts by subjects that it appears that many rulers virtually had to reconquer the empire to keep it together. Retribution was swift and brutal. The Black Obelisk of Shalmaneser III, for example, reported, "Marduk-bêl-usâte revolted against Marduk-zâkir-shumi, king of Karduniash [Babylon]. I pursued him. I cut down with the sword Marduk-bêl-usâte and the rebel army officers who were with him. While I was staying in Nimrud, word was brought that the people of Hattina [Syria] had slain Lubarna their lord and had raised Surri to the kingship over them. The people of Hattina were afraid before the terror of my mighty weapons; they seized the sons of Surri, together with the 'sinners,' and gave them to me. I impaled them on stakes." And the Prism of Sennacherib related, "The officials, nobles, and people of Ekron had thrown Padi their king into fetters of iron. I approached Ekron and slew the governors and nobles who had rebelled, and hung their bodies on stakes around the city."

The Assyrian concept of divine right to conquest foreshadowed the use of divine mandates by Muslims and Crusaders as a justification for conquest.

In order to maintain control of the empire and to keep the income flowing in, the empire was constantly on a war footing. The Assyrian nation came to consist of the people under arms. Even Assyrian religion was militaristic. The primary Assyrian god, Assur, was a war god. Ishtar was imported from Babylon as the goddess of not only fertility but also war. For the Assyrians, conquest was a "mission from god"; the empire simply was not designed to operate in peacetime.

The Assyrian administration of its conquered territories is best known for its ruthless oppression. The only method that the Assyrians had for maintaining control of their subject peoples was by using terror tactics. One problem confronted by any large empire is how to deal with the great religious, political, and cultural heterogeneity of its peoples. Assyrian policy was to try to destroy local identities by deporting large numbers of newly conquered people, especially the well to do, far across the empire, where they would be completely intimidated and less likely to cause trouble. The Assyrian capital at Nimrud, for example, was populated with deportees and captives. These relocations also promoted Assyrian ideas of economic development, for skilled persons, such as artisans and merchants, were transferred to economically underdeveloped regions. The deported populations became so demoralized that they no longer threatened Assyrian security; most soon lost their cultural identity and became integrated into the population where they were settled. In general, the least sign of unrest was met by harsh punishment, expulsion, enslavement, and execution. For example, when some Phoenicians objected to their taxes, Assyrian soldiers "made them jump around" with their spearpoints. And a rebel Syrian leader was captured and skinned alive. But these measures could not prevent constant unrest in the provinces, and Assyrian kings were confronted by repeated revolts.

Assyrian Government

In order to administer their empire, the Assyrians created the first unified imperial government. Past empires had consisted of one-on-one relations between each conquered people and the imperial authority, whether Akkadian, Babylonian, or Egyptian. The Assyrians created a consolidated administrative system that applied equally to all territories that became part of the empire. It was a "top down" system focused on meeting Assyrian political and economic needs, with no concern for winning the hearts and minds of the subject peoples. The most economically and politically important conquered territories were annexed, made into provinces, and placed under Assyrian provincial governors. Under Tiglath-Pilezer III the provinces were subdivided to reduce the governors' authority. More distant or marginal defeated peoples were allowed to govern themselves as Assyrian vassals so long as they behaved and paid tribute. Although the Assyrians were unwilling to extend Assyrian rights to conquered peoples, trading peoples who helped meet Assyrian demand for luxury goods, such as the Phoenicians and Aramaeans, had a privileged status. But even they were drained dry.

At the peak of the Assyrian administrative organization was the king. Like all Mesopotamian kings, the Assyrian king did not rule in his own right but as the representative of the god, in this case Assur. But Assur was not there, so the king was the supreme political, military, and religious leader, and all of the important functions of the state were manifested in him. As ruler of an empire under perpetual martial law, the king's primary role was as the leader of the Assyrian military. Each year the army was assembled and made the rounds of conquered and neighboring peoples, extorting donations along the way.

THE TEN LOST TRIBES OF ISRAEL

The Assyrians subdued conquered peoples, and especially those who had caused problems in the past, by deporting large numbers of their privileged classes to distant parts of the empire. Thus it was with residents of the northern Hebrew kingdom of Israel, who, according to the Bible, repeatedly revolted against the Assyrians. Circa 740 BCE (1 Chronicles 5:26), "So the God of Israel stirred up the spirit of King Pul [Tiglath Pileser] of Assyria, and he carried them away, namely, the Reubenites, the Gadites, and the half-tribe of Manasseh, and brought them to Halah, Habor, Hara, and the river Gozan, to this day." Several years later (2 Kings 15:29), "In the days of Pekah (740–732 BCE), king of Israel, came Tiglath-Pileser king of Assyria, and took Ijon, and Abelbethmaachah, and Janoah, and Kadesh, and Hazor, and Gilead, and Galilee, all the land of Naphtali, and carried them captive to Assyria." Finally, twenty years later (2 Kings 18:9–11), "In the seventh year of King Hosea (732–723 BCE), King Shalmaneser of Assyria came up against Samaria, besieged it, and in the ninth year of king Hosea, Samaria was taken. The King of Assyria carried the Israelites away to Assyria, settled them in Halah, on the Habor, the river of Gozan, and in the cities of the Medes."

Assyrian soldiers of Sennacherib deport the population of the Hebrew city of Lachish during the Assyrian conquest of Israel in 721 BCE. These exiles later were known as the "ten lost tribes of Israel."

Grandiose inscriptions were erected cataloguing the loot that the king raked in. After several successful campaigns, one Assyrian king gloated, "I carried away their possessions, burned their cities with fire, demanded from them hostages, tribute, and contributions, and laid on them the heavy yoke of my rule." Assyrian rulers are often depicted in artwork hunting the most dangerous quarry, lions, which still roamed wild in the Near East. The king hunted with a bow either on foot or horseback. Units of the Assyrian army accompanied him and served as beaters, driving the lions in the direction of the king. One king boasted that on a single hunt he killed not only 120 lions on foot and 800 from his chariot but also ten elephants.

The king was like a spider in the center of an increasingly centralized administrative web. All imperial officials, including nobles and priests, were servants of the king, appointed by him and responsible directly to him. The king kept close tabs on government officials with a system of royal messengers reporting directly to him. Assyrian "overseers" were stationed at the courts of

The biblical accounts neglect to note that Samaria actually fell, in 721 BCE, to Shalmaneser's successor Sargon II, who just had come to the throne. Inscriptions from Sargon's palace at Dur-Sharrukin (modern Khorsabad) give a more laconic account of the campaign: "In the beginning of my reign, in my first year [December, 722], Samaria I besieged, I captured. Twenty-seven thousand two hundred and ninety persons of its inhabitants I took captive; I made it greater than it had been before; people of the lands I had conquered, I settled there. I appointed my governor over them. Tribute, taxes, I imposed upon them as upon Assyrians." Tens of thousands of the Hebrews thus were deported to as far away as Media in western Iran, and Israel was made into an Assyrian province, known as Samerina, and populated by deportees from other places.

The deported Israelites became known to history as the "Ten Lost Tribes of Israel," although it would appear that only nine tribes were deported, for three of the original twelve tribes, Judah, Benjamin, and Simeon, continued to live in Judah. Some traditions, however, count the northern tribe of Mannaseh in two parts, which thus would make ten. In addition, the numbers cited by Sargon indicate that far from the entire population was deported; most likely only influential or well-to-do persons thought likely to cause trouble in the future were exiled. Halah apparently was in western Assyria, and Gozan is identified as the ancient site of Tell Halaf on the Habor River in northeastern Syria. The exiles sent here, therefore, would not have had far to go. Only those sent to Media, in eastern Iran, would have been far from home.

The fate of these exiles long has been debated. Although some suggest that they returned home after the Babylonian Captivity, this is unlikely, given that the Samaritan exiles were sent to Media, not to Babylonia, and Cyrus' ruling applied only to the Jews of Judah. Jewish tradition also speaks of the flaming river Sambaton, perhaps located in Arabia, behind which the Hebrews were exiled. And modern traditions identify various of the lost tribes as surviving in Ethiopia, India, Pakistan, Persia, Nigeria, Ghana, Afghanistan, China, North or South America, and many other places. But no material connection has ever been made between any people and the deported tribes, making it most likely that the exiles were assimilated into the local populations and that the only survivors of the ten tribes who can be identified are the Samaritans, Israelites who continued to inhabit what had been the kingdom of Israel.

vassals to ensure that they remained loyal. At home, traders and craftsmen were organized into government-run guilds. And an efficient class of scribes used standard Mesopotamian cuneiform to keep chronicles of events, such as the "**Limmu Lists**," in which the year was named eponymously (named after something) after officials in charge of the annual New Year's festival at the beginning of spring. The Limmu Lists also included brief references to annual military campaigns and eclipses; for example, under the year equivalent to 746 BCE, the lists note, "During the eponomy of Nergal-nasir, the governor of Nisibis, revolt in Kalhu." Thus, the lists permit modern historians to establish a very accurate Assyrian chronology.

Assyrian kings built magnificent palaces at capital cities such as Assur that functioned as the administrative, economic, and social centers of the empire, and loot and luxury goods were funneled into them. Assur-Nasir-Pal II (884–859) established a new capital city at Kalhu (modern Nimrud)]], and, using the loot from his conquests, Sargon II built a new palace called Dur-Sharrukin

("House of Sargon"), in modern Khorsabad, although it was abandoned soon after his death. Sennacherib made **Nineveh**, hitherto a sleepy provincial city, the primary capital of the empire, completely rebuilding it, with newly laid-out streets and the great "palace without a rival," 600 by 630 feet large. Later kings built additional palaces in Nineveh, along with temples to gods such as Nanna, Sin, Ishtar, and Nergal.

The palaces housed a great many people, including the king's family, which included multiple wives and many children. There were constant intrigues as the king's sons connived to be chosen as his successor. Foreign rulers and nobles also lived in the palace as honored hostages who ensured the good behavior of their people. The Assyrians also invented the concept of libraries, for they considered books to be another form of plunder. The palace at Nineveh also contained a library established by Sargon II and enlarged by **Assurbanipal** (668–627 BCE), who assembled an massive collection of texts dealing with mythology, religion, grammar, law, history, mathematics, astronomy, and, in particular, magic. Some twenty thousand clay tablets were discovered in the ruins of Nineveh, and it is thanks to Assyrian kings such as Assurbanipal that many ancient Mesopotamian literary works were preserved until the modern day.

The Decline and Fall of the Assyrian Empire

As a consequence of its shortsighted policies, the Assyrian Empire was threatened both inside and out. Because most of the profits of the empire benefited only the king and his court, rural nobles and free citizens, who made up the bulk of the Assyrian army, often went unrewarded. One of the results of oppressing their own people was that Assyrian kings sometimes were faced by internal unrest. During the reign of Shamsi-Adad V, for example, rural nobles and free citizens revolted against the privileges granted to nobles at court; the revolt was put down but no reforms were made. And in 745 BCE King Assur-Nirari V (754–745 BCE) and the entire royal family were assassinated.

In addition, given the oppressive nature of Assyrian rule, only Assyrians really could be trusted to serve in the Assyrian army. For three hundred years, the army was summoned nearly every year, and the continual warfare was a constant drain on manpower. The army became spread more and more thinly as the empire grew larger. In addition, being on campaign made it difficult for the farmers serving in the army to work their land back home, and the local Assyrian agricultural economy thus fell into severe decline. Tiglath-Pilezer III attempted to confront the problem by creating a permanent standing army from troops recruited in the provinces and from vassals such as the Medes, as well as from mercenaries hired from among the steppe nomads of Central Asia. This provided a larger but inferior army. The army became less homogeneous, less dependable, and less Assyrian.

Under Esarhaddon's successors, the Assyrian Empire crumbled. Egypt did not rest easy under Assyrian rule. In 663 Assurbanipal had to put down an Egyptian revolt; Thebes was sacked and never recovered. A plea from King Gyges (687–652 BCE) of Lydia in northwestern Anatolia for help against the Cimmerians went unanswered. In 655, the Assyrians were expelled from Egypt by the pharaoh Psamtik I (Greek Psammetichus) (664–610 BCE), who was aided in gaining power by Greek mercenaries, known as "men of bronze," sent from Lydia by Gyges, who had managed to defeat the Cimmerians on his own.

By then, however, Assurbanipal's hands were tied, for there was worse trouble closer to home. In the same year, Babylonia again had been invaded by the Elamites. Assurbanipal chased them off, capturing the Elamite capital at **Susa** in 653. Another Babylonian revolt, aided by Elam, was suppressed in 648. Elam, however, was not finally defeated until 639, when Susa was thoroughly sacked and the Elamite ziggurat destroyed, bringing the Elamite kingdom effectively to an end.

Save for the loss of Egypt, it appeared that the Assyrians had recovered, but all still was not well. The "Annals of Assurbanipal," an account of Assurbanipal's reign, for example, spoke of "strife and hatred in the land." After Assurbanipal's death in 626 BCE, the empire collapsed. In 626, the Chaldean Nabopolassar seized control of Babylon. At about the same time, the fragmented groups of Medes were united by Cyaxares, became fully independent, and allied themselves with the Chaldeans against the Assyrians. In 614, the Medes captured Assur, but the Assyrians escaped this threat by hiring the Scythians to attack the Medes. But the final blow came in 612. The Scythians changed sides, and an army of Chaldeans and Medes captured and sacked Nineveh. The remnants of the Assyrian government and army fled west to Syria. In 605, the last Assyrian army, assisted by the pharaoh Necho II (610–595 BCE), who was concerned about Chaldean expansion, was attacked by the Nabopolassar's son Nebuchadrezzar (Nebuchadnezzar in the Bible). At the battle of Carchemish, the Assyrians were completely defeated. With the destruction of the Assyrian army, the Assyrian Empire vanished. The empire had been held together by military force. When that force was gone, so was the empire, and with it the last of the ancient river valley empires.

THE SUCCESSORS OF THE ASSYRIANS (605–550 BCE)

The elimination of the Assyrian Empire left a power vacuum in the Near East. Four smaller but still potent powers briefly emerged in its place, the New Babylonian Empire, the Saïte Dynasty of Egypt, the Empire of the Medes, and the kingdom of Lydia. Neither the Medes nor the Lydians came from major river valleys, demonstrating the increasing importance of peoples from outside the Bronze Age river valleys in the rise of Iron Age civilization.

The New Babylonian Empire

In Mesopotamia, the Chaldeans established the **New Babylonian Empire** (612–539 BCE), which extended from the Persian Gulf to the Mediterranean. In Judah, the prophet Jeremiah predicted the destruction of Jerusalem as a consequence of Jewish failure to abide by the covenant. He prophesied that the Jews would be scattered and persecuted, but that eventually Yahweh would raise up a savior for them. Soon thereafter, the Chaldean king Nebuchadrezzar (605–562 BCE) attacked the southern Hebrew kingdom of Judah. According to a patriotic Jewish tradition, Nebuchadrezzar's general Holofernes led the Babylonian army. The Jewish heroine Judith charmed Holofernes, got him drunk, and then sliced off his head. To no avail, for in 587, Nebuchadrezzar took a page from the Assyrian book. He captured Jerusalem, tore down its walls, and deported large numbers of influential Jews to Mesopotamia in what was later known as the **Babylonian Captivity** of the Jews. Some of the exiles became very well to do. They were allowed freedom of religion, and temple worship was replaced by study of the Torah in **synagogues**, the name for Jewish places of worship. The belief arose in a **messiah** who would appear and be Yahweh's instrument in bringing victory to his chosen people. The exile caused the Jews to focus even more on keeping themselves separate in the midst of foreign influences. It was forbidden to marry non-Jews or to work on the Sabbath. This was the only way to express themselves after they had lost their political independence. In their subsequent history, the Jews were able to survive oppression because of their conviction that God was with them.

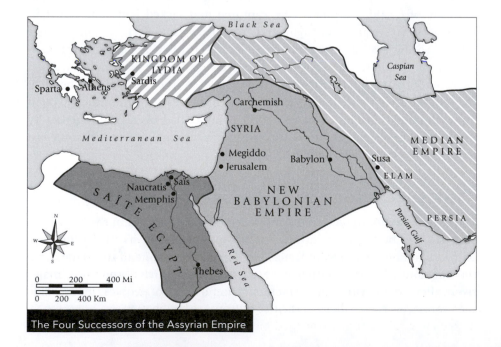

The Four Successors of the Assyrian Empire

Nebuchadrezzar strengthened the walls and made Babylon virtually impregnable. An elaborately decorated and fortified main gate was dedicated to the goddess Ishtar. He also built the famous Hanging Gardens of Babylon, later included among the Seven Wonders of the World, for his queen. Although no remains of the gardens survive, they may have incorporated a terraced arrangement associated with the rebuilt ziggurat of Marduk. Nebuchadrezzar's successors, however, faced native opposition when they tried to consolidate their authority at the expense of the influential Babylonian priests. The priests were famous for their knowledge of astronomy and **astrology**, for they believed that the gods placed messages in the heavens that had to be decoded. They devised the **zodiac**, the ring of twelve constellations through which the sun, moon, and planets move, and were able to calculate the positions of the moon and planets and to predict eclipses. But they had no concept of the scientific method, and their observations were inextricably intertwined with mystical interpretations.

The Empire of the Medes

Meanwhile, the Medes, with their capital at Ecbatana, attempted to consolidate their authority in Iran. But the **Empire of the Medes** (612–550 BCE), even though it was the largest of its time, had no past history of unity and remained a loosely organized coalition of clans. King Cyaxares (ca.625–585 BCE) occupied the old kingdom of Urartu, northern Assyria, and additional territory extending well into Anatolia; to seal an alliance with the Chaldeans, he married one of his daughters to Nebuchadrezzar. Divisions of the kingdom, called *satrapies*, were governed by **satraps** who had great personal authority. Their priests, known as **Magi**, were reputed to have tremendous powers. To the southwest the Medes competed with the Chaldeans, whom they cut off from trade to the east. This created even greater hardships for the Chaldean Empire. And the Medes' long skinny empire, which extended north of Mesopotamia all the way to Anatolia, also brought them into contact with Lydia.

The Magi gave their name to the modern word "magic."

The Kingdom of Lydia

Their cities on the Aegean Sea gave the kingdom of **Lydia** (ca. 690–547 BCE), a powerful and rich trading state located in northwestern Asia Minor with its capital at **Sardis**, access to the markets of the Mediterranean. Initially, trading competition led to warfare between Lydia and the Medes, but a battle in 585 was halted by an eclipse of the sun, and the two sides made peace. Subsequently, via the Medes, the Lydians were able to trade throughout the Near East. The Lydians acquired great wealth by mining electrum, an alloy of gold and silver, from the Pactolus River. The Lydians made one of the most significant economic innovations of all time when they invented **coinage**. Gold and silver always had been recognized by traders as being of great value but always had been traded simply by weight. Around 625 BCE the Lydians realized that exchanges could

An electrum stater (a word meaning "standard") issued by the kingdom of Lydia bears on the obverse ("heads") a lion's head symbolizing the authority of the Lydian king, and on the reverse ("tails") simply the mark of the punch that was used to drive the coin blank into the die that bore the obverse image.

be greatly facilitated by using lumps of gold and silver of the same weight. These lumps, which we now call "coins," thus all had the same value and could be used to create any amount of money that a merchant desired. Other traders soon adopted them, and coinage spread rapidly throughout the Near Eastern and Mediterranean world. A complicating factor, however, was that not everyone agreed what the standard weights for coins should be. Thus, the Lydians had one weight standard, the Phoenicians another, and so on, and this had the effect of complicating financial transactions.

The Saïte Dynasty of Egypt

The fourth Assyrian successor state was ancient Egypt, which enjoyed a new spirit of nationalism after the Assyrian expulsion and a momentary revival of influence under the Twenty-Sixth Dynasty, also known as the **Saïte Dynasty** (671–525 BCE), from the nome of Saïs in the northwestern delta. The Egyptians made a belated entrance into Iron Age commercialism by establishing a Greek trading colony at Naucratis in the Nile Delta, where they received Greek silver in exchange for wheat, papyrus, and linen textiles. The pharaoh Necho II (610–595 BCE) even began the construction of a canal to link the Mediterranean and Red Seas. And a report that Necho sent a Phoenician exploration expedition all the way around Africa just may be true, because the author reported, with disbelief, that on the southern part of the voyage the sun was in the north, rather than the south, something that could only happen south of the equator. During this period, a simplified form of hieratic script called **demotic** replaced the cumbersome hieroglyphic and hieratic scripts for official, legal, and commercial documents, thus making writing accessible to a much larger segment of the population. The Egyptians created a modern army by hiring Jewish and Greek mercenaries. Under Amasis II (569–526 BCE), Egypt made treaties with the New Babylonians and Lydia. Once again, Egypt looked like a major player in the Near Eastern world.

Demotic was the second script on the Rosetta Stone and was deciphered before hieroglyphics.

THE PERSIAN EMPIRE (550–331 BCE)

Just over fifty years after the fall of the Assyrian Empire a greater Iron Age empire appeared, the **Persian Empire**. The Persian Empire was very different from the Assyrian Empire in many ways. For one thing, the Persians came from southern Iran, not from a major river valley, and indicate even more clearly how new political and economic developments in the Iron Age were occurring outside the old Bronze Age centers of activity. In addition, the Persian Empire was much larger even than the Assyrian Empire had been.

And, in particular, the Persians were much more successful in conciliating their subject peoples and convincing them that they shared in the benefits of the empire.

Cyrus and the Creation of the Persian Empire

Both the Persians and the Medes were descended from the Aryans, Indo-Europeans who had moved into Iran beginning around 2000 BCE. Some of these peoples then filtered into western Mesopotamia and established the kingdom of Mitanni around 1500 BCE, whereas others migrated into India, where they may have eliminated the last survivors of the Bronze Age Harappa civilization. Those who remained became the ancestors of the Medes in western Iran and the Persians in the south. By 700 BCE, the Persians were sufficiently united to choose their first king, Achaemenes, and all later Persian kings were descended from him, forming the **Achaemenid Dynasty**. But for the next hundred and fifty years the Persians were vassals of the Medes.

In 550 BCE the Persian king **Cyrus** (559–530) turned the tables. He defeated the Medes and became King of the Medes and Persians, thus creating the Persian Empire. As had happened with Sargon of Akkad and Moses, popular legends grew up about Cyrus' childhood. Astyages, the king of the Medes, was said to have had a dream that a huge vine grew out of the womb of his daughter Mandane and covered the earth. The Magi took this to mean that Mandane's son would overthrow him. When Mandane gave birth to a son, Cyrus, Astyages ordered the noble Harpagus to kill him, but the shepherd that Harpagus hired to do so substituted his wife's stillborn infant, and they raised the child themselves. Eventually, Cyrus' royal character revealed itself, and the true story came out. When Astyages discovered that his orders had been disobeyed, he served Harpagus the head of his own son on a platter. Harpagus gained his revenge by encouraging Cyrus to revolt.

It might seem curious that Cyrus next turned his attention far to the west, to the kingdom of Lydia. But, from an Iron Age perspective, this was not so strange. Like the Assyrians, the Persians were interested in economic development. Given the lack of river valleys in Persia, the only way to expand the Persian economy was through commercial activity. An outlet to the Mediterranean was necessary. In 547, therefore, Cyrus attacked King **Croesus** (560–547) of Lydia, who was said to be the wealthiest man in the world. At the Battle of Thymbra in 547 BCE, the Lydian horses smelled camels from the Persian baggage train and fled. Soon afterward, Cyrus besieged and captured Sardis and took Croesus captive. As a consequence, the Persians occupied not only Lydia but also the Greek trading cities established by the Mycenaeans on the western coast of Anatolia.

Croesus' legendary wealth still is reflected in the saying to be "rich as Croesus."

Cyrus then turned his attentions to Mesopotamia, where the Babylonians were very unhappy with Chaldean rule. King Nabonidus (556–539 BCE), like the pharaoh Akhenaton before him, had attempted to implement a controversial program of religious reform. For reasons that are unclear, Nabonidus favored the moon god Sin over the primary Babylonian god Marduk. He may have done so out of religious zealotry, or perhaps from a desire to weaken the influence of the powerful priests of Marduk. In any event, he faced great popular opposition. Early in his reign, Nabonidus went on a religious retreat to a desert oasis and left his son Balshazzar, who later gained a reputation as a dissolute pleasure seeker, in charge of Babylon. The Bible tells the story of Balshazzar's Feast, a great banquet, perhaps related to the daily ceremonial food offerings to the god Marduk, for a thousand Babylonian nobles at which the treasures taken from the Jewish temple in 587 BCE were desecrated. It was said that a hand wrote unintelligible words on the wall, words that were interpreted by the Jewish prophet Daniel as meaning, "You have been weighed in the balance and been found wanting." When Cyrus threatened to invade, the Babylonian people saw him as their savior. In 539, he captured the city without striking a blow.

Rather than imposing himself as a conqueror, Cyrus claimed to be favored by Marduk and had himself crowned king of Babylon. In order to demonstrate continuity with the past, he also took the ancient Mesopotamian titles of King of Sumer and Akkad and King of the Four Quarters of the Universe. His spirit of conciliation led the cities of Palestine and Syria to acknowledge his authority. He showed further sympathy for his subjects by allowing the Babylonian Jews to return home. As a result, Cyrus was praised in the Bible, which noted, "Thus says Cyrus, king of Persia: The Lord has given me all the kingdoms of the earth. Whoever is among you of his people, let him go up to Jerusalem and rebuild the house of the Lord." And this is exactly what happened. And under Persian rule, the Jews of Judaea, as the Jewish homeland now was called, were permitted, and even encouraged, to pursue their worship with little or no interference from the government.

> **CAUSALITY QUESTION**
>
> What were the effects of Cyrus' treatment of Babylon in 538? How did these policies set the stage for the way the Persian Empire functioned?

Some Jews chose to remain in Babylon at the same time that Jewish communities developed in other places, as in Egypt. The result was the beginning of a Jewish **diaspora** (Greek for "scattering") throughout the Near Eastern world. The diaspora created a people based not on place of residence but on belief and cultural identity, for they were just as Jewish as the Jews of Palestine. Individual Jews did quite well for themselves under Persian rule. According to Jewish tradition, Esther, a Babylonian Jew, married a Persian king whom she convinced to change his mind after he had been tricked into ordering the destruction of the Jews. And in 445 BCE, another Babylonian Jew, Nehemiah, was made Persian governor of Judah and allowed to rebuild the walls of Jerusalem. At the same time, under the prophet Ezra, the Jewish Torah assumed its final canonical form. Because of its preservation in a written form, many Jewish concepts thus were transmitted to Christianity and Islam. In addition, work to rebuild the temple was undertaken, and the second Jewish temple was completed in 521 BCE.

The Persians, therefore, unlike the Assyrians and Chaldeans, gained a reputation for leniency and accommodation toward their subject peoples. This included the retention of native officials in the Persian administration, for there simply were not that many Persians, and they realized that they could not hope to rule effectively without local cooperation. Their empire quickly became so large that they could not hope to manage it, as the Assyrians had tried to do, by using native Persians only.

Cyrus expanded the empire all the way to the frontiers of India. In 530 BCE he attacked the Scythians, who regularly raided Persian territory and disrupted eastern trade routes. After Cyrus captured the son of the Scythian queen Tomyris, she told him, "If you return my son to me you may leave my land unharmed, but if you refuse, I swear by the sun, the lord of the Scythians, that I will give you your fill of blood." Cyrus refused and was killed in the ensuing battle. To fulfill her promise, Tomyris dipped Cyrus' head into an animal skin filled with blood, saying, "Thus I give you your fill of blood." And the Scythians continued to menace the Persians' northern frontier. The Persians later looked back on the reign of Cyrus as a Golden Age, and many legends sprang up about his life and his rule.

Cyrus was succeeded by his son **Cambyses** (531–522 BCE), who picked up where his father had left off by invading Egypt in 525 BCE. The Saïte pharaoh Amasis II was defeated, Memphis and Thebes were captured, and Cambyses was installed as the first pharaoh of the Twenty-Seventh Dynasty, thus demonstrating, once again, Persian respect for native customs. But his attempts, like earlier pharaohs, to reduce the influence of the priests gave him a bad reputation in

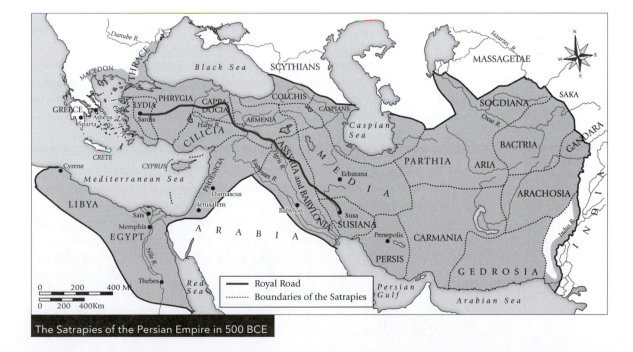

The Satrapies of the Persian Empire in 500 BCE

Egypt. In 522, after hearing of unrest back in Persia, Cambyses was on his way home when he reportedly fell on his sword while getting off his horse and died. One might wonder whether someone was holding the sword at the time.

The conquest of Egypt left Persia as the only power in the Near East. Cyrus and Cambyses had constructed the largest empire the world had yet known. But the past history of the Near East was littered with able rulers who had built empires that their successors could not hold together and that soon collapsed. The question now was whether the Persians would be any different. Could these territorial acquisitions be consolidated to create a more stable, long-lasting state in which the conquered peoples were not constantly on the verge of revolt?

DARIUS AND THE OPERATION OF THE PERSIAN EMPIRE

Cambyses was succeeded by **Darius I** (522–486 BCE), whose claim to the throne lay in being a distant fourth cousin of Cambyses. Like his predecessors, Darius did his own share of expanding the empire, for this was how early Persian kings demonstrated that they deserved the job. In particular, following an exploratory mission by the Greek explorer Scylax, he conquered the Indus River valley in India, marking the first time that three major river valleys had been brought under a single authority. But what Darius primarily is known for is establishing the administrative infrastructure that tied the empire together and gave it the ability to survive over the long haul, even when it had lackluster rulers. Underlying Darius' organizational policies were a respect for the traditions and religions of native peoples and a willingness to allow them to share in both the benefits and the responsibilities of the empire.

The Persians expected two things from their subject peoples: taxes and troops. Unlike Assyrian taxes, Persian taxes were relatively moderate. As for the army, in order to keep costs down, the Persian Empire had no professional army except for the king's own personal bodyguard, ten thousand elite Persian soldiers known as the **Immortals**. The rest of the army was recruited on an as-needed basis from the subject peoples, who provided specialized contingents. For example, Phoenicians provided warships, Mesopotamians infantry, Iranians cavalry, and so on. The fact that the bulk of the Persian army was composed of levies from the subject peoples demonstrates the degree to which the Persians trusted them. This arrangement put huge military forces at the Persians' disposal. When fully mobilized, the Persian Empire could raise an army of a quarter of a million men. The most effective soldiers were the archers, both mounted and on foot, for infantrymen were lightly armed and armored, often being protected just by wicker shields. The army's lack of homogeneity and fighting skill was balanced by its size. The Persians usually overwhelmed their enemies by sheer weight of numbers. But a built-in weakness of this system is that it took up to two years to mobilize the full Persian army. This was fine when the Persians were attacking someone else,

---

A PICTURE IS WORTH A THOUSAND WORDS

THE BEHISTUN INSCRIPTION

In order to get the news out about important events during their reigns, Persian kings had huge rock reliefs carved onto the sides of cliffs. For Darius I (522–486 BCE), the most important event of his reign was the very first, his proclamation as Great King, which occurred under somewhat irregular circumstances. Rather than being a direct descendent of the first Persian king Cyrus, Darius was a distant cousin. It therefore was crucially important that he establish his legitimacy, and one of the means he employed to do this was the creation of this rock carving that told the story of his rise to power; it not only showed him fully enthroned as king but also had an accompanying inscription, with copies in Persian, Babylonian, and Elamite, that began with Darius' statement of his claim to the throne: "King Darius says: My father is Hystaspes; the father of Hystaspes was Arsames; the father of Arsames was Ariaramnes; the father of Ariaramnes was Teispes; the father of Teispes was Achaemenes. King Darius says: That is why we are called Achaemenids; from antiquity we have been noble; from antiquity has our dynasty been royal. King Darius says: Eight of my dynasty were kings before me; I am the ninth. Nine in succession we have been kings. King Darius says: By the grace of Ahura Mazda am I king; Ahura Mazda has granted me the kingdom."

The monumental depiction shows Darius with his bow carrier Intaphrenes and his lance carrier Gobryas standing behind him. Intaphrenes had played an important role in Darius' accession, having not only helped to kill Gaumâta the usurper, who had seized the throne while Cambyses was in Egypt, but also raised an army to put down a revolt of Babylon against Darius. For a time he was the most powerful noble in the empire. After the creation of the monument, Darius decided it prudent to eliminate the powerful Intaphrenes and had him and all of his family executed on suspicion of treason. Gobryas, too, had helped to defeat Gaumâta, but nothing more of him is known.

Darius looks out over nine enemies bound at the neck, who can be identified based on Darius' statement in the inscription, "I overthrew nine kings and I made them captive." These are cited as Gaumâta the Magian, Nidintu-Bêl the Babylonian, Martiya the Persian, Phraortes the Mede, Tritantaechmes the Sagartian, Frâda of Margiana, Vahyazdâta the Persian, and Arakha the Armenian, all of whom had opposed Darius at the beginning of his reign. According to the inscription, all the rebels met a bad end; regarding the fate of Phraortes the Mede and his followers, Darius reports: "Then did I crucify him in Ecbatana; and the men who were his foremost followers, those at Ecbatana within the fortress, I flayed and hung out their hides, stuffed with straw." Darius rests his foot on a tenth unidentified captive lying in front of him. The monument also announces Darius' support of the Zoroastrian religion, with the symbol of the god Ahura Mazda occupying a prominent place above the procession; throughout the inscription, Darius calls on the support of Ahura Mazda, who is represented as a winged sun disk out of which a bearded man emerges.

The Persian Immortals continue to stand guard at Darius's palace at Persepolis.

The motto of the Persian messengers, "And neither snow nor rain nor heat nor gloom of night will prevent these couriers from completing their tasks," has been adopted by the U.S. Postal Service.

but it could cause problems if they were confronted by an invader who would be reluctant to give the Persians time to assemble their army.

As the Assyrians had done, the Persians organized their subject peoples into two categories: annexed territories and vassals. Vassals were permitted to remain under native rulers as long as they stayed loyal. Most defeated peoples, however, were annexed. The annexed territory was divided up into twenty very large administrative units called satrapies. For example, Egypt, Lydia, and Babylonia each were separate satrapies. Each satrapy was governed by a satrap appointed by the king. Sometimes the satraps were local people, but more usually they were Persians who belonged to an elite group of noble families known as the Seven. Satraps were powerful and ambitious, and it took a very strong-willed king to keep them in line. But when a king died, the next king was chosen by the Seven. Sometimes they chose a weakling so that they could have more freedom of action.

The Persian Empire, therefore, was much more loosely organized than the Assyrian Empire. Local officials, who might be thousands of miles away from the king's court, had a great deal of autonomy. Darius did what he could to try to consolidate the authority of the king. In order to keep the satraps honest, Darius appointed a chief military commander and financial officer in each satrapy who were responsible directly to him. He also created spies, known as the **Eyes and Ears of the King**, who were sent out to observe what was going on in the satrapies and then reported back to him. But there was still no day-to-day oversight of a satrap's activities, and a wise king always had to be ready to deal with misbehaving satraps.

Darius and later kings did much to try to unify their huge empire. Laws were codified in order to reduce confusion about what laws applied to whom. A simplified cuneiform system reduced the number of signs to forty-two alphabetic symbols and made record keeping much easier. Aramaic provided a universal language of diplomacy. Good communications were crucial. Darius developed the **Royal Road**, the first large-scale road system in antiquity, running sixteen hundred miles from Susa in Persia to Sardis in Lydia. Imperial couriers carried messages back and forth across the empire and could traverse it in a week, changing horses at regular stops using a system very much like the American pony express. Persian commercial interests were supported by the completion of a canal connecting the Mediterranean and Red Seas, permitting merchant ships to sail from the Mediterranean to India. Economic exchange and productivity also were facilitated by Darius' introduction of a standardized coinage system. The

SETTING THE VALUE OF THE COINS

A Persian gold daric depicts, on the obverse, the king running and shooting a bow, the characteristic Persian weapon. The reverse is just a simple punchmark, demonstrating that the propaganda value of the coinage had not yet been implemented.

The concepts that lay behind the development of coinage were fairly smple. First, identify a metal that was acknowledged by everyone to have an accepted value. Then create pieces of this metal, coins, that all had the same weight and therefore the same value. Then use these coins as a medium of exchange, so that goods and services were exchanged for coins and not for each other. In addition, coins were a simple method of storing and keeping track of wealth, especially for governments, which also could use coins for large transactions and could profit from their monopoly on the right to issue coins.

But putting these principles into action was not always easy, and problems arose in the practical implementation of coinage. For one thing, the first experiments in coinage by the Lydians, just before 600 BCE, were based on a naturally occurring alloy of gold and silver known as **electrum** that was found in the Pactolus River, but the ratios of gold to silver, nominally around 50:50, were not the same in all the coins. In addition, the standard weights of Lydia were not necessarily the standard weights of its trading partners. For example, Lydia used a talent weighing 83 pounds, whereas Babylonia had two different talents, a "Heavy"

one at 134 pounds, also used in Phoenicia, and a "Royal" one at 67 pounds. This required a conversion process from one weight standard to another, a transaction for which moneychangers exacted a fee. Another problem involved making the coinage accessible: a full-weight gold stater, the nominal standard denomination, could be worth three months' wages, so tiny denominations as small as 1/96 stater (only 0.004 oz.) were created, but these tiny coins just were not practical. Around 560 BCE, therefore, the Lydians adopted a bimetallic system, with coins being minted from either pure gold or pure silver and with an exchange formula based on an assumed 13:1 value differential between gold and silver. The silver coins—one was worth about a day's wages—thus could be used for smaller value transactions. But a continuing problem was that the ratio between the market values of gold and silver fluctuated, and cagy arbitragers (traders who benefit from fluctuations in the value of currency) could make a killing by buying the undervalued metal and exchanging it for the overvalued one.

The bimetallic problem was solved by the Persians, who also adopted a bimetallic system of interchangeable gold and silver coins. The gold coin, the daric, weighed 8.4 gm (0.3 oz.), and the silver coin, the siglos, weighed about 5.6 gm (0.2 oz.). Twenty sigloi, weighing 112 gm (3.95 oz.), equaled one daric, a 13:1 weight ratio. The Persian Empire was so huge, and the Persian government controlled so much of the money supply, that the government itself, which kept huge reserves of gold and silver, could adjust the gold and silver supply to ensure that the relative values of gold and silver did not get out of balance. Other states, however, such as the later Greek cities, did not have this much economic clout and thus were compelled to adopt a single-metal coinage, usually based on silver. In the future, only the Roman Empire would have sufficient economic power to be able to maintain a viable interchangeable gold and silver coinage.

gold daric and silver siglos circulated throughout the Near Eastern world. Persian kings amassed and stored huge gold and silver reserves in palace treasuries. In fact, they often were more concerned with hoarding their money than with spending it, even when necessity demanded it.

Persian Society and Religion

At the peak of the Persian social structure stood the king. The Persians raised the concept of absolute monarchy to a higher level. The Persian king was not just the king, he was the Great King, the **King of Kings**. Nor was this just an empty boast, as grandiose titles often had been in the past. He sat on a golden throne, wore elaborate gold and purple robes, and was attended by a court of worshippers. Reliefs lining the walls of the palace at **Persepolis** display the Persian court in action: rows of suppliant rulers bring offerings, and the ten thousand immortals still stand on guard. The palace was manned by eunuchs, the only men permitted in the personal chambers of the women of the royal family. Everyone living in the Persian Empire was a "slave of the king." Those introduced into his presence were expected to prostrate themselves face down on the floor in the ceremony of **proskynesis**. In order to publicize their great deeds, Persian rulers had huge murals carved out on the sides of cliffs. In one, for example, Darius established his legitimacy by telling a detailed story of how he had become king by putting down a revolt by the Medes (see the box "A Picture Is Worth a Thousand Words" in this chapter)[As absolute monarchs, Persian kings had the opportunity to behave capriciously and often cruelly: the favorite Assyrian punishment of impalement was often used on those who had especially gained the king's anger. Yet, in spite of their grandiose pretensions, the Persian kings, like earlier Mesopotamian monarchs, did not see themselves as gods; they rather were the earthly representatives of Ahura Mazda, the god of light. But this did not keep their subjects from treating them, or them from behaving, as if they were gods.

Persian social organization was based on the family. Persian families were patriarchal, and fathers had absolute authority over their children. Men could have several wives to ensure the birth of legitimate heirs. According to a the Greek historian Herodotus, young Persian nobles were taught "horse-riding, archery, and speaking the truth." Persian soldiers were assigned land by the king in exchange for military service. The Persians viewed crafts work as demeaning, so for this kind of work they generally employed their subject peoples. As with the Assyrians, scribes were valued for their ability to keep royal records of such things as military recruitment and tax payments. Most of the Persian population, however, consisted of herders and small farmers. And a large population of slaves acquired in the course of the wars performed many kinds of menial labor, serving on building projects, in the mines, on the vast imperial estates, or in the imperial palaces.

Native Persian religion was **dualistic**, that is, it viewed the universe as being in perpetual conflict between good ("the truth') and evil ("the lie"). It had two kinds of deities: *divas*, sky gods who were often bad, and *asuras*, abstract moral qualities, who usually were good. The chief Persian deity was the asura **Ahura Mazda**, a god of light worshipped at fire altars who represented truth and justice. **Ahriman**, a diva, represented darkness and evil. Around 750 BCE, the Persian prophet Zoroaster (or Zarathustra) formalized the teachings of Persian religion. Zoroaster taught that it was a person's individual responsibility to be good rather than evil. Spiritual things represented good and material things evil. At end of time everyone would be judged in the fire by Ahura Mazda: the good would be rewarded and the wicked punished.

Zoroaster's teachings, later known as **Zoroastrianism**, were preserved by Persian priests known, like the priests of the Medes, as Magi. With the Persian king at its head, Zoroastrianism became the Persian state religion. For example, a huge rock carving proclaimed: "King Darius says: By the grace of Ahura Mazda I became king; Ahura Mazda granted me the empire. I always acted by the grace of Ahura Mazda. Ahura Mazda brought me help because I was not wicked, nor was I a liar, nor was I a tyrant. I have ruled according to righteousness. Neither to the weak nor to the powerful did I do wrong. Whoever helped my house, him I favored; he who was hostile, him I destroyed. You who shall be king hereafter, protect yourself vigorously from lies; punish the liars well." The kings' desire to rule justly has been cited as one of the reasons why the Persian Empire was administered generally more effectively than earlier empires.

The tone poem "Also sprach Zarathustra" ("Thus spoke Zarathustra") by Richard Strauss provided one of the themes for the movie 2001: A Space Odyssey.

Zoroastrianism still survives in small pockets of the Middle East.

Persia and the West

Like his predecessors, Darius was confronted by problems with the Scythians, who continued to be a general nuisance by raiding Persian territory. Darius decided to deal with the Scythian problem by mounting a massive invasion of Central Asia. His plan was to attack via the back door by advancing up the west coast of the Black Sea, turning east, and then returning south to Persia. After assembling the full Persian army, Darius began his invasion in 513 BCE. Like many other would-be conquerors of Asia, however, Darius soon learned that Central Asia was a big place. The Scythians declined to stand and fight and lured the Persian army farther and farther into the steppes. Low on supplies, Darius finally was forced to turn back, and the only way out that the Persians knew was the way they had come. In an exercise of good generalship, Darius got his army out intact, just barely. Even though the Scythians had not been defeated, they had been demoralized and no longer were a serious menace. And even though the Persians had not fulfilled all the expectations of the Scythian campaign, they did acquire **Thrace** (modern-day Bulgaria), south

THE LEGACY OF ANTIQUITY

Can you think of any other religions that share the Persian concepts of the end of the world, a final judgment, and salvation though a savior god, all promulgated by one particular prophet?

of the Danube River, as a new satrapy, marking the first time a Near Eastern empire had incorporated European territory.

LOOKING AHEAD

The Persian Empire would last until 331 BCE, but before its subsequent history can be discussed, our attention must turn to the west, for the Persian occupation of Thrace brought the Persians into contact with the mainland Greeks, who represented the first European civilization. The question then arose of what the relationship between these two cultures would be. Before that issue can be discussed, we must pick up the history of the Greeks back at the end of the Mycenaean period and bring it up to the time of the Greek confrontation with the Persians.

FURTHER READING

Briant, Pierre. *From Cyrus to Alexander: A History of the Persian Empire.* Winona Lake, IN: Eisenbrauns, 2002.

Brosius, Maria. *The Persians: An Introduction.* London: Routledge, 2006.

Bryce, Trevor. *The Kingdom of the Hittites.* New York: Oxford University Press, 2005.

Curtis, John E., and Nigel Tallis, *Forgotten Empire: The World of Ancient Persia.* Berkeley: University of California Press, 2005.

Dercksen, Jan Gerrit. *Old Assyrian Institutions.* Leiden: Nederlands Instituut voor het Nabije Oosten, 2004.

Healy, Mark. *The Ancient Assyrians.* London: Osprey, 1991.

Hunter, Erica C. D. *Ancient Mesopotamia.* New York: Chelsea House, 2007.

Olmstead, A. T. *History of the Persian Empire.* Chicago: University of Chicago Press, 1959.

Polk, Milbry, and Angela M. H. Schuster, eds. *The Looting of the Iraq Museum, Baghdad: The Lost Legacy of Ancient Mesopotamia.* New York: Abrams, 2005.

Rea, Cam. *The Assyrian Exile: Israel's Legacy in Captivity.* Wordclay, 2008.

Schaps, D. *The Invention of Coinage and the Monetization of Ancient Greece.* Ann Arbor: University of Michigan Press, 2004.

Swerdlow, Noel. *The Babylonian Theory of the Planets.* Princeton, NJ: Princeton University Press, 1998.

Vanderhooft, David Stephen. *The Neo-Babylonian Empire and Babylon in the Latter Prophets.* Atlanta, GA: Scholars Press, 1999.

Wiesehöfer, Josef. *Ancient Persia: From 550 BC to 650 AD.* London: Tauris, 1996.

THE GLORY THAT WAS GREECE

CHAPTER 6

GREECE IN THE DARK AND ARCHAIC AGES
(1100–500 BCE)

The origins of the ancient Greek culture of the fifth century BCE, a period generally recognized as the Golden Age of Greece, are to be found during the periods known as the Dark and Archaic Ages, which lasted from roughly 1100 to 500 BCE. During these periods, the Greeks recovered from the decline and fall of the Mycenaean civilization to create an even more complex and sophisticated civilization based on the political institution known as the *polis*, or city-state.

THE GREEK DARK AGES (1100–776 BCE)

After the final collapse of the Mycenaean civilization around 1100 BCE, Greece began the Iron Age with a period called the **Greek Dark Ages**. The complex administrative and economic system developed by the Myceneans vanished, taking with it urbanization, stone architecture, a trading economy, sculpture, and the knowledge of writing. As a result, we have only a meager knowledge of post-Mycenaean Greece. There are few material remains, and only hints of the oral traditions of the times are preserved in myths and legends, written down centuries later, that do have some basis in fact but also are weighed down with such a superstructure of exaggerations and elaborations that the kernel of historical truth either is often difficult to identify or really does not tell us what we think it does. For example, the *Iliad* and the *Odyssey*, poems about the Greek war against Troy, do contain some recollections about the Mycenaeans but are probably more reflective of life during the post-Mycenaean period. The most we can do, therefore, is to identify several general developments—in particular, developments that were crucial for the construction of Greek identity—that occurred during this dimly known period.

Many think that another Dark Age occurred in western Europe after the fall of the Roman Empire.

The Coming of the Dorians

Greek legends tell of an invasion by the **Dorians**, warlike northern Greeks, that supposedly happened sixty years after the fall of Troy, or about 1120 BCE. The Dorians were said to have destroyed the Mycenaean civilization and occupied the most fertile agricultural lands of southern Greece. One tale told of the return of the Heracleidae, three grandchildren of the Greek hero Hercules, whose sons had been forced to withdraw to northern Greece, where they became rulers of the Dorians. After conquering the **Peloponnesus**, the southernmost part of Greece, these three divided the territory by lot: Temenus received **Argos**, Cresphontes obtained **Messenia**, and the sons of Aristodemus gained **Laconia**. A fourth descendent of Hercules, Aletes, later captured Corinth. There also were legends of Mycenaean emigration: the Neleids, a noble family from Pylos, for example, was said to have fled to **Athens**, which held out against the Dorians. It is difficult, however, to find any archaeological signs of massive invasions, although iron swords, tools, pins, and buttons, and cremation as opposed to inhumation burials, do begin to appear as of about 1100 BCE, a date surprisingly consistent with the legends.

Regardless of whether the Dorian settlement happened as a massive invasion, as once was thought, or as a gradual infiltration, the end result was that Dorian speakers eventually displaced the earlier Mycenaean populations and occupied nearly all of southern Greece. And given that the Dorians usually made the people whose land they occupied into agricultural slaves, it should be no surprise that those Myceneans who had the opportunity to escape did so. A few Mycenaeans held out on the acropolis of Athens. Others left Greece altogether and established colonies in **Ionia**, the name for the western coastal area of Anatolia, in what we call the First Wave of Greek Colonization, ca. 1100–1000 BCE. They soon lost contact with mainland Greece.

Some historians use a transliterated Greek spelling of Greek names, e.g., Herakles rather than Hercules, but for the sake of consistency, the more generally used Latin spellings are employed here.

Social Organization

Greek society of the Dark Ages was a far cry from the sophisticated social organization of the Mycenaean period. People lived in a rural village known as a *kōmē* or *dēmos*. Agriculture was virtually the sole basis of economic life. People now lived in a **subsistence economy**, where all the resources necessary for survival, including grain (wheat, barley, oats), animal products (from sheep, goats, pigs, cattle), pottery, textiles, and home-smelted iron, were locally produced. People lived in mud-brick huts with central hearths that vented through thatched roofs. Social organization was based on the family. The smallest family unit was the *oikos*, or household. Several households made up an extended family, or *genos* (pl. *geneis*). Families were organized into larger units, the *phratria* (**phratry**, or brotherhood) and the *phylē* (clan), whose identity came from having the same legendary ancestor. The entire people was known as the *laos*. A person's status in society was determined largely by which household,

THE HISTORY LABORATORY

USING DIALECT PATTERNS TO RECONSTRUCT THE DARK AGES

The history of the Greek Dark Ages, which brought the disappearance of the use of writing and a scanty archaeological record, is very poorly attested. Historians, therefore, must use any method they can to try to reconstruct this period. One means of doing so is based on an analysis of later patterns of the distribution of Greek **dialects**, that is, different versions of Greek spoken by Greeks from different historical backgrounds.

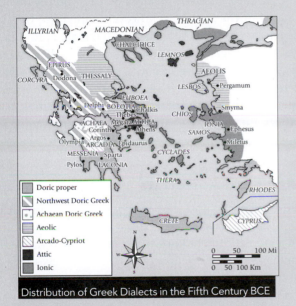

Distribution of Greek Dialects in the Fifth Century BCE

The earliest attested form of Greek was used in Mycenaean times, as recovered from the Linear B tablets. Mycenaean Greek, however, is quite different from the various Dorian dialects spoken by the Dorian settlers, which were used in western Greece, the Peloponnesus, and Crete. This geographical distribution fairly well maps out the settlement pattern of the Dorians and is consistent with the records from the Mycenaean city of Pylos telling of invaders coming down the western coast. Little Doric writing survives; a literary form of Doric was used only by poets such as Pindar of Thebes. The fate of the Mycenaeans, on the other hand, is suggested by the distribution pattern of dialects connected to Mycenaean Greek. The Greek dialect closest to Mycenaean is Arcado-Cypriote, which was spoken in the rough hinterland of Arcadia in the central Peloponnesus, an area that the Dorians did not think suitable for occupation, and on the island of Cyprus, where Mycenaean settlements had existed as of around 1400 BCE. Virtually no Arcado-Cypriote documents survive. Other descendents of the Mycenaeans, who came to speak the Ionic-Attic dialect, survived in Athens or escaped to establish colonies in Ionia. Homer's *Iliad* and *Odyssey* were written in an early version of this dialect, which also is known as Homeric or Epic Greek. The Attic dialect eventually became the main literary language of ancient Greece. And Aeolic (from Aeolis in Thessaly in northeastern Greece) was spoken especially by Greeks in **Thessaly** and **Boeotia** (where, in legend, a group of Aeolians settled), where Greek culture developed less in the sphere of the Mycenaeans. Some of these Greeks, likewise fleeing the Dorians, carried their dialect to the central part of Ionia, where it became the literary language of Sappho, Alcaeus, and other poets from the island of Lesbos off the northern coast of Anatolia.

The later distribution pattern of Greek dialects therefore confirms the view that Mycenaean refugees escaping the Dorians fled to Ionia and established colonies where they could be free from Dorian oppression. And in later times, Greeks could recognize each other's origins by their dialects. Thus, where a Doric speaker would say *damos* or *klaros* ("village" or "allotment"), an Attic speaker would say *dēmos* or *klēros*.

extended family, phratry, and clan that he or she belonged to, and a person's personal commitment and loyalty was focused on his or her family.

The different dialectical groups had different clan structures extending back into the Dark Ages. Ionian communities, for example, had at least four clans whose names suggest that their original purpose was based on their occupations: *Geleontes*, which means "the Shining Ones," suggests rulers; *Hoplētēs*, from the word for weapons, could mean soldiers; *Aigikoreis*, from the word for goat, implies shepherds; and *Argādes*, from the word for "broad fields," would designate farmers. By historical times, however, these four Ionian clans had lost any occupational connections. Dorian communities, on the other hand, generally had three clans, the names of two of which may recall the original Dorian conquest. The *Hylleis*, for example, were thought to have been named after Hyllus, a son of Hercules, and the *Pamphyloi*, meaning "all the people," could be an allusion to a body of invaders. The meaning of the name of the *Dymanes*, however, which the Greeks naïvely derived from a legendary Dorian ruler named Dymas, is not easily interpreted. Remnants of the original occupants of lands settled by the Dorians sometimes were given disparaging names: at Argos, for example, they were the *Gymnasioi* (naked people), and in Epidaurus they were the *Konipedes* (dusty-footed people). In both Ionian and Dorian societies, the clans were the basis of the military organization, and soldiers fought in units organized by clan.

Greek dialects differed from each other in a similar way to which a Brooklyn accent in the United States might differ from a southern accent.

Kings and Aristocrats

Most villages were isolated from each other and were independent political units. In Dorian communities, citizenship was based on land ownership. Dorian families controlled a land allotment known as a *klaros*, the possession of which gave family members full citizenship rights. The land was worked by agricultural slaves conscripted from the indigenous populations who had limited or, more usually, no legal rights. Other original residents, known as *perioikoi* ("dwellers around") retreated into marginal lands in the hills.

Each village was administered by a petty king known as a *basileus*, whose original function had been to serve as a war leader who oversaw attempts to acquire additional land or the defense against attacks by other communities. The standard form of Greek government at the beginning of the Dark Ages, therefore, was **monarchy** (from Greek for "rule by one"). The king resided in a rather larger mud-brick building known as a megaron, a rectangular hall with a front porch. Kings tended to come from a royal family and kingship was hereditary, but the selection of a new king also was validated by the *ekklēsia*, a warrior Assembly composed of all free men eligible to serve in the army. The Assembly also ratified (but could not introduce or discuss) decisions made by the king.

As time went on, some individuals, by means of their social connections, political astuteness, or just by being good farmers, gained control of the best land. Greek society thus became differentiated into the rich, who owned the best land, and the poor, who owned either poorer land or no land at all. Economic power fell into the hands of the richest families, who called themselves **aristocrats**, Greek for "the best people." The heads of the aristocratic families were members of a Council known as a *boulē* that advised the king, who needed the support of the richest and most influential people to remain in power. The social class of aristocrats became completely closed, as the aristocrats attempted to protect their own interests. To be an aristocrat one had to be born an aristocrat. The free male population over about the age of eighteen continued to belong to the Assembly, whose primary duties were to elect new kings and to ratify any proposals submitted by the king (negative votes were against the rules).

The more peaceful times following the initial Dorian settlement meant that there no longer was a need for a king whose primary responsibility was to serve as a war leader. As a result, nearly all of the Greek monarchies were replaced by a new kind of government called an **aristocracy** (Greek for "rule by the best people"), in which aristocrats shared the most important offices. Athens, for example, was said to have made the switch as early as 1000 BCE, although others changed later, such as Argos ca. 600 BCE, and one, **Sparta**, retained its kings; northern frontier areas such as Epirus and Macedonia also kept their kings. In an aristocracy the king was replaced by a chief magistrate often known as an *archōn* ("ruler," or **archon**), who served a limited term of one or more years. Typically, the authority of the chief archon was limited by other kinds of annual archons who divided up the powers of the king, such as the *archōn polemarchos* ("war-leader archon," or polemarch), who served as general, and the *archōn basileus* ("king archon"), a chief priest who performed the religious duties that had been performed by the old king. Aristocrats shared these offices among themselves in order to ensure that there was no return to monarchy. In some cities, there was only a single aristocratic family, such as the Bacchiadae at Corinth, whereas in others, there was an aristocratic phratry composed of several aristocratic families.

Aristocratic society and government was based on control of land, for Greece still had an almost exclusively agricultural economy. The wealth of

In the **geometric style** of pottery painting, figures were composed of simple geometric components, such as triangles and lines. This Greek krater (pot used for mixing wine and water), from Athens ca. 750 BCE, depicts aristocratic warriors who, after riding onto a battlefield in chariots, have dismounted in order to fight.

each aristocratic family was provided by its *klaros,* or landed estate. The aristocrats monopolized all the sources of authority in a society. Only aristocrats could serve in the **boulē**, which now became the primary executive and legislative institution: it supervised the archons and oversaw the daily activities of the city, and new legislation could only be introduced and discussed there. Only aristocrats could hold office, because government officials were selected by the *boulē.* Only the aristocrats knew what the laws were. In addition, because of the cost involved in maintaining a full set of arms and armor, and even a horse and chariot, the aristocrats bore the brunt of the fighting in warfare. The remainder of the free male population perhaps accompanied the aristocrats to war, but often was not well armed and rarely participated in actual military action. All free males belonged to the Assembly, which saw a lessening of its power; it no longer had the right to elect anyone and only could vote "yes" on measures that already had been approved by the *boulē.*

Besides the aristocrats, other free members of dark-age communities included farmers (*georgoi*), who scratched a living from their own small plots of land. Still other free men rented land from the aristocrats or worked as shepherds, farmhands, or craftspersons (*demiourgoi*). Those with the least privileges were a few slaves—most Greek societies of this period could not afford to support very many of them—who were not always well treated.

Our word politics comes from the Greek word politeia, *which means "citizenship in a city."*

As the years went by, populations expanded. Through a process called *sympoliteia* ("shared citizenship"), groups of neighboring villages tended to coalesce into a *polis* (plural *poleis*), or city-state. Each polis was wholly independent, with its own government and laws. A polis often was centered on a fortified high point called an "acropolis" that served as a place of refuge and overlooked a centralized city marketplace called an "agora." At Athens, for example, neighboring villages were incorporated into a single city by about 1000 BCE, supposedly by the Greek hero Theseus. Not long afterward, at some point before 800 BCE, five villages joined to form Sparta, and by 750 BCE eight villages combined to create **Corinth**. Over a hundred other cities were created in a similar manner. Eventually, all of Greece was divided up into city-states. As a consequence of Greece's mountainous geography, the poleis tended to develop in isolation from each other and to have little direct contact.

The polis became the center of Greek political life. Citizens' allegiances increasingly focused on the polis, which came to compete with the family for loyalty. Greeks were very proud of their cities, even though some covered less than one hundred square miles of territory and contained just a few thousand people. One of the consequences of this chauvinism was that, left to themselves, Greek cities never were able to unite politically, for Greeks living in one secluded polis found it distasteful to put themselves under the authority of another one. And another is that Greek cities actively competed against each other, even to the point of open warfare, to gain the best land, the most wealth, and the most glorious reputations.

THE CONSTRUCTION OF GREEK IDENTITY

During the Dark Ages, typical Greek characteristics developed that defined Greek identity. These included not only an adversarial spirit of competition that deeply imbued all Greek society and politics but also a culture that united the Greeks at the same time that they remained disunited politically.

The Competitive Spirit

Another Greek characteristic that was in place by the end of the Dark Ages was a fundamental competitive spirit that manifested itself in almost every aspect of Greek life. As a result of *stasis*, that is, constant competition and conflict, Greeks were unable to get along with each other. Individuals competed with individuals and families with families for wealth, power, status, and influence. Social classes clashed as aristocrats tried to protect their interests against everyone else. And cities competed with cities for resources and status. Athletic competitions were held even at funerals and religious ceremonies. The Greeks also believed that there was no joy in victory unless an opponent was completely humiliated. In Greek *aspondos polemos* ("unconditional warfare"), the losing side could expect no mercy. Even if it did not often happen, it was perfectly acceptable for defeated men to be executed and women and children to be sold as slaves. The Greeks never had the concept that "everybody could be a winner." Nor was there any such thing as a "good loser" or a "moral victory."

The only kind of victory that counted was one that was public, obvious, and apparent to all; no points were gained by subtlety. And the easiest way to gain social approval was by excelling in some sort of competitive endeavor, such as politics, speech making, warfare, or athletic competition. Greeks in general, and aristocrats in particular, were expected to demonstrate their *arētē* ("excellence") in some outward form, for it was only external appearances that mattered, not intentions. Only form counted, not content. The Greeks had no concept of "inner beauty" and would have laughed at the idea that "beauty is only skin deep"; one was expected to be *kalos k'agathos*, that is, "beautiful and virtuous." Respectable Greeks demonstrated their virtuousness by ostentatiously providing for their parents, worshipping the gods, and being hospitable to strangers. In general, therefore, the feelings of individual Greeks about themselves came from outside rather than from within. The Greeks lived in a **shame culture**, in which one's feelings about oneself were determined by how one appeared to other people, as opposed to a guilt culture, in which people can feel guilty about something regardless of what others think. Thus, according to Greek legend, after the death of Achilles, there was a competition between the Greek heroes Ajax and Odysseus for Achilles' armor. When the armor was awarded to Odysseus, Ajax was so distressed that he became temporarily insane and killed a flock of sheep, thinking that they were Trojans. When he came to his senses, there was no way for him to recover from the shame of what he had done, and he had no recourse but to commit suicide.

For Greek aristocrats, bravery in war was glorified more than anything else, whereas cowardice, such as throwing away one's shield, resulted in the greatest disgrace. The Greek hero Achilles, for example, made it clear that he would prefer to have a short, glorious life rather than a long, colorless one. Moreover, a Greek was not judged to have lived a truly glorious life until he was dead, for one never knew when disgrace and dishonor might creep up. This Greek competitive spirit would be both a blessing and a curse for the Greeks. It was a blessing in that it encouraged them to greater heights of achievement in intellectual endeavors such as literature, art, and architecture. But it was also a curse in that the inability to get along resulted in constant conflict and warfare and even a willingness to make common cause with foreign invaders in their efforts to gain an advantage over their neighbors.

Gender Roles

The Greek world was a man's world, and Greek men kept Greek women as an underclass in both public and private life. Women often were portrayed as a poorly understood and stereotyped "other" category. Men were favored from birth, and it was not uncommon for female infants to be abandoned. It was understood, however, that abandoned infants were free for the taking, and they often were taken in and raised as slaves. The sexes were rigorously separated: a man's place was in public life; a woman's was in the home. Even though men and women both could have citizen status, in practice women had no opportunity to exercise citizen rights. In public life, women could not attend legislative meetings or hold office, nor could they serve in the military. Their only public role was in a few religious rites limited to women.

In private life women were equally disadvantaged. Only sons or the eldest male in a family could inherit property. Married women were permitted to control only as much money as it took to buy a bushel of grain. Respectable women were secluded in the home and spent most of their time with other women. It thus was not uncommon for women to form very close friendships, including sexual ones, with other women. In addition, no respectable, well-to-do woman appeared outside the home without being accompanied by some male, even if just a boy. Women who did appear in public, in particular slaves, often were poorly treated. Prostitution was an

A terracotta figurine from Boeotia dated to ca. 500 BCE portrays a woman fulfilling a typical Greek gender role, baking cakes.

occupation that engaged many women, and it was not uncommon for men to visit prostitutes or to keep a mistress.

A woman's main duties were to take charge of the household and, in particular, to bear and raise children. Women were married as young as fourteen years old, often to a man of forty or fifty. Childbearing was the most fearsome task that most women faced, for medical care was minimal and women often died in childbirth. Greek women also could be mistreated by their husbands, especially if the husband was doing badly in his perpetual competition with other men.

Greek men were equally segregated and spent little time with women who were not mothers, wives, or prostitutes. Well-to-do men spent most of their time outside the home, exercising together

In a homoerotic scene on the inside of this red-figure kylix (drinking cup) of ca. 480 BCE from Athens, a standing older man propositions a seated young man. The inscription reads, "The boy is beautiful."

in the *gymnasion* (gymnasium), serving together in the military, and participating in politics. Poorer men worked as artisans, farmers, or laborers. In male society, homosocialization was promoted by a practice in which a thirty-year-old man instructed a fourteen- or fifteen-year-old youth in what it meant to be a male citizen of the city. This bond often involved sexual activity, although actual penetration was frowned on because it disqualified a man from citizenship. A popular male activity was the symposium, or banquet. Female company was provided by elegant and sophisticated prostitutes known as as **hetairai**, or "companions," who often were well educated and trained in activities such as music and dance, not to mention more intimate forms of entertainment.

The base meaning of the Greek word gymnasion *is "a place to be naked" because of the Greek practice of exercising in the nude.*

A Shared Culture

If the Greeks were politically and socially disunited, when it came to culture, they were very unified and very aware of being Greek. Collectively, they thought of themselves as the **Hellenes**, that is, those who came from Hellas, as Greece was called. Hellenes were defined as those who spoke Greek. The Greeks always had a chip on their shoulder about their cultural superiority and thought that they were better than everyone else. No matter how highly cultured Egyptians or Phoenicians or Persians were, in the minds of the chauvinistic Greeks they would always be **barbarians** because they did not speak Greek (their speech sounded like "*bar-bar-bar*") and thus could never engage with Greek culture.

Hellas is still the modern name for Greece.

Another thing that united the Greeks was their shared religious beliefs and practices. In Greek mythology, the twelve **Olympian gods**, headed by **Zeus**, the god of lightning and thunder, and his wife Hera, goddess of marriage and childbirth, met atop Mt. Olympus in northern Greece, even if all of them did not actually live there. Poseidon ruled the sea and earthquakes; and Hades was in charge of the underworld. Demeter controlled the harvest and Hestia the hearth. **Aphrodite** was goddess of sex and love, and Artemis was goddess of the hunt. Artemis' brother Apollo represented the sun, prophecy, music, and medicine; Hephaestus was god of crafts; and Hermes was the messenger god and god of commerce; and **Dionysus**, also known as Bacchus, was the god of wine and ritual madness. Ares was the god of war and **Athena** the armored goddess of wisdom. Greek cities chose one guardian deity: Athena, for example, looked over both Athens and Sparta.

Greek gods were **anthropomorphic**, human not just in shape but also in behavior. In Greek mythology, the gods got into the same kinds of mischief and had the same kinds of friendships, animosities, and personal relationships as humans. In addition, mortals interacted with the gods—Zeus, for example, fathered any number of sons by mortal women and also was fond of boys. There thus was an intermediary category of demigods (half-gods), whose parents were a human and a god, including heroes such as **Hercules** or Perseus. But by the Dark Ages, the gods had become distant. They no longer appeared on earth. Unlike Mesopotamians and Egyptians, the Greeks never had a separate class of priests, and religion was not nearly as much of an everyday presence as it was in the Near East. The gods rarely intervened in human affairs. People were on their own. The gods had put order in the world, but they were not micromanagers. Indeed, they favored take-charge individuals who essentially made their own good fortune. Nevertheless, the Greeks did believe that the gods were just and would punish evildoers, particularly anyone who did not do the will of the gods.

The gods were worshiped in a sacred space known as a *temenos* that sometimes included a grove of trees and often had a shrine or temple. An enclosed *naos*, or sanctuary, could be either round (a *tholos*), rectangular, or rectangular with semicircular apses. During the earlier part of the Archaic Age, until ca. 600 BCE, mud-brick walls were replaced by rows of wooden columns, and little remains of these. Subsequently, rectangular temples with tile-covered roofs became the norm, with outer rows of stone columns often over sixty feet surrounding the inner *naos*. Most temples were built using a 9:4 ratio for length versus width, known as the golden section. The altar on which sacrifices of animals or plant matter were made stood in the open air in front of the temple, whereas the temple proper often held an image of the god and votive offerings left by people either to gain favor from the god or in acknowledgment of some favor received from the god. The inner *naos* also served as a storage place for the temple treasury, and temples could accumulate great wealth.

By the middle of the sixth century BCE, two standard orders of Greek architecture had emerged, generally identified by the styles of their columns.

The simple, fluted Doric style, with a simple undecorated capital, originated on the Greek mainland in the west and is exemplified by the temple of Hera at Paestum in southern Italy dated from ca. 550 BCE. The Ionic style, with a capital consisting of two opposed spiral rolls, originated in Ionia, and its earliest known example is the temple of Hera on Samos dated to ca. 570–560. Only in the late third century BCE did a much more elaborate third alternative develop, the Corinthian style, with elaborate floral capitals.

The gods were worshipped in public religious rituals carried out by priests who were civic officials and not part of a priestly class as in the Near East. An animal would be sacrificed to the god, who then presumably would look favorably on the city, or at least do no harm to the city. A religious festival also was an occasion to have a banquet, for the only parts of the sacrificed animal that were actually presented as burnt offerings to the gods were bones wrapped in fat. The rest was consumed by the worshippers. In other regards, however, Greek temples usually were not places that were greatly frequented for religious purposes.

No written literature survives from the Dark Ages, but this was nevertheless a time of much composition and preservation of oral literature. Cycles of myths described how the gods had themselves been created and then created the world. Additional cycles of legends described the deeds of demigod and human heroes. The Greeks considered these legends, such as one about the Greek attack on Troy, to be their ancient history. During the Dark Ages, these tales were put into verse and memorized by wandering poets who were welcomed wherever they went because they provided one of the few forms of outside entertainment available. And because these stories were so well known, they could be used in art and literature and be immediately recognized by any Greek.

By the eighth century BCE, Greek cities were becoming less isolated and began to engage in shared activities. By 800 BCE, for example, the **oracle of Apollo** at Delphi had acquired international renown. Not only Greeks but even foreigners sent ambassadors seeking the oracle's advice—for a price, of course—on matters such as settling quarrels and engaging in wars. The priestess of Apollo known as the **Pythia** inhaled volcanic fumes and then delivered a cryptic response that often had several meanings. For example, when King Croesus of Lydia was considering an attack on the Persians in 547 BCE, he first

The three orders of Greek architecture, Doric, Ionic, and Corinthian. The column shafts were fluted, that is, had vertical grooves, and the primary differences were in the capitals at the top of the columns.

An Athenian scene of ca. 510 BCE depicts the sort of Greek athletic activities that took place at the Olympic games. Two wrestlers square off as, behind them, one athlete prepares to do the standing broad jump and another smoothes the landing pit.

consulted the oracle at Delphi, who responded that if he did so, "a great empire would be destroyed." Heartened by this response, Croesus attacked, only to be defeated and taken captive. When he then rebuked the oracle for giving a false response, he was told that he had neglected to ask which empire would be destroyed—it was, in fact, his own.

Many Greek cities stored and showed off offerings to Apollo at minitemples at Delphi. Twelve cities and peoples even formed an **Amphictyonic** (from a word meaning "neighboring peoples") **League** that could declare a Sacred War to protect the sanctuary and even attempted to establish guidelines for warfare, such as that no member should be completely destroyed and that water supplies should not be cut in wartime. Members included the cities of Athens, Sparta, Thebes, and Delphi. Because of the oracle's **pan-Hellenic** (Greece-wide) reputation, consulting the oracle provided a means whereby local quarrels, such as crimes involving blood guilt, could be resolved.

In 776 BCE, the first firm date in Greek history, the Greeks began to keep records of the meetings of a pan-Hellenic festival held at Olympia in the northern Peloponnesus in honor of the god Zeus. Subsequently, the Olympic games were held every four years, and the names of the winners were carefully preserved. In non-Olympic years, other pan-Hellenic games also were held: beginning in 573 BCE, the Nemean games, also in honor of Zeus, were held at Nemea, southwest of Corinth, in the second year of an Olympic cycle; in the third year of the cycle, as of 582 BCE, the Pythian games, which also included contests in music and poetry, were held at Delphi in honor of Apollo; and in the fourth year, also commencing in 582 BCE, the Isthmian games convened at Corinth in honor of Poseidon. In theory, at least, warfare was supposed to cease when these games rolled around so that athletes and spectators could attend without being attacked. At the same time there arose the custom of people whose personal safety was at risk being able to claim *asylia* (**asylum**, a word meaning "freedom from seizure") at temples; those who violated the right of asylum were cursed by the gods. These pan-Hellenic customs gave the Greeks an even stronger sense of what it meant to be Greek.

THE ARCHAIC AGE (776–500 BCE)

By the eighth century BCE, Greece clearly was emerging from its period of depression. There were signs of economic recovery everywhere, and the aristocracies of the Dark Ages evolved into oligarchies. At the same time, Greek culture became increasingly complex, based largely on Greek interactions with the more sophisticated cultures of the ancient Near East. This period is generally known as the **Archaic Age**.

The Revival of Trade and Evolution of Culture

The year 776 BCE also marks the beginning of the Archaic Age, which brought a revival of Greek trade and culture as the Greeks became one of the major economic and political forces in the Mediterranean world. This happened for several reasons. For one thing, the Dark Ages had seen a constant population increase, and Greece, with its great expanses of rocky and hilly soil, simply could not grow enough agricultural staples to support a large population. Methods for dealing with the extra mouths were needed.

The term Archaic Age originated with art historians who thought that the art of this period looked more old-fashioned—that is, worse—than the art of the fifth century BCE.

One response was to import food. As a consequence, Greek trade and manufacturing expanded. In exchange for olive oil, fine pottery, silver, and slaves, the Greeks acquired grain in Egypt and in the lands on the Black Sea coast. This expansion of Greek commerce brought the Greeks into conflict with the current Mediterranean trading power, the Phoenicians. The thirty-oared Greek galleys, known as triakonters, of the ninth and eighth centuries BCE were replaced by fleets of 90-foot long iron-beaked fifty-oared pentakonters. The clumsy Phoenician two-decked warships were no match for the more maneuverable Greeks, and the Greeks soon wrested control of much of Mediterranean trade from their Phoenician competitors, who at this time also were under attack by the Assyrians.

The revival of Greek trade also had other consequences. The Greeks also brought back culture, and as a result Greek culture evolved based largely on borrowings from the much more ancient and sophisticated cultures of the Near East. From the Phoenicians they borrowed the alphabet, for they now had just as great a need to keep records. In order to adapt the Phoenician alphabet, which had been designed to write Semitic languages, to write their own language, the Greeks added new letters representing vowels to make it more clear which word was meant.

In the late seventh century BCE, the Greeks of Ionia picked up coinage from the Lydians. In the early sixth century, coinage spread to the mainland, with the island city of Aegina issuing *staters* (coins of a standard weight) bearing a turtle on one side and a simple punch mark on the other. Around 570 BCE, Corinth issued coins bearing an image of Pegasus, the winged horse thought to have alighted at Corinth to drink from a sacred well; and about 525 BCE Athens began issuing its famous "Owls," bearing the head of Athena on one side and Athena's owl on the other. A multitude of other Greek cities also issued coins as a means of asserting their status and independence. The coins of important trading cities such as Aegina, Corinth, and Athens became standard currency in the Mediterranean world because of their extensive circulation. One

Because they are so widely accepted around the world, U.S. coins and paper money likewise rarely change their designs.

An Orientalizing Boeotian pithos (storage jar) of the early seventh century BCE depicts a prowling lion in the midst of the traditional geometric patterns.

problem, however, was that the Greeks could not agree on standard weights for all their coins. As a consequence, trading cities attempted to carve out their own spheres of economic influence by favoring the use of coins with their own weights. This resulted in a complicated mathematical calculation if, say, someone wanted to use Corinthian coins to pay for something with a price expressed in Athenian coins.

The Greeks also assimilated ideas about artistic expression from the east. During the Dark Ages, artistic designs had consisted of simple geometric patterns. The Archaic Age introduced a multitude of eastern styles. Greek sculpture assumed a very Egyptian look, and, in the Orientalizing style, at its height around 750 BCE, Greek pottery depicted many eastern motifs, such as lions, bulls, and sphinxes. But Greek artists soon developed their own idiosyncratic style by incorporating into their designs scenes drawn from their own myths and legends. Greek potters competed with each other to perfect different manufacturing techniques and artistic styles, and they soon were the acknowledged Mediterranean masters of pottery making.

The Second Wave of Greek Colonization

The Greek need to feed extra mouths could not be met simply by expanded trade. As a result, the Greeks devised other means of dealing with overpopulation. A second option was to migrate elsewhere in search of new homes, which also could be done to escape from foreign or domestic enemies at home, and to establish overseas trading relations. This led to a Second Wave of Greek Colonization lasting roughly from 750 to 550 BCE. Emigrants from the Greek mainland and Ionia established Greek **colonies** around the shores of the Mediterranean and Black Seas. Greek colonies were modeled on the cities that founded them. They had the same culture, social structure, and government. They maintained sentimental ties to their **metropolis**, or mother city, but otherwise each was a completely independent polis, just like the cities back home.

Only a few colonies were founded in North Africa. The Greek historian Herodotus related how the colony of Cyrene, on the coast of Libya, was founded by the island of Thera circa 630 BCE. In response to a Delphic oracle, a certain Battus was sent off to establish the colony with two pentakonters. The colonists eventually settled near a spring dedicated to Apollo called Cyre, which gave its name to the city of Cyrene. Subsequently, the Cyrenaeans offered land to

---

HISTORICAL CONTROVERSY

"BLACK ATHENA"

Some modern authors, in their attempts to glorify the Greeks, have largely ignored the great debt that later Greek culture owed to the much more ancient civilizations of the Near East. Others, however, have attempted to present a more balanced view. The most extreme effort to acknowledge non-Greek aspects of early Greek culture is found in a book by Martin Bernal, titled *Black Athena: The Afroasiatic Roots of Classical Civilization,* published in 1987 and subsequently enlarged to three volumes. Bernal argued that the Asiatic and African influence on ancient Greek culture had been largely downplayed or ignored by western scholars. Based on a Greek legend that the Phoenician Cadmus founded the city of Thebes and brought the Phoenician alphabet to Greece, Bernal argued that in the early second millenium BCE, Indo-European invaders from the north found Greece already occupied by Phoenician colonists. As early as the eighteenth century BCE, these backward northerners then adopted Semitic and Egyptian words (for example, Greek *bia* ["force"] being derived from Egyptian *ba* ["soul"]) and many other aspects of Near Eastern culture that underlay the later flowering of classical Greek culture. Bernal even downplays borrowings from western Asia and focuses on an Egyptian African origin for ancient Greek culture, suggesting that Egyptians invaded Greece in the sixteenth century BCE. And by claiming that the ancient Egyptians were in fact a Black African people, Bernal concludes that Greek civilization can be traced to Black Africa, hence his title,

"Black Athena." In this view, Greeks ranging from Socrates to Cleopatra were in fact Black.

Bernal's thesis about the Near Eastern origins of Greek culture has been challenged on several grounds, ranging from questionable linguistic interpretations to the lack of any archaeological evidence for his hypotheses. For example, in order to minimize the role of the early Mycenaean Greek civilization, Bernal dated the introduction of the Phoenician alphabet to ca. 1600 BCE (as opposed to the generally accepted date of ca. 750 BCE) and claimed that many Greek words were based on Semitic or Egyptian as opposed to the commonly accepted Indo-European origins.

On the other hand, Bernal's other claim, that in the past, and especially in the nineteenth century, the contributions of Near Eastern cultures were downplayed by pseudo-racist western scholars, is noncontroversial and is widely accepted. For example, for over a century Greek art of the Archaic Age has been described as "Orientalizing" as a result of the widespread adoption of Syrian, Phoenician, Assyrian, and Egyptian motifs during the eighth and seventh centuries BCE; other elements of the Greek adoption of eastern cultural attributes likewise have long been acknowledged.

The "Black Athena" hypothesis has had a great influence on modern Afrocentrism, which focuses on the role and significance of the cultures of Black African peoples, and the idea that Greek culture grew out of Africa continues to have many supporters.

---

any Greek who wished to settle there, and the city grew. When the Libyans saw themselves being "robbed and insulted by the Cyrenaeans," Herodotus relates, they put themselves under the protection of the Egyptian pharaoh Apries (589–567 BCE), who sent a huge army against Cyrene. But the militaristic Greeks marched out and completely defeated the Egyptians. Cyrene then established a prosperous mercantile economy based on the exploitation of the now-extinct silphium plant, which was widely used both as a condiment and for medicinal purposes ranging from a treatment for coughs to use as a contraceptive.

At the Greek trading colony of Cyrene in Libya, King Arcesilaus II (ca. 560–550 BCE) sits on the deck of a merchant ship and oversees the weighing of silphium, which is put below deck under the king.

The founding of other Greek colonies followed a similar pattern. Greek colonists from both the mainland and Ionia, led by an *oikistēs* (founder) and often following directions from an oracle, sought out coastal locations—the philosopher Plato described the Greeks as "frogs around a pond"—that would support mercantile activities. The colonists often had to seize territory at the expense of the peoples they settled among. And because they were mostly male, they also found wives, not to mention slaves, among the local population.

This Second Wave of Colonization was much more extensive than the first. Colonies also were established in the north. For example, on the northern coast of the Aegean Sea, a source of gold and silver, Corinth founded Thasos circa 700 BCE and Potidaea around 600 BCE. Even further north, many coastal colonies were established near the grain-rich lands surrounding the Black Sea, as at Sinope by the Ionian city of Miletus in the seventh century BCE. To the west, colonies were founded on the island of Corcyra on the eastern coast of the Adriatic Sea in 735; by Eretria on the island of Euboea; in France at Marseille; at the mouth of the Rhône River by the Ionian city of Phocaea ca. 600 BCE; and even on the eastern coast of Spain at Emporion circa 575 BCE, likewise by Phocaea.

But the most extensive Greek emigration was to southern Italy and western Sicily, an area that came to be called **Magna Graecia** ("Great Greece") because so many Greek colonies were founded there. Circa 757, the city of Chalcis

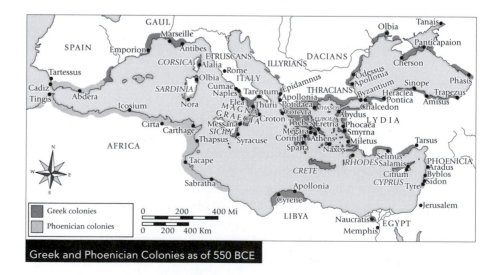

Greek and Phoenician Colonies as of 550 BCE

on the island of Euboea founded Cumae on the Bay of Naples in west central Italy; in 733, Corinth established the great city of **Syracuse** in Sicily; and in 706 and Sparta sent illegitimate children to found Tarentum in southern Italy. Some colonies even founded their own colonies; for example, Heraclea Pontica, established on the southern coast of the Black Sea circa 560 BCE by Megara, shortly thereafter founded Cherson, in the far northern reaches of the Black Sea.

A consequence of the spread of Greek people was the spread of Greek culture, which not only became a common culture in the Mediterranean world but also spread into southern Russia via the Black Sea colonies and into central Europe through Marseille.

The Consequences of Warfare

A third means by which a city could cope with overpopulation was to increase its own territory in Greece by military means. As a result, the Archaic Age also saw the growth of warfare. In the southern half of the Peloponnesus, for example, Sparta conquered the fertile plains of Laconia between ca. 800–730 and Messenia ca. 740–720; the rocky and rough territory of Arcadia in the central Peloponnesus, however, was bypassed. The Lelantine War, fought ca. 700/650 BCE between Chalcis and Eretria over the fertile Lelantine Plain on the long island of Euboea, involved many cities being drawn in on one side or the other. Miletus, Aegina, and Megara, for example, sided with Eretria, and Samos, Corinth, and the Thessalians with Chalcis. Although Chalcis eventually gained the upper hand, the hard fighting seriously weakened both sides.

Conflict also arose over the control of lucrative trade routes. The powerful trading city of Corinth ejected colonists from Corcyra after 735 BCE to gain control of the route into the Adriatic Sea and by 700 had defeated Megara to seize the shortest passage across the narrow Isthmus of Corinth, which connected northern and southern Greece. Corinth thus became the most wealthy and powerful trading city in Greece. The growing rounds of warfare benefited some cities, such as Sparta and Corinth, but disadvantaged others, such as Megara, Chalcis, and Eretria, whose losses of land and resources resulted in declines in these cities' influence.

The growth of trade and warfare had important, and probably unanticipated, consequences for Greek society and government. The great expansion in trade also resulted from the desire of nonaristocrats to better their economic and social standing. Because the aristocrats controlled the best land, engaging in manufacturing and trade was the most effective way of doing this, and this led to the rise of a new well-to-do class in Greek society. But no matter how wealthy or influential an artisan or merchant became, he could never become an aristocrat, for aristocratic status was limited to those who had been born aristocrats. And because participation in government was limited to aristocrats, the newly rich had no public voice. Wealthy merchants thus felt very unhappy about not being able to participate in decisions that seriously affected their ability to do business and that were being made by landowners who were not at all sensitive to their needs and who often were jealous of their wealth and prestige.

The newly rich got a chance to better their positions as a consequence of the new rounds of warfare. Previously, aristocrats had done most of the fighting in wars. There were two reasons for this. First of all, there was no government funding of warfare, and soldiers were expected to provide their own arms and armor, or even a horse and chariot. Only aristocrats could afford to do so. And second, the aristocrats realized that they were vastly outnumbered by the rest of the population. It made good sense for them not to give nonaristocrats an important military role if they wanted to maintain their own preeminent position. In warfare, individual aristocrats would ride out onto the battlefield in their chariots, identify an opponent on the other side, jump to the ground, and fight a duel. These aristocratic warriors would be accompanied into battle by their dependents, who usually would provide moral support but would not participate in the actual fighting. In the Lelantine War, the last major aristocratic war in Greece, the city of Eretria fielded sixty chariots, and the combatants genteelly agreed not to use arrows, which permitted disgraceful killing from a distance. Honor was just as important as state policy.

But this all changed when profits from commerce flowed into Greek trading cities. Cities that feared they would lose a war began to allow those who could afford their arms and armor into the army. As a result, large numbers of rich merchants became full-fledged infantrymen known as **hoplites** (from *hoplon*, "weapons"), and armies became much larger. A fully armed hoplite carried equipment made from bronze or iron, including a shield, sword, spear, helmet, cuirass (chest protector), and greaves (shin guards). The primary weapon was an eight-foot spear. These larger armies abandoned the chariots and old aristocratic duels and fought as a massed **phalanx** that was about six ranks deep.

There was no way that a city whose fighting strength was composed only of aristocrats could hope to compete with a city using the phalanx. Between around 700 and 650 BCE cities such as Sparta, Argos, Corinth, and Athens all created hoplite armies. The rest of the Greek cities did likewise, and by 650 BCE all of the Greek cities on the mainland and in Ionia had adopted the phalanx system by letting everybody who could afford their arms and armor into the army. Cities were not slow to use these new armies; in 669 BCE, for example, the city of Argos used the new phalanx to defeat Sparta at the Battle of Hysiae. A larger scale war involved the attempts of the city of Cyrrha, on the north coast of the Gulf of Corinth, to tax and control access to the shrine of Apollo at Delphi. In the First Sacred War (595–585 BCE) the Amphictyonic League was advised by the oracle of Apollo to undertake *aspondos polemos* (unconditional warfare), a war of total destruction without any rules, against Cyrrha. In the first known use of chemical warfare, Cyrrha's water supply was poisoned with hellebore, a poisonous plant that causes, among other things, stupor, vomiting, and cardiac arrest. The Cyrrhans were rendered so weak that the city was captured, cursed, and destroyed, and the entire population slaughtered.

One consequence of the military buildup was that the Greeks gained well-deserved reputations as excellent soldiers. Thus another way of dealing with overpopulation was for adventurous Greeks to go overseas to serve as mercenaries, who first appeared in the mid-seventh century BCE when they helped to restore the Egyptian pharaoh Psamtik I (664–610 BCE), who had been advised by an oracle to hire "men of bronze," to his throne.

Lawgivers, Oligarchy, and Tyranny

The rise of hoplite armies also resulted in the decline of aristocracies. When well-to-do merchants gained not only a place in the army but also military leadership positions based on their ability, their desire to participate in the political process became all the more acute. They demanded greater political rights. When the aristocrats resisted, the merchants made common cause with other disadvantaged groups, including the urban unemployed and poor farmers. In most of the Greek cities, discontent reached the point at which, in order to avoid open rebellion, the aristocrats felt compelled to respond. A primary grievance of nonaristocrats was that only the aristocrats knew the laws. For centuries, going back into the Dark Ages, the laws had been in the hands of aristocratic law rememberers, who had a tendency to remember the law one way one time and another way another time. Sometimes, and especially between 650 and 600 BCE, in an effort to lessen discontent, the aristocrats appointed **lawgivers** to write down the laws. Some of these laws attempted to reduce community strife by assigning to the city duties that in the past had been the responsibility of families. For example, government-run courts to try crimes such as murder, which in the past had been dealt with by personal retribution, helped to end destructive cycles of blood feuds between families. This was but one of the ways that the polis, as an institution, came to predominate over the aristocratic families. But other laws were intended to protect the interests of the aristocrats, especially their control of their *klaroi*, and to keep them in power. It was common practice, for example, to allow citizens who had fallen on hard times to be sold as slaves for debt. The law codes, therefore, did little to reduce the discontent.

Sometimes, moreover, the aristocrats attempted to salvage as much of their privileges as they could by making common cause with the most wealthy of the newly rich persons and appointing a lawgiver to create a new form of constitutional government called **oligarchy** ("the rule of the few"). This name is a bit misleading, because the "few" in this case

> **HISTORICAL CAUSALITY**
>
> How was overpopulation in Greece a factor that eventually led to changes in Greek government?

A PICTURE IS WORTH A THOUSAND WORDS

GREEK HOPLITES ON THE MARCH

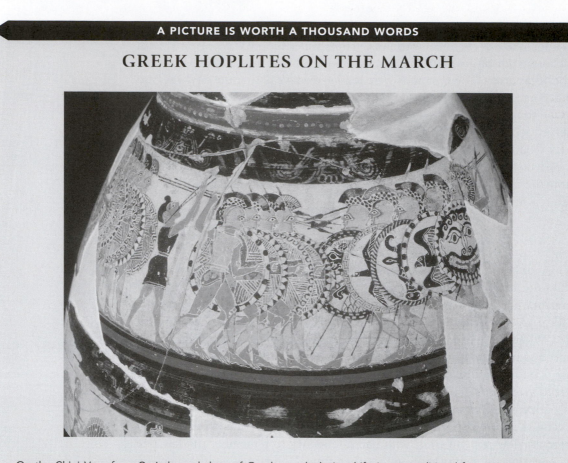

On the Chigi Vase from Corinth, a phalanx of Greek hoplites advances in formation. Each hoplite holds a spear in his right hand and a shield in his left. The music of a flute player helps them to keep in step. When a phalanx engaged an enemy, it was crucial for the hoplites to remain in position. A hoplite's own shield protected his left side, but his right side, where he held his spear, had to be protected by the shield of the man next to him. Thus the soldiers had to depend on each other. Battles between two phalanxes would begin like big shoving matches, with the two sides pushing against each other. Because the right side of the last hoplite on the right flank was unprotected, the right flank of a phalanx would tend to retreat and the left flank to advance, and the two phalanxes would slowly circle clockwise around each other. In order to counteract this clockwise drift, it was traditional for armies to station their most experienced men on the right flank, which was the place of honor, and the least experienced on the left. Otherwise, nothing much would happen as long as each phalanx maintained its discipline. But eventually, a section of one phalanx would begin to lose its cohesiveness and break apart, or a gap would open in the line. The other phalanx would make its way into the breach, and the undisciplined phalanx would disintegrate. When a hoplite's phalanx crumbled, his only concern was to save his own skin. He would discard his heavy shield and try to escape. And that was when the slaughter started, as the pursuing hoplites cut down their fleeing enemies from behind. It was not unusual in such battles for the losing side to have hundreds of casualties and the winners to have very few.

ended up including many more people than had been included in the earlier aristocratic governments. In this case, "the few" meant "the rich." Structurally, an oligarchy looked very much like an aristocracy, the primary difference being that the degree to which a person could participate in the government was determined not by his birth but by his wealth. The richer someone was, the more participation he had. Thus some were only wealthy enough to be able to serve on the *boulē*, which continued as the chief executive and legislative body, whereas richer citizens were able to hold offices such as archon. Oligarchy turned out to be the most stable form of Greek government. Even though the membership of an oligarchy continued to be very exclusive, its ability to incorporate new members based on their ability provided a safety valve that usually prevented worse things, such as violent rebellion, from happening.

But in cities in which the aristocrats resisted making any changes at all, it was only a matter of time until there was an overthrow of the state. Disadvantaged groups, such as rich merchants, ruined farmers, or the urban poor, would sponsor an illegal ruler called a **tyrant**, and the period 650–500 BCE is known as the **Age of Tyrants** because so many Greek cities used this means of dealing with intransigent aristocrats. Not all tyrants were bad, as the modern sense of their name would suggest. There were good tyrants, bad tyrants, and mediocre tyrants.

The establishment of most tyrannies followed the same general pattern. Tyrannies often were created because the aristocrats themselves could not maintain their own solidarity and one of them set himself up as tyrant. Most tyrants begin their attempts to seize power by hiring a bodyguard composed of either local people or foreign mercenaries. Sometimes there was an actual violent revolution, but just as often the aristocrats caved in without a fight. Tyrants could remain in power only if they kept their supporters, and in particular the underprivileged, happy. They did this by giving tax breaks to merchants in order to encourage economic development, by sponsoring extravagant building projects that kept the poor employed, and by distributing free seed grain to small farmers. These kinds of favoritism gave previously disadvantaged groups a sense of empowerment.

But tyrants also treated their enemies harshly, especially aristocrats, who at best were disrespected or forced into exile, and at worst were executed. A tyranny also gave previously oppressed groups the opportunity for some payback. At Sicyon, after a tyranny had

A modern reconstruction depicts the western end of the *diolkos*, a stone roadway built by the tyrant Periander that allowed ships to be dragged across the Isthmus of Corinth.

been established by a revolt of underprivileged people against Dorian aristocrats, the tyrant Cleisthenes insulted the three Dorian clans by renaming them
the "pig men," "swine men," and "ass men" and renamed his own clan from
the *Aigiales* ("goat men") to the *Archelaoi* ("rulers of the people").

The big commercial cities, such as Corinth, Megara, Miletus, Mytilene, and
Samos, in which there was a rich merchant class chafing under aristocratic
rule, were the ones most liable to produce tyrants. At Corinth, for example, an
aristocratic woman named Labda who had married a commoner bore a son
named Cypselus. The oracle at Delphi had prophesied that Cypselus would
overthrow the aristocratic Bacchiadae family, so the family hired two thugs
to murder him, but when the infant Cypselus smiled at them, they lost their
resolve. Cypselus grew up to become polemarch, and in this capacity he seized
power, exiled the aristocrats, and established a hereditary tyranny.

In 627 BCE, Cypselus was succeeded by his son Periander, who followed
the standard tyrannical policy of commercial expansion. He built a stone
ramp called the *diolkos* ("portage through") across the Isthmus of Corinth and
charged tolls for dragging ships between the Gulf of Corinth and the Aegean
Sea, thus eliminating the dangerous voyage around the Peloponnesus. Corinth
became so rich that Periander eliminated taxes. To protect the city's trade,
he created a powerful navy. And he increased the city's status in the Greek
world by establishing the Isthmian Games, which were held the year before
the Olympics. But he also became a model of an evil tyrant. He murdered his
wife and sent three hundred boys from the rival city of Corcyra to Lydia to
be made into eunuchs. But in spite of his bad reputation, Periander's motto,
"Forethought in all things," led to his later inclusion among the Seven Wise
Men of Greece.

But tyranny, because it was unconstitutional, was fundamentally unstable.
A tyrant looked too much like a king, and no city would permit a return to
monarchy.

No matter how popular or effective a tyrant was, he always feared assassination, and tyrannicides (the assassins of tyrants) were viewed as great heroes.
This anxiety was portrayed in the story about a flatterer named Damocles who
often praised Dionysius, the tyrant of Syracuse in Sicily, for his luxurious lifestyle. Dionysius allowed Damocles to be tyrant for a day and had him preside
at a great banquet. Damocles enjoyed himself tremendously until he noticed
a sword suspended by a single horsehair over his head. He then realized that
there could be no pleasure for someone who was always living under the
shadow of sudden death. And, in fact, with the major exceptions of Syracuse,
which kept its tyrants until it was conquered by the Romans, and Athens,
which developed a democracy, nearly all of the Greek cities with tyrants eventually replaced them with stable oligarchies. In Corinth, Psammeticus, the
nephew of Periander, was assassinated ca. 582 BCE; Aeschines of Sicyon was
driven out by the Spartans in 555 BCE; and Polycrates of Samos was executed,

IN THEIR OWN WORDS

THE EDUCATION OF A TYRANT

The Greek historian Herodotus, writing in the middle of the fifth century BCE, discussed how Periander, son of Cypselus, learned from Thrasybulus, tyrant of Miletus in Ionia, a valuable lesson on how to be an effective tyrant:

> When he became tyrant, Cypselus was a man of this character: he drove many of the Corinthians into exile and deprived many of their wealth and very many more of their lives. And when he had reigned for thirty years and had brought his life to a prosperous end, his son Periander became his successor in the tyranny. Now Periander at first was milder than his father; but after he had had dealings through messengers with Thrasybulus the tyrant of Miletus, he became far more murderous even than Cypselus. For he sent a messenger to Thrasybulus and asked what course of action was the safest for him to make, in order that he might best govern his state. Thrasybulus led the messenger who had come from Periander out of the city and entered a field of growing wheat, and as he passed through the crop of wheat, while inquiring and asking questions repeatedly of the messenger about the occasion of his coming from Corinth, he kept cutting off the heads of those ears of grain that he saw higher than the rest. As he cut off their heads he cast them away, until he had destroyed in this manner the finest and richest part of the crop. So having passed through the place and having suggested no word of counsel, he dismissed the messenger.
>
> When the messenger returned to Corinth, Periander was anxious to hear the counsel that had been given, but the messenger said that Thrasybulus had given him no counsel, and added that he wondered why Periander had sent him to such a man, for the man was out of his senses and a waster of his own goods, relating at the same time what he had seen Thrasybulus do. But Periander, understanding what had been done and perceiving that Thrasybulus counselled him to put to death those who were eminent among his subjects, began then to display all manner of evil treatment to the citizens of the state; for whatsoever Cypselus had left undone in killing and driving into exile, this Periander completed.

and his body then crucified, by the Persians in 522 BCE. Thus the tendency in Greece was always toward oligarchy; some cities went through an intermediate stage with tyrants, and others went there directly, but by one means or another, oligarchy became the most common form of Greek government.

Literature and Thought

These social, economic, and political developments occurred at the same time as a great revival of Greek literary culture. Along with keeping business records, the Greeks also used writing to create literature. Between 800 and 750 BCE, the most treasured of Greek legends, involving the Trojan War, were committed to writing by the blind poet **Homer**, who probably came from Ionia. The epic poem the *Iliad* told part of the story of the Greek attack on the city of Troy, and

An Athenian red-figured kalathos (bowl) of around 470 BCE depicts Alcaeus, holding a lyre, and Sappho. The two were reputed to have been lovers.

The lyre playing and singing associated with lyric poetry is analogous to songs accompanied by a guitar in the modern day.

LEGACY OF ANTIQUITY

How did the speculations of Ionian Greek philosophers foreshadow our modern understanding of the universe?

the *Odyssey* told how the Greek hero Odysseus struggled for ten years to get back from Troy while his wife Penelope fended off hordes of suitors. And around 700 BCE, the poet Hesiod, from Askra in Boeotia, composed works such as the "Theogony," a story of the origin of the gods, and the "Works and Days," advice about farming.

Not long afterward, Greeks began to write lyric poetry, which gets its name because it was sung while playing on a lyre, as a means of self-centered personal expression that stressed the value of the individual. For example, we find here expressions of heterosexual and homosexual love that look surprisingly modern. Ca. 600 BCE, Sappho of Lesbos said of a young man whom she fancied: "The youth who sits next to you seems to me to be the equal of the gods. My tongue grows numb; a subtle fire runs through my body. I sweat, I tremble, I turn pale, I faint." And in the late seventh century BCE, Anacreon of Teos in Ionia wrote, "Boy with a maiden's looks, I love you but you heed me not."

Some poems praised the good life, and especially wine drinking. Alcaeus of Lesbos, for example, wrote, "Let's drink! Why are we waiting for the lamps? Mix one part of water to two of wine, pour it in up to the brim, and let one cup push the other along." Other poets not only idealized warfare as a means of demonstrating excellence but also stressed the growing importance of loyalty to one's polis. Ca. 650 BCE, Callinus of Ephesus contrasted the brave man and the coward, saying, "Let one hurl a javelin even as he dies. Honor and glory are the lot of a man who fights for his country, for death is inescapable. Many a man flees the battle only to be met by death in his own home; but for such a man the city feels no love or regret. It is the valiant man whose fall is lamented by all." Around 635 BCE, the Spartan poet Tyrtaeus wrote, "A man does not prove himself good in war unless he can endure the bloodshed of battle and take his stand against the enemy with eagerness. It is a noble thing for a brave man to die falling in the front ranks struggling for his own land." And Solon of Athens wrote ca. 600 BCE, "Our polis is destined never to perish." But at the same time, there was a contrary trend toward realism and to express things the way that they really were.

Around 650 BCE, the poet Archilochus, from the island of Paros, violated all of the conventional aristocratic standards by writing, "Some Thracian now enjoys the shield I left in the bushes. I didn't want to lose it, but I got away alive." Archilochus also was the first Greek poet to write in the first person.

The Archaic Age also saw the rise of Greek scientific thought known as *philosophia* ("love of wisdom," or **philosophy**), influenced by contact with the astronomical and mathematical thought of the much more ancient civilization of Babylonia. Ionian pre-Socratic philosophers (who lived before the famous philosopher Socrates of Athens), several of whom came from Miletus, a major point of commercial contact with the Near East, speculated on issues such as cosmogony (the creation and composition of matter and the universe) and the nature of the gods. Rather than attributing the origin of the universe and the world to the activities of gods, as in mythology, philosophers looked for rational explanations that usually did not involve gods directly at all. Thales of Miletus proposed, ca. 585, that the world had originated from water; but his pupil Anaximander of Miletus suggested ca. 560 that everything came into existence by the separation of opposites (such as hot and cold) in the *apeiron* ("unlimited"), an infinite original mass; and ca. 550 BCE, Anaximander's pupil, Anaximines of Miletus, suggested the world arose from air. Rather later, ca. 400 BCE, Democritus of Abdera on the Thracian coast believed that matter was made up of *atomoi* ("things that cannot be split," or *atoms*), tiny particles that could not be divided, and introduced the concept of empty space unfilled by matter.

Democritus' theory of atoms provided the origin of modern atomic theory.

Pythagoras of Samos, who, like many Ionians, fled the Persians and migrated to Croton in southern Italy ca. 530 BCE, understood the universe in terms of mathematical harmony. He not only invented the Pythagorean Theorem, used for calculating the lengths of the sides of triangles, but he also believed in reincarnation. A story was told that once when he saw a dog being whipped, he took pity and said, "Stop, that dog has the soul of an old friend. I recognized him when he barked." In the late sixth century, however, Heraclitus of Ephesus rejected the concept of harmony and viewed the world as perpetually in flux. Nothing was constant, and his famous slogan was, "everything flows." But he did believe that there was some overall rational governing force, the **logos**, behind the universe, and the search to identify and define this *logos* would challenge philosophers well into the Christian period.

Nor were the gods themselves immune from philosophical study. Xenophanes, from Colophon in southern Italy, proposed around 500 BCE that the gods were anthropomorphic because people had invented gods in their own image. He reasoned, "The Ethiopians say that their gods are snub-nosed and black, and the Thracians believe that theirs have blue eyes and red hair. If horses could draw gods, they would look like horses." But questioning the nature of the gods was not always safe. Anaxagoras, an Ionian who settled in Athens, was exiled ca. 450 BCE for teaching that the sun and moon were material objects and not divinities. For all of these philosophers, it was enough simply to propose a theory and make the most rational argument that one could in its favor. None of them devised any experiments to prove or disprove their theories, and thus there was no way to tell which of them, if any, was right.

LOOKING AHEAD

During the Archaic Age, Greek cities were able to recover from the Dark Ages and create their own culture largely without outside interference. But the ensuing Classical Age would bring not only a major confrontation with the Persian Empire but also increasing attempts by the most powerful Greek city-states, Sparta and Athens, to impose their authority over other Greeks.

SUMMARY OF GREEK TERMINOLOGY

Aigiales   "Goat men"; an indigenous clan at Sicyon

Aigikoreis   An Ionic clan

Apeiron   "Unlimited"; an original mass that Anaxagoras suggested was the origin of all things.

Archelaoi   "Rulers of the people," an indigenous clan at Sicyon

archōn   Archon ("ruler"), the highest-ranking magistrate

archōn basileus   "King archon," a chief priest

archōn polemarchos   "Polemarch," or "war-leader archon"

arētē   Personal excellence

Argades   An Ionic clan

aspondos polemos   Unconditional warfare

asylia   "Freedom from seizure," the right of asylum at temples

atomoi   "things that cannot be split," or atoms

basileus   King

boulē   Legislative Council

damos, dēmos   Village, or "the people"

demiourgoi   Crafts persons

Dymanes   An Ionic clan

ekklēsia   Political assembly composed of all free men

Geleontes   An Ionic clan

georgoi   Farmers

Gymnasioi   "Naked people"; a clan of indigenous people

Hoplētēs   An Ionic clan

hoplon   Weapon

Hylleis   A Dorian clan

kalos k'agathos   "Handsome and virtuous," an aristocratic ideal

klaros/klaroi, klēros   Land allotment

kōmē   Rural village

Konipedes   "Dusty footed people"; a clan of indigenous people

laos   An entire Dorian, Ionian, etc. Greek people

naos   "Dwelling place," the inner sanctuary of a Greek temple

oikistēs   Founder of a colony

oikos   Household

Pamphyloi   An Ionic clan

perioikoi   "Dwellers around"; indigenous peoples living on the outskirts of a Dorian city

phylē   Clan; a large group of Greek families

polis   An independent Greek city state

philosophia   "Love of wisdom"; philosophy

temenos   A sacred space where gods were worshipped

tholos   A round temple sanctuary

Greek pronunciation: a = "ah" as in "shah"
ē = "a" as in "cake"
ō = "o" as in "vote"
γ = "oo" as in "room"

FURTHER READING

Andrewes, Antony. *The Greek Tyrants.* London: Hutchinson's University Library, 1956.

Bernal, Martin. *Black Athena: The Afroasiatic Roots of Classical Civilization.* East Brunswick, NJ: Rutgers University Press, 1987.

Boardman, John. *The Greeks Overseas: Their Early Colonies and Trade.* 4th ed. London: Thames & Hudson, 1989.

Burkett, Walter. *The Orientalizing Revolution: Near Eastern Influence on Greek Culture in the Early Archaic Period.* Cambridge, MA: Harvard University Press, 1992.

Burnett, Anne Pippin. *Three Archaic Poets: Archilochus, Alcaeus, Sappho.* London: Bristol Classical Press, 1998.

Dayton, J. C. *The Athletes of War: An Evaluation of the Agonistic Elements in Greek Warfare.* Toronto, ON: Edgar Kent, 2006.

Dover, Kenneth J. *Greek Homosexuality.* 2nd ed. Cambridge, MA: Harvard University Press, 1989.

Greenhalgh, P.A.L. *Early Greek Warfare: Horsemen and Chariots in the Homeric and Archaic Ages.* Cambridge: Cambridge University Press, 1973.

Gunter, Ann C. *Greek Art and the Orient.* Cambridge: Cambridge University Press, 2009.

Guthrie, William K. C. *The Greek Philosophers from Thales to Aristotle.* London/New York: Routledge, 1989.

Hammond, Nicholas G. L. *A History of Greece to 322 B.C.* 3rd ed. Oxford: Oxford University Press, 1986.

Hanson, Victor D. *Hoplites: The Classic Greek Battle Experience.* London: Routledge, 1991.

Lefkowitz, Mary, and Guy M. Rogers, eds. *Black Athena Revisited.* Chapel Hill: University of North Carolina Press, 1996.Morris, Sarah P. *The Black and White Style: Athens and Aigina in the Orientalizing Period.* New Haven, CT: Yale University Press, 1984.

Ostwald, M. *Oligarchia: The Development of a Constitutional Form in Ancient Greece.* Stuttgart, Germany: Steiner, 2000.

Pomeroy, Sarah, Stanley Burstein, Walter Donlan, and Jennifer Roberts. *Ancient Greece: A Political, Social, and Cultural History.* Oxford: Oxford University Press, 1998.

Ridgway, David. *The First Western Greeks.* Cambridge: Cambridge University Press, 1992.

Stewart, Andrew. *Art, Desire and the Body in Ancient Greece.* Cambridge: Cambridge University Press, 1997.

Woodard, Roger D. "Greek Dialects." In *The Ancient Languages of Europe,* edited by R. D. Woodard, pp. 51ff. Cambridge: Cambridge University Press, 2008.

CHAPTER 7

SPARTA, ATHENS, AND THE CLASSICAL AGE
(500–387 BCE)

By the end of the Archaic Age, ca. 500 BCE, the Greeks had become the greatest economic and even cultural force in the Mediterranean world. But politically they continued to be disunited and spent much of their time squabbling with each other. Up until this point, the Greeks had confronted no serious foreign threats and had been able to develop socially and politically without outside interference. But the following **Classical Age** of Greek history (500–323 BCE) brought the Greeks into conflict with the greatest power in the world, the Persian Empire. The Greeks later looked on their successful resistance to the Persians as their defining moment. By this time Sparta and Athens, moreover, had become the two most powerful Greek cities. During the rest of the century, competition between them eventually resulted in a ruinous war that benefited no one except the Persians and served only to weaken the Greeks. But at the same time, the Greeks created a level of cultural achievement known as the Classical Age that continues to be admired in the modern day.

THE SPARTAN WAY

Sparta was one of the Dorian city-states that had developed in the Peloponnesus during the Greek Dark Ages. Unlike other important Greek cities, it was inland, far from the sea. Sparta never engaged in trade and always retained a purely agricultural economy. Thus, when other Greek cities became wealthy through commerce, Sparta remained poor. The Spartans were so economically unsophisticated that for money they used cumbersome iron rods instead of coins. Sparta's military was based solely on its army, for it could not afford an expensive navy. The only way that the Spartans could expand their economy was by using their army to take land from their neighbors. As often was the case with farmers, the Spartans remained very conservative and were always wary of foreigners and new ideas.

The Good Rule of Sparta

According to Spartan tradition, about 700 BCE the Spartan lawgiver **Lycurgus** devised a constitution known as the **Great Rhetra** that established the uniquely Spartan system of life known as the *eunomia* ("**Good Rule**"). Given that Lycurgus is dated to a period before the system he supposedly devised had come into being, the attribution of the Rhetra to him might be doubted and would have been intended to provide it with an antiquity that gave its measures an unquestioned authority. The Rhetra was intended to create unity by eliminating the political importance of family-based units such as the phratry, by making all male citizens equal, and by focusing everyone's loyalty on the polis. The Spartan commitment to simplicity was reflected in the belief, for example, that Lycurgus had prohibited gold and silver coinage in an effort to curtail greed. Spartans were taught to speak in terse, pithy, ironic sentences, a speaking style that came to be known as "laconic" (from Laconia, the Spartan home territory).

Greece During the Classical Age

Sparta was the only Greek polis that retained its kings. According to Lycurgus' constitution, two kings were elected from the two leading aristocratic families, the Agaids and Eurypontids, by a vote of the male citizens. The kings alternated as chief magistrate, and in order to avoid disagreements when the army was on campaign, one or the other of the kings was required to remain in Sparta at all times. The kings were supervised by a group of five *ephoroi* ("overseers," or **ephors**) who were elected each year and managed the day-to-day activities of the city. The ephors also were in charge of foreign policy, so no war could be declared without their majority vote, and two of them went on campaign with the king to ensure that he did not exceed his authority. Every month, the kings swore to uphold the laws and the ephors to uphold the authority of the kings, but if the ephors believed that a king was violating his trust, they had the right to impeach him. The kings, therefore, were very aware of the need not to antagonize the ephors, and ultimately the ephors even challenged the authority of the kings.

The chief law-making body was the *gerousia* (from a word meaning "old men"), a Council of Elders that was the Spartan version of the *boulē*; along with the two kings it was composed of men over sixty years old elected by the citizen body for life, making it even more conservative than Councils in other cities. Recommendations of the *gerousia*, known as rhetras, were passed on to the *apella* (*ekklēsia* in other cities), an Assembly of all male Spartan citizens over thirty and presided over by an ephor. But the *apella* merely rubber-stamped these measures and had no true role in decision making, as made clear ca. 635 BCE by the poet Tyrtaeus, who wrote, "The kings, whose care is the lovely city of Sparta, shall have the first voice in council; and after them the men of older birth, the elders; and the men of the people shall give their assent to their just ordinances." The *gerousia* also served as a high court; it tried murder cases and had the power to execute, exile, or fine those found guilty. It even had the power to put the kings on trial. The powers of the kings, therefore, were greatly hampered by the ephors and the *gerousia*, and in many ways the primary responsibilities of the kings came to be to command the army and perform certain religious ceremonies.

Lycurgus established a very militaristic society that was designed solely to raise good soldiers. Whereas the soldiers of other Greek cities were essentially a citizen militia, drilling and practicing only in their spare time, the Spartans were professionals and spent their lives in military service. Like other Greek armies, the Spartan army fought as a phalanx about ten ranks deep. Along with the usual spear, shield, and other accoutrements, the Spartans favored a very short sword, not much larger than a dagger, for close combat. It was said that when a young Spartan complained to his mother about his sword being too short, she dismissively replied, "Then add a step ahead to it!" The Spartans were so confident in the army's ability to defend the city that they declined to build a wall. And this confidence was justified, for the city was not captured by a foreign enemy until 222 BCE.

Spartan Society

In the modern day, the term Spartan *refers to anything that does not have any frills.*

Boys were trained to be soldiers in a system known as the ***agogē***, or "upbringing." A child's participation in the *agogē* began at birth, when infants were inspected by the ephors. If they seemed unhealthy or malformed, they were abandoned to die on the slopes of neighboring Mt. Taÿgetus. Young children were taught not to be afraid of the dark and or be finicky about their food. Boys left home to begin their military training when they were seven years old. They were organized into *ilai* ("packs") and learned to fight in any kind of weather and terrain, to live off the land by stealing or foraging for whatever food was available, and not to complain. A typical story told of a Spartan boy who had stolen a fox. As he was walking along, holding the snarling animal at arm's length, he saw an adult Spartan man approaching him, and to avoid the disgrace of being apprehended having stolen the fox, he hid it under his tunic. In the course of a friendly conversation with the man, the boy had his innards torn apart by the fox and died, a paramount example of what it really meant to be Spartan.

When they reached the age of twenty, the young men would be elected into a *sussition* ("eating together"), a men's mess that also served as a Spartan army unit. The election was very serious business, because a single negative vote would mean that a man would not become a citizen. If that happened, he would become a sort of unperson, continuing to live in Sparta but having no place in the community. At thirty, after further seasoning, a young man became become one of the *homoioi*, or "equals," the full citizens of Sparta also known as **Spartiates**. At this point, the new Spartiate was able to take full control of a *klaros*, a plot of land, that had been assigned to him while still a child, making him economically independent and able to provide his contribution to the *sussition*, thus freeing him to concentrate on his military training. Men were encouraged to marry by the age of thirty in order to produce offspring to supply the Spartan army. Technically, they were not supposed to visit their fiancées before that time, but it was expected that they would sneak off to do so. They then were allowed to live at home but were liable to be called back into active service at any time until they were sixty, when they finally were allowed to retire. The most honored of the Spartan soldiers were the *hippeis*, a royal bodyguard of three hundred elite soldiers chosen annually from men who already had sons.

This kind of cradle-to-grave social system meant that Spartan society was very closed. It was impossible, under normal circumstances, for anyone not born as a Spartan citizen to become one. There were never more than about six thousand Spartan men, and as that number declined over the years due to incessant warfare and with no established means of creating new citizens, the Spartans' ability to maintain their viability as a strong city was challenged.

Spartan women were the most liberated women in Greece. Instead of wearing the swaddling clothing typical of other Greek women, they only wore a single tunic slit down the side, giving them the nickname "thigh-flaunters." They, too, were part of Lycurgus' militaristic system. Girls remained at home but were trained as athletes and learned to be as tough as the men. Unlike other Greek women, who often were married by fourteen, Spartan women usually did not marry until eighteen, an age that was considered more suitable for childbearing. They oversaw the household economies and were responsible for providing each Spartiate's contribution to his army mess. They were the only women in Greece who could inherit property; indeed, nearly half of the land in Sparta eventually belonged to women. Even though Spartan women, like other Greek women, could not hold public office, they were the only Greek women who appeared openly in public and even had a voice in matters of politics.

Spartan women had a reputation for fearlessness. In a work called "The Sayings of Spartan Women," the Greek writer Plutarch reported that a Spartan woman who was being sold as a slave was asked by her buyer what she knew how to do. "To be free," she answered. When he ordered her to do things not fitting for a free woman, she committed suicide. Spartan mothers promulgated the Spartan disdain for defeat. When a mother handed her son his shield before he went off to war, she told him, "Come back with this or on top of it."

IN THEIR OWN WORDS

THE EDUCATION OF SPARTAN WOMEN

The second-century CE Greek writer Plutarch composed a series of biographies of famous Romans and Greeks. His life of Lycurgus described the upbringing and role of Spartan women, which was quite different from that of women in other Greek cities.

In order to establish the good education of their youth, he went so far back as to take into consideration their very conception and birth, by regulating their marriages. He ordered the maidens to exercise themselves with wrestling, running, throwing, and casting the dart, to the end that the children they conceived might, in strong and healthy bodies, take firmer root and find better growth, and that they, with this greater vigor, might be the more able to undergo the pains of child-bearing. And in order that he might take away their excessive tenderness, and fear of exposure to the air, and all acquired womanishness, he ordered that the young women should go naked in the processions, as well as the young men, and dance, too, in that condition, at certain solemn feasts, singing certain songs, while the young men stood around, seeing and hearing them. On these occasions, they joked about those men who had misbehaved in the wars; and again sang praises for those who had done any gallant action, and by these means they inspired the younger men to emulate their glory. Nor was there anything shameful in this nakedness of the young women; it taught them simplicity and a care for good health, and gave them some taste of higher feelings, admitted as they thus were to the field of noble action and glory. Hence it was natural for them to think and speak as Gorgo, for example, the wife of [the Spartan king] Leonidas, is said to have done, when some foreign lady told her that the women of Lacedaemon were the only women in the world who could rule men; "With good reason," she said, "for we are the only women who give birth to men." These public processions of the maidens, and their appearing naked in their exercises and dancings, were incitements to marriage. But besides all this, to promote marriage yet more effectually, those men who continued bachelors were in a degree disfranchised by law, for they were excluded from the sight of those public processions in which the young men and maidens danced naked, and, in winter, the officers compelled them to march naked themselves round the marketplace, singing as they went a certain song to their own disgrace, that they justly suffered this punishment for disobeying the laws.

Being brought back dead was felt to be better than abandoning one's shield in order to escape alive. On one occasion when the Spartan army was away at war, a Greek general used the opportunity to attack the city. While the men debated whether to send the women to Crete for safety, a sword-bearing woman entered the *gerousia* and asked if the men expected the women to continue living if the city were captured. The women then fortified the city, and the young men defeated the invaders.

Spartan Foreign Policy

The reason for this military life was that Sparta had a very large unfree population, the **helots**, descendents of the peoples defeated when Sparta conquered Laconia and Messenia. Their legal status was between slave and free; on the one

In this painting by Edgar Degas (ca. 1860–1880), with Mt. Taÿgetus in the background, Spartan girls, wearing characteristic slit tunics, challenge Spartan boys during their physical training. The whole Spartan population had to be well trained to defend the Spartan way of life.

hand, they had no freedom of movement, but on the other hand they could not be arbitrarily sold to anyone else. Most helots worked in agriculture, tilling the *klaroi* (land allotments) that were assigned to Spartiates for their support. These helots were required to turn over a certain amount of produce in grain, olive oil, and wine but were allowed to keep the excess for their own sustenance, and some helots became quite prosperous, even being able to buy their freedom. In times of emergency, helots who volunteered for military service also could be freed. Helots also could serve as body servants, traders, and artisans. In addition, as a result either of personal desire or state policy, Spartan men often formed liaisons with helot women that produced male offspring, known as *mothakes*, who served in the Spartan army but did not become full Spartan citizens. Another source of additional manpower in the Spartan army was units recruited from the free *perioikoi* who dwelt in the Spartan uplands.

The Spartans were greatly outnumbered. Only about 5 percent of the total population was Spartan; about 15 percent were free noncitizens, and the remaining 80 percent were helots. As time went on, this disparity became even greater as the number of Spartiates fell and that of the helots rose. The Spartans kept the helots firmly under their thumbs: Plutarch also commented, "Those who were free were the most free anywhere, and those who were slaves were the most enslaved." The helots constantly chafed in Spartan servitude and were ready to revolt at a moment's notice. On one occasion, after an earthquake had leveled Sparta, the helots immediately rose in revolt. Only because one dazed Spartan had the presence of mind to sound the assembly trumpet did the Spartan discipline take over and permit the army to muster just in time to beat off the attack.

The primary goal of the Spartans was to keep the helots in their place. Every year, the ephors ritually declared war on the helots, reminding the Spartans of the potential dangers the helots posed. In their late teens, chosen Spartan men participated in the *krypteia* ("secret affair"), when in the fall the ephors declared ritual war on the helots and the young men went out to spy on the helots and were authorized to kill any of them who appeared disloyal or to have good leadership skills. This duty impressed on young Spartans the degree to which they were outnumbered and justified the sacrifices they had to make in the service of the city.

Fear of the helots had a direct effect on Spartan foreign policy. For one thing, the Spartans disliked sending their army very far away from home lest the helots take advantage of the absence to revolt. The Spartans' interests thus were limited primarily to the Peloponnesus, where they wanted to be the strongest power. They first accomplished this goal with the defeat of Argos in 546 at the Battle of Thyrea. The Spartans also preferred cities that had aristocratic or oligarchic governments and that kept power in the hands of a few, as opposed to tyrannies, which sought the support of the underprivileged. Thus, during the first half of the sixth century BCE, the Spartans took it upon themselves to expel tyrants from Corinth, Sicyon, and Megara. And the Spartans also organized the **Peloponnesian League**, an alliance of Greek cities in the Peloponnesus. Any member who was attacked could call on the help of the other members. As a result, the Spartans had a core of local allies to help them in case of a helot revolt.

THE RISE OF ATHENS

The territory of Athens, known as **Attica**, covered over a thousand square miles and in the mid-fifth century BCE had a total population of around four hundred thousand. It was second in size only to the territory controlled by Sparta. In some ways, such as controlling large territories, Athens and Sparta were similar, but in most ways, the two were opposites. The Athenians were Ionian

Greeks, descendents of the Mycenaeans, whereas the Spartans were Dorians. Unlike landlocked, agricultural Sparta, but like nearly all other Greek cities, Athens was located near the coast and developed an economy based heavily on trade. Whereas Sparta was poor, Athens was rich. The Spartans had a closed citizen body, whereas, at least for a time, Athens welcomed new citizens. Athens was walled, Sparta was not. Athens' military might lay less in its army than in its navy, which was funded by silver mines and large mercantile profits. Whereas Sparta kept its foreign policy interests close to home, the Athenians developed political interests throughout the Mediterranean. And whereas Sparta was exceptionally conservative, Athens developed the most liberal political ideology of all the Greek cities.

From Aristocracy to Oligarchy

With respect to its political evolution, Athens followed the usual Greek pattern. By 800 BCE the monarchy had been replaced by an aristocracy, in which only the aristocrats, known as *hippeis* from the word for "horse," who owned the best land, could participate in the government. Each year, nine archons were selected from among the aristocrats as chief magistrates. These included a head archon, who served as chief executive officer; the king archon, or chief priest; the polemarch, or war leader; and six thesmothetes, or "law-recorders." Originally, new archons were selected every ten years, but as of 683 BCE they were replaced annually, and the chief archon became an **eponymous** archon who gave his name to the year. Ex-archons became members of the **Areopagus** (named after its meeting place on the Hill of Ares), a Council that initiated legislation, supervised the conduct of the archons, served as a supreme court that tried serious crimes such as treason, and chose the archons. This meant, of course, that aristocrats were choosing the archons, and they only chose other aristocrats. All male citizens belonged to the *ekklēsia*, or **Assembly**, but all the Assembly could do was rubber-stamp by acclamation measures already passed by the Areopagus.

Things began to change as of about 700 BCE, when increasing engagement in trade, based largely on the production of olive oil, made Athens very wealthy. Because aristocrats tended to concentrate their interests on agriculture rather than trade, this led to the rise of a new moneyed merchant class. By 650 BCE, when all the Greek cities were developing hoplite armies, any nonaristocrat who could afford his own weapons was eligible to serve in the army. This created two new social classes, the *zeugitai* ("yoke-men," a reference to being yoked together in the phalanx), merchants and small farmers who could afford army service, and the **thetes**, the landless poor, who could not.

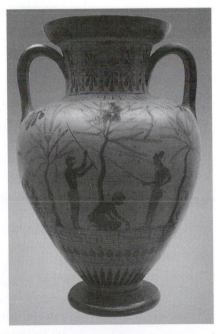

Athenians harvest olives, the mainstay of the Athenian agricultural economy, on a black-figure vase of ca. 520 BCE.

Athens was confronted by many kinds of strife. Aristocratic families competed with each other for power, wealth, and influence. Wealthy traders resented the aristocrats because, no matter how rich the traders became, they could never become aristocrats and therefore could never be part of the government. Immigrant foreigners who had settled in Athens, known as **metics**, also were unhappy, for citizenship was based on belonging to an Athenian family, phratry, and clan. This meant that there was no way for newcomers, and in particular immigrant merchants and craftspersons, to become citizens. The residents of different regions of the city—the traders of the coast, the aristocrats of the plain, and the rural poor of the hills—each pursued their own agendas. And another unhappy segment of the population was the small farmers, who had a hard time making ends meet. If they fell into debt to an aristocrat and could not repay the loan, they were in difficult straits. They usually could not sell their land because the land technically belonged to the phratry and was inalienable. So some debtors promised to repay a loan with one-sixth of their crops every year and became *hektemoroi*, or "one-sixth partners." But others, who had used their own bodies as collateral, could be sold into slavery. Nor were the urban poor, who needed jobs, always happy with aristocratic administration.

In 632 BCE, an ambitious aristocrat named Cylon attempted to establish himself as tyrant after his father-in-law, Theagenes, the tyrant of Megara, provided him with a bodyguard. When his attempt failed, he and his supporters took asylum in the temple of Athena on the city's acropolis. Although Cylon escaped, his supporters were tricked by the archons into leaving the temple and killed; the chief archon Megacles was later exiled for this heinous violation of sanctity.

Nine years later, in 621, hoping to avoid further unrest, the aristocrats responded to one of the sources of discontent by appointing an aristocratic lawgiver named Draco to write down the laws. Draco's law code attempted to focus loyalty on the city by distinguishing between intentional murder and involuntary homicide—something Near Eastern codes such as that of Hammurabi had not done—and taking the authority for judging murder cases out of the hands of families, which had led to **vendettas**, or blood feuds, and gave it to the Areopagus. In other regards, however, the written laws merely repeated the existing laws and protected the rights of aristocrats. For example, the power to enslave debtors was preserved. The harshness of the law code became legendary; it was said that when asked why so many crimes were punished by death, Draco responded that lesser crimes deserved it and that he could find no more severe penalty for serious crimes. The result was that discontent simply escalated.

The level of unrest became so great that the aristocrats realized that there would be a revolt if they did not do something more substantive. Therefore, in 594 they gave the archon Solon full authority to deal with the social and

Draco's code was so severe that the word Draconian still describes excessively harsh measures.

economic complaints. Solon's program of *seisaktheia*, or "Lifting of Burdens," abolished all of Draco's laws, except for the homicide court, and replaced them with more humane measures: for example, rather than death, the penalty for theft became ten times the value of an unrecovered item. Solon also outlawed debt slavery and set free those who had been enslaved for debt, allowed metics to become citizens, prohibited grain exports in order to preserve the food supply, and even established standard weights and measures to stimulate economic development. These reforms helped to deal with the economic unrest and went a long way toward making Athens into a major commercial center that could compete with Corinth.

The success of these measures led to Solon's appointment in 592 as Reformer of the Constitution with Full Powers to deal with political discontent. Solon's response was to do what many other Greek cities were doing—to change the form of government from an aristocracy to an oligarchy. To do so, he divided the Athenian citizen body into four groups based on their annual income as expressed in bushels of grain: (1) the *pentakosiomedimnoi*, or "500-bushel men," (2) the *hippeis*, a term that now applied not just to aristocrats but to anyone who earned 300–499 bushels annually, (3) the *zeugitai*, who made 200–299 bushels, and (4) the thetes, who earned less than 200 bushels. One's ability to participate in government now became based on one's wealth and financial contribution to the city. The *tamiai*, the treasurers of the temple of Athena, were chosen from the top group. Archons were chosen from the top two groups. The right to issue new legislation was removed from the Areopagus and given to a *boulē*, the Council of Four Hundred, made up of one hundred men from each of the four Ionic clans chosen from the top three groups. The Areopagus retained an overall "guardianship of the laws," the authority to try cases of murder and arson, and the oversight of certain religious rituals. All male citizens continued to serve as members of the Assembly, whose only right continued to be to approve by acclamation laws already passed by the Council of Four Hundred. But, in fairness to the poor for their lack of privileges, only the three top classes were taxed. Solon also introduced the *heliaia*, a popular court open to all citizens that heard appeals of magistrates' verdicts and protected the people from arbitrary actions of magistrates. The final court of appeal was the citizen Assembly.

Then, so as not to exercise further undue influence, Solon left Athens and traveled about the known world. During these travels he had a famous meeting with King Croesus of Lydia. When Croesus asked him who was the happiest man he had ever seen, rather than flattering Croesus by naming him, Solon gave a typically Greek response that "no one could be called truly happy until after they were dead," for who knew when disaster could strike, as indeed happened to Croesus when his kingdom was conquered by the Persians, and when repeating this story to the Persian king Cyrus saved his life. For this and other wise acts, Solon later was numbered among the Seven Wise Men of Greece.

From Oligarchy to Tyranny

In Athens' case, however, the transformation from aristocracy to oligarchy was not enough. Its large territory meant that it also had regional differences. Three groups had their own interests and agendas. The *eupatridai*, the rich, aristocratic, and conservative inhabitants of the *pediakē*, the rich agricultural Plain, wanted to retain an aristocratic constitution; the *agroikoi*, the poor farmers living in the *diakria*, or Hill, desired employment and greater democracy; and the *dēmiourgoi*, the liberal artisans, merchants, and sailors living on the *paralia*, or Coast, favored oligarchy, overseas ties, and increased trade.

These kinds of conflicts were the perfect breeding ground for tyranny. In 561 the polemarch Peisistratus, the leader of the Hill and a hero of the recent war to seize the island of Salamis from Megara, gained the support of new citizens and debtors, was voted a bodyguard, and seized power as tyrant. He was expelled in the following year but regained power in 556, again for just a year. In 546 BCE, he returned again, with a large force of mercenaries. To enhance popular support, he found a husky maiden, dressed her up as the goddess Athena, and rode in a chariot with her into Athens, preceded by heralds proclaiming, "O Athenians, welcome Peisistratus, who is accompanied into her city by Athena herself." Enough of the population went along with this farce, not to mention being overawed by the mercenaries, so that Peisistratus was installed as tyrant for good.

Rather than being oppressive, Peisistratus was an enlightened and largely popular tyrant. He claimed to be adhering to Solon's constitution; indeed, the philosopher Aristotle later wrote, "his administration was more like constitutional government than a tyranny." Archons continued to be appointed and then to serve on the Areopagus, even though it still was Peisistratus who chose them and other magistrates. His policy for staying in power was simple: keep the support of the coast and hill at any cost. Funded by silver mines at Laurion, he provided seed grain to small farmers, jobs to the poor, and loans to merchants. Under his rule, Athens captured the vase market from Corinth. He sent Miltiades the Elder to northwestern Anatolia to occupy the strategic Thracian Chersonese, now the Gallipoli peninsula, which controlled traffic through the Hellespont, the narrow strait between Anatolia and Europe, and thence to the Black Sea. To ensure that there were no unemployed malcontents, he sponsored building projects, including a temple to Athena, Apollo, and Zeus, and an aqueduct to bring fresh water to the city. And to instill pride in the city, he created the Dionysia, an annual festival in honor of Dionysus at which dramatic productions—tragedies and comedies—were performed. Nominally religious, the real purpose of such festivals was to keep the people happy. Typically, given the Greek competitive spirit, after the performances the top three plays were selected.

The Athenian festivals foreshadow the later Roman policy of "bread and circuses" to keep the people happy.

After Peisistratus' death in 527 BCE, he was succeeded by his sons Hippias and Hipparchus, who continued their father's policies. But it always was open season on tyrants, and the Athenian tyranny soon fell on hard times. In 514, as a result of a lover's quarrel, Hipparchus was assassinated by Harmodius and Aristogeiton. The two went down in history as the "liberators" and the "tyrannicides" and later served as models for others who assassinated illegal rulers. Hippias responded with a much more oppressive rule. In 510 BCE his opponents, including the exiled ex-archon **Cleisthenes**, the grandson of the tyrant Cleisthenes of Sicyon, allied themselves with the tyrant-hating Spartans. They seized Athens and expelled Hippias, who took refuge with the Persian king Darius. Athens then nominally returned to its oligarchic constitution but fell into political turmoil as the aristocrats Cleisthenes and Isagoras competed for authority. Isagoras recalled the Spartan king Cleomenes I, an old friend, and expelled Cleisthenes. But Isagoras proceeded to rule harshly, exiling hundreds of his opponents, restricting citizen rights, and even attempting to dissolve the *boulē*. The people revolted, blockaded Isagoras on the Acropolis, and forced him to leave the city. Three hundred of Isagoras' supporters were executed, and Cleisthenes was recalled, elected archon, and given the authority to rewrite the constitution.

After John Wilkes Booth assassinated Abraham Lincoln in 1865, he reputedly said, "Sic semper tyrannis" ("And thus always to tyrants"), recalling the Greek attitude toward tyrants.

The Evolution of Athenian Democracy

Like Solon, Cleisthenes' goal was to end factional strife and focus everyone's loyalty on the state. To achieve this, Cleisthenes devised a new form of government, which he called *isonomia* ("equal rights") but which later was called *dēmokratia*, or **democracy** ("rule by the people"). In order to break down geographical and familial loyalties, he allocated the Athenian citizen body among three regions, the *asty* (City), composed of craftsmen and merchants; the *paralia* (Coast), made up of sailors and fishermen; and the *mesogaion* (Interior), the aristocrats and other farmers. He then distributed the roughly 150 small territorial districts known as **demes** equally among the three regions, giving each region about 50 demes. Within each region, noncontiguous demes were assembled into ten *trittyes* ("thirds"), giving each *trittys* about five demes. To provide the basis for political organization, Cleisthenes then abandoned the four old Ionic clans and created ten new clans, each comprised of one *trittys* from each of the three regions. Each new clan, therefore, represented a cross-section of the geography and population of Athens, and it became much harder for regionalism or family factionalism to find expression in politics. Each clan had its own assembly and officers, and elected its own *stratēgos*, or general.

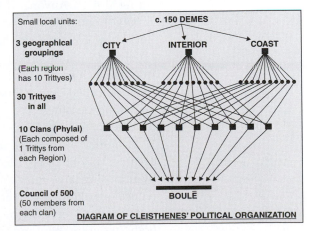

Small local units:

3 geographical groupings
(Each region has 10 Trittyes)

30 Trittyes in all

10 Clans (Phylai)
(Each composed of 1 Trittys from each Region)

Council of 500
(50 members from each clan)

c. 150 DEMES

CITY　　INTERIOR　　COAST

BOULĒ

DIAGRAM OF CLEISTHENES' POLITICAL ORGANIZATION

Under Cleisthenes' new constitution, all full citizens had an equal chance to serve in any number of capacities. The old Council of Four Hundred was replaced by a Council of Five Hundred, which met every day and to which each clan contributed a **prytany** consisting of fifty members. Members of the Council were chosen by lot from among citizens over thirty years of age to serve for one year. The Council proposed legislation to be presented to the Assembly and acquired the authority to oversee tax income, expenditures, and foreign relations. Each *prytany* ran the government for one-tenth of the year, and at any given time one-third of the *prytany* members, about seventeen men, lived in the *tholos*, or city hall, so someone was on duty all the time. The *prytany* on duty prepared the agenda for the daily meetings of the Council, and every day a new *epistatēs*, or president, was chosen by lot to preside over the meetings of the Council and, if it met, the Assembly. The archons likewise were chosen by lot and, as before, became members of the Areopagus, which initially retained judicial responsibilities. All male citizens over eighteen years of age were eligible to attend the meetings of the Assembly, which customarily met four times during each *prytany*. The Assembly had the right to pass, emend, or reject measures introduced by the Council, and it also could require the Council to introduce measures. It thus became the primary legislative body of Athens. The *heliaia*, meanwhile, now had juries with hundreds of members, selected from a panel of six thousand jurors. Initially, the *heliaia* judged cases involving accusations against archons and other public officials.

Because of its radical nature, the Athenian democracy was very cumbersome to operate. Meetings of the Assembly could have more than six thousand men present, each with an equal right to speak and introduce legislation. Discussion began with a herald asking, "Who wishes to speak?" Men over fifty spoke first, and no one under thirty could speak at all, although men as young as eighteen could attend. Also barred from speaking was anyone convicted of not supporting his parents, of throwing away his shield in battle, or of prostituting himself. Anyone advocating an unpopular opinion ran the risk of being simply shouted down, and voting was done by a show of hands, so everyone knew how everyone else had voted. The majority of the Assembly was made up of thetes, landless poor who often would vote for any measure that would improve their economic circumstances. Knowing this, good speakers with glib tongues, called demagogues, could sway the Assembly by introducing moneymaking measures. As a consequence, Athenian government sometimes was little better than mob rule.

A number of policies were introduced in order to keep the system manageable. For one thing, the introduction of frivolous legislation was inhibited by imposing large fines on those whose bills did not pass. And in order to reduce quarreling, each year the Assembly decided whether to hold an **ostracism**. Anyone receiving more that one-tenth of the vote of the entire citizen body, about six thousand votes, was ostracized and compelled to leave Athens

THE NATURE OF ATHENIAN DEMOCRACY

It has been suggested, on the basis of rather slim evidence, that Athens did not have the first Greek democracy. The best possibility of an earlier manifestation comes from the island of Chios, where an inscription dating to the first half of the sixth century BCE refers to a "boulē dēmosiē," or People's Council, consisting of two hundred members, and to officials called *dēmarchoi* ("leaders of the people") and *basileis* ("kings"). The details of this government, however, are too poorly known—in fact, it is not even clear that the inscription comes from Chios at all—and alternate suggestions include the possibility that the inscription refers not to a democracy but to an act of *sympoliteia,* the union of several villages into one city, or to another version of oligarchy. Thus, even though there may have been prior examples of cities that adopted various principles relating to democratic government, such as Solon's own occasional use of selection by lot, Athens remains not only as the earliest attested clear example of democracy but also as the city that took the concept of democracy the farthest.

Athenian democracy is known as a **radical democracy**, because all citizens were equally responsible for participating in the government. The writer Peter John Rhodes, in *Athenian Democracy,* for example, notes, "The classical [Athenian] democracy was based as far as possible on active involvement of the citizens." Radical democracy thus is much more participatory than American representative democracy, in which people elect representatives to serve in the government on their behalf. In the modern day, Athenian democracy has been held up as a model of ancient government; regarding democracy as one of several forms of government, Rhodes notes, "In the twentieth century it became the one of which almost all claim to approve, though they adjust the definition to fit their own particular regime."

Athenian democracy also was different from modern democracies in that, in spite of its reputation, it was much less "democratic." In the mid-fifth century BCE, for example, it has been estimated that Athens had a total population of about 400,000 persons. Of these, 40,000 were metics, or resident foreigners, and 200,000 were slaves. These individuals, some 60 percent of the population, had no citizenship rights at all. Of the remaining 160,000 citizens, about half, or 80,000, would have been women, and of the 80,000 male citizens, only about half, or about 40,000, would have been age eighteen or over and have had the right to attend the Assembly. Thus only about 10 percent of the Athenian population, never more than around 40,000 men, could actually participate in the democracy. This may not seem like many, but it was still a much greater percentage than in any nondemocratic Greek city. In Greek oligarchies, for example, only about 1 percent of the population had full participation rights. Thus the 6,000 maximum number of Spartiates was only 15 percent the size of the male citizen body of Athens.

---

for ten years. Ostracism became a way for crafty politicians to get rid of their enemies.

The Athenians also recognized that, selection by lot was not the best method for chosing military commanders. The office of *stratēgos*, which replaced the polemarch as general, therefore was the only elective Athenian office. The problem with this system, however, was that ambitious politicians without any military abilities got themselves elected as *stratēgos*, and Athens often was saddled with bad generals. In addition, quarrels could arise among the ten generals because each was of equal authority. Another problem with the

The Greek word for general, stratēgos, *gives us our word* strategy.

Athenian democracy was that, as it was initially established, not all Athenian citizens had the liberty to participate in government, which could be a very time-consuming business. Only the very rich or the unemployed had the leisure time to do so; other Athenians had to work for a living.

THE GREEKS AND PERSIA (547–465 BCE)

At the beginning of the fifth century BCE, the mighty Persian Empire still was expanding, and during the course of two wars the Persians attacked the Greek mainland. Led by Sparta and Athens, the Greeks were able to repel the invaders, and in the mind of the Greeks this was their finest hour. But instead of helping to unify the Greeks, the Greek victory only served to create jealousy and hostility between Athens and Sparta.

The Ionian Revolt

As the Persian Empire expanded westward during the second half of the sixth century BCE, it incorporated more and more Greeks. After the Persian conquest of Lydia in 547, for example, the Persians turned to reducing the Greek cities of Ionia. The Ionians appealed to Sparta, then the strongest city in Greece, but when the Spartans complained to Cyrus, the latter responded simply, "Who are the Spartans?" By 540, all the Ionian cities had fallen, and the Persians installed tyrants loyal to them. Initially, this policy worked, and during the attack by the Persian king **Darius** on the Scythians in 513, Histaeus, the tyrant of Miletus, persuaded the Greeks guarding the bridge over the Danube River not to destroy it and thus saved Darius and his army during their retreat.

But relations between the Persians and their Greek subjects soon turned sour. For one thing, given that Greeks considered all foreigners to be barbarians, no Greek could tolerate being ruled by any non-Greek for long. Nor were the Ionians happy about being ruled by unconstitutional tyrants whose first loyalty was to Persia. In 499 Aristagoras, tyrant of Miletus, persuaded Darius to attack the Greek island of Naxos. When the attack failed, Aristagoras knew that he would be held responsible, so the next year he resigned as tyrant and aroused the Ionians to revolt. The tyrants were expelled and replaced by democracies.

Realizing that they could not hope to hold out for long against the full might of the Persian Empire, the Ionians appealed for help to the mainland Greeks, but the Spartans declined, and the only response was twenty ships from Athens and five from Eretria. At first the rebels were successful. They captured and burned the Persian capital of Lydia, Sardis, but failed to capture the acropolis and had to retreat. At that point the Athenians and Eretrians lost interest and withdrew, leaving the Ionians to their fate. It took Darius until 495 to raise his army, which the Ionians could not hope to resist. The Greeks thus put their hope in their navy, but when the ships from Samos and

Lemnos deserted to the Persians in exchange for easy terms, the Ionian fleet was defeated at the Battle of Ladē and the revolt collapsed. Miletus was burned and its inhabitants deported to the frontiers of India. This was not a usual Persian practice, and it shows how angered the Persians had been by this revolt. But the Persians otherwise were lenient with the rebel cities, who were permitted to keep their democracies and were assessed a more moderate tribute, an indication that the Persians realized that their control over the Greek cities, which were on the very fringes of their empire, could never be very tight under any circumstances.

The First Persian Invasion of Greece

Many mainland Greeks now feared a Persian attack on the Greek mainland. In Athens, the radical democrat **Themistocles** was elected archon for 493; foreseeing the value of sea power in any confrontation with the Persians, he oversaw the construction of a fortified naval base on the coast at the Piraeus. In the same year, Miltiades, the grandson of Miltiades the Elder, arrived in Athens after being expelled from the Thracian Chersonese by the Persians. After being acquitted of a charge of being a tyrant, he was elected *stratēgos* of one of the ten clans. And the poet Phrynicus was convicted and fined for presenting a tragedy titled *The Taking of Miletus*, which reminded the Athenians of their disastrous involvement in the Ionian revolt. Public opinion was turning toward resisting the Persians.

Darius, meanwhile, citing the interference of Athens and Eretria, now had a justifiable pretext for attacking the mainland Greeks. In a cunning attempt to exploit Greek stasis, he sent ambassadors to the Greek cities demanding "earth and water," the Persian sign of surrender. Some Greek cities, such as Athens' rival Aegina, saw an alliance with the Persians as a means of gaining an advantage over their Greek rivals and immediately went over to the Persians. This gained them the nickname Medizers, or supporters of the Medes, for the chauvinistic Greeks could never tell the difference between Medes and Persians. Athens refused to surrender and when the Persian ambassadors arrived at Sparta, the Spartans simply killed the ambassadors by pitching them into a well and telling them to get the earth and water themselves. This was not good, for ambassadors were under the protection of the gods. The Greeks

On this red-figured Athenian plate from just before 500 BCE, a lightly protected Persian archer, no match for an armored Greek hoplite, runs to the left, looking back over his shoulder as he draws an arrow from his quiver.

knew the Persians were coming but made no plans for any joint resistance; it was every Greek city for itself.

The first Persian invasion of Greece came in 490 BCE. A Persian force of two hundred ships and twenty-five thousand soldiers sailed across the Aegean Sea and, after capturing several Greek islands, laid siege to Eretria. The city soon was betrayed and burned, and Athens was next on the menu. The Athenians sent to Sparta asking for help, but the Spartans were engaged in one of their many religious ceremonies and could not leave for several days; only the neighboring city of Plataea sent one thousand hoplites. The Persians landed on the plain at **Marathon**, about twenty-six miles from Athens on the opposite side of Attica, where the flat terrain would allow them to exploit their cavalry. The Athenians then debated whether they should hold out inside their walls or advance to meet the Persians in the field. Miltiades, who had had experience fighting the Persians in Asia Minor, convinced the Athenians that the Persians were beatable. As a result the Athenian army of ten thousand heavily armed hoplites advanced to meet the twenty-five thousand Persians. After waiting several days until a moment when the Persian horses were away being watered, Miltiades attacked.

Pheidippides' run to Athens inspired the race now known as the marathon.

In the ensuing **Battle of Marathon** it became clear how superior the trained Greek hoplites were to the much more lightly armed and inexperienced Persian infantrymen. The Athenians posted most of their troops on their flanks and allowed the Persians to push through the center of their line. The Athenian flanks then closed in behind the Persians. Completely outmaneuvered, the Persians fled to their ships, and many were cut down as they tried to escape. The final toll was 6,400 Persian dead compared with only 192 Athenians. It was a tremendous Athenian victory. The runner Pheidippides was sent to Athens with the news and fell in the marketplace, gasping *"nika"* ("victory"). The Spartans did not finally arrive until the next day and could only congratulate the Athenians and regret that they had not been there to share the glory. The Battle of Marathon had shown that the Persians were not invincible, but it was by no means the end of Persian attempts to conquer Greece. It was just the opening skirmish.

The Second Persian Invasion of Greece

Galley slaves, whom one often sees in the movies, were never used in antiquity.

The Greeks understood that it was only a matter of time before the Persians returned. When a huge new silver mine was discovered at Laurion, the Athenian *stratēgos* Themistocles convinced the Athenians to invest the money in two hundred **triremes** (warships with three banks of oars), giving Athens a new, state-of-the art navy. The thetes supported this measure because each ship was manned by 180 rowers recruited from thetes too poor to serve in the army and well paid by the government.

Persian plans to attack Greece in force were postponed when Darius died in 486 BCE. But his son Xerxes (486–465 BCE),, well aware that Persian kings were expected to expand the empire, soon took up the cause and began to prepare openly for a massive invasion of Greece by land and sea. In preparation,

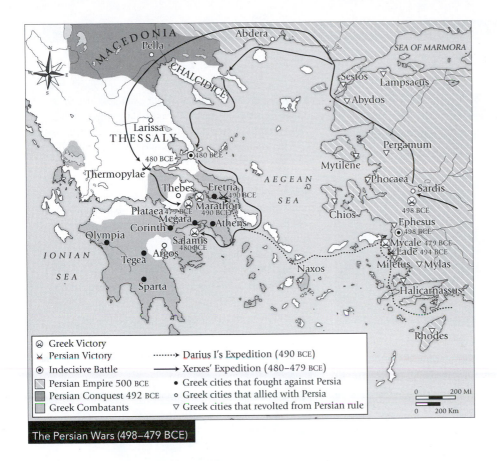

The Persian Wars (498–479 BCE)

a pontoon bridge over the Hellespont and a canal behind the dangerous promontory of Mt. Athos were constructed, leading to Greek claims that Xerxes "was trying to turn the sea into the land and the land into the sea." In 481, the southern Greek cities assembled in a Pan-Hellenic **Congress at Corinth** to discuss what to do; the northern cities, fearing that they would not be defended, declined to participate. The Greeks immediately began to quarrel over who would be in charge, and the powerful cities of Argos and Syracuse refused to participate because they could not share in the command.

Meanwhile, again hoping to benefit from the Greek inability to get along, Xerxes sent ambassadors to all the Greek cities except for Sparta and Athens, offering good treatment in exchange for earth and water. Xerxes' plan succeeded. About one-third of the Greek cities surrendered to the Persians. Another one-third decided to wait to see who was going to win. Ultimately, only Sparta and Athens and their trustworthy allies committed to resistance. The Athenians put aside old quarrels and allowed the Spartans the command not only on land, where the Spartans were undeniably supreme, but also at sea, because the Spartan allies refused to serve under an Athenian. Things looked bleak for the Greeks. Even the Delphic oracle appeared to favor the Persians, prophesying to

THE CONSTRUCTION OF A GREEK TRIREME

a modern attempt to reconstruct a full-size trireme at Piraeus outside Athens was made in the mid-1980s. The trireme, named the "Olympias," was built from Oregon pine and Virginia oak and had a bronze bow ram that weighed 200 kg. During an exercise in 1987 the ship was crewed by 170 volunteer male and female rowers and reached a speed of 9 knots (11 miles per hour), being able to make 180-degree turns in one minute within only two and a half ship-lengths. These results demonstrate that with an experienced crew, a trireme would have been truly formidable.

In 2004, the *Olympias* was used to transport the Olympic flame from the port of Keratsini to the main Athenian port at the Piraeus. The ship now is on exhibit in dry dock at the old Athenian port of Phaleron.

The Greek trireme was easily the most terrifying and effective warship of antiquity, requiring some 180 rowers organized at very close quarters into three banks of oars, one atop each other, to row effectively in perfect rhythm. In the past, many theories have been proposed about how the Greek trireme functioned, in part because there are so few surviving detailed descriptions or illustrations of triremes in action. In fact, only a single artifact, the so-called Lenormant relief, shown here, from Athens ca. 410 BCE, shows the middle section of a trireme being rowed.

Using the most up-to-date scholarly analyses, which suggested that the top tier of oars jutted over the side of the ship as a sort of outrigger arrangement and that the two lower tiers were inside the hull,

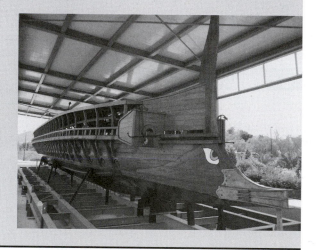

the Spartans that "they must lose their city or one of their kings" and advising the Athenians to "flee to the ends of the earth." When the Athenian ambassadors, afraid to return with such a negative response, asked for a second opinion, they were mysteriously told to "trust to their wooden walls."

In May of 480 BCE a Persian force numbering about 250,000 soldiers (the Athenian historian Herodotus' estimate of 1,700,000 is clearly exaggerated) and 1,200 warships advanced out of Anatolia by land and sea in the second Persian invasion of Greece. Accompanying Xerxes were a number of Greek exiles, including the sons of the Athenian tyrant Hippias and the Spartan king Demaratus, whose presence allowed Xerxes to claim that he was actually supporting Greek interests. Xerxes hoped simply to overwhelm the Greeks by sheer force of numbers. The Greeks realized that the best way to try to neutralize the Persian numerical superiority would be to fight in confined quarters.

As a first line of defense the Greeks chose a narrow pass in northern Greece between the mountains and the sea, only about one hundred yards wide, at **Thermopylae**, a Greek word meaning "hot gates." The Spartan king Leonidas, accompanied by the three hundred *hippeis* and seven thousand other Greeks, marched north to try to delay the Persian advance. It was said that as the Spartans prepared to meet the Persian attack on the pass, a local farmer attempted to frighten one of the Spartan soldiers by saying that the sky would go dark when the Persian archers loosed their arrows. The Spartan bravely replied, "Well, then, we'll get to fight in the shade." The **Battle of Thermopylae** began with an initial Persian failure to break the Spartan line. Eventually, Xerxes sent the flower of his army, the Persian immortals, against the Spartans holding the pass. They, too, were repulsed by the well-trained Spartans, and Xerxes began to despair of ever getting his army through. But then the Greek traitor Ephialtes offered to show the Persians a mountain trail around behind the Spartans. Betrayed, the Spartans were surrounded. But even then the Persians could not defeat them. Eventually, Xerxes called off his infantry and ordered his archers to send volleys of arrows onto the Spartans until all were dead. King Leonidas was killed, and the oracle's prophecy thus was fulfilled. The Greeks later erected an epitaph to the three hundred Spartans that read, "Stranger, go tell the Spartans that we lie here, obeying their orders." At just about the same time as Thermopylae, moreover, the elements also conspired to reduce the Persian forces when storms twice destroyed one hundred Persian warships as they attempted to negotiate the rocky eastern coast of Greece.

The Persians then advanced south, and all the cities of central Greece capitulated. The Greek opposition withdrew to a line of defense across the Isthmus of Corinth, leaving Athens undefended. The Athenians withdrew their population just off the coast to the island of **Salamis**, and Athens was captured without a fight and burned in retaliation for the burning of Sardis. The Greeks then debated their next step. The Peloponnesians favored withdrawing the Greek fleet to defend the Peloponnesus, but the Athenian general Themistocles, by threatening to withdraw the Athenian fleet and population and flee to Sicily, convinced the Greeks to resist the Persian fleet at Salamis. He also sent a secret message to Xerxes advising him that the demoralized Greeks were about to try to escape. Xerxes, believing this ruse and seeing this as his chance to destroy Greek naval power, ordered an attack.

In the ensuing **Battle of Salamis**, the Persian ships had to sail through the narrow strait between Salamis and the mainland in order to come to grips with the Greeks.. Seated on a specially constructed high point, Xerxes watched

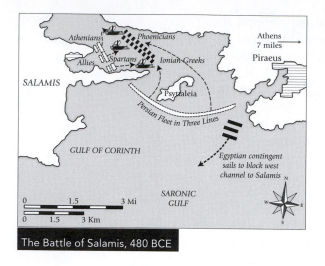

Athenians
Phoenicians
Athens
7 miles
Piraeus
Allies
Spartans
Ionian Greeks
SALAMIS
Psytaleia
Persian Fleet in Three Lines
GULF OF CORINTH
Egyptian contingent
sails to block west
channel to Salamis
0   1.5   3 Mi
0   1.5   3 Km
SARONIC
GULF

The Battle of Salamis, 480 BCE

the well-drilled Greek ships pick off the Persians one by one. When the ships rammed each other, heavily armed Greek marines stormed aboard the Persian ships and made short work of the Persian archers. The Greeks won a spectacular victory, losing only forty ships to the Persians' two hundred, and it now was clear what the oracle had meant by "wooden walls." Having lost the better part of his navy, Xerxes' communications back to Persia were severely compromised. Xerxes therefore left his army in Greece, sent his fleet to defend the Hellespont, and returned to Persia by land. Meanwhile, in the west, on the same day as the Battle of Salamis, it was said, Gelon, tyrant of Syracuse, defeated the Persians' ally Carthage at the Battle of Himera in Sicily.

In the following year, the Persian army, still numbering about seventy-five thousand Persians and Greeks, faced forty thousand hoplites of Sparta, Athens, and their allies at the Battle of Plataea. The Spartans, led by King Pausanias, stood stoically under Persian arrow fire until it was their turn to go into action. At about the same time, or even, again, on the same day, the Athenians destroyed the Persian fleet at the Battle of Mycale on the Ionian coast, and the Ionian cities again revolted. These Persian defeats marked the last attempt of the Persians to conquer the Greek mainland or anyplace else, for that matter. Later in their history, the Greeks considered the defeat of the Persians to have been their finest hour, forgetting that most of them had not participated. The Greek victories left the Greeks with the upper hand and Sparta and Athens as the most powerful cities in Greece.

After the Persian defeat, many Greeks, and especially the Athenians, wanted to follow up on their success. But almost immediately, Greek dissension interfered with any ability to cooperate. There had been little enough unity in the wars themselves, and once the Persian invasion had been defeated, the fundamental inability of the Greeks to get along became increasingly apparent. The unity between Athens and Sparta began to crumble as each city pursued its ambition to become the most powerful and influential polis in Greece. From the very beginning, the Athenians were worried about Spartan ambitions. A year after Plataea, while Themistocles was negotiating at Sparta about future strategy, the Athenians hastily refortified the city after the Spartans had demanded they not do so. The Athenians, using their naval strength, wanted to carry the attack to the Persians and to set free the cities of Ionia, but the Spartans, leery of fighting too far from home, favored Ionian emigration somewhere else. And within Athens and Sparta themselves, political intrigues emerged as politicians attempted to increase their own status at the expense of their rivals. In 476, Pausanias, after further successes against the Persians, was executed on trumped-up charges of intrigue with Persia and conspiring with the helots. And the Athenian hero Themistocles was convicted by his enemies of collaboration with the Persians and ostracized; he fled in exile to Xerxes, who made him governor of several Anatolian cities. And many other able Greeks, hounded out of their own cities by political intrigue, likewise were welcomed into exile by the Persians. In these cases, it was clear that the Greek rule for success was not to be too successful.

Athens and the Delian League

In 478, after Sparta had withdrawn from the naval offensive, Athens organized a league of Greek cities to continue the fight against Persia with the goal of setting free the Ionian Greeks. Headquartered on the island of Delos, it now is known as the **Delian League**. Its members contributed either money or military forces, especially warships; most opted for the simpler monetary contributions. Under Athens' leadership, the Persians were repeatedly defeated. They first were expelled from Thrace and the north Aegean. Then, in 466, the Athenian general Cimon destroyed 350 Persian ships at the Battle of the Eurymedon River in southern Anatolia. In a similar engagement near Cyprus in 460, the Persians lost another 200 ships.

As the power of Athens increased, Athens began to treat the members of the League as if they were Athenian subjects. Contributions intended for the league were used to pay not only for the Athenian navy but also for the expensive Athenian democracy. When the island city of Naxos attempted to resign in 471, the city was captured, its walls were torn down, and it was forced to accept a democratic constitution. It was clear that league membership now was mandatory. Other cities that attempted to resign were equally harshly treated. Thasos, in the northern Aegean, was captured in 463 after a two-year siege and forced to give up its walls, navy, and silver mines. Free-will contributions now became compulsory **tribute.** What had begun as a voluntary league of equals had become an **Athenian Empire**.

THE GOLDEN AGE OF ATHENS (465–431 BCE)

The fifth century BCE is generally known as the "Golden Age of Greece" and more specifically as the "**Golden Age of Athens**," for it was Athens that most represented the cultural developments of this period. Using the profits from its empire, Athens manifested a massive amount of architectural construction and literary productivity. But at the same time, the Athenians' overweening sense of chauvinism and entitlement led them into ever greater and more dangerous foreign confrontations, confrontations that eventually would destroy the city's political authority and economic prosperity.

The Radicalization of Athens

As Athens' prestige had increased, the Spartans had grown ever more jealous, and there were increasingly hard feelings between the two cities. In 464, disaster struck Sparta; an earthquake leveled the city, and the helots immediately revolted. Honoring the former alliance, the Athenians immediately sent soldiers in support of the Spartans. In 462, the Spartans again appealed to Athens for help, and after an acrimonious debate in which the land-owning conservatives, led by Cimon, argued that the Athenians should abide by their old treaty with Sparta and the radical democrats, led by the *stratēgos* Ephialtes and his ally **Pericles**, pointed to the natural rivalry between the two cities, the Athenians decided to send Cimon and four thousand hoplites. But the Spartans, fearing that the democratic Athenians might take the side of the helots, dismissed the Athenians as soon as they arrived. Humiliated, Cimon returned to Athens, and the conservatives were completely disgraced.

Under Ephialtes, the Athenian democracy became even more radical. Nearly all power was removed from the Areopagus—which was the last bastion of oligarchic and aristocratic sentiment because archons still had to belong to the two top economic classes—and transferred to the Council, the Assembly, and the *heliaia*. The right to try cases involving *eisangelia* (impeachment), *dokimasia* (ascertaining eligibility for public service), and *euthynai* (the examination of the accounts of ex-officials) was transferred to the Council of Five Hundred. The *heliaia* took over the legal role of the Areopagus and became the high court of Athens, judging the constitutionality of laws and almost all civil and criminal cases. There were no lawyers, and litigants were expected to present their own cases, although it was acceptable to read speeches written by rhetoricians and legal experts. Soon afterward, the archonship was opened up to *zeugitai* and then even to thetes. The Areopagus thus lost its elite status and was reduced to trying murder and arson cases and overseeing some vestigial religious duties. In addition, in order to give all citizens an equal opportunity to participate, members of the *heliaia* now were paid to serve, at the rate of an obol, a small silver coin worth one-sixth of a drachm, per day. Soon afterward, members of the *boulē* also were paid, and by the end of the century so were those attending the Assembly.

Roman marble copy of an Athenian bust of Pericles, in the helmet of a *stratēgos*, of 440–430 BCE.

The Athenian democracy therefore became very expensive to operate. In addition to being paid for participating in government, the thetes also looked for income from work on building projects and service in the navy and rarely saw a spending project that they did not like. This meant attempting to squeeze even more out of the empire and engaging in ill-conceived military campaigns. And this helps to explain why Athenian-style democracy was so rarely adopted by Greek city-states not under the influence of Athens: not only was there always the threat of having the populace swayed by glib-tongued but irresponsible demagogues, but it also was simply too expensive to operate. Only an economic powerhouse like Athens could afford it, and Athens continually was looking for ways to raise money to pay for it.

In 461, Cimon was ostracized for acting as a "friend of Sparta," Ephialtes was assassinated, and the radical democrats, now led by Pericles, were left in firm control of the city. Pericles' mother was Agariste, the niece of Cleisthenes, and his mistress Aspasia was not at all like other Athenian women, for she appeared regularly in public, spoke her mind, and was greatly envied for her political influence. Pericles held the office of *stratēgos* every year but one for the next thirty-two years, implemented a policy of "power to the people," and kept the unruly Athenian populace under control by giving it everything it wanted, including full employment and extravagant entertainments. But Pericles' policies also carried with them the seeds of the city's destruction, for the Athenians privileged short-term gains over long-term strategies for survival. For example, in 451 BCE, with Athenian citizenship carrying ever greater personal benefits, Pericles gained the passage of the restrictive **Athenian Citizenship Law**, according to which both of a citizen's parents had to be citizens, not just the father, as had been customary. This had the result of lessening the numbers of citizens at the very time that Athens' expanding horizons required greater manpower.

LEGACY OF ANTIQUITY

How are modern concepts of sea power similar to those of the Greeks?

Athens Overreaches Itself

Militarily, Athens expanded its efforts to increase its political prestige among the Greeks and to raise additional funds. At the same time that Athenian campaigns against Persia became more and more extravagant, Athens also attempted to extend its influence on the Greek mainland, a policy that brought the city into direct contact with Sparta. By making an alliance with Argos, Sparta's main rival in the Peloponnesus, by inducing Sparta's ally Megara to form an alliance with Athens instead, and by giving sanctuary to refugee helots, Athens challenged the Spartans on their home turf. In 457, Athens expanded northwest and overran all of Boeotia except for **Thebes** and forced the cities into the Delian League. And in the same year, Athens conquered the powerful island city of Aegina, which was reduced to a tribute-paying ally. In addition, the Athenians prudently built the five-mile "long walls" running down to the port of the Piraeus, allowing them access to the sea even if the city were under attack by land.

But Athens now was seriously overextended. In 455, after an initial Athenian attack on Cyprus, an Athenian invasion of Egypt failed miserably: as many as twenty thousand sailors and soldiers and one hundred ships were lost. And in

451 another Athenian attack on Cyprus likewise achieved nothing. In 454, in the midst of these difficulties, Athens moved the treasury of the Delian League from Delos to Athens, where the income from the league became just one more component of the income of Athens and was duly recorded in the **Athenian Tribute Lists**. The Athenian Empire on the Greek mainland also collapsed. In a five-year truce with Sparta in 451, Athens gave up its alliance with Argos. In 448, the Boeotians revolted and soon regained their independence; under the leadership of Thebes, a **Boeotian League** was created. Megara also revolted and rejoined the Peloponnesian League. The Spartans even invaded Attica but then withdrew amid rumors of bribery by Pericles.

As a result of these and other setbacks, the Athenians were completely exhausted and decided to cut their losses and recover their strength. In 448, hostilities between the Athenians and Persians finally came to an end with the Peace of Callias, named after the Athenian ambassador to Persia. Both sides simply recognized the status quo. The Persians gave up their claim to the Greek cities of Ionia, and Athens acknowledged Persian control of Cyprus and Egypt.

Once the war with Persia had ended, many cities of the Delian League stopped making their contributions. When Athens forced them to continue paying, the transition of the Delian League into an Athenian Empire was complete. And on the mainland, in 446, Athens and Sparta entered a Thirty Years' Truce, during which the fighting would stop, at least for a while. Athens and Sparta recognized each other's alliances, but any residual goodwill between the two cities now had been lost, and an objective observer would have realized that the truce settled none of the underlying rivalries and hard feelings between the two cities.

Periclean Athens

Once Athens had extricated itself from its foreign military adventures, things looked much better for the city. The proceeds of the empire made it very wealthy. This period became known as the **Golden Age of Athens** (465–431 BCE). It was a time of extravagant building projects. In 449, Pericles introduced a law allocating 9,000 talents of silver to finance a massive building program, especially on the **Acropolis**, the high point of Athens. The creation of Periclean Athens not only glorified the city but also gave work to multitudes of thetes who were left unemployed as the Athenian military escapades wound down.

Construction of the **Parthenon**, a new temple of Athena Parthenos (Athena as a virgin) to replace the one that had been destroyed by the Persians, cost 469 silver talents and began in 447. Built in the Doric style, with seventeen columns on the long sides and eight on the short, all except the terracotta roof was of fine-grained white Pentelic marble from Mt. Pentelikos near Athens. It

A PICTURE IS WORTH A THOUSAND WORDS

THE ATHENIAN TRIBUTE LISTS

One-sixtieth of all the tribute from the Delian League was dedicated to the Temple of Athena in Athens, and these contributions were recorded by the *tamiai* (treasurers of Athena) on stone tablets, now known as the Athenian Tribute Lists, erected from 454, the year the treasury of the Delian League was moved to Athens, until 415 BCE. Each list presented the name of the contributor and the amount, in silver drachms (there were 120 drachms in a mina and 7200 in a talent, which weighed 67 lb.). The numbers are presented in the acrophonic number system, in which the number is represented by the first letter of the word for the number. Hence, Π (pi) or Γ (gamma) for *pentē* or *gentē* (an early form of *pentē*, analogous to Latin *quinque*, 5), Δ (delta) for *deka* (10), Η (eta) for *hekaton* (100), and X (chi) for *xilioi* (1,000), along with the obvious single stroke I for "one." There also were combinations, such as delta-pi = 15, or pi-delta = 5 times 10 = 50. Thus, in this section, the amount dedicated from ΓΡΥΝΕΙΕΣ = Gryneion was 50 + 5 + 5 = 60 drachms (from a total assessment of 3,600 drachms), that from Isindos was 15 + 5 + 4 = 24 drachms (from 1,440 total); that from Karpathos was 50 + 100 + 100 + 100 = 350 drachms (from 21,000 total), and so on.

Although each of the yearly lists as it survives is incomplete, enough of the different yearly versions survive so that detailed reconstructions can be made of the members of the Delian League at any given time and the amounts of their contributions. As of 425 BCE, there were about three hundred members of the league, allocated among seven geographical districts: Ionia, Hellespont, Thrace, Caria (southern Anatolia), the Islands, Pontus (the Black Sea), and Acte (the northern Aegean Sea). The payments were due in March, and any arrears were collected by warships in the summer. The total income from the League was about 400 talents per year, and other sources of income, such as taxes on metics and silver mines, brought the annual Athenian income to about 1,000 talents (about 67,000 lb.) of silver. Given that one trireme cost about three talents per year to operate, the sixty-ship standing navy would have eaten up 180 talents of this income, with much of the rest going to pay for overseas officials and garrison troops, shipyard workers, building projects, the costs of the democracy, and the reserve fund kept in the temple of Athena.

was 221 feet long by 101 wide and thus adhered to the standard 9:4 golden section ratio for Greek temples. The work was supervised by the sculptor **Phidias**, who designed the gold-plated statue of Athena housed in the *naos*, or central sanctuary, of the temple. Phidias' pupils created the many marble sculptures that also decorated the temple. The ninety-two metopes (sculptured blocks running under the eaves of the temple) depicted the war between the gods and giants on the east side, battles with Amazons on the west, battles with centaurs on the south, and the Trojan War on the north. The 115 plaques of the frieze, relief sculptures along the top of the outer wall of the *naos*, portrayed scenes from the processions of the summer Panathenaic festival, the most solemn religious ceremony of the Athenian year, celebrating the birthday of Athena. The eastern pediment (the triangular area above the main entrance) depicted the birth of Athena, and the western one showed the mythological conflict between Athena and Poseidon over who would have the right to give his or her name to the city.

In the 430s BCE, the Propylaea, a monumental gateway to the Acropolis, was built. It consisted of a central building flanked by two lateral wings with rows of Doric and Ionic columns. Behind the Propylaea stood Phidias' thirty-foot-tall bronze statue of Athena Promachos (Athena as a warrior goddess). Subsequently, two more temples were added. Ca. 420, the Erechtheum was

The Acropolis of Athens as of ca. 420 BCE, with the Propylaea in the foreground, the tiny Temple of Athena Nike at the right, the Parthenon at top right, and the Erechtheum at the left. The older temple of Athena stood between the Erechtheum and the Parthenon.

constructed in the Ionic style. The *naos* was divided into two sections, one honoring Athena Polias (Athena as guardian of the city) and the other Poseidon Erechtheus, a combination of Poseidon and a legendary early Athenian king. The Erechtheum also included the famous porch of the caryatids, with columns shaped as maidens. And at the same time the small temple of Athena Nike (Athena as bringer of victory) was built, likewise in the Ionic order. A statue of Athena Nike holding a helmet stood in the small *naos* (only five by five meters). Collectively, these monuments made the Acropolis the most famous temple complex of the ancient world.

THE PELOPONNESIAN WAR (431–387 BCE)

The fundamental incompatibilities between Sparta and Athens—one a conservative agricultural land-based monarchy-cum-oligarchy, the other a radical mercantile sea-based democracy—eventually manifested themselves in escalating degrees of open warfare. The resultant Peloponnesian War eventually involved nearly all of the major powers of the Mediterranean and Near Eastern worlds and resulted only in the Greeks destroying themselves as a major world power.

The Buildup to War

The Athenians were far from the most popular Greeks of the fifth century BCE. The cost of the Athenian democracy came at a great cost that was borne largely by the members of the Delian League, who were unhappy not only because of the financial burdens but also because of their loss of autonomy. In addition, the Athenians simply could not resist interfering in the affairs of other Greek cities, and especially cities allied with Sparta. In the course of gratuitous meddling in a war between Miletus and Samos in 440, Athens captured Samos, tore down its walls, took hostages, destroyed its fleet, and imposed a penalty of 1,276 silver talents. In addition, now that Athens was prohibited by the terms of the truce with Sparta from expansion on the Greek mainland, the city looked for new opportunities on the northern Aegean coast, establishing a colony ca. 435 BCE at Amphipolis in close proximity to rich silver mines.

Athens' most serious offense in the eyes of the Spartans was the city's renewed interference in mainland affairs. In 434, during a war between Corinth and the western island city of Corcyra, Athens allied itself with Corcyra and gained a base in western Greece. Two years later, the Athenians issued the Megarian Decree, which forbade Athens' trading rival Megara from trading in markets controlled by Athens, effectively shutting Megara out of the entire Athenian Empire. At this, Corinth, Megara, and Aegina (which still was paying tribute to Athens) all complained to Sparta. In 432, the Peloponnesian League voted for war against Athens on the grounds that Athens had violated the Thirty Years' Truce by interfering with Spartan allies, and Sparta demanded that Athens cancel the Megarian Decree and grant autonomy to Aegina. If they were to preserve

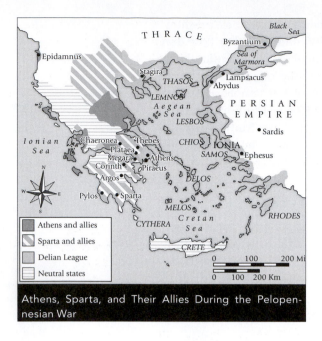

Athens, Sparta, and Their Allies During the Pelopennesian War

the status of Athens among the Greeks, this was a demand that Pericles and the Athenians could not possible accept, and in 431 the Athenians voted for war. Thus began the **Peloponnesian War**, the most disastrous conflict the Greeks would ever fight.

The Peloponnesian War was, in effect, the first world war. On one side were Sparta and her allies, representing conservativism and oligarchy, which included not only most of the Peloponnesian cities except for Argos but also Boeotia, led by the city of Thebes, and the powerful Sicilian city of Syracuse. The Spartans, with their scant financial resources, could raise an army of fifty thousand hoplites but only about one hundred ships. Athens, representing liberalism and democracy, was supported by the Athenian Empire of some three hundred cities. With seven thousand talents of silver in reserve in addition to its annual income, Athens could muster about thirty thousand hoplites and over four hundred ships. In addition, a third party that was very interested in the outcome of the war was Persia, which was waiting in the wings, not willing actually to fight but ready to use its hoarded wealth to gain its most important goal: the recovery of the Greek cities of Ionia.

The Archidamian War

The first phase of the war, the **Archidamian War** (431–421 BCE), is named after the Spartan king Archidamus, whose initial strategy was to lead the Spartan army, which had uncontested superiority on land, into Attica each year and destroy the crops and olive trees. Pericles' policy, on the other hand, was to withdraw the Athenian population behind their walls and refuse to fight until the Spartans withdrew their forces in the fall, for, lacking effective siege technology, the Spartans (and all the Greeks) had no way to capture a walled city except by surrender or starvation. Pericles hoped simply to hold out by supplying the city by sea, keeping control over the empire, and using Athens' control of the sea to raid the Peloponnesus. Neither side, therefore, had a policy that was designed actually to win the war, nor, indeed, had either side actually wanted the war: the Spartans were reluctant warriors, having been drawn in only by the appeals of their allies, and the Athenians, who were the injured party, having suffered the initial attack by Sparta, had not wanted war, either; all Pericles hoped to do was to avoid dangerous encounters.

The literary evidence suggests that the plague was typhus, but recent DNA analysis indicates typhoid fever.

The situation immediately turned worse for the Athenians because they had not counted on a terrible plague caused by the unsanitary conditions resulting from so many people crowded into the city. According to the historian Thucydides, an unsuccessful Athenian general who had been exiled in the late 420s, "Many who were in perfect health, all in a moment and without any apparent reason, were seized with illness. The breath became unnatural and fetid. The disease moved to the stomach and brought on vomiting of bile. The body broke out in pustules and ulcers. The internal fever was intense; sufferers could not bear to have on the least garment and insisted on being naked. They were tormented by unceasing thirst and could not sleep. Either they died on the seventh or ninth day, or the disease then descended into the bowels and produced violent ulceration and severe diarrhea. Severe exhaustion then usually carried them off. If a person got over the worst, the illness then often attacked the genitals and the fingers and toes. Some escaped with the loss of these, others with the loss of their eyes." One of the victims carried off by the plague was Pericles himself, and after his death, Athenian demagogues egged the Athenian mob into increasingly extravagant campaigns. His successor, Cleon, had worked as a tanner and provided an example of how the democracy allowed less privileged, and less experienced, persons to rise to the top.

The war progressed without any major decisions. The Spartans stopped invading Attica for fear of the plague and turned on Athens' allies. In an instance of *aspondos polemos*, after the Spartans captured Plataea in 427, the defenders were simply executed. In the north, the Spartans allied themselves with the Macedonians and captured Amphipolis in 424, cutting the Athenians off from their sources of silver and ship timber and killing the Athenian general Cleon. On the other hand, in 425 the Athenians trapped and captured 120 Spartiates on the island of Sphacteria, the first time that a Spartan army had ever surrendered, a huge blow to Spartan morale. The Athenians threatened to execute their captives if the Spartans again invaded Attica.

By 421, both sides only wanted peace. In Athens, the usually democratic small farmers were concerned about the regular destruction of their crops, and in Sparta there was a great concern with the decline in the citizen population and a possible helot revolt. Sparta and Athens therefore concluded the Peace of Nicias, named after the Athenian general who negotiated for Athens. The terms were simple: the Spartan prisoners were returned, Athens lost Plataea but gained a port city from Megara, and otherwise there was a return to the status quo at the beginning of the war. The war therefore settled nothing, and left Sparta's Peloponnesian allies unhappy at having gained nothing after ten years of warfare.

The Expedition Against Syracuse

Thus began a period of cold war, during which the Athenians were led by the opportunist Alcibiades, who, after orchestrating the failure of a further settlement with Sparta, was elected *stratēgos* and sought to renew the war solely as a

Herms, sacred to the messenger god Hermes, were used as milestones and boundary markers in Attica and were thought to bring good luck. When many of them were mutilated just before the departure of the fleet for Syracuse, it was seen as a very bad sign.

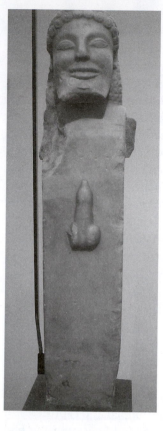

means of furthering his personal ambitions. By making an alliance with Argos and other cities in the Peloponnesus, Alcibiades struck directly at Spartan insecurities. In order to oppose this unexpected coalition, the Spartan king Agis II mobilized not only the entire army of Spartiates but also the *neodamodais*, a force of freed helots. At the Battle of Mantinea in 418 BCE, the Athenians, Argives, and their allies were completely routed, and Spartan morale and reputation for invincibility were restored.

In spite of this setback, Athens continued to pursue its imperialist ambitions. In 416, the Athenians laid claim to the island city of Melos, which hitherto had avoided entanglement in the conflict, demanding that it join the Delian League and pay tribute to Athens. The Melian Dialogue reported by the historian Thucydides exemplifies Athens' arrogant "might makes right" policy at this time: the Athenians argued that they were being "humanitarian" by offering the Melians the chance to surrender rather than undergoing a siege they could not win. When the Melians refused, the Athenians captured the city with the assistance of Melian traitors and made good their threats, killing all the men and selling the women and children into slavery.

Meanwhile, a new opportunity for Alcibiades to pursue extravagant military adventures had appeared in 415, when the Sicilian city of Segesta asked to hire sixty Athenian warships for use in a local conflict. Alcibiades saw this as a foot in the door and tantalized the Athenians with visions of greater sources of income, an even larger empire in Sicily and southern Italy, and the easy conquest of the powerful Sicilian city of Syracuse. In an attempt to dissuade the Athenians from such a rash plan, the pacifist Nicias proposed sending an impossibly large force, over 100 warships, 130 supply ships, 5,000 heavily armed hoplites, and 1,300 light-armed troops—the largest Greek expedition ever attempted—on the assumption that such an absurd plan would be voted down. But Nicias had miscalculated. The Athenian thetes, always looking out for their own self-interest, not only adopted the proposal but also put Alcibiades and Nicias in command. Bad omens appeared before the expedition could set sail when the **herms**, sacred stones with erect phalluses set up around Athens, were mutilated. Alcibiades was falsely accused by his enemies of the crime, but only after he had arrived, with all of his supporters, in Sicily was he ordered to return to Athens to stand trial. Knowing that he would be convicted, he fled, leaving the overly cautious Nicias in charge of the expedition. Back in Athens, Alcibiades was indeed condemned to death in absentia and thus took refuge with the Spartans, whom he now advised regarding the best way to defeat Athens.

Initially, the Athenians caught Syracuse by surprise. Few had believed that the Athenians would be so foolish as to attack, and Syracuse was almost completely besieged before the city appealed to Sparta, which in 414 BCE sent a single Spartiate, Gylippus, to organize the Syracusan defenses. Syracuse gradually gained the upper hand, and Athens sent massive reinforcements. But to no avail. In 413 BCE, after several naval defeats, the Athenians attempted a hopeless overland retreat. The entire Athenian force was either killed or captured, and over the course of the expedition Athens lost a total of two hundred ships, thirty thousand sailors, and ten thousand hoplites. Athens had sustained not only a crippling loss to its ability to wage war but also a devastating blow to its international prestige, and many members of the Delian League now revolted.

The Decelean War

As if this were not bad enough for Athens, the Spartans in the same year had renewed the land war in Greece in what is known as the **Decelean War** (413–404 BCE). Here, the Spartans showed uncharacteristic flashes of imagination. For one thing, they had taken the advice of the traitor Alcibiades and fortified the village of Decelea in northern Attica, thus establishing a permanent military base from which they could attack and harass the Athenians, preventing both agriculture and the exploitation of the Laurion silver mines. At the same time, they realized that to defeat Athens they would need a navy. Navies were expensive, and Sparta was poor. The Spartans therefore made an alliance with Persia. In exchange for Persian money, the Spartans agreed to let Persia reoccupy Ionia if they won the war. But the Spartan allies were slow to mobilize their forces, and Persian support was slow in forthcoming, and the Spartans thus lost the chance to make a quick strike at the Athenian Empire. The Athenians, meanwhile, desperately tried to restore their army, rebuild their fleet, and train new sailors. In a moment of prudence at the beginning of the war, Athens had set aside special funds and one hundred ships to be used only in an emergency; these resources were now released.

The situation became so bad at Athens, with increasing resentment among the conservative well-to-do against what they considered to be the irresponsible behavior of the mob that controlled the democracy, that in 411 the democracy was overthrown and replaced by an oligarchy of the wealthy known as The Four Hundred, who briefly replaced the democratically chosen Council of Four Hundred. But a few months later, after oligarchic extremists not only proposed making peace with Sparta but also even may have planned to surrender the city, the Four Hundred were overthrown and replaced with The Five Thousand, an equally short-lived, more inclusive oligarchy that even included *zeugitai*. A similar revolution at Samos, where the Athenian fleet was stationed, failed, and the democrats there swore to defend the democracy and continue the war against Sparta. The Samian fleet was persuaded by the general Thrasybulus to support the restoration of Alcibiades, who boasted that he would be able to turn Persian support from Sparta to Athens. At Athens, The Five Thousand were quickly overthrown, and the democracy was restored.

At sea, the war continued. In 411, Athens finally received some good news when, at Cynossema, an Athenian fleet under Thrasybulus narrowly defeated a Spartan fleet that had seized the Hellespont and blocked the Athenians from access to the grain-producing lands of the Black Sea, on which Athens had become increasingly dependent as the empire crumbled. A Spartan victory here, with Athens controlled by an oligarchy favorable to the Spartans and the city still reeling from the defeat at Syracuse, almost certainly would have ended the war, but Athens now had time to recover its strength and continue to fight. Indeed, in 410, in naval battles at Abydos and Cyzicus under the Athenian generals Alcibiades, Thrasybulus, and Theramenes, the Spartans lost a total of 110 ships, and Sparta, now weary itself of the long war and hating to fight so far from home, offered peace based on the status quo. But the Athenians, full of themselves once again after their recent victories, refused the overture, so Sparta rebuilt its fleet and the war continued.

Athens proceeded to win additional naval victories and recover much of its empire. These and other Athenian victories allowed Alcibiades to return to Athens in triumph in 407. All charges against him were dropped, and he was elected *stratēgos*. But at the same time Athens continued to be its own worst enemy. In 406, for example, after a great naval victory over Sparta at the Arginusae Islands, near the island of Lesbos, in which the Athenians destroyed seventy-five Spartan warships, a severe storm came up, preventing the Athenian admirals from recovering shipwrecked, wounded, and dead Athenians. Six admirals were tried and executed. It was never more clear how fickle the Athenian mob could be and how the Athenians repeatedly worked against their own best interests. The Spartans again offered to make peace based on the status quo, this time offering to surrender the fort at Decelea, and once again the Athenians refused.

Alcibiades, now in command of the Athenian navy, badly needed another victory to secure his position. And meanwhile, the command of the Spartan fleet had passed to Lysander, who, although born of a poor Spartan family, had risen to high military command. Unlike other Spartan commanders, who were generally blunt-spoken if not just plain rude, Lysander was an excellent diplomat and had obtained funding from Cyrus the Younger, the son of the Persian king Darius II (423–404 BCE) and the new Persian commander in Anatolia. At the Battle of Notium, near Ephesus, in 406 BCE, Lysander lured the Athenian fleet into battle while Alcibiades was away and destroyed twenty-two Athenian ships. Even though this was a relatively minor setback, Alcibiades, aware of the unpredictability of the Athenian electorate, went into voluntary exile, and the remaining experienced Athenian admirals, such as Theramenes and Thrasybulus, were indeed dismissed. The Athenians thus were deprived of nearly all their effective commanders.

In 404, Lysander made renewed attacks on the Hellespont, Athens' lifeline to the grain of the Black Sea. The Athenian fleet under the admiral Conon could not allow this and tried unsuccessfully to lure the Spartans into battle. Only after the Athenians had beached their warships one day and gone off to forage for food did the Spartans attack, thus changing a sea battle into a land battle. At the ensuing Battle of Aegospotami, 150 Athenian ships were destroyed, and three thousand captured sailors were subsequently executed. Conon escaped to Cyprus with a few ships and took refuge with the Persians. Athens thus lost all capability to resist the Spartans.

With the destruction of the Athenian fleet, the Spartans now were free to deliver the final blow to Athens. Later in 404, the Spartan king Pausanias besieged the city by land, while Lysander blockaded it by sea. Starved into submission, the Athenians had no choice but to agree to Spartan terms for surrender: they tore down the long walls to the Piraeus, gave up the Athenian Empire, gave up all but twelve of their remaining ships, and were compelled to obey Spartan foreign policy. Given the hard feelings that had characterized the war, the Spartans were surprisingly lenient, and it was only through the negotiating skills of the general Theramenes that the city was not destroyed and the population enslaved, as had in fact been recommended by the city of Thebes in retaliation for Athenian interference in Boeotia. And on the other side of the Aegean, the Greek cities of Ionia were abandoned to the Persians.

The Spartans also forced the Athenians to abandon their democracy and to accept an oligarchic government, which later was known as The Thirty and was led by Theramenes and Critias, a former supporter of Alcibiades. Some Athenians had their wealth confiscated, hundreds were executed by being made to drink hemlock, and nearly all lost their citizenship rights. Meanwhile, Athenian democrats who had been occupying the empire returned home, and the general Thrasybulus led a democratic revolution in which the forces of the oligarchs were twice defeated and Critias was killed. In 403 BCE the oligarchs recalled Pausanias and another battle ended with a narrow Spartan victory, but the Spartan losses were so great that Pausanias agreed to a restoration of the democracy, no doubt believing that Athens had been so greatly weakened that it would never again prove a threat to Sparta. The end result of the Peloponnesian War and its immediate aftermath, therefore, was that both Sparta and Athens had exhausted many of their resources after some twenty-seven years and more of warfare. Athens was completely ruined, having lost its empire, its financial resources, its walls, and tens of thousands of its inhabitants. Sparta, too, had suffered citizen losses that it could not replace and now was reduced to not much more than two thousand citizens. The one thing that all the cities of Greece desperately needed was time to recover their strength. But this was not to be.

The Aftermath of the War

The end of the Peloponnesian War meant that Sparta now was the strongest city in Greece. This put the Spartans in an unaccustomed and awkward position of dominance known as the **Spartan Hegemony** (404–371 BCE). During the course of the war, all that most Spartans had wanted to do was bring an end to hostilities and return to cultivating their purely local interests. But their new role made this difficult, as Sparta, having usurped the international role of Athens, now was continually called on to intervene in matters far from home.

When the Persians began to reoccupy Ionia, the Ionians appealed to Sparta for help, and Sparta was put in a bind. In order to uphold their new status as the leaders of the Greeks, the Spartans felt compelled to abandon their agreement with Persia and send an army to Ionia. In 400, the Spartans invaded Anatolia under King Agesilaus, whose campaigns took him well into the Persian Empire. In the Aegean Sea and Ionia, the Spartans replaced Athenian-style democracies with ten-man oligarchies strengthened by Spartan military governors called *harmosts*. Back in Greece, the wars soon resumed. In 395, allies of Sparta dissatisfied with Spartan high-handedness revolted and withdrew from the Peloponnesian League. With Persian support, Athens began to rebuild its walls, and Thebes, Corinth, Argos, and Athens banded together in an anti-Spartan coalition and launched the **Corinthian War** (395–387 BCE). Agesilaus was recalled to Greece, and in 394 the Spartans defeated all comers at the Battle of Coronea, where only the Thebans stood up to the Spartan attack.

The Persians, meanwhile, had used their inexhaustible financial resources to construct a fleet of three hundred warships. The Athenian exile Conon was placed in command, and in 394, at the Battle of Cnidus, off the southwestern coast of Anatolia, the entire Spartan fleet was captured or destroyed, and the Persians proceeded to reoccupy the Greek cities of Ionia and the Aegean. Conon then sailed to Athens and, with Persian funding, completed the rebuilding of the long walls, meaning that Athens once again could defend itself and was able to regain its position as the greatest sea power in Greece.

The war between Athens and Sparta was thus renewed, but neither side was strong enough to raise a large force. Both sides were exhausted and only wanted peace, but neither would allow the other to make the terms. Finally, the Persian king Artaxerxes II (404–359 BCE) was prevailed on to act as an arbitrator to settle the disputes between Sparta and Athens. At a conference at Sparta in 387, the King's Peace, also known as the Peace of

Antalcidas after the Spartan ambassador, was issued by Persian ambassadors who stated, according to the historian Xenophon, "King Artaxerxes thinks it just that the cities in Asia should belong to him, and that the other Greek cities, both small and great, should be left independent. But whichever of the two parties does not accept this peace, upon them I will make war, both by land and by sea, with ships and with money." Thus, after over forty years of almost incessant warfare, the Greeks had only weakened themselves. The only one to gain anything from the conflict was the king of Persia. The previous century had demonstrated the basic inability of the Greeks to unite, even when faced with the most serious threats. The Greeks were their own worst enemy.

Greek Society and Culture: Unity in Disunity

At the same time that the Greeks were destroying themselves politically, they were engaged in their most brilliant period of artistic and literary production, and it would be in this regard that they would have their greatest impact on the future. Because of the funding opportunities that were available, many of the new developments took place in Athens. The discussions of philosophers turned from the nature of the universe to the nature of human interactions. Itinerant educators known as **sophists** (from *sophos*, or "wise"), who claimed to be able to teach *arētē* (virtue), charged a fee to teach methods of effective argumentation and believed not only that it was possible to find the true answer to any question by means of reasoned dialogue but also that being able to make a good argument was an end in itself. In order to do this, sophists had to be able to argue both sides of a question and "to make the weaker argument appear to be the stronger." This led some, such as the philosopher **Plato**, who taught in Athens between ca. 390 and 350 BCE, to view the sophists as being rather immoral for denying the existence of absolute truth. It probably would be closer to the truth, however, to say that sophists acknowledged the relativity of human culture, believed that questions of ethics and morality needed to be discussed in their own contexts, and accepted that there could be more than one side to a question. Sophists could earn a very good living in a city such as Athens because it was crucially important for individuals to be able to make good arguments both in political debates in the Assembly and in private lawsuits, in which litigants had to represent themselves. Indeed, it has been suggested that the sophists' focus on the ability to make effective decisions based on reasoned arguments contributed to the growth of Athenian democracy.

Socrates, the most famous user of sophistic rhetoric (although not a sophist himself because he accepted no fees and made no promises), taught in Athens during the Peloponnesian War. Socrates left no writings of his own, so his teachings have come down to us secondhand through the writings of his pupil Plato, who criticized what he called the sophists' desire to seek power

A mosaic of the early first century BCE from Pompeii depicts Plato's Academy.

rather than truth. Plato established a school of philosophy known as the Academy, named after a grove of olive trees dedicated to Athena just outside Athens. His written works, many of which re-create discussions supposedly held by Socrates, indicate that Socrates' teaching involved attempts to understand universal moral concepts that all humans comprehend. In order to understand these concepts and the human interactions that they affect, Socrates asked questions such as, "What is justice?" His question-and-answer way of attempting to gain insight into these questions is still known as the Socratic Method. Socrates also rather simplistically assumed that if one could by this method define concepts such as "virtue," then one would necessarily be virtuous and that lack of virtue was simply the result of ignorance.

Plato, meanwhile, taught that the world is a very imperfect reflection of the perfect forms that exist in the perfect static universe and that humans should strive to copy this perfection. His own attempt to create perfection in the real world was manifested in his most influential book, *The Republic*, which presented his model of a perfect human society that lacked the constant strife that was so characteristic of the Greeks. Everyone living in Plato's Republic had a fixed place, assigned by the government, that could not be changed. Some people were soldiers, some were workers, and the rulers, of course, were the philosophers, who could just as easily be women as men.

Plato's desire to create a perfect society was conditioned by his disillusionment with the way the Athenian democracy treated his mentor Socrates. In 399 BCE, Socrates had been charged with corrupting the youth and atheism, that is, teaching that the gods did not exist. What probably really troubled the Athenians, however, was Socrates' penchant for teaching people to question their beliefs about such issues as the proper role of government. In the uneasy times after the end of the Peloponnesian War, these were touchy issues. At his trial before the *heliaia*, instead of respectfully defending himself, Socrates insulted the jury by using the occasion to present his teachings. He was convicted by a vote of by vote of 280 to 220, and the death sentence was imposed by an even greater vote, probably in the hopes even of his supporters that he would follow the usual course of action by those sentenced to death and go into exile. Socrates refused even to make an appeal, which might well have been granted, stating that Athens could kill his physical body but never his soul. On the appointed day, with his friends and pupils around him, Socrates carried out his own execution by drinking hemlock, and a fatal numbness crept up from his legs to his vital organs.

The Golden Age of Athens also marked the high point of Greek **drama**, which had two forms, tragedy and comedy. The difference, simply put, was that a tragedy had a sad ending, whereas a comedy had a happy ending. In the context of Athenian democracy, tragedy and comedy dealt with important matters, but tragedies did so in a very serious way, and comedies did so light-heartedly. The underlying theme of tragedies was the necessity of obeying the will of the gods and adhering to traditional values; anyone who failed to do so suffered grievously. The plots of tragedies were drawn from the myths and legends that all the Greeks knew so well. That meant, of course, that the audience of a Greek tragedy already knew the ending. The dramatic tension resulted from the way in which the characters in the play were inexorably drawn to discover what their awful fate was going to be. In a series of three plays known as the *Oresteia*, which won first prize at the Dionysia in 458 BCE, the playwright Aeschylus dramatized the revenge taken by Orestes for the betrayal and murder of his father, the king of Mycenae, Agamemnon, by his wife Clytemnestra and her lover Aegisthus. Sophocles told how the king of Thebes Oedipus married his mother Jocasta and blinded himself. And Euripides described how the eastern enchantress Medea got even with her wayward husband, the Greek hero Jason, by killing her own children, and how Agave unwittingly tore her own son Pentheus, king of Thebes, to pieces. Because of their serious nature, tragedies were not viewed as an effective vehicle for discussing Athenian politics. In 493, as already seen, the poet Phrynicus produced a tragedy called *The Fall of Miletus* that detailed the Persian suppression of the Ionian Revolt the year before. The Athenians were so distressed at being reminded of this disaster that Phrynicus was fined 1,000 drachms and the play was forbidden from being again performed.

Comedies, on the other hand, were risque and full of sexual innuendo. Because they purportedly were not meant to be taken seriously, comedies provided a safety valve whereby current events and politically incorrect ideas that were on peoples' minds could be safely engaged with. On several occasions, the expression of what were considered to be absurdly hilarious ideas about women served as a blind for engaging more serious matters. For example, in 411 BCE, in the middle of the Peloponnesian War, the poet **Aristophanes** produced the *Lysistrata*, in which the women of Athens, Sparta, and other Greek cities, led by the Athenian Lysistrata, crafted a plan for ending the war: they all would refuse to have sex with their husbands until the men stopped fighting. It would not have been safe to express an unpatriotic desire about ending the war openly in the Assembly, but in a comedy, this delicate topic could be brought up. And in a play called the *Ecclesiazusae*

All parts of conium maculatum, or poison hemlock, contain a fast-acting alkaloid neurotoxin, similar to curare, that causes muscular paralysis and eventual respiratory collapse.

Because Greek tragedies deal with timeless themes of human emotion, faith, and morality, they still are meaningful in the modern day, whereas the focus on contemporary issues in comedy strikes less of a chord with contemporary audiences.

CROSS-CULTURAL CONNECTIONS

How was the function of Greek literature different from that of Near Eastern literature?

("The Assemblywomen"), presented in 390 BCE, Aristophanes alluded to dissatisfaction with Athenian government after the resumption of the war with Sparta with a comedy that had Athenian women disguising themselves as men and taking control of the government, arguing, among other things, "that they are mothers and will therefore spare the blood of our soldiers." The women then created an even more extreme form of democracy in which the government confiscated all property and fed and housed every Athenian and every woman could sleep with every man—on condition that the woman slept with an unattractive man first and vice versa. The message here was simple: something had to change. In addition, no public figure was safe from being lampooned. In one play of Aristophanes, for example, Socrates was depicted as living in "cloud cuckoo-land."

Another literary genre for which the Greeks of this period are very well known was history, which was invented by Greeks who were the first to see that by studying the past we can learn from it and not only avoid the mistakes of the past but also anticipate how similar circumstances could lead to similar results in the future. The three most influential early Greek historians worked in Athens. During the 440s, **Herodotus**, who was given the nickname "the father of history" by the Romans, composed a massive history based on the Persian Wars, which he thought was the most important event in Greek history. Even though he portrayed the war as a conflict between civilization and barbarism, he nevertheless painted a very sympathetic picture of Persian and Egyptian culture. He was the first known historian to use the "historical method," in which historians gather evidence, make hypotheses, and reach conclusions by testing their hypotheses against the most reliable evidence. But Herodotus' historical model was also rather unsophisticated. Like the writers of tragedy, he believed that fundamentally the gods were responsible for what happened and that they punished the wicked and rewarded the good. For Herodotus, there was a clear distinction between right and wrong, with no middle ground.

In early modern times, some of Herodotus' extraordinary reports about the customs of non-Greek peoples, many now known to have been based on fact, also led to his being called "the father of lies."

Thucydides, an Athenian general who had been exiled after losing a battle, wrote a history of the Peloponnesian War. In his view of history, the gods had nothing to do with making history; people did, and they were responsible for their own actions. For Thucydides, the most fundamental factor in making history happen was a struggle for power. He believed that there were underlying patterns of cause and effect in events, and it was his hope that a critical study of the factors surrounding the Peloponnesian War could help to prevent future wars. Thucydides also took a more sophistic approach than Herodotus and suggested that every quarrel had two sides, without any absolute right or wrong.

Following Thucydides, historical writing was represented by the Xenophon, another Athenian general who later took to writing history. Xenophon picked up the history of Greece after the Peloponnesian War. Unlike either Herodotus or Thucydides, however, Xenophon's history is primarily straight narrative—first this happened, then this, then this—without any attempt to make events fit a particular model. Most subsequent historians followed the narrative style of Xenophon.

LOOKING AHEAD

The events of the fifth century demonstrated that no matter how cultured the Greeks became, when it came to politics they were their own worst enemies. In the years after the Peloponnesian War, the Greeks continued to bicker among themselves. The increasingly powerful kings of Macedonia soon would assert their authority over Greece and bring the age of the polis to an end.

SUMMARY OF GREEK TERMINOLOGY

agogē   The "upbringing" of Spartan boys

agroikoi   Poor farmers

apella   The Assembly of all male Spartan full citizens

aspondos polemos   Unconditional warfare

asty   The "city" region of Athens

boulē   Political "Council" of Greek cities that initiated legislation

dēmiourgoi   Craftsmen and merchants

dēmokratia   "Rule by the People"; democracy

dokimasia   Athenian process for determining eligibility for office

ephoroi   Ephors, "overseers"; Spartan magistrates

eisangelia   Athenian impeachment procedure

ekklēsia   Political Assembly of all male full citizens of a Greek polis

epistatēs   President of Athens who served for one day

eunomia   The "Good Rule" established at Sparta by Lycurgus

eupatridai   Another term for aristocrats

euthynai   Examination of the accounts of Athenian officials

genos   "Extended family," a unit of Greek society

gerousia   Spartan council of elders

hektemoroi   Athenians sharecroppers who owed one-sixth of their crop

heliaia   An Athenian law court

hippeis   Aristocrats; also Athenians making 300–499 bushels of grain

homoioi   "Equals," the full Spartan citizens

ilai   "Packs" of Spartan boys training to be soldiers

klaros   An inalienable plot of farmland

krypteia   Spartan secret service used to terrorize the helots

mesogaion   The "interior" region of Athens

mothakes   Sons of Spartiates and helot women who served in the Spartan army

naos   Central sanctuary of a temple

neodamodais   Freed helots who fought for Sparta

paralia   The coast region of Athens

pediakē   The rich agricultural "plain" of Athens

diakria   The "hill" region of Athens

phratry   "Brotherhood," a unit of Greek society

pentakosiomedimnoi   Athenians with an annual income of over five hundred bushels of grain

phylē, phylai   "Clan," a unit of Greek society

polis   An independent Greek city state

prytany   Fifty-man unit of Athenian government

sussition   Dining group, and army unit, of Spartan men

seisaktheia   The "Lifting of Burdens" implemented by Solon

stratēgos   General

tamiai   Treasurers of the temple of Athena

thetes   Landless citizens; Athenians making less than two hundred bushels of grain

tholos   City hall of Athens *trittys*

trittyes   An Athenian "third," with equal parts city, coast, and hill

zeugitai   Hoplites; also Athenians making 200–299 bushels of grain

FURTHER READING

Bagnall, Nigel. *The Peloponnesian War: Athens, Sparta, and the Struggle for Greece.* New York: Thomas Dunne Books, 2006.

Bodel, John. *Epigraphic Evidence: Ancient History from Inscriptions.* London: Routledge, 2001.

Hammond, Nicholas G. L. *A History of Greece to 322 b.c.* 3rd ed. Oxford: Oxford University Press, 1986.

Hanson, Victor Davis. *A War Like No Other: How the Athenians and Spartans Fought the Peloponnesian War.* New York: Random House, 2005.

Just, Roger. *Women in Athenian Law and Life.* London: Routledge, 1989.

Kagan, Donald. *The Peace of Nicias and the Sicilian Expedition.* Ithaca, NY: Cornell University Press, 1981.

Kallet, Lisa. *Money and the Corrosion of Power in Thucydides: The Sicilian Expedition and Its Aftermath.* Berkeley: University of California Press, 2001.

Keuls, Eva C. *The Reign of the Phallus: Sexual Politics in Ancient Athens.* New York: Harper & Row, 1985.

Krentz, Peter. *The Thirty at Athens.* Ithaca, NY: Cornell University Press, 1982.

Lazenby, J. F. *The Defence of Greece 490–479 BC.* **Oxford:** Aris & Phillips, 1993.

McGregor, Malcolm F. *The Athenians and Their Empire.* Vancouver: University of British Columbia Press, 1987.

Meritt, Benjamin Dean, H. T. Wade-Gery, and Malcolm F. McGregor, *The Athenian Tribute Lists,* 4 vols. Cambridge, MA: Harvard University Press, 1939–1953.

Pomeroy, Sarah, Stanley Burstein, Walter Donlan, and Jennifer Roberts, *Ancient Greece: A Political, Social, and Cultural History.* Oxford: Oxford University Press, 1998.

Raaflaub, Kurt A., Josiah Ober, and Robert Wallace, eds. *Origins of Democracy in Ancient Greece.* Berkeley: University of California Press, 2008.

Reeder, Ellen. *Pandora: Women in Classical Greece.* Princeton, NJ: Princeton University Press, 1995.

Rhodes, Peter John, *Athenian Democracy* (Oxford Univ. Press: New York, 2004), pp. 3, 6.

Robinson, Eric W., ed. *Ancient Greek Democracy: Readings and Sources.* Bognor Regis, UK: Wiley-Blackwell, 2004.

CHAPTER 8

ALEXANDER THE GREAT AND THE HELLENISTIC AGE
(387–31 BCE)

During the Classical Age (500–323 BCE), the Greeks had the opportunity to become the preeminent military and political power of the Mediterranean world, but their inability to get along eventually weakened them and left them open to attack from outside. Unity was finally imposed on Greece by the kingdom of Macedon to the north, whose king Alexander the Great conquered the known world from Greece to beyond the Indus River. But after Alexander's death, his empire crumbled and was divided among his generals. Alexander's conquests opened Greece up to much greater interaction with the eastern world and brought about the Hellenistic Age (323–31 BCE), during which Greek and eastern culture merged to create a composite culture that incorporated aspects of both worlds in the spheres of literature, religion, science, and technology.

GREECE AFTER THE PELOPONNESIAN WAR (387–336 BCE)

During the last phase of the Classical Age, after the King's Peace of 387 BCE, the Greek cities continued to bicker among themselves. By then, the cities of Sparta and Athens had been so weakened that other cities, such as Thebes, had the opportunity to lay claim to greater authority, and conflict continued. Eventually the northern kingdom of Macedon, whose king, Philip II, had created the most powerful army on earth, imposed its authority over Greece.

Greek Mercenaries

One result of the end of the Peloponnesian War in 404 BCE had been that many Greek hoplites were out of work. This significance of this was not lost on the Persians, who long had realized the superiority of Greek hoplites over Persian infantry. The Persians therefore instituted a policy of hiring Greek mercenaries to man the armies of their western satrapies. Large numbers of Greeks were recruited into Persian service, and especially into the army of Cyrus the Younger, who in 401 BCE revolted against his brother, Artaxerxes II of Persia. Even though the Greeks defeated Artaxerxes near Babylon in the Battle of Cynaxa, Cyrus was killed. In "The March Upcountry," one of the greatest adventure stories of all time, the historian Xenophon, who was one of the mercenary commanders, described how the Greeks then fought their way to the Black Sea. Their cry when they finally reached it, *"Thalatta, thalatta"* ("The sea, the sea"), is one of the most memorable scenes in historical writing. As Greek cities suffered increasing losses of citizens as a result of constant warfare during the first half of the fourth century BCE, it became more and more common for them, too, to hire mercenaries rather than to risk further citizen casualties.

The Rise and Fall of Thebes

The decline of Sparta and Athens as major powers gave other Greek cities an opportunity to pursue their own ambitions. The most important of these was Thebes, which dominated the cities of Boeotia, northwest of Athens, and thus became a strong regional power, as Athens had done in Attica and Sparta in the Peloponnesus. The Thebans already had held their own against Sparta in the Corinthian War, but the city was disadvantaged by the King's Peace, for its hegemony over the Boeotian League was dissolved when the peace declared all the Greek cities independent. In addition, in 382 the Spartans unexpectedly and without cause occupied Thebes, much as they had occupied Athens in 404. But

Greece and the Aegean Sea During the Theban Hegemony

the Spartan garrison was expelled three years later by Pelopidas, and he and the Theban general **Epaminondas** then led Thebes in an increasingly aggressive foreign policy now that Athens and Sparta were no longer the supreme powers in Greece. Thebes reconstituted the **Boeotian League**. The Theban army now was based on a professional core of 150 superbly trained male couples, each consisting of an older and a younger man, known as the Sacred Band, which in 375 BCE became the first Greek army unit to defeat a larger army of Spartans.

Meanwhile, in 378, the Spartan general Sphodrias had launched an unprovoked attack on Athens that had been repelled; this led the Athenians not only to ally themselves with Thebes but also to create an alliance of Aegean and mainland city-states, known as the **Second Athenian League** or the Second Athenian Empire (378–355 BCE). Its stated purpose was to ensure that Sparta would not interfere in the government of any Greek city. As a result of what had happened with the Delian League, the terms of membership were very clear that Athens was not permitted to interfere in the government of any member or to control, or to station soldiers in, the territory of any member. There was no tribute; only the Athenians made regular contributions, and any contributions by the allies were voluntary.

Athens' position changed in 373 BCE, however, when Thebes attacked and destroyed Plataea, an Athenian ally that just had been refounded. The Athenians then changed sides and made an alliance with Sparta, which attacked Thebes in 371 in an attempt to regain its own hegemony. At the **Battle of Leuctra** in Boeotia, the Spartans were confronted with a new military tactic introduced by Epaminondas. Instead of forming a uniform phalanx of about twelve hoplites deep with their best troops on the right flank, the Thebans created from their best troops a massive column fifty hoplites deep on their left flank, which advanced against the Spartan right flank, where the Spartiates and the Spartan king were stationed, with their allies on their left. The remainder of the much thinner Theban line, composed of echelons of allied troops, extended diagonally to the rear and initially did not even engage the enemy. The Spartan phalanx was unable to resist this enormous column and disintegrated. With the defeat of the Spartan contingent, Sparta's allies fled. Sparta lost four hundred of the one thousand Spartiates there, including their king, and the Spartan loss of manpower and prestige were so great that Sparta no longer could maintain its position as the leading power in Greece, a role that was taken over by Thebes in a period known as the **Theban Hegemony** (371–338 BCE).

In an attempt to reduce Sparta to second-class status, Epaminondas then invaded the Peloponnesus to free the Messenian helots and the Arcadians from Spartan domination. In Arcadia, Epaminondas oversaw the founding of a new city, Megalopolis, intended to serve as a focal point for Peloponnesian opposition to Sparta. Subsequently, Pelopidas defeated the Thessalians to the north and even invaded Macedonia, where Philip, the brother of the Macedonian king Amyntas III, was taken to Thebes as a hostage. While there, Philip became fully educated in the new Theban military tactics. In

364, meanwhile, Pelopidas was killed in a northern skirmish. The Spartans cobbled together another army that included the Athenians, who also were concerned about the rising power of Thebes. Epaminondas again invaded the Peloponnesus in 362 and, aided by the Arcadians and using the same tactics as at Leuctra, defeated the Spartans again at the Battle of Mantinea, but the losses were very heavy on both sides, and Epaminondas himself was killed.

As a result of this warfare, Thebes and Sparta had both weakened themselves to the extent that neither had the resources to undertake any further serious military campaigns. This, then, gave Athens an opportunity to expand its authority, which it attempted to do by behaving more autocratically toward its own League. But after the defeats of Sparta, the League had lost its purpose, and, provoked by Athens' increasingly domineering attitude—whereby Athenian generals extorted money from league members—in 357 BCE a number of the allied cities broke away from the league in the **Social War** (357–355). Things did not go well for Athens. One Athenian fleet was destroyed in 357 BCE, and in 356, at the decisive Battle of Embata, much of the rest of the Athenian fleet suffered the same fate. After a failed attempt to gain support from the Persians, who responded by ordering Athens to remove its forces from Anatolia, the Athenians had no choice but to give up all of its claims to its allies and make peace in 355 BCE.

By the mid350s BCE, it was clear that the Greeks not only would never be able to unite themselves but also that they were their own worst enemies and never would even be able to get along with each other. The only result of round after round of incessant warfare was that any Greek city that appeared to be on the verge of dominating Greece excited so much opposition from other Greek cities that all of the Greek cities succeeded only in weakening themselves. In addition, the support given by Persia to whomever appeared to be the weaker parties in Greece further ensured that no single Greek city or confederation would ever prevail. As a consequence, Greece became more and more vulnerable to external threats of the sort that the Greeks had been able to overcome in the early fifth century. If such a threat ever came again, the Greeks would not have nearly the same resources to resist.

The term Social War *has nothing to do with social issues, but comes from the Latin word for "ally," and thus means "War of the Allies."*

The Rise of Macedon

The term **Macedonia** *refers to the geographical region and Macedon to the ancient kingdom.*

For more than six hundred years, from 1100 BCE until 490 BCE, the Greeks had had little to fear from outside invaders and thus had been able to develop their culture in peace. One of the reasons the Greeks had had this luxury was that their northern cousins, the Macedonians, whose earliest kingdom was centered on the Haliacmon River, had helped to provide a buffer zone between the Greeks and any hostile peoples to the north, such as the Illyrians, Thracians, and **Celts**. Like the Assyrians, the Macedonians had been open to almost constant attack on all sides. And like the Assyrians, they eventually created a powerful and effective army. Because they never lost their need for military leaders, the Macedonians always retained their kings, who were chosen from a royal

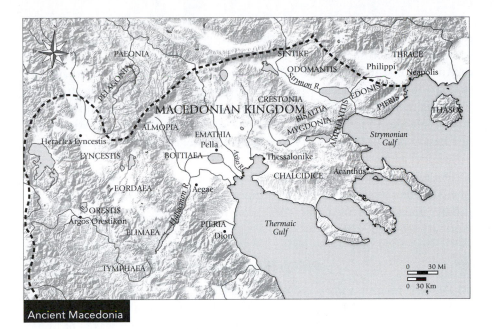

Ancient Macedonia

family known as the Argeadae (because they were thought to be descended from kings of Argos) by an assembly made up of the Macedonian army.

The nobles, called the king's *hetairoi,* or "companions," held their land from the king in a very personal relationship. They provided the Macedonian cavalry, which was famous for its wedge-shaped charge and initially was the only effective arm of the Macedonian military. The Macedonian king typically was in the forefront of military action, usually leading the cavalry. In addition, the king granted conquered territory known as "spear land" to Macedonian peasants in exchange for service in a poorly trained infantry. They became known as the *pezhetairoi,* or "foot companions."

Macedonian life was a world of hunting, drinking, and blood feuds. The Macedonians also had a very comfortable relationship with their king and were free to speak their minds. Some Macedonian nobles, and especially Macedonian royalty, also were very attracted to Greek culture and became patrons of Greek poets and teachers. In the late fifth century BCE, Socrates declined an invitation to Macedonia. The poet Euripides, however, accepted and even wrote a play about a Macedonian king. But he met his death when he was attacked and torn apart by savage Macedonian hunting dogs. And Macedonian documents were written in Attic Greek.

Around 510 BCE, in the aftermath of the Persians' Scythian campaign, the Macedonians became Persian vassals. In addition, the Macedonian kingdom initially was too weak to prevent Greeks from the south from founding colonies on their coast. The Greeks also were not quite sure what to make of the Macedonians. They were not even sure whether they were Greeks, for their northern Dorian-based dialect was virtually incomprehensible. In 496 BCE, the Macedonian king Alexander I (498–454) had his Greekness challenged when he tried to participate in the Olympic games. Only by proving his descent directly from the Greek hero Hercules was he allowed to compete, and he tied for first in the foot race. In the late 490s, when the Persians began to prepare for their attacks on Greece, Alexander secretly supported the Greeks by warning them about Persian plans and supplying Athens with ship timber. In exchange, Alexander was made a *proxenos*, an honorary citizen of Athens, the greatest honor that a Greek city could bestow. After the Battle of Plataea in 479, Alexander ambushed the retreating Persians and took advantage of the Persian defeat to expand the kingdom. But before and during the Peloponnesian War, the Macedonians again were victimized when Athens, needing both ship timber and silver, seized Macedonian territory, creating a long-term sense of antipathy toward Athens.

Philip II of Macedon

Macedonia became a major power during the 350s BCE under the leadership of **King Philip II** (359–338 BCE). Philip molded the untrained foot companions into a professional fighting force, at least part of which was kept under arms year round, by rigorously drilling it and arming it with the sarissa, an 18-foot-long double-pointed pike. The Macedonian phalanx, with ten ranks of pikemen, looked like a porcupine, with the spears of the men in the front ranks pointed forward and those of the men in the rear held upward to deflect arrow fire and just to keep them out of the way. The pikes of the first five ranks reached beyond the front of the formation, meaning that there were many more points than possible targets, and it therefore was impossible for an enemy to break through a well-drilled phalanx. The phalanx could go only in

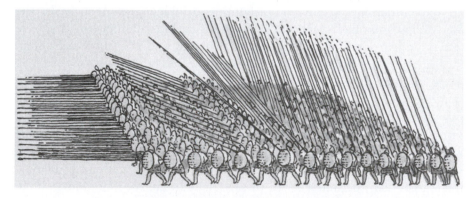

A Roman general later called the charge of the Macedonian phalanx, with its impenetrable barrier of spear points, the most terrifying sight he had ever seen.

one direction, forward, and it cut like a knife through anything in its path. An elite unit of infantry known as the hypaspists served as a royal guard and was generally stationed on the right flank. With the heavy cavalry and hypaspists guarding its flanks, the Macedonian army was the most fearsome fighting machine in the ancient world.

Philip used this new army to extend his control further and further from Macedonia and to incorporate additional peoples, such as the Thracians and Thessalians, under his authority. He seized the Athenian colony of Amphipolis and thus gained access to the gold and silver of Thrace. Philip was an excellent diplomat and understood that, rather than risking his army unnecessarily, there were other means that could be used to achieve his military goals; like the Persians, he became adept at buying the adherence of potential enemies and was reported to have claimed that "walls also can be climbed with gold." At the same time, Philip consolidated his personal authority by granting land to a new class of nobles who were loyal directly to him and lessened the influence of the old nobility.

In 354 BCE, Thebes, seeing that Athens had been rendered powerless, undertook the Third Sacred War (356–346 BCE) against the Phocians, who had seized control of the shrine of Apollo of Delphi and used the temple treasures to hire a large and expensive mercenary army. Once again, the Greeks chose sides. Argos, Megalopolis, and the former allies of Athens sided with Thebes, whereas Athens and Sparta favored the Phocians. But neither side, in their weakened conditions, was able to make any headway against the other. While the Greeks were distracted by their own continuing quarrels, Philip occupied **Thessaly**, a large region in northern Greece, and became the new *tagos* (head) of the Thessalian League, effectively uniting Thessaly with Macedonia. And when the northern city of Olynthus made an alliance with Athens, Philip captured and completely demolished it and sold the population into slavery. Philip himself then became involved in the Sacred War when Thebes invited him to intervene. In 346, Philip invaded, and the Phocians surrendered without a fight. Philip now controlled the seats of both Thessaly and Phocis on the Amphictyonic Council, which gave him respectability in the Greek world, and his conquest of Greece had begun.

Meanwhile, as the Greeks continued to bicker among themselves, and as each city attempted to gain some small advantage over its rivals, some Greek intellectuals realized that the constant Greek conflicts were counterproductive. Unlike earlier philosophers, who functioned in a world of theory, these Greeks attempted to find solutions in the real world to the problem of Greek disunity. There was a rising concept of **pan-Hellenism**, a belief that Greeks ought to unite politically, as well as culturally, and should use this unity to show their superiority over the Persians, whom the Greeks considered to be effeminate and luxury loving. For the one thing that all the Greeks could agree on was that they disliked the Persians. The famous teacher Aristotle, for example, suggested that non-Greeks such as the Persians were suited only to be slaves. The Athenian orator Isocrates thought he had the solution to the problems caused by overpopulation and continuing warfare in Greece: "On no other condition could the Greeks find peace unless the leading Greek cities can put an end to their quarrels and carry the war into Asia, and take from the barbarians what they now think to take from each other." And Philip of Macedon, whom he described as himself "the ruler over many barbarians," was just the kind of person that Isocrates thought could unite the Greeks. In 346 BCE, he said to Philip, "My intention is to advise you to take the lead both in securing the harmony of Hellas and in conducting the expedition against the barbarians." Philip was happy to oblige in both regards.

Philip then was drawn further into conflicts in Greece. In 340, he attempted to seize control of the straits connecting the Aegean and Black Seas and may even have been entertaining the idea of invading Persian-held Anatolia. The Persian king Artaxerxes III (358–338 BCE), who controlled the straits, therefore intervened militarily in Europe for the first time in 140 years by sending a mercenary army against Philip. At the same time, Athens, whose food supply depended on free use of the straits, declared war after Philip had seized more than two hundred Athenian grain ships. Philip was forced to withdraw, one of his very few defeats, and the Athenian navy blockaded the Macedonian ports. This gave Philip an excuse to make a full-scale invasion of Greece in 338. Athens could not hope to resist the Macedonians by itself. The Athenian orator Demosthenes, who opposed to Philip in a series of speeches known as the *Philippics*, in which he described Philip as "a pestilent scoundrel from Macedonia, where it was never possible to buy a decent slave," persuaded Thebes to assist Athens in the resistance. The decisive engagement took place at the Battle of Chaeronea in Boeotia, where thirty-two thousand Macedonians faced thirty-seven thousand Athenians, Thebans, and allies. The Greek citizen troops were no match for Philip's well-trained phalanx, and the decisive Macedonian cavalry charge was led by Philip's impetuous eighteen-year-old son, Alexander. The Theban Sacred Band was the only Greek unit to hold its ground, and nearly all perished. Philip removed control of Boeotia from Thebes, but treated Athens gently, probably in hopes of being able

A gold stater attesting to Philip II's Greekness shows on the obverse the head of Apollo, whose support Philip claimed, and on the reverse a two-horse chariot, an allusion to the victory of Philip's race horse at the Olympic games in 356. The legend reads simply "Of Philip," indicating that Philip ruled on his own authority, not that of the Macedonians. Hundreds of thousands of such coins were issued and helped to finance Philip's expansion of the Macedonian kingdom.

to use Athens' fleet in a future attack on Persia. The Greeks were unable to offer any further resistance. Greece finally had been conquered by a foreign power, and for two thousand years Greece would, in whole or part, be ruled by outsiders.

Declining the impossible task of governing the Greeks directly, Philip placed Macedonian garrisons in a few key cities, such as Thebes, Corinth, and Chalcis, and formed the **League of Corinth**, a coalition of nearly all the Greek cities except for now impotent Sparta, with himself at its head. All the members were to remain autonomous, and the Macedonian king was to command the League's army. The ostensible purpose of the League was something nearly all Greeks would agree with: an attack on the Persian Empire, not only to set free the Greek cities of Ionia but also in retribution for the destruction of Athens' temples by Xerxes in 480 BCE. Philip guaranteed that fighting among the Greek cities finally would stop, which resulted in multitudes of out-of-work Greek mercenaries now heading to Persia to work for the Persian king, who was well aware of Philip's plan to conquer Anatolia.

But in 336, just after Philip had sent a Macedonian expeditionary force into Anatolia, he was assassinated by a member of his personal bodyguard for reasons that remain unclear. Theories regarding the cause range from a lover's quarrel to a plot by Philip's ambitious wife Olympias, who was jealous because Philip had taken a new wife and wanted to ensure that her son Alexander became king. Irrespective of the reasons for the assassination, it would have appeared to the Greeks, the Persians, and perhaps even the Macedonians that all bets were off and that Philip's grand plans had come to an end.

THE AGE OF ALEXANDER (336–323 BCE)

After the death of Philip II, his son **Alexander III** led a Macedonian and Greek attack on the Persian Empire. During thirteen years of campaigning, from Anatolia to India, Alexander showed himself to be the greatest military commander of all time and created the greatest empire that the world had yet seen.

Young Alexander

After the assassination of Philip, his son Alexander III became king of Macedonia. It was presumed by almost everybody that this young man, barely twenty years old, would scarcely be able to put his father's grandiose plans into effect. Alexander proved the doubters wrong. In 335, several Greek cities, including Thebes and Athens, immediately revolted. Alexander stormed, sacked, and razed Thebes; it was said that only one house, that of the poet Pindar, was left standing. According to Plutarch, "Alexander hoped that a severe example might terrify the rest of Greece into obedience. Thirty thousand were publicly sold for slaves and upwards of six thousand were put to the sword." Plutarch was right:

THE PERSONALITY OF ALEXANDER

The nature of Alexander's personality has intrigued historians ever since antiquity, and there have been many interpretations of the character of the man who became the most famous general of all time. Many tales were told about the development of his personality. When he was ten years old, for example, it was said that he tamed the supposedly untamable huge wild warhorse Bucephalus by recognizing that the horse was afraid of its shadow. At thirteen, Alexander began to be tutored by the philosopher Aristotle and was joined by other noble Macedonian boys, such as Cassander, Hephaestion, and Ptolemy, who would accompany him for the rest of his life. At sixteen, Alexander began his military career, being entrusted with campaigns against the Thracians and Illyrians by his father. By the time he became king at twenty in 336, Alexander was a seasoned general, with a supreme confidence in himself and his abilities.

Much modern speculation has involved analyses of the nature of Alexander's personality, what influenced its development, and how it was manifested. He was undoubtedly one of the most charismatic leaders of all time, being able to command the loyalty of tens of thousands of men during eleven years of campaigning, covering thousands of miles of some of the most difficult territory in the world. It also has been suggested that Alexander was obsessed by a sense of competition with his father, Philip, whose own extraordinary achievements must have seemed nearly impossible to outdo; according to Plutarch, "He believed that everything he received from his father diminished and prevented his own future achievements." And, certainly, without Philip, there never could have been an Alexander. This insecurity came to a head in 328 when, in a drunken rage, he killed his old comrade-in-arms Cleitus the Black, who had saved his life at the Granicus River, after Cleitus said that all Alexander's achievements were due to his father. His traditional Macedonian tendency to excess use of alcohol was balanced by a reasonable side, no doubt influenced by his schooling with Aristotle, that was willing to listen to rational arguments.

Speculation also has surrounded Alexander's sexuality, and especially the nature of his relationship with his close boyhood friend Hephaestion, who, according to the historian Curtius, was "by far the dearest of all the king's friends and shared all his secrets." Ancient sources do not specifically confirm that they were lovers, but given Greek tolerance of homosexuality, there would have been no reason to expect them to, and Alexander's and Hephaestion's identification of each other as Achilles and Patroclus indicates a very close relationship. Hephaestion's death in 324 plunged Alexander into a deep depression that may have contributed to his death.

As he moved from success to success, moreover, Alexander behaved more and more autocratically, even

this show of force sufficiently overawed the Greek cities, and they caused no more problems for Alexander.

Alexander's Persian Wars

In 334 BCE, Alexander picked up where his father had left off and led his army into Anatolia. He faced a daunting task. His forces, which included twenty-five thousand Macedonian infantry, seven thousand Greek infantry, and five thousand Macedonian cavalry, were all he had. He could not afford to lose any battles. Against him the Persians could raise a total of two hundred fifty toward his closest associates. After the hitherto reliable commander Philotas had been executed for conspiracy, Alexander also executed Philotas' father, his second-in-command Parmenion. Alexander also exhibited signs of megalomania by behaving more and more like an actual deity. His mother Olympias, a princess from Epirus and the fourth of Philip's eight wives, had encouraged him in the belief that he was the son of Zeus, not the son of Philip II, saying that on the night before her wedding to Philip she had dreamed that her womb was struck by Zeus' thunderbolt. Given that his father's family claimed descent from Hercules and his mother's from Achilles, both sons of Zeus, Alexander's claim was not as unusual as it might seem. He was so fascinated by the exploits of Zeus' son Achilles that he even kept on his night table a copy of the *Iliad* given him by Aristotle. Alexander's visions of godhood were one factor that led him to believe that he could conquer not just the Persian Empire but the entire known world, all the way to the great ocean that geographers believed lay just east of India. After a visit to the oracle at the Siwa Oasis in Egypt, where he was welcomed by the oracle of Amon as the son of Ra, Amon, and Zeus, Alexander identified himself as the son of Zeus-Ammon; a ten-drachm coin issued after the Battle of the Hydaspes shows Alexander holding the thunderbolt of Zeus. He also attempted to impose the Persian custom of proskynesis, in which subjects prostrated themselves on the floor, as if before a god, before him, something the down-to-earth Macedonians simply refused to do.

The riddles of Alexander's personality will never be solved, and no doubt will continue to mystify generations of students of antiquity.

In this relief from the temple of Amenhotep III at Luxor in Egypt, Alexander at right is portrayed as the pharaoh standing before the god Amon-Ra, thus demonstrating his respect for Egyptian customs.

thousand soldiers. But Alexander had chosen a good time for his attack. He had taken the Persians by surprise, and they did not have time to assemble their army. And to make matters worse, the Persian king, Darius III (336–330 BCE), had just led a successful revolt to seize the throne, but had not yet consolidated his power.

Alexander's strategy was to conquer the empire bit by bit. First on the agenda was Anatolia, which was all his father had ever wanted and which was defended by an army of some five thousand Greek infantry, twelve thousand Persian infantry, and fifteen thousand cavalry. In the ensuing Battle of the Granicus River, Alexander was in the forefront

HISTORICAL CAUSALITY

How did Alexander take advantage of the weaknesses of the Persian Empire?

of the fighting. The Persians attempted to use their superiority in cavalry to mount a direct attack on Alexander himself; according to Plutarch, a Persian nobleman gave Alexander, who already had killed several nobles, "such a blow with his battle-axe on the helmet that he cut off its crest and the edge of the weapon touched the hair of his head." After a desperate fight, the Persians were defeated. Afterward, reflecting his distrust of Greeks, Alexander had four thousand of the Greek mercenaries slaughtered and two thousand enslaved. Alexander then proceeded to occupy the rest of Anatolia. At the city of Gordion, where an oracle had predicted that whoever could untie a very intricate knot binding an oxcart to a post would become king of Asia, Alexander solved the riddle by cutting the knot with his sword.

In the modern day, finding an imaginative solution to a complicated problem is said to be "cutting the Gordian knot."

Once again, the Ionian Greeks had been freed from Persian control, but this time they were free only to join the League of Corinth and become Macedonian allies. As Alexander marched farther and farther from home, maintaining his lines of communications, by which he received news, supplies, and reinforcements, became of paramount importance. Not fully trusting Greeks, he dismissed his Greek fleet and adopted a policy of controlling the Mediterranean Sea by controlling the land and port cities that surrounded it.

By 333, even though Darius had been able to raise only the army of the western half of his empire, his one hundred thousand troops still substantially outnumbered Alexander's forty thousand. Initially Alexander was outmaneuvered, for the Persian army got between him and Macedonia. All the Persians now needed was a draw, and Alexander would be trapped. The two armies met at the **Battle of Issus** in northern Syria, where the small size of the battlefield inhibited the Persians from utilizing their superiority in manpower. Once again, Alexander was in the thick of the fray, first leading the hypaspists on foot to break through the Persian line and then leading a cavalry charge against the Persian center that killed Darius' bodyguard and sent Darius himself fleeing. His army took off after him. Among the captives taken by the Macedonian were the mother, wife, and daughters of Darius, and Alexander gained much credit for his humane treatment of them. Plutarch reports, "He allowed them to bury whom they pleased of the Persians, and to make use for this purpose of what garments they thought fit out of the booty. He diminished nothing of the respect formerly paid them, and allowed larger pensions for their support than they had had before."

After the battle, Darius offered to make peace, to surrender to Alexander all the territory he had occupied, and to pay him ten thousand talents of silver for the return of his family. Significantly, Alexander kept this offer a secret, for this was all that Philip II had ever wanted, and many Macedonians might have been content to stop here. But not Alexander, who had a much greater ambition—the conquest of the whole Persian Empire. Before pursuing Darius into Asia, Alexander prudently determined to occupy the eastern Mediterranean coast and Egypt so as not to leave any enemies behind him. Most cities surrendered without a fight and were well treated, but, trusting to Alexander's lack of a navy, the island city of Tyre held out. After the Tyrians murdered Alexander's peace negotiators, a terrible breach of diplomatic etiquette, Alexander spent eight valuable months of 332 BCE building a kilometer-long stone causeway out to the city, which was stormed and sacked. As punishment for their resistance, Alexander crucified two thousand men and sold thirty thousand others into slavery. Gaza, the only other city that resisted, was treated similarly after it was captured: the male population was executed and the women and children sold into slavery. The remaining cities of the Levant, such as Jerusalem, surrendered peacefully and were treated benevolently. By late 332 BCE Alexander had occupied Egypt. At this point, Darius offered to surrender all of the empire west of the Euphrates River. According to a famous story, Alexander's second-in-command Parmenion said to Alexander, "If I were Alexander, I would accept that offer," to which Alexander snidely replied, "And if I were Parmenion, so would I."

Alexander advanced into Mesopotamia in 331 with some fifty thousand soldiers, including thirty thousand heavy infantry and seven thousand cavalry. By then, Darius had been able to assemble an army of nearly one hundred thousand, including ten thousand Greek mercenaries, his own ten thousand Immortals, forty thousand cavalry, especially Iranians and Scythians, and even two hundred scythe chariots. At the **Battle of Gaugamela**, a name meaning "House of the Camel" (also known as the Battle of Arbela), the two armies met on a large flat plain, which had been specially smoothed by the Persians for their chariots and cavalry, that would allow Darius to use his numerical seniority to full advantage. Alexander ordered the phalanx to advance in echelon formation, just as Epaminondas had done forty years earlier. The apparently disordered nature of the Macedonian advance lured the Persian cavalry to attack.

Meanwhile, Alexander led the companion cavalry to his right, requiring the Persian line to extend to protect its flanks. This opened up a gap between the Persian left flank and center, where Darius was stationed with the Immortals. Alexander wheeled his force about and, leading the characteristic Macedonian wedge formation, threw himself into the gap. On the other Macedonian flank, meanwhile, the Persian cavalry had driven off the greatly outnumbered Macedonians and broken through the Macedonian line. The battle now hung in the balance. If the Persian cavalry had turned and attacked the Macedonians from the rear, Alexander's army would have been destroyed. But the Persians snatched defeat from the jaws of victory. Thinking the battle was won, they rode off to loot the Macedonian camp. Back in the Persian center, Alexander's cavalry destroyed the Immortals. Cut off, the commander of the Persian left wing, Bessus, the satrap of **Bactria** in northeastern Afghanistan, began to withdraw his forces. The troops around Darius likewise began to break up, and Darius fled with Bessus. Darius' army disintegrated, and the Persians had lost their last chance for large-scale opposition.

Alexander then proceeded to occupy the remainder of the Persian Empire, seizing Babylon before moving into Persia and taking Susa, one of the capitals. On the way to the main capital of Persepolis, however, Alexander was ambushed in the Zagros Mountains in a narrow pass called the Persian Gates. In this Persian equivalent of the Battle of Thermopylae, the Persian defenders nearly defeated and killed Alexander, and they held the pass for thirty days before Persian traitors showed Alexander a secret path behind the defenders. Persepolis was looted for four months, the men were killed, and the women enslaved. When the city then burned, some claimed that it was in retribution for the Persian burning of Athens. Others said it was just a drunken prank. Hoarded in the Persian treasury at Persepolis, Alexander discovered nine thousand talents of gold coins and forty thousand of silver ingots (about 270 and 1,200 tons, respectively). This treasure, which could have been used to defend the empire, now was used by Alexander to pay his own mounting expenses.

In 330 BCE, Alexander continued east in his pursuit of Darius. As Alexander closed in, Bessus murdered Darius and named himself King Artaxerxes. Alexander, however, claiming that Darius had named him his successor with his dying breath, laid claim to the throne. Like previous foreign conquerors, he assumed all the titles of Near Eastern kings. He became the *Shahanshah* (King of Kings), the King of Sumer and Akkad, and the King of the Four Quarters of the Universe.

The Campaigns of Alexander the Great

Alexander spent the next four years conquering the rest of the Persian Empire. Bessus was surrendered by his own people and executed. Bactria proved especially difficult, but Alexander eventually won over the Bactrians by his bravery and his magnanimity. Alexander even married an Afghan princess named Roxanne. In 327, not content with the Persian Empire, Alexander invaded India. The Indians defended themselves desperately, village by village. Alexander himself often was in the thick of the fighting and was wounded many times; on one occasion, he was the first over the wall of an Indian fortress and barely escaped with his life, surviving a barbed arrow sunk deep in his chest. In 326 BCE at the hard-fought Battle of the Hydaspes (modern Jhelum) River, the Macedonians were confronted by the war elephants of the Indian king Porus. After another desperate battle, Alexander again emerged victorious and proposed next to attack the powerful kingdoms of the Ganges River valley.

But the constant fighting was taking its toll. The Macedonian army, or those who had survived, had been away from home for eight years. The soldiers had had enough of war. With every hill they crossed, instead of the eastern ocean all they saw were more hostile Indians. They were ready to go home. Finally, at the Hyphasis River (modern Beas), the army mutinied and refused to take one step farther east. After sulking in his tent for three days, Alexander finally agreed to turn back, but to avoid the appearance of a retreat, the Macedonians returned along the Indus River valley, fighting every inch of the way. After finally reaching the Indian Ocean, Alexander made a foolish and harrowing trek in 325 across the Gedrosian Desert of southern Iran to get back to Persepolis. Many never made it back at all.

Alexander's Empire

Alexander returned to Babylon in 324. In only ten years he had created the largest empire that the world had yet known. The questions now were what was he going to do with it, and how could he hope to hold it together? In order to establish a Greek presence in the conquered territories and to deal with thousands of army veterans, Alexander founded over 70 colonies, all named **Alexandria**, except for one named Bucephala after his horse. The colonies extended from Alexandria in Egypt to Furthest Alexandria in Afghanistan. This process can be characterized as the Third Wave of Greek colonization, although, unlike the first two, which resulted in many seacoast colonies, this was a colonization by land. Alexander thus fulfilled Isocrates' plan for how to deal with excess Greek population, and his colonies brought Greeks and their culture to the far reaches of the Asian world.

Alexander knew that there were far too few Greeks and Macedonians to rule his empire directly and that he would need the cooperation of the conquered peoples. He therefore adopted the Persian model, based on showing respect for native customs, of how a small kingdom can effectively govern a large empire. He retained the Persian satrapies and integrated native peoples into his government. In distant India, for example, Porus was allowed to remain satrap of his own kingdom. He recruited thirty thousand Afghans into the army and trained them to fight as Macedonians. He himself adopted Persian dress and customs. In an even more extreme attempt to create a unified people, he took a second wife, Statira, also known as Barsine, the daughter of Darius, and married five thousand Macedonians to five thousand Persian women.

For the conservative Macedonians, some of this was too much. They thought that Alexander had gone too far. When Alexander suggested that he would welcome the ceremony of proskynesis, in which the subjects of the Persian king prostrated themselves before him, they simply refused. But the genie could not be put back into the bottle. These Macedonian farmers had experienced a wider world that was very different from what they had known. Many of them would no longer be happy with life on ten acres back in Greece. So most remained. Those who did return home brought eastern culture with them. Whether they liked it or not, the Greeks now were experiencing the full force of eastern culture.

In 323 BCE Alexander established the capital of his empire at Babylon, at the meeting point of the eastern and western parts of his empire. Ambassadors from a multitude of peoples came to congratulate him on his victories and sought good relations with him. There were representatives not only from the powerful western trading city of Carthage but also from Rome, a central Italian city that was just beginning to expand. Meanwhile, Alexander's own plans to conquer the known world continued unabated. He planned first to attack the Arabs of Arabia to the south, and then to move into the western Mediterranean, all the way to the straits of Gibraltar.

Meanwhile, Alexander's Babylonian astrologers had received disturbing omens and went so far as to arrange a ruse in which they sat a commoner on the throne to absorb the bad luck they saw coming Alexander's way. To no avail. After another Macedonian drinking party, Alexander fell ill, and he died a few days later. His death has been attributed variously to the cumulative effects of alcoholism and war wounds, to poison (including excessive medicinal use of hellebore, thought to cure gout and insanity), and to malaria, typhoid fever, and even West Nile virus. After his death, Alexander assumed legendary status. He became forever after **Alexander the Great**. Exotic tales of his adventures in just about every corner of the world were widely circulated as the "Alexander Romance" and enjoyed a popularity that extended into the Middle Ages. One tale involved a love affair with Thalestris, the queen of the Amazons, regarding which Alexander's general Lysimachus joked, "And where was I when that happened?"

ALTERNATIVE HISTORY QUESTION

What do you think would have happened if Alexander had gone west instead of going east?

THE HELLENISTIC KINGDOMS (323–120 BCE)

After Alexander's death, his generals divided up his empire. Ultimately, the families of Ptolemy, Antigonus, and Seleucid established Hellenistic kingdoms that survived until the coming of the Romans beginning in the second century BCE. This period is known as the **Hellenistic Age** (323–31 BCE).

The Divisions of Alexander's Empire

One thing Alexander had neglected to do was to provide an heir to his throne. When he was asked, as he was dying, who should succeed him, some thought that he answered, "The strongest man." Roxanne did not bear his only son, Alexander IV, until after his death, and this infant and Alexander's half-brother Philip Arrhidaeus, mentally incapacitated as a result of a botched poisoning attempt, were named joint kings, although neither was in any position actually to govern. Alexander's generals, known as the **Diadochi**, or "successors," began to squabble among themselves in attempts to carve out chunks of the empire for themselves.

Soon after Alexander's death, his generals were named satraps throughout the empire to rule in the name of the two kings. Antipater, for example, received Macedonia and Greece; Lysimachus received Thrace; Antigonus I Monopthalmos ("the One-Eyed") gained most of Anatolia; **Ptolemy** received Egypt; **Seleucus** received Babylonia; and so on. A series of Wars of the Diadochi then ensued, in which Alexander's generals attempted to expand their holdings and even to restore the empire. This was an age of great generals and elaborate campaigns. Because armies now were largely **mercenary armies**, warfare took on a different perspective. Rather than fights to the death, as often had happened among the Greeks, Hellenistic commanders and soldiers alike were much more attuned to reaching accommodations and preserving their forces. It was customary for battles to be rather genteel affairs. As soon as one side had the upper hand, fighting would cease, and the commanders would reach an agreement in which the winner got something, the loser lost something, and most everybody lived to fight another day. As a result, with the exception of Egypt, the wealthiest and most easily defended satrapy, which remained firmly in the hands of Ptolemy, territories repeatedly changed hands.

In Macedonia, Antipater was replaced by his son Cassander, who governed in the name of Philip III but was opposed by Alexander's still-ambitious mother Olympias, who supported the infant Alexander IV. In the course of the conflict, Olympias had Philip executed, but Cassander soon turned the tables, executing first Olympias and then, in 309, Roxanne and Alexander IV. In 305, Cassander had himself declared king of Macedon. Further east, Antigonus the One-Eyed, aided by his able and ambitious son Demetrius, had managed to gain control of the entire empire from Anatolia to Persia by 316. But this caused Cassander, Ptolemy, and Seleucus (whom Antigonus had expelled from Babylonia) to ally against him, and the tide of battle flowed back and forth. Ptolemy defeated

Demetrius in 312, and Seleucus reoccupied Babylonia. But in 306, Ptolemy, attempting to attack Anatolia, was defeated in a naval battle by Demetrius, who occupied Cyprus. Antigonus then declared himself *basileus*, king, a move that removed any fiction that there still was a united empire, and was copied by Cassander, Lysimachus, Seleucus, and Ptolemy.

The fighting continued. In 305, Demetrius mounted a great siege of the island city of **Rhodes**, located off the southwestern coast of Anatolia, the primary stopping point for commercial traffic traveling along the Anatolian coast. Demetrius constructed siege engines of such great size that he gained the nickname Poliorcetes, or "Besieger of Cities." But the siege failed, and the Rhodians melted down the metal from the siege engines to create a 110-foot-tall statue of the sun god Helios known as the Colossus of Rhodes, which stood at the entrance to their harbor and became one of the Seven Wonders of the World. The city then became rich on harbor tolls, and, in order to protect its trade, it developed a powerful navy for the suppression of piracy.

In 301, Antigonus was attacked by the combined armies of Lysimachus and Seleucus and at the Battle of Ipsus was defeated and killed at eighty-one years of age. His kingdom was divided by the victors. But Demetrius still had his own ambitions. In 297 Cassander died, and Demetrius saw his opportunity. In 294 he seized Athens, murdered the son of Cassander, and established himself as the king of Macedon, only to be expelled in 288 while in the process of making plans of his own to recover Alexander's empire. Lysimachus then occupied Macedonia. The last of the Diadochi to strive to reclaim Alexander's empire was eighty-year-old Seleucus, who in 281 defeated and killed Lysimachus, also eighty years old, at the Battle of Corupedium in Lydia. Seleucus thus united Macedonia and Thrace to his dominions in Asia and had recombined nearly all of Alexander's empire except for Egypt. But this was a short-lived triumph, for later in the same year Seleucus, the last living comrade of Alexander, was assassinated by Ptolemy Keraunos ("The Thunderbolt"), an adventurer son of Ptolemy I. The age of the Diadochi was over.

Egypt—where Ptolemy II had succeeded his father, who died at eighty-four in 283—Palestine, and Cyprus now were controlled by the **Ptolemaic Dynasty** (323–31 BCE); and Anatolia and all the rest of the Asian satrapies were ruled by Antiochus I, the son of Seleucus, and the **Seleucid Dynasty** (312–63 BCE). Only Macedonia remained to be resolved, but not for long. In 279 a huge army of Gauls, as the Celts from the Danube were known, invaded Macedonia, defeated and killed Ptolemy Keraunos, and looted Macedonia and northern Greece. Two years later, a large contingent of Gauls was ambushed and destroyed by

A tetradrachm of Antigonus Gonatas displays on the obverse the horned head of the god Pan, who inspired the Gauls with panic terror at the Battle of Lysimacheia, surrounded by Macedonian shields; the reverse depicts a fighting Athena with the legend "of king Antigonus," for by now all of the Hellenistic monarchs had adopted the royal title.

Antigonus Gonatas, the son of Demetrius Poliorcetes, at Lysimacheia. Gonatas then laid claim to the throne of Macedonia as Antigonus II (277–239 BCE) and established the **Antigonid Dynasty** for good.

Hellenistic Government and Economy

In general, during the Hellenistic Age everything was done on a grand scale. Concepts of rule were quite different from those of earlier forms of Greek government, in which greater or lesser numbers of the general population had shared in the government. Hellenistic kings and queens were absolute monarchs. As a consequence of their great authority, they, like Alexander, were believed to have certain godlike qualities. This idea was foreign to Greek ideas of rule but quite consistent with Near Eastern practices. Kings and queens often were accorded divine honors not only after they were dead but even while still alive. And their subjects, not only easterners but Greeks as well, were only too willing to believe that their rulers did in fact have elements of godhood in themselves.

Hellenistic economic life also functioned on a bigger scale. The huge infusion of Persian gold and silver into the Mediterranean economy brought both inflation—when the amount of gold and silver in circulation was more than the economy could absorb and the value of gold and silver therefore plummeted—and increased prosperity resulting from the much greater availability of money to many more people. Many more people than in the past became wealthy. There was increased focus on a market economy, with the production of crops and manufactured items for export. This became the age of huge estates in places such as Anatolia and Sicily, which were worked by hundreds or thousands of slaves. At the same time, new opportunities for trade opened up as communications between the Mediterranean world and areas as far away as India and beyond were suddenly opened up to economic development and exploitation. Indeed, it has been said that the Hellenistic Age brought with it the first large-scale economic boom in the history of the world. But not everyone benefited; at the same time that successful entrepreneurs acquired huge fortunes and many riches flowed into the cities in particular, the poor, and especially the urban poor, gained little, and the life of agricultural slaves became even more desperate, with the result that social unrest always was a concern.

Antigonid Macedonia and Greece

In the third century BCE, Macedonia now was just a shadow of its former self. The constant departure of soldiers to fight in the wars had left the land depopulated, and the economy likewise had been drained to pay for decades of warfare. Macedonia no longer was a world power. The best that the Antigonid kings could hope to do was to be the strongest power in Greece, and they accomplished this by establishing strategic fortresses, the so-called "Fetters of Greece," at Corinth, Chalcis, and Demetrias, to keep the Greeks under control.

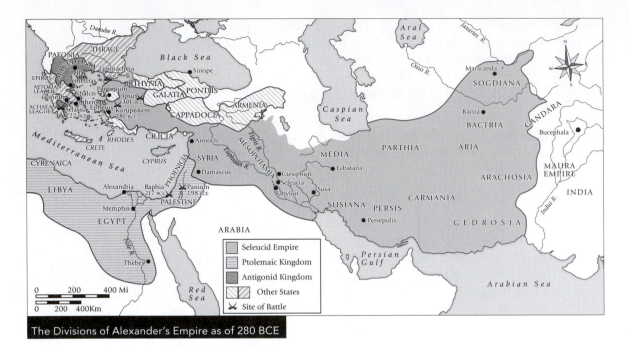

The Divisions of Alexander's Empire as of 280 BCE

The efforts of the Antigonid kings to maintain their authority in Greece were countered by a growing tendency among Greek cities at long last to work together by forming federations. In central Greece, north of the Gulf of Corinth, the **Aetolian League** was formed in the mid- to late fourth century in opposition to the growing power of Macedonia. Perhaps largely because of the poor, rural nature of their territory, the Aetolians had a reputation for banditry and piracy. And in the central and northern Peloponnesus, the **Achaean League** was formed in the early third century BCE, likewise to resist Macedonian expansion. Under its leader, Aratus of Sicyon, the league expanded to incorporate Corinth, seized from the Macedonians, Megalopolis, and Argos.

Eventually, the Achaean League fell afoul of a revived Sparta. In the 240s, King Agis IV (245–241 BCE) had attempted to revive the Good Rule of Lycurgus after the number of full Spartiates had fallen to only seven hundred, with most of the land in the hands of only a few families. Agis proposed that Spartan lands be redistributed not only among all the Spartiates but also among suitable *perioikoi* and even strangers. But the rich ephors, who opposed these reforms, had Agis executed. Subsequently, King Cleomenes III (235–222 BCE), who had married Agis' widow, continued Agis' reform attempts. After winning several military victories against the Achaeans to consolidate his support, he had the ephors murdered. He then divided the land equally among the remaining Spartiates and enfranchised enough of the *perioikoi* to give Sparta

Visual evidence, presented here in full color, depicts the great variety of material culture—including burials, architecture, pottery, coinage, sculpture, mosaics, and paintings—that can help historians to understand and reconstruct the past.

The earliest known male elite burial, from Varna, a Neolithic settlement on the Black Sea coast of Bulgaria, dates to the late fifth century BCE. It contains over three pounds of gold beads, bracelets, and ornaments, along with copper and stone axes, that attest to the accumulation of wealth by the more privileged elements of society. The man holds a war mace and wears a gold penis sheath that, along with bull-shaped gold ornaments, may have represented virility.

The function of the so-called "Standard of Ur," dated to ca. 2500 BCE and now in the British Museum, is unknown, and interpretations of its design vary. It consists of a thin wooden box inlaid on both sides with bits of shell, red limestone, and lapis lazuli. One side seems to depict the city at peace, with the ruler in the top register overseeing a banquet while a musician at the far right plays a lyre; in the lower two registers farmers and merchants engage in their daily activities, perhaps paying their taxes. The other side, perhaps representing the city at war, portrays a victorious army —with some soldiers wearing cloaks and armed with spears walking and others riding in carts— trampling defeated enemies and rounding up captives being delivered to the king at the top

The three largest Egyptian pyramids, from left to right, those of the pharaohs Menkaure, Khufu (the "Great Pyramid"), and Khafre, date to the twenty-sixth century BCE. In front are two smaller satellite pyramids intended for other family members, who shared in the afterlife of the pharaohs. In spite of ingenious devices, all the pyramids were looted in antiquity.

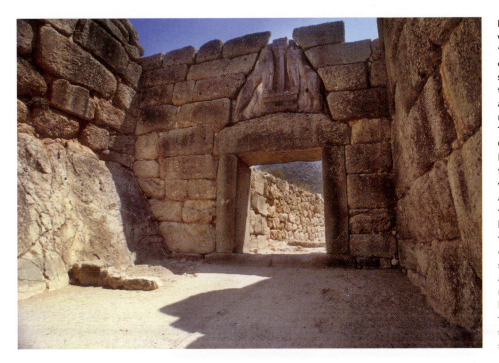

Mycenaean cities were protected by "Cyclopean" walls, constructed of huge stone blocks and up to forty feet tall, that attest to a society in need of protection. The ceremonial "Lion Gate" of the city of Mycenae, about ten feet high and ten feet wide and dating to about 1250 BCE, had to be approached between flanking walls from which defenders could hurl down spears, stones, and boiling oil and water. The original metal heads of the lions, which attest to the warlike Mycenaean spirit, no longer survive.

The Ishtar Gate of Chaldean Babylon, as reconstructed in the Pergamon Museum in Berlin, was built around 575 BCE and is nearly fifty feet tall. The superb fired tile facade, with golden lions (which represented the goddess Ishtar and the power that lay in the city's rulers), dragons, and bulls on a blue background, belies the gate's impregnable fortifications: defenders could pour arrows, stones, and boiling tar from three sides on anyone assaulting the main gate.

The Olympian gods were identified by their attributes. In this scene from an Athenian black-figured amphora of ca. 540 BCE, Athena is shown being born, fully armed, from the head of Zeus, who holds a thunderbolt. The Olympian gods Hermes, with wings at his ankles, and Apollo, holding his lyre, stand to the left, and Aphrodite, holding a flower, and Ares, fully armed, are on the right.

The temple of Athena Parthenos in Athens, now known as "The Parthenon," was built in the 440s BCE and was the focal point of Athenian civic religion. After antiquity, the Parthenon served as both a church and a mosque and survived remarkably intact, but in 1687 it was used as a gunpowder magazine by the Turks and exploded, destroying much of the temple. Restoration work in recent years, as seen here in 2007, has attempted to restore the temple to some of its former glory.

The depiction of the Battle of Issus of 333 BCE in this fresco of ca. 100 BCE from Pompeii shows a determined Alexander the Great, at left, riding his famous horse Bucephalus and advancing toward a worried looking Darius, who already is fleeing in his chariot toward the right as the chariot driver frantically whips the horses in an attempt to escape.

The marble sculpture known as "The Dying Gaul," a Roman copy of a Hellenistic original of about 225 BCE, depicts a Celtic warrior in typical battle dress, with limed hair and wearing only a torque around his neck. The common artistic theme of "death to the Celts" reflects typical Roman fears going back to the sack of Rome by the Gauls in 390 BCE.

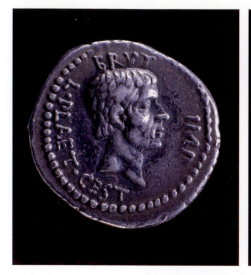

A denarius issued in 42 BCE gives Caesar's assassin Brutus the title IMP(erator) (victorious general) on the obverse and graphically displays on the reverse direct references to Caesar's assassination, including the daggers that were used, a freedom cap, and the legend "EID MAR" ("Ides of March"). The name L. Plaetorius Cestius refers to the young mint official who was responsible for issuing the coin.

In this scene from Augustus' Altar of Peace, completed in 9 BCE, members of the imperial family take part in a religious procession. On the far left, Agrippa is veiled as a Roman state priest. In the background, a woman sometimes identified as Augustus' wife Livia puts her finger to her lips to quiet the children, one of whom wears a torque and has been identified as an honored Celtic hostage.

In a mosaic of the third century from a cemetery beneath St. Peter's basilica in Rome, Christ is depicted as the sun god driving a four-horse chariot across the sky, reflecting the popular association of Christianity with sun worship. The solar radiate crown evolved into the Christian halo.

In this mosaic made from pieces of inlaid marble, the newly installed consul Junius Bassus celebrates his office in 331 CE with an adventus, or "arrival ceremony," in which, wearing a gold embroidered consular toga, he parades in a chariot through the streets of Rome on his way to opening the circus games. The four horsemen, wearing blue, green, red, and white colors, represent the four chariot racing teams of Rome.

A mosaic from the apse of the church of San Vitale in Ravenna dated to the mid 540s CE depicts the emperor Justinian participating in a communion procession. Justinian, whose halo signifies his near divinity, progresses toward the altar carrying the communion bread in a golden paten. He is flanked by secular officials and soldiers to his right and clerics on his left; the shields of the soldiers on the far right bear the Christogram. On the emperor's left, the bishop of Ravenna, Maximianus, who had underwritten the cost of the church and mosaic, is the only person actually named.

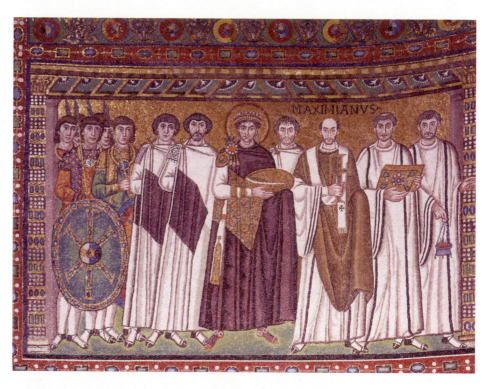

On the other side of the apse from Justinian in the church of San Vitale in Ravenna is a matched mosaic of the court of the empress Theodora. Like the emperor, she has a halo and wears an elaborate diadem. She has the three magi embroidered on the hem of her purple cloak and carries a communion chalice. To her left are elaborately garbed ladies of her court, and two high-ranking palace eunuchs stand to her right.

an army of four thousand hoplites. He also restored Spartan military discipline and adopted the use of the Macedonian phalanx. Aratus was reduced to calling on the Macedonian king, Antigonus III Doson (229–221), for help against Sparta. Doson reestablished the League of Corinth and resoundingly defeated the Spartans in 222 at the Battle of Salassia; for the first time in history, Sparta was captured by a foreign enemy. Cleomenes fled into exile, and Doson was able to recover the Macedonian position. Doson's successor, Philip V (221–179 BCE), continued Doson's initiatives, but his ambitions eventually were checked by the rising power of Rome, just across the Adriatic Sea.

Ptolemaic Egypt

Immediately after Alexander's death his general and childhood friend Ptolemy became satrap of Egypt, the most economically productive and easily defended part of the empire, and he held onto it for dear life. As Ptolemy I (323–283), he became the first of fourteen Ptolemaic kings of Egypt, all named Ptolemy. The Ptolemies had to rule over both Greek and Egyptian populations. To Greeks, they were Macedonian successors to Alexander. But to Egyptians, they were a Ptolemaic Dynasty of pharaohs, and, up to a point, they behaved like pharaohs. They built new temples to the ancient Egyptian gods, married their sisters, and were worshipped as if they were gods. Ptolemaic queens named Arsinoë, Berenice, and Cleopatra continued the tradition of strong Egyptian female rulers; some ruled in their own names, and others exerted a strong influence over their brothers or sons.

Even though the Ptolemies outwardly adopted aspects of Egyptian culture that suited their political agendas, culturally they remained completely Greek; indeed, only the last Ptolemaic ruler, Cleopatra VII, was even said to have learned Egyptian. As their capital the Ptolemies chose the great port city of Alexandria, located on the Mediterranean coast west of the mouths of the Nile. The city was officially divided into five districts, numbered alpha through epsilon, and popularly designated quarters also existed, populated by different categories of people; for example, Jews lived in the Delta district, native Egyptians in the Rhakotis quarter, and the wealthy in the Bruchion quarter. Although there were many Greek towns, there were few other cities. Naucratis continued to prosper, and at the other end of Egypt, four hundred miles up the Nile, the Ptolemies founded the city of Ptolemaïs, named after Ptolemy I, a model Greek polis complete with *boulē* and *ekklēsia* that served as a focal point of Greek administration and culture. And the prosperous port city of Berenice, founded by Ptolemy II on the Red Sea in Upper Egypt, served as a center for trade with Arabia and India.

In the countryside, in order to attract Greek settlers, the Ptolemies offered land grants in exchange for military service. Thus, as was typical of the Macedonian homeland, the army used the Macedonian phalanx and consisted of Greek and Macedonian peasant soldiers rather than mercenaries. These

A PICTURE IS WORTH A THOUSAND WORDS

PTOLEMY II AND ARSINOË II

The Ptolemaic rulers of Egypt made a special effort to conciliate their Egyptian subjects by portraying themselves as just the most recent of a long line of pharaohs. Ptolemy II (283–246 BCE), for example, took the Egyptian name "Loved by Amon, Chosen by Ra." A relief from a shrine in Tanis and now in the British Museum depicts Ptolemy II and Arsinoë II, who were full brother and sister, both being the offspring of Ptolemy I and Berenice I. Ptolemy is shown as the Egyptian pharaoh, holding the long was-scepter, with a stylized animal head at one end and a fork at the other, symbolizing dominion over the world, wearing a collar and short kilt and crowned with the *pschent*, the double crown combining the low red crown of Lower Egypt and the tall white crown of Upper Egypt with the uraeus, a protective female cobra. In a nod to Ptolemy's Greek origin, he holds in his left hand the thunderbolt of the god Zeus. Arsinoë, on the left, wears a long form-fitting robe and is portrayed as the goddess Isis, holding the papyrus scepter of goddesses in her left hand and the sign of eternal life, the ankh, in her right, and bearing on her head the vulture headdress of the mother goddess Mut and, atop the red crown of Lower Egypt, the plumes of Mut and the horns and sun disk of the cow goddess Hathor.

The hieroglyphic inscriptions identify Ptolemy as the pharaoh and Arsinoë as the daughter of Amon. Arsinoë is thus given the same divine status as Ptolemy, the divine pharaoh, and this depiction demonstrates the degree to which the Ptolemies assimilated the culture of ancient Egypt. For their Egyptian subjects, Ptolemy and Arsinoë were the pharaoh and his sister/wife, both living gods. After her death in 271 BCE, Arsinoë was officially deified by her brother and continued to be named in royal decrees.

Greek settlers were scattered throughout Egypt, some in military garrisons and Greek towns, but multitudes of others mingled with the native population. As a consequence, there was increasing integration between the Greek and Egyptian populations, and aspects of Greek culture eventually spread even to Upper Egypt. To provide common ground, the Ptolemies even created a composite god, Serapis, who was a combination of the Greek Zeus and the Egyptian Osiris. But integration was never fully achieved: native Egyptians rarely held high office, and the Greek population continued to have its own laws and to preserve its own language.

The Ptolemaic administration was very centralized. The most senior officials were Greeks, but lower level bureaucrats, such as scribes and translators—who were needed because most Greeks did not speak Egyptian—were mostly Egyptians. The economy was closely supervised to ensure the maximum return. Like the earlier pharaohs, the Ptolemaic kings sponsored irrigation, drainage, and land reclamation projects. The government revived the old Phoenician coinage weights to issue a very stable gold and silver coinage that inhibited the use of coins of its mercantile competitors—in particular Seleucids and Antigonids, who used the weight standards of Athens—in its markets. But at the same time, the Ptolemies catered to their conservative Egyptian subjects by issuing gigantic copper coins to satisfy the desire to have the value of small change be determined by its actual metal content. Ptolemy II also reopened a canal from the Nile River to the Red Sea, allowing merchant ships free passage from the Mediterranean to Arabia, India, and other points east.

The "pharos", or lighthouse, of Alexandria, here depicted in a sixth-century CE Byzantine mosaic from Libya, was one of the Seven Wonders of the World. It stood at the entry to the harbor of Alexandria and was about 450 feet high; a large fire reflected by a great mirror was visible from up to thirty miles out to sea.

The height of Ptolemaic Egypt came under Ptolemy III (246–221), whose army and fleet advanced as far as Babylon and Thrace. In order to compete with the military forces of the Seleucids, which greatly exceeded their own, the Ptolemies not only used their wealth to hire mercenaries but also accepted tens of thousands of Jews as military settlers and integrated Egyptian natives into the phalanx. This force was used to very good effect in 217 at the Battle of Raphia against the Seleucid king, Antiochus III. There, the weak-willed Ptolemy IV (221–205 BCE) was overshadowed by his sister and wife, Arsinoë III. The Jewish book of Maccabees reports that when the battle was going badly, Arsinoë "went to the troops with wailing and tears, promising to give them each two minas of gold if they won the battle. And so it came about that the enemy was routed in the action, and many captives also were taken." Subsequently, however, the Ptolemies were confronted by several native Egyptian revolts, to some degree facilitated by the admission of native Egyptians into the army, and Ptolemaic military strength rapidly declined. As a result of a secret treaty in 203 BCE, the Macedonian king Philip V seized Ptolemaic holdings in Thrace and Anatolia, and the Seleucid king Antiochus III defeated Ptolemy V (205–181) at the Battle of Panium in 198 BC and captured Syria and Judea. Much of the next 160 years was beset by dynastic quarreling that sapped the kingdom's ability to restore its political position. In addition,

The Suez Canal, a modern version of Ptolemy II's canal, was completed in 1869.

as of the 140s BCE, Ptolemaic Egypt came increasingly under the influence of Rome, and the top priority of Ptolemaic rulers became keeping the Romans happy.

Seleucid Syria and the East

Unlike the Antigonids and Ptolemies, the Seleucids controlled many different peoples, and thus they ruled an empire rather than a kingdom.

The Seleucid Empire, known to the Seleucids as Asia and extending from Anatolia to India, was easily the most heterogeneous of the successor states and the most difficult to hold together. It contained a huge non-Greek population, and it was difficult to attract additional Greek settlers. Thus the Seleucids realized they had to conciliate their subjects. After Alexander died, for example, most Macedonians divorced their Persian wives, but Seleucus remained married to Apama, and their son, Antiochus I (281–261), therefore was half Persian. In Mesopotamia, the Seleucids made common cause with priests who feared a renewed Persian takeover. Native rulers were allowed to remain in office, even as satraps, so long as they paid tribute and provided military aid. Seleucus even allowed the Persian Bagadates to serve as satrap of Persis, the Persian homeland, a conciliatory move that backfired when Bagadates revolted against the Seleucids. More distant territories to the east were managed by making alliances with local potentates. Extensive international trade focused on the eastern trade routes to India and China, which brought silk to the Mediterranean world.

Realizing that their Greek population was far too small to scatter about the countryside as had been done in Egypt, the Seleucids continued Alexander's policy of colonization and established hundreds of colonies as focal points of Seleucid rule. In Syria, which became the core of the empire, Seleucus founded the great city of Antioch, named after his father Antiochus, on the Orontes River, and in Mesopotamia, Seleucia on the Tigris River was the center of Greek culture and administration; Seleucus also was said to have founded sixteen other Antiochs. Whereas in the cities native peoples, even some Jews, became Hellenized, Greek culture scarcely penetrated into the countryside.

Although the Seleucid Empire, like the Antigonid and Ptolemaic kingdoms, maintained the Macedonian phalanx as an important arm of its army, the Seleucids also adopted the Persian practice of raising native contingents from among the many different peoples of the empire, and thus they had a much more disparate kind of military force that included Iranian archers, war elephants, Gauls, and even war chariots.

The Seleucids faced almost constant military threats, and from the very beginning, the Seleucid Empire began to shrink at its outer margins. After an inconclusive battle in 305 with the Indian king Chandragupta, founder of the Maurya Empire, Seleucus gave up his Indian territories in exchange for five hundred war elephants. In Anatolia, Cappadocia (301), Pontus (ca. 300), and Bithynia (297) were occupied by native dynasties, and in 278 invading

Gauls began carving out the independent territory of Galatia in the central highlands.

In western Anatolia, the kingdom of **Pergamum** was established in 281 BCE by Philetaerus, a eunuch who had been given custody of Lysimachus' treasury of nine thousand talents of silver at Pergamum. Philetaerus then revolted, took the money, and established his own principality under the nominal authority of the Seleucids. He was succeeded in 263 BCE by his adopted son, his nephew Eumenes, who was succeeded in turn by his own adopted son Attalus I, who finally took title of king in 238 BCE and gave his name to the Attalid Dynasty (238–133 BCE). The Attalid kings established a philhellene monarchy with close connections to the culture of the Greek mainland. They made bequests to the temples of Apollo at Delphi and Delos and even modeled their own Acropolis on the Acropolis of Athens. The most noteworthy monument in the capital city, also known as Pergamum, was a massive marble altar constructed by King Eumenes II, perhaps after a victory over the Galatians, in the early second century BCE. It depicted a Gigantomachy, or battle between gods and giants. Pergamum became a major center of learning and boasted a famous school of medicine and a library second only to that of Alexandria. Pergamum also was known for the invention of *pergaminus*, or **parchment,** a writing material made from stretched and cured sheep skins that reduced the Pergamene dependence on Egyptian papyrus. In the second century BCE, the Attalids assiduously allied themselves with Rome as a means of defending themselves against their more powerful neighbors. And in the easternmost reaches of the empire, the satrap Diodotus of Bactria revolted ca. 245 and established an independent kingdom.

The Altar of Pergamum, now reconstructed in Berlin, was described in the Christian book of Revelation as "Satan's Throne."

But the primary competitors with the Seleucids were the **Parthians**, Indo-European invaders from the steppes who settled in, and got their name from, the satrapy of Parthia in northeastern Iran. In 247 BCE, under King Arsaces, the Parthians declared their independence, created the Arsacid Dynasty of kings, and proceeded to chip away at Seleucid territory. Parthian society was structured into four classes: (1) the royal family, (2) nobles and priests, (3) merchants, and (4) farmers and herders. The nobility controlled large estates and were responsible for raising the Parthian army and for selecting the king, who often had difficulty keeping the independently minded nobles under control. In fact, in order to maintain their own authority, the nobles sometimes would consciously select a weak king. Militarily, the Parthians continued to be threatened on their northern frontier by steppe nomads such as the Scythians, a factor that might have inhibited them from military activities against their western neighbors.

Although the Parthian economy was primarily rural, Parthian trade benefited from the expansion of the Chinese "silk road" by the Han Dynasty all the way to Parthia in 114 BCE as a result of the work of the Chinese explorer Zhang Qian, who referred to the Arsacids as the "Anxi." Around 100 BCE, the

Parthians responded by sending an embassy of their own to the Chinese court. Although a few documents written in the Parthian language survive, the Parthians became heavily Hellenized, and much of their writing and record keeping was done in Greek. Parthian coins, for example, were modeled on Greek coins and had legends in Greek.

The reign of Antiochus III (224–187 BCE), who had ambitions to restore the empire of Alexander, brought a resurgence of Seleucid authority. In the west, Antiochus ended a century of Syrian wars with Ptolemaic Egypt by gaining control of Palestine after native uprisings in Egypt had weakened the Egyptian military. And during an extensive eastern campaign, Antiochus restored Seleucid authority over Parthia and Bactria, invaded India, and was on his way to restoring the empire of Alexander. But an ill-considered attempt to invade Greece brought Antiochus into conflict with the Romans, who brought a speedy end to Antiochus' ambitions.

Despite occasional attempts to recover past glory, the remainder of Seleucid history was a sad tale of continued losses of territory to the Parthians and repetitious dynastic quarrels. In 168, Antiochus IV (175–163) was on the verge of occupying all of Egypt before he, too, was foiled by the Romans, who forced him to leave; in the course of the last Seleucid expedition to the easternmost parts of the realm, he was killed in battle against the Parthians. The final attempt to restore Seleucid power came under Antiochus VII (139–129), who briefly recaptured Mesopotamia and Media from the Parthians but was likewise killed in 129 BCE by the Parthians, who now occupied nearly all of the former Seleucid Empire, from the western Euphrates all the way to the borders of India. Henceforth the Seleucid kingdom, now no longer an empire, was limited to Syria.

A silver tetradrachm issued by the Indo-Greek king Archebios (ca. 80–60 BCE) attests to the integration of Greek and Indian culture, displaying on the obverse the king wearing an Indian helmet, with the Greek legend "Of the Victorious and Just King Archebios," and on the reverse the god Zeus holding a thunderbolt with a similar legend in the Indian Karosthi script used for writing Sanskrit, "Archebios, victorious king of the Dharma."

Bactria and India

Greek expansion into Afghanistan and India brought the Greeks into even more intimate contact with eastern culture. After 250 BCE, the easternmost Greek cities were effectively cut off by the Parthians from the rest of the Greek world, and the satrap Diodotus formed the kingdom of Bactria. The Bactrian Greeks had no hope of reinforcements from the west and, indeed, were virtually forgotten by their western cousins. Against all the odds, they maintained their Greek way of life, largely by enlisting native help and assimilating native customs much more extensively than any other Greek rulers. For example, their coins carried lettering in Greek on one side and in Indian on the other. Greek culture was preserved in cities established by Alexander—including Alexandria on the Oxus (Ai-Khanum), Alexandria in the Caucasus (Bagram), Alexandria Eschata ("Furthest Alexandria," Khojent), and Antioch in Margiana (Merv), rebuilt by Antiochus I (281–261)—not to mention in the native city of Maracanda (Samarkand).

Around 180 BCE the Bactrian king Demetrius invaded India, conquered the satrapy of Gandara on the Indus River, and established an Indo-Greek kingdom that included Greeks who had resided there ever since the days of Alexander and Seleucus. Gandara became a Hellenized center of Greek language and art. King Menander (ca. 155–130 BCE) supported local Buddhists who had been oppressed by the Indian Hindus; according to tradition, Menander even became a Buddhist himself and was named among the four great Buddhist rulers of India. But Bactria fell to the Tocharians, a blue-eyed Indo-European people of Mongolia, around 120 BCE, and later became incorporated into the Kushan Empire. About 10 CE the last Greek rulers of India succumbed to the Saka, Scythian invaders from central Asia who established an Indo-Scythian kingdom. The Greek rulers of Bactria and India were largely lost to western Greek history, and most are known to us only by the thousands of coins that they left behind.

Beyond the Frontiers

At the same time that Greco-Macedonian states were being carved out of the old Persian Empire, there was a great increase of interest in the Greek world in even more exotic and distant places, peoples, and cultures. As a result, the Hellenistic period also saw an expansion of geographical exploration, and a literary work known as a *periplus* (a narrative of a voyage) described strange places and peoples. The *periplus* often was practical, commissioned by rulers to aid them in gaining knowledge about their domains, or compiled by merchants to identify good places to trade and the safest ways to get there.

Much of the impetus for these accounts came from the eastern campaigns of Alexander the Great. In 325 BCE, Alexander instructed his admiral Nearchus to survey the coast between India and Persia, and after his return Nearchus wrote an account of India, some of which was preserved in the *Indica*, a work about India, by the second-century CE author Arrian. Nearchus reported on many aspects of local color, for example, "If there is an intelligent animal, it is the elephant. I myself saw an elephant clanging the cymbals while other elephants danced; two cymbals were fastened to the player's forelegs and one on his trunk. As he rhythmically beat the cymbal on either leg in turn the dancers danced in circle." Nearchus traveled so far south in the Indian Ocean that at noon, he reported, the sun cast no shadow, and at night some of the northern stars could not be seen. When the rowers of his warships became distressed by the sight of a pod of spouting whales, Arrian says, "Nearchus signaled them to

THE PERIPLUS OF THE RED SEA

The Periplus of the Red Sea, an account of the route from the Red Sea to India, was written in the first century BCE by a merchant who listed market towns and goods that could be traded. Heading down the African coast, the merchant traveled no farther than modern Somalia, commenting, "beyond these places the unexplored ocean curves around toward the west, and running to the south of Africa it mingles with the western sea." In the other direction was the route going east; every summer, trading ships would make use of the annual etesian winds out of the southwest to strike out across the open sea from southern Arabia and western Africa for India:

Now to the left of Berenice is the adjoining country of Arabia, in its length bordering a great distance on the Erythrean [Red] Sea. Different peoples inhabit the country, differing in their speech. The country inland is peopled by rascally men speaking two languages, who live in villages and nomadic camps, by whom those sailing off the middle course are plundered, and those surviving shipwrecks are taken for slaves. And so they too are continually taken prisoners by the chiefs and kings of Arabia. Navigation is dangerous along this whole coast of Arabia, which is without harbors, with bad anchorages, foul, inaccessible because of breakers and rocks, and terrible in every way. Therefore, we hold our course down the middle of the gulf and pass on as fast as possible by the country of Arabia.

After Eudaemon Arabia [Aden] there is a continuous length of coast, and a bay extending two thousand stadia [230 miles] or more; just beyond the cape projecting from this bay there is another market-town, Cana, of the Kingdom of Eleazar, the Frankincense Country [Yemen]. The frankincense is gathered by the king's slaves and those who are sent to this service for punishment. For these places are very unhealthy, and pestilential even to those sailing along the coast; but almost always fatal to those working there. The inhabitants are foreigners, a mixture of Arabs and Indians and Greeks, who have emigrated to carry on trade there. Sailing along the coast, which trends northward toward the entrance of the Persian Sea, there are many islands known as the Calxi. The inhabitants are a treacherous lot, very little civilized. There follows not far beyond the mouth of the Persian Gulf. Sailing through the mouth of the Gulf, after a six-days' course there is a market-town of Parthia called Ommana [Oman].

Beyond this region, the continent making a wide curve from the east, there follows the coast district of Indo-Scythia, the whole marshy,

turn the ships' bows towards the whales as if to give battle and to raise their battle cry. When they neared the monsters, they shouted with all the power of their throats, and the bugles blared, and the rowers made the greatest splashing with their oars. So the whales were frightened and dove into the depths." And in the early third century BCE, Megasthenes, an ambassador from Seleucus to the court of Chandragupta, also wrote an *Indica* that discussed the Himalayas and the Indian caste system and likewise was used by many later authors.

At the same time that some Hellenistic sailors were exploring and seeking new markets in the east, others went westward, out of the Mediterranean and into the Atlantic. For example, Pytheas, a Greek sailor from Marseille, reported on a voyage made about 300 BCE on a shoestring budget from the Phoenician from which flows down the river Sinthus [Indus], the greatest of all the rivers that flow into the Erythrean Sea. This river has seven mouths, very shallow and marshy, except one by whose shore is the market town, Barbaricum [Karachi in Pakistan]. Inland is Minnagara, the metropolis of Indo-Scythia; it is subject to Parthian princes who are constantly driving each other out. There are imported into this market figured linens, topaz, coral, sweetgum, frankincense, vessels of glass, silver and gold plate, and a little wine, and there are exported ginger, myrrh, wolf-berry, incense, turquoise, lapis lazuli, Chinese skins, cotton cloth, silk yarn, and indigo. Sailors set out thither with the Indian etesian winds, about the month of July: it is more dangerous then, but through these winds the voyage is more direct, and sooner completed. The whole country of India has very many rivers, and very great ebb and flow of the tides; increasing at the new moon, and at the full moon for three days, and falling off during the intervening days of the moon.

This whole voyage, from Cana and Eudaemon Arabia, they used to make in small vessels sailing close around the shores of the gulfs; and Hippalus the pilot first discovered how to lay his course straight across the ocean. For at the same time when with us the etesian winds are blowing, on the shores of India the wind blows in from the ocean. From that time to the present day ships start, some direct from Cana and some from the Cape of Spices [Cape Guardafui in Somalia]; and those bound for Damirica [the Malabar coast of southern India] throw the ship's head considerably off the wind; whereas those bound for Indo-Scythia hold the same course straight out to sea, quite away from the land.

Beyond this, the course turns toward the east again, and sailing with the ocean to the right and the shore to the left, the territory of Ganges comes into view, and near it the very last land toward the east, Chryse [Malaysia]. There is a river near it called the Ganges, and it rises and falls in the same way as the Nile. After this region under the very north, the sea outside ending in a land called This [China], there is a very great inland city called Thinae, from which raw silk and silk yarn and silk cloth are brought on foot through Bactria to Barygaza [Bharuch on the northwestern Indian coast], and are also exported to Damirica by way of the river Ganges. But the land of This is not easy of access; few men come from there, and seldom. The regions beyond these places are either difficult of access because of their excessive winters and great cold, or else cannot be sought out because of some divine influence of the gods.

colony of Gades (Cadiz) in Spain up the Atlantic coast to Albion, as he called Britain, and the Cassiterides, or "Tin Islands" (probably modern Cornwall). Along the way, he took careful measurements, and he was the first Greek to connect the tides with the motion of the moon. He reported that six days north of Britain was an island called Thule, identified as the Shetland Islands or the Orkneys, where navigation was rendered nearly impossible by a weather condition with no distinction between the air, sea, and earth, probably a reference to thick fog. He also reported that on the summer solstice, June 21, the day was twenty-four hours long, suggesting the Arctic Circle. Pytheas also made the geographically impossible claim to have surveyed the northern coast of Europe to the east as far as Tanaïs, the Don River in Russia, in the course of which he found a source of amber. But this would have been based on the standard misconception of the time that the known world was surrounded by a single great ocean. What he thought was the Don probably was the Elbe or another river that flowed into the North Sea or the Baltic Sea.

HELLENISTIC RELIGIONS

The expansion of their world during the Hellenistic period brought the Greeks into contact with a multitude of different peoples, cultures, and beliefs. These contacts, especially with the Persian and even Indian worlds, engendered a new period of Greek culture during which the Greeks lost their insular view of the world and accepted the value of peoples and cultures outside of their own. The old distinction between Hellenes and barbarians now was less clear, as populations and cultures became mixed from Greece to the Indus River valley. As during the Archaic Period, oriental influences in art, religion, government, and thought flowed into Greece. Greek culture now became an amalgamation of eastern and western culture that also served to give western and eastern people common ground that they had not had before. For many Greeks, the Hellenistic period also created a crisis of identity. The city-states that previously had been major actors on the world stage now were just bit players. The importance of Greece had declined to the point at which being Greek no longer produced the same sense of smugness as before. Both Greeks and non-Greeks felt lost and adrift in the new Hellenistic multicultural world. In order either to find a new sense of identity or to hold on to their old identity, many people turned to religion and philosophy.

An Age of Anxiety

The Hellenistic period brought with it the end of the age of the polis. The days were long past when a single city, such as Athens or Sparta, could be a major player on the world stage. The Hellenistic age was a time of kings and empires. Cities were shuffled around from one kingdom to another like so many pawns on a chessboard. Greeks who in the past had focused their sense of identity on their cities now felt adrift. Being a subject of a king could not replace the feeling of security that one had from being a citizen of an independent city. Rather than being primarily a citizen of a polis, the feeling arose that one now was a citizen of the **cosmopolis**, a Greek word meaning "world-city." But being a citizen of the world did not provide one with any meaningful sense of personal identity. It was no longer possible to live out one's life in a single city, essentially oblivious to what was going on elsewhere. People encountered the wider world every day: in the street, in the marketplace, and in the classroom. At the same time, the old Greek sense of cultural supremacy was threatened by outside influences, and Greeks no longer could remain blissfully ignorant of the cultures of other peoples. They were constantly bombarded with the artifacts of foreign cultures, some of which in fact had a great attraction for them.

This made Greeks very uncomfortable. They were used to feeling integrated into a comprehensible world. Now they felt lost. It was commonly felt that the world was controlled by *tychē*, blind chance, which could bring either good fortune or complete ruin. As a consequence, Greeks desperately sought to get their world back under control. Many did so by supernatural means and embraced some of the same Near Eastern ideas that had made them uncomfortable. Babylonian astrology, which taught that a future ordained by the gods could be read in the stars, gained many followers in Greece. In the early third century, the Babylonian priest Berossus wrote a *Babyloniaca*, a history of Babylonia, and opened a school of astrology on the Greek island of Cos. In addition, the use of magical spells gave average people a sense of empowerment. It was believed, for example, that speaking a god's secret name gave a person control over the god. An Egyptian charm

A zodiac mosaic from a third-century CE Jewish synagogue at Beth Alpha in Israel attests to the popularity of the belief that peoples' lives were governed by the motions of heavenly bodies.

read: "Hear me, I am going to say the great name, Aoth, before whom every god prostrates himself and every demon shudders. Your divine name is Aeeioyo Iayoe Eaooyeeoia. I have spoken the glorious name, the name for all needs." In addition, there survive large numbers of curse tablets that were buried near a place in contact with the gods, such as a sacred well, an execution site, or a grave, and that invoked a god to bring misfortune on a wrongdoer, such as a thief, an opponent in a lawsuit, or a rival lover.

Not surprisingly, people also looked for help from the gods in curing their maladies. Incubation, or sleeping in the temple of a god known for healing, such as Asclepius, was done to treat maladies ranging from psoriasis to cancer, and temple walls were hung with plaques recording cures. A soldier left one that read, "As he was sleeping in the Temple the god extracted the spearhead and gave it to him into his hands. When day came he departed cured." Dreams also could convey signs of cures. According to another report, "Arata, a woman of Sparta, suffered from dropsy [an accumulation of fluid]. While she remained at home, her mother slept in the temple and saw a dream. It seemed that the god cut off her daughter's head and out came a huge quantity of fluid matter. Then he fitted the head back on the neck. Afterward she went home where she found her daughter in good health." People also attempted self-medication. And an ancient pregnancy test advised, "You should make the woman urinate on the Great-Nile plant. When morning comes, if you find the plant scorched, she will not conceive. If you find it green, she will conceive."

Hellenistic Mystery Cults

Given the uncertainties of life on earth, people became increasingly concerned about what would happen to them after death. As a result, **mystery cults** (from Greek *mysterion*, or "secret"), which promised a happy afterlife, gained great popularity. Participants went through an **initiation** rite in which they learned the secrets that would grant them eternal life. All of the mystery cults involved the worship of a god or goddess who suffered, died, and was resurrected. During the ceremony, the human participant in some way shared the identity of the god and as a consequence shared in the god's immortality. If the god could be resurrected, then so could you. Different cults created this mystical union with the god in different ways. Initiates were sworn to secrecy, but enough of the ritual slipped out for us to be able to form a general picture of what happened. The ceremony usually began with a purification ritual that enabled the initiate to come into contact with the deity. It then entailed sitting through, or actually participating in, an elaborate performance explaining the cycle of life and death.

In order to be initiated into most mystery cults, all people had to do was show up, although some cults made greater demands than others. Whereas some initiations, such as into the Eleusinian mysteries in Athens, occurred only in single location, others could occur anywhere. For example, the ancient Egyptian cult of Isis, in which Osiris was brought back from the dead after being dismembered and thrown into the Nile, was refurbished to make it more attractive to a mass audience. The account given by the third-century CE writer Apuleius provides the most accurate account of the initiation process. First of all, those desiring initiation were expected to live in the temple for a while with the priests and to attend temple rites. Eventually, participants received during the night a sign from the goddess that they were ready to proceed. The next morning the initiates were instructed from an ancient book written in strange characters, probably a reference to hieroglyphs. Then, asking pardon from the gods for their sins, they were baptized with water identified as sacred water from the Nile and were reborn just as Osiris had been reborn from the Nile. Following their baptism, the initiates remained pure for ten days by refraining from drinking wine, eating meat, and having sex. The final initiation rite began at sunset on the tenth day, when the candidates were taken to the innermost part of the temple and metaphorically became Osiris, undergoing a ritual death, traveling to the underworld, and seeing the gods; in one account, Isis herself said to an initiate, "When you descend to the underworld, there you will see me shining and you will worship me as the one who has favored you." The initiates then were reborn with the rising sun the next morning.

In the initiation into the cult of the wine-god Dionysus, a son of Zeus known as the "twice born" because Zeus had recreated him after he was eaten by the Titans, participants first drank wine, which represented the god's blood. The next sacrament was the "feast of the raw flesh" in which they tore apart and ate raw a wild animal, such as a fawn, which represented Dionysus himself. By sharing Dionysus' flesh and blood, initiates partook of his divinity and immortality. On some occasions, Dionysian rites known as the Bacchanalia (after Bacchus, another name for Dionysus) turned into sexual orgies brought on by the wine and religious ecstasy.

The most demanding mystery cult was that of **Cybele**, an Anatolian mother goddess. In myth, Cybele fell in love with her son Attis, a vegetation god, but when the young man preferred a local princess, the goddess drove him mad, and he castrated himself with a sharp stone and died under a pine tree. But Cybele brought him back to life in the spring, and, like vegetation, he was ready to die again. The annual festival of Cybele, celebrated in March, recreated the death and rebirth of Attis. A pine tree representing the dead Attis was brought to the temple of Cybele, and devotees then mourned his death by abstaining for a day from drinking wine and from eating fruits and vegetables. The climax came on March 24, "the Day of Blood." Participants worked themselves into a frenzy by madly dancing to the sound of clashing cymbals, blaring horns, and beating drums. They also slashed themselves with knives, sprinkling fertilizing blood on the pine tree in order to restore Attis to life. The Greek satirist Lucian described what then could happen: "Frenzy comes upon many who have come simply to watch. The initiate throws off his clothes, takes up a sword, and castrates himself. Then he runs through the city holding the parts he has cut off. He takes female clothing and adornment from whatever house he throws the parts into." By this means, the initiate not only became Attis, the consort of Cybele, but also, in a sense, became Cybele herself, and thus was able to gain immortality. Having taken this irrevocable step, the initiate, if he survived, also became one of the wandering priests of Cybele known as the Galli.

There was nothing complicated about mystery cults. People gained salvation simply by having a brief devotion to a mystery deity and by engaging in the appropriate rituals. There was no need for any long-term commitment or any continued ritual. Nor were the cults exclusive, and people could be initiated

This scene from the Villa of the Mysteries in Pompeii depicts an initiation into the cult of Dionysus involving pain followed by pleasure. The woman on the left is being whipped, whereas the two women on the right, having completed the initiation, strike the cymbals and brandish a thyrsus, a staff wound with vine leaves and topped by a pine cone, the symbol of Dionysus.

into any number of mystery cults. These were the first religions of redemption open to all, and they were extraordinarily popular. Thus there was a widespread belief in the Hellenistic period that it was possible to gain a life after death by following the model of a god who had done the same thing and by participating in a ceremony that mimicked the experiences of the god.

Hellenistic Philosophy

People who preferred to have a more intellectual basis for understanding their place in the world and the universe could turn to philosophy. But the teachings of the pre-Socratic philosophers and their successors, such as Plato, who had attempted to explain the workings of the universe and human society writ large, did not respond to the needs of individual people. The Hellenistic period thus saw the introduction of philosophical systems that gave people the opportunity to define their own personal place and role in the world. The philosopher Diogenes of Sinope, for example, taught that the best way to avoid being at the mercy of either blind chance or a distant king was by discarding all human conventions and "living according to nature." His followers were called **Cynics**, from the Greek word for "dog," because, like dogs, they felt no shame about performing all their bodily functions—eating, sleeping, defecating, and having sex—out in the open. This made them self-sufficient, indifferent to what anyone thought of them, and unconcerned with status. And their disregard of authority made them willing to speak their minds on anything to anybody. Thus, it was said, when Alexander the Great asked Diogenes, who lay naked sunning himself, what he could do for him, Diogenes replied, "You could move to the side and stop blocking the sun."

The philosopher Epicurus of Samos, who founded a school called the Garden in Athens ca. 300 BCE, took a materialistic approach to understanding one's personal role in the world. His teachings, which came to be known as **Epicureanism**, proposed that there were no gods or good or bad luck and that the universe consisted simply of atoms randomly falling through space without any guiding principle. Sometimes the atoms swerved, clumped together, and created the material world, including people. The swerve also gave people the free will to pursue the Epicurean goal of gaining *ataraxia*, peace of mind, by pursuing hedonism, or pleasure. But for Epicurus, pleasure meant preventing one's atoms from getting jangled, and this meant avoiding pain. Thus pleasures that caused pain, such as overeating or drunkenness, were to be avoided. To attain *ataraxia*, one needed to avoid being affected by circumstances. Epicurus thus recommended avoiding public service and pursuing a life of seclusion spent with like-minded friends. Epicurus' school was unusual in that it admitted women.

Zeno, a native of Citium on Cyprus who also settled in Athens about 300 BCE, had a different view that came to be called **Stoicism** because he

The focus on "pleasure" led to a modern misunderstanding that Epicureans overdo their seeking of pleasure, exactly the opposite of what Epicurus meant.

taught in the *Stoa Poikilē*, or Painted Portico. His teachings, like those of Epicurus, were centered on a materialistic universe, but for Zeno the universe was highly structured into a pattern that was established by a rational governing force called the *logos*. The universe was like a finely tuned machine that repeated itself about every twenty-six thousand years. Every person represented one part of the machine, and it was everyone's duty to perform the role that they had been assigned by god. The Stoic creed was, "Lead me, O Zeus, wherever you will, and I will follow willingly, and if I do not, you will drag me." The only choice a Stoic had was either to accept the inevitable, which already had been determined by the *logos*, or to fight against it and inevitably be destroyed. The importance given to the performance of duty made Stoicism well suited for individuals committed to public service.

Hellenistic Judaism

Another religion affected by the Hellenistic Age was **Judaism**. After Judaea was absorbed into Alexander's empire, the Jews continued to enjoy the same freedom of worship as under the Persians, but later, unlike the Ptolemies and other Greco-Macedonian rulers, the Seleucids sometimes tried to force Hellenism on their subjects as a means of unifying their kingdom. Many Jews, mostly well-to-do and engaged in public life, embraced Hellenistic culture. They learned Greek, studied Greek literature, and adopted Greek religious and philosophical beliefs. This may have led King Antiochus IV Epiphanes (175–164 BCE), whose epithet meant "God Made Manifest," to believe that other Jews also could be Hellenized. But his efforts to impose Greek culture aroused great opposition, especially among less privileged Jews led by the Hasidim ("the pious ones"), who feared that any adoption of Greek culture could lead to their destruction. Antiochus responded by actively attempting to undermine Jewish practices. He not only prohibited circumcision, studying the Torah, and observing the Sabbath, but he even instituted ritual prostitution in the Temple in Jerusalem, where he also placed a statue and altar to Zeus on which pigs, which the Jews believed were unclean, were sacrificed, something the Jews called the "abomination of desolation." Rebellion broke out led by Judah, nicknamed Maccabee ("The Hammer"); the rebels' goal was not just religious freedom but also political independence. Against all odds, Judah defeated Antiochus in 165 BCE and liberated Jerusalem, marking one of the very few times in antiquity that a popular revolt succeeded in gaining a people's independence. The following year, the temple was cleansed and reopened. In 140 BCE, Simon, the brother of Judah, was named both high priest and king of the Jews, thus reestablishing a Jewish kingdom. This marked the beginning of the Hasmonean Dynasty (140–37 BCE), which would last for another hundred years and would be the last independent Jewish nation until 1949 CE.

The reconsecration of the Jewish temple is still commemorated each year in the Jewish festival of Hanukkah ("the Dedication").

Jewish independence did not, however, mean an end to disagreements among the Jews. Hellenism still attracted many Jews, such as members of the **Sadducees**, who oversaw the temple in Jerusalem. The Sadducees interpreted Jewish law narrowly, relying solely on written scriptures. The **Pharisees**, on the other hand, the successors of the Hasidim, supported a rigorous enforcement of Jewish religious law and oversaw the study of scripture in the synagogues. During the reign of Queen Salome Alexandra (76–67 BCE), the Pharisees gained enormous authority and produced a new body of law, the **Mishnah**, oral interpretations of Mosaic law (Law of Moses) that vastly increased the numbers of prohibitions and regulations that were necessary for living a life acceptable to Yahweh.

At the same time, the Jewish diaspora continued the spread of the Jewish population throughout the Mediterranean world, especially in Mesopotamia and in Alexandria, where a large population of Jews made up of exiles, merchants, and mercenaries eventually outnumbered the Jews of Palestine. These foreign Jews were remarkably successful at being able to preserve much of their culture in the midst of foreign customs. But with respect to language, the Jews of Alexandria eventually functioned in Greek rather than in Hebrew. To make scripture available to them, beginning in the third century BCE a Greek version of the Old Testament was created, known as the **Septuagint**, from the Latin word meaning "seventy," because it supposedly had been made by seventy translators.

HELLENISTIC THOUGHT

The Hellenistic period saw a major shift toward the practical as scientific thought turned from the production of theories, which were argued but never put into practice, to experimentation, proofs, and applications in the real world.

Aristotle and Scientific Philosophy

In the Hellenistic period, Greek scientific thought turned from theories based on imaginative hypotheses and convincing argumentation to theories based on observation and experimentation. The first great practical philosopher was **Aristotle**, a native of northern Greece whose father was the personal physician of King Amyntas III of Macedonia. After studying medicine with his father and philosophy with Plato in Athens, he moved to Ionia, where he made biological observations with his friend Theophrastus. After being employed by Philip II of Macedon as the tutor of Alexander the Great, he returned to Athens in 335 BCE and founded his own school, called the Lyceum, named after the grove of Apollo Lyceus, the Greek wolf god, where the school met.

Aristotle opposed the belief that scientific controversies could be solved simply by thinking about them. His method for understanding the world was to collect evidence, analyze it, categorize it, and only then come to conclusions. Rather than focusing on pure theory devoid of proof, Aristotle studied the real world of nature and real human interactions. Whereas Plato had looked for a unified system based on perfect forms that would explain everything in the world, Aristotle took the opposite approach and looked for unity by searching for the essence of individual categories of things and looked at each one individually. He and his pupils subdivided and categorized many aspects of philosophical study, and a multitude of books, which might have been intended more as lecture notes than for widespread circulation, appeared under his name.

In what he called "natural philosophy," relating to the natural world, Aristotle considered biology, zoology, astronomy, and chemistry. His biological studies, for example, resulted in the identification of different species. Aristotle took Greek philosophy out of the think tank and into the laboratory of the real world. His empirical approach to understanding the universe, based not on theory but on observation, resulted in the introduction of the **scientific method**, in which evidence is collected, studied, classified, and analyzed and conclusions are determined by the evidence, not by who can make the best argument. This approach was adopted by later Hellenistic scientists, whose advances in mathematics, physics, astronomy, and medicine were not superseded until the early modern period.

Aristotle also considered abstract topics, such as rhetoric, poetry, and ethics. He invented the field of formal logic, involving the use of deductive reasoning. And in his *Politeia* (*Politics*), Aristotle formulated his own concept of an ideal society that was not based on pure hypothesis, like Plato's, but on a collection of the constitutions of a multitude of real human governments, including even that of the barbarian Carthaginians. Aristotle believed, for example, that virtuous people could govern themselves. More theoretically, whereas Plato had denied the significance of change by arguing that the transitory worldly things are merely imperfect reflections of perfect unchanging forms, Aristotle taught that the world was defined by how things change. Nothing happens without a material cause, and every change occurs for some reason and purpose. He had little room for gods in his universe. Although he acknowledged that some kind of divinity had gotten the universe going, once started, it was self-perpetuating. His model of the universe was based on observation, logic, and common sense and could be replicated by someone else. All of this made Aristotle's approach very different from the methods and models of earlier philosophers.

Hellenistic Science

Alexander the Great himself was a product of the new age of scientific investigation, and he took with him on his eastern campaigns a staff of scientists to observe and record discoveries in fields ranging from botany to geography. The Hellenistic monarchs were great supporters of scholarly studies, and several

The works of Alexander's botanist, Aristotle's friend Theophrastus, served as the foundation for modern botany.

Hellenistic cities gained reputations as major centers of learning. Athens, of course, continued as one of the intellectual centers of the Greek world. And Pergamum boasted a library and a famous school of medicine.

But it was Alexandria in Egypt that became the cultural capital of the Hellenistic world. There, Ptolemy I and II founded a university called the **Museum**, or home of the Muses. Next door was the great Library of Alexandria, where hundreds of thousands books were deposited from throughout a Hellenized world that now extended from Spain to India. A large community of scholars pursued many sorts of scientific studies. Alexandria was especially famous as a scientific center. The mathematician **Euclid,** who worked ca. 300 BCE, was the most famous mathematician of all time. His textbook on plane geometry not only presented the standard geometric axioms, such as that only one line parallel to another line can be drawn through a point, but also demonstrated how these axioms could be used to present proofs of geometric theorems.

With more than one thousand editions, Euclid's textbook is said to be, after the Bible, the most influential book ever published. Modern geometry textbooks do little more than reproduce Euclid's theorems.

The Hellenistic period also brought advances in medicine, a field that had been largely invented in the early fourth century by **Hippocrates** of Cos, the first Greek physician to reject the common belief that illness was caused by, and could only be cured by, the gods. He and his pupils taught that sickness was caused by environment and diet and that it was important to observe symptoms, so that similar illnesses could receive similar treatments. But in other regards, he was reluctant to administer medicine out of a belief that the body was usually able to heal itself simply with rest. During the Hellenistic period, the Alexandrian school of medicine expanded the knowledge of human anatomy by dissecting the bodies of executed criminals. As a result, Alexandrian physicians discovered the function of nerves and that blood flowed through vessels.

The medical ethics introduced by Hippocrates are preserved in the modern Hippocratic Oath.

Alexandria also was home to a host of famous astronomers, who investigated the position of the Earth in the universe. Aristotle and others had presumed that the heavenly bodies revolved around the Earth. But about 250 BCE, Aristarchus proposed a heliocentric ("sun-centered") universe, with the sun rather than the Earth at the center, and with a rotating Earth. But he was unable to provide any proof for his hypothesis. Not only was his theory not accepted, but he himself was accused of disrespecting the gods. Shortly thereafter, Eratosthenes calculated the circumference of the Earth at 24,887 miles, nearly exactly correct, by comparing the different lengths of shadows cast at noon at different places in Egypt. He also predicted that there were other continents in the southern hemisphere.

The accusations against Aristarchus are eerily similar to the accusation of heresy against Galileo in the seventeenth century for proposing the same theory.

By suggesting that one could reach India by sailing west from Spain, Eratosthenes made the same mistake Columbus made 1700 years later.

Around 140 BCE, Hipparchus, the most influential Hellenistic astronomer, created the field of observational astronomy by producing the first western star catalogue. Using an astrolabe, a long, thin tube, to identify a star's location, he established the exact positions of five hundred stars. Hipparchus also devised a standard reference system that used lines of latitude and longitude to define positions on the Earth and in the sky. Rejecting Aristarchus' heliocentric system as unprovable, Hipparchus returned to the geocentric system, with the sun, moon, and planets revolving around the Earth. But in order to explain the looping motion of the planets as viewed against the stars, he was forced to hypothesize a system whereby the planets did not move in perfect circles around the Earth, but in a complicated pattern of circles within circles. Hipparchus' concept of an Earth-centered universe, later called the **Ptolemaic System** after the Roman astronomer Ptolemy, was so convincing that it remained the standard belief for the next seventeen hundred years.

Hellenistic Technology

In antiquity, technological advances generally came slowly, but the Hellenistic age was different and was the greatest period of ancient technological advances. Machines were invented that served both practical purposes and as curiosities and that surprisingly prefigured many modern technological developments. The first great Hellenistic inventor was Ctesibius of Alexandria. In the years after 250 BCE, he realized that air was a substance that could be manipulated, and he invented a number of devices using water pressure and compressed air, such as a water clock that used valves to turn the water on and off, an organ that used water pressure to create air flow through sets of pipes that was the first keyboard instrument, and a high-pressure pump to shoot streams of water at fires.

Three centuries later, Hero of Alexandria, nicknamed "the machine man," created other machines based on air and water pressure. One caused a hollow sphere to rotate using steam jets on the sides of a hollow sphere, but it was used only to make puppets dance. More practical inventions included hydraulic devices to force the oil out of olives, automatic door openers for temples, and an odometer, a system of gears connected to a wheel, to measure distances. The odometer later was used to place the mile markers on the Roman road system.

The most famous Hellenistic inventor of all was **Archimedes**, a native of Syracuse, who invented the field of mathematical physics and developed a number of physical theorems, such as that a body will displace its own volume of water. The application of this concept allowed for the calculation of specific gravity based on the weight and volume of water displaced by any object. Perhaps his most useful invention was the Archimedes screw, which was used in pumping water out of rivers and canals for irrigation. And although Hellenistic inventions rarely were used for warfare, in 212 BCE Archimedes used his engineering skills to defend Syracuse when it was being attacked by the Romans. According to Plutarch, "Huge poles thrust out from the walls over the ships sunk some by the great weights that they dropped down upon them; others they lifted up into the air by an iron hook and whirled about. A ship was frequently lifted up to a great height in the air and kept swinging until the mariners were all thrown out, when at length it was dashed against the rocks

LEGACY OF ANTIQUITY

In what ways did Hellenistic science and technology anticipate the discoveries of the modern day?

The principle of Hero's steam engine is used in the modern jet engine.

THE HISTORY LABORATORY

THE ANTIKYTHERA DEVICE

The most complex machine to be preserved from antiquity, now in the Athens National Museum, was discovered in 1900 by a Greek sponge diver near the island of Antikythera off the coast of Crete, and it is thus known as the Antikythera device. It was built around 80 BCE and is the first known mechanical computing machine. It is preserved in the same encrusted condition it was in when pulled from the sea, but close examination, assisted by X rays, shows that the surviving section (part of it was missing) contains no less than thirty-two gears. It is based on the astronomical theories of Hipparchus about the movement of astronomical bodies around the Earth and can display the position of the sun, moon, and planets in the zodiac, along with the phases of the moon, at any time, past or future. It is accurate to one part in eighty-six thousand. The ability to make such predictions had very practical significance for astrologers, for it allowed them to cast precise horoscopes for any date.

below." He even was said to have built a system of mirrors that set Roman ships afire by concentrating sunlight on them.

Art and Literature

Whereas classical Greek culture had been marked by homogeneity and standardization, Hellenistic culture was characterized by heterogeneity and syncretism. The simplicity, restraint, and clean lines of classical art were replaced by the baroque and emotional extravagance of Hellenistic art. One example of this change is seen in architecture. By the mid-fourth century BCE, the simple Doric and Ionic capitals had been largely replaced by the elaborately floral Corinthian capitals as the preferred building style. Huge elaborate public buildings and monuments replaced the simplicity of Classical temples such as the Parthenon.

Hellenistic literature, moreover, produced little that could challenge the literature of the Archaic and Classical periods. In the middle of the third century BCE, under Ptolemy II, Alexandria became the literary capital of the classical world. The pithy epigrams of Callimachus of Cyrene exhibited the Hellenistic preference for brevity, a focus more on quality than quantity, and an aversion to long epics such as those of Homer; his famous motto was that "a big book is

a big evil." But Callimachus authored a big book of his own, a 120-volume catalogue of the holdings of the Library of Alexandria. Even though Callimachus'
rival, Apollonius of Rhodes, the librarian of Alexandria, did compose an epic
poem, the *Argonautica*, a story of Jason's search for the Golden Fleece, it still was
only a third the length of the *Iliad*. And at same time the Sicilian Theocritus
settled in Alexandria and created the genre of bucolic poetry, set in the countryside and replete with shepherds and singing matches. All of these poets were
beholden to the Ptolemies as their patrons and praised them assiduously in
their works. Callimachus' poem the *Coma Berenices*, for example, described
how a lock of hair of Queen Berenice II, wife of Ptolemy III, became the astronomical constellation of the same name. And Theocritus earned his keep by
writing a poem praising the tyrant Hiero II of Syracuse and a poetic hymn in
honor of the marriage of Ptolemy II and his sister Arsinoë II in 277 BCE.

At the same time, there was a greater concern with appealing to a mass audience, and form became more important than content. The late fourth-century
comedies of Menander, for example, no longer dealt with current events but
were full of slapstick and had plots often revolving around romantic love and
marriage. A new dramatic genre was the **mime**, a brief portrayal of a scene from
domestic life with no more real content than a modern sitcom. Stories combining love and adventure resulted in the creation of the romance novel. The end
result was that little Hellenistic poetry or drama has stood the test of time, and
perhaps the most notable representative of Hellenistic literature is its histories,
such as that of the Greek Polybius.

In academic circles, creative literature was often replaced by scholarship.
Authors were more interested in showing off how much they knew than in
dealing with timeless issues of morality and ethics. Not, however, that this
was necessarily a bad thing, for Hellenistic scholars created editions of the literature of Greek antiquity, such as the Homeric epics, that, by and large, still
remain standard. Likewise, grammars and dictionaries created in Hellenistic
times served as the ancestors of all later ones. Hellenistic literature also is
known for its attention to practical applications. Geographical treatises, school
handbooks, and philosophical systems had a great influence on later western
culture. At the same time, a form of Greek known as *koinē* ("common form")
became the standard literary language throughout the Mediterranean and Near
Eastern worlds, which became culturally united in a way that they never had
been before and never would be again.

LOOKING AHEAD

Before we can continue our discussion of the Hellenistic kingdoms, we must
turn to the west, for at the same time that Hellenistic politics and culture were
evolving in the Near East and the eastern Mediterranean, a new power had
arisen in the western Mediterranean, the city of Rome. Over the course of

250 years, Rome had grown from a small village in central Italy to the most powerful state in the Mediterranean world. The eastern powers, however, did not yet know this, and in the third century BCE, Antigonid Macedonia and Seleucid Syria would have a rude awakening when Roman armies appeared on their doorsteps.

FURTHER READING

Aperghis, G. G. *The Seleukid Royal Economy: The Finances and Financial Administration of the Seleukid Empire.* Cambridge: Cambridge University Press, 2004.

Beck, Hans. *Central Greece and the Politics of Power in the Fourth Century BC.* Cambridge: Cambridge University Press, 2008.

Bingen, Jean. *Hellenistic Egypt.* Edinburgh: Edinburgh University Press, 2007.

Buckler, John. *The Theban Hegemony, 371–362 BC.* Cambridge, MA: Harvard University Press, 1980.

Burkert, Walter. *Ancient Mystery Cults.* Cambridge, MA: Harvard University Press, 1987.

Cargill, Jack. *The Second Athenian League: Empire or Free Alliance?* Berkeley: University of California Press, 1981.

Chauveau, Michel. *Egypt in the Age of Cleopatra: History and Society under the Ptolemies.* Translated by David Lorton. Ithaca, NY: Cornell University Press, 2000.

Dijksterhuis, E. J. *Archimedes.* Princeton, NJ: Princeton University Press, 1987.

Engel, Donald W. *Alexander the Great and the Logistics of the Macedonian Army.* Berkeley: University of California Press, 1978.

Errington, R. M. *A History of the Hellenistic World.* Oxford: Blackwell, 2008.

Gabbert, Janice. *Antigonus II Gonatas: A Political Biography.* London: Routledge, 1997.

Grabbe, Lester L. *A History of the Jews and Judaism in the Second Temple Period.* Vol. 2, *The Coming of the Greeks: The Early Hellenistic Period (335—175 BCE).* London and New York: Clark, 2008.

Green, Peter. *Alexander to Actium: The Historical Evolution of the Hellenistic Age.* Berkeley: University of California Press, 1990.

Hammond, Nicholas G. L. *The Macedonian State.* Oxford: Oxford University Press, 1989.

Kuhrt, Amelie, and Susan Sherwin-White. *From Samarkhand to Sardis: A New Approach to the Seleucid Empire.* Berkeley: University of California Press, 1993.

Lloyd, G. E. R. *Greek Science after Aristotle.* New York: Norton, 1973.

Reitzenstein, Richard. *Hellenistic Mystery Religions: Their Basic Ideas and Significance.* Pittsburgh, PA: Pickwick Press, 1978.

Stanwick, Paul Edmund. *Portraits of the Ptolemies: Greek Kings as Egyptian Pharaohs.* Austin: University of Texas Press, 2002.

THE GRANDEUR THAT WAS ROME

CHAPTER 9

THE RISE OF ROME AND THE ROMAN REPUBLIC

(753–121 BCE)

During the course of the Iron Age, the centers of new cultural and political development continued to move ever farther to the west. The third and final great center of cultural development in the ancient world, after the Near East and Greece, was Rome. After its foundation as a small farming village on the Tiber River in the mid eighth century BCE, Rome assimilated both population and culture from its neighbors, creating a truly multicultural society. Then, over the course of the Roman Republic, Rome expanded to become the greatest power of the ancient Mediterranean world.

THE CULTURAL ENVIRONMENT OF EARLY ROME

One of the most noteworthy characteristics of the ancient Romans was their ability to assimilate aspects of the cultures of other peoples while at the same time maintaining their own unique identity. One of the reasons for this, no doubt, is that from the very beginning of their history, the Romans were in close contact with neighboring peoples with very different cultural traits. Rather than fearing foreign contacts, the Romans readily borrowed from the cultures of their neighbors.

Indo-European Movements

In the years after ca. 2000 BCE, at the same time that some groups of Indo-Europeans were moving off the southern Russian steppes into Iran and Anatolia, others began to filter into Europe. They merged with the indigenous European peoples who were the descendents of those who had created the Megalithic culture. According to one model, there were at least two movements into Italy of peoples identified by their Indo-European dialects. The first was by the "Q speakers," for whom, for example, the number "five" was "quinque." Subsequently, the "P speakers," for whom "five" was "pompa," arrived and

This distinction survives in Irish (Q) and Breton and Welsh (P) speakers

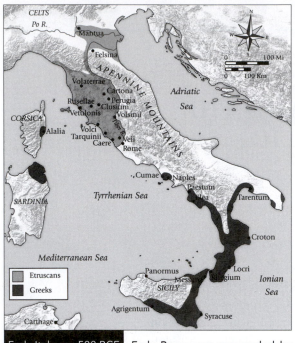

Early Italy, ca. 500 BCE   Early Rome was surrounded by different peoples and cultures, which would have a tremendous impact on the subsequent evolution of Roman culture.

pushed in on the Q speakers. By ca.1000 BCE, the Q speakers, whose dialect became Latin, inhabited only the rich agricultural plain of Latium, south of the lower Tiber River, and included primarily the people known as the **Latins**. The P speakers, whose dialects included Oscan and Sabellian, developed into the **Italic peoples,** such as the **Samnites**, Campanians, and Lucanians, who dwelt in the mountainous areas of central and southern Italy.

The Celts

In inland Europe, the Hallstatt culture appeared in the lower Danube area ca. 800 BCE. It was characterized by burials of important persons in wagons in log-lined underground chambers. It eventually spread along the Danube and Rhine rivers and encompassed all of Europe except for Greece and Italy. The people associated with this culture came to be called either **Celts** or Gauls.

In some ways, the Celts were like the Greeks. Rather than being united into a single country or nation, they were composed of many different groups. Each was governed either by a *rix* ("king") or by a council of warrior aristocrats. The Celtic economy was primarily agricultural, but the Celts also maintained a complex trading network, and Celtic metalwork was highly prized.

Also like the Greeks, the Celts often engaged in conflict. But Celtic warfare was undisciplined and very unlike Greek warfare. Celtic warriors had metal rings called torques, often of gold or silver and very ornate, forged around their necks. The only way to remove a torque was by decapitating a slain warrior, a practice for which the Celts were famous. Celtic fighters made themselves look more terrifying before a battle by smearing wet lime into their hair to make it stand straight back when it dried. Some Celtic warriors fought in the nude, believing that the magical powers of their torques would protect them. A battle began with Celtic soldiers jumping about and shouting insults at their enemy. After they had worked themselves up into the famous "Celtic fury," they charged. In their initial encounters with the Celts, no Mediterranean people could resist the terrifying assault of hordes of naked six-foot Celts wildly swinging their yard-long swords.

Carthage

In the late ninth century BCE, the Phoenician city of Tyre founded **Carthage** as a trading post on a well-protected harbor on the coast of modern Tunisia in North Africa. By the sixth century BCE Carthage had grown into a rich and powerful trading city in its own right. It controlled the western third of Sicily, and its influence extended into southern Spain and as far as the western coast of Africa. Carthaginian merchants traded by land and sea with sub-Saharan Africa to the south, whence they obtained peacocks, apes, ebony, and ivory; in the sixth century BCE, for example, the Carthaginian sailor Hanno wrote a periplus describing a journey down the west coast of Africa at least as far the Congo River on which hippopotamuses and hairy creatures called "gorillas" were sighted. To the north, Carthaginian traders brought back silver from Spain, and a virtual monopoly on trade in tin from the British Isles was a major source of the city's wealth. Other trade goods included the purple dye brought from Tyre, fine textiles, incense, perfumes, jewelry, inlaid furniture, wine, and horses. The Carthaginian economy also benefited from extensive exploitation of the surrounding rich agricultural lands, utilizing crop rotation and advanced irrigation techniques; a treatise on agriculture written in Punic by the Carthaginian Mago later was translated into Latin and became a standard work on the topic.

Because of the need to protect its seaborne commerce, the Carthaginians possessed a powerful navy of over three hundred warships, kept ready to go to sea in a specially constructed circular war harbor. The navy, which was responsible for protecting the Carthaginian homeland, was recruited primarily from native Carthaginians, and, as at Athens, provided a livelihood for the poor. The Carthaginian army, on the other hand, was used primarily for foreign wars and relied heavily on mercenaries, including cavalry from Numidians, a people of northwestern Africa, and several hundred African war elephants.

Carthage was ruled by an oligarchy of the rich; each year two Suffets ("judges") were elected to head the government, and the most significant legislative body was a *gerousia* ("Senate") chosen from the wealthiest and most influential families. As in Greece, a popular Assembly confirmed the decisions of the Senate. The Carthaginian constitution was even included by Aristotle in his collection of constitutions, something quite unusual given that the Greeks otherwise considered the Carthaginians to be "barbarians."

Along with the creation of the typical purple dye, the Carthaginians preserved many Phoenician traditions, and Carthaginian religion was very similar to that of the Phoenicians. At the head of the pantheon was a divine couple composed of the fertility goddess Tanit (who in Ugarit was an eater of flesh and blood) and the creator god Ba'al Hammon (the Carthaginian version of the Phoenician El). Later Roman sources reported that in times of stress Carthaginian parents sacrificed their infant children to these two, and these reports are confirmed by the finding of several cemeteries containing the cremated bodies of infants.

The Western Greeks

Cities such as Naples, Syracuse, and Marseilles still are major commercial centers.

During the Second Wave of Greek Colonization, mainland Greeks established several colonies on the southern Italian coast, the most prominent being Capua, Naples, and Tarentum. Other colonies were founded on the coasts of Sicily (such as Syracuse) and southern France (Marseilles). In the course of their extensive trade, these colonies served as a conduit both for the spread of Greek culture into the European hinterland and for the reception of native culture into the Mediterranean area. During the fifth century BCE, native peoples of the Italian uplands began to move toward the coast, occupying some of the Greek colonies and creating an amalgamation of Greek and Italian culture.

The Etruscans

The Etruscans gave their name to modern Tuscany.

The civilization of the **Etruscans** arose in northwestern Italy. The Etruscans did not form a unified nation but consisted of a dodecapolis of twelve independent cities. Each was ruled by a *lucomo* (king), who was supported and advised by a warrior aristocracy. The highly developed Etruscan economy was based on trade and manufacturing; the Etruscans were particularly admired for their metalwork. They used an alphabet developed from that of the Greeks to write a language that still is undeciphered.

Etruscan religion made heavy use of **divination**, whereby one attempted to foretell the future based on signs received from the gods. For example, Etruscan priests took the *auspices* (inspecting flights of birds) and the *haruspices* (examination of sheep livers) for indications of the outcome of future events. The Etruscans also had a cult of the dead that was superficially similar to that of the Egyptians: they believed that "you could take it with you" and that life after death was a perpetuation of all the best aspects of life on earth. They constructed elaborate cities of the dead marked by groves of cypress trees and composed of hundreds of multiroomed stone-cut underground tombs. The walls had carved into them implements that were used in everyday life, and marble coffins, or sarcophagi, contained the remains of married couples who remained united in death just as they had been united in life. Etruscan funerals were marked by athletic contests, such as wrestling matches, in honor not only of the dead but also of the gods of the underworld.

Much Etruscan trade was with the Greeks, and some of the best-preserved Greek pottery comes not from Greece but from Etruria. In the seventh century

A scene from the Etruscan Tomb of the Augurs of about 530 BCE in Tarquinia depicts athletic contests at funerals that later evolved into Roman gladiatorial games.

BCE, the Etruscans expanded south across the Tiber River and as a result came into conflict with the Greeks of southern Italy. Around 535 the Etruscans joined with the Carthaginians to resist Greek intrusions into their markets and defeated the Ionian Phoecaeans at sea at the Battle of Alalia off the coast of Corsica. Carthage then occupied the island of Sardinia and shared Corsica with the Etruscans. At about the same time, the Etruscans expanded into the Po River valley of northern Italy and began to exploit the rich soil there.

In the late sixth century BCE, however, the fortunes of the Etruscans began to deteriorate. They suffered several defeats at the hands of the Greeks, and they lost their holdings south of the Tiber River. By 400 BCE, Celts from across the Alps had forced them out of the Po Valley, which became known as Cisalpine Gaul, or "Gaul on this side of the Alps." This decline in their political affairs was reflected in their funeral practices, which assumed a more sinister tone. The Etruscans feared that the uncertainty in their earthly lives might follow them after death, and they therefore developed rituals intended to placate the demons of the underworld. The lighthearted funeral games evolved into ritual combats to the death, and even were accompanied by human sacrifice.

MYSTERIES OF HISTORY

THE ORIGIN OF THE ETRUSCANS

The Lemnos inscription, thought to preserve a form of the Etruscan language.

For at least two reasons, the ancient Etruscans often are referred to as a "mysterious" people. For one thing, their language, although written in a form of the Greek alphabet, is undeciphered, meaning that their history has to be reconstructed from archaeology and the accounts of their enemies, the Greeks and Romans. And secondly, an enduring controversy has arisen regarding the Etruscans' origin because different historians give different versions. Around 10 BCE, Dionysius of Halicarnassus believed that the Etruscans were native Italians who developed their own idiosyncratic civilization. Nowadays, this version tends to be preferred by Italian historians, who suppose that Italian ancestors of the Etruscans assimilated foreign cultural attributes, much as the Greeks had done during the Archaic Age. But other ancient writers thought differently. At about the same time, the Roman historian Livy had the Etruscans originally coming from the Danube region. And in the fifth century BCE the Greek historian Herodotus wrote that the Etruscans had migrated to Italy from Lydia around 800 BCE. This view is consistent with inscriptions found on Lemnos, an island off the coast of Lydia, dating to the sixth century BCE and written in an alphabet almost identical to the Etruscan alphabet. An eastern origin for the Etruscans also would be consistent with the Etruscans being identified as the descendents of the Tursha, one of the Sea Peoples who were scattered after their defeat by Ramses III, and also could help to explain the many eastern motifs in Etruscan art.

ROME OF THE KINGS (753–509 BCE)

This multicultural Italian environment saw the rise of Rome, a city that was to establish the most successful Mediterranean Empire of all time. In its early days, however, Rome was but one of thousands of small, undistinguished agricultural villages scattered about the Mediterranean, and no contemporary records of its foundation and early history survive. As a result, one must rely on archaeological evidence, legends, and later traditions for evidence about this period. According to Roman tradition, Rome was founded in 753 BCE and first was ruled by kings. For reasons that are not yet clear, the Roman monarchy ended in 509 BCE and was replaced by an aristocratic form of government known as the Roman Republic.

The Founding of Rome

Several legends told of the foundation of Rome. A Greek version had Rome being founded by Trojans, led by the hero Aeneas, the son of the goddess Aphrodite (Roman Venus) and the Trojan Anchises, who had fled ca. 1184 BCE from the burning city of Troy. But another, more popular local legend had the city established on April 21, 753 BCE. In order to deal with this inconsistency, later Roman historians had Aeneas founding a city at Alba Longa, not far from the later site of Rome, and Rome actually being founded by his distant descendents. Thirteenth in descent from Aeneas were the brothers Numitor, the legitimate king of Alba Longa, and Amulius. The ambitious Amulius drove out his brother and usurped the throne. In order to prevent Numitor's daughter Rhea Silvia from having any sons, Amulius compelled her to become a Vestal Virgin, one of the priestesses responsible for keeping the sacred fire burning. Rhea nevertheless became pregnant and blamed the god Mars. In time she gave birth to twins, Romulus and Remus, whom Amulius ordered to be killed so they could not lay claim to the throne. But their executioner did not have the heart to kill them, so he sent them down the Tiber River in a basket. Downstream, a shepherd found them being suckled by a wolf (*lupa*, the Latin word for wolf, also was the word for prostitute, and could suggest that the twins' birth was not as august as the legend claimed), and they were raised as shepherds.

The story of Romulus and Remus being set adrift reflects a common folk-tale motif, as seen in similar stories about Sargon and Moses.

As young men, the two discovered their true heritage and killed their uncle. But because they had incurred blood guilt for murdering a relative, they were compelled to leave town, and they therefore decided to found a new city on a site with seven hills on the southern bank of the lower Tiber River. After an argument over which twin would have the right to found the city, Romulus killed Remus, and hence the new city was named Rome, after him. Romulus then became the first of seven kings of Rome. He and his successors established **Rome of the Kings** and were believed to have introduced many of the most time-honored customs of Rome. Very little evidence survives from the regal period, and many later legends grew up about the kings, whose existence we can accept even if we doubt many of their supposed activities. For example, it seems clear that later views about the kings were largely based on folk etymologies of their names, such as that Numa (derived from *numen*, or "divine power")

RECONSTRUCTING EARLY ROME

One of the things that makes it difficult to recover the earliest history of Rome is that no written records survive from that period. The Romans did have legends about early Rome, but they did not begin to write them down until around 200 BCE, and by that time the legends had become greatly embellished and largely if not completely fictional. The best opportunity to try to reconstruct early Rome comes from archaeology. Excavations on the Palatine Hill have recovered artifacts from the very earliest history of Rome. For example, post holes show where the poles that supported the sides and roofs of huts were set into the ground. This discovery allows historians to establish the floor size of early Roman homes. In addition, excavations of early Roman cemeteries have recovered pottery urns that held the bones and ashes of the cremated dead. These urns were sometimes made in the shape of the huts in which the people they contained had lived when they were alive. By combining the shape of the cremation urns with the dimensions provided by the post holes, archaeologists can reconstruct with a great degree of accuracy what the simple houses of the early Romans looked like, demonstrating that, at that time, there was nothing to mark Rome for future greatness.

A reconstruction of early Rome based on archaeological evidence.

had organized Roman religion; that Tullus Hostilius (from *hostilis,* "hostile") had been a successful warrior; and that Servius Tullus (from *servus,* "slave"), originally had been a slave. But even though the belief that Tarquinius Priscus came from the Etruscan city of Tarquinii might be pressing the evidence too far, his name is, in fact, Etruscan. In general, it is simply impossible to say with any certainty what any particular king did or did not do.

Based on what can be projected back from later times, however, we know that the kings had the powers of **imperium,** which gave them authority to lead armies, and **auspicium**, the right to assess the will of the gods. According to legend, the city initially was populated by a variety of bandits, Latins, and Italic peoples; stories such as this gave rise to traditions of Roman willingness to incorporate newcomers. For example, it was believed that, in order to find wives, the early Romans kidnaped women from a neighboring Italic people, the Sabines (an event later known as the "rape of the Sabine women"), whose king, Titus Tatius, later joined forces with the Romans.

TABLE 9.1   THE KINGS OF ROME AND THEIR LEGENDARY DATES AND DEEDS (ALL DATES BCE)

Native Kings		
Romulus	753–716	Established Senate and important institutions
Numa Pompilius	716–672	Established religious institutions
Tullus Hostilius	672–640	Engaged in warfare
Ancus Martius	640–616	Engaged in warfare and built bridges
Etruscan Kings		
Priscus Tarquin	616–578	First Etruscan king, built the *Cloaca Maxima*
Servius Tullius	578–533	Built the first wall, took first census
Tarquin the Proud	533–509	Last king, built the Capitoline temple

Rome Becomes a City

In addition, regardless of how much one credits the patriotic legends, archaeological excavations show that the first settlements on the hills of Rome do in fact date to around 750 BCE. At this time, moreover, Rome was a very modest place, consisting of straw huts perched on the tops of hills. For some 150 years, the inhabitants of Rome were subsistence farmers, grubbing a scanty sustenance from the soil. They were not yet even unified into a single community, although they did share some religious festivals.

According to Roman historical traditions, this situation changed drastically just before 600 BCE, when Rome was occupied by the Etruscans, who provided the last three kings of Rome and who are credited with making Rome into a city. These accounts are generally consistent with archaeological evidence indicating that Rome became a city at this time. The swampy land between the hills was drained (the legends spoke of the construction of the building the *Cloaca maxima*, or "big sewer"), and the first pebble pavements, the first stone buildings, including a temple of Jupiter atop the Palatine Hill, and the **forum**, or central meeting place, were constructed.

At the same time, many aspects of Etruscan culture, such as divination and the Etruscan version of the Greek alphabet, were imported into Rome, and new occupations, including trading (according to legend, King Tarquin the Old originally had been an Etruscan trader) and pottery manufacturing, were adopted. Other Roman concepts that had an Etruscan origin included the *fasces* (bundled rods with axes) that symbolized a high

The *lapis niger* (black stone), dating to the sixth century BCE and the earliest surviving Roman document, was found buried in a shrine in front of the senate house and contains the word PECEI (standard Latin "regi"), "for the king."

magistrate's power; and Luceres, the name of an ancient Roman tribe, derived from *lucumo*, Etruscan for "king." Even the Latin word *populus*, "the Roman people," was the name of an Etruscan god. Thus, even though some would argue that the Romans simply adopted aspects of Etruscan culture on their own, the extent of the assimilation suggests that it was the Etruscans who brought urbanization and civilization to Rome; indeed, the very name Roma may have been Etruscan.

Early Roman Society

The terms patrician and plebeian still refer to "upper-" or "lower-" class people.

This period saw the development of several characteristic Roman institutions. As a result of economic differentiation, a process by which a few families gained control of most of the wealth, the citizen body evolved into two social orders, or classes: the **patricians** and the **plebeians** (or plebs). The patricians were the Roman equivalent of the Greek aristocrats. They controlled the best land, and about one hundred of them belonged to the **Senate** (from the word for "old men"), which advised the king. The plebeians were mostly peasant farmers who worked either their own small plots or land that belonged to the patricians. Some, however, followed the Etruscan example and became well to do in trade and crafts. But no matter how rich they became, there was no way for plebeians to enter the hereditary patrician order, for the distinction between patricians and plebeians was not about wealth, but about social status.

The Roman character was fundamentally conservative and was based on the concept of *mos maiorum*, "the ways of our ancestors." In general, the Romans felt that the older something was, the better it was. Thus Roman legends tended to retroject into the past some of Rome's most hallowed traditions, in much the same way that the Spartans had done, so as to endow them with greater antiquity and authority. The Romans valued moral qualities such as stability, discipline, industry, frugality, temperance, and fortitude. They had a down-to-earth character that rejected the idealized portraiture of the Greeks, preferring a realistic style that depicted themselves as they were, warts, wrinkles, and all. Intellect, innovation, and imagination were generally not high on the Roman list of virtues.

The Romans' concern over status also went far beyond the distinction between patricians and plebeians. Everyone knew his or her place in Roman society. Family life was structured and authoritarian. Within each family the *paterfamilias*, or "father of the family," had life-and-death authority over the household. Fathers undertook the responsibility for educating their sons by taking them along as they fulfilled their own responsibilities in the daily round of public and private life. Most sons lived at home under paternal authority, even after they were married, until their

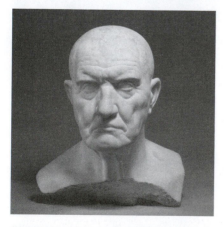

For a typical Roman *paterfamilias*, life was serious business, as suggested by the expression on this portrait from the later Republic.

fathers died, and they then became "fathers of the family" in their own right. But there was a way to do this in advance: if the father fictitiously sold his son and set him free three times in a row in a process called *emancipatio* (emancipation), the son then was *sui juris*, that is, under his own legal authority.

All women were under the *manus* (legal authority) of some man except for the six **Vestal Virgins**, whose duty was to keep the sacred hearth fire of the goddess Vesta burning. Daughters were generally expected to marry and assume control over a household. Having a marriage recognized under Roman law was very important, because it allowed property and Roman citizenship to be inherited by one's children. Early Rome had three different kinds of marriage, two of which were *in manum*, that is, they transferred *manus*, or legal authority, over the wife from the father to the husband. *Confarreatio* ("with spelt") was the most restrictive form and occurred only between patricians. The wedding consisted of the couple sharing a cake made of spelt (a type of wheat) in the presence of ten witnesses, and the woman then passed into the *manus* (authority) of her husband. It was required that those wishing to become certain kinds of priests, such as Flamen Dialis (high priest of Jupiter), or Vestal Virgins have parents who were married by *confarreatio*, and divorce was almost impossible. *Coemptio*, or "purchase," was a much more common form of marriage, usually involving a dowry, in which a father fictitiously sold his daughter as a means of transferring *manus* over her to the husband. The third form of marriage, *usus* ("usage"), involved simple cohabitation, equivalent to a modern "common law" marriage. If the woman remained in the husband's home for a year without interruption, she passed into his *manus*, but if she stayed out of his house for three nights during the year, she remained under the more distant *manus* of her father (or another male member of her father's family). Many women preferred the *usus* form of marriage as a means of maintaining some semblance of independence in the marital home.

Roman social relations involved the concept of bilateral duty and responsibility with respect to the gods, the state, family, friends, and benefactors. If anyone did a Roman a favor, the Roman was beholden to that person until the favor had been repaid. **Senators** felt that it was their duty to participate in public life, and they expected to be rewarded by recognition and office. The same values were manifested in religion, in which it was believed that various inchoate *numina*, or forces of nature, controlled the environment. Contractual rituals were developed to ensure that each **numen** performed its function. In the sphere of personal religion, for example, every year farmers would sacrifice a red dog at a crossroads to ensure that the red rust, which was controlled by the *numen* Robigus, did not strike their crops. Religious practices to ensure the well-being of Rome were overseen by a chief priest known as the **Pontifex Maximus**, who supervised the Vestal Virgins and other state priests. The chief state gods consisted of the Capitoline Triad of Jupiter Optimus Maximus (Jupiter the Best and Greatest), Juno, and Minerva (Greek Zeus, Hera, and

The title Pontifex Maximus still is borne by the Pope in Rome.

Athena). From their temple atop the Capitoline Hill, they oversaw the welfare of Rome as a whole. State religion adopted several Etruscan practices, such as the performance of the *auspices* and *haruspices* by state priests before important undertakings.

One of the most important Roman social institutions was the system of **clientela**, in which a patron and a client rendered mutual services to each other and were bound to each other in a quasi-religious union. At this time, the patrons were usually patricians, who would have many plebeian clients. A patrician patron provided physical protection, legal services (only the patricians knew the laws), and economic support, including foodstuffs and seed grain when times were tough and even land to rent if a pleb lost his own. What the patron received in return was an entourage to accompany him when he went to war—for the aristocrats did most of the actual fighting—or even when he went into Rome, for one of the measures of the status of an aristocrat lay in the number of clients who accompanied him. Clients also provided a little help in raising a ransom or dowry. This system of reciprocal responsibility bound Roman society together in a way that Greek society never was, with the result that Romans were inhibited from resorting to violence when disputes arose. But it also was designed to maintain the status quo and to preserve the privileges of the patricians.

LEGACY OF ANTIQUITY

In what ways do you think that our own values are more like those of the Romans or those of the Greeks?

The Fall of the Monarchy

Patriotic legends reported that in 509 BCE Sextus Tarquin, the dissolute son of the autocratic Etruscan king Tarquin the Proud, raped the virtuous and aristocratic Roman matron Lucretia, who then committed suicide for dishonoring her family. The native Roman aristocrats then rose in revolt and expelled the kings. Although this legend tells us more about Roman attitudes toward women than about historical processes—the most fitting place for a woman was at home spinning wool to make clothing for her family—it correctly reports, at the right point in time, the transition from a monarchical to an aristocratic form of government. This transitional model also is analogous to political evolution in Greece, where monarchies had been replaced by aristocracies around the ninth century BCE. But another suggestion rejects the historical account and suggests that the last few kings of Rome—whose legendary backgrounds included being a slave and a merchant—were not Etruscans at all but were, in fact, native Romans who, akin to Greek tyrants, came to power by appealing to the underprivileged and that their overthrow resulted from an aristocratic revolution. A problem with this interpretation, however, is that other examples of this kind of political devolution are difficult to find—in Greece, for example, tyrannies always followed on aristocracies, not monarchies, and were always replaced by oligarchies and never regressed to aristocracies. However that may be, it is clear that the monarchy did disappear, to be replaced by the *res publica* ("public thing"), or **Republic**, a form of government designed to prevent the Romans from ever having a *rex* ("king") and in which sovereign authority lay with the people.

THE EARLY ROMAN REPUBLIC (509–246 BCE)

The government of the Roman Republic began as an aristocracy in which only the aristocratic patricians could participate. Political and social development was marked by a drawn-out struggle by nonaristocrats, the plebeians, to gain more rights and privileges, and in particular the right to hold political office. By 366 BCE, the most influential of the nonaristocrats had joined with the aristocrats, the patricians, to form a much more stable oligarchy.

Republican Government

The administration of the Republic was based on the concept of **collegiality**: no office was overseen by a single person. The king was replaced by two **consuls** who were elected each year. Like the king, they had the powers of *imperium* and *auspicium* and were accompanied by twelve lictors carrying the fasces who symbolized the consul's power. They also had the right to oversee the administration of justice and to name new senators and citizens. Other yearly magistrates were the Quaestors, who originally assisted the consuls in enforcing the laws and later oversaw financial matters. Only in times of dire emergency—if, for example, the state was on the verge of being defeated by a foreign enemy—did the Romans permit a very limited form of one-man rule in which the consuls appointed a **Dictator**. But there were severe limitations on the Dictator's authority: he could serve only until the emergency was over, and never longer than six months.

Most of the population consisted of citizens, for at this time the slave population was quite small because Rome was not yet very prosperous. Citizens enjoyed private rights, which allowed them to carry on business and to marry under Roman law, and public rights, which permitted them to vote and to run for public office. A significant difference from other ancient societies was that freed slaves became endowed with full Roman citizen rights. The entire citizen body, or *populus*, was organized into three ancient **tribes** (from Latin *tribus*, a third)—the Ramnes (from Romulus), Tities (from Titus Tatius), and Luceres (from Etruscan *lucumo*)—supposedly descended from the Romans, Italians, and Etruscans, respectively, and representing the multiethnic nature of the Roman people. Each tribe consisted of ten *curiae* (singular *curia*), or clans, and the *curiae* were composed of *gentes* (sing. *gens*), extended families. Each *gens* was made up of individual *familiae* (singular *familia*), or families, each under the authority of a *paterfamilias*. Roman men bore a first name, such as Gaius, a *gens* (gentilic) name, such as Julius, and a family name, such as Caesar. Family names often were based on an attribute of a distant ancestor (Caesar, for example, meant "hairy"). Women, on the other hand, had a gentilic name, such as Julia, and an iteration number, such as Secunda ("the second").

The thirty *curiae* were organized into a popular (from *populus*) assembly called the **Curiate Assembly**—or assembly organized by *curiae*—which was the sovereign political body of the Roman state. Each *curia* had one vote. Like all later popular assemblies as well, the Curiate Assembly did not have initiative authority. It only considered motions that previously had been approved by the Senate, which grew to about three hundred members (who served for life) and became the primary governing body of Rome. This left the patricians effectively in control of the government. Not only were all the members of the Senate patricians, but patricians also could instruct their clients how to vote when a measure was being considered in a popular assembly. Likewise, the patricians also could control who was elected to the magistracies: even though there was no rule against plebeians running for office, they could not hope to muster sufficient votes to be elected. And, given that the Senate was composed of persons appointed by the consuls, there was little chance that a plebeian could become a member. At the beginning of the Republic, therefore, the patricians held virtually all the social, political, and economic privileges.

The Conflict of the Orders

The early years of the Republic were a struggle for survival as the Romans not only fought off Etruscan attempts to retake the city but also competed with neighboring Latins and Italic peoples for control of **Latium**. The situation was exacerbated by a long period of nonviolent domestic unrest known as the **Conflict of the Orders** (500–287 BCE), during which plebeians attempted to obtain expanded rights and opportunities. The plebeians had several complaints against the patricians. They had no officials to look out for their interests. They did not know what the laws were. Well-to-do plebeians had no realistic chance of being elected to office or becoming members of the Senate. Poorer plebeians could be sold into slavery if they defaulted on loans, which usually were made by patricians. The patricians, however, were determined to maintain the status quo and resisted calls for change.

Two factors helped the plebeians to pursue their goals. For one thing, it soon became apparent to the patricians that they could not hope to defend Rome without plebeian assistance. According to Roman tradition, for example, 306 members of the patrician Fabian family had been killed in 479 BCE in a battle with the city of Veii. Therefore, soon after 500 BCE, the **Servian Reforms**—later named after King Servius in order to endow them with even greater antiquity—were implemented. They allowed the wealthiest plebeians to serve in the army, for only those Romans who could afford to purchase their own weaponry were allowed to be soldiers. The citizen body was divided into 193 units, called "centuries," that were distributed among different classes based on wealth. Thus the highest ranking class, the *equites* (equestrians, or **knights**), was assigned eighteen centuries and consisted of those who nominally were rich enough to afford not only a full panoply of arms and armor but also a horse. Class I, eighty centuries, contained men who could afford a complete panoply; the men of Class II, twenty centuries, could manage not quite an entire panoply; and so it went, down to Class V, thirty centuries, men who could afford just a single weapon. The largest group, the **proletariate**, were those who had no property and could provide only their offspring (*proles*) to support the state; they were assigned five centuries and did not fight. The citizenry under arms then became another popular assembly, the **Centuriate Assembly**—or assembly organized by centuries—which assumed several of the duties of the old Curiate Assembly, such as declaring war and electing the consuls. Each century had one vote even though the poorer centuries contained many more people than the rich ones. Thus, the patricians were able to control the votes, because, as long as the knights and Class I, which contained all the patricians, voted together—as they initially always did—their ninety-eight votes outnumbered the ninety-five votes of everybody else. But at the same time, wealthy and influential plebeians in the knights and Class I who were in the army served side by side with patricians and had the opportunity, based on their military ability, to serve as military tribunes in command of army units. In addition, army service meant that the patricians now needed the collective cooperation of the plebs to a far greater extent than they had before.

The plebeians also found strength in numbers and organization in another way. They formed their own assembly, known as the **Council of the Plebs**. Its organization was based on twenty geographical tribes into which the people were divided based on where they lived; each tribe had one vote. It issued pronouncements, or **plebiscites**, that were binding only on the plebeians, although they could be ratified by the Senate and one of the other popular assemblies. Each year the plebeians also elected ten **Tribunes of the Plebs**, whose responsibility was to defend the interests of the plebeians against patrician oppression. The plebs swore to avenge themselves on any patrician who ever harmed a tribune. The tribunes appropriated the authority to say **"veto"** ("I forbid") if the patricians ever did anything against plebeian interests. On such occasions, the plebs went on strike until the tribune could be induced to remove his veto. In extreme cases the plebs could threaten to secede from the state and to withdraw to the Aventine Hill and establish their own nation. The plebs sometimes did so when Rome was under military threat as a means of coercing the patricians into making political concessions.

TABLE 9.2   THE CENTURIATE ASSEMBLY

Class	Number of Centuries/ Votes
Knights	18
Class I	80
Class II	20
Class III	20
Class IIII	20
Class V	30
Proletariate	5
Total Centuries/Votes	193

In the United States, only chief executive officers, such as the president and governors, have veto power.

Social Reforms

One of the plebeians' earliest demands was to know the laws. As a result, in 451 BCE the patricians appointed a board of ten men, the **decemvirs**, who, analogous to the Greek lawgivers, were charged with writing down the laws. After being reappointed for a second term in 450 BCE, the decemvirs issued the famous **Twelve Tables** of Roman law, which, with few exceptions, did not create new law but merely recorded existing law. They stated the fundamental concepts of Roman law, such as *mancipatio* (transferring ownership over property), *stipulatio* (making a contract between two parties), *emancipatio* (freeing someone from slavery), and *nexum* (reducing someone to slavery). The code also covered criminal law, with crimes such as arson, casting spells, and stealing crops being punishable by death, but because there were no state police or prosecutors, criminal prosecutions had to be instituted by the wronged parties themselves.

The laws offered little redress for plebeian complaints. For example, they still permitted those who fell into debt to be sold as slaves; the law even specified that a defaulted debtor had to be bound with at least fifteen pounds of chains. And to add insult to injury, one of the new laws added in 450 prohibited marriages between patricians and plebeians and thus blocked the only means by which members of a plebeian family could enter the aristocracy, for if a plebeian woman married a patrician man, their children would be patricians. The plebeians were sufficiently incensed by such laws that they seceded. In 449, the patricians responded with the Valerio-Horatian Laws (named after the consuls Valerius and Horatius, who had introduced them), which acknowledged the validity of plebiscites, subject to ratification by the Senate; guaranteed the *sacrosanctitas* (sacrosanctity, or personal security) of the Tribunes of the Plebs; and allowed the Council of the Plebs to appoint two aediles, who oversaw the markets, streets, and public buildings. At the same time, it seems, a new popular assembly, the **Council of the People by Tribes**, was introduced, modeled on the Council of the Plebs but also including the patricians. It was more inclusive than the Curiate Assembly because it

TABLE 9.3   COMPOSITION OF ROMAN POPULAR ASSEMBLIES

Name	Members	Units	No. units	Membership Basis
Curiate Assembly	All citizens	curia	30	family
Centuriate Assembly	All citizens	century	198	property
Council of the Plebs	Plebeians	tribe	20/36*	residence
Council of the People	All citizens	tribe	20/36*	residence

*The number of geographical tribes grew from 20 to 36 as Rome expanded.

automatically included new citizens who did not belong to one of the family-based *curiae*.

Continued agitation by the most influential plebeians brought the Canuleian Law, named after a tribune of the plebs, Canuleius, which in 445 repealed the ban on intermarriage. But the patricians balked when the plebeians insisted on being given a realistic opportunity to be consuls. Being unable to contemplate the idea of having a plebeian consul, the patricians responded in 444 by abolishing the consulate altogether and replacing it with the office of Military Tribune with Consular Powers. At least two, and as many as six, were appointed each year. The new office absorbed the military functions of the consuls and could be held by plebeians, who, after their terms of service, then entered the Senate. Meanwhile, other consular duties were transferred to another new official, the *censor*, two of whom were appointed every five years. They served for eighteen months and ranked above the consuls. It was their responsibility to take the census of citizen property, to appoint new members to the Senate, to let out contracts for public works construction, and to oversee public morality. Only patricians were chosen for this office. Thus, even though the patricians were willing to make concessions to plebeian demands for increased opportunity when circumstances demanded, they did so only grudgingly and in small doses.

The Censors' moral duties survive in modern "censoring."

Nevertheless, as the years went by, many influential plebeians became members of the Senate and were able to participate in truly substantive decision making. Eventually, this factor, combined with intermarriage, led the patricians and these powerful plebeians to make common cause. In 367, the **Licinio-Sextian** Law restored the consulate: henceforward one of the consuls would be a plebeian. But here, too, the patricians fought a rear-guard action to retain something of their past privileges. They introduced at the same time two new aediles to oversee public works and the urban **praetor**, an official with imperium who had jurisdiction over legal cases involving Roman citizens. Initially, the new offices introduced by the patricians were open only to patricians as a means of limiting plebeian authority, but such ploys were short-lived. In 356 BCE, the first plebeian Dictator was appointed; in 351 BCE, the office of censor was opened to plebs; and in 337 the praetorship was, too. The plebeians achieved final victory in 287, when the **Hortensian Law** made the plebiscites issued by the Council of the Plebs' independent authority binding without the need to get Senate approval. By then, the Conflict of the Orders was unquestionably at an end.

The end result of these developments was an evolution from an aristocracy, in which Rome was governed essentially just by the patricians, to an oligarchy, in which patricians and influential plebeians served together in the Senate and shared the rule. Eventually, all ex-office holders became members. Within the Senate, senators

CROSS-CULTURAL QUESTION

In what ways was the transition from aristocracy to oligarchy similar and different in Greece and Rome?

TABLE 9.4 OFFICIALS OF THE ROMAN REPUBLIC (AS OF 197 BCE)

Title	No.	Duties	Term of office
Annually elected officials (in rank order)			
Consul	2	Lead Roman army, preside at assemblies	1 year
Praetor	6	Oversee law courts, govern some provinces	1 year
Aedile	4	Oversee public works and markets in Rome	1 year
Quaestor	6	Oversee treasury and financial matters	1 year
Tribune	10	Preside over Council of the Plebs	1 year
Nonannual officials			
Dictator	1	Replace consuls in grave emergencies	6 months maximum
Censor	2	Property assessments, appoint Senators	18 months
Proconsul	varies	Has the authority but not title of a consul	varies

jockeyed for status. Those whose ancestors had ever been consuls became an inside group called the **Nobles**, who jealously guarded access to the consulate. Only the most able and ambitious non-nobles were able to become consuls, and this was so unusual that one who did so was designated a *novus homo*, or **New Man**. Every five years, the censors drew up a list of the Senate in rank order. Every senator's ambition was to be named the *Princeps senatus*, or First Man of the Senate, for all of the other senators then would have to yield precedence to him. The key to the successful functioning of the government lay in the willingness of the senators to share the rule among themselves.

Roman Law

In the Republic, only the popular assemblies had the constitutional authority to issue laws binding on the entire Roman state, but the powers of the assemblies were very limited. They could not initiate legislation, which was presented to them by their presiding magistrates, either a consul or tribune; nor could they discuss or emend measures presented to them. All they could do was vote "yes" or "no." Real lawmaking went on behind the scenes, and real legislative power lay in the hands of the Senate. Although the Senate had no constitutional authority to issue legislation—that right belonged only to the popular assemblies—it had a very powerful advisory position. A consul or tribune who wanted to introduce a law was expected to receive Senate approval before presenting it to an assembly. And the Senate thus issued *senatus consulta*, Decrees of the Senate, which were advice to magistrates or interpretations of existing Roman law. In practice, the advice was almost always followed, and these Decrees of the Senate gained the de facto force of law. The Senate also performed important executive functions, including overseeing state expenditures and managing foreign policy. As a consequence, the Senate was the real governing body of the Republic.

Roman private law was administered by the urban praetor, who heard cases involving citizens, and the peregrine praetor, an office introduced in 246 BCE to hear cases involving foreigners. The urban praetors put into practice the concepts embodied in the private law of the Twelve Tables and developed standard *formulae* (legal forms) for different kinds of contracts and lawsuits

Technically, Roman ius civile (civil law, or "the law of citizens") applied to what we in the modern day would consider to be both civil and criminal law.

involving, for example, purchases, sales, contracts, property disputes, and so on. If a *formula* did not already exist for a particular kind of case, the praetor created one. All of the *formulae* were collected into a constantly expanding Praetor's Edict. Lawsuits took place in two phases: in the *actio* (action) phase, the praetor himself drew up the *formula*, which included the plaintiff's claim and the penalty that the accused stood to suffer. For the *judicium* (judgment) phase, the praetor then appointed a *judex* (judge), who could be anyone, to try the case based only on what was in the *formula*. At the trial, litigants and lawyers called witnesses, presented evidence, cited legal precedents, and made their arguments. The final decision lay solely in the hands of the judge, and there was no appeal.

ALL THOSE WARS (390–133 BCE)

During the course of the Roman Republic, the Romans engaged in wars that took them farther and farther from Rome. Although, unlike in Greece and the Near East, these wars were not fought for imperialistic purposes, as a consequence of them the Romans gradually acquired more and more overseas territories that they were responsible for governing; and thus, paradoxically, what we call the Roman Empire largely developed during the Roman Republic.

The Gallic Sack of Rome

During the fifth century BCE, the combined army of patricians and plebeians defended Rome against attacks from Etruscans, Latins, and Italian peoples such as the Aequi, Volsci, and Hernici. Many heroic legends arose. In or about 498, the Romans engaged in the Battle of Lake Regillus with the Latin League, a confederation of Latin cities, for control of Latium. According to legend, the Romans were on the verge of defeat when the heroes Castor and Pollux came to their rescue. In the resultant Cassian Treaty, the first treaty made by the Romans, the Romans and Latins agreed to be equal partners in any future wars, to share any war booty, and to share legal rights. There also was the tale of the ex-consul Cincinnatus, who was plowing his fields in 458 BCE when word came that a Roman army was trapped by the Aequi and that he had been appointed Dictator. Cincinnatus raised a force of old men and boys, rescued the army, and then went back to plowing his fields after only sixteen days as Dictator, the very model of Roman virtue.

It was not until 396 BCE, with the defeat of the Etruscan city of Veii, that the Romans were able markedly to increase their territory. The newly won land was distributed to landless plebeians in order to make them eligible for military service and remove a potential source of unrest from Rome. Immediately after this victory, however, Roman fortunes took a decided turn for the worse. In 390 BCE a raiding party of Gauls from the Po River valley attacked Rome. The Roman army, packed together in the traditional phalanx formation, was completely flabbergasted by the horrifying, undisciplined

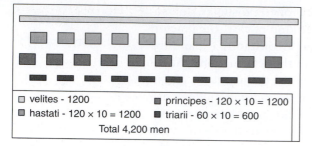

□ velites - 1200 ■ principes - 120 × 10 = 1200
■ hastati - 120 × 10 = 1200 ■ triarii - 60 × 10 = 600
Total 4,200 men

The battle formation of Roman **legions** had two lines of 120-man maniples and one line of 60-man maniples. The first line of young *hastati* ("spear men") went into action first. If things got tough they could withdraw through the second line of more experienced men, the *principes* ("leading men"), who then went into action. If they could not win the battle, then the *hastati* and *principes*, armed with the pilum (throwing spear) and gladius (short sword), would withdraw behind the veteran *triarii* ("third-line men"), armed with the long hasta, or thrusting spear, who would simply try to hold the enemy off. A screen of young *velites* ("speedy men") serving as skirmishers started out in front of the formation; they withdrew to the rear as soon as the real fighting started.

The Roman equivalent of the English saying "We've got our backs to the wall" was "We're back to the triarii."

charge of the howling Celtic warriors. The Romans turned tail and ran, leaving the Gauls to occupy, sack, and burn the city of Rome, destroying in the process any records, such as the original copy of the Twelve Tables, that existed. Only by paying a hefty ransom were the Romans able to induce the Gauls to depart. According to one account, after the Romans complained that the ransom paid to the Gauls was too great, the Gallic chieftain Brennus threw his sword onto the scales and said, *"Vae victis,"* that is, "Woe to the conquered."

The sack of Rome in 390 BCE by the Gauls subsequently was commemorated yearly as a *dies ater,* or "dark day." The Romans swore that such a humiliation would never happen again, much as the Egyptians had done after the expulsion of the Hyksos. To this end, they constructed a large defensive wall around the city and restructured the army, abandoning the old phalanx in favor of a more flexible tactical structure based on 120-man units known as **maniples**, which could act independently and accommodate themselves to the landscape.

Roman Motives for Going to War

The Gallic sack also engendered in the Romans a virtually paranoid fear of strong neighbors. This led to a policy of **defensive aggression**, as a result of which the Romans would sometimes preemptively attack neighbors whom they felt were becoming potential threats. Other factors that could encourage the Romans to go to war included a desire by consuls to gain military glory, wishes to obtain land for land-hungry plebeians, dutiful responses to pleas for assistance from their neighbors, and genuine threats. There is little indication, however, that before around 150 BCE the Romans engaged in calculated imperialism out of a desire for large-scale political, financial, or territorial gain.

Wars in Italy

It took the Romans about fifty years to recover from the Gallic sack. They then became engaged in a protracted series of Italian military conflicts lasting from 343 to 268 BCE that eventually gave them control of all of Italy south of the Po River valley.

A PICTURE IS WORTH A THOUSAND WORDS

THE SERVIAN WALL

One of the consequences of the Gallic sack of Rome was that it made the Romans even more sensitive to the threats that foreign enemies could present and to the need to defend the city. Unable to deal with such a huge undertaking themselves, the Romans hired Greek stonemasons from Campania to build a stone wall to enclose a city that had greatly expanded since the regal period. The Greek masons used huge polygonal (squared off) stone blocks of yellowish tuff (a volcanic rock) imported from Veii to construct the wall. The blocks were laid as headers (lengthwise) and stretchers (with the butt end out) to strengthen the wall. The finished wall had sixteen gates, was seven miles long, and up to thirty-three feet high and twelve feet wide. Parts of the wall had either a ditch in front or an earthen ramp behind to increase its effective height.

Later in their history, the Romans, out of their desire to retroject great events from their history as far into the past as possible, called the wall the Servian Wall, attributing it to King Servius back in the sixth century BCE. The wall was put to its best use in 211 BCE, when it prevented the Carthaginian general Hannibal from capturing the city, and it continued to be maintained until the end of the Roman Republic. The next wall built to protect Rome would not be constructed for another 650 years, attesting to the future success the Romans had in protecting themselves from foreign threats.

The First Samnite War (343–341 BCE)

In 343 BCE, the city of Capua in Campania requested Roman assistance against attacks by the Samnites, an Italic mountain people that was expanding west toward the Bay of Naples. In spite of the fact that in 354 the Romans had concluded a mutual defense treaty with the Samnites, they now were fearful of growing Samnite strength and accepted the invitation. This First Samnite War (343–341 BCE) ended in a draw in 341 BCE when the Romans had to withdraw because of a mutiny in the Roman army by soldiers unhappy at being away from home, mutinied. But, as often was the case with the Romans, this initial involvement set a crucial precedent, and the Romans now found themselves committed to maintaining a presence in Campania; they may even have annexed Capua and made its citizens *cives sine suffragio*, that is, "citizens without the vote," a form of partial citizenship that included only the private rights of a Roman citizen.

The Great Latin Revolt (340–338 BCE)

In the short term, however, the Romans were confronted in 340 BCE by the Great Latin Revolt (340–338 BCE) after the Latins felt that they were being drawn into Rome's wars and that the terms of the Cassian Treaty were not being observed. After the defeat of the Latins in 338, the Romans dissolved the Latin League and simply annexed the Latin towns. Those living closer to Rome were made full Roman citizens, and those farther away were granted the *ius Latinum*, or "Latin Rights," a form of partial Roman citizenship that gave the Latins all the private rights of a Roman citizen plus the right to vote if they happened to be in Rome, but denied them the right to hold office. By these means, the Romans began the process whereby they shared their citizenship rights with increasing numbers of other peoples, something that was unheard of among the Greeks.

The Second Samnite War (326–304 BCE)

In 326 BCE the Romans entered the Second Samnite War (326–304 BCE) after the Samnites had occupied the Greek city of Naples. The war was marked by repeated Roman defeats. In 321, a Roman army was trapped and captured at the Battle of the Caudine Forks and then forced to suffer the humiliation of "passing under the yoke," where defeated soldiers were compelled to bow as they went underneath a gateway made of their own captured spears that represented the yoke connecting a pair of oxen, as if the soldiers had become dumb beasts of burden. In 315, the Romans again were again routed at the Battle of Lautulae. The Romans did, however, get some good news with the defeat of the Etruscans, who had allied themselves with the Samnites, at the Battle of Lake Vadimon in 310. And at the same time that the Romans were losing battles against the Samnites, they were establishing their strategic superiority. They began the construction of military colonies on the borders of Samnium: destitute Roman citizens gave up their citizenship in exchange for the opportunity to receive land grants and a new start. And in 312 BCE the censor Appius Claudius Caecus began the construction of the Appian Way, an all-weather military road from Rome to Capua, which allowed for the speedy concentration of troops and supplies in the south. At the same time, the Romans recaptured territory gained by the Samnites outside of Samnium. By 304, the Samnites were hemmed in and exhausted and sued for peace, which was made based on a return to the status quo before the war and a renewal of the treaty of 354.

The Third Samnite War (298–290 BCE)

The Third Samnite War (298–290 BCE) commenced in 298 BCE after the Samnites formed a great Italian coalition against the Romans. The decisive encounter occurred at the Battle of Sentinum in 295, where a combined force of Samnites, Etruscans, and Gauls was on the verge of defeating the Romans when Decius Mus, the Roman consul, performed the ancient ritual of *devotio*. He dedicated himself to the gods, charged into the enemy ranks, and was killed. Instead of causing demoralization, his brave act gave courage to the soldiers, who, confident that the gods now would do their part and grant the Romans victory, rallied to defeat the enemy. In 290, the Samnites submitted to Rome and, although allowed to remain independent, were made into dependent Roman *socii*, or allies.

As an epilogue to the Samnite wars, in the 280s the Romans conducted reprisals against the Gauls of northeastern Italy, defeating them, again at Lake Vadimon, in 283 BCE and laying waste to an area called the *ager Gallicus* ("Gallic field") that remained a desert for the next fifty years.

The Pyrrhic War (280–275 BCE)

In 282, Rome came into conflict with the Greeks of southern Italy after the city of Tarentum sank a small Roman scouting fleet and, what was worse from the Roman perspective, spattered mud on the togas of some Roman ambassadors, an act that grievously offended the Roman sense of *dignitas* (dignity). Knowing they could not stand up to Roman retaliation by themselves, the Tarentines appealed for help to the most able Greek general of the day, King Pyrrhus of Epirus. Pyrrhus, who had notions of his own about expanding his influence into Great Greece in southern Italy and Sicily, accepted the challenge, and in 280 BCE he sailed to Italy with his army, which included war elephants. During the Pyrrhic War (280–275 BCE), the Romans fought three arduous battles with Pyrrhus, at Heraclea in 280, Asculum in 279, and Beneventum in 275. Even though Pyrrhus won the first two and the third was indecisive, his losses were very heavy; after one battle, he commented, "Another victory like this and I shall be totally ruined." The losses of the Romans were even greater, but unlike typical Hellenistic states, they simply refused to come to negotiate. One of Pyrrhus' ambassadors returned from Rome complaining that the Senate acted like an "assembly of kings." By 275 BCE Pyrrhus had had enough and returned to Greece, supposedly with the words, "What a battlefield I am leaving for Rome and Carthage." This left the Greeks of southern Italy unable to resist, and by 268 BCE all had surrendered to Rome.

In these campaigns, the Romans often prevailed primarily because of their persistence, their willingness to suffer great losses, and their ability to create long-term

The term Pyrrhic victory still refers to a victory with enough losses to qualify as a defeat.

An Etruscan dish depicts a western war elephant. Never having seen elephants before, the Romans called Pyrrhus's war elephants "Lucanian cows," after the region of Italy in which they were fighting.

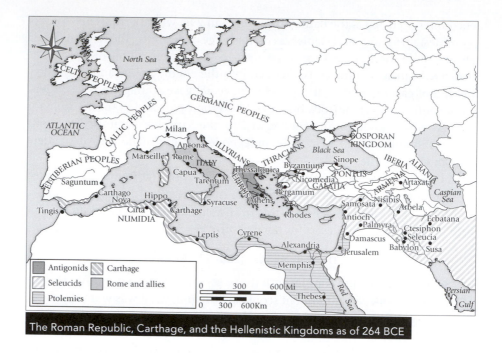

The Roman Republic, Carthage, and the Hellenistic Kingdoms as of 264 BCE

strategies for defeating enemies by constructing roads and military colonies. In their wars during this period, they usually lost more battles than they won, often because their generals, who were in office for just a single year, were amateurs and had a tendency to take risks in a rush for personal military glory. Senatorial generals strove to gain the greatest honor that a senator could be granted, a **triumph** after a military victory. In a triumph, the victorious general, painted red like the god Jupiter, led a procession of cheering soldiers, disconsolate captives, and wagons piled with loot along the Sacred Way through the forum in Rome and up to the Capitoline temple.

By 268, Rome had become the dominant power in Italy south of the Po River valley. Curiously, however, aside from confiscating tracts of land called *ager publicus* ("public land") in strategic areas, the Romans showed little interest in actually taking over the territory of their defeated neighbors. Part of the public land was used to establish military colonies at strategic points, such as river fords and mountain passes. The colonies also allowed the Romans to make land grants to landless plebeians and thus make them eligible for military service.

The Romans' primary concern was to weaken potential adversaries in Italy to a point at which they no longer posed a threat to Rome. Their usual policy was to impose a bilateral treaty on a defeated enemy, with Rome as the patron and the enemy as the client. The former enemy became a Roman *socius*, or ally. It relinquished its independent foreign policy and was required to have "the same friends and enemies" as Rome. Whenever Rome went to war, its allies were expected to contribute manpower for the Roman armies. The result of this **Italian Alliance** was that, even though Roman territory did not expand greatly after these victories, Rome gained access to a manpower reserve of over half a million soldiers. And Roman society now consisted of two groups of people: senators and plebeians, who had Roman citizenship, and Italian allies and slaves, who did not.

Wars in the Western Mediterranean

It was only a short time before Rome became entangled in additional wars on an even greater scale, especially, between 264 and 201 BCE, with the powerful North African city of Carthage. Early in its history, Rome had entered into several treaties with Carthage in which each recognized the sphere of influence of the other: Rome in Italy, and Carthage in the Mediterranean. Carthage was especially interested in expanding its authority over the Greek cities in eastern Sicily, and it was this ambition that brought it into conflict with Rome.

The First Punic War (264–242 BCE)

In the 280s BCE a band of Campanian mercenaries called the Mamertines, or "Sons of Mars," seized the Sicilian Greek city of Messana, located on the Strait of Messina just nine miles from Italy. In 265 they were attacked by the powerful city of Syracuse. Fearful of being defeated and executed, the Mamertines accepted aid from the Carthaginians, who were delighted to gain a foothold in eastern Sicily. The Carthaginians then refused to leave, and the Mamertines responded by offering to become allies of Rome.

Even though the Romans had no obligation at all to these disreputable mercenaries, the matter was debated in the Senate. The Senate, however, could not decide what to do and, in an unprecedented move, passed the motion to the Centuriate Assembly without any recommendation. The consul-elect Appius Claudius Pulcher, eager to win personal glory in a war, played on fears of strong neighbors and argued that the Romans "could fight the Carthaginians either in Sicily or before the gates of Rome." War was declared, and Rome became committed to its first overseas conflict, the First Punic War (264–241 BCE), from *Poenus*, the Latin word for Phoenician.

Sicily was an island. So the Romans, who had little seafaring experience, were compelled to construct a navy from scratch. It was said that they copied a wrecked Carthaginian warship that had washed up on shore and practiced rowing on benches set up on the beach. The Carthaginians, of course, were much better sailors than the Romans, so the Roman tactic was to turn a sea battle into a land battle. They outfitted each warship with a long plank with a spike at the end. At the Battle of Mylae in 260 BCE, the Roman captains maneuvered their ships close to the overconfident Carthaginians and dropped the gangplanks. Roman troops swarmed over the surprised Carthaginians. The result was an overwhelming Roman victory. Although the Carthaginians were not fooled again, this unexpectedly easy triumph only strengthened the Roman commitment to fight on until they had won.

Meanwhile, in Sicily, the war bogged down into largely unproductive siege warfare, the only result being the devastation of much of the Sicilian countryside. An attempted Roman invasion of Africa under Marcus Regulus in 256 BCE was defeated by the Spartan mercenary Xanthippus, and the Carthaginian commander in Sicily, Hamilcar Barca, consistently outwitted the Romans. Finally, in 241, faced with a renewed Roman offensive, the Carthaginians decided to cut their losses and sue for peace. Carthage evacuated Sicily and agreed to pay a war **indemnity** of 3,200 talents of silver (a talent being about fifty-six pounds), for the Romans expected defeated foreign enemies to pay the costs associated with the war.

In the very next year, the Carthaginians faced a new threat when their mercenaries, who formed the backbone of their army, mutinied because they had not been paid. Unable to deal with them, the Carthaginians appealed to their new Roman patrons for help, and the Romans assisted in the suppression of the revolt. In 238, however, this friendly Roman attitude changed after Hamilcar Barca, their nemesis in Sicily, undertook to restore Carthaginian military strength. When the Carthaginian mercenaries in Sardinia offered to turn the island over to Rome, the Romans accepted. The Carthaginian protest was met by a Roman declaration of war. The weakened Carthaginians had no choice but to accept a revised treaty that added an extra 1,700 talents to the indemnity and required them to evacuate Sardinia and Corsica as well. This callous Roman opportunism offended many Carthaginians.

The question remained of what to do with the territories Carthage had abandoned. Fearful of having the rich island of Sicily fall into the wrong hands, the Romans annexed it and in 227 made it their first **province,** or foreign territory over which Rome assumed direct control. In the same year, Sardinia and Corsica became a second province. Having no method of governing these new territories, the Romans created two new praetors to serve as governors. But otherwise, the Roman policy toward the provinces might be best described as benign neglect.

The Illyrian and Celtic Wars (229–219 BCE)

Hitherto, the Romans had confined their attentions almost exclusively to the western Mediterranean and had shown little interest in the Greek world. This changed in 229, when pirates from Illyria, roughly modern Albania, killed a Roman ambassador on the Adriatic Sea. That was all it took for the Romans to declare war on the Illyrian queen Teuta, initiating the First Illyrian War (229 BCE). The Illyrians could not hope to resist. Teuta promised not to do it again, and the Roman fleet departed, but not before acknowledging as *amici* ("friends") some of the Greek peoples near the Adriatic coast. In 219 BCE, after another spate of piracy, the Romans had to return to Illyria in the Second Illyrian War (219 BCE). These rather inglorious episodes had the effect of giving the Romans a precedent for future involvements on the Greek mainland.

This decade also saw the last Gallic invasion of Italy when in 225 a coalition of some seventy thousand Gauls from the Po River valley, augmented by Gallic mercenaries from Transalpine Gaul ("Gaul across the Alps"), advanced south. They were met at the Battle of Telamon, on the coast of Etruria, by two Roman armies who caught them from both sides. After a savage battle, the Gauls were defeated, and thousands were sold into slavery. Subsequently, the Romans decided to deal with the problem of the north Italian Celts once and for all and invaded the Po Valley. By 220, nearly all the Italian Gauls had been defeated, and the Romans established military colonies to keep a further eye on them.

The Second Punic War (218–201 BCE)

In the interim, the Carthaginians had been recovering their strength in Spain, where whey found silver and **Celtiberian** (the name given to the Celts of Spain) mercenaries under the leadership of Hannibal, the son of Hamilcar Barca. It was later thought by the Romans that in his youth Hannibal had sworn to his father that he would destroy Rome. In the Ebro Treaty of 226, Rome prohibited the Carthaginians from going north of the Ebro River in Spain but acknowledged Carthaginian authority south of the Ebro. Nevertheless, in 219, when the city of Saguntum, well south of the Ebro, appealed to Rome for help against a besieging Carthaginian army, the Romans ordered Hannibal to withdraw. Hannibal refused and captured Saguntum, along with a vast amount of booty. The Romans thus sent the ambassador Quintus Fabius Maximus to the Carthaginian Senate with a demand that Hannibal be handed over to Rome, but when the Carthaginians blamed the Romans for the violation of the Ebro Treaty, Fabius reached into a fold in his toga and said, "I have here peace and war, which do you choose?" When the Carthaginians responded, "War," Fabius replied, "Then war it must be." And Hannibal himself, having observed many examples of unwarranted Roman interference in Carthaginian affairs, saw no alternative to war and determined to attack the Romans on their home territory and to try to break up Rome's Italian Alliance, which he saw as the real source of Rome's strength.

Therefore, in 218 BCE Hannibal led his mercenary army of Celtiberian infantry and Numidian

This Carthaginian gold shekel of ca. 222–205 BCE, depicting the goddess Tanit on one side and a North African horse on the other, would have been used to fund the cost of the Second Punic War and attests to Carthage's economic power.

cavalry, accompanied by seventeen war elephants, out of Spain, through the Alps, and into Cisalpine Gaul, where he expected that the Cisalpine Gauls would flock to join him. Thus began the Second Punic War (218–201 BCE). But the Gauls, who recently had been defeated by the Romans, were reluctant to take up arms. In 218, 217, and 216, Hannibal inflicted three devastating defeats on the Romans at the Battle of the Trebia River in Cisalpine Gaul, the Battle of Lake Trasimene in Etruria, and the Battle of Cannae in southeastern Italy. For the last of these, the Romans had raised a double consular army of over fifty thousand men, but Roman operations were paralyzed by bickering between the consuls Varro, a New Man, and his patrician colleague Paullus. In the ensuing battle, the Roman army was virtually annihilated after being surrounded by Hannibal's smaller thirty-thousand-man army. Paullus died with his men; eighty other senators were killed. This was the worst disaster Rome had ever suffered. When Varro, who survived and saved as much of the army as possible, returned to Rome, he was met by the Senate, who publicly thanked him for not despairing of Rome. And as for Hannibal, he was rebuked for not immediately attacking Rome by Maharbal, one of his cavalry commanders, with the famous words, "You know how to win a victory, Hannibal, but not to use it." But at that point, Hannibal's army was too exhausted to go anywhere. And these spectacular victories now did induce some of Gauls to join Hannibal.

Fabian strategy still refers to a tactical avoidance of battle, as George Washington did at Valley Forge.

The Senate responded by appointing a Dictator, Quintus Fabius Maximus, who refused to fight Hannibal in the field but shadowed him so closely that Hannibal could controlled the patch of ground on which his army was camped. At one point, Hannibal actually did march his army up to the gates of Rome, but, safe behind the Servian Wall, the Romans refused to fight him; in fact, it was said that the Roman who owned the land on which Hannibal camped sold the property that day and made money on the deal. Rather than giving in, the Romans showed their commitment to persevere by raising additional armies and widening the scope of the war. They sent armies to Sicily, where Syracuse had revolted; to Spain, the primary source of Carthage's financial and manpower reserves; and to Greece, where King Philip V of Macedon (220–179) had allied himself with Hannibal, resulting in the the First Macedonian War (214–205).

Gradually, the Romans disentangled themselves from the other theaters of the war. Syracuse was betrayed and sacked in 211. In 210 the command in Spain was given to Publius Cornelius Scipio, who as a young military tribune had survived the Battle of Cannae and whose father and uncle had been killed in Spain the previous year. Even though Publius was only a twenty-five-year-old ex-aedile, there was so much popular sympathy for him that he was granted the *imperium* of a proconsul (an ex-consul). Mimicking the tactics of Hannibal, he was able to achieve total victory in Spain by 206. And in 205 the Romans extricated themselves from Greece by negotiating the Peace of

Phoenice with the Macedonians, in which they abandoned their Greek friends: this thus became the only Republican war that the Romans lost. But Hannibal still was unopposed in Italy.

At this point, Scipio, as consul for the year 205, with only reluctant support from the Senate took an army consisting primarily of the defeated legions from Cannae to Africa to attack the Carthaginian homeland. Scipio found a local ally in Masinissa, an ambitious Numidian chieftain who supplied the Roman army with much-needed cavalry. In 203 the Carthaginians were defeated at the Battle of the Great Plains and finally recalled Hannibal from Italy. The final showdown came the next year at the Battle of Zama Regia, in which the Roman and Numidian cavalry was able to slip behind and surround the Carthaginian army. Hannibal finally was defeated, and Scipio gained the victory title Africanus, or "conqueror of Africa." The Carthaginians had no choice but to make peace. They were compelled to relinquish all claims to Spain, to reduce their navy to ten warships, and to pay an indemnity of twenty thousand talents in fifty annual installments. They also were prohibited from making war or even defending themselves without the consent of Rome. Carthage never again would be a strong military power.

The Second Punic War involved the entire western Mediterranean, just as the Peloponnesian War had involved nearly the entire Greek world. It demonstrated the strength of Rome's Italian Alliance, for nearly all of Rome's Italian allies had held firm. The Romans later looked back to their defeat of the terrifying Hannibal as their defining moment, and they never forgot it; for hundreds of years, Roman mothers would frighten their children into obedience by saying, "Hannibal's at the gates!" Its victory left Rome as the only power in the western Mediterranean, and one of its unanticipated consequences was that the Romans felt compelled to lay claim to Spain, if for no other reason than to keep the Carthaginians away from it. In 197 BCE two new provinces were created there, Nearer and Further Spain, governed by two additional praetors, although at this time Rome controlled only the coastal areas.

Warfare Spreads to the East

The end of the Second Punic War found Rome absolutely drained. Tens of thousands of soldiers had been killed, and the property losses in Italy were staggering. One would have thought that the Romans would have wanted nothing more than to rest and recover their strength. But this was not to be. In addition to continuing wars in the west, between 200 and 146 BCE Rome also was drawn into involvements with the Hellenistic states that had succeeded to the empire of Alexander the Great. These included not only Antigonid Macedonia, Seleucid Syria, and Ptolemaic Egypt but also a number of smaller states, such as Pergamum in western Anatolia, the island of Rhodes, and the Achaean and Aetolian Leagues of Greece.

The Second Macedonian War (200–197 BCE)

The first of these wars involved unfinished business. The Romans had not forgotten the unsatisfactory conclusion of the First Macedonian War. In addition, the Roman fears about strong neighbors were revived when Rhodes and Pergamum reported that Philip V, ruler of Macedon, and King Antiochus III, ruler of the Seleucid Empire, had concluded a "Secret Treaty" whereby they planned to carve up the possessions of the Ptolemaic kingdom of Egypt. With the full support of the consuls, who would have the opportunity to gain military glory, the Senate therefore recommended that war be declared on Macedonia. But then something completely unprecedented happened. The Centuriate Assembly, tired of war, rejected the revised motion. Only after a revised motion exempted military veterans from service was war declared. Even though the Macedonians could not hope to resist the full might of the Roman army, it was not until 197 BCE that the Romans found a capable general, Titus Quinctius Flamininus, who ended the Second Macedonian War (200–197 BCE) by defeating the wily Philip at the Battle of Cynoscephalae (Dogs' Heads). But rather than occupying any Greek territory, the Romans were content to weaken Macedonia by requiring Philip to pay a war indemnity, give up his navy, and evacuate his holdings in Greece. They declared the Greek cities "free," and then returned home.

The Syrian War (192–188 BCE)

At this point, King Antiochus III (223–187), ruler of the vast Seleucid Empire of Syria and western Asia, saw an opportunity to gain control of much of the empire of Alexander. In 192 he invaded Greece, and the Romans were compelled to send another army to the east to deal with what they perceived as a grave threat. The Syrian War (192–188 BCE) was decided in 190 BCE at the Battle of Magnesia, where the well-trained Romans, commanded by the consul Lucius Cornelius Scipio, who was advised by his brother Scipio Africanus, demolished the motley Seleucid army, which still employed war elephants and even scythe chariots. In the Treaty of Apamea in 188 BCE, the Romans once again occupied no new territory, but they did compel the Seleucids to pay a war indemnity of fifteen thousand talents over the course of twelve years and to evacuate most of their holdings in Anatolia, which the Romans granted to Pergamum.

The Third Macedonian War (170–168 BCE)

During the succeeding years, Macedonia regained its strength. A new king, Perseus (179–168), began to expand his influence to the north. A rumor reached

Rome that he planned to hire the Bastarnae, a Celtic people living near the Danube, to attack Rome. Fears of a new Macedonian threat led the Romans again to declare war in 171 BCE. The Third Macedonian War (171–168 BCE) played out much like the second. Not until 168 BCE did a competent general emerge, Lucius Aemilius Paulus, who defeated Perseus at the Battle of Pydna, a set battle that definitively demonstrated the superiority of the Roman legions over the Macedonian phalanx. This time the Romans took more serious measures to prevent future problems. They did not take over any territory, but they divided Macedonia up into four independent republics, which were forbidden contact with each other. They then departed, confident that the Macedonian threat had been eliminated.

After the Third Macedonian War, the Romans began to act like the bullies of the Mediterranean, as they became increasingly aware that no one could resist them. On the way home from Macedonia in 168 BCE, the Roman army pillaged Epirus, enslaving 150,000 inhabitants of Epirus in belated retaliation for the Pyrrhic War. In the same year, the Seleucid king Antiochus IV (215–164 BCE) conquered Ptolemaic Egypt. On being notified that a Roman ambassador had arrived in Alexandria, Antiochus honored him by greeting him on the beach. But the ambassador, an old friend of Antiochus, formally notified him, "The Senate and the Roman people want you to get out of Egypt." When Antiochus asked time to think it over, the ambassador replied he could have as long as he wanted so long as he did not leave a circle the ambassador drew around him in the sand. Antiochus, offended by Roman arrogance but very aware of Rome's power, had no choice but to comply.

TABLE 9.5	ROMAN WARS (390–146 BCE)
390	Gallic sack of Rome
343–341	First Samnite War
340–338	Great Latin Revolt
326–304	Second Samnite War
298–290	Third Samnite War
280–275	Pyrrhic War
264–241	First Punic War
229–227	First Illyrian War
219–218	Second Illyrian War
218–201	Second Punic War
215–204	First Macedonian War
200–197	Second Macedonian War
192–188	Syrian War
181–179	First Celtiberian War
171–168	Third Macedonian War
154–133	Second Celtiberian War
149–146	Third Punic War
149–148	Fourth Macedonian War
146	Achaean Revolt

The Third Punic War (149–146 BCE)

Carthage, too, which had rebuilt itself as an economic, although not as a military, powerhouse, experienced Roman high-handedness. The hawkish senator Marcus Porcius Cato the Elder, a New Man, was jealous of Carthage's wealth and ended his speeches in the Senate with the words, "And in other regards, I think that Carthage must be destroyed." In 150 BCE, the Carthaginians paid off the last of the installments of the indemnity of 201. The next year, the Romans declared war after the Carthaginians violated the treaty of 201 by defending themselves against attacks by the Numidians. This began the Third Punic War (149–146 BCE), which dragged on until the Romans found a skilled general in Scipio Aemilianus, the adoptive grandson of Scipio Africanus. In 146 BCE the city was captured in desperate house-to-house fighting, during

The popular story that the Romans sowed the site of Carthage with salt is an urban legend dating to the eighteenth century.

This portrait bust of the fourth century BCE known as the Dama de Elche portrays a Celtiberian woman wearing an elaborate coiled headdress and reveals the difference between Greco-Roman and Celtic conceptions of good style.

which many Carthaginians threw themselves into the burning temple of Tanit rather than be taken captive.

The Fourth Macedonian War and Achaean Revolt (149–146 BCE)

In 149 Rome also faced a Fourth Macedonian War (149–148 BCE) in Greece, where a pretender to the Macedonian throne had reconstituted the kingdom. He was defeated in 148, but in 146 BCE the Achaean League, manifesting increasing Greek discontent with Roman high-handedness, also revolted. The Roman general Mummius swiftly suppressed the Achaean revolt, and in the same year the Romans decided that a lesson had to be provided to those who contemplated resisting the will of Rome in the future. Thus, in 146 BCE the Romans destroyed two of the most famous cities of the Mediterranean world, Corinth in Greece and Carthage in North Africa. In addition, Macedonia and Achaea were annexed as the new province of Macedonia, and the territory of Carthage became the province of Africa. The Roman lesson finally was learned, and there was no further serious resistance against the Romans in the Mediterranean.

These acquisitions brought to an end the Roman reluctance to acquire foreign territory, and the Romans soon began to annex additional overseas provinces. Thus, when King Attalus III of Pergamum died in 133 and, lacking an heir, willed his kingdom to Rome, the Roman government accepted the offer. After a short-lived popular revolt led by a certain Aristonicus, who claimed to be Attalus' long-lost brother, had been easily suppressed, Pergamum was incorporated as a new province grandiosely named **Asia**. And in 121 BCE, to facilitate land communications to Spain, the province of Narbonese Gaul was annexed in southern Gaul.

Narbonese Gaul came go be known simply as provincia *("the province"), leading to the modern designation Provence.*

The Wars in Spain (181–133 BCE)

Meanwhile, endemic warfare in Spain continued to drain Roman resources and manpower as the Romans gradually extended their control over the peninsula. Two Celtiberian Wars (181–179, 154–133 BCE) were interspersed with incessant guerilla warfare, and any general who wanted military glory could always look for it in Spain if there were no wars going on anywhere else. The losses suffered have led to Spain being referred to as "the Graveyard of the Roman Republic." The conflict came to head in the 140s with joint rebellions in north central Spain, centered on the *oppidum* (hill fort) of Numantia, also known as the Numantine War, and in Lusitania (modern Portugal) in the west, led by the charismatic chieftain

Viriathus. After winning several victories, Viriathus was betrayed and killed in 139. Meanwhile, the Numantines were besieged on and off beginning in 143 BCE. After several inglorious episodes in which defeated Roman generals were forced to grant the Numantines a treaty only to have it repudiated by the Senate, Scipio Aemilianus, the victor at Carthage in 146, was given the command. The following year, after Scipio had constructed a five-and-a-half-mile-long ring of fortifications around the city, the inhabitants, realizing their cause was hopeless, burned the city and largely committed suicide. Only a few hundred survived. This was the last organized local resistance against Rome, and the pacification of Spain then proceeded more smoothly.

THE IMPACT OF EXPANSION ON ROME

By 120 BCE, Rome controlled territory extending from Spain to Anatolia, giving rise to what has been known as the **Republican Empire.** This expansion had far-reaching economic, social, and cultural effects.

Economic Developments

Roman expansion created the need for an effective monetary system to pay for it. The earliest Roman money had consisted of large copper bricks known as *aes signatum* ("stamped copper") with symbols, such as a cow, pig, or elephant, imprinted on them. Indeed, the Latin word for money, *pecunia*, was derived from *pecus*, or herd of cows, suggesting that the Roman economy initially was on the cow standard. Copper coins, first issued in 289 BCE, were cumbersome and crude: the *as*, a coin valued at a pound of copper, actually weighed a pound. Soon afterward, a silver coinage, based on Greek models, was created. The standard Roman silver coin, the **denarius,** was introduced around 212 BCE, when tremendous amounts of coinage were needed to pay the expenses of the Second Punic War. A gold aureus, which was issued only in times of great emergency, also was issued as the Romans consolidated their resources in the fight against Hannibal. By then, moreover, the Romans also had become more financially sophisticated, and they realized that by linking the value of the copper and silver coinages—one silver denarius was initially valued at ten copper

The word penny *comes from* denarius.

TABLE 9.6   COIN DENOMINATIONS OF THE ROMAN REPUBLIC

Metal	Denomination	Value
Gold	Aureus (aurei)	First 18, then 20 denarii
Silver	Denarius (denarii)	First 10, then 16 asses
Silver	Quinarius	½ denarius: 5, then 8 asses
Silver	Sestertius (sesterces)	¼ denarius: 2 ½, then 4 asses
Copper	As (asses)	12 unciae
Copper	Semis	6 unciae, ½ as
Copper	Triens	4 unciae, ⅓ as
Copper	Quadrans	3 unciae, ¼ as
Copper	Sextans	2 unciae, ⅙
Copper	Uncia	1 uncia (ounce)

asses—they could float a loan on the population by using smaller, cheaply produced copper coins in place of silver ones. Once the Romans had gained political control of the Mediterranean world, their economic influence became so great that the silver denarius likewise became the standard currency of the Mediterranean world.

A consequence of having larger economic resources was the growth of both building projects and public entertainments. Aqueducts, beginning with the Aqua Appia built in conjunction with the Appian Way in the late fourth century BCE, brought fresh water into Rome. Old-fashioned buildings, such as the temple of Jupiter on the Capitoline Hill, were remodeled, and new public buildings, such as basilicas, where the praetors could hear legal cases, were constructed. More imaginative forms of architectural construction used bricks and concrete, as well as stone, to build the arch, the vault, and the dome and replaced the rather predictable Greek marble-block, rectangular-temple format. And people came to expect elaborate entertainments, such as chariot racing and gladiatorial combats, to commemorate festivals and special events. Regular chariot races, borrowed from the Etruscans and Greeks and held on racecourses known as circuses, were held as of 211 BCE in a festival honoring Apollo. And gladiatorial contests, likewise borrowed from the Etruscans, were presented at the funerals of important persons commencing in 174 BCE. Eventually, however, they were put on purely for entertainment.

CROSS-CULTURAL QUESTION

What do you think was the greatest similarity between the culture and values of the Greeks and the Romans? What was the greatest difference?

A social consequence of Rome's economic expansion was the rise of a new social class, the knights (or equestrians) who adopted the name (but not the function) of the old top class of the Centuriate Assembly and ranked between the senators and the plebeians. These opportunistic individuals made their fortunes in trade, manufacturing, money lending, and tax collecting, activities that were considered unsuitable for conservative senators, who believed that land was the only respectable kind of investment. Indeed, a law of 218 BCE even prohibited Senators from owning seagoing merchant ships. Roman political control over the Mediterranean world gave the knights business advantages over non-Romans, such as access to large financial resources and legal preference in Roman courts.

Cultural Consequences

Roman expansion also exposed the Romans to many foreign cultural influences, especially from Greece. Indeed, the poet Horace later wrote that "captured Greece overcame her savage conqueror and introduced the arts into rustic Latium." Greek theories of rhetoric found a receptive audience among the Romans, for whom public speaking was a necessity of political life. Greek philosophical beliefs also made their way into Rome. Stoicism, which taught that doing one's duty was the highest virtue, found many Roman followers, although Epicureanism, with its focus on self-indulgence, was so offensive to some influential Romans that at one point Epicurean teachers were expelled from Rome. Roman playwrights such as Plautus and Terence wrote Latin comedies modeled on Greek originals. In the years after 200 BCE, the first histories of Rome were written in Greek by both Romans and Greeks, most notably Polybius, a Greek hostage who accompanied Scipio Aemilianus at the fall of Carthage and wrote by far the best surviving account of Rome's third-century BCE wars. The adaptation of Greek literary styles and genres to Roman purposes was supported by influential senators such as Scipio Aemilianus, whose Scipionic Circle included not only writers such as Terence, Polybius, the satirist Lucilius, and the Stoic philosopher Panaetius of Rhodes but also senatorial patrons of the arts, such as C. Laelius Sapiens.

But other Romans were chary of the adoption of too much Greek culture. The conservative senator Cato the Elder, fearing that Rome would be overwhelmed by Hellenism, insisted on writing his own history of Rome in Latin, and later writers followed in his footsteps. At the same time, the Romans developed their own national literary genre, satire, introduced by the writer Lucilius, which took a critical but humorous look at society, morality, and personal behavior. It was written in both poetry and prose and was full of parody, obscenity, and invective. By the end of the second century BC, Latin had become an established literary language in its own right. And Greece, having lost its political significance, became a place where young Romans went to continue their studies in subjects such as rhetoric and philosophy, especially in Athens.

Satire continues to be popular, as still seen in political cartoons.

Religious Assimilation

The Romans not only enthusiastically adopted Greek myths and legends, but also assimilated eastern religious practices. Sometimes this was done officially, as when during the closing days of the Second Punic War, with Hannibal at the gates of Rome, the Romans consulted the Sibylline Oracles and were told to bring the "Great Mother" from Anatolia. As a result, the eastern mother goddess Cybele was introduced into Rome. But on other occasions, the importation of eastern religions created official anxiety. In 186 BCE, the consul Spurius Postumius received a report from Hispala, an ex-slave, that worshippers of the wine god Bacchus were holding secret orgies. According to the later historian Livy, "There was nothing wicked that was not practiced among them. There was more frequent pollution of men with each other than with women. If any were unwilling to commit vice, they were sacrificed as victims." The Senate not only feared a threat to conventional morality but also was concerned that the clandestine gatherings might lead to conspiracies against the

LEARNING FROM HISTORY

Many Romans would have liked to maintain their old established customs at the same time that they were extending their authority throughout the Mediterranean. Do you think that a world power can keep culture isolated from politics as it expands to absorb other peoples?

THE DECREE OF THE SENATE ON THE BACCHUS WORSHIPPERS

One of the very few original decrees of the Senate to survive from the Republican period was "The Decree of the Senate Concerning the Worshippers of Bacchus," issued to the consuls in 186 BCE. It demonstrates that even though the Senate was just an advisory body, it often acted as if it had direct authority to issue regulations and to instruct magistrates to take specific actions. This copy was inscribed on bronze and set up for all to see. It included the actual minutes of a meeting of the Senate:

> Quintus Marcius, the son of Lucius, and Spurius Postumius, consulted the Senate on the Nones [7th] of October, at the temple of the Bellonae. Marcus Claudius, son of Marcus, Lucius Valerius, son of Publius, and Quintus Minucius, son of Gaius, were the committee for drawing up the report. Regarding the Bacchanalia, it was resolved to give the following directions to those who are in alliance with us: No one of them is to possess a place where the festivals of Bacchus are celebrated; if there are any who claim that it is necessary for them to have such a place, they are to come to Rome to the Urban Praetor, and the senate is to decide on those matters, when their claims have been heard, provided that not less than one hundred senators are present when the affair is discussed. No man is to be a Bacchantian, neither a Roman citizen, nor one with Latin Rights, nor any of our allies unless they come to the Urban Praetor, and he in accordance with the opinion of the senate expressed when not less than one hundred senators are present at the discussion, shall have given leave. Carried.
>
> No man is to be a priest; no one, either man or woman, is to be an officer (to manage the temporal affairs of the organization); nor is anyone of them to have charge of a common treasury; no one shall appoint either man or woman to be master or to act as master; henceforth they shall not form conspiracies among themselves, stir up any disorder, make mutual promises or agreements, or interchange pledges; no one shall observe the sacred rites either in public or private or outside the city, unless he comes to the Urban Praetor, and he, in accordance with the opinion of the senate, expressed when no less than one hundred senators are present at the discussion, shall have given leave. Carried.

government. Many of those convicted of engaging in these Bacchanalian rites were condemned to death, with women turned over to their families "so they could inflict the punishment in private." And as a reward for coming forward, Hispala was granted the unusual privilege of being permitted to marry a man of higher social status.

The example of Hispala demonstrates that by the second century BCE, women were becoming more outspoken and assertive. Women gained additional influence in other ways, too, with a liberalization of some of the more restrictive aspects of Roman treatment of women. Some women became so dissatisfied that they took matters into their own hands. In a celebrated case of 331 BCE, 170 women were convicted of trying to poison their husbands. On another occasion, in 195 BCE, women protested against a law commanding that no woman should own more than a half ounce of gold, or wear multicolored clothing, or ride in Rome in a carriage. They blockaded the forum and confronted the senators. This kind of political activism by women was absolutely unprecedented. Even though the conservative consul Cato the Elder complained, "Our freedom is conquered by female fury; we even now let them meddle in the Forum and our assemblies," the offensive law was repealed.

Other demands by women no doubt were pursued behind the scenes, and over the course of time women gained additional rights. The "usage" type of marriage began to be replaced by a marriage *sine manu*, "without authority," in which a woman technically remained under the authority of her father and her property was kept separate from that of her husband. When her father died she then became *sui juris*, "under her own authority," with independent ownership of her own property. Women also obtained the right to initiate various kinds of legal proceedings, such as divorces, buying and selling property, or making wills, although they still needed a cooperative male "guardian" to conduct the legal formalities.

LOOKING AHEAD

By the middle of the second century BCE, the big question was whether the Romans would be able to preserve the way of life that had made Roman government work ever since 509 BCE, a system based on senators working to distribute power and authority among themselves in a way that kept powerful, status-conscious senators sufficiently happy that they were willing to continue to bring all their many resources to bear in support of the government. The rise of Rome as a world power brought many disruptive influences into Rome: great wealth, the opportunity for great military power, and the realization that there were additional sources of wealth, culture, authority, and prestige outside of Rome. Would powerful senators be willing, or able, to continue to put Rome first?

FURTHER READING

Barker, G., and T. Rasmussen. *The Etruscans*. London: Blackwell, 1998.

Boatwright, Mary T., Daniel J. Gargola, and Richard J. A. Talbert. *The Romans: From Village to Empire*. New York: Oxford University Press, 2004.

Byrd, Robert C. *The Senate of the Roman Republic.* Honolulu: University Press of the Pacific, 2001.

Cary, M., and H. H. Scullard. *A History of Rome down to the Reign of Constantine,* 3rd ed. New York: St. Martin's Press, 1975.

Cornell, Tim. *The Beginnings of Rome: Italy and Rome from the Bronze Age to the Punic Wars (c. 1000–264 BC).* New York: Routledge, 1995.

Crawford, Michael H. *Coinage and Money under the Roman Republic.* London: Methuen, 1985.

Cunliffe, Barry. *The Ancient Celts.* Oxford: Oxford University Press, 1997.

Errington, R. M. *The Dawn of Empire: Rome's Rise to World Power.* Ithaca, NY: Cornell University Press, 1972.

Gabba, Emilio. *Republican Rome, the Army, and the Allies.* Berkeley: University of California Press, 1976.

Harris, William V. *War and Imperialism in Republican Rome 327–70 B.C.* Oxford: Oxford University Press, 1979.

Raaflaub, Kurt, ed. *Social Struggles in Archaic Rome: New Perspectives on the Conflict of the Orders.* Berkeley: University of California Press, 1986.

Rosenstein, Nathan S. *Imperatores victi: Military Defeat and Aristocrati Competition in the Middle and Late Republic.* Berkeley: University of California Press, 1990.

Warmington, B. H. *Carthage.* New York: Praeger, 1960.

CHAPTER 10

THE DECLINE OF THE REPUBLIC AND THE FOUNDING OF THE PRINCIPATE
(149–21 BCE)

During the second century BCE, Rome became the most powerful state in the Mediterranean world, and, even though we still call it the Republic, it amassed an empire of provinces extending from Spain to Anatolia. The creation of this empire placed tremendous stress on administration and politics. Rome's city-state form of government was not equipped to handle the administration of an overseas empire. The need to raise large professional armies was inconsistent with the Roman tradition of armies recruited from peasant farmers. And powerful ambitious senators, in command of these large armies, increasingly tended to put their own personal ambitions ahead of the best interests of the Roman state. Combined, these factors eventually led to the fall of the Republic as it initially had been established.

FROM ONE CRISIS TO THE NEXT (149–88 BCE)

During the second half of the second century BCE, a number of problems that had been developing over the course of the previous century, such as the failure of Roman methods for administering the provinces and a crisis in military recruitment methods, became so serious that they threatened the very existence of the Republic as it initially had been established.

Provincial Administration

The establishment, between 227 and 121 BCE, of provinces that extended from Spain in the west to Asia in the east created critical pressure for the Roman administration, which had been instituted to govern a small city-state, not a Mediterranean-wide empire. The strain became so serious that in many ways Rome was simply unable to cope with the consequences and responsibilities that

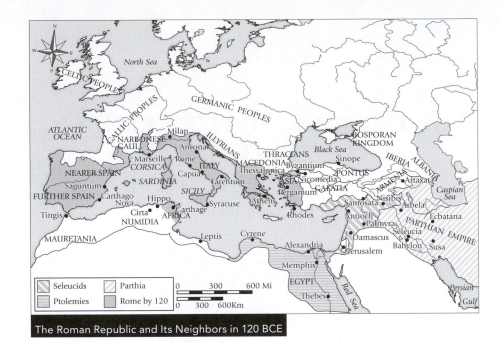

The Roman Republic and Its Neighbors in 120 BCE

came with these new territories. Never having really wanted most of them in the first place, and often having acquired them simply to keep them out of the hands of potential enemies, the Romans saw little reason to alter their city-state form of government in order to accommodate them. As a result, direct Roman administration was very minimal. Provinces were governed by **proconsuls** (who in the past, usually the year before, had been consuls) and by praetors. Proconsuls had the same imperium as consuls, and thus could issue laws and lead armies, which generally were stationed in the provinces only on an as-needed basis because of the expense involved. Provincial governors generally served for one year and had only a very small staff, consisting of a quaestor to handle the finances and a few legates to whom authority (and *imperium*) could be delegated.

Many cities created in western Europe by the Romans continue to be important cities in the modern day.

A governor's main responsibilities were to oversee the administration of justice, provide military defense, and collect the taxes. Their small staffs meant that nearly all the aspects of day-to-day local administration were left in the hands of locals. This was done by dividing up the province into smaller territorial units, each administered by the city council of a *civitas* (city). If a province did not already have cities, as was the case in western European regions such as Spain, the Romans created them and, for purposes of local administration, divided up the province's territory among them. In many cases, the territory of a *civitas* capital roughly matched the territory of the previous Celtic peoples, although the actual city was established not at one of the old hill fort sites but at a more accessible place. Governors made a regular circuit of the cities in their provinces to remind the **provincials**, the inhabitants of the provinces who did not have Roman citizenship, of the Roman presence and to adjudicate legal disputes that could not be settled locally.

Even though the Romans did not intend to exploit or misgovern the provinces, there were potential problems with Roman policies and administrative methods. For example, the provincials had no established means of interaction with the Roman government. There was no centralized office of provincial administration either in Rome or in the individual provinces, the provincials had no rights in Rome, and the governor was the last court of appeal. In addition, there was no regular means by which provincials could become Roman citizens, although governors, by virtue of their power of imperium, did have the right to create citizens in an ad hoc way.

TABLE 10.1	ROMAN PROVINCES 227–121 BCE	
Province	**Date**	**Governor**
Sicily	227 BCE	Praetor
Sardinia and Corsica	227 BCE	Praetor
Nearer Spain	197 BCE	Praetor
Further Spain	197 BCE	Praetor
Africa	146 BCE	Proconsul
Macedonia	146 BCE	Proconsul
Asia	129 BCE	Proconsul
Narbonese Gaul	121 BCE	Proconsul

The greatest complaint with provincial administration, in some provinces at least, involved the taxes. Not that Roman taxes were excessive; indeed, sometimes they were lower than before the Roman conquest. The problem, in some provinces, had to do with how the taxes were collected. Taxes were assessed by two different processes, depending on the system that had been in place at the time the Romans created a province. In economically sophisticated provinces where there already was extensive exploitation of agriculture, such as Sicily and Asia, the taxation system known as the **tithe** was in effect. In the tithe system, farmers paid one-tenth of their annual crop in taxes. This meant that in a good farming year taxes would be high, and in a bad year they would be low. This could have been a fair system, but in practice, because of the lack of Roman administrative oversight, there were many opportunities for abuse, as when the locally hired tax collectors, known as *publicani* ("publicans"), seized large quantities of crops and called it "a tenth." As a result, *publicani* developed a most unsavory reputation. In provinces that were less economically developed, a form of tax known as *tributum,* or *tribute,* was assessed. This was a fixed amount that was paid each year irrespective of how economically productive a province had been during the year. The tribute system was less liable to corruption because there was no uncertainty about exactly how much each taxpayer owed.

Because the government did not have staffing to arrange to collect the taxes itself, the right to do so in various regions was auctioned off to "tax-farming" companies. These paid the Roman government a lump sum and then extorted as much as they could from the provincials. Even if a governor protested against or tried to limit abuses, he often had little ability to prevent it. And to make it even more difficult to restrain unscrupulous tax collectors, the tax-farming companies were increasingly operated not by wealthy provincials but by even wealthier Roman knights, who often were the only ones with financial resources sufficient to raise the huge amounts of money needed to bid. The knights' connections in Rome made it even more difficult for provincial governors to repress corruption in the provinces, given that the knights were behind the corruption, and once a governor's term of service was up he could expect resentment and resistance from ambitious knights and their senatorial allies back in Rome.

In most regards, the Roman government paid little attention to the provinces. It did not intend to exploit the provinces, and it rarely made money. Any corruption that arose through the sale of justice or problems in tax collection benefited individual profiteers or governors, not the Roman government. The government just had no procedures for policing the provinces. A senatorial *Quaestio de repetundis,* or **Extortion Court**, established in 149 BCE, was meant to try governors for corruption but often ended up being used to trump up charges against a senator's political enemies, and as a consequence good governors sometimes ended up being the ones charged with "corruption." One of the main failures of the Republic was that it never found a way to integrate the provinces and the provincials into Roman government, administration, and society.

Tiberius Gracchus and the Agricultural-Military Crisis

The provinces also created problems in other ways. The very act of acquiring them necessarily involved another Roman institution: the army. Ever since the Samnite Wars (343–290 BCE), Roman armies had been fighting farther from home for longer periods. This created problems for the agricultural economy. The ancient military recruiting policies specified by the Servian Reforms required soldiers to be property owners. This meant that rather than tilling the soil, thousands of small farmers were far from home fighting Rome's wars. Many of them did not return, and those who did often had little desire to return to tedious farm life and were happy to sell their plots to senators, who always were looking to acquire additional land. As a consequence, the recruiting base for the army became ever smaller, leaving Rome facing an **agricultural-military crisis**.

It would seem that there would have been two possible solutions to this dilemma: either to abandon the property requirement altogether or to distribute state-owned *ager publicus,* or "public land," to landless plebeians and thus make them eligible for military service. In typical fashion, however, the conservative Senate opposed any attempt at reform: in 140 BCE, the consul Laelius was dissuaded from introducing a land distribution law and as a result gained the nickname Sapiens ("The Wise"). The problem thus continued to fester.

In 133 BCE a tribune of the plebs, **Tiberius Gracchus**, attempted to deal with the recruitment crisis after observing that most of the land in Etruria was being worked not by Roman peasant farmers eligible for military service but, as reported by Plutarch, by "barbarian slaves working as cultivators and shepherds." Now, Tiberius came from the most blue-blooded of Roman senatorial families. His mother, Cornelia, was the daughter of Scipio Africanus, and his sister, Sempronia, was married to Scipio Aemilianus. After the death of her husband, Cornelia turned down an offer of marriage from Ptolemy VII, king of Egypt, and raised and educated Tiberius, Sempronia, and their brother Gaius by herself. She became a classic model of Roman female virtue. According to one story, when she was questioned by fancily adorned Roman matrons about why she, too, was not showing off her jewelry, she called in her sons and stated, "These are my jewels." Tiberius embarked on the standard senatorial career. As a military tribune, he was the first over the wall in the final Roman assault on Carthage in 146 BCE, and as quaestor in Spain in 137, he rescued a defeated Roman army by negotiating a treaty with the Celtiberians. Tiberius thus could have looked forward to an outstanding traditional political career including, no doubt, the consulate. But he instead chose to become a reformer by introducing legislation in the Council of the Plebs to distribute plots of thirty *jugera* (a *jugerum* was about two-thirds of an acre) each of public land to the poor, thus increasing the number of Romans eligible to serve in the army.

Even though Tiberius was supported by some of the most influential senators, the sticking point in his bill was that much of the public land already was being rented by powerful, land-hungry senators who had come to look on it as their own, and this in spite of a law dating back to 367 specifying that no one could lease more than 500 *jugera* of public land. In an attempt to defuse senatorial objections, Tiberius' law granted 500 *jugera* to each senator and 250 to each son of a senator free and clear. But even that was not enough to gain Senate support. When hostile senators induced another tribune to veto Tiberius' law, Tiberius simply had him deposed and then took the extraordinarily divisive step of failing to gain prior Senate approval and taking his law directly to the Council of the Plebs, where it was duly passed. The opportunity to do this had been enhanced just six years earlier with the passage of a law replacing the old method of verbal voting with secret ballot voting, which weakened the patronage hold of senators on plebeian voters.

When the Senate then refused to allocate any funding to put the **land law** into effect, Tiberius threatened to introduce a law assigning it the wealth of the newly acquired kingdom of Pergamum, and the Senate was forced to yield, only exacerbating the hard feelings of many senators toward Tiberius. The law then took effect, and public land began to be allocated to landless plebs. But when Tiberius announced a provocative intention to run for reelection as tribune, so as to ensure the success of the land law, conservative

A denarius issued in 113 BCE by the moneyer Nerva depicts on the obverse the head of Roma and a * (shorthand for XVI), reflecting the revaluing of the denarius from 10 to 16 asses. On the reverse, it recalls the introduction of the secret ballot in 139 BCE with a voting scene depicting one plebeian placing a ballot in a ballot box and another receiving a ballot.

senators had had enough. Tiberius had violated too many time-tested traditions. On election day, rioting broke out. In the Senate, the senator Scipio Nasica, an ex-consul and the cousin of Tiberius, declared, "All who want to save the state, follow me." A number of senators, using pieces of broken furniture, then clubbed Tiberius and three hundred of his supporters to death. The willingness of the senators to violate the principle of *sacrosanctitas*, which made the persons of tribunes inviolate, demonstrates the degree to which they were prepared to violate past traditions in pursuit of their agendas. Subsequently, senatorial kangaroo courts executed or exiled many of Tiberius' supporters.

The murder of Tiberius and his supporters marked the first appearance of serious **violence** in Republican politics. And the tactics used by both Tiberius and the Senate marked the beginning of the breakdown of the carefully nurtured cooperation among senators that had made the Republic work. Senators now increasingly looked out for their own self-interest. They adopted different strategies for doing so. Some, known as the **optimates** ("the best people"), preferred to work within the Senate, often in an obstructionist manner, in an attempt to prevent any reform of the Roman political, economic, and social system. Others, the **populares** ("men of the people"), sought support for political programs directly from the people and were characterized by programs intended to gain popular support, such as land distribution or subsidized foodstuffs. Populares also made common cause with the knights, and even with Italians, in an attempt to find support outside the Senate. But the distinction between optimates and populares refers strictly to the kinds of political methods they used and should not be confused with political parties, for those who used these different tactics did not have any common political agendas. All would have claimed that they supported the rights of the Senate and were working for the greater glory of Rome as each politician pursued his own immediate personal ambitions, not the long-term goals of any group.

What to Do with the Italian Allies?

In the aftermath of Tiberius' murder, other Roman politicians, usually using popular tactics, also attempted to deal with some of the problems confronting Rome. Military recruitment policies also created another kind of problem. Over time, Rome's Italian allies had provided an ever-greater percentage of Rome's armies, rising from half in the third century BCE to two-thirds by the early first century. The Italians felt that they were bearing more and more of the burden for Rome's wars but were sharing less and less in the benefits. Not only that, but the Roman government was behaving more and more high-handedly toward them. On one occasion, the wife of a Roman magistrate wanted to use the men's baths at an Italian town. The chief magistrate was publicly flogged when he was slow in clearing out the baths. And after the passage of Tiberius

Gracchus' land law, the Romans attempted to confiscate Italian land for distribution, giving rise to howls of protest.

Italian concerns coalesced into demands to be granted Roman citizenship. But these demands were resisted both by senators, who feared that the addition of hundreds of thousands of new citizens would weaken their ability to use their ties of patronage to control the voting in the popular assemblies, and by plebeians, who feared that the dilution of the citizen ranks would lessen the privileges that they gained from citizenship. In 125 BCE the consul Fulvius Flaccus, an ally of the Gracchi, introduced a bill to make Italians citizens, but he was induced by the Senate to withdraw the measure by the offer of an attractive military command in Gaul. When Flaccus' bill was rejected, the Latin town of Fregellae attempted to withdraw from its alliance with Rome. The Roman response was quick and deadly: Fregellae was razed to the ground by the praetor Opimius.

Gaius Gracchus and the Expansion of Popular Tactics

These events set the stage for the rise to prominence of Tiberius' younger brother **Gaius Gracchus**, who was elected tribune of the plebs for the year 123 BCE. Gaius made no attempt to hide his antipathy toward the Senate, which he viewed as being directly responsible for his brother's death. As one of the most preeminent orators of Rome, Gaius was able to influence the Council of the Plebs to approve many reform measures. He reaffirmed and expanded the program of land distribution, increasing the size of the plots and founding colonies for those who wanted to settle together. He even attempted to found an overseas colony in Africa, near, but not on, the site of Carthage. Back in Rome, in order to maintain his support among the urban mob, Gaius passed legislation providing subsidized foodstuffs to needy plebeians. Having secured his electoral base, Gaius then took his revenge on the Senate, transferring control of the Extortion Court from the Senate to the knights, the very people who were the cause of most of the extortion. This meant that a governor who actually suppressed extortion in a province could be put on trial and convicted for extortion back in Rome, as happened in 92 BCE when the ex-consul Rufus, a New Man, was convicted of extortion in Asia after he had gallantly suppressed the abuses of the knights. He spent his exile in Asia, where he was welcomed with open arms. Gaius was said to have called this law "a dagger in the side of the Senate." This act also acknowledged the knights as an important political entity and marked another step in the weakening of the Senate's authority. Gaius also favored the knights with a law stipulating that the right to collect the taxes for the entire province of Asia was to be auctioned off in Rome, something that only opportunistic knights could afford.

Gaius was reelected as tribune for 122 and was joined by Fulvius Flaccus, who took the unprecedented step of running for tribune after already having been consul. The two revived the plan to grant Roman citizenship to the Italians, but they were opposed by another tribune, Drusus, an ally of the Senate. Drusus' strategy was to out-Gaius Gaius by making even more popular proposals, such as a plan to found twelve colonies for the poorest Roman citizens, that he and his senatorial allies never intended to implement. Drusus then vetoed Gaius' franchise bill, and Gaius felt too weakened to do anything about it. When Gaius ran for a third tribunate, he was soundly defeated. He and Flaccus then occupied the Aventine Hill, the traditional place of plebeian resistance, with armed bands, at which the Senate passed the *Senatus consultum ultimum,* the "**Last Decree of the Senate,**" which commanded the consuls to take whatever measures they thought were necessary to see to it that the state came to no harm. At this, the consul Opimius—who as praetor had destroyed Fregellae—raised an armed band of citizens. Flaccus was killed in the general melée, Gaius ordered a trusted slave to stab him to death, and in the aftermath three thousand of Gaius' followers were executed.

The end of Gaius and his supporters made it even more clear that the old Roman Republican "gentlemen's agreements" among senators—to work together to avoid dissension and to keep power in the hands of the Senate and preserve old traditions while at the same time favoring the ambitions of a few preselected nobles—just was not working anymore. Cagy politicians had learned that they could achieve their goals by looking for support further down the social scale, from knights, plebeians, and even Italian allies. No matter how much senatorial Optimates attempted to close ranks, resist change, and hold on to authority, the united front on which they had prided themselves so much in the past was broken.

Marius and the Volunteer Army

The new land distribution policy was not sufficient to stem the reduction in the recruiting pool. The Romans limped along using the old system, which continued to be marginally functional as long as there were no large recruiting demands. But it broke down completely in the years after 113 BCE, when the Romans were compelled to fight no less than three crucial campaigns at the same time. The first crisis began when two large groups of Celts from northern Europe, the **Cimbri**, under King Boioris, and the **Teutones**, under King Teutobod, were forced to leave their homes because of flooding on the Baltic Sea and arrived in southern Gaul looking for new homes. Peoples friendly to Rome called on Roman assistance, and the Romans sent several armies north. By now, however, the Celts were even more formidable fighters

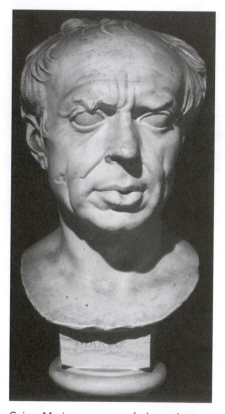

Gaius Marius, creator of the volunteer army.

than before. Rather than fighting naked with just a longsword, as they had in Italy, they now wore metal helmets and armor and were organized into phalanxes. In 113 BCE they defeated the consul Carbo at the Battle of Noreia in the territory of Noricum near the Danube River. In 109 they requested land to settle on in exchange for military service, and when that offer was refused, they destroyed the army of the consul Silanus at an unidentified place in Narbonese Gaul. Other peoples, such as the Tigurini, also joined in the attacks. In 107 BCE, at the Battle of Agen, near Bordeaux, the consul Longinus was killed, and the Roman survivors were disgraced by being forced to pass under the yoke. But the biggest disaster occurred in 105 BCE, when at the Battle of Arausio (Orange) the aristocratic proconsul Caepio refused to cooperate with the consul Maximus, a New Man. The Romans suffered their worst defeat since Cannae; the two generals and a few hundred men escaped, but the Romans lost eighty thousand men that they could ill afford to lose. It was only their own lack of direction that kept the Cimbri and Teutones from invading Italy.

During the same period, in 111 BCE, Rome also declared war on Jugurtha, a Numidian king whose army had massacred some Italians in North Africa. Roman armies had little success in the guerilla war that Jugurtha pursued. And the military situation was made even worse in 103 BCE by a second slave revolt in Sicily (a revolt in 135 BCE had taken three years to suppress), led by a slave named Salvius, who took the name Tryphon, the name of an earlier Seleucid rebel general, and raised an army of more than twenty thousand men. The Roman recruiting base simply could not bear the load.

A solution to the problem came from another ambitious New Man, Gaius **Marius**, a knight from southern Latium who, after distinguished military service in Spain in the 130s, embarked on a political career and was elected consul for 107 BCE. He was assigned the war in Africa, and to raise an army he resorted, on his own authority, to enlisting men who had no property at all. This created the **volunteer army**, in which soldiers were not fighting for the greater glory of Rome, as the Senate liked to think, but to gain personal profit. Nor did the Senate then assume responsibility either for funding this new army or for rewarding the soldiers with land after the war was over. This was left to the general, which raised a disturbing possibility that such armies would have more loyalty toward their generals than toward the state.

Marius also reorganized the army tactically, abandoning the old maniples in favor of more stable six-hundred-man **cohorts**, each consisting of six one-hundred-man centuries. Ten cohorts made up a legion of six thousand men. Each soldier was equipped with a *pilum* (javelin), a *gladius* (a short Spanish sword useful for both hacking and thrusting), and two six-foot wooden stakes used for constructing palisades around camps while the army was on the march. The soldiers, now laden with fifty pounds of equipment, referred to themselves as "Marius' mules."

With his new army, Marius was able to hem Jugurtha in, but not to defeat him—that was accomplished only by treachery, when Marius' lieutenant

Lucius Cornelius **Sulla**, a member of an old patrician family fallen on hard times, induced the Mauretanian chieftain Bocchus to hand Jugurtha over. Marius then spent three years training his army for the expected next attack by the Cimbri, Teutones, and Tigurini. This came in 102 BCE, when the Celts finally had a plan, a three-pronged attack on Italy. Later in the year, Marius fell upon the Cimbri as they approached through southern France. At the Battle of Aquae Sextiae (Aix), they were completely defeated, and thousands were enslaved. The following year, when the Teutones invaded northern Italy, Marius met and defeated them at the Battle of Vercelli. Although some of the women killed themselves and their children to escape slavery, thousands more were enslaved. In the same year Sulla drove off the Tigurini, and the barbarian threat was ended. Finally, in 100 BCE, the Sicilian slave revolt was suppressed by Manius Aquillius, a protégé of Marius.

Thus the recruitment needs of the Roman army had been met, and the agricultural-military crisis had been solved. But Rome now was left with an even more perilous problem: armies whose loyalty to the Roman government was dependent on the good will of the senatorial generals who commanded them. Indeed, when the Senate resisted granting land to Marius' veterans, Marius was compelled to ally himself with two rabble-rousing tribunes, Saturninus and Glaucia, and to call in his troops to ensure that the law was passed. But when Saturninus and Glaucia began to use open violence to secure their political goals, the Senate issued the Last Decree of the Senate and ordered Marius to deal with the crisis. Marius obeyed, and both tribunes were killed in the subsequent rioting. As a consequence, Marius—a much better general than politician—lost credibility as a popular leader, and his political career was ruined. He also provided a lesson to later politicians about the need to hold on to their political power base.

A denarius issued by the Italians during the Italian Revolt. The obverse bears the head of the personification of Italy and the legend "Italia"; the reverse depicts eight Italian soldiers sacrificing a pig and swearing an oath not to surrender to the Romans.

The Revolt of the Italian Allies

Meanwhile, Italian discontent about being forced to serve in Rome's wars without the opportunity to become Roman citizens finally boiled over in the 90s BCE. In 95 BCE, Italians living in Rome were expelled, and in 91 BCE another reforming tribune of the plebs, Drusus, the son of Gaius Gracchus' opponent, once again proposed to enfranchise the Italians. He was assassinated, and Roman supporters of the Italians were put on trial. For the Italian allies, this was the last straw, and in 90 BCE a massive coordinated revolt of the Italian Allies, also known as the **Social War**, from the Latin word *socii*, or "allies," broke out. The Italians established their own country, called **Italia**, with its own Senate, modeled on that of Rome, and a capital city at Corfinium, and raised one hundred thousand soldiers.

The Romans mobilized armies in northern and southern Italy but could not hope to win such a war quickly, if at all, so, in typical fashion, when they were forced to introduce change, they were quite willing to do so. In the first year of the revolt, the consul L. Julius Caesar issued the Julian Law, which granted Roman citizenship to all Italian cities that were not yet in revolt. And in the next year the tribunes M. Plautius and C. Papirius sponsored the Plautian-Papirian Law granting citizenship to all rebels who laid down their arms and reported to a Roman praetor within 60 days. The vast majority of the Italians now had what they wanted, and by 88 BCE the revolt had collapsed; only the Samnites continued to hold out. The result was another alteration in the structure of Roman society. The status of Italian ally disappeared, and all the free population of Italy became Roman citizens. The composition of the army necessarily also changed. Italians now enrolled in the legions, and there were no more units of allied Italians. This compelled Roman generals to look further afield, out into the provinces, when it came to recruiting bands of auxiliary soldiers.

AN AGE OF GENERALS (88–60 BCE)

At the end of the Italian Revolt, the Roman government was confronted by three overwhelming problems: the ineffective administration of the provinces, the need to control a volunteer army that was loyal to its generals, and the increasing disinclination of ambitious senators to get along with each other. The ineffectiveness of the Senate in dealing with these problems ultimately would lead to the demise of the Republic itself as a viable form of government.

The *Regnum Sullanum*

Dissatisfaction with provincial administration continued to fester and was particularly rampant in economically developed provinces such as Asia and Sicily, which offered greater opportunity for corruption. In 88 BCE resentment boiled over into open revolt in Asia. This provided an opening for **Mithridates VI** (119–63 BCE), a supposed descendent of Darius I and the ambitious king of Pontus, located on the southeastern coast of the Black Sea, to expand his territory. After first occupying the neighboring kingdom of Bithynia, he then invaded the Roman province of Asia. In the so-called "Asiatic Vespers," it was said that eighty thousand Romans were murdered on a single day, and the Roman legate Manius Aquillius, the victor over the Sicilian slaves in 100 BCE, was executed by having molten gold poured down his throat with the words, "And now let the Roman thirst for gold be satisfied."

Mithridates VI of Pontus portrayed as Hercules wearing a lionskin, attesting to his claims to divine status.

IN THEIR OWN WORDS

SULLA'S MARCH ON ROME

In 88 BCE the Consul Sulla assembled an army in Campania for the war against King Mithridates of Pontus. But before he could depart, politics intervened when Marius attempted to take over Sulla's command. The Greek biographer Plutarch relates what happened next:

At the time of which I speak, Sulla's thoughts soared to the Mithridatic war. But here he found a rival in Marius, who was possessed by ambition and a mad desire for fame. And when Sulla had set out for his camp, Marius contrived that most fatal sedition, which wrought Rome more harm than all her wars together had done, as indeed the heavenly powers foreshowed to them. Marius now made alliance with Sulpicius who was a tribune of the plebs, a man second to none in prime villainies. This man was now let loose upon the people by Marius, and after confounding all things by force and the sword, he proposed certain vicious laws. Sulpicius did not take the consulship away from Sulla, but merely transferred the expedition against Mithridates to the command of Marius. He also sent Military Tribunes at once to Nola, who were to take over the army there and conduct it to Marius. Sulla succeeded in reaching the camp first, and his soldiers, when they learned what had happened, stoned the Tribunes to death. The Senate, when it learned that Sulla was marching against the city, sent two Praetors to forbid his advance. These men addressed Sulla with too much boldness, whereupon his soldiers would have gladly torn them to pieces, but contented themselves with breaking their fasces, stripping them of their senatorial togas, insulting them in many ways, and then sending them back to the city. Here a terrible dejection was produced by their announcement that the sedition could no longer be checked.

Sulla, at the head of six full legions, moved from Nola, his army, as he saw, being eager to march at once against the city. It is said, also, that to Sulla himself there appeared in his dreams a goddess who stood by his side and put into his hand a thunderbolt, and naming his enemies one by one, bade him smite them with it. Encouraged by the vision, at break of day he led on towards Rome. He sent forward Lucius Basillus and Caius Mummius, who seized for him the citygate and the walls on the Esquiline hill; then he himself followed hard after them with all speed. Meanwhile Marius made a proclamation calling the slaves to his support under promise of freedom; but the enemy coming on, he was overpowered and fled from the city. Sulla now called together the Senate, and had a sentence of death passed on Marius himself and a few others, among whom was Sulpicius the tribune of the plebs.

In Rome, the command of the war against Mithridates was given to the consul Lucius Cornelius Sulla, an experienced general who had served in North Africa and defeated the Tigurini. In 88 BCE, Sulla had recruited his own volunteer army and was on the point of departure when he learned that Marius had induced the Senate to transfer the command to himself. Rather than passively acquiescing to this setback, Sulla appealed to his soldiers. With their support, he marched on Rome. In a virtual coup d'état, he put Marius to flight, seized the city, and forced the government to give the command back to him. He then sailed off to do battle in the east.

Meanwhile, back in Rome Marius returned, raised an army, and instituted a reign of terror against Sulla's supporters, with the heads of executed enemies displayed in the Forum. Even though he himself soon died, his adherents, such as the consuls Cornelius Cinna and Papirius Carbo, continued to oppose Sulla and even planned to send an army against him to Greece; but Cinna was murdered by his own soldiers because they did not want to engage in a profitless civil war. In 83 BCE, Sulla returned to Italy and, over the course of the following year, defeated all of his enemies, including the Samnites, who in 82 BCE made a last-ditch stand and died to a man at the Battle of the Colline Gate outside Rome. Sulla's first order of business was to reward his troops, and in doing so he also was able to revenge himself on his enemies. He published lists of enemies known as **Proscriptions**: both the lives and the property of those on it were forfeit, and several thousand wealthy persons throughout Italy perished. By these means, which amounted to little more than state-sanctioned murder, Sulla found land for 120,000 of his army veterans.

Ambitious Republican politicians often sponsored the construction of public works in order to gain popular support and demonstrate their public spirit. One of the few such buildings to survive is the "tabularium," or government archives, built by the consul Catulus in 78 BCE. It was built from travertine, tufa, and concrete and preserved records formerly stored in the Temple of Saturn. In the modern period, an upper story was removed by Michelangelo, and what remains now is part of the City Hall of Rome.

In spite of his unconstitutional actions, Sulla, as a Roman, desired to find some quasi-constitutional method for holding absolute authority. He therefore had himself appointed Dictator for Restoring the Republic, but without the customary six-month limitation, a decidedly unconstitutional situation. Sulla then governed so high-handedly that his regime was known as the *Regnum Sullanum*, or "Rule of Sulla." He attempted to ensure that no one else would do what he had just done by imposing reforms that attempted to weaken the power of popular politicians and strengthen the authority of the Senate. He restored the Senate's right to preapprove measures submitted to popular assemblies, and he transferred jurisdiction over criminal cases from the assemblies to the Senate. To make the office of tribune less attractive, the tribunician veto was outlawed, and tribunes were not permitted to run for higher office. He increased the number of quaestors and praetors in order to expand the membership of the Senate and thus make it more representative of the optimates. In 78 BCE Sulla retired, and, racked by illness, he died the following year.

Although Sulla tried to undo what he had done and restore power to the Senate, his most important legacy was his example of using his army to take control of the state and to subvert constitutional government. Others were quick to follow his precedent. Marcus Aemilius **Lepidus**, one of the consuls for

78 BCE, for example, attempted to gain power by adopting a popular program, such as offering to restore land confiscated by Sulla. Assigned the province of Narbonese Gaul, Lepidus raised an army, and when the Senate ordered him to return to Rome, he brought his army with him, intending to do what Sulla had done and seize control of the government. But Catulus, the other consul, defeated him on the outskirts of Rome. Lepidus fled and soon died of disease.

It now had reached the point at which it was almost a necessity for senators who wanted to have influential positions in the state to control large armies, for one's soldiers could be used not only to win glory away from home but also to manipulate votes in the Senate and popular assemblies. The only way to gain control of an army was to be assigned a province where there was a war going on. Therefore, ambitious senators became even more eager for military commands than they had been before. The question now was no longer which faction in the Senate would have political predominance, but which individual would. In the post-Sullan period, three senatorial generals in particular were to engage in a tumultuous struggle for power: Crassus, Pompey, and Caesar.

Crassus and the Revolt of Spartacus

One of the consequences of Rome's many wars was a large increase in the slave population of Italy and Sicily, where war captives labored on large senatorial estates called *latifundia*, a word meaning "wide fields." These agricultural slaves were not always well treated. Because they cost so little, the senator Cato the Elder recommended working them to death and then buying new ones. Sicilian slave revolts in 135 and 103 attested to the discontent that could arise among the slave population as a result of such attitudes.

An even more serious problem arose in 73 BCE, when **Spartacus**, a Thracian slave being trained as a gladiator at Capua, led an insurrection among the slave population of Italy. The slave army, which numbered more than seventy thousand and included many former soldiers, defeated several Roman armies sent against them. Spartacus' plan was to lead the slaves north out of Italy, whence they could disperse to their homes, but the slaves chose to continue looting in Italy. Ultimately, Marcus Licinius **Crassus** Dives ("The Rich") was given the military command. Most of Crassus' noble family had been killed during the Marian purge, but Crassus' support of Sulla had allowed him not only to recover the family wealth but also to become the richest man in Rome. After restoring discipline in the Roman army, in part by using the old Roman military punishment of **decimation**, wherein every tenth man in a disgraced army unit was executed, Crassus hemmed in the slaves in southern Italy. The slave army was defeated in 71 BCE, and the rebels were mercilessly punished: six thousand were crucified at one-hundred-yard intervals on the Appian Way outside Rome. There were no further large slave rebellions after this. On the other hand, however, the treatment of slaves also improved, in part because the Romans had learned their lesson about what could happen if slaves were treated too badly.

His suppression of the slave revolt made Crassus into one of the most powerful senators in Rome, but it also left the Senate reluctant to grant him another command that would allow him to acquire even greater glory and power.

The Rise of Pompey

Another ambitious senator was Gnaeus **Pompey**, the son of the consul Pompey Strabo, a New Man who had distinguished himself in the Italian Revolt. After his father, a supporter of Sulla, died of the plague in 87, nineteen-year-old Pompey kept his father's army together. In 83 BCE he offered his own support to Sulla, who sent him to Sicily; there, Pompey's enthusiastic execution of one of Sulla's enemies gained him the nickname *Adulescens carnifex*, or "the Teenage Butcher." Pompey realized very early in his career the importance of controlling an army in order to gain political advancement, and he did everything he could to obtain military commands. During the 70s BCE, he put down the revolt of Sertorius, a supporter of Cinna who had established a separatist state among the native peoples of Spain, and he returned just in time to claim the credit for mopping up the last of the defeated slaves in 71 BCE. A major quarrel with Crassus over this was averted when both were named consuls for 70 BCE.

In 67 BCE, the Gabinian Law gave Pompey an extraordinary command, on the sea and fifty miles inland, against the pirates who then infested the

A fresco by Cesare Maccari (1840–1919) in the Palazzo Madama in Rome depicts Cicero denouncing Catiline, seated by himself at the right, before the Senate. In reality, however, Catiline was not actually present when Cicero delivered his Catilinarian speeches.

Mediterranean. In a well-organized campaign he swept from Gibraltar to the Levant, mopping up the pirates as he went and eventually settling them in a city in southern Anatolia named Pompeiopolis. In the following year, the Manilian Law put Pompey in charge of another war against Mithridates. He used this as an opportunity to settle the affairs of the entire eastern Mediterranean. In 63 BCE he abolished the Seleucid Empire and made Syria, the most Hellenized part of the old Seleucid kingdom, into a Roman province; this left Ptolemaic Egypt, a slavish adherent to the Roman line, as the last independent Hellenistic kingdom. At the same time, Pompey offended the Jews by entering the sanctuary of the temple in Jerusalem, although he declined to occupy the Jewish kingdom. When he returned to Rome in 62 BCE, he had the potential of becoming the most politically powerful senator in Rome, but he turned out to be as naive a politician as he was a shrewd general. Pompey found the Senate jealous of his great successes and unwilling to approve his eastern settlement or to pass a law granting land to the veterans of his army.

Another influential politician of this period, Marcus Tullius **Cicero**, was something of a throwback and an anomaly. He made his reputation not by his military prowess but by his legal and oratorical talents. Cicero came from a family of knights from Arpinum, a town south of Rome. After a token attempt to pursue a military career under Pompey Strabo and Sulla during the Revolt of the Italian Allies, he studied rhetoric and philosophy in Greece and followed a legal career. After a string of successful defenses and prosecutions of influential senators, as a result of which many powerful senators became indebted to him, Cicero ran for consul for 63 BCE. He gained election when the senatorial Optimates, with whom he wished to associate himself but who never really accepted him, were forced to back him against Crassus' candidate Lucius Sergius Catilina, or **Catiline**, who was proposing an extensive reform program. The disappointed Catiline then raised an army, and in a series of famous Catilinarian speeches Cicero warned that Catiline planned to overthrow the state. The Senate issued the Last Decree of the Senate, and Cicero had Catiline's supporters arrested and executed without a trial, an act that later would come back to haunt Cicero. Shortly thereafter, Catiline's ragtag army was defeated, with Catiline himself dying in the front ranks.

Julius Caesar

The third powerful general of this period was a late bloomer. Gaius Julius **Caesar**, a member of a patrician family supposedly descended from

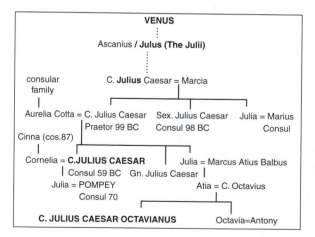

Venus, had been named in Sulla's proscription lists—his aunt was married to Marius, and he himself was married to the daughter of Cinna—and had barely escaped with his life. His political career, therefore, got off to a slow start. As aedile in 65 BCE, he lay claim to popular support by restoring the trophies of his uncle Marius to the Capitoline temple and sponsoring the most elaborate public entertainment yet, with no less than 320 pairs of gladiators fighting in silver-gilt armor. His first military command did not come until 62 BCE, when he served as a praetor in Spain, but in 60 BCE he was forced by the Senate to give up his claims on a triumph in order to run for, and win, the consulate. Like any ambitious senator, Caesar then wished to receive a province, where, as proconsul, he could recruit a large army and acquire glory and power. The Senate, however, was reluctant to permit him to pursue his ambitions and insultingly allocated to him "the foot paths and cattle trails of Italy."

Portrait bust of Julius Caesar.

THE TRIUMVIRATES (60–31 BCE)

The final collapse of the Roman Republic was hastened along by means of two triumvirates, groups composed of three ultra-powerful senators who banded together in pursuit of their own interests. With authority based on their possession of large armies, these senators effectively removed whatever vestiges of independent authority the Senate possessed.

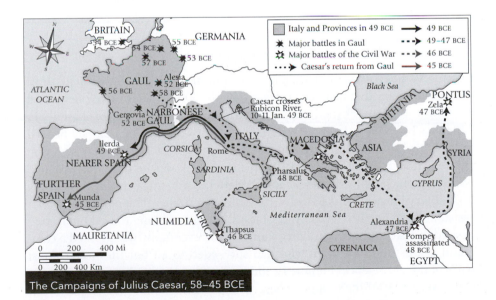

The Campaigns of Julius Caesar, 58–45 BCE

CAESAR'S SIEGE OF ALESIA

A reconstruction of Caesar's siege works at Alesia.

Caesar's attempt to suppress the Gallic revolt of Vercingetorix in 52 BCE began badly with a defeat at the hill fort of Gergovia, near modern Clermont-Ferrand.

But because Vercingetorix had not yet assembled all of his forces, he withdrew to the hill fort of Alesia with eighty thousand troops to await the arrival of

The First Triumvirate

Crassus, Pompey, and Caesar then made common cause. The desires of all three in one way or another had been thwarted by the Senate. They therefore formed an unofficial alliance called the **First Triumvirate** (a "group of three men") in which each agreed to look out for the interests of the others. Pompey needed to have his legislation passed, and Caesar, as consul in 59 BCE, saw to it that this was done. Caesar wanted a suitable province, and he now was assigned both Cisalpine and Narbonese Gaul, the latter of which gave him an opening for military interventions to the north, where a number of appeals for Roman assistance had been received. And Crassus, fearful of being the odd man out, desired to restore his own military standing. He eventually was granted a command against the Parthians, who had succeeded to all but the westernmost parts of the old Seleucid Empire. In addition, Cicero was exiled for having illegally executed Catiline's supporters.

one hundred thousand reinforcements. Caesar knew that he could not permit the two forces to unite, so he besieged Vercingetorix in Alesia with his army of sixty thousand Romans. Caesar was vastly outnumbered, so he did what the Romans did best: he built fortifications, which Caesar himself described in great detail in his *Gallic War*. First, over a period of three weeks a line of circumvallation eleven miles long and thirteen feet high, fronted by a ditch fifteen feet wide and deep and with towers at intervals, was built around Alesia to prevent the besieged Gauls from escaping and to starve them out. Caesar took great pains to discuss all of the work that his men put into building booby traps to keep the Gauls from even reaching the walls. Sharpened stakes placed in pits were jokingly called *lilia* ("lilies") by the men, groups of brambles were called *cippi* ("gravestones"), and *stimuli* ("spurs") were wooden blocks with iron hooks in them extending just above ground level. Then an even longer, similarly designed, fourteen mile wall of contravallation was constructed to keep the relief force from attacking Caesar's rear.

The final showdown came in September of 52 BCE. After a furious battle in which one area of the Roman fortifications was almost completely overrun and in which Caesar himself led the Roman cavalry reserves in a desperate attempt to save the day, the Gauls were finally forced to retreat. That decided the issue, for Alesia could no longer hold out, and Vercingetorix surrendered the next day.

In later French history, the heroic resistance of Vercingetorix served as an example of French resistance to invaders, and ever since the nineteenth century attempts have been made to identify the site of the battle. In the 1860s, when France was threatened by an attack from Germany, the French emperor Napoleon III (1852–1870) sponsored excavations at Alise-Sainte-Reine near Dijon that claimed to have found remains of the battle, and a great monument was erected. The only problem was that the site did not match Caesar's description very well. But many other possible sites also have been proposed, as at Alaise in the Franche-Comté, or near either Chaux-des-Crotenay or Salins-les-Bains in the Jura Mountains in eastern France, or atop Mont-Auxois, where an artifact with the words "in Alisiia" ("In Alesia") was found.

Although the dispute over the location of the battle no doubt will continue, Caesar's careful descriptions allow his fortifications to be reconstructed with a fair degree of accuracy, and many models, large and small, have been made. One can only imagine the degree of apprehension the Gauls must have felt when attempting to attack such formidable defenses.

In 58 BCE Caesar, having raised ten legions, went to Gaul, where he remained for nine years. He reported the progress of his campaigns in a series of dispatches that collectively became known as the *Gallic War*, one of the most famous historical accounts to survive from antiquity. By making effective use of the Roman maxim "Divide and conquer," he played off one Celtic people against another and by 53 BCE, having made expeditions into Germany and Britain, appeared to have conquered all of Gaul up to the Rhine River. But then, as in the case of Spain, a charismatic leader, **Vercingetorix**, arose and united the Gauls in a great revolt against Rome in 52 BCE. Only after a tremendous battle before the hill fort of Alesia were the Gauls definitively defeated. As a result of his Gallic campaigns, Caesar built up not only a massive amount of wealth but also an effective and battle-hardened army.

Meanwhile, in 54 BCE Crassus went off to fight the Parthians. The campaign was a disaster. Crassus' soldiers became bogged down in the sands of

The Parthian Kingdom at the Time of Crassus

Mesopotamia. Unable to bring the Parthian horse-archers to battle, all they could do was hunker down behind their shields while their water ran out. Eventually, Crassus attempted to parley with the Parthians but was butchered and beheaded instead. Most of his soldiers were captured and enslaved, and his head was used as a stage prop in a production of *The Bacchae*, a Greek tragedy by Euripides, in Ctesiphon, the Parthian capital. The triumvirate thus became a less stable duovirate.

The Civil War

Back in Rome, senators such as Cicero had been playing on Pompey's vanity and naïveté in an effort to detach him from his ally Caesar. After the death of Pompey's beloved wife Julia, Caesar's daughter, in 54 BCE, they were successful. In 50 BCE, Caesar was refused the right to run for consul in absentia and ordered to return to Rome as a private citizen. He realized that doing so would be political suicide, for it would leave him open to trumped-up charges by his rivals. He therefore felt that he had no recourse but to return—not without his army, but with it. In 49 BCE, saying, "The die is cast," he crossed the shallow **Rubicon River**, the boundary between Cisalpine Gaul and Italy. Doing so automatically put him into rebellion against the Roman state.

Pompey was caught largely unprepared. He fled to Greece with his senatorial supporters in order to gather his resources and strengthen his army. After being duly legitimatized by what was left of the Senate in Rome, Caesar too crossed to Greece. At the Battle of Pharsalus in 48 BCE the army of Pompey was defeated, and Pompey fled to the opulent kingdom of Ptolemaic Egypt in a last effort to rebuild his forces. He was met by King Ptolemy XII (51–47 BCE), who, thinking to do Caesar a favor, beheaded him. Caesar, who arrived soon thereafter, was not amused by the idea of an Egyptian king decapitating a distinguished Roman general who also was his son-in-law, and he deposed Ptolemy in favor of his twenty-year-old sister and co-regent, Cleopatra VII (51–30 BCE).

Caesar was forced to remain in Egypt for the winter, and nine months later Cleopatra bore his son, Caesarion. In the spring of 47 BCE, Caesar returned to Rome after making a detour to Anatolia, where Pharnaces, the son of Mithridates, was attempting to expand his territory. After a five-day war and a quick victory at the Battle of Zela, Caesar issued his famous words *"veni, vidi, vici"* ("I came, I saw, I conquered"). He spent the next two years mopping up his remaining rivals at the Battles of Thapsus in Africa and Munda in Spain.

Caesar attempted to preserve his position as head of state by regularly serving as consul and by holding the quite unconstitutional position of *Dictator perpetuus*, or Dictator for Life. In order to maintain popular support for his admittedly irregular position, he made many benefactions to the Roman people. Using spoils from the Gallic wars (unlike Sulla, Caesar did not confiscate wealth from his personal enemies), Caesar undertook a large-scale renovation of the forum. He constructed a new law court, the *Basilica Julia* ("Julian basilica"), reconstructed the rostra, or speaker's platform, and began a reconstruction of the curia, or Senate house, in a new form, the *Curia Julia* ("Julian curia"). He also built the first new forum to take some of the pressure off the old Republican forum, which no longer had sufficient capacity to meet the needs of the growing population of Rome. The highlight of the Forum of Caesar was a temple of Venus Genetrix, "Venus the Ancestress," an allusion to Caesar's putative descent direct from the goddess Venus; the temple also contained a statue of Cleopatra.

Caesar's position of supreme authority also gave him the power to attempt to deal with some of the problems facing the Republic. For example, his extension of Roman citizenship to some cities outside Italy assisted in the integration of the provinces into the Roman world, as did his creation of overseas colonies at Seville in Spain, Arles in Gaul, Carthage in Africa, and Corinth in Greece to provide land for one hundred thousand army veterans. He attempted to reduce extortion by replacing the Asian and Sicilian tithe with tribute. He made the Senate more representative by expanding it to nine hundred members and including some non-Italians. And, because the Roman calendar had gotten out of synch, with December occurring in the summer, he introduced the **Julian calendar** of 365 days, with a leap year every fourth year; the month

MYSTERIES OF HISTORY

CLEOPATRA, THE LEGEND AND THE REALITY

In the modern day, Queen Cleopatra VII Philopator (69–30 BCE) is legendary for her beauty and sexuality. She has been the *femme fatale* of the cinema for over a hundred years, and the French philosopher Blaise Pascal, alluding to her beauty, even argued, "If Cleopatra's nose had been shorter, the whole face of the world would have been changed."

And there is no doubt that Cleopatra is one of the most romantic and enigmatic personalities of the Roman past, not to mention one of the most misrepresented. As Egyptian pharaoh (and the only one of the Ptolemies to learn to speak Egyptian), last Macedonian queen of Egypt, and paramour of two of the most powerful Romans of her day, she moved among three different social and cultural worlds. Indeed, her status as a native of North Africa even has given rise to modern beliefs that she was of sub-Saharan Black African descent.

As the eldest child of Ptolemy XII, Cleopatra was named joint ruler with her father at the age of fourteen, but at his death in 51 BCE his will made her joint ruler with her twelve-year-old brother Ptolemy XIII, whom Cleopatra also married. Cleopatra soon seized sole power and issued coins solely in her own name. A palace revolt expelled her from power, but she quickly gained reinstatement by gaining the favor of Julius Caesar, who had pursued Pompey to Egypt in 48 BCE. Plutarch reports that "Caesar was first captivated by this proof of Cleopatra's bold wit, and was afterwards so overcome by the charm of her society" that he eventually supported her claims and made her queen of Egypt. In 44 BCE, Cleopatra visited Caesar in Rome, creating a scandal when Caesar put a golden statue of her as the goddess Isis in the temple of his own ancestress Venus.

But Cleopatra's true claim to fame lay in her role in Mark Antony's attempts to seize control of the Roman world during his rivalry with Octavian. Ancient writers portrayed Antony as Cleopatra's lackey. According to Plutarch, in 42 BCE, when Cleopatra was summoned to meet Antony at the outset of his Parthian war, "She had faith in her own attractions, which, having formerly recommended her to Caesar, she did not doubt might prove yet more successful with Antony. Caesar's acquaintance was with her when a girl, young and ignorant of the world, but she was to meet Antony in the time of life when women's beauty is most splendid, and

Sextilis also was renamed "July" in his honor. Caesar's short period of rule and repeated military distractions meant that he did not have the opportunity to introduce any systematic or comprehensive reforms, but he did demonstrate that a single ruler could deal with problems much more effectively and efficiently than the Senate had.

One of Caesar's policies had been to show *clementia* (clemency) and to pardon defeated enemies in an attempt to restore normalcy to the state. These magnanimous gestures came back to haunt him when, on the **Ides of March** (March 15) in 44 BCE, just before his departure for a war against the Parthians, he was stabbed to death at a meeting of the Senate by a group of conspirators who objected to his unconstitutional holding of power. Ironically, he died in a theater built by Pompey at the feet of a Pompey's statue. And his assassins included a number of pardoned enemies, such as Marcus Brutus and Gaius Cassius.

ALTERNATIVE HISTORY

Are there any other ways that Caesar could have modeled his position in the state that might have worked more effectively? How would Roman history have played out if Caesar had not gone to the Senate meeting on the Ides of March?

their intellects are in full maturity." Antony's preparations to attack Parthia, Plutarch continues, "Were all rendered useless to him because of Cleopatra. For, in order to pass the winter with her, the war was pushed on before its due time, as by a man who had no power of control over his faculties, who was under the effect of some drug or magic and whose object was much more to hasten his return than to conquer his enemies."

This tetradrachm of Cleopatra and Mark Antony, probably issued in Antioch around 36 BCE, depicts an elaborately dressed Cleopatra in the position of honor on the obverse, and a bare-headed Antony on the reverse. Cleopatra clearly was a woman of great character, but hardly the great beauty of legend.

Soon afterward, Cleopatra and Antony, seated on two golden thrones, divided up the eastern world among their three children: the twins, Cleopatra Selene and Alexander Helius, and Ptolemy Philadelphus. According to Plutarch, "Cleopatra was then, as at other times when she appeared in public, dressed in the habit of the goddess Isis, and gave audience to the people under the name of the New Isis." But these grand plans were not to last. Cleopatra and Antony were defeated at the Battle of Actium in 31 BCE, and a year later both committed suicide. Thus died the last true pharaoh of Egypt, bringing the Ptolemaic Dynasty, and the last of Alexander the Great's successor kingdoms, to an end.

But the real Cleopatra might not in fact have been the great beauty of legend, as suggested by the comparison between her and Antony's Roman wife Octavia, the sister of Octavian: "the Romans who had seen Cleopatra could report that she in no way had the advantage of Octavia either in youth or in beauty." It may be, then, that to Julius Caesar and Mark Antony she was more attractive for her wealth than for her physical charms. And it was only by an accident of history that her offspring—by either Caesar or Antony—did not end up ruling the Roman Empire.

Caesar was the second senatorial general to use his army to seize control of the state. Neither he nor Sulla had been able to find an effective way to maintain his authority except by making unconstitutional uses of the archaic office of Dictator, the only Republican office that provided for any sort of one-man rule. Both of them had aroused extreme jealously among other senators, who felt, quite justifiably, that these two generalissimos were monopolizing too much of the influence and authority for themselves in a decidedly unrepublican manner and were not sharing enough of the rule with other senators. Neither Sulla nor Caesar, therefore, was able to solve any of the greatest problems that bedeviled the late Republic, especially the problem of ambitious senators who put their own interests ahead of the interests of the state.

It soon became clear that Caesar's assassins had no idea about how to deal with any of these difficulties, either. They apparently presumed that after Caesar was gone, the old Republic again would begin to function. They were mistaken. Two of Caesar's favored generals, Marcus Aemilius Lepidus and Marcus Antonius, better known as **Mark Antony**, retained the loyalty of much of Caesar's army. Lepidus, the son of the Lepidus who had led an insurrection in 78 BCE, had managed to restore the family fortunes and risen to the position of Master of Horse, or deputy dictator, under Caesar in 44 BCE. And Antony, the grandson of a famous orator and a distant cousin of Caesar, spent a dissolute youth gambling and drinking. After showing military talent in the east, he attached himself to Caesar. As a tribune in early 49 BCE he tried to veto the Senate's actions against Caesar and was forcibly expelled from Rome, and in 47 he, too, was made Caesar's "Master of horse." He was married to Fulvia, the granddaughter of Gaius Gracchus and a politician in her own right; indeed, it was reported that she preferred politically active husbands so she, too, could engage in politics. Her first husband was the demagogue Clodius, who had served as Caesar's man in Rome. After Clodius' murder, she then married Curio, another ally of Caesar's, and after his death in Africa she married Antony. At the time of Caesar's assassination in 44 BCE, Antony was sharing the consulate with Caesar.

A newcomer to the scene was Gaius Octavius, Caesar's eighteen-year-old grandnephew who had been adopted in his will and thus become C. Julius Caesar Octavianus, or **Octavian**. At the time, Octavian was studying in Apollonia in western Greece, but he immediately returned to Italy to lay claim to Caesar's legacy. Initially, the hardened Italian politicians thought little of him, but he soon showed that he possessed a sense of political astuteness well beyond his years. He began by using the name of his adoptive father, C. Julius Caesar, and by making his own play for the loyalty of Caesar's troops, many of whom flocked to his standard.

The Second Triumvirate

After some initial bickering, Antony, Lepidus, and Octavian joined forces against Caesar's assassins by forming the **Second Triumvirate** in 43 BCE, and the time had come for them to revenge themselves on their enemies. Cicero, who had delivered a series of speeches called the "Philippics" (an allusion to Demosthenes' speeches against Philip II of Macedon) against Antony, was murdered, and his head was displayed in the forum with a golden hairpin stuck through its golden tongue by Fulvia. And Caesar was officially **deified**, that is, made into a god. The chief assassins, meanwhile, had fled east, Brutus to Macedonia and Cassius to Syria, where they raised armies of their own. In 42 BCE, the armies met at the Battle of Philippi, in Macedonia, with Octavian facing Brutus and Antony opposing Cassius, Lepidus having been left back in Italy. In the first encounter, Brutus repelled Octavian, but Cassius was defeated and committed suicide. In a second battle three weeks later, Brutus was defeated and likewise killed himself.

There then commenced yet another struggle among senatorial generals to see who would end up on top. The triumvirs divided up the Roman world, with

Lepidus receiving Spain and Africa, Octavian Italy and Gaul, and Antony the east. In 41, in an effort to further Antony's claims, Fulvia raised eight legions in Italy and seized Rome, but eventually she was forced to surrender and soon died in exile. Fulvia also became the first Roman woman to have her portrait displayed on the coinage. Meanwhile, Sextus Pompey, the son of Pompey the Great, had raised a powerful navy and seized Sicily. Two attacks by Octavian failed, and only in 36 BCE was Sextus defeated by Octavian's loyal and able general Marcus Agrippa. Sextus' illegal execution without a trial the following year brought opprobrium upon Antony. The victory over Sextus left Octavian strong enough to force Lepidus into retirement after the latter attempted to seize Sicily; he was exiled to a small town in Latium where he survived until 13 BCE.

The Roman world then was repartitioned, with Octavian receiving authority in Italy and the west and Antony in Syria and the east. Both knew that it was only a matter of time before a final showdown came, and both raised enormously bloated armies of about forty legions each. Even though Egypt was still an independent state ruled by its queen (or pharaoh) Cleopatra, Antony spent most of his time there exploiting its resources and building up his forces. In the west, Octavian commenced a propaganda war in which Antony was depicted as Cleopatra's lackey. The slanders against Antony seemed to be confirmed when Octavian illegally seized Antony's will from the Vestal Virgins and revealed that, after his death, Antony wished to be buried in Egypt alongside Cleopatra.

In 31 BCE Octavian marched east and Antony west. The two armies met at Actium, on the western coast of Greece. The result of this encounter was something of an anticlimax. Antony's soldiers began to lose heart and to desert to the side of Octavian, who was assisted by the strategy and generalship of Agrippa. Eventually, Antony decided that the most he could hope to do was to flee back to Egypt and live to fight another day. He and Cleopatra attempted to break out by sea, and the result was the **Battle of Actium**. Antony lost most of his fleet, although he and Cleopatra did make good their escape.

Octavian, now in possession of an overwhelmingly large military force, occupied Egypt in the following year. Antony and Cleopatra, not wishing to be humiliated by being led in chains in Octavian's triumph, took the honorable way out and committed suicide, and young Caesarion was put to death. And once again, an ambitious senatorial general had used his army to eliminate his rivals and to gain control of the Roman world. The question now was, what was he going to do with it?

> **LEARNING FROM HISTORY**
>
> What does Roman history teach us about the role of self-interest in politics? Even though they claimed to be "supporting the Republic," did these Roman leaders really have the best interests of Rome at heart? Can you think of any politicians in the history of the world who sacrificed their own ambitions for the good of the country?

THE ESTABLISHMENT OF THE PRINCIPATE
(31–21 BCE)

Fortunately for Rome, Octavian was a much better administrator than he was a general. This was just what Rome needed. Octavian had two primary goals in

A PICTURE IS WORTH A THOUSAND WORDS

CAESARION AND CLEOPATRA

This relief from Dendera in Egypt portrays the continued respect of the Ptolemaic Dynasty for Egyptian customs even in the mid-first century BCE. On the left stands the cow goddess Hathor, a goddess of motherhood, wearing a headdress of a sun disk and cows' horns and holding the ankh, symbol of eternal life, in her right hand, and a long was-scepter, a symbol of power often associated with pharaohs, in her left. On the far right stands Cleopatra, portrayed as Isis, wearing the same cow horns with sun disk, topped by the double plumes of the mother goddess Mut. In front of her, a teenaged pharaoh Caesarion stands in the full regalia of a pharaoh, wearing the double crown of Upper and Lower Egypt. Cleopatra and Caesarion both make offerings to Hathor. The identity of the small figure in front of Hathor wearing the regalia of a pharaoh is uncertain; it may be the deified Ptolemy XIV, Cleopatra's brother, who died in 44 BCE. The identity of the even smaller figure between Caesarion and Cleopatra is even more mysterious.

Caesarion, the son of Cleopatra and Caesar, was born in 48 BCE: according to Plutarch, "Caesar left Cleopatra as queen of Egypt, who soon after had a son by him, whom the Alexandrians called Caesarion." Cleopatra made Caesarion coruler of Egypt at the age of three after Caesar's assassination and gave him the tongue-twisting title Ptolemy Theos Philopator Philometor Caesar; in modern parlance he is known simply as Ptolemy XV. By doing so, Cleopatra hoped to create a dynasty of rulers who would combine rule of Egypt with rule of the Roman world. But this vision was complicated by Cleopatra's liaison with Mark Antony, with whom she had three more children, who replaced Caesarion in her plans for dominion. After the occupation of Egypt by Octavian in 30 BCE, the eighteen-year-old Caesarion was executed because, in spite of Caesar's will, he could have challenged Octavian's status as the successor to Julius Caesar. The death of Cleopatra and Caesarion brought an end to the last of a line of independent pharaohs going back to 3000 BCE.

mind. First of all, he wanted to end the civil wars while at the same time ensuring his own personal security. Second, he wished to deal with the problems that had plagued the Republic and make the Roman state into a more stable, enduring establishment.

From Octavian to Augustus

Most important, Octavian had to find a way to maintain control of the army. To relinquish his military command would only mean a revival of the internecine warfare of the past and would permit another ambitious senator to do to him what he had just done to everyone else. He realized that the solution of Sulla and Caesar, holding the dictatorship, was too unconstitutional and too high profile and simply would not work. He determined to be more circumspect and at least to give the appearance of working within republican constitutional traditions.

Indeed, Octavian worked hard to convey the impression that all he wanted to do was to restore the Republic. He made sure that all of his actions were done legally, by due process. Even though, paradoxically, he knew that any organized opposition was likely to come from the Senate, he went out of his way to consult with it and to respect its ancient perquisites. He understood that without the cooperation of the senators, who embodied all of the civil and military experience and controlled most of the wealth in the Roman world, he could not hope to govern effectively.

In 28 BCE, Octavian and his trusty comrade Agrippa were named censors. Using their authority to expel and add senators, they reconfigured the Senate membership to Octavian's liking. Then, the next year, Octavian went so far as to offer to relinquish all of his powers. The Senate, however, not only declined this magnanimous proposal but also piled new honors on Octavian, including a new title, that of **Augustus**, which was not an office or even a power but only a mark of very great respect and admiration, meaning something like "the one who is revered." Octavian was so proud of his new title that he used it as his name. The title of Augustus continued to be used by the individuals we now identify as Roman emperors, although it must be stressed that Augustus himself claimed neither to have established the Roman Empire nor to have become Roman emperor. These are modern-day concepts, for we know very well that regardless of what Augustus (as he now can be called) said it was, the Roman Republic was dead, and one individual, the Augustus, now controlled the army and otherwise oversaw the affairs of state.

The Principate

We therefore say that the Roman Empire began in 27 BCE. In the form in which it was established by Augustus, it is called the **Principate**. It was based on the assumption that the emperor and the Senate worked in partnership to govern the Empire, for the emperor also was the *princeps*, the First Man of the Senate.

There was nothing new here; there always had been a *princeps*. This meant that even though the emperor took precedence in the Senate, he still could be perceived as just another senator.

In order to avoid repeating the mistakes of the past, Augustus had to determine exactly what his official role would be. Initially, he served as one of the two consuls every year. This gave him the *imperium*, which allowed him to retain command of his armies. Soon, however, this monopolization of the highest magistracy aroused the same jealousy that Sulla and Caesar had encountered. In addition, the official duties became rather burdensome for the rather sickly Augustus.

Therefore, in 21 BCE Augustus adopted a new solution. Based on precedents going back to Scipio Africanus, he had the Senate grant him the power of a proconsul, which gave him the *imperium* that allowed him to control certain key provinces and the armies stationed in them. To be on the safe side, he held an *imperium proconsulare maius*, a **greater proconsular imperium**, which allowed him to outrank all generals and officials. In one fell swoop, therefore, Augustus not only kept control the army but also ensured that there would be no other senator ever to supersede him.

In addition, Augustus received annually the *tribunicia potestas*, the **tribunician power**. By receiving only the powers and not the actual office, Augustus, a patrician, was able to sidestep the requirement that Tribunes of the Plebs had to be plebeians. The tribunician power permitted Augustus not only to introduce legislation but also to veto the actions of any other magistrate. The mere knowledge that he had this power meant that he never had to use it, for any senator contemplating a legislative initiative made sure to consult Augustus in advance. Another power that Augustus appropriated was the censor's right to **adlect** (appoint) new members of the Senate, and in so doing to control its composition. In 13 BCE he also assumed the title of *Pontifex Maximus*, and thus became the head of the Roman state religion, there being no separation of church and state in the Roman Empire.

The greater proconsular imperium and the tribunician power became the two sources of the authority of the Roman emperors during the Principate. They permitted emperors to get things done on the one hand and to keep a low profile on the other. This enabled them to avoid, as much as possible, arousing jealousy, resentment, and opposition in the Senate. Everything the emperor did was done under the rubric of the old Republican constitution, and he was able to claim that no matter what extraordinary authority he had, he was working in partnership with the Senate.

Politicians at Leisure: The Republican Golden Age of Literature

The late Republic also saw the full flowering of Latin literary culture. As before, some writers, particularly poets, made their reputations primarily on the basis of their literary efforts. Catullus, writing in the 60s and 50s BCE, was known primarily for his love poetry, addressed to a fictitious lover named Lesbia. But he also wrote other kinds of elegiac poetry, ranging from a tender "farewell" to his deceased brother to various kinds of invective, as when he lampooned a Romanized Celt for supposedly engaging in the Spanish practice of brushing his teeth with urine. Catullus was one of the first Latin writers to apply Greek lyric verse meters to Latin. And the poet Lucretius, about whom very little is known, authored a poem *On the Nature of Things* written in the 50s BCE, which described the Epicurean view of the universe and was intended to free one from fear of death.

At the same time, the senatorial ideal now included the expectations that a senator would not only participate in public life but would also engage in leisure activities that included both reading and writing various kinds of literary works. Indeed, the most famous late Republican prose writers, Caesar, Cicero, Sallust, and Varro, all were very active in politics. Caesar, of course, wrote the *Gallic War* and the *Civil War,* both intended to portray his own political actions in the most positive light. And Cicero published not only his speeches and letters, likewise intended to enhance his personal reputation, but also works on oratory and philosophy. In later years, Cicero set the standard of Latin prose writing against which all other authors were measured.

In addition, Sallust, a supporter of Caesar during the civil war who used ill-gotten gains in the provinces to create famous gardens on the Quirinal Hill in Rome, wrote surviving historical accounts of the *War against Jugurtha* and the *Conspiracy of Catiline;* his *Histories* of the post-Sullan period, however, have been lost. Rather than merely narrating events, Sallust attempted to explain the human motivations and weaknesses and the historical processes lying behind them, and thus he set the stage for a more nuanced writing of Roman history. And Varro, a supporter of Pompey pardoned by Caesar, was believed to have written no less than 620 books, most of which do not survive, on various topics. In the field of history, he developed the standard historical chronological framework for Roman history based on lists of consuls beginning in 509 BCE and on the foundation of Rome in 753 BCE; in this scheme, dates were expressed in years "AUC," or *Ab urbe condita* ("from the foundation of the city"). Two of his works, practical in nature, survive: *On the Latin Language,* a grammatical treatise, and *On Agricultural Matters,* a handbook on farming. Influential Roman senators in public life thus also saw themselves as the representatives of Roman culture and values.

LOOKING AHEAD

By 21 BCE, Augustus had solidified his political control over the Roman government in a way that earlier generals in his position, such as Sulla and Caesar, had not been able to do. In so doing, he had largely solved the problem of keeping ambitious senators under control. But the other problems that had led to the fall of the Republic—poorly administered and unintegrated provinces and an unruly quasi-mercenary army—remained to be dealt with. Unless Augustus could do so, the Roman world would be neither prosperous nor peaceful.

FURTHER READING

Badian, Ernst. *Roman Imperialism in the Late Republic.* Ithaca, NY: Cornell University Press, 1971.

Badian, Ernst. *Sulla, the Deadly Reformer.* Sydney: Sydney University Press, 1970.

Bradley, K. R. *Slavery and Rebellion in the Roman World 140 B.C.–70 B.C.* Bloomington: Indiana University Press, 1989.

Brunt, P. A. *The Fall of the Roman Republic.* Oxford: Clarendon Press, 1988.

Brunt, P. A. *Italian Manpower 225 b.c.–a.d. 14.* Oxford: Clarendon Press, 1971, rev. ed. 1987.

Canfora, Luciano. *Julius Caesar: The People's Dictator.* Edinburgh: Edinburgh University Press, 2006.

Evans, Richard J. *Gaius Marius: A Political Biography.* Pretoria: University of South Africa, 1994.

Gardner, J. F. *Women in Roman Law and Society.* Bloomington: Indiana University Press, 1986.

Goldsworthy, Adrian. *Caesar: Life of a Colossus.* New Haven, CT: Yale University Press, 2006.

Keaveney, A. *Sulla: The Last Republican,* 2nd ed. Oxford/New York: Routledge, 2005.

Kleiner, Diana E. E. *Cleopatra and Rome.* Cambridge, MA: Harvard University Press, 2005.

Lintott, A. *Violence in Republican Rome.* Oxford: Clarendon Press, 1968.

McCullough, Colleen. *First Man in Rome.* New York: Avon Books, 1991. A historical novel about the days of Sulla and Marius.

Mouritsen, H. *Plebs and Politics in Late Republican Rome.* Cambridge: Cambridge University Press, 2001.

Rawson, E. *Intellectual Life in the Late Roman Republic.* Baltimore: Johns Hopkins University Press, 1985.

Scullard, H. H. *From the Gracchi to Nero: A History of Rome from 133 BC to AD 68,* 5th ed. Oxford: Routledge, 1982.

Stockton, D. L. *The Gracchi.* Oxford: Clarendon Press, 1979.

Syme, Ronald. *The Roman Revolution.* Oxford: Oxford University Press, 1939.

Taylor, Lilly Ross. *Party Politics in the Age of Caesar.* Berkeley: University of California Press, 1961.

Yakobson, A. *Elections and Electioneering in Rome: A Study in the Political System of the Late Republic.* Stuttgart: Steiner, 1999.

CHAPTER 11

THE ROMAN PEACE
(27 BCE–192 CE)

The Principate—the Roman Empire as established by Augustus—inaugurated a period of more than two hundred years of peace and prosperity for the Roman world. For the most part, the Roman army not only was successfully kept out of politics but also maintained a secure frontier defense system that prevented foreign invasions at the same time that it permitted commerce and immigration across the borders. As the Roman Empire became more socially, culturally, and economically integrated, it embraced all of the manifold peoples living within its diffuse frontiers and provided opportunities for advancement to all of its residents. The evolution of a Mediterranean culture created the most cohesive and successful empire that the world had yet known. In general, the first and second centuries are known as the period of the *Pax Romana*, or Roman Peace. A unified culture and society was created that extended from Britain to Arabia.

THE AGE OF AUGUSTUS (27 BCE–14 CE)

By finding a way to continue to hold supreme power without looking like a dictator or autocrat, Augustus was able not only to ensure his personal security but also to deal with the problem of ambitious senators that had contributed so greatly to the fall of the Republic. Once he was fully in control, he was able to turn to the two other problems that the Republic never had been able to solve: how to deal with the provinces and how to keep the army under control. By dealing with these two problems, he would make the Roman Empire into a better governed and more integrated whole that would have the staying power to last over the long term and not just for his own lifetime. The most complex problem that Augustus confronted was dealing with the provinces, which had suffered more than two hundred years of neglect. Augustus' initiatives in the provinces had three components: (1) crafting a coherent imperial policy with respect to expansion and defense, (2) creating an effective system of provincial administration, and (3) finding a way to integrate the millions of provincials into the Roman world.

The Provinces: Expansion and Defense

During the Republic, provinces had been annexed more or less at random, and there had been no consistent concept of systematic expansion or border defense. To correct this, Augustus pursued a policy of consolidating the territories that Rome already controlled and seeking borders that were easy to defend. Regarding consolidation, Augustus did some infill and annexed marginal regions in areas already under Roman control, usually in uplands such as northwestern Spain or the Alps. And as to defensible frontiers, different sections of the empire required different approaches. In the south was the Sahara Desert, which, given the lack of invasion threat, required but a single legion to defend. Egypt, a special case because of its great wealth, became the personal property of the emperor. To the east lay the Parthian Empire. After the Republican debacles, which had resulted from personal ambition rather than state policy, Augustus accepted that there was nothing to be gained by campaigning there, so he pursued a policy of peace and negotiated a favorable treaty. Border areas not considered strategically significant enough to annex were left under **client kings**, such as **Herod** in Judaea, Juba II in Mauretania in western North Africa, and Archelaus in Commagene in Anatolia, who were allowed to rule so long as they remained loyal and did not antagonize Rome.

Paradoxically, nearly all of the conquests that created the Roman Empire occurred during the Roman Republic or under Augustus.

The most serious problem was in the north, where Germanic peoples threatened the security of the frontier. Augustus proposed to create a defensible border by expanding to the Danube River and was successful doing so until the revolt of the Illyrian leader Bato in 6 CE. Once the revolt had been subdued by Augustus' stepson Tiberius, the annexation then proceeded smoothly. Augustus also wanted to expand beyond the Rhine to the Elbe River in Germany and create a shorter Elbe-Danube frontier by annexing a new province of Germania (Germany). By 6 CE, after initial successes by Tiberius and Augustus' stepgrandson Drusus, Augustus declared victory and appointed Quinctilius **Varus**, an experienced general and administrator, as governor. But in 9 CE, the Germans made a last stab at independence led by **Arminius**, a German in Roman service who had risen to the rank of knight. Varus, trusting Arminius' loyalty, was led into an ambush in the **Battle of the Teutoburg Forest**, where he and three Roman legions were slaughtered. What became known as the "Varian disaster" went down in Roman history, with the sack of Rome by the Gauls in 390 BCE and the Battle of Cannae in 216 BCE, as one of the worst Roman defeats ever. According to the biographer Suetonius, this setback left Augustus momentarily so deranged that he wandered the palace at night, pounding his head on the wall and groaning, "Varus, Varus, give me back my legions!" Unable to face starting afresh, Augustus withdrew to the Rhine River, and the Rhine and Danube thus became the northern frontier. The reentrant angle between their upper reaches later would serve as a staging ground for barbarian attacks.

The site of the Battle of the Teutoburg Forest was discovered in the late 1990s at Kalkriese Hill in Lower Saxony.

Augustus ended the runaway, reckless expansion of the Republic. He concentrated on protecting the frontiers, overseeing interactions with the outside, and consolidating Roman territory. His policy of no further large-scale foreign conquest was followed by nearly all of his successors, and it created an empire that was more concerned with effectively governing the areas that it controlled than with conquering and exploiting additional foreign territories.

Provincial Administration

The empire now consisted of some twenty-five provinces with a total population of between seventy and one hundred million persons. In order to give substance to his partnership with the Senate, Augustus shared the responsibility for provincial administration. He retained under his own control provinces such as northern Spain, Gaul, Illyricum, and Syria, where the bulk of the Roman army was stationed. The remaining provinces, such as southern Spain, Sicily, Africa, Achaea in Greece, and Asia, were returned to administration by the Senate. The governors of senatorial provinces still were known as proconsuls, whereas those of imperial provinces were called *Legati Augusti*, **legates of Augustus**, because, as during the Republic, they were acting as legates to whom a proconsul had delegated his imperium—although the Republican constitution, of course, had not anticipated that a single person would have proconsular authority in several provinces. Even though any policies that Augustus introduced were directly applicable only to the provinces under his own control, the Senate generally followed his lead.

Augustus chose governors who either were senators or who became senators on the basis of their ability, especially where military operations were at issue. He allowed them to serve for extended periods of several years, and he paid them a salary so as to lessen the temptation toward corruption. He also established a permanent civil service with offices in Rome and the provinces, in which members of the **equestrian class**, the knights, served as lifetime civil servants. Typical equestrian officials included **prefects**, who held positions deemed too sensitive for senators to hold, and **procurators**, supervisors of tax collection. Both, moreover, sometimes served as governors of small provinces that did not merit a senatorial governor.

To cope with inequities in provincial tax assessment, Augustus followed Caesar's lead and completely eliminated the variable tithe, replacing it with fixed tribute. To ensure an equitable imposition of taxes, Augustus instituted

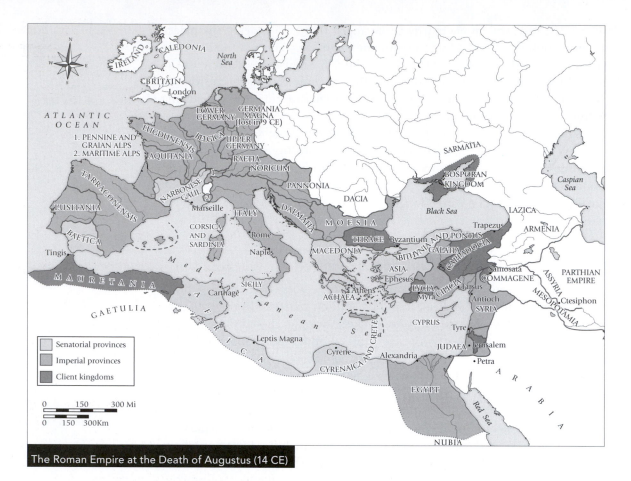

The Roman Empire at the Death of Augustus (14 CE)

a regular census in which all provincials registered their property; this provided the basis for fair tax assessment. Italy, where the vast majority of Roman citizens lived, received special treatment: it had no taxes and no governors. And Egypt, the financial base of Mark Antony and a possible source of trouble should it fall into the wrong hands, also was special; rather than being made into a typical province, it became the personal property of the emperor and was administered by an equestrian prefect; any senator wishing to visit Egypt needed permission from the emperor.

Winning the Hearts and Minds of the People

Augustus' greatest achievement lay in his creation of a sense of internal cohesiveness in the provinces where none had existed before. He introduced many policies intended to create both the appearance and, to a large extent, even the reality of unity in the diverse Roman world. For example, a standardized coinage system, based on gold, silver, and copper coins, facilitated financial transactions throughout the Roman world and became a standard currency even beyond the frontiers. And the construction of the elaborate Roman road system, initially designed for military transport, was utilized primarily for personal and commercial traffic and gave the hinterland of the Roman Empire the kind of access to communication with the outside world that in the past had been available primarily to coastal areas.

The U.S. interstate highway system, begun in the 1950s, also was intended as a military transport system but ended up with mostly civilian use.

But Augustus' greatest achievement in creating unity involved the people of the empire. In the past, Italy, the home of most Roman citizens, had had a privileged position in the Roman world, with the provinces treated, at best, with benign neglect. But Augustus realized that for the empire to succeed, the inhabitants of the provinces would have to be integrated into the Roman world and made to feel that Rome's best interests were their best interests as well. Augustus thus did much to unify the chaotically organized territories he inherited from the Republic.

In particular, Augustus wanted to integrate the inhabitants of the provinces into the Roman world, to create in them a sense of participation, and to convince them that they and Rome had the same interests. He established annual provincial councils, where representatives from cities met to receive messages from the emperor and to convey their concerns to him. Provincials also participated in the imperial cult, also known as the **Cult of Rome and Augustus**, where by dropping incense into a fire on an altar they symbolically renewed their loyalty to the emperor and state.

But the primary means of integration lay in grants of **Roman citizenship**, which had been virtually impossible to obtain during the Republic. Augustus established two methods for obtaining citizenship. Local governments were modeled on that of Rome. Each city had its own local senate, or *Curia*, whose members, the **decurions**, could make a pro

The Maison Carrée ("square house") at Nîmes in southern France was a temple of the imperial cult dedicated by Agrippa to his sons Gaius and Lucius, the adopted sons of Augustus. It survives because of its use as a church in the Middle Ages.

TABLE 11.1   COIN DENOMINATIONS OF THE ROMAN EMPIRE

Metal	Denomination	Value
Gold	Aureus (aurei)	25 denarii
Gold	Quinarius	12 ½ denarii
Silver	Denarius (denarii)	16 asses = 4 sesterces
Copper	Sestertius (sesterces)	4 asses
Brass	Dupondius	2 asses
Copper	As (asses)	1 as
Brass	Semis	½ as
Copper	Triens	⅓ as
Copper	Quadrans	¼ as

forma request for citizenship from the emperor. This had the effect of encouraging all local elites to identify their interests with Rome. In addition, provincials who served for twenty-five years in the **auxilia**, army's auxiliary forces, which backed up the citizen legions, also received citizenship upon retirement. The children and wives of these new citizens likewise became citizens. But because Augustus viewed citizenship as a reward, he slowed down the entry of slaves into the citizen ranks, creating an intermediate status of *libertus/liberta*, **freedman** or **freedwoman**, for freed slaves. Freedmen were prohibited from becoming knights or senators and from holding most offices, although Augustus did create priests of the imperial cult known as the *Seviri Augustales* ("Six men of Augustus"), who could only be freedmen. The offspring of freedmen and -women then became full Roman citizens.

Once a male had become a citizen, either by direct grant or by being the son of a citizen, there were other opportunities for social advancement. New plebeians could enlist in the Roman legions and work their way up in the ranks, perhaps even attracting the attention and patronage of the emperors, who often endowed favored army veterans with sufficient money to make them eligible for membership in the knights. Wealthy citizens became members of the **equestrian class** if they possessed four hundred thousand **sesterces** worth of property. Senators, moreover, were drawn from the **senatorial class**, which required property totaling at least one million sesterces for membership. Actual membership in the Senate was gained either by holding one of the old Republican magistracies or by direct adlection by the emperor. And Augustus controlled who was selected to hold magistracies by the practices of *nominatio*, in which he supported a candidate's nomination, thus ensuring their election, and *commendatio*, whereby an individual was simply appointed to the office. In this way, Augustus was able to preserve the form of Republican political institutions while at the same time keeping complete control over who served in these institutions.

LEARNING FROM HISTORY

What does our study of history teach us about the respective roles of culture and politics in society? Does having political authority always establish cultural authority, too? Or are there political rulers of a nation or empire who did not try or were not able to impose their culture on the people they ruled, or even saw no value in doing so?

Dealing with the Army

Augustus also had to contend with the army, which was responsible for defending thousands of miles of frontier and for maintaining civil order. It was by far the largest drain on the imperial treasury, eating up 70 percent or more of the empire's yearly expenditures, and, most important, it was the basis of the emperor's political authority. In order to minimize its cost, Augustus cut the army back to the bare bones, reducing it from eighty legions at the end of the civil war to a mere twenty-five legions (the three lost by Varus were not replaced). He considered the bare minimum necessary to defend the frontiers and perhaps to undertake one campaign against a foreign enemy. Most of the army was spread out along the frontiers, creating a **shell defense system** intended to prevent potential invaders from breaking through into the undefended inner regions of the empire. Distributing the army along the frontier also lessened dangerously large concentrations of troops and kept the army far from Rome and, one hoped, out of politics. So as not to completely lose touch with his military support, Augustus stationed in the towns outside Rome an elite body of ten thousand soldiers known as the Praetorian Guard. They were commanded by an equestrian **praetorian prefect** because Augustus felt it would have been far to dangerous to have a senator commanding the only sizable body of troops not on the frontier. In general, as a result of the implementation of Augustus' policy of no further foreign conquests, the Roman army became a garrison army and was often kept busy on construction projects such as building roads, bridges, and, especially, fortifications.

Because Augustus himself had come to power using his army, it always was possible that someone else would try to do the same. It thus was a top priority of Augustus and later emperors to maintain the army's loyalty. Augustus adopted several means of doing so. For one thing, the only person an emperor could really trust to lead a large army was himself, or, failing that, a close relative. Augustus therefore used his relatives by marriage, Agrippa, Drusus, Tiberius, and Germanicus, as his must trusted generals. He also professionalized the army by creating a standing army that was not disbanded after each campaign, as had been the case during the Republic. The core of the command structure lay in the centurions, senior noncommissioned officers who commanded units of one hundred men. Army discipline was strictly enforced; the most serious punishment was known as decimation, in which every tenth man in a disgraced unit was executed by the nine other men in his selection group. A strong sense of esprit de corps developed, and a unit's military standards were accorded a religious reverence.

Soldiers in the legions, who had to be citizens, were paid 225 denarii a year, and it also became customary for emperors, upon their succession, to bestow a **donative** of several gold pieces on the troops to solidify the loyalty of the army. After seventeen years of service, legionaries retired with a bonus of either three thousand denarii or a land allotment, perhaps twenty acres, often in military colonies established around the empire; during his reign, Augustus had to find land for some one hundred fifty thousand veterans. Whereas the legions were stationed at strong points on the frontier, the auxiliary forces, roughly equal in number to the legions and composed mostly of provincials paid only marginally less than the legions, were spread out in smaller garrisons, often in

Unlike the modern day, the Roman Empire had no police force; serious breaches of the peace had to be dealt with by detached units of the Roman army.

forward positions. Auxiliary forces also included most of the cavalry, along with specialized units such as slingers and archers. Soldiers' sons often followed in their fathers' footsteps. The rewards bestowed by emperors on the army fostered the natural patron-client relationship between the commander and the troops, meaning that if an army was loyal to the father, it also would be loyal to the family. And yet, in spite of the attractions of army service to both citizens and provincials, emperors always were concerned about finding enough recruits.

The army also carried Roman culture to the frontiers of the empire and thereby became one of the main purveyors of **Romanization**, or the extension of Roman culture into the provinces. For example, the first thing an auxiliary soldier had to learn was the Latin language, a later consequence of which was the development of the modern Romance languages of Italian, French, Spanish, Portuguese, and Romanian. In addition, during Augustus' reign, eighty colonies were established for army veterans in Spain, North Africa, and Greece, creating centers of Roman administration, society, and culture in the provinces. And at the same time that Greek and Roman culture was spreading into the provinces, provincial culture was making its way into Rome, just as eastern culture had been propagated into Greece during the Hellenistic period.

Propaganda

Augustus and subsequent emperors used several methods for advertising their achievements, justifying their own existence, and linking the image of the emperor with that of Rome. For mass media, the emperors used the coinage to proclaim their deeds in a manner designed to reach the widest possible audience. Coins could be used to disseminate either specific information, such as a military or diplomatic victory, or general ideologies relating to the emperor's piety or generosity.

Augustus sponsored the construction of a multitude of monuments in Rome to commemorate special events and to demonstrate his generosity. Indeed, according to the second-century biographer Suetonius, Augustus claimed to have changed Rome from a city of brick into one of marble. Augustus' *Ara pacis*, or Altar of Peace, for example, completed in 9 CE, portrayed Augustus as the one who had brought peace to the Roman world; few could contest this claim. A triumphal Arch of Augustus erected in the forum had on one side the official *Fasti consulares*, a list of all the consuls going back to 509 BCE, and on the other the official *Fasti triumphales*, a list of all the generals who had been granted a triumph. Augustus also built in the forum a temple of *Divus Julius*, "the deified Julius," in honor of Caesar, whose deification had made Augustus into "*divi filius*," the son of the god. Like Caesar, Augustus built a new forum, the Forum of Augustus. This forum contained a temple of Mars Ultor, "Mars the Avenger," which Augustus had vowed to build when he took up arms against the assassins of Caesar. Elsewhere, Augustus built the Theater of Marcellus in honor of his nephew and the great temple of Apollo on the Palatine Hill; in general, he claimed to have built or restored no less than eighty-two temples. Finally, Augustus constructed a mausoleum, an elaborate tomb designed, like Etruscan tombs, to be covered with a mound of earth planted with cypress trees, to hold the remains of himself and his family.

Augustus and his successors also provided the people with entertainment, most popularly in the form of gladiatorial combats and chariot races. Augustus took control of who sponsored popular entertainments, many of which he underwrote himself, so as to prevent senators from using the sponsorship of games to gain popularity. He sponsored as many as twelve chariot races a day in the *Circus Maximus*, or "Greatest Circus," which could seat up to one hundred fifty thousand spectators. There were four chariot racing teams, named after their team colors, the "blues," "greens," "reds," and "whites," each of which had fan clubs, one of the few forms of permitted public organizations. The fan clubs sometimes had political overtones; the members of a circus faction would shout out slogans intended for the ears of the emperor. Augustus also claimed to have provided *annona* (grain doles) for more than one hundred thousand persons. And the emperors were the only source of "disaster relief" in the Roman world. For example, after a great earthquake in the province of Asia devastated Sardis and eleven other cities, Augustus' successor Tiberius granted ten million sesterces for the relief of the city, and all twelve cities had their taxes remitted for five years.

As *pater patriae* ("Father of the Country"), Augustus felt that it was his duty to restore the moral fiber of a people who had become disheartened after so many years of civil war and lost sight of the values that had made the Romans great. He opposed extravagance in favor of living a simple life. Being something of a prude, he attempted to intrude himself into the most intimate aspects of people's lives. On the one hand, he encouraged marriage and childbearing (which was good for army recruitment)—women with three or more children received legal privileges, and men were free of civic obligations—but childless persons were prohibited from receiving inheritances. He also restricted marriages between persons of different social classes, prohibiting slaves and freedwomen from marrying senators. At the same time, he prohibited soldiers from getting married while on active duty. He taxed prostitutes, punished homosexuality, and banished adulterers. Indeed, Augustus' own daughter Julia fell afoul of Augustus' moral agenda when she was convicted of adultery and banished to the tiny island of Pandataria, where she was forbidden to see any men.

In general, the emperor served as both a patron and a unifying element for the entire Roman world, whose population became his clients. The old Roman tradition of *clientela* was therefore brought into service as a model for creating a kind of imperial state that the world had never seen before. The emperor provided offices and honors for the senators, salaries and bonuses for the soldiers,

RECONSTRUCTING THE DEEDS OF THE DEIFIED AUGUSTUS

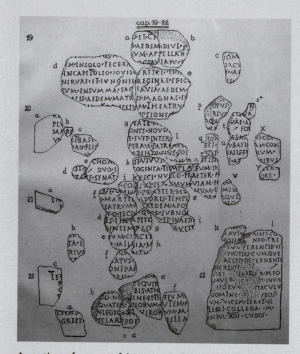

A section of a copy of Augustus's *Res gestae* found in Ancyra (Ankara) in Turkey.

Most of the lengthy literary texts that survive from antiquity were preserved as texts written first on papyrus scrolls and then later copied onto parchment manuscripts. But some texts were preserved as inscriptions cut into stone. This form of preservation, of course, was much more costly than writing on a perishable text and was usually done under government auspices—one recalls the decree of the Senate on the worshippers of Bacchus in 186 BCE. During the Roman Empire, the government oversaw the preservation of other documents on stone, including a speech of the emperor Claudius (41–54) and the Edict on Maximum Prices issued by Diocletian in 301. One of the most historically significant texts preserved on stone, and one of the most effective pieces of propaganda ever produced, is the *Res gestae divi Augusti,* or "Deeds of the Deified Augustus," an autobiographical account of his own achievements that Augustus wrote when he was seventy-six and instructed the Senate to post throughout the empire, in both Latin and Greek, after his death. This was done, but the *Res gestae* do not survive intact anywhere. The original bronze copy from the forum in Rome is lost, and the surviving version had to be pieced together from stone fragments found at Ancyra, where the best copy was found; at Apollonia; and at Antioch.

and edibles and entertainment for the urban mob of Rome. As the years went by, more and more power fell into his hands. Bit by bit, the authority of the Senate, which historically had been unwilling to change with the times, dwindled. Sometimes, the only real opportunity the Senate had to express its opinion about an emperor came after the emperor had died, and the Senate could choose to deify him, to do nothing, or, if it really disliked him, to issue a decree of *damnatio memoriae,* **Damnation of Memory**, which permitted the mutilation of his images, ordinarily an act of high treason.

The Augustan Golden Age of Literature

In other ways, too, Augustus propagated the idea of a mystique of Rome, with himself as the divinely ordained leader. Poets and writers recruited by Augustus' adviser Maecenas perpetuated the **Golden Age of Roman literature** that had

The reconstructed document is in thirty-five paragraphs preserved on eight tablets. Paragraphs 2–14 record Augustus' political career and are consistent with how Roman senators traditionally were remembered. Paragraphs 15–24 go on to catalogue Augustus' benefactions to the people of Rome, demonstrating that he behaved like a responsible patron. Paragraphs 25–33 detail Augustus' military activities, showing how he had dutifully defended and expanded the empire. And the final two paragraphs summarize Augustus' important role in the state:

> In my sixth and seventh consulates (28–27 B.C.E.), after putting out the civil war, having obtained all things by universal consent, I transferred the state from my power to the dominion of the Senate and Roman people. And for this merit of mine, by a senate decree, I was called Augustus and the doors of my temple were publicly clothed with laurel and a civic crown was fixed over my door and a gold shield placed in the Julian senate house, and the inscription of that shield testified to the virtue, mercy, justice, and piety, for which the senate and Roman people gave it to me. After that time, I exceeded all in influence, but I had no greater power than the others who were colleagues with me in each magistracy. When I administered my thirteenth consulate (2 BCE), the Senate and Equestrian Order and Roman people all called me Father of the Country (*pater patriae*), and voted that the same be inscribed in the vestibule of my temple, in the Julian senate-house, and in the forum of Augustus under the chariot that had been placed there for me by a decision of the senate. When I wrote this I was seventy-six years old.

A brief appendix, added posthumously, summarized Augustus' benefactions to the people, for example, "All the expenditures which he gave either into the treasury or to the Roman plebs or to discharged soldiers: 2,400,000,000 sesterces."

By controlling the flow of information about his own reign, Augustus was able to predetermine how he would be perceived by future generations. Both in antiquity and in modern times, the *Res gestae* have been used as a primary source for the reign of Augustus, and much of Augustus' own spin about himself has been accepted into the scholarly and popular tradition. And by reconstructing original documents of this sort, historians sometimes are able to get much closer to the thoughts and intentions of ancient peoples than they can by studying written traditions that have been recopied, rewritten, and revised over the course of many centuries.

begun in the late Republic. Horace became the poet laureate of Augustan Rome and in 17 BCE wrote a hymn in honor of the Secular Games, which took place only every 110 years and marked the beginning of a new age. And the historian Livy authored a massive 142-volume history of Rome, of which about one-quarter survives, that began with the city's foundation and ran up to his own day.

The most famous Augustan poet was Publius Vergilius Maro, or Vergil, who wrote *Georgics* and *Eclogues* on the joys of the rural life, a theme that Augustus wished to promulgate after so many years of war. The Fourth *Eclogue*, later known as the "Messianic" *Eclogue*, told about the birth of a boy who would bring a new Golden Age. Vergil, of course, intended this to be interpreted as Augustus, but in later centuries Christians saw this poem as a foreshadowing of Jesus Christ, and as a result Vergil was viewed as a Christian poet, and his works were preserved. But Vergil's greatest work, the *Aeneid*, became the Roman national epic, and sections of it were memorized by every Roman schoolchild.

THE GEMMA AUGUSTEA

The Gemma Augustea, a 7.5- by 9-inch cameo carved from a piece of two-layered white and blue Arabian onyx, now in the Kunsthistorisches Museum in Vienna, probably was made by Dioscorides, Augustus' favorite gem cutter, for display at the imperial court. It is one of the most effective pieces of political propaganda ever made. The identifications of some of the figures are heavily debated, so one can always feel free to suggest alternate interpretations. According to some interpretations, the upper register depicts Augustus posing as Jupiter, just as on the ubiquitous coins of Alexander the Great, seated partially nude on a throne, holding a *lituus,* a curved stick symbolic of the power of *auspicium,* in his right hand and a scepter, the symbol of his earthly *imperium,* in his left. The eagle of Jupiter stands underneath and Augustus' astrological sign, Capricorn, is above to his left. Oikumene (the whole world), wearing a turreted crown and veil, stands behind him and crowns him with the "corona civica," an oak wreath awarded to those who saved Roman lives. In front of her, at the far right, stands Neptune, signifying dominion over the sea, and Italia sits in front of him, accompanied by children representing fertility, the same theme that appeared on Augustus' Altar of Peace. Seated next to Augustus, the goddess Roma, made to look like Augustus' wife Livia, is ready for war, with one hand on a spear and the

other on a sword. At the far left, Tiberius, Augustus' stepson and eventual successor, descends from a chariot driven by the goddess Victory, in which he had just triumphed in 12 CE. He already is garbed in the toga after laying down his command, and he is the only other figure holding a scepter, representing the imperium already granted him by Augustus. The young military garbed figure on Roma's right seems just to have dismounted from the horse behind and perhaps represents Germanicus, son of Tiberius' brother Drusus and consul in 12 CE.

The lower register presumably portrays the victory celebration after a battle on the northern frontier and is linked to the upper register by the shields under Augustus' feet. It depicts the power on which Augustus' rule was based and advertises the emperor's role as the one who protected the empire against threatening barbarians. On the left, soldiers raise a trophy of captured weapons above a seated pair of dejected Germanic or Celtic captives, with the man's hands bound and the woman weeping, and to the right additional captives begging for mercy are brought in. According to one interpretation of this scene, the Romans are Roman soldiers, and the different styles of the soldiers' helmets and dress indicate that both Roman legionaries and auxiliary troops are represented. But other scholars interpret the Roman figures as the

---

It told the story of the Trojan hero Aeneas, who, with his wife Creusa, son Ascanius (also known as Iulus), and father Anchises, had escaped from burning Troy and had wandered for ten years before founding a city a short way away from the future site of Rome. Aeneas was famous for his *pietas,* or sense of duty, and he foreshadowed later Romans, culminating in Augustus himself, who had dutifully expanded the grandeur of Rome.

Greek writers also participated in the Augustan Golden Age of literature and proclaimed the glories of Augustan Rome. Dionysius of Halicarnassus in Anatolia settled in Rome after the civil wars, studied Latin, and wrote a massive Greek work called *Roman Antiquities* covering Roman history from Aeneas and Greek mythology until the First Punic War. His work was intended to convince

gods Apollo (at the far left in a Thracian cap), Mars (helmeted), Castor and Pollux (lifting the trophy), Diana (carrying two spears and in hunting clothes), and Mercury (wearing a *petasus,* or sun hat). At the far left, moreover, the shield bears the sign of Scorpio, the sign of Tiberius. The victory has been interpreted as that of Tiberius over the Dalmatians in 9 CE, with the triumph having been delayed as a result of the Varian disaster, or that of Tiberius over the Germans in 12 CE.

Greeks of the positive aspects of Roman rule and that the Romans were, in fact, an ancient part of the Greek world. Dionysius and Livy provide the only surviving narrative accounts of early Roman history.

There also was a second flowering of Latin love poetry by poets such as Propertius, another client of Maecenas; Sulpicia, a niece of the patron of the arts Messalla and the only female poet whose work survives; Tibullus, a client of Messalla; and Ovid, whose poem *The Metamorphoses* explained Greek mythology in Roman terms and who was banished to distant Tomis on the Black Sea as a result of what he described only as "a poem and a mistake." Their poems, lacking the imperial jingoism of the court authors, provide insights into the personal and private leisure lives of the Roman educated elite.

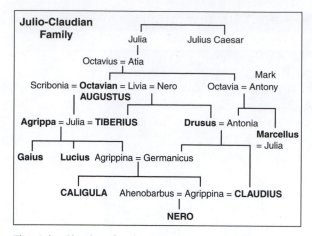

The Julio-Claudian family tree depicts one of the great ironies of Roman imperial history: the last Julio-Claudian emperors were direct descendents of Mark Antony.

Note: Failed successors of Augustus are in bold lowercase and emperors are in bold uppercase.

The Imperial Succession

One final problem that Augustus faced was the choice of a successor. Given that there was no constitutional position of emperor, there was no constitutional means of choosing a new emperor when the current one died. This quandary created the problem of the **Imperial Succession**. Augustus dealt with it in two ways. He granted to the person he wanted to succeed him all the powers that he had. This made the Senate happy, because the transfer was thus done legally. And he adopted him. This made the army happy, for in Rome loyalties were inherited. But this was only an ad hoc solution and was to result in problems when future emperors did not have the foresight to put their successors in place before they died. Augustus also had decidedly bad luck when it came to choosing successors. One by one, those he chose, including his nephew Marcellus, his friend Agrippa, his grandsons Gaius and Lucius, and his stepson Drusus, all died. Some have attributed this unfortunate chain of events to the machinations of his wife Livia, although there is no direct evidence for this.

The last thing that Augustus did to ensure the success of his settlement was to live a long time. In spite of his poor health, he died in 14 CE at the age of seventy-six. He immediately was deified by the Senate. It had been more than sixty years since the Republic had operated as such. Few remembered it as anything but ancient history.

THE JULIO-CLAUDIAN AND FLAVIAN DYNASTIES (27 BCE–96 CE)

Augustus was the first in a long line of emperors of what modern historians call the Roman Empire. As a means of organizing the emperors, emperors who were related in some way to one another are grouped, as were the Egyptian pharaohs, into dynasties. During the first century CE, two imperial dynasties, the **Julio-Claudian Dynasty** (27 BCE–68 CE) and the **Flavian Dynasty** (69–96) established the policies and principles that would guide the Roman Empire through its first three centuries.

The Julio-Claudian Dynasty

The Julio-Claudian emperors all were related in some manner to Augustus. Under the Julio-Claudians, the Principate as established by Augustus was consolidated. Emperors obtained their powers in a package consisting of the greater proconsular imperium and the tribunician power. Political and social privilege gradually began to move out of Italy into the provinces. And an imperial bureaucracy that actually could manage the administration of the huge empire gradually coalesced. But problems arose with the lack of an established succession system; indeed, one of the curiosities about the Julio-Claudians is that even though the ideal succession pattern, from the point of view of the army, would have been for a son to succeed a father, none of the four Julio-Claudian emperors who followed Augustus was succeeded by a blood son.

Tiberius (14–37)

Ultimately, the only choice left for Augustus was Livia's son and Augustus' stepson and adopted son, Tiberius. After Augustus' death in 14 CE, Tiberius offered to return to the Senate all the powers that Augustus had granted him. The Senate not only declined but granted to Tiberius all of the powers for life in a single package. This became the standard method by which later emperors received their authority. As a consequence, the historian **Tacitus** later claimed that the Senate had "rushed into servitude."

Like Augustus, Tiberius was an effective administrator. He also was an excellent general, having campaigned extensively on the Danube and Rhine. He was efficient, capable, and had a strong sense of duty. On the other hand, however, he had difficulty getting along with people, and his long experience as the odd man out in the imperial selection process had given him a suspicious nature. Initially he worked well with the Senate, expanding their powers at the expense of the increasingly vestigial Republican popular assemblies. He did this, however, for his own convenience, deeming it easier to work with the Senate rather than with the more rambunctious, cumbersome, and unpredictable assemblies.

By 26 CE the situation had changed. Like Augustus, Tiberius had been having problems finding a successor who could outlive him. His popular nephew Germanicus died in 19 amid rumors of poisoning, and his son Drusus died in 23. Nero and another Drusus, the elder sons of his stepniece Agrippina, then were tabbed. Meanwhile, the praetorian prefect **Sejanus** began to exercise increasing influence over the emperor. To increase his own influence, Sejanus moved the guard into the *Castra praetoria*, the Praetorian Camp, right outside Rome. He convinced Tiberius to retire to the island of Capri, and the emperor never returned to Rome. By the year 30, Agrippina, Nero, and Drusus III all were dead, and Sejanus, even though just a knight, plotted to seize the throne himself. Only in 31 did Tiberius learn of

TABLE 11.2 IMPERIAL DYNASTIES OF THE ROMAN PEACE

Julio-Claudian Dynasty

Augustus (27 BCE–14 CE)

Tiberius (14–37)

Caligula (37–41)

Claudius (41–54)

Nero (54–68)

Flavian Dynasty

Vespasian (69–79)

Titus (79–81)

Domitian (81–96)

Antonine Dynasty

Nerva (96–98)

Trajan (98–117)

Hadrian (117–138)

Antoninus (138–161)

Lucius Verus (161–169)

Marcus Aurelius (161–180)

Commodus (180–192)

Sejanus' schemes. He recruited Macro, another knight who served as prefect of the night watch, to arrest and execute Sejanus and then promoted Macro to be praetorian prefect.

Tiberius' suspicions then grew by leaps and bounds, and he set an unfortunate precedent of giving a ready ear to **delators**, or informers, who received one-fourth of the estate of any condemned person they had informed on. When Tiberius died in 37, no successor had been named. Macro submitted the name of Gaius, the surviving youngest son of Agrippina, to the Senate, which had little choice but to concur. The young man had been born in the army camp of his father, Germanicus, and the little boots that the soldiers made for him resulted in the nickname by which he is better known: Caligula.

Caligula (37–41)

Caligula initially showed promise, recalling those who had been exiled by Tiberius. He also granted a double donative to the soldiers, a dangerous precedent that could suggest financial incentives in making new emperors. But Caligula then became seriously ill, and afterward he exhibited some bizarre behavior. Believing himself to be the god Jupiter, he decreed divine honors for himself. Caligula also ignored the Senate and, it was said, even made his horse, Incitatus, a consul.

Eventually Caligula made an emperor's most fatal error: he antagonized the army. A commander on the Rhine was executed for treason, and a proposed invasion of Britain failed dismally. In the latter case, tales that Caligula sent soldiers gathering seashells so he could claim victory over Neptune probably misrepresent the use of crushed shells in cement for building lighthouses and seaport facilities. Early in 41 even the Praetorian Guard turned against him after he insulted a guard officer, and he was assassinated, marking the first time that the army had rid itself of an unwanted emperor. It would not be the last.

Claudius (41–54)

Once again, the army took matters into its own hands. While the Senate dithered, it declared as emperor Caligula's lame and stammering old uncle Claudius, who as a youth had been afflicted with some type of disability, perhaps infantile paralysis, and had been kept very much in the background. As a result, Claudius had taken up the study of ancient history, writing histories of the Carthaginians and Etruscans. In the interest of running the state more efficiently, Claudius put his studies to good use. He extended Roman citizenship to peoples north of Italy and even admitted some Gauls into the Senate. He also relied on ex-slaves to fill important positions in the imperial bureaucracy, reasoning that they would be more loyal to him than powerful senators would be. Claudius also finished some of Caligula's unfinished business by commencing the conquest of Britain in 43.

But Claudius also had domestic difficulties. In 48, his third wife Messalina was implicated in a conspiracy and executed, although their son Britannicus survived. Claudius then married his niece, another Agrippina, who had imperial ambitions for her own son, who took the name Nero after being adopted by Claudius. In 54, Claudius died, after eating poison mushrooms, some said. Agrippina then persuaded the Praetorian Guards to proclaim Nero as the next emperor. Young Britannicus survived only until the next year.

Nero (54–68)

Nero was only sixteen years old when he became emperor. He had had no administrative experience; indeed, his primary interests included singing accompanied by a lyre, acting, poetry, and chariot racing, and he regularly entered competitions in these fields, including the Olympic Games. He invariably won the crown of victory, even if, as in the case of the Olympics, he was thrown from his chariot. Such activities, frowned on by the Senate, endeared him to the general populace. In spite of his lack of aptitude for rule, Nero, like Caligula, began his reign auspiciously. Under the guidance of the philosopher Seneca and experienced administrators, informers were restrained, and the government ran efficiently. Soon, however, the situation worsened, as Nero increasingly gave ear to those who catered to his more prurient interests. In 64, a great fire destroyed a section of Rome just where Nero had wanted to build a new palace known as the Golden House. Seeking a scapegoat, Nero blamed the Christians, many of whom then were executed in what came to be known as the first imperial persecution of Christians. A senatorial conspiracy led by the senator Piso was squelched in the next year, and Seneca and many others were invited to commit suicide—an option that saved them from theatrical executions and preserved their property for their families.

Ultimately, problems with the army led to Nero's downfall. A revolt in Britain in 60 organized by Queen **Boudicca** was followed in 66 by the "Great Revolt" of the Jews. Both campaigns required large armies to be assembled under generals with no family connections to the imperial house. The British revolt was quickly suppressed, and, as in Spain, Gaul, and Pannonia, the occupation of Britain then proceeded relatively peacefully; but the revolt in Judaea dragged on. A revolt on the Rhine in 68 was subdued, but the Praetorian Guards then shifted their support to Galba, a governor in Spain. Nero fled to the countryside, where, assisted by a last loyal slave, he took the only honorable way out and committed suicide.

The Year of the Four Emperors

After the death of Nero, there were no family members left as obvious candidates for the throne, and the Roman Empire was up for grabs. According to Tacitus, the army now learned the "secret of Empire: that emperors could be made in other places than Rome," and the year 69 became known as the **Year of the Four Emperors**. The first claimant was Galba, but the Rhine legions refused to recognize him and nominated their own commander, Vitellius, instead. Meanwhile, at Rome, Galba's onetime supporter Otho bribed the Praetorian Guard to lynch him, and Otho immediately was recognized as emperor by the Senate. Soon thereafter, Vitellius' army arrived in northern Italy and defeated Otho, who committed suicide, and Vitellius was duly acknowledged as emperor. But meanwhile the eastern armies had named their own candidate, Vespasian, who had been ordered to suppress the revolt of the Jews. The powerful Danubian legions followed suit and seized Rome. Vitellius was killed, and Vespasian then was named emperor.

The Flavian Dynasty

Vespasian established the Flavian Dynasty (69–96), which consisted of himself and his two sons, Titus and Domitian. This marked the first father-to-son succession to the throne. Vespasian was a new kind of emperor. He was not descended from an old-line senatorial family, but rather came from an Italian equestrian background and had risen to power in the army. The Flavian Dynasty thus represents an opening up of all of the political and military offices, even the emperorship, to an increasingly broader spectrum of individuals.

The triumphal arch erected by the emperor Titus in commemoration of the suppression of the Jewish revolt depicts the sack of the Jewish temple in Jerusalem, including the carrying off of the great seven-branched Menorah and the Table of Showbread, or offering table.

Vespasian (69–79)

By building a Forum of Peace at Rome, Vespasian, like Augustus before him, portrayed himself as one who had brought peace to the Roman world after a period of civil war. But the most enduring monument constructed by the Flavians was the Flavian Amphitheater, or Colosseum.

Vespasian and his sons were competent administrators. Their reign saw an expansion of the professional bureaucracy. Secretarial and finance work now tended to be done by knights rather than by ex-slaves. This bureaucracy eventually became large and entrenched enough to be able to survive relatively catastrophic changes at the top. At the same time, the status of the Senate continued an inexorable decline. The emperors' consultations came to have more show than substance. The increasing incorporation of non-Italians and proven administrators, who were beholden to the emperors, meant that the Senate had less internal cohesiveness and fewer anti-imperial sentiments.

Titus and Domitian (79–96)

Vespasian (69–79) was succeeded by his popular but short-lived son Titus (79–81), who had been left with the task of suppressing the Jewish Revolt after his father had departed for Rome. In 70, he captured Jerusalem and destroyed the **Jewish temple**. Titus' reign also was marked by a massive eruption of Mt. Vesuvius that buried several cities, such as **Pompeii** and Herculaneum, on the Bay of Naples in Italy.

The Jewish temple in Jerusalem was never rebuilt, although its western foundations, called the "Wailing Wall," continue as the most sacred site in modern Judaism.

Titus was succeeded by his younger brother Domitian (81–96), a good administrator who was popular with the soldiers—he raised their pay to three hundred denarii—and the provincials. Under Domitian, the empire reached its farthest extent in Britain. In 84 CE, general Agricola was on the verge of conquering the last bit of Caledonia (Scotland) when he was recalled because of troubles on the Danube. The territory between the Rhine and Danube then was occupied and fortified and rendered mostly peaceful for the next 150 years.

In Rome, however, Domitian was not loved by the Senate, who saw him as excessively suspicious and autocratic. He was said to have liked being addressed as "lord and god." A failed revolt in 88 led to a return of the delators, and in 95 Domitian's two cousins were executed for conspiracy. In 96, his wife Domitia, fearing for her own safety, induced a palace servant to stab Domitian to death while he was engrossed in reading a report of a bogus conspiracy.

THE ANTONINE DYNASTY (96–192)

The **Antonine Dynasty**, also known as the period of the Adoptive Emperors or the **Five Good Emperors**, represented the period of the *Pax Romana* during which the Roman Empire was absolutely at its height. Peace prevailed from Scotland to the Nile cataracts, from Gibraltar to the Caucasus Mountains; the empire was well governed and economically prosperous, and it offered opportunities to residents of all sections of the empire. Indeed, Edward Gibbon, who in 1776 published *The Decline and Fall of the Roman Empire,* opined that this was the best time to have lived in the whole history of the world.

The Five Good Emperors

One of the reasons that the empire was well administered under the Antonines was that the first four had no blood sons, meaning that they could groom their successors and then adopt them to placate the army. The first five Antonine emperors thus went down in history as the Five Good Emperors.

Nerva (96–98)

After the assassination of Domitian, the Senate was prepared. It immediately granted imperial powers to the elderly senator Nerva (96–98) and affixed a decree of Damnation of Memory upon Domitian. Nerva, realizing that to survive he needed army support, adopted as his successor the popular army general Trajan (98–117), who duly succeeded him in 98. A native of Spain, Trajan was the first emperor of non-Italian origin, and power continued to

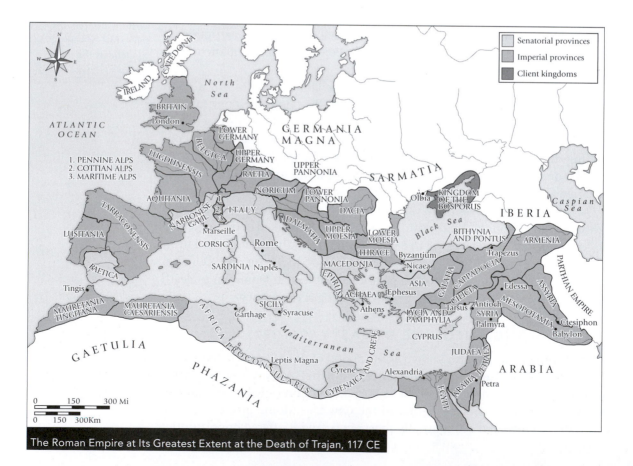

The Roman Empire at Its Greatest Extent at the Death of Trajan, 117 CE

diffuse out of Italy and into the provinces. Nerva and Trajan mark the beginning of a period in which emperors were chosen on the basis of their ability and were adopted by their predecessors in order to give the army the sons it loved.

Trajan (98–117)

Trajan was a popular emperor. He often consulted the Senate and received from it the title the Best Prince. His building program in Rome included the construction of a huge bath complex and the vast Trajan's Forum, which included a marketplace for the distribution of free food, a basilica, libraries, and a temple in his own name, anticipating his own deification. His reign was looked back on as the second Golden Age of the Roman Empire, the reign of Augustus having been the first. Trajan was the only emperor to undertake large-scale violations of Augustus' policy of nonexpansion. Between 101 and 107 he conducted two wars in Dacia (101–102 and 105–106 CE), on the north of the lower Danube River, and annexed it as a new province. In 115 he invaded the Parthian empire. He captured the capital city of Ctesiphon on the Tigris River and became the only Roman emperor to go wading in the Persian Gulf. He then created a new province of Mesopotamia. But Trajan then died unexpectedly in 117. His wife, Plotina, declared that just before his death Trajan had named another Spaniard, Hadrian, an experienced soldier and administrator, as his successor. This was a popular choice, and the claim went unchallenged.

Hadrian (117–138)

Hadrian (117–138) immediately returned to Augustus' policy of establishing strongly defended borders and avoiding adventures of foreign conquest. He made a treaty with Parthia that returned most of Trajan's conquests and gained very favorable trading privileges for Roman merchants. The exposed province of Dacia, however, was retained, for its gold mines were needed to replace the output of the depleted gold and silver mines of Spain, Egypt, and Anatolia. Hadrian spent much of his reign on the road, visiting nearly every province. He built a stone fortification known as Hadrian's Wall across northern Britain and another between the upper Rhine and Danube. He also suppressed the **Bar Kochba Revolt** (132–135), the second revolt of the Jews, in which the Jews went so far as to establish their own country. He adorned Rome with additional public buildings, including a Temple of Venus and Rome and the circular temple called the Pantheon, Greek for "All the Gods," not to

Hadrian constructed the Pantheon, or temple of "All the Gods," a round temple added to a porch built over a century earlier by Agrippa, the friend of Augustus.

AELIUS ARISTIDES, "PRAISE OF ROME"

During the Roman Empire, it was common for orators to present speeches to emperors on special occasions, such as birthdays or anniversaries of accession to power. These speeches not only expressed lavish praise and often said what the emperor wanted to hear but also expressed popular views of how influential individuals thought the empire was being or should be governed. One such orator was Aelius Aristides, a Greek orator who represented the Second Sophistic period of Greek literature. Many of the beneficiaries of these educational practices went on to serve in the imperial administration, giving imperial administrators a kind of common culture. Aristides' teacher Fronto was the teacher of the future emperor Marcus Aurelius, whose friend he himself later became, and he became the most famous orator of his age, traveling from city to city making speeches. In about 144 CE, Aristides delivered an oration called "Praise of Rome" to the emperor Antoninus Pius, with Marcus

In the British Empire of the nineteenth and early twentieth centuries, British overseas administrators shared the common classical culture taught them in the British "public" (actually private) school system

Aurelius probably also in attendance, in which he fulsomely praised the advantages and opportunities offered by Roman rule. In the course of his speech Aristides also expressed the growing commonplace that Rome in fact ruled, or ought to rule, the entire world.

> Far from being able to talk adequately about Rome, one cannot even get an adequate view. For what man could accurately take in so many hilltops comprised under the name of one city, so many tracts of plain built up, so much land enclosed? No one can say this immense city has not acquired the power that befits such size. If you look at the whole empire, you marvel at the city, to think that a tiny part rules all of the earth. But if you see the city herself, you can marvel no longer that the whole world is ruled by a city of this size. The empire has boundaries too far-flung to be belittled, or even for the area within them to be defined by measurement. Extensive and sizable as the empire is, perfect policing does much more than territorial boundaries to make

mention a new mausoleum for himself, all of the previous emperors having been interred in the tomb of Augustus.

The imperial bureaucracy continued to expand. Hadrian formalized the policy of using knights rather than ex-slaves in midlevel government posts in the central government and preferred to consult more with *amici* ("friends") and a private *consilium* ("council") made up of high officials and jurists rather than with the Senate. And when it came to the succession, Hadrian was a micro-manager. After his first choice, Lucius Aelius, died, Hadrian not only adopted the middle-aged senator Antoninus but he also required Antoninus to adopt both Aelius' eight-year-old son Lucius Verus and seventeen-year-old Marcus Aurelius Antoninus, a talented member of a distinguished senatorial family. Hadrian also required Antoninus to marry his daughter Faustina, when the time was right, to Verus.

it great. For there are no Mysians, Saka, Pisidians, or others usurping territory in the midst of the empire, whether by forcible invasion or unsuppressed revolt. The whole world speaks in unison, more distinctly than a chorus; and so well does it harmonize under this director-in-chief that it joins in praying this empire may last for all time. Like one continuous country and one race, all the world quietly obeys. Everything is carried out by command or nod, and it is simpler than touching a string. If a need arises, the thing has only to be decided on, and it is done. While your empire is so large and you rule it with so much statesmanship and authority, the following is by far your greatest triumph, and one quite peculiar to you: You are the only ones ever to rule over freemen. Your state is administered like a single city, and you choose governors for the whole world as if it were one city holding an election. They are to protect and care for the governed, not to be their masters. All come as though to a public market place where each will get fair measure. What a city is to its countryside and environs, this city is to the whole world. It is set up as the urban center, with the world for its countryside. You might say that all mankind lives on the outskirts of Rome, or in scattered country villages, and gets together at this one citadel. Rome has never said, "No more room!" Even as the earth's surface holds all men, so Rome takes them in from every country, like the sea welcoming the rivers. In your grandeur you have reckoned your state on a grand scale. You have not made it a world's wonder by conceit, by letting nobody else share in it. No, your effort has been to give it the population it deserves. You have made the word "Roman" apply not to a city but to a whole nationality. You have stopped classifying nationalities as Greek or barbarian, and have proclaimed a classification safe from ridicule, because you have produced a city-state more populous than the whole Greek race, so to speak. You have redivided mankind into Romans and non-Romans! So far have you extended your civic name. Under this classification, there are many in each town who are no less fellow-citizens of yours than of their own blood, though some of them have never seen this city.

Antoninus Pius (138–161)

On Hadrian's death in 138, **Antoninus** smoothly succeeded as emperor. He ruled over the Roman Empire during its most flourishing period and gave his name to the Antonine Dynasty. Another curious consequence of Antoninus' success is that little of interest to sensation-seeking historians occurred, and the historical record of Antoninus' reign thus is rather scanty. He demonstrated fiscal responsibility by cutting back on the extravagant building programs that had characterized the reigns of his predecessors. He was popular with the Senate, which granted him the epithet *Pius* ("The Dutiful"), a title that, like *Augustus*, was so popular that it also was adopted by many subsequent emperors. After his death, a temple honoring him and his wife Faustina was constructed in the Roman forum.

Marcus Aurelius (161–180)

Antoninus Pius was succeeded in 161 by his own adopted sons, **Marcus Aurelius** (161–180) and Lucius Verus (161–169), marking the first time the empire had been ruled by more than one emperor at the same time. Even though Marcus was the senior, and much more able, member of the partnership, he accorded Verus full equality in the rule. Marcus was devoted to Stoic philosophy, which inculcated the necessity of doing one's duty. He even composed a book called the *Meditations* that preserves some of his personal thoughts on what it meant to be emperor. He had little chance, however, for private reflection, because several problems arose that required his full attention. For one thing, the empire was afflicted by a devastating plague brought back from a Parthian War in the mid 160s. In 169, Verus died, leaving Marcus as sole emperor.

In addition, for the first time, there were significant threats on the northern frontier. Germanic peoples such as the Marcomanni and Quadi were seeking to move south of the Danube. Marcus was compelled to spend most of his reign on campaign. By 180, the Germans had been pushed back, and the frontier was again secure. Individual defeated barbarians were settled on depopulated Roman land in exchange for their military service. At the time of his death, Marcus was on the verge of creating two new provinces on the northern banks of the Danube and the Rhine, but his desire to fulfill Augustus' plan to shorten the northern frontier died with him.

The Evolution of Roman Law

The *Pax Romana* saw significant developments in Roman law as emperors assumed a personal role in issuing legislation, absorbing the Republican roles of the Senate, the popular assemblies, and the magistrates. At the beginning of the Principate, emperors introduced legislation by presenting an *oratio* (speech) to the Senate, which dutifully issued a Decree of the Senate that was rubber-stamped at a pro forma meeting of the Council of the People. But the popular assemblies soon lost all of their powers. The rights of the Centuriate Assembly to declare war, elect magistrates with imperium, and try cases were transferred to the emperor, Senate, and jury courts, respectively. The Council of the Plebs lost all power to the emperor by virtue of his tribunician power. And the Council of the People stopped meeting under Nerva. By the second century, moreover, approval of imperial legislation by the Senate was assumed, and the imperial *oratio* itself gained the force of law.

Private legal cases were streamlined by combining the action and judgment phases of a case into a single hearing before a judge appointed by a Roman magistrate such as a provincial governor. The administration of private law also became more complicated because of the need to maneuver through a welter of provincial legal customs according to which noncitizen provincials still functioned. In the provinces, criminal law was overseen by the provincial

THE DARK SIDE OF ROMANIZATION

The Romans were not loath to use violence to terrorize peoples who resisted them, as seen in this scene from the Column of Marcus Aurelius, in which defeated Germans are forced to decapitate each other.

In the past, historians customarily saw the creation of a common Greco-Roman culture in the Roman Empire as a process of Romanization whereby the benefits of Roman culture were happily assimilated by provincial populations. But two Jewish revolts suggest that not all the provincials were happy with Roman occupation. Indeed, the Romans themselves realized that the situation on the ground was not so simple. On several occasions, the historian Tacitus presented the other side. For example, in explaining why the Britons revolted under Boudicca in 60 CE after the death of King Prasutagus, he noted, "His kingdom was plundered by centurions, his house by slaves, as if they were the spoils of war. First, his wife Boudicca was scourged, and his daughters outraged. All the chief men of the Iceni, as if Rome had received the whole country as a gift, were stripped of their ancestral possessions, and the king's relatives were made slaves. Roused by these insults and the dread of worse, they flew to arms. It was against the veterans that their hatred was most intense. For these new settlers drove people out of their houses, ejected them from their farms, called them captives and slaves, and the lawlessness of the veterans was encouraged by the soldiers, who lived a similar life and hoped for similar license." And in his account of the Battle of the Graupian Mountain in Scotland in 84, Tacitus put words into the mouth of Caledonian leader Calgacus that again showed that peoples about to be incorporated into the empire might have a different perspective on the benefits of Roman rule: "There are no peoples beyond us, nothing indeed but waves and rocks, and the yet more terrible Romans, from whose oppression escape is vainly sought by obedience and submission. Robbers of the world, having by their universal plunder exhausted the land, they rifle the deep. If the enemy be rich, they are rapacious; if he be poor, they lust for dominion; neither the east nor the west has been able to satisfy them. Alone among men they covet with equal eagerness poverty and riches. To robbery, slaughter, plunder, they give the lying name of empire; they make a desert and they call it peace."

governor, whereas in Italy, the praetorian prefect began to assume criminal jurisdiction.

The Principate also saw the rise of legal scholars known as **jurists** who either authored commentaries on Roman law or served as legal advisers to emperors. If a jurist was approved by the emperor, his legal opinions or commentaries could be cited as precedents in courts of law. Hadrian, in an attempt to consolidate legal authority in the emperor's hands even further, removed from the praetor the right to issue new formulae and appointed the jurist Salvius Julianus to codify the Praetor's Edict into a standard, permanent format. In addition, every citizen had the right to appeal directly to the emperor, who responded to thousands of petitions a year. Thus, even more authority coalesced in the hands of the emperor. By the end of the Antonine Dynasty it was possible to say, as did the jurist Ulpian, that "whatever the emperor authorizes has the force of law." Imperial legal enactments, which had the generic name **constitutions**, included not only edicts—laws binding on the entire empire—but also mandates, instructions to imperial officials, decrees, decisions in court cases rendered by the emperor, and rescripts, replies to petitions.

The modern term constitution, *the general guiding legal principles of a country or organization, has a meaning quite different from the ancient term.*

The End of the Antonines

There were five good emperors, but there were six members of the Antonine Dynasty, the last of whom was problematic. Unlike his predecessors, Marcus Aurelius had a son, Commodus (180–192), whose claims to the throne could not be ignored. Like Domitian, Commodus was popular with the army and in the provinces. He made a favorable peace with the Germans and supported the rights of oppressed tenant farmers.

But Commodus also had a yen for luxurious living, including sponsoring extravagant circus and gladiatorial games, and his expenses could not be met by an empire still recovering from plague and invasion. He went so far as to portray himself as the Greek hero Hercules. His excesses led to plots against him. He responded by giving a ready ear to delators and by using *frumentarii*, imperial foragers, as a sort of secret police. In 192 his mistress, Marcia, and several high officials, afraid for their lives, induced a professional athlete to strangle Commodus in his bath. Once again the empire was left adrift.

This statue portrays the emperor Commodus wearing Hercules' lion skin and carrying Hercules' club. This kind of identification of living emperors with divinities was very unusual at this time but common a hundred years later.

THE WORLD OF THE *PAX ROMANA*

The *Pax Romana* fully manifested Augustus' promise to bring peace and prosperity to the Roman world. New opportunities became available to greater numbers of people for social advance, for economic prosperity, and even in religious worship.

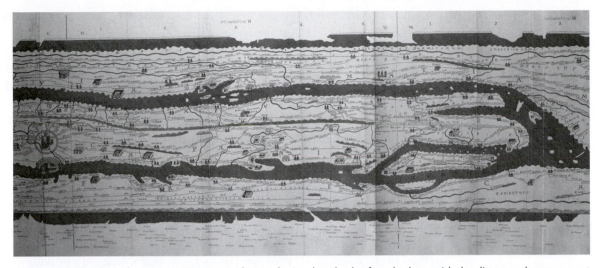

Peutinger Table, the only surviving Roman road map, depicts hundreds of roads along with the distances between rest stops from Britain to India. The Italian section shows the goddess Roma, representing the city of Rome, in a large circle at left, with Ostia, the port city of Rome, immediately below. The Apennine Mountains run the length of the peninsula. In this squeezed and flattened format, Greece is at the top and North Africa at the bottom.

Those living during this period would have had every reason to believe that the good fortune of the Roman Empire would last forever.

Society

By the end of the second century CE, Roman citizenship had been extended to as many as half of the free inhabitants of the empire. The Senate represented more of a cross-section of the population and now included many North Africans and Greeks along with Italians and other western Europeans. Non-Romans, such as Greeks and Syrians, benefited from the economic opportunities available in the free market provided by the *Pax Romana*. Segments of the population that had been lacking in privilege in the past gained new rights. Under Hadrian, for example, the old authority of the "father of the family" was weakened, and the status of women and slaves was improved.

Indeed, women came to have greater rights than in any ancient civilization. By the first century CE, marriages *sine manu* ("without authority"), in which women did not come under the legal jurisdiction of their husbands as was the case during the Republic, had become standard. Women retained control over their own property (usually their dowry) after the deaths of their fathers, and as a result a marriage consisted of not one but two economic units. Women also could manage their own property; they still needed a male to do the paperwork, but if one was not available, the court would appoint one. A divorce could be effected by a simple notification—saying "I divorce you" three times in front of witnesses—of a desire to dissolve the marriage. This is not to say, of course, that wives and husbands did not live amicably. Generally, women managed the household while their husbands oversaw business outside the home. Men often did not marry until after the age of thirty, but wealthy women, who would have slaves to assist them, married as young as twelve or thirteen and shared the rank and status of their husbands. They were well educated and participated in social and cultural activities as much as any man.

Slaves now were valued much more than they had been in the late Republic, for the wars of conquest and the days of cheap slaves were long gone. Regulations on one imperial estate worked by slaves stated that hospitals and baths were to be provided and that slave women were to be freed after bearing so many slave children. Indeed, by this time many imperial and senatorial estates were managed by slaves, for senators, too, found it to their advantage to leave their estates in the hands of a few trusted slaves.

The most visible aspects of Roman life during the *Pax Romana* were centered on the city. Urban life expanded immensely. Rome boasted a population of about one million, and Alexandria, Antioch, and Carthage each checked in at over a quarter of a million. On the frontiers, Roman garrison posts became cities such as Mainz, Strasbourg, Bonn, Vienna, Budapest, and Belgrade. Members of city councils, the decurions, manifested their civic responsibilities by vying with one another to endow their cities with amenities including theaters, amphitheaters, temples, town halls, libraries, and aqueducts. The emperors often contributed imperial assistance for public works projects, and army troops sometimes provided the labor. Sometimes, however, cities overspent on grandiose construction projects and fell into debt. If they were lucky, the emperor would bail them out.

The Economy

The *Pax Romana* also saw an expansion in manufacturing and commerce. Ease of travel by water, either by sea or by river, made it possible to ship small-value items great distances, and the Roman road system made land transport much less expensive. The unified currency system eliminated complicated monetary transactions. Tolls and port dues were low, banditry had been suppressed, and piracy had been virtually eliminated. Much of the trade was in the hands of easterners, resulting in a shift of the economic center of gravity of the empire toward the east.

Different regions came to be known for different kinds of manufactured products and trade goods. Italy and Gaul were known for their ceramics; Sidon in Phoenicia and northern Gaul were famous for glassblowing; Spain and Britain were centers of mining; and Britain also was a source of wool. Amber was imported from the Baltic Sea area, and exotic animals from sub-Saharan Africa. But the most extensive foreign trade was with the east, to India and even China. Roman gold, silver, glassware, fabrics, and wine were exchanged for gems, silks, spices, and perfumes. Trajan reopened a canal between the Nile River and the Red Sea, and every year over one hundred trading ships set out from Egypt for the east. The journey from Italy, through the canal, and on to India took about sixteen weeks. A second-century Indian poet wrote, "Drink the cool and fragrant wine brought by the Yavanas (Ionians) in their vessels." In 166, envoys claiming to be the representatives of the emperor "An-Tun," apparently a reference to Marcus Aurelius Antoninus, visited the Chinese court. One consequence of the eastern trade was a huge balance-of-payments deficit, which Pliny the Elder estimated at 550 million sesterces per year (enough to pay the annual expenses of the entire Roman army). The result was a growing scarcity of gold and silver in the empire that gradually made it more difficulty for the government to issue sufficient numbers of coins to meet its expenses.

The ancient canal from the Nile to the Red Sea silted up in the Middle Ages and was not reopened, as the Suez Canal, until 1869.

Even though the cities had great visibility, and in spite of the expansion in manufacturing and trade, the Roman economy remained essentially agricultural, and the great bulk of the population lived in rural areas. The cities always were parasites on the countryside. The second-century physician Galen, for example, reported that as a consequence of the great urban demand for foodstuffs, country dwellers sometimes were reduced to eating grass and acorns just to survive. The primary grain-growing areas were Egypt, North Africa, which was heavily irrigated, and Sicily. Each year a huge grain fleet departed from Alexandria and headed across the Mediterranean for Rome to help to meet Italy's insatiable need for grain. In addition, certain areas became known for particular kinds of agricultural products. Olive oil came from North Africa, Italy, and Spain; wine from Italy and southern Gaul; and a popular fish sauce known as *garum* from Spain.

Some farmland was held by small subsistence farmers, but huge *latifundia* were owned by senators. Initially, the *latifundia* were farmed mainly by a combination of slave and day labor, but by the second century tenant farmers known as **coloni** were increasingly used. They remitted a portion of their crops to the landowner and kept the rest for themselves. The biggest landowner was the emperor himself, whose estates grew ever larger as a result of purchases, bequests, and confiscations.

The Silver Age of Roman Literature

Latin literature continued to thrive. Whereas the literature of the late Republic and Augustan period is called Golden Age Latin, that of the remainder of the first and the second century is called the Silver Age. Many Silver Age writers came from outside Italy, reflecting the much more representative nature of the post-Augustan empire. The expansion of literary culture resulted partly from a growing state-sponsored education system, for the expanding imperial bureaucracy had a constant and growing need for educated civil servants. Grammarians and rhetoricians were funded by cities and the imperial government. The education was purely literary, with little exposure to science and mathematics. Law was the most popular field for advanced study: even if orators had much less opportunity to engage in politics than in the Republic, they still could argue cases in court or enforce the law as imperial administrators, and many silver-age writers practiced law at some point in their careers.

The Thracian slave Phaedrus wrote poetic fables under the first four Julio-Claudian emperors. Under Nero, Persius, a native of Etruria, wrote verse satire in the manner of Horace in which, among other things, he espoused Stoic philosophy and complained about a general decline in morality. Petronius, a member of Nero's court, was called Nero's "judge of elegance" and usually is identified as the author of a partly surviving novel, *The Satyricon*, which relates the attempts of Encolpius, an ex-gladiator, to keep his sixteen-year-old boyfriend Giton faithful to him. The *Satyricon* includes the famous "Trimalchio's Dinner," an account of the extravagant, but ultimately tedious, attempts of a social-climbing newly rich freedman to fit into Roman society. The rhetorician and philosopher Seneca, a Spaniard, wrote nine surviving tragedies, such as "The Madness of Hercules," and 124 letters on moral topics, such as "On Anger." In the late 40s he became the tutor of the young Nero, and early in Nero's reign was one of his chief advisers. And Lucan, a Spanish nephew of Seneca, initially was a good friend of Nero's and wrote an epic poem, the *Pharsalia*, about the war between Pompey and Caesar. In 66, Petronius, Lucan, and Seneca all were implicated in the conspiracy of Piso and allowed to commit suicide. Clearly, writers who interacted too closely with emperors were risking their lives.

Nevertheless, in the Flavian period, Latin writers continued to play with fire. The Spanish orator Quintilian wrote a rhetorical handbook, the *Institutes of Oratory*, and was made consul by the emperor Vespasian in acknowledgment of his efforts to educate the Roman governing class. Statius, the author of a book of occasional verse known as the *Silvae* ("Groves"), flourished during the reign of Domitian, who presented Statius with a golden crown. And Pliny the Elder, who rose from a cavalry commander in Germany to command of the Roman fleet stationed on the Bay of Naples, wrote a *History of the German Wars* and a *History of His Times*, both lost, and a surviving massive thirty-seven-book *Natural History* that summarized all of ancient knowledge, including geology, geography, zoology, botany, agriculture, architecture, and medicine. Along the way, Pliny added his own pithy observations, such as, "by a marvelous disease of the human intellect, it pleases us to record bloodshed and slaughter in histories, so that the wickedness of men might become known to those who are ignorant of the real world." During the eruption of Vesuvius in August of 79, Pliny accompanied ships from the Roman fleet on a rescue mission, and in the course of his scientific observations he was asphyxiated by the volcanic gases. Other practical writers included Columella on agriculture and Frontinus on aqueducts, not to mention Vitruvius, who wrote on architecture a century earlier.

In the modern day, the most explosive volcanic eruptions are termed Plinian eruptions.

Pliny the Younger, the nephew and adopted son of Pliny the Elder, advanced through the Republican magistracies and became consul in 100 CE. He subsequently served on the *consilium* of Trajan and died while serving as governor of Bithynia and Pontus. He is known primarily for a panegyric, or speech of praise, in honor of Trajan and for a collection of nine books of personal and official letters, which provide priceless insights into both private lives and administrative procedures during this period. His most famous two letters describe the eruption of Vesuvius and his own soul-searching about whether or not to prosecute Christians in 112.

Under the early Antonine emperors, writers who had felt inhibited under emperors such as Nero and Domitian felt that they could express themselves more freely. Tacitus, arguably the greatest of Roman historians, held several traditional Republican senatorial offices and married Julia, the daughter of the famous general Agricola. After being implicated himself in some of Domitian's purges, Tacitus, drawing on the histories of Pliny, turned to writing history under the Antonines. Surviving works include the *Germania*, a sympathetic account of the peoples and customs of Germany; the *Agricola*, a biography of his father-in-law; and longer historical narratives—the *Annals*, going from the death of Augustus to the death of Nero, and the *Histories*, covering the Flavian period. Tacitus carefully researched his source material, but although he claimed to be writing *"sine ira et studio"* ("without rancor or favoritism"), he pitched his presentation is such a way so as to make clear his general unhappiness with how the empire was governed. Like the Greek historian Thucydides, Tacitus provides insights into the nature of the acquiring and wielding of power and has little confidence that powerful persons, such as emperors, will do the right thing. Tacitus also believed that the Senate was largely complicit in the whittling away of Roman liberties.

Outspoken in another way was Suetonius, who served as directory of the imperial archives under Trajan and as personal secretary to Hadrian. He therefore had access to a full range of imperial documents, which he put to good use in his *On the Life of the Caesars*, biographies of rulers from Julius Caesar through Domitian that overlap with much of Tacitus' material. Although Suetonius cites a wealth of detail, he also retails a great deal of salacious court gossip. Yet another outspoken writer was the satirist Juvenal, who may have lived into the reign of Hadrian. Juvenal criticized Roman customs and morals, sometimes in such an extravagant way that it is difficult to assess how much he should be believed. For example, he described the influx of easterners into Rome as "the waters of the Orontes [a river in Syria] flowing into the Tiber."

From later in the second century comes another writer of possible African origin, Aulus Gellius, whose work *Attic Nights*, written ca. 170 CE, is a collection of literary extracts, many from authors who do not survive, made for his children. It provides precious insight into literary life and literary education at this time. At about the same time, the North African lawyer and writer Apuleius composed the only Latin novel to survive in full, a bawdy farce known variously as the *Metamorphoses* or the *Golden Ass,* in which a certain Lucius experiments with magic, is turned into an ass, and has a series of adventures. The grammarian Fronto, yet another North African, gained fame as an orator and became the teacher of Marcus Aurelius and Lucius Verus, being rewarded with a consulate in 142. Fronto is best known for his surviving private correspondence with Antoninus Pius, Lucius Verus, and Marcus Aurelius, which paints a sympathetic picture of the relations between a teacher and his imperial pupils and patrons.

In the Greek east, the writers of this period represent the Second Sophistic period (harking back to the first Greek sophists of the fifth century BCE) of Greek literature, representing a return to a higher standard of education and rhetorical exposition. Around 100 CE, for example, **Plutarch**, a native of Greece, wrote *Moralia* ("Customs"), a collection of seventy-eight works dealing with matters such as "Brotherly Affection" and "On Peace of Mind," but he is best known as the most famous biographer of antiquity: his *Parallel Lives* contain comparative biographies of famous Greeks and Romans, such as Alexander the Great compared with Julius Caesar. In the mid-second century, Arrian of Nicomedia, a Roman governor and general, wrote the most thorough surviving account of the life of Alexander the Great. Appian of Alexandria, a lawyer who argued cases before emperors, wrote a *Roman History* covering Rome's wars from the founding of Rome until Trajan's Dacian wars. And Lucian of Samosata in Anatolia wrote wildly popular satires, such as "Praise of a Fly," "The Rooster's Dream," and "The Sky-Man," about a man who made a pair of wings, flew up to the gods, and discovered that Zeus intended to destroy all philosophers.

RELIGION AND THE RISE OF CHRISTIANITY

Religions always had had a place of prime importance in the lives of ancient peoples. This remained the case during the Roman Empire, which saw the development and rise of one of the most significant religious movements in the history of the world, Christianity. During the first few centuries of its existence, Christianity had some difficult times with the Roman government, but, even so, there were those who argued that without the existence of the Roman Empire, Christianity never could have grown to become the most influential religion that the Mediterranean world had ever seen.

Traditional Religious Practices

As was the case throughout antiquity, there were two fundamental kinds of religion in the Roman world: state religion and personal religion. During the Roman Empire, state religion focused on the imperial cult, participation in which was one's way of pledging allegiance to the empire and the emperor. As *pontifex maximus,* the emperor was responsible for maintaining the *pax deorum* (peace with the gods), which entailed carrying out appropriate sacrifices, such as the *suovetauralia,* the sacrifice of a pig, a ram, and a bull, before the army set out on campaign. In addition, an increasing catalogue of deified emperors could be depended on to continue to watch over the well-being of the empire.

Personal religion was much more varied. The Hellenistic mystery cults, such as those of Isis and Cybele, maintained their popularity, although in the case of Cybele, the staid Romans preferred to substitute bulls' testicles for their own as an offering. These were joined by the cult of the Persian god sun god **Mithras**, the origins of which have aroused much controversy. Some would argue that the cult of Mithras was directly descended from the sun god Mithras, who was part of the Zoroastrian pantheon of the old Persian Empire and whose continued worship in the Hellenistic period was reflected in the royal name *Mithridates* ("Given by Mithras"). But given that the first solid evidence for Mithraism in the Roman world does not first appear until the first century CE and comes almost exclusively from the western Mediterranean, it also has been suggested that Mithraism as a mystery cult was essentially a Roman invention based on Roman understandings of eastern religions.

In this relief from Rome, the emperor Marcus Aurelius, veiled and acting as *Pontifex maximus,* sacrifices a bull in front of the temple of Capitoline Jupiter in Rome.

Initiates into Mithraism met in an underground shrine known as a Mithraeum, and much of what little can be deduced about Mithraic theology is inferred from the Tauroctony ("bull killing"), a standard depiction of Mithras slaying a sacred bull in a cave. Other scenes show the sun god Helius kneeling before Mithras, Mithras and Helius sharing a meal of bull parts, and Mithras riding to heaven in a chariot. Mithraism demanded lifetime participation and thus was different from other mystery cults that required no more than a few days of initiation rituals. Seven degrees of initiation, ranging from Corax ("raven") to Miles ("soldier") to Pater ("father"), gave worshippers greater ranks and privileges in the cult. The initial stage included a simulated murder of the initiate, which reinforced the salvific aspects of the cult, followed by baptism and a communal meal. Before moving up in rank, the initiate was required to meet tests of endurance, including not only ritual flogging, but also water, fire, cold, hunger, and thirst. Initiates believed they were guaranteed immortality, for after death they would be judged by Mithras himself, whose tests they already had passed. For several reasons, the cult was especially popular in the Roman army: it only admitted men; the slaying of the bull was a brave manly activity; and soldiers related to a religion that offered an afterlife based on the continued exercise of virtue, as opposed to a one-time initiation. Small Mithraic shrines holding no more than a hundred worshippers became a common attribute of military bases, especially in Europe.

Other kinds of personal religious practices, of course, continued to include magic and astrology. Of the philosophical schools, stoicism, with its focus on duty and responsibility, had the greatest attraction for the Roman ruling elite. In addition, by the third century there was a growing sense that all of the traditional gods were representatives of a single overarching deity. It was especially common to see the sun as the manifestation of this "**pagan monotheism**."

Judaism in the Roman World

The most structured personal religion continued to be Judaism, and in the Jews' organization lay potential problems for the imperial government, for the Jews manifested occasional signs of discontent. A passage from the Jewish Talmud, a guidebook for Jewish life, portrays a divergence of Jewish opinion about Rome: "Rabbi Judah said, 'How excellent are the deeds of this nation. They have instituted market places, they have instituted bridges, they have instituted baths.' Rabbi Simeon ben Yohai answered, 'All that they have instituted they have instituted only for their own needs. They have instituted market places to place harlots in them, baths for their own pleasure, bridges to collect toll.'" In general, the Roman government was tolerant of Jewish religious sensibilities and, based on their traditional and well-known monotheistic beliefs, exempted the Jews from making sacrifices to the emperors and to Rome. Nonetheless, the Jews were the only annexed people who ever engaged in large-scale organized resistance to Rome, in 66 and again in the Bar Kochba revolt in 132, in which the Jews reestablished their own separate nation. But the Jews could not hope to resist the might of the imperial armies, and after the suppression of the revolt, thousands of Jews were expelled from Judaea, resulting in an expansion of the Jewish diaspora throughout the Mediterranean world.

The Origins of Christianity

It was in this heterogeneous religious context, in a world of peace, prosperity, and easy communications for thousands of miles, that a new religion arose in the early years of the Roman Empire: Christianity. The Roman client king Herod (41 BCE–4 CE) ruled the Jews during a period when many Jews were expecting the arrival of a messiah, the **Christ** ("the anointed one"), who would lead them to glory. One of several who were identified as such was **Jesus of Nazareth**, a distant descendent of the Hebrew King David. Jesus' teachings that he was the son of God, that the kingdom of God was open to all equally, including the unprivileged, and that the old covenant with Yahweh now was to be replaced by a new covenant based on faith in God, brought the enmity of the Sanhedrin, the Jewish governing council, who saw him as a frightening revolutionary. Although he was found innocent of the charges against him by the Roman prefect **Pontius Pilate**, Pilate nonetheless consented to his execution ca. 27 CE in order to avoid offending the fractious Jews. After he rose from the dead, it was said, Jesus' followers, who came to be known as Christians, that is, the followers of Christ, continued to proselytize on his behalf.

The early Christians retained much in common with their Jewish forebears. They prospered in urban environments: soon, many large cities had Christian communities led by a **bishop**. They had an ethical and moral code for guiding one's life. They preserved their beliefs in written scriptures, now known as the **New Testament**. And Christianity provided a social support system for the underprivileged and a community that held regular communal worship services. Unlike Jews, however, Christians competed with non-Christian mystery cults with their promise of a happy life after death. Their concept of forgiveness for sins also was very popular. And, under the leadership of the apostle Paul, Christians opened up conversion to gentiles, or non-Jews. Doing so gave Christianity the potential to become an empire-wide religion embracing all of the manifold peoples of the empire.

Initially, the Romans had a hard time distinguishing Christians from Jews, and they took little notice of them. In the Roman sources, the earliest possible surviving reference to Christians comes from the Suetonius, who reported that during the reign of Claudius, "The Jews made disturbances at the instigation of Chrestus" and were expelled from Rome. Their next appearance comes in Tacitus' account of how Nero accused them of setting the "great fire" in Rome in 64 and severely punished them. The general Roman population also had many misconceptions about Christian worship, believing, for example, that they were cannibals because they ate the flesh and drank the blood of their god and that they practiced incest because they called each other "brother" and "sister."

The Christians and Rome

Once the Romans realized that Christians were not Jews, problems sometimes arose. Many Christians, as a consequence of their belief in only a single god, refused to participate in the state loyalty exercise, which involved sacrificing to the state gods. This was viewed by the government as

> ### HISTORICAL CAUSALITY
>
> To what extent do you think that the spread of Christianity was affected by the nature of the Roman Empire at the time it arose?

This graffito from Rome depicting a donkey-headed man being crucified reads "Alexamenos worshipping his god" and reflects the popular misconceptions about Christians that circulated in the first century CE.

high treason, and Christians were accused of "superstition," that is, of not believing in the gods. In addition, the tendency of Christians, unlike participants in polytheistic religions, to worship in private, out of the public view, led to their being seen as a secret society engaged in subversive activities.

In spite of these perceptions, the Roman government was generally tolerant of the Christians, and action was taken against them only rarely. Circa 111, for example, Pliny the Younger, the Roman governor of Bithynia and Pontus, consulted the emperor Trajan regarding how to deal with several Christians he had apprehended. Trajan responded that they were not to be sought out and that anonymous accusations were to be ignored. Christian **apologists** such as Justin Martyr and Athenagoras of Athens, many of them converts from polytheistic religions, rebutted misconceptions about the Christians in tracts addressed to the emperors. In an "Apology" of 197 CE, for example, the African Tertullian complained, "If the Tiber rises too high or the Nile too low, the cry is 'The Christians to the lions.'"

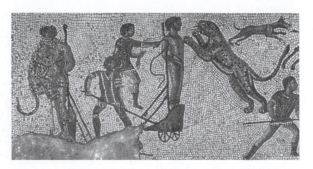

This mosaic of ca. 200 CE from Zliten in North Africa shows the kind of punishment reserved for noncitizens—such as most Christians—sentenced to death.

The occasional spates of prosecutions of Christians came to be known as **persecutions**. Some Christians suffered torture or were sentenced to the mines and became known as confessors. Others were executed and became **martyrs**, with many dying in the arena, because Christians often were of low social status, although those who held Roman citizenship, like the apostle Paul, were sent to Rome for trial and suffered an honorable beheading on conviction. Both martyrs and confessors often were recognized as Christian **saints** in recognition of their steadfastness in their faith. The court records of their trials were sometimes preserved and served as the basis for popular biographies known as saints' lives, which provided models for how to lead a Christian life. As of the late second century, however, there was still no indication that Christianity would ever be much more than just another eastern fertility cult.

LOOKING AHEAD

Until the late second century, the history of Rome and the Roman Empire had been one of increasing consolidation of authority over an expanded Mediterranean world that extended to Scotland in the northwest and Arabia in the southeast. This consolidation brought with it a concomitant extension of social status and economic opportunity to all persons living under Roman authority, creating a degree of social, cultural, and political unity never before seen in the ancient world. As of the year 192, the Roman Empire looked deceptively stable. A few civil wars and barbarian invasions had been quite easily weathered. The economy was sound, the administration efficient. But forces had been at work that were undermining the Principate as it had been established by Augustus, and few living at the end of the second century would have guessed that there were some very tough times coming.

FURTHER READING

Anderson, G. *The Second Sophistic: A Cultural Phenomenon in the Roman Empire.* London and New York: Routledge, 1993.

Ando, Clifford. *Imperial Ideology and Provincial Loyalty in the Roman Empire.* Berkeley University of California Press, 2000.

Balsdon, J. P. V. D. *Roman Women: Their History and Habits.* Westport, CT: Greenwood Press, 1962.

Bauman, R. *Women and Politics in Ancient Rome.* New York: Routledge, 1992.

Champlin, Edward. *Fronto and Antonine Rome.* Cambridge, MA: Harvard University Press, 1980.

Duthoy, Robert. *The Taurobolium: Its Evolution and Terminology.* Leiden, Netherlands: Brill, 1969.

Fishwick, D. *The Imperial Cult in the Latin West: Studies in the Ruler Cult of the Western Provinces of the Roman Empire,* 4 vols. New York: Brill, 1987.

Gradel, Ittai. *Emperor Worship and Roman Religion.* Oxford: Oxford University Press, 2002.

Keay, S., and N. Terrenato, eds. *Italy and the West: Comparative Issues in Romanization.* Oxford: Oxbow, 2001.

Lambert, R. *Beloved and God: the Story of Hadrian and Antinous.* New York: Viking, 1984.

MacMullen, Ramsay. *Enemies of the Roman Order: Treason, Unrest and Alienation in the Empire.* New York: Routledge, 1993.

Millar, Fergus. *The Emperor in the Roman World.* London: Duckworth, 2003.

Price, J. J. *Jerusalem under Siege: The Collapse of the Jewish State.* Leiden, Netherlands: Brill, 1992.

Severy, Beth. *Augustus and the Family at the Birth of the Roman Empire.* Oxford: Routledge, 2003.

Smallwood, E. Mary. *The Jews under Roman Rule. From Pompey to Diocletian.* Leiden, Netherlands: Brill, 2001.

Webster, Graham. *The Roman Imperial Army of the First and Second Centuries* A.D. Norman: University of Oklahoma Press, 1998.

Webster, J., and N. Cooper, *Roman Imperialism: Post-Colonial Perspectives.* Leicester, UK: University of Leicester Press, 1996.

Whitmarsh, Timothy. *The Second Sophistic.* Cambridge: Cambridge University Press, 2006.

Zanker, P. *The Power of Images in the Age of Augustus,* trans. A. Shapiro. Ann Arbor: University of Michigan Press, 1990.

THE WORLD OF LATE ANTIQUITY

CHAPTER 12

CRISIS AND RECOVERY

The Formation of the
Late Roman Empire
(192–337)

Beginning in the third century, the homogeneous world of the Roman Empire began to disintegrate as a result of economic, political, and military problems that the Roman government found increasingly difficult to deal with. A fifty-year Imperial Crisis that brought a breakdown of the hard-won unity that had been created over the previous two centuries finally was brought to an end when Diocletian and Constantine reestablished the empire in a new form. The **Late Roman Empire** was very different from the Principate, and the changes it brought marked the onset of **Late Antiquity**, the fourth and final phase of the ancient world. The world of Late Antiquity would be characterized by the breakdown of the unity of the Mediterranean world that had evolved ever since the days of the ancient Phoenicians and Greeks. At the same time, many of the defining characteristics of the modern world, such as the genesis of western European nations and the appearance and expansion of new religious movements, such as Christianity and Islam, also are to be sought here.

THE SEVERAN DYNASTY
(193–235)

Commodus had failed to name a successor, and after his assassination in 192 there were no obvious candidates for the throne. So once again, as after the death of Nero in 68, the empire was up for grabs. The lack of a constitutional method for choosing new emperors meant that a series of claimants arose all around the empire. The eventual victor, the Libyan Septimius Severus, instituted policies that made it clear that the empire as it had been established by Augustus had become less and less relevant to the social and political realities of the time.

TABLE 12.1	DYNASTIES AND RULERS (193–275)

Severan Dynasty

Septimius Severus (193–211)

Caracalla (211–217)

Macrinus (217–218) (usurper)

Elagabalus (218–222)

Severus Alexander (222–235)

Imperial Crisis (selected)

Maximinus the Thracian (235–238)

Philip the Arab (244–249)

Trajan Decius (249–251)

Valerian (253–260)

Gallienus (253–268)

Soldier Emperors (selected)

Claudius II Gothicus (268–270)

Aurelian (270–275)

The Severan tondo, one of the few panel paintings to survive from antiquity, shows the Severan family ca. 200: the empress Julia Domna and emperor Septimius Severus stand behind their sons, the Caesars Geta and Caracalla. Geta's face has been obliterated because he suffered "damnation of memory" after being murdered by his brother.

Jockeying for Power

The choice of Commodus' assassins fell on Pertinax, an old lieutenant of Marcus Aurelius. Pertinax, however, attempted to restore discipline among the Praetorian Guards and was murdered early in 193. The Guards then sank to a new low and auctioned off the emperorship. The high bidder was Didius Julianus, whose only qualification lay in being filthy rich. He paid each guardsman twenty-five thousand sesterces (the modern equivalent of about $250,000) for the dubious privilege of becoming emperor during these troubled times.

At this, the frontier legions became disgusted and named their own candidates: Clodius Albinus in Britain, Septimius Severus on the Danube, and Pescennius Niger in Syria. Severus dashed on Rome and demanded recognition from the Senate. The senator and historian Dio Cassius, who was present, later reported, "Silius Messala, who was then Consul, assembled us. We thereupon sentenced Julianus to death, named Severus emperor, and bestowed divine honors upon Pertinax." Thus proper procedures were followed in this case and other similar ones, and the praetorians then murdered the hapless Julianus. After disingenuously designating Albinus as his successor by giving him the rank of **Caesar**, or junior emperor, Severus headed off to the east where he defeated Niger. He then returned west and in 197 polished off his erstwhile ally Albinus. Severus then created the **Severan Dynasty** (193–235).

The Reign and Policies of Septimius Severus

Severus faced several problems in attempting to consolidate his authority. For one thing, he had no connection to the previous dynasties, although he attempted to remedy that issue by having himself posthumously adopted by Marcus Aurelius, giving himself and his sons the name Antoninus. He also was definitely not what the Italian senators had in mind. He was a native of Libya, he had been a mere knight before gaining senatorial rank, and his wife, Julia Domna, came from Syria. The snobbish Romans made fun of his Libyan-accented Latin. In addition, many senators had preferred the more cultured Albinus. Severus' career had been solely in the army, and he understood very well where his real support lay.

Severus, therefore, had little reason to cooperate with the Senate, and the carefully maintained united front presented by the emperor and the Senate began to crumble. Severus created several new provinces (by subdividing existing ones) and army units, placing knights rather than senators in charge of them. Senators accused of crimes lost the right to be tried before the Senate; they now were heard before the praetorian prefect, who assumed legal jurisdiction over all of Italy. Severus also packed more provincials into the Senate; by the end of his reign, it was only about one-third Italian and even less cohesive than before. As the status of the Senate declined, the empire became more and more an open military dictatorship. One of the consequences of the emperor's distancing himself from the partnership with the Senate was that many senators no longer saw the empire as acting in their best interests. As a consequence, there was an increasing tendency for senators to withdraw their own support from the state and to pursue purely local interests and to consolidate their local authority.

In 208, Severus traveled to Britain to deal with local unrest. After advancing into Scotland and repairing Hadrian's Wall, he withdrew to York, where he died in 211. His last words were, "Anything else to do? Give it here!" He was succeeded by his sons Marcus Aurelius Antoninus, better known by his nickname Caracalla (the word for a long Gallic cloak) and Geta, whom he already had named Caesar. This marked the first time that an emperor had been succeeded by multiple natural sons at the same time. Later in the year, however, Caracalla, the elder son, murdered his younger brother.

A Restive Army

Severus bequeathed to his sons an empire that once again had well-protected borders and was financially solvent. But he also left the seeds of some serious problems, one of which involved the army. By the Severan period, the army had assumed a different character from the army of Augustus. Few Italians enlisted anymore. The army became heavily provincialized, with large numbers of recruits coming from the hinterlands of the Rhine and Danube rivers. To meet chronic manpower shortages, emperors increasingly recruited barbarian units from across the frontiers. The soldiers had little in common with their educated and cultured senatorial commanders and often went out of control. Emperors who wished to remain in power would have to know how to maintain control over their increasingly unruly troops.

Severus reportedly advised his two sons to "treat the soldiers well, despise everybody else." He followed his own advice by extending several privileges to soldiers. He allowed them to marry while still in service. This made them happier, but it also made them less mobile, for they became reluctant to leave home and travel to some far-flung sector of the empire. He recruited the Praetorian Guard from provincials instead of from Italians. And he raised army salaries from 300 to 500 denarii a year.

> **LEARNING FROM HISTORY**
>
> Government actions often can have disastrous effects on the economy, and manipulating the quality of the coinage and the money supply can have consequences that go far beyond the initial intentions of such actions. The Severan monetary experiments brought inflation and financial collapse. Can you think of any times in the modern day when the value of the money has been compromised because the amount of money in circulation was dramatically increased by a government? What can happen as a result?

Caracalla (211–217) continued this trend by raising the salaries to 750 denarii per year. These increases were far more than the imperial treasury could bear.

Financial Collapse

The Roman Empire operated on a mandated balanced budget. There was no national debt and no paper money. Expenditures, primarily in silver, simply could not exceed income. And income, based primarily on the land tax, was essentially constant: the best that it could do was to remain the same. Until the reign of Severus, emperors, perhaps only by sheer good fortune, had been able to live within their financial limits. But the exorbitant pay increases granted by Severus and Caracalla broke the bank. The soldiers' salaries, the major imperial expenditure, had more than doubled, but there were no large new sources of income in sight.

In 212, Caracalla did his best to make up the difference by issuing the **Antonine Constitution**, a law that made all the inhabitants of the empire, except for slaves and certain freedmen, into Roman citizens. He did so not from a far-seeing desire to make everyone equal under the law but for more mundane reasons. For one thing, only citizens were required to pay certain kinds of taxes, such as an inheritance tax, which made the citizenship grant a moneymaking initiative. In addition, by now so many Romans were already citizens anyway that making nearly everyone a citizen streamlined civil legal processes that otherwise would have had to take into account differences in legal status between citizens and provincials. In addition, from the perspective of criminal law, Roman citizenship no longer determined how a person was treated, for another kind of legal distinction had taken its place. A person now was automatically classified either as one of the *honestiores*, "more distinguished people" (senators, knights, decurions, and soldiers), or as one of the *humiliores*, "more humble people" (everyone else). If arrested, *honestiores* retained the right of appeal to the emperor and could not be tortured. If convicted of a capital crime, they suffered a simple execution rather than being thrown to the wild beasts in the arena.

To deal with the monetary crisis, the emperors had no choice but to **debase** the currency, that is, to mix copper in with the silver. Caracalla, after his 50 percent pay increase to the soldiers, realized he could not add more copper, as this would make the debasement even more obvious, so he came up with an ingenious solution that permitted him to pay out the increase without

An antoninianus of Julia Domna issued ca. 215 gives to her the same titles, "Pia, Felix, Augusta," given to male emperors, attesting to the status of Severan women. The reverse legend, "Venus the Ancestress," asserts Julia's almost divine origins. The antoninianus' value as a double denarius was indicated by a radiate solar crown for men and by a crescent moon under the bust for women.

further debasing the coinage: he issued a new coin called the **antoninianus** (after his name, Antoninus) that was officially valued at two denarii but only weighed as much as 1½ denarii. These measures fooled no one, and as the weight and silver content of the coins decreased, so did their value. Perhaps the emperors anticipated and were willing to accept this on the assumption that the drop in value would be balanced by the increase in salary. But what they would not have foreseen was the effect of pouring into circulation more than double the accustomed number of coins every year. This brought the law of supply and demand into play: as money became more and more plentiful than goods and services, the value of the goods and services increased and the value of the money decreased, resulting in spiraling inflation. Nor would the emperors have anticipated that Gresham's Law, a modern economic proposition that "bad money drives good money out of circulation," would go into effect: people hoarded the older good silver coins and paid their taxes with the new debased ones. The result was that when the incoming coins were melted down to make new coins, there was less and less actual silver to use. In addition, another unforeseen factor was that as the value of the silver coinage plummeted, it no longer served to shore up the value of the fiduciary bronze coinage, which soon lost all of its good faith value and eventually stopped being issued altogether.

In the modern day, money has no intrinsic value at all, and its value comes from government manipulation of the money supply.

All of these factors resulted in financial disaster for the Roman government. Accelerating cycles of debasement and inflation irretrievably ruined the old Roman coinage system based on the silver denarius. By mid-century, the silver coinage had fallen to 5 percent silver. This meant that the soldiers' salaries, rather than being increased, became nearly worthless: soldiers complained that they spent their entire salary on a single purchase. The only remaining money of any value was the gold coinage, which was distributed only in the form of donatives on the accession of a new emperor. It would not be long before the soldiers put this knowledge to use.

Local administrative and economic problems also were exacerbated by the expanding financial catastrophe. Cities had been overspending and misspending as a consequence of poor management and the lack of an effective accounting system. Many had undertaken massive building projects, such as amphitheaters, aqueducts, and baths, that they could not complete. The emperors often were called on to step in. They often made up the shortfall, resulting in another expense to the treasury, and appointed curators to oversee the city's finances. This fed the increasing bureaucratization of the government.

Another problem involved tax collection, which was a responsibility of the decurions. In the case of shortfalls, the decurions had to make up the difference. In addition, what had once been voluntary municipal philanthropy by the mid-second century had become mandatory, a burden on the members of city councils. As a result, being a decurion sometimes was no longer the great honor it once had been, and decurions increasingly looked for ways to

THE HISTORY LABORATORY

THE DEBASEMENT OF THE SILVER COINAGE

In the past, emperors had debased the coinage on a small scale without doing any harm to the value of the money, but Severus reduced the coinage to only 50 percent silver, creating gray-colored denarii as opposed to shiny silver ones. Later emperors were forced to debase the coinage even further. Chemical analysis of Roman silver coins of the third century graphically depicts the effect of debasement on the silver content of the coins. Up until 192, the denarius retained its old quality of nearly 90 percent silver, but the debasement caused by Severus' massive military pay increase quickly brought the silver content down almost to only 50 percent. Caracalla's sleight of hand with the antoninianus meant that he, and the immediately following emperors, could hold the line for a time at 50 percent, but soon thereafter there commenced a catastrophic decline to only about 5 percent silver by the year 260. As a consequence, the once mighty denarius lost nearly all of its purchasing power.

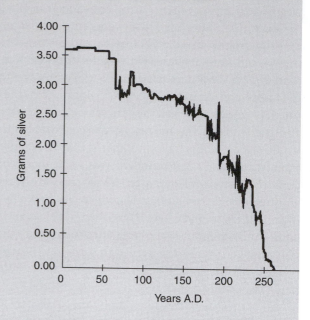

Emperor	Date	Total Weight	Purity	Wt. of Silver
Pertinax	193	3.16 gms.	87.0%	2.75 gms.
Septimius Severus	196–211	3.22 gms.	56.5%	1.81 gms.
Caracalla	212–217	3.23 gms.	51.5%	1.66 gms.
Macrinus	217–218	3.15 gms.	58.0%	1.82 gms.
Elagabalus	219–222	3.05 gms.	46.5%	1.41 gms.

The decline in value of the silver money brought with it rampant inflation. As debasement increased, the value of the money declined, and prices consequently increased. In the modern day, U.S. currency went off the silver standard in 1964, when paper money was no longer exchangeable for silver. It was at about the same time that inflation in the United States took off and was brought back under control only when the government learned to balance the amount of money in circulation against the availability of goods and services that the money could purchase.

evade their responsibilities. The injudicious Severan military salary increases therefore had far-reaching effects that contributed to the ruin of the Roman economy in many different venues.

Imperial Women and Boy Emperors

In 217, Caracalla was assassinated by a conspiracy of ambitious army officers. The praetorian prefect Macrinus (217–218) became emperor, marking the first time that a knight had done so. To indicate his disdain for the Senate, Macrinus did not even bother to request recognition from the Senate. But the dynastic principle soon reasserted itself. Severus' wife, **Julia Domna**, and her sister, Julia Maesa, passed off Maesa's fourteen-year-old grandson, Elagabalus, a pleasure-loving priest who had taken the name of the eastern sun god Elagabal, as a son of Caracalla. The army went over, and Macrinus was murdered. Elagabalus then adopted his nine-year-old cousin, Severus Alexander, as his successor. Elagabalus soon was lynched by the Praetorian Guard and dumped into the Tiber River. The government then was taken over by Julia Maesa and Alexander's mother, Julia Mamaea, who, like Julia Domna, received the title of **Augusta**.

This was the closest that Rome ever came to having real empresses. Mamaea attended meetings of the Senate and tried to restore its authority in order to counter the growing power of the army. She included senators in the emperor's *consilium* and opened up the office of praetorian prefect to senators. In the end, however, the army had its way. In 234, army discipline became so bad that German raiders had to be bought off. In the next year, Alexander and his mother were killed during an army mutiny.

THE IMPERIAL CRISIS (235–284)

The murder of Severus Alexander marked not only the end of the Severan Dynasty but also the beginning of a very difficult period for the Roman Empire, the **Imperial Crisis**, also known as the **Military Anarchy**. In addition to economic collapse, armies throughout the empire named their commanders emperor, marched on Rome to force the Senate to recognize them, and received their donatives. No single emperor was able to end the disorder or to reestablish normal dynastic succession. At the same time, the frontiers were menaced by foreign enemies. Germanic people coalesced into large and formidable coalitions: on the lower Rhine, there were the **Franks** (named after the *francisca*, their favored throwing axe), and on the upper Rhine and upper Danube the **Alamanni** ("all men") appeared. Moreover, on the north shore of the Black Sea the **Goths** appeared. And in the east, in 227 the Parthians were overthrown by a Persian dynasty, the **Sasanids**, who created the **New Persian Empire** and laid claim to all the territories of the Old Persian Empire of the fifth century BCE at its fullest extent, including Egypt, Palestine, and Anatolia, resulting in a state of war with the Roman Empire. All of these peoples were eager to take advantage of Roman weakness, and the empire was beset by simultaneous attacks from without. Indeed, it was a wonder that the empire survived at all. It is not easy to reconstruct the political history of this chaotic period, for it is discussed at length in only one connected ancient source, the "Augustan History," a work of historical fiction written in the 390s.

A Multitude of Emperors

Between 235 and 284 there were more than fifty emperors, some very short-lived. One was said to have "been proclaimed one day, reigned the next, and been assassinated the next." Few left much mark on history, but some are worthy of mention. Maximinus the Thracian (235–238), the second nonsenatorial emperor after Macrinus, was denigrated by effete senators as a seven-foot barbarian, a description no doubt resulting from his provincial origin and army career. And Philip the Arab (244–249) treated Christians fairly and even was considered to be a crypto-Christian; he demonstrated that the emperorship was indeed open even to those from a distant frontier. In 247, he presided over secular games in honor of the one thousandth anniversary of the founding of Rome, but his attempt to equate the eternity of Rome with that of his own dynasty failed dismally.

In 249, Decius, commander of Roman armies on the lower Danube, was proclaimed emperor by his soldiers after inflicting a defeat on the Goths. After Philip the Arab was defeated and killed, Decius was acknowledged as emperor by the Senate. In order to gain legitimacy and inspire confidence, Decius also assumed the name Trajan Decius (249–251), harking back to the glorious Roman past. He then proposed to reunify the empire using religion as a common denominator by requiring all citizens to attest to their loyalty by sacrificing to the state gods. In return, they received a certificate: one reads, "I have always sacrificed to the gods, and now, according to the order, I have made sacrifice and libation, and tasted the victim's flesh." This was the first empire-wide ruling that, potentially, could affect all Christians. Many Christians apostatized by sacrificing, but others, such as bishop Fabian of Rome, were martyred. In 251, Decius was killed in a desperate battle against the Goths and Carpi on the lower Danube, becoming the first Roman emperor to be killed in battle. Rejoicing Christians saw this as the judgment of God and gleefully described Decius' body being devoured by wild animals on the battlefield.

Emperors such as Maximinus I, Philip the Arab, and Trajan Decius desperately tried to reestablish constitutional normality by creating new dynasties. Each of them appointed their young sons as either Caesars or Augustuses—indeed, Trajan Decius made three of his sons co-emperors. But these young men were obvious figureheads, and all but one (who died of the plague) were killed along with their fathers. In 253, the senator Valerian (253–260) was made emperor, and he immediately named his thirty-five-year-old son, Gallienus (253–268), as his colleague. Gallienus was the first son to be named coemperor who was actually able to share the rule. The empire was faced with perils on all sides. The frontier defense system of Augustus collapsed, and foreign invaders broke through.

Valerian took charge of the east, which was threatened by Goths and Persians, but to no avail. In 260 he was defeated and captured by the New Persian king Shapur. He spent the rest of his life as Shapur's slave, and the Persians invaded the eastern provinces. In the aftermath of this disaster, bands of Goths and Heruls devastated Greece and the Black and Aegean seacoasts, and the rich and powerful Roman caravan city of Palmyra, in the Syrian desert, declared its independence. The city's queen, **Zenobia** (267–274), created a Palmyrene Empire that included the Levant, part of Anatolia, and Egypt, and she eventually took the unprecedented title of Augusta, empress of the Roman Empire not just in name but in fact.

In the west, Gallienus defeated the Alamanni in northern Italy in 259, but in the following year the defensive structure between the upper Rhine and Danube rivers collapsed, and the Alamanni permanently occupied the Roman territories on the far side of the rivers. Further west, the Franks broke through into central Gaul and northern Spain. As a result, the army in Gaul, trusting that it could defend itself better than the emperors of Rome could, acclaimed its general Postumus (259–268) as emperor. A breakaway Gallic Empire, consisting of Gaul, Spain, and Britain, was created. Postumus restored the frontier, but the unity of the empire had been shattered. On top of all this, the empire was decimated by another onslaught of the plague. By 260, Gallienus was left with only the core of the empire: Italy, North Africa, and the Balkans. The empire was disintegrating around him.

Faced with apparently insurmountable difficulties, Gallienus did the best he could with what he had. He transferred the command of armies from senators to knights, who came from social and cultural backgrounds more similar to those of the men in the ranks. He made greater use of cavalry, part of a trend to quality over quantity as recruitment problems continued. And he experimented with a **defense in depth** policy with a mobile field army stationed well behind the frontiers that could respond more quickly to hotspots on and inside the frontiers. Eventually, however, he fell victim to a conspiracy among his own officers, and was murdered in 268.

This Persian sardonyx cameo shows the Persian king of kings Shapur capturing the Roman emperor Valerian, all without even having to draw his sword, a tremendous propaganda coup for the New Persians.

An antoninianus of Zenobia, queen of Palmyra, with the title of Augusta ("Empress"); Zenobia was the only woman actually to have ruled with this title during the Roman Empire.

The Soldier Emperors

Gallienus was succeeded by a series of emperors who came from the backwoods of Illyria. They had risen in the ranks of the army by dint of their own ability, and they were better able to relate to and control the troops. They came to be known as the **Soldier Emperors**. The first of them, Claudius II (268–270), was faced by a huge invasion of Goths intending not merely to raid but to settle

An antoninianus of Severina, probably issued after Aurelian's assassination, has a male rather than a female reverse, depicting not Venus, Juno, or other feminine design but the goddess Concord holding two military standards and the typical male legend, "Concord of the soldiers."

in Roman territory. Assembling the last remnants of the Roman armies, Claudius dealt the Goths a devastating defeat in 269. The survivors were settled as tenant farmers near the Danube, and Claudius gained the nickname Gothicus, or "slayer of the Goths." He then succumbed to the plague in 270 and became the only emperor of this period to die in his bed.

Claudius was succeeded by another Illyrian, Aurelian (270–275), whose nickname "Hand on Sword" attested to his military prowess. Aurelian completed the task of reconstituting the empire. He drove the **Vandals**, a Germanic people from the area of modern Poland who had been spreading southward, back across the Danube, but, realizing that the province of Dacia could no longer be held (and that the gold mines had played out), he withdrew those of the Roman inhabitants who wanted to leave and abandoned it. He then marched east. Palmyra was destroyed and its proud queen Zenobia taken captive. Then, in 273, Aurelian likewise defeated the Gallic emperor Tetricus. The empire had been recovered, and Aurelian gained a new nickname, "the Restorer of the World." In a show of magnanimity, Aurelian allowed his defeated rivals to live: Zenobia was given an estate outside Rome and became a Roman socialite, whereas Tetricus was appointed a provincial governor.

Like Gallienus, Aurelian attempted to deal with some of the problems that bedeviled the empire. He tried to restore the value of the currency by giving the essentially copper antoninianus a thin silver wash. It looked impressive, but the coating soon rubbed off, and few were fooled for long. He attempted to give some religious unity to the empire by favoring the worship of the god **Sol Invictus** ("The Unconquered Sun"). Moreover, recognizing the army's inability to defend even the inner reaches of the empire, Aurelian built Aurelian's Wall, the first new wall around Rome in 550 years. But he then suffered the same fate as Gallienus and was assassinated in 275 by a group of disgruntled army officers. Confusion then reigned. No successor was chosen, perhaps because the army was ashamed of its actions, and his wife Severina took charge of the government during the brief interregnum. Finally, the Senate, showing uncharacteristic initiative, named the elderly senator Tacitus (275–276) as emperor, although, typically for Senate choices, he died the next year.

Hopeful Signs

In spite of problems restoring continuity in the emperorship, the empire was surviving the Imperial Crisis. One reason for this was that, even though there were many changes at the top, the Roman bureaucracy continued to operate at both the empire-wide and local levels. Imperial bureaucrats continued to be appointed and to carry out their duties, taxes were collected and distributed, and the government continued to function. Western European cities still were prosperous enough to be able to construct expensive walls, some with elaborate decorations, that served not only for defense but also as a means of showing off. In addition, not all areas of the empire were equally distressed. Indeed, some regions, such as Britain and North Africa, positively prospered during the third century.

Nor was the frontier as dangerous a place as might be thought. Yes, there were spates of raids and invasions, but by and large, frontier life not only remained relatively peaceful but also remarkably integrated. The frontier, rather than being a line in the sand, was a very fluid place, with constant coming and going and incessant interaction. It often would have been difficult to know just what side of the border one was on, for at the same time that barbarians were adopting Roman customs, the reverse also was true. Barbarian hairstyles and dress, such as trousers and footgear, became the height of Roman fashion, and the barbarian custom of raising a newly named ruler on a shield was adopted by the Roman army. And barbarians on the other side of the frontier likewise picked up Roman culture: Dio Cassius remarked, "The barbarians were adapting themselves to the Roman world. They did not find it difficult to change their life, and they were becoming different without realizing it."

Now, as then, it is customary to use the term barbarian *in a generic nonpejorative way to refer to peoples who lived beyond the Roman frontiers.*

In addition, there was a long tradition of barbarian settlement within the empire, usually organized by a Roman government that always was struggling to find enough farmers to till the soil (and thus ensure the payment of the land tax) and enough soldiers to man the army. It was especially common to settle defeated barbarians, as individuals rather than groups, on Roman land that had been deserted and gone out of production for any number of reasons, such as falling into tax arrears, being abandoned by decurions who could no longer afford the costs of office, being overfarmed or ruined by drought, or even being devastated by barbarian raids. Augustus, for example, settled fifty thousand Getae, Tiberius found land for forty thousand Germans, Nero brought in more than one hundred thousand Transdanubian immigrants, and Trajan imported thousands of defeated Dacians. Most barbarians, it seems, were happy to have this opportunity, for, after all, throughout the history of Rome, a peaceful and prosperous life within the imperial frontiers had been the dream of many barbarians. As a consequence, these barbarian settlers soon were indistinguishable from their Roman neighbors, and after the issuing of the Antonine Constitution, they, too, became Roman citizens.

Initially, literary activities continued to be pursued as before, although very often in Greek, a sign that the intellectual balance in the empire was shifting toward the east. The senator **Dio Cassius** prospered under emperors from Commodus through Severus Alexander, but he ran into problems in 229 when he was given command of two legions and received death threats from the unruly soldiers. He then went into retirement and authored, in Greek, a massive *Roman History* in eighty books covering the period from the arrival of Aeneas in Italy until his own consulate in 229. In the 240s, a *History of the Roman Empire since Marcus Aurelius* was written, also in Greek, by Herodian, who may have been a minor government official. Subsequently, however, literary productions tailed off; perhaps the political uncertainties reduced the number of patrons willing to underwrite literary efforts. One notes the Platonic philosopher Plotinus, a friend of the emperor Gallienus who did much to establish a new philosophic system known as **Neoplatonism**, and the Greek historian Callinicus, who lived at the court of Queen Zenobia of Palmyra and was executed by Aurelian. And the patriotic Athenian Dexippus, who as archon in the late 260s had raised an army to help drive off attacking Heruls, wrote a *Chronica*, a complete history up until the time of Claudius Gothicus, and a

A porphyry sculpture brought from Constantinople to Venice in the thirteenth century depicts the four tetrarchs with their arms around each other, to show that even if there were four emperors, there was still only one empire, and their hands on their swords, to demonstrate the source of their authority.

Scythica, on Rome's wars with the Scythians, as the Goths were poetically called.

That said, however, the empire still was confronting serious political, military, and economic problems that would have to be dealt with. The emperors may have been getting the situation back under control, but much work clearly remained to be done. It was clear that the Principate as established by Augustus was no longer working and that radical changes would have to be made if the empire were going to return to normalcy.

SAVING THE EMPIRE: THE REFORMS OF DIOCLETIAN AND CONSTANTINE

In 284, **Diocletian**, another Illyrian soldier, was named emperor. Like Augustus, he was a better administrator than general, but the empire had an abundance of generals; a good administrator was what it needed. Also like Augustus, Diocletian set about not only to safeguard his own position but also to implement reforms that would solve the problems that were facing the empire. Diocletian's attempts, however, were not uniformly successful, and the efforts of one of his successors, **Constantine**, bore greater fruit. Some of their reforms had an effect different from those of Augustus: instead of creating unity, they resulted in increasing fragmentation. The Roman Empire as it was reorganized by Diocletian and Constantine goes under several names, such as the Dominate, the Late Roman Empire, and, ultimately, the Byzantine Empire.

Diocletian and the Dominate

When Diocletian (284–305), a career soldier and another of the Soldier Emperors, assumed the throne, the Roman Empire faced a multitude of problems that had accumulated during the Principate, had worsened during fifty years of civil war, and had threatened to undermine the unity that Augustus and his successors had worked so hard to create. These included an army that was difficult to control, a lack of an effective method for choosing emperors, threats of foreign attacks, a society in which certain classes felt disadvantaged or alienated, an economy in ruins, an expanding and expensive bureaucracy, and a state religion that engendered less and less devotion. To restore normality, Diocletian wanted to accomplish two things. On the one hand, in order to deal with the Imperial Crisis and ensure his own longevity, Diocletian desired to take complete control of the empire and end the civil wars. And on the other, he wished to implement reforms that would result in the long-term success and security of the empire.

Diocletian's first priority was to consolidate his own authority. He tried to do so in several ways. He altered the way that the emperor was perceived. The last vestiges of the fictional partnership with the Senate were abandoned. Rather than being just another senator, he became the **Dominus**, or "Lord and Master," a godlike person elevated far above other men. He replaced the general's cloak with a floor-length purple robe and the laurel wreath for a pearl diadem. Everything associated with his person became "sacred." Those who met with him performed proskynesis, prostrating themselves face down on the floor. These practices made it more difficult for potential rivals to envisage themselves bridging the gap between subject and emperor. As a result the empire was transformed from the Principate of Augustus to the **Dominate**, and we now move into what is called the Late Roman Empire.

Diocletian attempted to gain more direct control of the administration by greatly expanding the imperial bureaucracy. He regularized the custom of having multiple emperors that had come into use in the third century. He introduced the **Tetrarchy**, or "Rule by Four," in which he appointed three other army officers as emperors to rule various sections of the empire. Two had the rank of Augustus, or Senior Emperor: Diocletian ruled the eastern provinces, and Maximianus administered Italy, Africa, and Spain. Two Caesars, or Junior Emperors, Galerius and Constantius, administered the Balkans in the east and Gaul and Britain in the west, respectively. Each emperor had his own **comitatus** (court, from the word *comites*, or comrades), consisting of his chief officials, bodyguard, and household personnel, and each established his own imperial capital—for example, Diocletian at Nicomedia in Anatolia and Constantius at Trier in northern Gaul. Rome, on the other hand, now far removed from the action, lost its status as an

TABLE 12.2   THE TETRARCHIES

First Tetrarchy

Diocletian (Augustus) (284–305)

Maximianus (Augustus) (285–305)

Galerius (Caesar) (293–311)

Constantius (Caesar) (293–306)

Second Tetrarchy

Galerius (Augustus) (305–311)

Constantius (Augustus) (305–306)

Maximinus II (Caesar, Augustus) (305–313)

Severus II (Caesar, Augustus) (305–307)

Later Additions

Constantine (Caesar, Augustus) (306–337)

Maxentius (Augustus) (307–312)

Licinius (Augustus) (308–324)

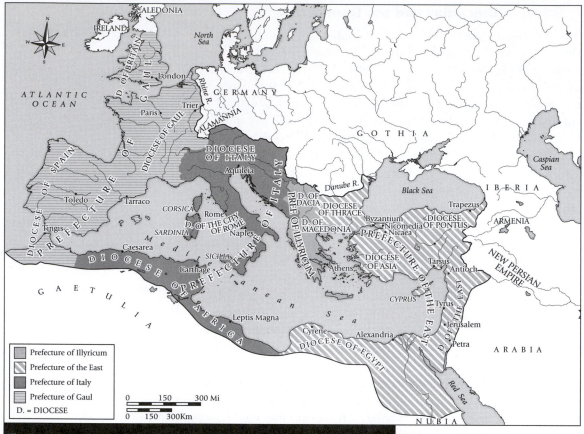

The Reorganized Empire of Diocletian, Divided into Prefectures and Dioceses

imperial capital. If an emperor went on campaign, he was accompanied by his entire comitatus, and the government set up shop wherever the emperor happened to camp. Diocletian proposed to solve the problem of the imperial succession by designating each Caesar as the successor of his respective Augustus. In this way he hoped to eliminate rival claimants to the throne after emperors died.

In order to reduce the possibility of anyone gaining enough power to lead a revolt, Diocletian subdivided the sources of authority. Gallienus' experimental defense in depth policy was formalized. The army was split up into the *limetanei*, or border army, stationed on the frontier and commanded by dukes, and the *comitatenses*, or field army, mobile units stationed in internal areas and commanded by counts. One consequence of this was that the border troops became even more tied to the regions in which they were stationed. They took up farming and lost their mobility, becoming little more than a citizen militia. Civil and military functions and offices were separated, so that generals did not govern provinces and provincial governors did not command troops. By a process of subdivision, the number of provinces was increased from fifty to one hundred, lessening the authority of each governor. In addition, Italy was demoted to the same status as the rest of the provinces, and

Diocletian expanded the third-century policy of restricting the entry of senators into high-ranking governmental posts, especially military ones.

New levels of bureaucracy were introduced. The provinces, whose governors had the positions of proconsul, consular, praeses, and corrector, were grouped into twelve **dioceses**, administered by **Vicars**, of about eight provinces each. And the dioceses were organized into four **Prefectures**, each administered by a praetorian prefect, who thus gained even greater authority. The praetorian prefect became the most powerful imperial official after the emperor: he was the only provincial administrator to report directly to the emperor and was permitted to wear a purple cloak extending to his knees. Measures such these not only brought an end to the repetitious cycles of revolts but also gave the imperial government an increased local presence—and greatly increased costs.

Strategies for Survival

Once Diocletian had put an end to the Military Anarchy, he could attempt to solve more long-term problems. The economy was in a very sorry state. The debased silver coinage was nearly worthless. Tax revenues could hardly meet expenses, and, in border areas, some land had gone out of cultivation as a consequence of fifty years of warfare. In an attempt to restore value to the currency, Diocletian reissued a good gold coin weighing one-sixtieth of a pound and known as the *aureus* or *solidus,* a good silver coin known as the *siliqua,* and a large silver-coated copper coin called the *follis* (a word meaning "bag of money"). But the follis fooled no one, and the attempt to reissue good gold and silver coins failed because there was not enough available metal. A Maximum Price Edict issued in 301 attempted to curb inflation by purely legal means by setting maximum prices that could be charged for goods and services. But this served only to drive goods onto the black market, and rampant inflation continued.

Diocletian finally accepted the ruin of the money economy and revised the tax system so that it was based on payments in kind, known as the ***annona***, rather than on payments in the worthless coinage: farmers, for example, now paid taxes in produce rather than silver currency. In order to take into account changes in productivity levels over time and changes in the imperial budget, the annona was recalculated in periodic reassessments, called indictions, every fifteen years. Produce was gathered into imperial storehouses, and imperial factories manufactured uniforms and weapons. Soldiers were paid in kind, in ration units that also were called the annona. The soldiers' only monetary salary became the gold and silver donative, which now was issued at five-year intervals rather than just at the beginning of a reign, a policy that now gave the soldiers an incentive to keep a good emperor in office.

In order to ensure the long-term survival of the empire, Diocletian also identified certain jobs, known as **compulsory services**, that had to be performed. These included the occupations of soldier, baker, decurion, and tenant farmer, to name just a few. These positions were made hereditary, and those

Wage and price controls often have been used to try to control inflation; they were last used in the United States by President Richard Nixon in 1971–1973 after inflation had remained above 4 percent for years.

DIOCLETIAN'S "EDICT ON MAXIMUM PRICES"

The preamble to Diocletian's *Edictum de pretiis rerum venalium* ("Edict on the Prices of Things for Sale"), issued in 301, provides insights into what the emperors thought the causes of inflation were and how it was their responsibility to solve them:

> Diocletian, Maximianus, Constantius, and Galerius declare: As we recall the wars which we have successfully fought, we must be grateful to the fortune of our state, second only to the immortal gods, for a tranquil world that reclines in the embrace of the most profound calm, and for the blessings of a peace that was won with great effort. That this fortune of our state be stabilized and suitably adorned is demanded by the law-abiding public and by the dignity and majesty of Rome. Therefore we, who by the gracious favor of the gods previously stemmed the tide of the ravages of barbarian nations by destroying them, must surround the peace that we established for eternity with the necessary defenses of justice. If the excesses perpetrated by persons of unlimited and frenzied avarice could be checked by some self-restraint, that

A section of Diocletian's Maximum Price Edict now in the Pergamon Museum in Berlin lists the prices for slaves, ranging from fifteen thousand denarii for boys and girls to thirty-five thousand for a male or eunuch aged sixteen through forty, with the proviso that "for a slave instructed in a skill, with regard to the type and experience and quality of the skills, it is fitting regarding the price to reach an agreement between the buyer and seller to the extent that a double price, at least, might exceed that established for the slave."

engaging in them were prohibited from changing their careers. The repeated reissuance of these laws, however, leads one to wonder just how widely they were obeyed.

Finally, like Augustus and Trajan Decius, Diocletian attempted to use traditional state polytheistic religion as a unifying element. But Christianity, which rejected participation in polytheistic sacrifices made for the safety of the empire, had become attractive not just to the less privileged but also to senators, officials, soldiers, and intellectuals, and now it was perceived by some as a direct threat to the empire's well-being. In a last-ditch effort to reverse the rise of Christianity and restore the polytheistic imperial cult, Diocletian, urged on by his Caesar Galerius, commenced the so-called **Great Persecution** in 303. A series of edicts began with a command to surrender Christian books, then ordered the arrest of Christian clergy, and culminated in an order to "sacrifice or die." But by now there was increased popular acceptance of and even avarice that rushes for gain and profit with no thought for mankind, or if the general welfare could endure without harm this riotous license by which, in its unfortunate state, it is being very seriously injured every day, the situation could perhaps be faced with dissembling and silence, with the hope that human forbearance might alleviate the cruel and pitiable situation. But the only desire of these uncontrolled madmen is to have no thought for the common need. Among the unscrupulous, the immoderate, and the avaricious it is considered almost a creed to desist from plundering the wealth of all only when necessity compels them. Through their extreme need, moreover, some persons have become acutely aware of their most unfortunate situation, and can no longer close their eyes to it. Therefore we, who are the protectors of the human race, are agreed, as we view the situation, that decisive legislation is necessary, so that the long-hoped-for solutions which mankind itself could not provide may, by the remedies provided by our foresight, be provided for the general betterment of all. We hasten, therefore, to apply the remedies long demanded by the situation, satisfied that no one can complain that our intervention with regulations is untimely or unnecessary, trivial or unimportant. These measures are directed against the unscrupulous, who have perceived in our silence of so many years a lesson in restraint but have been unwilling to imitate it. For who is so insensitive and so devoid of human feeling that he can be unaware or has not perceived that uncontrolled prices are widespread in the sales taking place in the markets and in the daily life of the cities? Nor is the uncurbed passion for profiteering lessened either by abundant supplies or by fruitful years. It is our pleasure, therefore, that the prices listed in the subjoined schedule be held in observance in the whole of our empire. It is our pleasure that anyone who resists the measures of this statute shall be subject to a capital penalty for daring to do so. We therefore exhort the loyalty of all, so that a regulation instituted for the public good may be observed with willing obedience and due scruple, especially as it is seen that by a statute of this kind provision has been made, not for single municipalities and peoples and provinces but for the whole world. The prices for the sale of individual items which no one may exceed are listed below.

sympathy with Christian teachings. Christians, for example, were popularly seen as sun worshippers because they met on Sunday, and Christ was seen as a manifestation of the unifying Sun god. Christian scripture, adopted from the Jews as the Old Testament, even referred to Christ the Messiah as the "sun of righteousness." There thus was little public support for the persecution, and in most of the empire the edicts were ignored, and Christians were permitted to worship in peace.

In 305, saying that he had ruled long enough, Diocletian took a step unprecedented for a Roman emperor. He retired, taking his colleague Maximianus along with him. Another of his motives would have been to ensure that his method for dealing with the imperial succession went into effect. A Second Tetrarchy was created: Galerius and Constantius became the Augustuses in the east and the west, and two new Caesars, Maximinus II and Severus II, were appointed.

A solidus issued by Constantine ca. 313 in commemoration of a defeat of the Franks depicts on the reverse a trophy of captured weapons and a grieving woman representing "Francia" (the land of the Franks). The legend reads, "The joy of the Romans," emphasizing the expectation that Roman emperors would win victories over threatening barbarians.

The Rise of Constantine

Constantius, however, died the very next year, and the Tetrarchy then collapsed. Its fatal error was that it could not supplant the army's preference for sons. The Second Tetrarchy had ignored Constantine and Maxentius, the sons of Constantius and Maximianus. Both were declared emperors by their fathers' soldiers, Constantine in Britain and Maxentius in Italy. Severus II was killed in 307 when he attacked Maxentius, and a new round of civil wars ensued. In 312, Constantine overcame Maxentius at the **Battle of the Milvian Bridge** underneath the walls of Rome and gained control of the entire western half of the empire. After a shaky period of peace with the eastern emperor Licinius (308–324), who had killed Maximinus II in 313 and taken control of the east, civil war again broke out. In 324, Constantine first defeated Licinius at the Battle of the Hellespont, the last major naval battle of antiquity, and then routed Licinius at the Battle of Chrysopolis. Once again the empire was controlled by a single emperor.

Constantine took a rather different approach to some of the problems confronted by Diocletian. Regarding the senators, Constantine, like Augustus, believed that the empire could not succeed without the support of its richest, most experienced, and most influential social class. Constantine thus reversed the third-century practice of alienating the senatorial aristocracy. He implemented a new accommodation with the senators: they were welcomed into imperial offices—mostly civil offices, although the occasional senator did become an army general—but the Senate, as a body, never regained its authority to name emperors; in the future its only role in the naming of emperors was to deliver congratulations.

With regard to the economy, Constantine decided that it was necessary to have credible hard currency to deal with imperial income and expenditures more efficiently. Instead of trying to revive the discredited silver coinage (a pound of gold now was valued at one hundred twenty thousand debased denarii), he put the imperial economy on the gold standard in 312 by introducing a new form of the gold **solidus**, larger but thinner and weighing less, only one-seventy-second of a pound. But in order for the solidus to succeed, the empire needed a constantly replenishable supply of gold. Because there were no new gold mines to exploit, the only way to do this was by getting hoarded gold back into circulation and keeping it there. The government thus implemented a multitude of measures intended to keep gold in circulation. Moneylenders and gold miners were compelled to sell their gold to the state. Merchants paid an income tax in gold. And taxpayers who preferred the convenience of cash to the cumbersome annona could pay in gold. These procedures resulted in a constant recycling of the gold coinage: it was paid out in expenses and received back in taxes and forced purchases. Constantine's solidus was so successful that it served as the main means of exchange in the Mediterranean world for nearly a thousand years.

Constantine observed most of Diocletian's administrative reforms, retaining all of the tactics used to split up the sources of authority. Indeed, Constantine furthered the process by removing all military authority from the praetorian prefects and entrusting it to masters of soldiers, who became the highest-ranking Roman generals. The praetorian prefects still were the highest-ranking officials after the emperor, but the potentially dangerous consequences of combined civil and military authority were thereby avoided.

Constantine also concurred with Diocletian's recognition of the growing importance of the east as the population, economic, and even cultural center of the empire. In 330 CE he therefore established a permanent eastern capital city on the Bosporus, the strategic strait between Anatolia and Europe, on the site of the old Greek city of Byzantium. Always the self-promoter, he named the new city **Constantinople**, after himself. In many ways, Constantinople was a copy of Rome. It supposedly was built on seven hills, and it soon had its own imperial court, its own new Senate, and its own circus (where the "blues" and "greens" became the favorite chariot racing teams). In order to emphasize the city's role as the New Rome, Constantine placed beneath the Column of Constantine the *palladium*, an ancient wooden statue of Athena said to have been brought from Troy to Rome by Aeneas himself, the legendary ancestor of the Romans. The city was decorated with monuments removed from other famous sites. In the hippodrome stood the famous serpent column that had been dedicated at Delphi after the Greek victory over the Persians at Plataea in 479 BCE. Many statues of polytheistic gods, including the Pythian Apollo from Delphi, the Hera from Samos, and the Zeus from Olympia, were removed from their temples and brought to the city. And a milestone known as the *milliarium aureum* ("Golden Milestone") was the point from which the distances of all roads in the east were measured.

Constantine handled the problem of the imperial succession by abandoning Diocletian's Tetrarchy and returning to **dynastic succession**: whenever possible, fathers were to be succeeded by sons. Sovereignty now rested in the hands of the emperor and the army. Only the reigning emperor or emperors could make new emperors. A usurper such as Constantine could become legitimate only if he defeated or was recognized by the existing legitimate emperors. If there were no reigning emperors, then only the army had the authority to name a new one. Male emperors bore the title Augustus and female members of the imperial family the title Augusta. Although women were not constitutionally barred from ruling, no woman ruled alone until Irene in 799. This method of succession was remarkably stable—between 364 and 802, there were only five imperial dynasties and only two brief periods of anarchy.

THE ARCH OF CONSTANTINE

Reused reliefs from a monument of the emperor Trajan.

The single monument most associated with the emperor Constantine is no doubt the arch that was built in Rome after his defeat of Maxentius in 312. In this case, one has not only an iconographical program establishing Constantine's legitimacy—for he was, after all, a usurper—but also a verbal inscription communicating the message that the Senate, which sponsored the building of the arch, wanted to promulgate. And the arch was full of levels of meaning. For one thing, the inscription ambiguously attributed Constantine's victory to "the movement of the divinity," without specifying just what that divinity was. A Christian, of course, could see it as the Christian god, but a polytheist could see it as any of the other monotheistic divinities, such as the sun god. And the artwork was a curious mixture of original art, depicting Constantine's victories and then his generosity, and of art taken from earlier monuments of the Antonine emperors. In the past, it was thought that the use of earlier artwork was a sign of the cultural bankruptcy of the late empire, that the best later emperors could do was cannibalize the monuments of earlier emperors, but historians now realize that the situation was much more nuanced; by connecting himself to the Antonine emperors, Constantine was not only stressing his legitimacy but also assuring the people that his reign would bring back the happy and secure times of the past. Thus, these reliefs from a monument of Trajan would have recalled to a viewer the Golden Age of the reign of Trajan, and their depiction of the emperor addressing the troops and engaging in a pagan sacrifice is something that would not have made Christian viewers happy.

Constantine and Christianity

Constantine's most significant legacy lay in his policies toward the Christian church, and he is best known as the emperor who began to make Christianity into the most dominant force in the Mediterranean world and beyond. In early 313, not long after his victory over Maxentius, Constantine and the eastern emperor Licinius issued the **Edict of Milan**, which decreed tolerance for all religions and ordered the restitution of Christian property that had been confiscated by the imperial treasury or acquired by private persons, with the latter being provided compensation by the state. This marked the first time that the imperial government recognized the Christian church as a lawful institution. Christianity thus was converted at one stroke from a persecuted to a favored religion.

LEGACY OF ANTIQUITY

Constantine believed that Christianity was the religion that most suited the needs of his times. Do you believe that Christianity is still a religion suited to the needs of the times?

Constantine agreed with Diocletian that religion could be used as a unifying factor, but realizing that traditional Roman polytheism was on the decline, he decided that Diocletian had chosen the wrong religion. Constantine saw in Christianity a religion that met the needs of his times much better than the traditional beliefs, for the organizational structure and standardized doctrine of the church, he believed, could be mobilized in support of imperial unity. In various ways, Constantine therefore threw his support to Christianity. He granted senior clergy the status of *honestiores*, exempted Christian priests from taxation, and made Sunday, the Christian day of worship, the official market day so that Christians would have liberty to attend church services. Constantine and his mother Helena also demonstrated their personal piety by building churches in Rome, Constantinople, and the Holy Land.

But Constantine also believed that his support for Christianity should bring benefits to the empire. For example, it allowed him to confiscate polytheist temple treasures and use the proceeds to issue large numbers of his new gold coins. Other benefits to the state included growing government reliance on Christian churches to provide social services, such as poor relief and the care of the incarcerated. In order to take some of the load off the Roman judicial system, Christian bishops even were granted legal jurisdiction in some cases, such as the manumissions of slaves.

But Constantine soon discovered that he had been wrong about just how unified the Christian church was. The years of seclusion and persecution had isolated the many Christian communities from each other and had prevented the development of the kind of homogeneity that Constantine hoped for. The church was plagued by disagreements over questions of belief, organization, and authority. Dissension raged over just what Christians were supposed to believe and who was to have the right to decide this. Constantine solved the second of these questions in one stroke: the emperor now took the responsibility for compelling fractious churchmen to reach agreement on any number of divisive issues. Just as, during the Principate, the emperor had siphoned authority off from the Senate, he now did so from the church, and even greater power coalesced into his hands. The first step toward **Caesaropapism**, in which the head of state also was the head of the church, had been taken.

Constantine mobilized state authority in an attempt to create Christian unity, sometimes by issuing imperial regulations, but the preferred method for settling major quarrels was to convene **ecumenical** (Greek for "the whole world") **church councils** comprised of bishops from all over the empire. The bishops were the heads of the church in each city; theoretically each was responsible only to God and had no earthly supervisor. An ecumenical council therefore represented the collective authority of the entire Christian church.

Some of the problems confronting the church involved church authority, especially the authority of priests and bishops. In North Africa, conflict arose when Christians known as **Donatists** (after their leader, bishop Donatus of Carthage) taught that *traditores* ("betrayers"), Christian bishops and priests who had turned over Christian books during Diocletian's Great Persecution, had lost their spiritual authority and could no longer hold church office. Others, however, believed that spiritual authority lay in the office, not the man, and that after doing penance, the *traditores* could continue in office. The dispute was referred to Constantine, who in 314 convened a church council at Arles in southern Gaul. Donatism was condemned and became the first official **heresy**, or illegal belief.

A much more serious controversy arose in Alexandria in Egypt, where the priest Arius taught that Christ the Son was different in substance from and subordinate to God the Father. This teaching, known as **Arianism**, struck a chord with those who viewed the Christian Trinity (the father, son, and holy spirit) as analogous to a human family but was rejected by Christians who believed that all three persons of the Trinity were of the same substance and thus equal in status. In 325, at the first ecumenical **Council of Nicaea**, in Anatolia just south of Constantinople, Constantine persuaded 318 bishops, assembled with government support from throughout the empire, to condemn Arianism. The council formulated the **Nicene Creed**, an official statement of belief that all Christians were expected to accept. But many Arians refused to concede, and the Arian controversy continued to simmer.

The Nicene Creed still is used in many modern Christian churches.

The Council of Nicaea also dealt with administrative issues, establishing the official date of Easter and formalizing an administrative model for the church based on the Roman provincial model. Within each province, the church in each *civitas* was under the authority of a bishop, and the bishop of the capital city of each province became an archbishop, who had a higher status than and a loose supervisory authority over the provincial bishops. The bishops of Alexandria, Antioch, and Rome were assigned the even higher status of **patriarch**, which conveyed great honor but not any additional authority; soon thereafter the bishops of Constantinople and Jerusalem received the same status. In addition, the bishops of Rome claimed to have the highest

HISTORICAL CONTROVERSY

CONSTANTINE'S CHRISTIANITY

One of the great controversies of ancient history is the extent to which Constantine was a true Christian and the extent to which his motives for supporting Christianity were personal as opposed to political. The official Roman version of Constantine's conversion, according to the Christian historian Eusebius, was that in 312, in the midst his war with Maxentius, he saw in the sky a cross of light above the sun, accompanied by the words *"In hoc signo vinces"* ("In this sign you shall conquer"). That night, the story continued, Christ himself came to Constantine in a dream and commanded him to create a standard bearing the overlapping letters X (chi) and P (rho), the first two letters in the Greek spelling of the name of Christ. After Constantine's victory at the Battle of the Milvian Bridge in October 312, the chi-rho sign became known as the **Christogram**, or sign of Christ, and Constantine's victory was attributed to the Christian God. Constantine not only did not contradict this opinion but also began to support Christianity openly and actively.

But Constantine might have been less the zealous believer and more a political opportunist. It would have been clear from the failure of Diocletian's Great Persecution that the old imperial cult was no longer feasible as a unifying factor; to a political pragmatist, Christianity might have seemed a more viable possibility. And there are, in fact, many ambiguities about Constantine's religiosity. For one thing, even though Constantine issued laws favorable to Christians, he never issued any antipagan legislation; even very late in his reign Constantine approved the construction of a temple in central Italy in honor of his own family, where stage plays and gladiatorial games were overseen by a pagan priest. And Constantine never seems to have abandoned his devotion to Sol Invictus, the Unconquered Son, whom many Romans, and especially Roman emperors, had looked on not only as the most important traditional god but even as the only god. At the same time that he issued coins bearing the Christogram, he continued to issue coins in honor of Sol Invictus, who also was portrayed rising to heaven on the Arch of Constantine. Even the chi-rho sign his soldiers placed on their shields had an alternate meaning as a sign of the sun god. But even here, Constantine's devotion to the Sun god need not mean that he was not a devoted Christian, for the common identification of Christ with the sun god would have made Constantine's solar monotheism very close to Christian monotheism.

---

status of all the bishops based on the argument that they were the successors of the apostle Peter. But other bishops also claimed to be the successors of apostles, and they, along with most other bishops, refused to acknowledge the primacy of the bishop of Rome.

Constantine died in 337. Only on his deathbed was he finally baptized as a Christian, with the ceremony being performed by an Arian bishop who had retained his belief and had risen in the emperor's favor. Constantine was buried in the Church of the Apostles in Constantinople and later became a Christian saint. Constantine's plan for dynastic succession then went into effect, and the empire was divided among his three sons.

The Legacy of Diocletian and Constantine

Curiously, even though Diocletian usually gets the credit for saving the empire after the imperial crisis, most of his reforms were dead ends. It was Constantine's initiatives, such as his establishment of a second capital, his introduction of the solidus, his rapprochement with the senators, his establishment of dynastic succession, and, in particular, his support of Christianity that were to be crucial in charting the future course of the Roman Empire. Once Constantine took sole control of the empire, the civil wars came to an end and stability returned.

LOOKING AHEAD

Diocletian and Constantine restored stability to the empire, but in the course of doing so they abandoned the Principate as established by Augustus and established a new form of imperial state in which the emperor's role was pre-eminent and the partnership with the Senate was definitively abandoned. Several problems that had arisen by the third century—such as the lack of a viable currency, the imperial succession, and keeping the army under control—were effectively solved. But the question remained of whether these would be long- or short-term solutions. And, just as Augustus' solution by its very nature brought problems with imperial succession, Constantine's plan to use the Christian church as a unifying factor in the service of the empire likewise did not work out as he had planned and brought with it new problems of its own.

FURTHER READING

Barnes, Timothy D. *The New Empire of Diocletian and Constantine.* Cambridge, MA: Harvard University Press, 1982.

Birley, Anthony R., *Septimius Severus: The African Emperor.* 2nd ed. New Haven, CT: Yale University Press, 1988.

Brauer, George C. *The Age of the Soldier Emperors.* Park Ridge, NJ: Noyes 1982.

Brown, Peter. *The World of Late Antiquity: From Marcus Aurelius to Mohammed.* New York: Harcourt, Brace, Jovanovich, 1971.

Corcoran, Simon. *The Empire of the Tetrarchs, Imperial Pronouncements and Government AD 284–324.* Oxford: Clarendon Press, 1996

de Blois, L. *The Policy of the Emperor Gallienus.* Leiden, Netherlands: Brill, 1976.

Drake, Harold A. *Constantine and the Bishops: The Politics of Intolerance.* Baltimore: Johns Hopkins University Press, 2000.

Garnsey, Peter, and Carolina Humfress, eds., *The Evolution of the Late Antique World.* Cambridge: Orchard Academic Press, 2001.

Potter, David S. *The Roman Empire at Bay: AD 180–395.* New York: Routledge, 2005.

Rees, Roger. *Diocletian and the Tetrarchy.* Edinburgh: Edinburgh University Press, 2004.

Turton, G. E. *The Syrian Princesses: The Women Who Ruled Rome,* A.D. *193–235.* London: Cassell, 1974.

Watson, Alaric. *Aurelian and the Third Century.* Oxford: Taylor & Francis, 2004.

Williams, Stephen. *Diocletian and the Roman Recovery.* New York: Routledge, 1997.

CHAPTER 13

THE CHRISTIAN EMPIRE AND THE LATE ROMAN WORLD
(337–476)

The late Roman world looked very different from the Principate. The most significant change was the evolution of Christianity into the primary religion of the Roman world. Even though emperors continued to be confronted by religious controversy, by the end of the fourth century, Christianity had prevailed and had become the only fully legal religion. Christianity muscled its way into every nook and cranny of the Roman world, and Christian culture became inextricably intertwined with virtually every aspect of Roman society, culture, and politics. At the same time, other trends led to a continued breakdown of the carefully constructed unity of the Principate. One of the greatest changes was the arrival and settlement of various barbarian peoples, who by the 480s had established independent kingdoms in the western half of the Roman Empire.

THE SUCCESSORS OF CONSTANTINE (337–378)

The successors of Constantine, including first his sons and then the families of the generals Valentinian I and Theodosius I, continued the policies that had been laid out by Diocletian and Constantine. At first, all appeared to be well, but the 370s brought the first of the barbarian invasions that eventually would spell the end of the western Roman Empire.

The House of Constantine

In 337, the empire was divided among Constantine's three sons: the eldest, Constantine II (337–340), obtained Gaul, Spain, and Britain; Constantius II (337–361), received all of the east; and Constans (337–350), the youngest, inherited Italy and North Africa. But Constantine II was killed in 340 when he unadvisedly invaded Constans' territory, and Constans in turn was killed by the Gallic usurper Magnentius (350–353) in 350. In 351, the armies of

397

TABLE 13.1   EMPERORS AND DYNASTIES OF THE LATE EMPIRE (337–480)

The Dynasty of Constantine

Constantine I (306–337)

Constantine II (337–340)

Constans (337–350)

Constantius II (337–361)

Julian (360–363)

The Dynasty of Valentinian and Theodosius

West

Valentinian I (364–375)

Gratian (367–383)

Valentinian II (375–392)

Honorius (393–423)

Valentinian III (425–455)

East

Valens (364–378)

Theodosius I (379–395)

Arcadius (383–408)

Theodosius II (402–450)

Marcian (450–457)

Shadow Emperors (selected)

Majorian (457–461)

Julius Nepos (474–480)

Romulus "Augustulus" (475–476)

A large copper coin portrays Julian on the obverse as a bearded philosopher and depicts on the reverse a bull, a characteristic symbol of traditional Roman religious practices. The legend, "Security of the Republic," indicates where Julian thought that the best interests of the empire lay.

Constantius and Magnentius met at the Battle of Mursa in modern Croatia. After a bloody engagement, Magnentius finally retreated; a total of fifty thousand soldiers had been lost, severely weakening the military forces of both sides. Magnentius finally was defeated in 353, leaving the entire empire in Constantius' hands. In the east, meanwhile, the drawn-out wars with the New Persians continued, now often focusing on sieges of fortified sites as both sides dug in and attempted to preserve what they had.

During Constantius' reign, eastern bishops who denied they were Arians but refused to accept the Nicene Creed and supported the Arian teaching that the father and son were not of the same substance gained the support of Constantius II and attempted to reach a compromise with Nicene Christians by proposing that the father and son were alike "according to the scriptures." This interpretation left it up to the individual to decide just what the degree of likeness was. Circa 340, an Arian Gothic bishop, **Ulfilas**, was dispatched to convert the Goths north of the Danube, some of whom already were Nicene Christians, to Arian Christianity. Not only they but other barbarian peoples as well, such as the Vandals, Burgundians, and Goths, adopted the Arian form of Christianity. For a time it looked as if some version of Arianism might yet prevail.

In 360, Constantius was faced by a revolt in Gaul by his nephew, **Julian**, whom he had raised to the rank of Caesar in 355 when barbarian problems arose in Gaul. The next year, however, Constantius died before the final confrontation, leaving Julian as sole emperor. Like all members of the imperial family, Julian had been raised as a Christian, but he harbored a secret devotion to Neoplatonic philosophy and traditional religious practices. He now showed his true colors, and, preaching "tolerance for all," he announced his desire to revive polytheism, thus gaining the epithet "the Apostate." In several ways, Julian attempted to weaken the hold Christianity had on the empire. He disparagingly referred to Christians as Galileans and prohibited Christian professors from teaching the ancient Greek and Latin classic authors, arguing that it was hypocritical to teach material discussing gods in which one did not believe. In order to gain Jewish support, he promised to rebuild the temple in Jerusalem. And, using Christianity as a model, he even sought to create an organized polytheistic church. But Julian's initiative fell on sterile ground. The days of large-scale state-sponsored polytheism were past. In 363, during a skirmish against the New Persians, he was killed, some said by a one of his own Christian soldiers. He then became a pagan saint, but Christianity clearly was the way of the future for both individual persons and the empire as a whole.

The House of Valentinian

The following year, the army selected one of its own commanders, **Valentinian I** (364–375), as emperor. He immediately made his younger brother, Valens (364–375), coemperor, assigning to him the eastern provinces while he took responsibility for the more demanding west. By doing so Valentinian continued the trend toward a de facto division of the empire into eastern and western halves. And whereas Valentinian generally kept out of Christian controversies, Valens was an open supporter of Arianizing Christianity.

The reign of Valentinian I later was looked on as the third and last Golden Age of the Roman Empire. The borders were secure, the economy relatively sound, and society reasonably harmonious. To outward appearances, the empire looked much like it had in the first century: its borders still extended from Scotland to the Euphrates. Rural life flourished on **villas** in Gaul, Spain, Italy, and North Africa, not to mention throughout the east. The imperial treasury, with the gold standard firmly in place, was solvent. Even quarreling among the Christians had died down. Disputes between pagans and Christians were carried out in a genteel, drawing-room atmosphere. There were no serious threats on the horizon to suggest that the empire would not continue to thrive for centuries to come.

Cracks in the Façade

On the other hand, however, this Indian summer of normality did not mean a return to the heyday of the *Pax Romana*. There were signs that all was not well. The expansion of life in the countryside had been matched by a retrenchment of urban life, which, although still vital, functioned at a reduced level. The areas enclosed within city walls constructed in the late third and fourth centuries was often as little as a tenth of what a city's area had been in the second century. And the gulf between the rich and poor was widening. Wealth was being concentrated in the hands of extremely wealthy senators who were intent on consolidating their rural estates. Their income could exceed a thousand pounds of gold a year. But at the same time, more and more of the poor were reduced to a state of dependency on powerful potentates.

Furthermore, even though the army was back under control, it was now a very heterogeneous crowd. The old monolithic legions had been discarded in favor of smaller units of about a thousand men each, scattered about the countryside and often billeted with the local population. This was made necessary by the implementation not only of the new defense in depth policy but also of the annona income and payment system and the concomitant need to spread the burden of supplying the army more evenly. The military, therefore, was much more of an everyday presence than it had been two hundred years before.

Manning the army continued to be a problem, especially after the loss of large numbers of troops in civil wars. Landowners responsible for furnishing recruits as part of their tax assessment either provided men unsuited for military service or chose to pay an exemption fee in gold. Men eligible for the draft sometimes cut off various body parts in an attempt to avoid it. As a result, the emperors had to dip even further down into the recruitment pool and engage greater numbers of barbarian soldiers, either in ethnic units under Roman command or incorporated directly into the legions. It even became common for barbarians to be named as masters of soldiers. Thus many barbarians, such as the Franks Richomer, Arbogast, Merobaudes, and Bauto, the father-in-law of the future emperor Arcadius (383-408), entered Roman service and reached high office. This **barbarization** of the Roman army was expanded by the hiring of *foederati* ("allies"), barbarian contingents serving under their own chieftains. It was assumed that the *foederati* would return home after the end of the campaign for which they had been hired. Usually they did, and they brought back with them not only elements of Roman culture but also tales of the wealth and opportunity that lay within the empire.

And a shift in the geographical balance of the empire came with Diocletian's and Constantine's choice to reside in the east, which reflected the increasing importance of this part of the empire. It was seen as more economically sound, more populous, more defensible, and even more civilized. Throughout antiquity, the center of gravity of civilization had been moving west, but during the Principate this process reached its high-water mark. A movement back toward the east accelerated, with Italy and the west losing their leading role as cultural incubators. Moreover, the two duplicate administrations contained the seeds of a future breach. Conflicts of interest became possible when the best interests of one half of the empire were not those of the other.

On this gold solidus, the emperor Valens, trampling a defeated barbarian and holding the labarum, advertises himself as the "Salvation of the Republic." His propaganda was of little use to him when he was killed at Adrianople.

The Arrival of the Visigoths

In 375 a group of defeated barbarians whom Valentinian I was interviewing became so insolent that Valentinian had an apoplectic fit and died. He was succeeded as western emperor by his son and coemperor Gratian (367–383), then only sixteen years old. The able Valentinian could not have died at a less opportune time. A year later, Valentinian's brother Valens was confronted by a difficult decision. Thousands of **Visigoths**—by that time the Goths had subdivided into the Visigoths, or Western Goths, and the **Ostrogoths**, or Eastern Goths—had appeared on the Danube. They were fleeing from the **Huns**, steppe nomads of Mongolian origin with a reputation for terrible ferocity who had created a barbarian empire north of the Black Sea that incorporated many defeated barbarian peoples living on the central Russian steppes, including Alans, Gepids, Rugians, Scirians, Heruls, and the Visigoths' eastern relatives, the Ostrogoths. In exchange for being allowed to settle on deserted lands located safely within the Roman frontier, the Visigoths offered to provide military service. In the past, the Romans had permitted, and even compelled, defeated barbarians to do this on a regular basis, but never before had they allowed a large, unified group into the empire. Yet doing so would help to solve two needs at the same time: finding enough army recruits and bringing more land onto the tax rolls.

Valens accepted the Visigothic offer on condition that they turn over their weapons and that the Romans provide them with food until they could harvest their own crops. The Roman officials in charge of the transfer, however, pocketed much of the food money and accepted bribes to allow the Goths to keep their weapons. It was said that the Visigoths were faced with such famine that they were forced to trade their children for dogs they could eat. Soon after, starving, armed Visigoths began rampaging about the Balkans. Valens was forced to assemble the eastern Roman army in an attempt to bring the Visigoths to heel. In 378, rashly declining to await the arrival of the western Roman army, he attacked the Goths in the **Battle of Adrianople**, northwest of Constantinople. The Roman army was virtually annihilated, and Valens was killed. An experienced general, **Theodosius I** (379–395), was named as new eastern emperor, but he was unable to expel, or even defeat, the Visigoths. The most he could accomplish was to agree to a treaty that recognized the Visigoths as Roman *foederati*. This subterfuge left the Visigoths free to wander about the empire, under their own chieftains, as they pleased.

THE TRIUMPH OF CHRISTIANITY AND THE WORLD OF THE CHURCH

During the course of the fourth century, Christianity triumphed and became not only the only fully legal religion in the empire but also a part of virtually every aspect of life. The overwhelming impact of the spread of Christian beliefs and practices was felt not only in private but also in public life. Christian ideologies became imperial ideologies, and powerful Christian clerics came to be major players as makers of public policy and could exercise great influence even over Roman emperors. The success of Christianity thus was inextricably bound up with the favor that the church received from the imperial government, and

Christian historians saw it as no accident that the rise of Christianity coincided with the rise of the Roman Empire, which, as attested by Christ's "render unto Caesar" and Paul's pride in his Roman citizenship, was an implicit part of the Christian world. According to **Augustine**, bishop of Hippo in North Africa, the creation of the Roman Empire was itself part of God's plan: "He, therefore, who is the one true God gave a kingdom to the Romans when He wished. He who gave power to Marius gave it also to Gaius Caesar; He who gave it to Augustus gave it also to Nero."

Christian Competitors

During the fourth century, other religions continued to compete with variant forms of Christianity for the hearts and minds of the people. Judaism, for example, continued to have a numerous and committed following in urban centers throughout the empire and beyond as a result of the diaspora. Despite previous expulsions, many Jews still lived in Palestine, where a Jewish patriarch served as a go-between with the imperial administration. To the east, by the fifth century over a million Jews, led by a "Prince of the Captivity," were living in Babylon under New Persian rule. Jewish scholars crafted the **Talmud**, a comprehensive guidebook for Jewish life that comprised oral tradition, interpretations of Mosaic Law, observations on faith and morality, bible commentaries, and historical narratives. One version of the Talmud was completed in the late fourth century in Palestine, and a Babylonian version was completed by ca. 500. Christian treatment of Jews ranged from tolerance to attempts to convert them to Christianity, by force if necessary. And Jews also were subject to legal restrictions imposed by the imperial government, such as prohibitions on their holding government offices, testifying in court, making wills, and receiving inheritances. Although some Jews did convert under coercion, most remained steadfast in their faith.

Nor was traditional polytheism by any means dead. Indeed, some of the most committed pagans of all were the senators of Rome and Italy, who believed that Rome's past greatness had resulted from Roman faithfulness to the traditional Roman deities. But otherwise, large-scale classical urban paganism was on the decline. Many temples were unfrequented and unmaintained, and enthusiasm for Christianity had largely overwhelmed any remaining passion for paganism. But polytheistic practices continued to be the norm in the countryside, where followers of polytheistic religious practices continued to cling to their ancestral traditions. Some mystery cults also continued to flourish, especially that of Mithras, which had much in common with Christianity, such as baptism, group worship, communal meals that included communion with bread and wine, a moral code, and a belief in a life after death. Mithras' birthday, December 25, even came to be accepted as the birthday of the Christian God. The ability of Mithraism to become a mainstream religion was greatly hindered, however, by its exclusion of women.

Pagan philosophy also retained a strong following, especially Neoplatonism, a variant of the teachings of the Athenian philosopher Plato. Neoplatonism, which developed during the third century with the teachings of the philosopher Plotinus, taught that the source of all existence was a single, transcendent, impersonal, divine principle called **The One**. Everything in the material world derived from The One in a series of hierarchical spheres, with the more distant sphere, earthly existence, reflecting the nature of The One only very imperfectly. From The One emanated the Divine Mind, known variously as the *logos*, *nous*, or demiurge, which contained the perfect forms of all existing things, and from the Divine Mind came the World Soul, which connected the intellectual world to the material world. A person's goal was to leave earthly existence behind, attain a higher consciousness through the World Soul, and thus gain a better sense of The One. Neoplatonism's stress on morality made it attractive to Christian intellectuals. Neoplatonism also had other several points of contact with Christianity, such as a disbelief in the independent existence of evil. In addition, Christians believed, based on the statement in the book of John, "In the beginning was the word (*logos*)," that the *logos* represented Christ.

One of the greatest competitors with Christianity at this time was another new religion, which likewise had arisen in the Near East, **Manichaeism**. The prophet Mani (ca. 215–275) was born in Babylon in the New Persian Empire. In his youth he received a divine revelation that led him to claim to be the successor of Zoroaster, Buddha, and Jesus. He incorporated aspects of all of these religions into Manichaeism, a new dualistic religion whose precepts, like those of Judaism and Christianity, were contained in books of sacred scripture. In essence, Manichaeism viewed the world as based on a constant struggle between God, representing the spiritual world of light and good on the one hand, and Satan, representing the material world of darkness and evil on the other. One's body was a battleground between good and evil, and a Manichaean's goal was to gain eternal life by setting the light part of the soul free from the matter-bound part. One purified oneself by living an ascetic life. There were two categories of Manichaeans: the Elect, who lived an ascetic life consisting of abstinence from meat, wine, sex, and property owning, and the Hearers, who accepted Manichaean beliefs but did not have the will power to become members of the Elect. The emphasis on a constant conflict between good and evil, in which both had an independent existence, was easier to understand than the Christian concept of evil as a perversion of good and helps to explain the attraction that Manichaeism had for many people. Like Christianity, Manichaeism suffered persecution, in its case from both the Roman and New Persian governments: as early as 297, for example, Diocletian ordered that Manichaean leaders were to be burned alive together with their scriptures.

The Political Victory of Christianity

But there was no stopping the rise of Christianity. After the death of Julian, Nicene Christianity consolidated itself in the face of both pagan survivals and competing Christian theologies. The eastern emperor Theodosius I was a devoted supporter of the Council of Nicaea and an avowed opponent of Arianism. In 381 he summoned the second ecumenical **Council of Constantinople**; it reaffirmed the condemnation of Arianism, which then withered among the Roman population even as it continued to spread among barbarian peoples. In the western empire, the senators of Rome continued to support their ancient polytheistic traditions. During the 380s, the focus of senatorial devotion was the **Altar of Victory**, which stood in the Senate house in Rome. Powerful Christian bishops such as **Ambrose of Milan**, himself a senator and ex-provincial governor, successfully lobbied the emperor Gratian to have this decidedly non-Christian relic removed, creating hard feelings among senators who felt that their traditions were not being respected. Soon, however, even diehard traditionalists began to convert to Christianity, often for a combination of both spiritual and political reasons. The prominent pagan senator of Rome Praetextatus, for example, realizing the power that came from being bishop of an important city, was heard to exclaim, "Make me bishop of Rome, and I'll become a Christian, too!"

After his defeat of the western usurper Magnus Maximus (383–388), which brought him to Italy, Theodosius became embroiled in a quarrel with Ambrose of Milan. Theodosius first angered Ambrose by ordering Christians who had destroyed a Jewish synagogue in Mesopotamia to rebuild it. Then, after a massacre of rioting citizens by the army in Greece, Ambrose excommunicated the emperor. Theodosius was not readmitted to Christian fellowship until after he had performed public penance. The emperor's humiliation served notice regarding the exalted status to which the Christian church now had risen. Suitably chastised, Theodosius also issued legislation further restricting pagan worship, culminating in a law of 392 that totally prohibited pagan practices and made Christianity the only legitimate religion within the empire. At the same time, Jews, who were grudgingly allowed to continue to worship, suffered legal disabilities, and followers of Christian variants that the government deemed heresies, such as Manichaeism, were treated even more harshly, often receiving the death penalty. As a consequence of his support for Nicene Christianity, Theodosius gained the epithet "the Great."

By the turn of fifth century, Christianity had emerged completely triumphant. In the course of less than a century it had gone from being a persecuted religion to the only legal religion, and its devotees enjoyed a number of religious and legal privileges. Once it had become a favored religion, Christianity adopted many of the trappings of the Roman Empire. Christ himself, for example, was portrayed as manifesting many of the attributes, such as the role of lawgiver, of the Roman emperor.

Now that the tables were turned, some fanatical Christians assaulted pagans with a vengeance. Many pagan temples were demolished, sometimes against the violent opposition of rural pagans who continued to be devoted to their gods. Others, like the Parthenon in Athens, were converted into Christian churches and thus escaped destruction. Pagan statues were either smashed or Christianized by having crosses etched on their foreheads. And, in an extreme case, in 415, **Hypatia**, the leading Neoplatonist philosopher at Alexandria, was gruesomely lynched by a band of rampaging monks; she was torn limb from limb and the flesh was scraped from her bones with shells.

As time went on, the bishops of Rome, the old capital of the empire, laid increasing claims to preeminent authority in the church. Although the pretensions of the popes, as the bishops of Rome came to be called in the sixth century, to supreme authority were generally ignored in the east, the bishops of Rome gained increasing power in the west based on their claims to be the successors of the apostle Peter and on their willingness to hear appeals from disgruntled bishops who had already been condemned of various infractions in their own provinces. Thus powerful Roman bishops such as **Leo the Great** (440–461), who was able to enlist the faltering authority of the Roman emperor on his behalf, gradually built up precedents for Rome as the greatest source of ecclesiastical authority in the west.

The sarcophagus of the Roman senator Junius Bassus, who converted to Christianity just before his death in 359, depicts Christ, portrayed like a Roman emperor, dispensing the law, demonstrating how Christian iconography often was modeled on Roman imperial iconography.

The Christian Life

The adoption of Christianity by greater and greater numbers of people brought changes in both public and private lifestyles. As in the modern day, some Christians expressed their devotion and spirituality more publicly than others. There were nominal Christians, who only made occasional appearances in church, and people who converted for political reasons. But most Christians enthusiastically expressed their faith. Going to church on Sunday not only served spiritual needs but also provided entertainment. Church services incorporated choirs, singing, chanting, and sermons by trained orators.

The Liberian basilica in Rome, begun by the bishop of Rome Liberius (352–366), was built on the Esquiline Hill atop a temple of the goddess Cybele and completed by the bishop of Rome Sixtus III (432–440). It now is the basilica of Santa Maria Maggiore.

Basilicas in large cities held up to a thousand persons—it was standing room only then, for laypersons stood to worship—and sported marble columns and frescoes or mosaics on the walls, but even smaller churches and chapels boasted as much decoration as their sponsors could afford. The church calendar contained many festivals honoring Christian saints and martyrs. Some saints, such as the apostles, had empire-wide prominence, but others were of purely local significance, perhaps someone martyred during an imperial persecution.

Social life—which never had been an important element of most polytheistic religions—also often centered on the church, and worshippers would mingle before and after a service. In their private lives, devoted Christians at least to some degree also were expected to engage in prayer, fasting, and good works, such as helping the poor or at least making offerings to their local church. An increasingly popular activity was the making of **pilgrimages** to sacred sites, such as the site of a martyr's death or even the **Holy Land** itself, for reasons of personal piety, in search of a cure for an ailment, or in fulfillment of a vow.

Steadfast Christians constantly expected the second coming of Christ, also known as the Apocalypse and the **Last Judgment**, which they thought would mark the end of the world as they knew it. The biblical book of Revelation and other apocalyptic writings attempted to predict when the Judgment Day would occur. One approach was to combine the seven days it took to create the world with the biblical passage that "every day is like a thousand years" to predict that the Last Judgment would take place six or seven thousand years after the creation. Others believed that the Last Judgment would be foreshadowed by evil signs. For example, bishop Cyprian of Carthage wrote, "It was foretold that evils would be multiplied in the last times. As the Day of Judgment is now drawing near, the censure of an indignant God will be more and more aroused for the punishment of humanity." To prepare themselves for the Apocalypse, many Christians went through second conversion, usually late in life, and adopted a life of penitence based on a constant, and public, repentance for the many sins they believed they had committed.

Asceticism and Monasticism

The most enthusiastic Christians practiced extreme **asceticism**, or physical self-denial, a practice that also had been used by pagans and Jews who desired to become closer to God and reach a higher level of spirituality. An ascetic life provided a substitute for martyrdom, which generally was no longer available in a Christian empire. Christian ascetics rejected worldly pleasures, such as comfortable quarters, expensive clothing and food, and, in particular, sexual relations, which carried a reminder of the **original sin** of Adam and Eve. Bishops were expected to conform to the ascetic ideal by embracing **celibacy** even if they were married. The greater the degree of self-deprivation that one suffered, the greater degree of holiness and spiritual authority that one was thought to have gained.

Some Christian ascetics remained at home, but during the fourth century increasing numbers, especially in Egypt, Palestine, Syria, and Anatolia, abandoned the secular world and adopted the isolated lives of hermits, living in huts and caves. At the same time, groups of ascetic-minded men and women became **monks** and lived together in single-sex monasteries directed by an abbot or abbess. In the late fourth century, ascetic and monastic practices also were embraced in the west not only by persons such as Martin of Tours, who abandoned a military career and became a hermit, but also by Roman aristocrats, who created pseudo-monasteries in their town and country mansions. Some monastic communities, with monks called *anchorites*, attempted to recreate the seclusion of the desert, whereas others, with monks known as *cenobites*, focused on performing charitable services. In the fifth century and later, written monastic rules were created that defined a nontraditional family-type life based on obedience to the abbot and fixed routines of prayer, worship, and labor. Monks also distanced themselves from the authority of bishops, who lived in cities, and in so doing contributed to a decentralization of church authority. In general, monasticism created a world that was separated from urban life and was analogous to the withdrawal to the countryside and focus on local interests that characterized Late Antiquity.

The most zealous ascetics gave up all their earthly possessions, if they had any, and attachments. Because these **holy men and women** were thought to be isolated from earthly concerns and close to God, they were seen as impartial counselors and arbitrators and were consulted by all segments of the population. Thus women, who were excluded from church offices, and unprivileged men could acquire great authority outside the normal channels of social privilege or government jurisdiction. The holy man Simeon, for example, the son of a shepherd, sat atop a column in all weather in northern Syria for thirty years and, like an ancient Greek oracle, was consulted by privileged and unprivileged alike on account of his reputation for holiness.

Women found the ascetic life attractive for a variety of reasons. Matrona of Constantinople, for example, escaped her abusive husband by disguising herself as a man, adopting the ascetic life, and entering a male monastery. After later becoming abbess of her own convent, she possessed great spiritual authority and even instructed the emperor on matters of church teaching.

Many of these ascetics were considered to be Christian saints either during their lifetimes or after their deaths. The Roman aristocrat Melania became an ascetic after her husband and two of her three children had died. During a pilgrimage to the Holy Land, she dressed in a slave's clothing so she could circulate freely among the poor and established two monasteries, one for men and one for women. She also convinced her daughter, also named Melania, and her husband to adopt the ascetic life. The two renounced sex and built monasteries in North Africa and the Holy Land for virgins and ex-prostitutes. Women may have been prohibited from holding ecclesiastical office, but by becoming ascetics they could still gain spiritual authority, and wealthy women could do so very visibly by expending their wealth on religious endeavors.

THE LATE ROMAN WORLD

The rise of the Christian church and the creation of a Christian empire was just one of the things that made the Late Roman Empire very different from the Principate. Many of the more secular aspects of the late Roman world also had their own idiosyncrasies. Indeed, many of the institutions and attributes that we in the modern day consider to be aspects of the Middle Ages can be seen to have had their origins in the world of Late Antiquity.

The Role of the State

In the Late Roman Empire, the emperor was the "decider" who had the final word on everything.

Late Roman emperors adopted the attitude that they had the authority to do whatever was necessary to get the empire back on its feet. This policy has resulted in a modern assumption that the late empire was an authoritarian, military despotism, in which the emperors, in a big-brotherly kind of manner, assumed cradle-to-grave responsibility for supervising the lives of all of their subjects. More recent study, however, demonstrates that the Late Roman world was a dynamically changing place, full of opportunity. Far from being unflaggingly oppressive, imperial humanity, as it was called, recognized certain personal rights regardless of an individual's gender or social status.

The characteristic late Roman method of attacking problems was to issue laws, thousands of which still survive. Every document issued by the emperor, even replies to memos, had the force of law. But this is not to say that emperors were out-and-out dictators. For one thing, it was understood that even emperors were subject to the increasingly extensive precedents of Roman law. Emperors also were careful to consult with an imperial advisory council known as the

A PICTURE IS WORTH A THOUSAND WORDS

A LATE ROMAN GOVERNOR HEARS A CASE

A sixth-century illustrated gospel written in Greek in silver ink on purple-dyed parchment and preserved in Rossano, Italy, recreates the trial of Christ before Pontius Pilate as if it were a late Roman courtroom scene. In late Roman law, the presiding magistrate, who would be a provincial governor in important cases, had complete authority to adjudicate all phases of the case, ranging from determining what the charges were to making the final judgment. Here, the governor, wearing a military robe pinned at his right shoulder—for even civilian officials were technically in *militia*, or military service—sits on a dais that raises him above the level of others in the courtroom. The governor holds in his left hand a scroll that may contain his official letter of appointment or be intended to record his official disposition of the case; other scrolls of either upcoming or resolved cases lie on the floor beneath him. The governor's rank is attested by the large colored patch on his uniform (in real life, the uniform probably would have been white and the patch purple, as in the San Vitale mosaic illustrated in the next chapter). Behind the governor stand two *apparitores* (bailiffs), also in military uniforms, who look warily at the postulants to their left and are flanked by standards bearing portraits of the two emperors; the emperors' portraits also appear on the cloth covering the desk in front of the governor. The imperial portraits serve as stand-ins for the emperors, just as portraits of the U.S. president are found in modern U.S. courtrooms. An inkpot and pens lie on the table, but the *tabellarius* (court stenographer) standing to the governor's left makes his transcript of the proceedings using a stylus to write on folding wax tablets. His own rank is attested by the colored patch on his uniform. On the right, litigants make their case to the governor, and on the left, members of the general public also express their opinion about how the case should be decided.

Consistory, which consisted of the highest ranking officials of state, including, along with the praetorian prefects and the masters of soldiers, the quaestor of the Sacred Palace, the chief legal official, who oversaw the drafting of laws; the master of offices, a factotum who oversaw the office staffs, received foreign ambassadors, and even commanded a unit of the bodyguard; and the two chief treasury officials, who oversaw the tax income and the administration of imperial property.

The voluminous legislation has the appearance of being terribly prescriptive and inflexible, for it proposed to regulate some of the most intimate and personal aspects of Romans' lives. If it all had been enforced, as once was supposed, the Late Roman Empire would in fact have been a totalitarian establishment. But it was not. What the legislation in fact represents is the emperors' perceptions of what the problems were and methods that could be used to solve them. Very often, the legislation represents what was not happening rather than what was happening: for example, reiterated directives that sons of soldiers must be soldiers suggest only that the laws were not being obeyed.

Late Roman Economy and Infrastructure

The late Roman imperial economy revolved around the gold coinage, based on Constantine's gold solidus. Gold coins were paid out in salaries, expenditures on public works, and subsidies to barbarian peoples, and were returned to the treasury in taxes, fines, and other forms of income. To ensure that taxes did not fall into arrears—for if that happened for too long a period, taxpayers simply stopped paying—the land tax was paid in three installments per year, and to facilitate the accounting, a one-third solidus piece, the tremissis, was extensively minted. The use of gold allowed the government to hoard large amounts of currency in good times that could later be used to meet unexpected large expenditures.

This form of economy was fine for the wealthy and for the government, which worked with huge amounts of money, but did little to benefit the poor, for whom three solidi could represent a year's wages. The lack of a viable silver or copper coinage, that is, one that was tied directly to the gold coinage, meant that local economies, and trade in small-value, high-volume items, suffered badly. Silver coins were never issued in large numbers, and the value of the copper coinage was allowed to float based on market forces, with the result that its value continued to plummet. The book value of the old denarius, no longer minted but still used to value the copper coinage, was 4,350 denarii per solidus in 324; 275,000 per solidus in 337; 4,570,000 per solidus in 360; and 45,000,000 per solidus thereafter. To counteract this inflation, the government attempted to revalue copper coins at higher values; for example, the *centenionalis* issued in the mid-fourth century may have been valued at 100 denarii. To meet the needs of local economies, some regions resorted to issuing their own small change in copper, to which the government turned a blind eye. Nor did long-distance trade completely stop. North African pottery known as red slipware, for example, was extensively exported until well into the seventh century.

Economic restructuring of the empire also was caused by the reorientation of the Roman army. With the decline of large frontier legionary forts and the dispersal of the army around the countryside, the large grain-producing villas of the northern frontier areas lost their economic underpinning. Those owned by absentee landlords were just abandoned, and those run by local senators were reoriented toward a more localized subsistence economy. Many villas were subdivided, occupied by local peasants, and given over to subsistence farming. This farming pattern, of course, looked very different from that of the Principate, but it was equally well suited to the needs of its times.

A mosaic of ca. 400 CE from Carthage in North Africa depicts the fortified villa of the estate-owner Julius and the kinds of activities associated with it, including farming, hunting, and herding.

On the other hand, however, the fourth century was the great age of senatorial villas in southern Gaul, Spain, and North Africa, which continued to prosper. Excavations at the villa of Chiragan near Toulouse, for example, brought to light hundreds of sculptures dating from the first through the fourth centuries, perhaps the private collection of the villa owner.

The nature of urban settlement also changed. The overall decrease in long-distance trade meant a reduced role for cities as major centers of manufacture and economic exchange, just as the reduced role of the Roman government meant a decline in Roman imperial administrative services. The increasing withdrawal of the Roman army from frontier areas brought a parallel drop in the prosperity and population of the cities that had arisen to support it. In addition, senators, decurions, and other large landowners concentrated more on expanding, consolidating, enhancing, and fortifying their country villas, which also could serve as refuges in times of trouble. City populations shrank as both rich and poor sought security in the countryside. The areas enclosed within city walls were as little as a tenth of some city's areas in the second century.

IN THEIR OWN WORDS

CLAUDIUS POSTUMUS DARDANUS AND THE RETREAT TO THE COUNTRYSIDE

During Late Antiquity, there was an increasing focus on local interests. Many senators retreated to the isolated splendor of their estates and consolidated their local authority by constructing fortified villas that not only allowed them to isolate themselves from political and economic changes but also protected them and their clients from more direct threats to personal security. During the second decade of the fifth century, the powerful senator Claudius Postumus Dardanus, who as praetorian prefect of Gaul had remained loyal to the Italian regime during several Gallic usurpations, withdrew with his family to a fortified estate at Sisteron in the French Alps. The construction of this refuge was recorded in a lengthy inscription that proudly listed all of the titles of Dardanus, his wife, and his brother, and acknowledged the role of patronage in local politics: Dardanus' refuge, which would have provided protection not only in times of civil war but also from marauding barbarians, was intended to shelter not only his own family, but also the local population:

> In the place that has the name Theopolis, Claudius Postumus Dardanus, an illustrious man and of patrician rank, ex-consular (governor) of the province of Viennensis, ex-master of the office of petitions, ex-quaestor, ex-praetorian prefect of Gaul, and his *materfamilias* ("mother of the family") Naevia Galla, also an illustrious woman, provided the use of roads, with the sides of the mountains pierced on both sides; they furnished walls and gates, which, established on their own estate, they wished to serve as a common refuge for everyone; with the assistance, indeed, of Claudius Lepidus, an illustrious man, a count, and the brother of the aforementioned man, ex-consular of the province of Germania Prima, ex-master of messages, ex-count of the private purse, they did this so that it would be possible that their enthusiasm for the safety of all and a record of their public devotion would be displayed.

Dardanus also corresponded with some of the most distinguished Christian authors of his day, including Jerome and Augustine. His choice to name his refuge Theopolis, Greek for "City of God," is almost certainly an allusion to Augustine's famous work *De civitate dei, On the City of God,* published at just the time Dardanus was building his private fort.

But cities by no means vanished. What economic life remained continued to be centered on cities, many of which, for example, still had communities of Jewish merchants and moneylenders. Town councils continued to function in many cities, even if at a reduced level. The decline in secular administration was at least partly compensated for by an increase in the role of bishops not only as ecclesiastical leaders but also, in the western provinces, as secular administrators. Funding that in the past had been allocated to the construction of temples, baths, amphitheaters, and buildings typical of the Principate was reallocated to church construction; indeed, churches, often built in the city suburbs and underwritten by the same public-spirited citizens who used to sponsor circus games, now became the most significant urban monuments. Many cities reoriented themselves to be centered on the churches; the old city centers were abandoned and used as stone quarries for material to build more churches. Some cities, such as Rome and the cities of the Holy Land, prospered as pilgrimage centers; people came from far and wide, for example, to be healed at the shrine of St. Martin of Tours.

Late Roman Society

The prescriptive nature of late Roman legislation suggests that late Roman society was very structured and stratified. But in other regards, there were new opportunities. When it came to getting things done, much happened outside the normal administrative, legislative, and judicial channels. Late Roman society and politics functioned through a complex process of behind-the-scenes interaction in which whom one knew often was crucially important. Influential individuals relied on each other to pursue their ambitions. The less privileged often attached themselves for dear life to someone of greater status, trading their independence of action for a legal and economic safety net. The institution of clientela remained just as pervasive in late Roman society as it had been during the Roman Republic.

As always, most of the social, economic, and even political power lay in the hands of the senatorial aristocracy. Unlike the Principate, during which there were only perhaps six hundred true "members" of the Senate, by the late Roman period thousands upon thousands of persons could lay claim to the title of "senator." One could become a senator by several means: by holding one of a multitude of civilian or military offices, by being a Christian bishop, or, most commonly, by being the son of a senator, for senatorial status was inherited. The old order of knights also was absorbed into the senatorial order.

For senators, their most important attribute continued to be their status, that is, how they ranked with regard to other senators. Status was measured by rank (usually obtained through office holding); by wealth (in the form of landed property); by the number of one's clients; and by *potentia* ("power"), the ability to "get one's way." One senator wrote, "The glory of my status flourished, furnished with submission and supported by a crowd of clients." The most obvious determinant of status was rank: all senators had the entry-level rank of *clarissimus* ('most distinguished"); the higher ranks of *spectabilis* (respectable), and *inlustris* ("illustrious") were obtained by holding high offices. And the highest rank, that of patrician, could be received only by a special grant from the emperor.

Senators cultivated their role as patrons by doing favors for their friends and their clients. Even emperors got into the act, for they realized that they could hope to maintain the support of senators only by granting them what they wanted: offices, ranks, and opportunities to accumulate even greater wealth. All in all, however, the senators were not nearly as dependent on the goodwill of the emperor as they had been during the Principate. They now knew that, if need be, they could do quite well without him.

The ideal life of a senator consisted of a balance between *militia*, or state service, and *otium*, or leisure. Senators still coveted the power and prestige that came from holding high office. A senator's fondest dream was to be appointed consul; not only would he give his name to the year, but he also would outrank nearly every other senator. But holding state office no longer was as important as before. Yes, it was a way to gain status, accumulate wealth, and advance the interests of one's family and friends, but a senator's real interests lay at home, somewhere in the provinces. The end result was a continuation of the withdrawal of senatorial support for the central government and the pursuit of local interests and authority. By retiring to the security of fortified villas on their estates, aristocrats could hope to isolate themselves from the vagaries of politics. In the western empire, where the Senate had a long tradition, most senators preferred to be big men in their home provinces rather than small fish, dependent on the goodwill of the emperor, in Rome. Some senators strengthened their local authority by recruiting bands of private retainers made up of mercenaries known as *bucellarii*, or "hardtack men." In the east, however, where the Senate had been created only in the mid-fourth century CE, senators continued to be less independent and more under the thumb of the emperors.

Now that the knights had been incorporated into the senatorial order, the lowest ranking members of the *honestiores* ("more distinguished people") were the decurions. They had the least *potentia* of all the aristocrats. Socially, they were squeezed between the senatorial elite and the mass of the unprivileged population. In a sense, they suffered the worst of both worlds, disdained by their senatorial superiors and distrusted by their plebeian or servile inferiors. More and more responsibilities for local administration, such as expensive road repairs, were foisted on them. And taxes that senators could evade or ignore would devolve on the decurions, who then were compelled to squeeze more out of the plebeian population. Municipal offices, once an honor, now often were a burden.

Decurions constantly confronted the possibility of falling into debt, losing their rung on the ladder of privilege, and falling into the ranks of the *humiliores* ("more humble people"). Yet, for the most ambitious and able, opportunities presented themselves. This was a world in which local interests were foremost, and decurions were experts at life on the local level. Audacious decurions sometimes even appropriated, quite illegally, the title of "senator." This allowed them to evade their municipal responsibilities, although their doing so only increased the burdens on their erstwhile brethren.

Lower still on the social scale was the majority of the population, the great mass of the "more humble" population, most of whom still were referred to generically as "plebeians." For most of them, little changed. The free plebeians, if anything, became even more dependent on either aristocrats or the church for support and continued employment. It remained possible to make a career in the army, but the opportunity to reach high political office by this means, as many had done in the third century, had largely vanished. Small peasant farmers who owned their own land still existed, but there often was pressure to sell out to land-hungry aristocrats, become their clients, and serve as tenants on what had been one's own property. The numerous tenant farmers, the *coloni*, often sank virtually to the level of *servi*, or slaves (the "serfs" of the Middle Ages); the restrictions on their legal freedom were balanced by the security they gained from being under the protection of a powerful aristocrat.

As for the slaves, the days of large slave gangs were gone. The number of agricultural slaves decreased as tenant farming became the preferred method of cultivating large estates. Many slaves were engaged in various kinds of personal services. Even persons of modest means, such as soldiers and schoolteachers, had a slave or two, whose de facto status was little different from that of free plebeians. An occupation that was legally restricted to slaves was that of eunuch. Castration was illegal within the empire, and eunuchs had to be imported, often from Persia. For some, this was a good career choice. The keeper of the sacred bedchamber in the imperial palace, for example, was a eunuch; he was in constant attendance on the imperial family and had very great influence.

Although this social system provided an economic and legal safety net for the less privileged (assuming they had a responsible patron), it also was designed to maintain the status quo. Not everyone was happy with the way that privileged persons often operated outside the legal system. One writer commented, "Who indeed is the rich man or noble who keeps his hands free from crime of all sorts? The socially great wish to have the privilege of committing the lesser crimes as of their right."

New Opportunities

The social, political, and religious transformations of Late Antiquity opened windows of opportunity for advancement and fulfillment to able and ambitious persons, from all segments of the population, whose aspirations might have been stifled or restricted in the past. These included lesser aristocrats, women, the poor, and even barbarians. In the past, for example, the highest-ranking state offices had been monopolized by the most influential senatorial families. Late Antiquity, however, saw old-guard aristocrats being challenged. It always was possible for a New Man, who came from the local landed gentry, if not from an even less privileged element of society, to gain the favor of the emperor, be granted a high office, and enter the aristocracy.

The expansion of Christianity also brought new career opportunities, and, for privileged persons, church office became an attractive alternative to state office. Christianity now attracted the brightest minds and most able individuals in the Roman world; indeed, it was not uncommon for individuals being tracked into government service, such as Ambrose of Milan and Augustine of Hippo, to do a sudden about-face and become bishops. Senators came to see the office of bishop as a way to culminate their careers. It not only permitted them to manifest their Christian piety but it also allowed them to display their public spirit, and to acquire the local authority that they cherished so much. Bishops oversaw the care of the poor, ill, and elderly, for whom the church was now responsible. They intervened on behalf of persons accused or convicted of crimes. They ransomed those captured by barbarians. Using the right of *episcopalis audientia* ("episcopal hearing") granted by the government, they judged civil and criminal cases. All these activities gained them both status and supporters. The office of bishop became so desirable that conflicts sometimes arose over episcopal elections, as rival factions supported their candidates. Further down the social scale, the less privileged likewise had the opportunity to enter ecclesiastical careers, not only as doorkeepers, readers, and gravediggers but also as deacons, priests, and even, on occasion, bishops.

Women, whose status generally was coupled with that of their fathers or husbands, also stood to benefit from the changing times. As always, women's activities usually took place in a family context, although some high-ranking women, both Romans and barbarians, played important roles in political and religious developments during Late Antiquity. Legally, women gained greater rights in choosing marriage partners; a law of the early fifth century stated, "If the suitors are equal in birth and character, the person whom the woman herself approves, consulting her own interests, shall be adjudged preferable." In addition, wealthy women had the opportunity to gain greater control over their own affairs, for by adopting the religious life and devoting themselves to charitable works or to church building, women could not only achieve spiritual fulfillment but also dispose of their property as they saw fit. No matter how much the family might want a rich woman to marry or remarry, it was impolitic to criticize women who expended their wealth on the church.

Imperial women provided role models for female philanthropy. For example, **Helena**, the mother of Constantine, rose from very humble beginnings as a stable girl to become a patroness of the church. After Constantine's adoption of Christianity, she made a pilgrimage to the Holy Land, during which she later was believed to have discovered the cross on which Christ was crucified.

She also built a church on the site of Christ's tomb in Jerusalem. And Anicia Juliana, granddaughter of the emperor Valentinian III, eventually settled in Constantinople, where she had the rank of patrician and married the barbarian general Areobindus. She displayed her religious devotion by building at least three churches, one of which was the largest church in Constantinople until the construction of the church of Hagia Sophia in the mid-sixth century. Other rich and influential women also devoted their lives to the pursuit of Christian piety. Some also built churches; others expended their wealth in other charitable acts, such as the care of the poor.

The patrician Anicia Juliana also was a patroness of the arts. Her portrait appears, garbed in wedding regalia and flanked by the personifications of Magnanimity and Prudence, on the dedicatory page of a copy of the *Herbal of Dioscorides*, one of the earliest surviving illustrated manuscripts.

Late Antique Literary Culture

Contrary to the old-fashioned commonplace that literary culture went into decline after the Principate, Late Antiquity in fact was a time of great literary productivity, with most of the literary works that survive being written by members of the senatorial aristocracy. In their pursuit of leisure, senators placed a great emphasis on their cultural activities. Their education was a literary one, focusing first on grammar and then on rhetoric. Their estates were decorated with sculptures, frescoes, and mosaics modeled on themes from the literature of the Greek and Roman past. They prided themselves on their ability to compose extemporaneous poetry, and made **manuscript** copies of the past literature with their own hands. It is due to their efforts that much of the literature of classical antiquity survived to the modern day.

In the world of secular literature, the last great Latin historian of antiquity, **Ammianus Marcellinus**, an ex-army officer who was part of many of the events he discussed, concluded his *Res gestae* ("Histories"), written in the 390s, with the Battle of Adrianople in 378. The "Augustan History," written at about the same time, is more a work of historical fiction and contains many absurd tales of various emperors' faults and foibles. Subsequent historical works consist primarily of jejune chronicles.

Writers in the traditional literary genres of the classical Greek and Roman past gradually were overwhelmed by those writing in Christian genres. In the fourth and fifth centuries, Christianity demonstrated its intellectual stature with the creation of literary masterpieces by some of the most skilled writers of all time. Christian writers now known as the **Church Fathers**, most of whom came from aristocratic or curial backgrounds, authored in Greek and Latin sermons, commentaries on scripture, theological treatises, letters, and Christian versions of Roman history that had a great effect on the future course of Christian belief and practice.

In the east, bishop Eusebius of Caesarea wrote a *Life of Constantine*, a *Church History*, and a massive *Chronicle* collating all the events of the human past up to the year 325. The theologian **Athanasius**, bishop of Alexandria, almost single-handedly preserved Nicene theology in the east during the period of Arian resurgence in spite of being sent into exile several times. He wrote several works against the Arians, including an "Apology" addressed to Constantius II, and his *History of the Arians* even portrayed Constantius II as the Antichrist. The "Cappadocian fathers," named after a province in Anatolia, also were strong supporters of Nicaea from the 360s into the 380s. They included Basil the Great of Caesarea, whose works included letters, sermons, and "On the Holy Spirit," which demonstrated the place of the Holy Spirit in the Trinity; Gregory of Nyssa, Basil's younger brother, whose important writings include a *Life* of his sister Macrina and works on the Trinity such as "Why There Are Not Three Gods"; and Gregory of Nazianzus, who likewise nuanced the nature of the Holy Spirit and is especially known for the orations he delivered during a brief tenure as bishop of Constantinople. And John Chrysostom, bishop of Constantinople from 398 until he was exiled in 403, authored the largest surviving collection of writings, including sermons, biblical commentaries, letters, and treatises such as "Against Those Who Oppose the Monastic Life."

The west produced equally talented Christian authors. **Jerome**, a native of Illyricum who settled as a monk near Bethlehem, wrote letters, scriptural commentaries, saints' lives and a catalogue of saints, and a Latin translation of the *Chronicle* of Eusebius that he continued up to 379. In addition, by the end of the fourth century, a standard **canon** of books of the Christian bible had been defined, and, after learning Hebrew, Jerome translated the Old and New Testaments from Hebrew and Greek into Latin in a form known as the "**Vulgate**," which gradually replaced the variant versions of the Latin Bible used by different churches. In Milan, Ambrose authored sermons, biblical commentaries, letters, some of the first Christian hymns, and tracts such as "On the Faith, to the Emperor Gratian" and "On Virginity."

To the south, Aurelius Augustine, a North African, was raised as a Christian but then became a Manichaean Hearer. As a young man, he pursued a secular career and served as the official orator of Milan, the imperial capital, in the 380s. But after receiving instruction from Ambrose, he was baptized as a Nicene Christian and adopted the Christian life, eventually becoming bishop of Hippo in North Africa. He was a strong proponent of the need for divine grace to be saved and of the theory of "predestination," whereby God knows in advance who will be saved and who will be damned, which severely weakened the role of free will. His literary output was prodigious: it later was said that "not only could no one ever write as many works as Augustine did, no one could even read that many." He wrote letters, sermons, biblical commentaries, and tracts both in support of his beliefs, such as "On the Trinity," and against a multitude of heresies. His account of his conversion experience, the *Confessions*, is the most important autobiographical account to survive from antiquity.

All of these Christian intellectuals had received the standard classical, and largely polytheistic, education, and they later debated the question of what role pagan literature might have in the Christian world. Some argued that the Greek and Latin classics were relics of paganism and should be simply abandoned. Jerome, who feared being condemned for his classical education, told of seeing himself in a dream standing before God in the Last Judgment and being told, "You are not a Christian. You are a Ciceronian." Augustine and Ambrose, on the other hand, believed that a classical literary education, with its emphasis on grammar and public speaking, could be used in the service of the church. When used cautiously, pagan wisdom likewise had value. Of course, in many instances Christian thinkers disagreed with their pagan predecessors. For example, in *The City of God*, Augustine promoted the Christian linear concept of history, which progressed from the Creation at the beginning to the second coming of Christ at the end, as opposed to the classical view that history was cyclical and repeated itself over and over.

Thanks to Christians who felt the same as Augustine, Greek and Latin classical literature was preserved in the Middle Ages and passed on to the modern day. Christian clerics and monks reproduced manuscripts that previously had been copied by and for cultured senators. And, in general, the preservation of both the pagan and Christian writings of antiquity was furthered by the use of the **codex**, or book format, which usually was made from virtually indestructible parchment, a writing material made from sheep and calf skins, as opposed to the old-fashioned scroll, which usually was made from papyrus and soon became fragile and disintegrated.

THE DECLINE AND FALL OF THE WESTERN ROMAN EMPIRE

The most pivotal political development of Late Antiquity was the dissolution of the western Roman Empire. By the 480s, by a process that still is not completely understood, bands of barbarians managed to carve the Roman west up into a number of independent kingdoms, some of which then served as the germ of the modern European nations.

The Final Separation

In 394, after suppressing a western revolt, Theodosius I became emperor of a united empire. He could not have known that this would be the last time that the Roman Empire would be united under a single ruler. He died in the

THE CREATION OF THE CHRISTIAN BIBLICAL CANON

In the modern day, most Christians assume that the Christian Bible, with its standardized contents of books, or "canon," has been around pretty much ever since the beginning of Christianity, but, at least as regards the New Testament, nothing could be further from the truth. The Old Testament was borrowed directly from the Jewish Septuagint, a Greek translation of the twenty-four books of the Jewish biblical canon that had been drawn up in Alexandria in the Hellenistic period. But the New Testament evolved in a more hit-and-miss fashion and went through many variations before achieving its final form. In the early church, books of scripture, including not only the modern Gospels and the letters of Paul but also a "Gospel of Peter," a "Gospel of Thomas," and the "Acts of Pilate," to name but a few, circulated independently in different churches. Churches often did not have the same collections of scripture.

Attempts to define a standard New Testament canon go back at least to the late second century and a fragmentary document called the Muratorian Fragment; it listed not only many of the modern books but also others, such as the "Revelation of Peter," and it rejected Paul's letters to the Laodiceans and Alexandrians. In the early third century CE, the Christian scholar Origen of Alexandria used a canon including all but four of the books in the modern canon, plus a book called "The Shepherd of Hermas." In 367,

Bishop Athanasius of Alexandria became the first known writer to cite the books of the New Testament in the modern Roman Catholic order, but his list was not yet fully accepted, as some eastern churches, for example, rejected the book of Revelation. And in the west, after much debate, the modern canon was approved at African church councils in the 390s and in a letter of bishop Innocent of Rome in 407. The book of Second Peter, for example, barely gained endorsement. By the fifth century, therefore, by which time most eastern churches had accepted Revelation, the orthodox churches of both the Greek east and the Latin west were in full agreement on which books to include in the Old and New Testaments, and this became the definitive ordering in Jerome's *Vulgate.* But that did not end disputes over the biblical canon, because splinter groups of Christians still preferred to use other noncanonical, or apocryphal (meaning "hidden"), books of scripture; the Egyptian Coptic church, for example, still includes two "Letters of Clement," and the Ethiopian Orthodox church continues to recognize "The Shepherd of Hermas" and the "Acts of Paul." In addition, during the Christian reformation, the biblical canon underwent several significant changes by Protestant groups, which reordered some of the New Testament books, eliminated some Old Testament books, and placed others in a special section, the *Apocrypha.*

following year and was succeeded by his two young sons. Arcadius (383–408), the elder, received the eastern part of the empire, whereas Honorius (393–423) received the west. Neither showed much aptitude for rule, and both came under the influence of ambitious courtiers, relatives, and masters of soldiers.

The forces of fragmentation now reached their logical outcome, and the split between the Greek-speaking east and Latin-speaking west became more than a merely linguistic one. Henceforward there would be an emperor in the east, at Constantinople, and an emperor in the west, usually headquartered at Rome, Milan, or **Ravenna**. Each emperor had sovereign jurisdiction in his own territories. Constitutionally, there continued to be only one empire, and the eastern and western emperors continued to issue coins and laws in each other's names. But in reality the two halves of the empire now went their own ways. Each administration looked out increasingly for its own interests.

One problematic issue had to do with finances. Even in the best of times, the west had barely been able to pay its own way. By the late fourth century, faced with mounting civil and military costs and reduced income, it was a financial liability. As long as there had been a unified rule, resources could be redistributed to prop up the unprofitable west. But the separate administrations changed this. Easterners were reluctant to subsidize the costly west. In addition, disagreement over who controlled the territories in the western Balkans and their rich military recruiting grounds resulted in open hostilities. In the fifth century, the west was largely left to deal with its problems as best as it could by itself. Except for a few uncharacteristic bursts of activity, the eastern government passively sat by as the west collapsed.

The Fall of the West

The barbarian invasions that first had afflicted the east soon had an even greater impact on the west. In 401, the Visigoths decided to go west and invaded Italy. For a time, the half-Vandal, half-Roman master of soldiers Stilicho was able to keep the Visigoths at bay. But the situation worsened in 405, when the barbarian adventurer Radagaisus assembled a huge army in the Danubian region and invaded Italy. In order to defeat him the following year, Stilicho was compelled to withdraw troops from the northern frontier. He could not have done so at a worse time. On the last day of 406, several barbarian peoples, including the Vandals, Alans, and Burgundians, crossed the undefended and frozen Rhine River. They traveled south, and in 409 the Vandals and Alans crossed into the fertile and largely ungarrisoned provinces of Spain. Meanwhile, back on the frontier, the Franks edged south of the Rhine, and Honorius told the isolated Britons to look to their own defense and to expect no help from the empire. Britain then soon was invaded by Angles, Saxons, and Jutes from the area of modern Denmark.

On the base of the Theodosian obelisk, erected in the hippodrome in Constantinople in 390 CE, Theodosius sits at court with the western emperor Valentinian II (375–392) at his left, and his two sons and successors, Arcadius and Honorius, at his right. The imperial family is flanked by military generals (with cloaks pinned at the right shoulder) and ex-consuls wearing decorated togas. Below, barbarian peoples offer tribute signifying their submission to the empire.

TABLE 13.2 THE BARBARIAN INVASIONS

376	Visigoths cross the Danube
378	Battle of Adrianople
401	Visigoths invade Italy
406	Barbarians cross the Rhine
409	Barbarians enter Spain
410	Visigoths sack Rome
429	Vandals invade Africa
451	Battle of the Mauriac Plain
455	Vandals sack Rome
468	Expedition against Vandals
476	Odovacar deposes Romulus

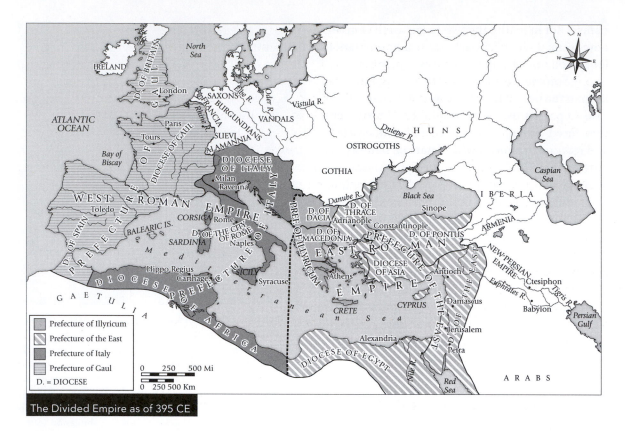

The Divided Empire as of 395 CE

Meanwhile, on August 24, 410, the Visigoths, under their chieftain **Alaric**, occupied and **sacked Rome**. It was a rather genteel sack, lasting only three days and leaving the churches untouched. But the point had been made. For the first time in eight hundred years Rome had fallen to a foreign enemy. Unconquered Rome, as it had been called, now had been conquered. The psychological damage was even greater than the material destruction. The emperor Honorius, safely ensconced in **Ravenna**, in the swamps of northeastern Italy, eventually rid himself of the Visigoths by ceding to them Aquitania in southwestern France. Technically still Roman allies, they soon established their own independent kingdom. The dismemberment of the west was under way.

In 425, Honorius was succeeded by his four-year-old nephew Valentinian III (425–455), whose mother, the Augusta Galla Placidia, served as regent and de facto ruler of the western empire. The political situation continued to worsen. The Vandals crossed to North Africa in 429 and ten years later occupied the great city of Carthage. The loss of North Africa was a disaster for the western empire. Not only did it put much of the grain supply of Italy into enemy hands, but it also gave the Vandals the opportunity to take to piracy. Vandal raiders fell upon

---

ALTERNATIVE HISTORY

Do you think it would have made any difference in the long run if Attila and the Huns had been able to conquer the western Roman Empire?

the coasts of Sicily, Italy, Spain, and even Greece. By the 440s, the treasury was empty, and the western army had disintegrated. What remained of the western empire was largely held together largely by the efforts of the master of soldiers **Aëtius**, often called the "Last of the Romans," who did his best at the dangerous game of playing one barbarian group off against another. When **Attila**, king of the Huns, invaded Gaul in 451, Aëtius cobbled together an unlikely alliance of Romans, Franks, and Visigoths. At the Battle of the Mauriac Plain in northern Gaul, the hitherto undefeated Huns were put to flight. The Roman coalition then collapsed, and the barbarians went back to expanding their holdings at Roman expense. In 452, Italy itself was invaded by the Huns, who, it was said, were turned back by the appeals of Leo, bishop of Rome. Plague and lack of supplies also played a role.

In 454 Aëtius was murdered by Valentinian, who in turn was murdered by two of Aëtius' comrades the following year. Although Valentinian was ineffectual as a ruler, his legitimate status and connection to the old ruling dynasty had provided a last vestige of unity for the increasingly fragmented Roman empire. After his death, the collapse of the west accelerated. In 455, Rome again was sacked, this time by the Vandals, who conducted a thorough and lengthy fourteen-day looting of the city, although Leo was said to have prevailed on king Geiseric not to burn the city. The Vandals returned to Carthage not only with the spoils taken by Titus from Jerusalem in the year 70—the ship carrying them was said to have sunk—but also with the empress Licinia Eudoxia and Valentinian's two daughters Placidia and Eudoxia; the former was married to a Vandal prince.

The term Vandalism *comes from the thoroughness of the Vandal sack of Rome.*

The different regions of the west went their own way, and the remaining nine western emperors are known variously as the **Shadow Emperors** (because of their obscurity) or the **Puppet Emperors** (because they were often manipulated by their masters of soldiers). Few merit mention. Majorian (457–461) forced the Gallic barbarians to terms, reoccupied Spain, and was on the verge of attacking the Vandals when his fleet was treacherously burned in harbor. He was compelled to return to Italy, where he was beheaded by **Ricimer**, his barbarian master of soldiers. And in 468, a huge joint eastern-western expedition against the Vandals failed dismally, and the emperor Anthemius (467–472) subsequently died during a civil war with Ricimer.

The last legitimate western Roman emperor was **Julius Nepos** (474–480), a Greek appointed by the eastern government. He was expelled in 475 by his master of soldiers Orestes, who once had been the secretary of Attila the Hun. Orestes named his son Romulus, nicknamed "Augustulus" ("the little emperor"), as emperor, but the child was deposed in 476 by **Odovacar**, another barbarian general. Odovacar informed the eastern emperor Zeno (474–491) that he would rule Italy in Zeno's name. Odovacar provides an excellent example of the barbarian adventurers who successfully pursued their careers in the midst of the decline of the western Roman Empire. Four years later the exiled

A nineteenth-century engraving depicts young Romulus Augustulus surrendering his diadem to Odovacar, marking the end of the western Roman Empire and the beginning of barbarian Europe.

Nepos died and, with him, any hope of reviving the western emperorship. But, even though the western Roman Empire legally lapsed in 480, Romulus' nickname—the same as the name of the founder of Rome—was too symbolic, and history generally views young **Romulus Augustulus** as the last western Roman emperor.

Perceptions of the Fall of the Western Roman Empire

Ideas about why the western empire fell have exercised the popular imagination ever since the fall of the western empire itself. In an illustrated treatise titled "On Warlike Matters," one contemporary writer recommended to the emperors a number of inventions that he thought could be used to great effect against barbarian invaders, including various kinds of spear chuckers and even an oxen-driven paddlewheel ship. Although none of these inventions is known to have been implemented, they demonstrate that Romans were aware of the problems facing the empire and were suggesting imaginative ways of dealing with them.

In a less practical vein, religious explanations for the Roman decline were common. Pagans blamed it on the abandonment of the old pagan gods. Augustine of Hippo responded to this charge in his *City of God* by arguing that what happened on Earth needed to be tolerated because it was God's will and much less important than what took place in the "heavenly city." Other Christians suggested that the disasters were God's punishment of Christians for their immoral lives.

In 1776, in his famous book *The Decline and Fall of the Roman Empire*, Edward Gibbon revisited the controversy and saw the fall of the western empire as the "triumph of Christianity and barbarism." He suggested that Christianity had attracted the best minds and that its message of love and peace had weakened the will of the Romans to resist, opening up the way for the more martial barbarians.

Among the inventions proposed to the emperors was a paddlewheel ship powered by oxen. This contraption, which would have saved the hundred-plus sailors needed to man the oars, is not known to have been constructed, but vessels of a similar design operated on the lakes of upstate New York in the nineteenth century.

This explanation, however, now is seen as too simplistic. After all, most of the barbarians were Christians themselves. And as for the barbarian invasions, for centuries the emperors had dealt with barbarian threats quite handily. In addition, aside from the Battle of Adrianople, it is difficult to identify many significant barbarian victories during their supposed military conquest. The barbarians occupied the west by means of infiltration, peaceful settlement, and persistence rather than by military superiority or right of conquest. The real question, it seems, is what factors made it possible for the barbarians to succeed at this point when they had been notable only for their failures in the past.

More recent thought identifies a multitude of interrelated causative factors. Some suggestions, ranging from climatic change to ethnic mixing to lead poisoning, can be easily dismissed. Others include the withdrawal of senatorial support, increasing administrative decentralization, barbarization of the army, the lack of organized resistance, economic collapse, overtaxation, corruption, manpower shortages, excessive bureaucracy, bad leadership, and just plain bad luck.

Furthermore, any satisfactory explanation for the fall of the west also must explain the survival of the east. It is clear, for example, that the east had more secure geographical frontiers, a stronger economy, a less well-entrenched senatorial order, a larger population, and a more dependable Roman military recruitment base, all of which increased the east's chances of survival. From this perspective, it may be that the once the empire split into two halves, the decline of the west was virtually foreordained.

LEGACY OF ANTIQUITY

The inventions suggested by the anonymous Roman reformer seem not to have been implemented in their own time. Can you think of other occasions on which imaginative ideas for weapons of war also have been ignored? Were any of them implemented at a later date?

THE BARBARIAN SETTLEMENT
CATASTROPHE VERSUS TRANSFORMATION

In a model prevalent since antiquity, which might be called the *Catastrophe Model*, savage barbarian hordes have been blamed for waves of invasion during the fifth century CE that were the primary cause of the decline and fall of the western Roman Empire. These uncouth barbarians have been held responsible for the destruction of the western Roman government, for a decline in levels of economic productivity, and for the material destruction of Roman art and architecture. They also have been blamed for attempting, consciously or unconsciously, to destroy classical civilization and for creating a period of cultural decline and barrenness known ominously as the Dark Ages, when only faint glimmers of classical civilization were preserved by a few dedicated monks. The Catastrophe Model sees a barbarian settlement characterized by violent conquest, material destruction, severe economic decline, social and religious animosities between Romans and barbarians, and, in general, many changes from the Roman world. This view sees the fall of the western empire as being primarily due to external factors—the barbarian invaders—and continues to have eloquent supporters in the historical community.

Recent decades, however, have brought the development of a different model regarding the causes and impact of the barbarian settlement on the Roman world. The *Ttransformation Model* posits largely peaceful integration and assimilation, punctuated only occasionally by bouts of violent conquest, in which, in most places, there was little actual violent conquest; minimal material destruction; economic decline caused not by the barbarians but by the general economic changes of the period; social and religious integration; and, in general, cultural, social, and administrative continuity from the Roman period. Proponents of the Transformation Model point out that it is difficult to find many battles that the barbarians won; indeed, most of the set battles were won by the Romans. It also is difficult to find signs of violent destruction in the archaeological record. The level of cultural decline, it is argued, was neither so precipitous nor so complete as once had been thought; indeed, there was an explosion of ecclesiastical writing. And religious animosities have been greatly exaggerated; except in Vandal Africa, Nicene Romans and Arian barbarians in fact got along very well, even attending each other's services. The real issue, in this view, is what kind of internal changes allowed the barbarians to succeed when in the past the Roman government had been quite able to deal with barbarian threat.

The proponents of both these views tend to be rather prescriptive in arguing their views. But what is more likely is that any ultimate answer to the question of the nature of the barbarian settlement, to the degree that one exists, will be a combination of elements drawn from both schools of thought.

And finally, it sometimes has been questioned whether the western Roman Empire actually did fall: politically, it did, as barbarians—often Romanized barbarians—assumed the responsibility for governing different areas of the west. But most aspects of Roman culture, including language, literature, administration, law, and, in particular, the Christian religion, survived and were transmitted to later ages. In addition, the western Roman Empire was revived under the Frank Charlemagne, who once again took the title of Augustus in the year 800, and the German-based Holy Roman Empire lasted from the eleventh century until its final dissolution in 1806.

Meanwhile, however, the title of Caesar had been revived as *czar* in Russia, which claimed to be the successor of the Roman Empire until the end of the Russian monarchy in 1917. The whole question of the causes of and even the date of the fall of the western Roman Empire is therefore full of complexity and nuance, and one can safely conclude that this controversy will never be definitively settled.

LOOKING AHEAD

As of the 480s, various barbarian peoples had established independent kingdoms in all of the western Roman Empire. Most surveys of Roman or ancient history stop at this point, if they get this far at all, leaving the reader believing that the barbarians had won and that the Roman Empire was effectively at an end. But by continuing the narrative of ancient history until the end of Late Antiquity, ca. 650, a very different picture is presented, as will be seen in the next, and concluding, chapter.

FURTHER READING

Arnheim, M. T. W. *The Senatorial Aristocracy in the Later Roman Empire.* Oxford: Oxford University Press, 1972.

Boak, Alfred E. R. *Manpower Shortage and the Fall of the Roman Empire in the West.* Ann Arbor: University of Michigan Press, 1955.

Bowersock, G. W. *Julian the Apostate.* London: Duckworth, 1978.

Bowersock, G. W., P. Brown, and O. Grabar, *Late Antiquity: A Guide to the Postclassical World.* Cambridge, MA: Harvard University Press, 1999.

Brown, Peter. *The Body and Society: Men, Women, and Sexual Renunciation in Early Christianity.* New York: Columbia University Press, 1988.

Brown, Peter. *Power and Persuasion in Late Antiquity: Towards a Christian Empire.* Madison, WI: University of Wisconsin Press, 1992.

Clark, Gillian. *Women in Late Antiquity.* Oxford: Oxford University Press, 1993.

Ferrill, Alfred. *The Fall of Rome: The Military Explanation.* London: Thames and Hudson, 1986.

Harrison, Martin. *A Temple for Byzantium: The Discovery and Excavation of Anicia Juliana's Palace-Church in Istanbul.* Austin: University of Texas Press, 1989.

Hoare, F. R., ed. *The Western Fathers: Being the Lives of Martin of Tours, Ambrose, Augustine of Hippo, Honoratus of Arles and Germanus of Auxerre.* New York: Sheed and Ward, 1954.

Jones, Arnold H. M. *The Later Roman Empire, 284–602: A Social, Economic and Administrative Survey,* 3 vols. Oxford: Blackwell, 1964.

Kelly, Christopher. *Ruling the Later Roman Empire.* Cambridge, MA: Harvard University Press, 2004.

Lenski, Noel E. *Failure of Empire: Valens and the Roman State in the Fourth Century a.d.* Berkeley: University of California Press, 2002.

Levine, L. I., ed., *The Synagogue in Late Antiquity.* Philadelphia: American Schools of Oriental Research, 1987.

Liebeschuetz, J. H. W. G. *The Decline and Fall of the Roman City.* Oxford: Oxford University Press, 2001.

Mathisen, R. W. *People, Personal Expression, and Social Relations in Late Antiquity.* 2 vols. Ann Arbor: University of Michigan Press, 2003.

Matthews, John F. *The Roman Empire of Ammianus.* Baltimore: Johns Hopkins University Press, 1989.

McCormick, Michael. *The Origins of the European Economy: Communications and Commerce, A. D. 300–900.* Cambridge: Cambridge University Press, 2001.

McLynn, Neil B. *Ambrose of Milan: Church and Court in a Christian Capital.* Berkeley: University of California Press, 1994.

O'Flynn, J. M. *Generalissimos of the Western Roman Empire.* Edmonton, Alberta, Canada: University of Alberta Press, 1983.

Pohl, Walter, ed., *Kingdoms of the Empire: The Integration of Barbarians in Late Antiquity.* Leiden, Netherlands: Brill, 1997.

Potter, David S. *The Roman Empire at Bay, AD 180–395.* London: Routledge, 2004.

Southern, P., and K. Dixon, *The Late Roman Army.* London: Batsford, 1996.

Ward-Perkins, Bryan. *The Fall of Rome and the End of Civilization.* Oxford: Oxford University Press, 2005.

Whittaker, C. R. *Frontiers of the Roman Empire: A Social and Economic Study.* Baltimore: Johns Hopkins University Press, 1994.

CHAPTER 14

THE END OF ANTIQUITY
(476–640)

By the end of the fifth century, the Roman world looked very different from the way it had appeared at the time of Augustus. The hard-won political unity of the Mediterranean world had been fractured. The western part of the empire had been partitioned among several barbarian peoples. But in the east, the Roman Empire, now known to modern historians as the Byzantine Empire, continued to survive and even flourish, adapting to changing times just as it had done in the past. During the seventh century, the ancient world was even more dramatically changed with the appearance of a new religion, Islam, in Arabia. The Persian Empire disappeared, and Muslims soon occupied much of the ancient world. The ancient world was drawing to a close, soon to be replaced by three separate political, religious, and cultural worlds of the **Middle Ages**.

THE BARBARIAN WEST

Even though the year 476 often is considered to mark the end of the Roman Empire in the west, some elements of the western Roman population continued to hold out. But by 500, all of the western empire had been incorporated into barbarian kingdoms, with the Visigoths in southwestern Gaul and Spain, the Vandals in North Africa, the Angles and Saxons in Britain, Burgundians in central Gaul, Alamanni on the upper Rhine, the Franks on the lower Rhine, and the Ostrogoths in Italy. One of the curiosities of historical writing is that most modern accounts of ancient history stop here, leaving the reader thinking that the barbarians had won and the Romans had lost. But by continuing forward in time for another few hundred years, one discovers that this was not the case. After not very long, the Romans had reconquered most of the western Mediterranean world, and smaller barbarian kingdoms had been gobbled up by larger ones. By the early eighth century, Spain had fallen to the Muslims,

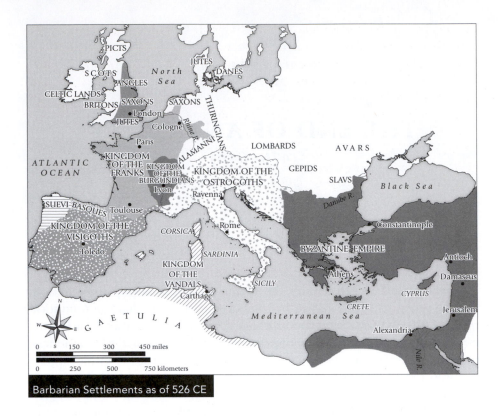

Barbarian Settlements as of 526 CE

and the only barbarian kingdoms left were those of the Franks in France and the Angles and Saxons in England.

Romans and Barbarians

Eventually, all the inhabitants of western Europe felt the effects of the barbarian presence. Some fled, others faced life as captives, but most had to make whatever kind of private peace they could. In some cases, powerful Roman magnates may have preferred a local barbarian ruler who acknowledged their property rights and did not ask too many questions to a distant yet intrusive emperor. In many regards, the barbarian settlement caused little disruption, and, on a local level, life went on much as before, with barbarians becoming not only political rulers but also neighbors and social acquaintances. Indeed, in some ways all that made the sixth century different from the fourth was that the supreme political authority was a barbarian king rather than a Roman emperor.

The barbarians could not escape the power and prestige of either the Roman Empire or classical culture—not that they would have wanted to. For, after all, most of the barbarian peoples who occupied the western empire had been living in close contact with the Roman world and had even been working inside the empire for centuries and had enthusiastically absorbed much of it even before they crossed the Roman frontier. Except in Britain, Roman culture continued as before. The Latin language was adopted by all of the barbarian settlers except for the Anglo-Saxons, and it gradually evolved into the modern-day **Romance** (from "Roman") **languages**, including Spanish, Portuguese, French, Italian, and Romanian. Classical literature was appreciated, engaged in, and preserved by the educated elite. Over the course of time, barbarians, too, were assimilated into the classical cultural tradition.

In addition, in most regards, barbarian kingdoms looked like small-scale models of the Roman government. All of the barbarian governments adopted, to a greater or lesser degree, Roman procedures, making use of Roman law and administrative practices and continuing to use Roman officials. Barbarian kings were kings of peoples, not of territories; but, like Roman emperors, they continued to issue laws that were binding on all of the people living in territories under their control and compiled law codes just as Roman emperors did. None of the barbarian kingdoms, however, had an economy or bureaucracy that was nearly as complex as the Roman one.

Older scholarly suggestions that there was one law for Romans and one for barbarians generally are no longer considered credible.

One concern that barbarian rulers had was how to maintain their individuality and authority in the midst of so many Romans, for the barbarians were but a drop in a Roman sea. In an attempt to preserve their identity and justify their authority, barbarians often created an origin myth that gave their ruling families, which often were of very recent derivation, the luster of great antiquity. The rulers of the Franks, for example, claimed to be descended from the Trojans. But even here, the best they could do was to try to work their way into the classical tradition. Barbarian rulers also realized that if they could not conciliate their Roman subjects, they risked provoking uprisings in which they could be overwhelmed. The only way to survive was by respecting Roman traditions and values and making common cause with the powerful Roman magnates, much as Augustus had ruled with the cooperation of the senators at the beginning of the Principate.

In particular, the Christian church thrived under barbarian rule. If barbarian peoples were not already Christian when they entered they empire, they soon became Christian. And Christian culture at this time involved not only the spiritual life but also secular life. In much of the western Mediterranean world, and especially in Gaul, Christian bishops had absorbed many of the duties of city councils and Roman local officials. This often left bishops as de facto secular administrators on the local level. Many Roman cities shrank to little more than episcopal centers, overseen by a bishop. Bishops administered justice, oversaw local public works, and were able to mobilize local populations. By the fifth century, Roman senators, who by then were focusing on pursuing local interests anyway, had come to monopolize episcopal office in many cities. Thus, when barbarian kings dealt with Christian bishops, they often were dealing with Roman senators. This made it even more important for barbarian rulers to be on good terms with powerful Roman senators and to respect their ancient rights.

This is not to say, of course, that there were not any difficulties during the course of the barbarian settlement. A very obvious possible source of conflict concerned property. Barbarian settlers, first and foremost, were seeking land on which to settle. Where was it to come from? Several solutions were implemented. Sometimes, barbarians were granted either land that in the past had belonged to the Roman government or shares in Roman tax receipts that could be used to purchase land. On other occasions, large Roman landowners shared their land with barbarian settlers, turning over to barbarians meadows that had not been leased out to tenants and keeping for themselves the more valuable rented lands. Despite some squabbling over how the division was to be made, the system was generally effective; after all, there were a great many Roman landowners and just not that many barbarians, and large landowners often saw the advantage in having barbarian neighbors who now had an interest in protecting local property.

Another potential incompatibility, at least in some places during the early years of the settlement, lay in the area of religion. Both Romans and barbarians were Christians, but the Romans followed the Nicene Creed, whereas most barbarians were Arians. Recent study, however, suggests that this dissimilarity usually was of little consequence. Arians and Nicenes generally were tolerant of each other, even going so far as to attend each other's church services and dinner parties. And when barbarians did become Nicene, as all of them eventually did, by choice or by compulsion, they, including their clergy, were incorporated into the Nicene church with a minimum of fuss.

A third factor that characterized the European post-Roman world was a general increase in the level of violence, for the reduced level of government oversight meant that powerful persons often ended up taking justice, and the pursuit of their own advantage, into their own hands. This meant that it was all the more important for unprivileged and powerless persons to become clients and put themselves under the protection of powerful persons—barbarian nobles, Roman senators, and bishops—who they hoped would look out for their interests.

The Visigoths

As the first barbarian invaders to settle and maintain their independence on Roman soil, the Visigoths adapted themselves readily to Roman practices. In 412, the Visigothic chieftain Athaulf even went so far as to marry the Roman princess Galla Placidia, who had been kidnapped during the sack of Rome in 410. The death of their infant son, Theodosius, ended the hopes of a joint Roman-Visigothic union.

After settling in Aquitania in 418, nominally as Roman allies, with their capital at Toulouse, the Arian Visigoths established an independent Kingdom of Toulouse that took advantage of Roman weakness to occupy more and

ETHNICITY VERSUS HISTORY VERSUS CULTURE

The Greeks and Romans left extensive literary remains, but other ancient peoples, especially those living beyond the frontiers of the Roman Empire, left no written records. These barbarian peoples are known only by occasional references in Greek and Latin authors, which historians use to try to establish when and where they lived. Archaeologists, on the other hand, use the material remains left behind by different peoples to identify characteristic archaeological cultures, whose extent in space and time likewise can be established. A popular armchair sport of scholars lies in attempting to match up the archaeological cultures with historical peoples. The fit often is less than perfect.

Others attempt to identify the ethnicity of peoples who left no written records on the basis of the material attributes—including elements such as hairstyle, dress, jewelry, and weapons—that are associated with them in both literature and archaeological excavations. But doing so can be tricky. Ancient authors loved to categorize different peoples and cultures based on their appearance. Diodorus of Sicily, for example, regarding the Celts, described "shirts that have been dyed and embroidered in varied colors, and breeches that they call in their tongue 'bracae,' and striped coats, fastened by a buckle on the shoulder." One can still recognize here the tartans of the modern Scots. Germans were known for dyeing their hair red. More specifically, Visigoths were said to favor mustaches, Suevi the "Suevic knot" in their hair (attested in literature, art, and physical remains), and *Longobardi* (Lombards), or "long beards," sported long unshaven beards. Barbarians also could be categorized based on their weaponry. Franks favored the *francisca,* a throwing ax that gave them their name, and the Saxons were named after the seax (also known as the scramasax), a large single-edged knife.

On the other hand, some historians have challenged the identification of ethnicity based on cultural attributes by citing counterexamples, such as a Frank who did not use the *francisca* or a Visigoth who did, but it is well known that people of one culture (including Romans) often used words and material used by other groups, a process linguists refer to as "code switching," and the act of doing do does not lessen the identification of the word or item with a particular ethnic group.

Nor are these merely academic discussions, for modern governments have attempted to lay claim to modern territory that their putative ancestors of thousands of years ago supposedly occupied. Thus in the 1930s the Nazi government of Germany used the findings of scientific archaeology to claim ownership of Poland because their ancestors, the Goths and Vandals, supposedly had lived there. Others, however, argued that it was the ancestors of the Slavs, not the Germans, who had dwelt in ancient Poland. And the debate continues.

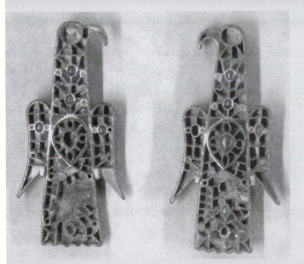

Different barbarian peoples favored particular styles of ornate *fibulae*, clasps used to hold garments together at the shoulder (note the jeweled fibula worn by Justinian in the mosaic pictured in the color plate following p. 240). For example, the Visigoths liked ornate "eagle" fibulae made from bits of colored glass set in a metal framework.

The opening section of the Breviarium of Alaric II, a compilation of earlier Roman laws and legal theory, preserved in a manuscript of the eighth century.

more Roman territory. Under King Theoderic II (453-466), for example, the Visigoths defeated the Suevi, who had occupied northwestern Spain and began to occupy Roman Spain. But the most able Visigothic king in Gaul was Euric (466-484), who conquered the remainder of southwestern Gaul, expanding from Provence to the Loire River and ruling the largest and most powerful barbarian kingdom in Europe. Unlike his Arian predecessors, Euric was increasingly harsh in his treatment of the Nicene church hierarchy. Some bishops were exiled, and cities that had lost their bishops were forbidden to ordain successors.

Euric's son Alaric II (484-507), however, was threatened by the Franks. In 506, he attempted to conciliate the Roman population by sponsoring a compilation of Roman law known as the *Breviarium* ("Summary"), and even permitting the Nicene bishops to hold a church council. But it was too little too late. The final confrontation came in 507 at the **Battle of Vouillé**, just outsider Poitiers, where Alaric was defeated and killed by Clovis and the Franks and the Visigoths lost nearly all their Gallic possessions. Subsequently, the Visigothic kingdom was limited to Spain and an adjoining narrow strip of southern Gaul.

The Visigothic kingdom in Spain, the Kingdom of Toledo, survived by making extensive use of Romans in both secular and ecclesiastical positions. Unlike Gaul, which returned to a largely agrarian society, Spain continued to have an active urban culture, and some of the Visigothic kings even founded new cities. The kingdom of the Suevi was completely absorbed, and in 589 the Visigoths officially converted from Arian to Nicene Christianity at the Third Council of Toledo. This created a uniform Nicene Christian world in western Europe, nominally all under the authority of the bishop of Rome. In the seventh century, Visigothic kings issued a massive legal compilation known as the Book of Judgments. The Visigothic kingdom survived until 711, when it fell to a Muslim invasion from North Africa.

The Ostrogoths

In 488, the Byzantine emperor Zeno rid himself of the troublesome **Ostrogoths** by sending them west to occupy Italy, which they and their king, Theoderic, were happy to do. Theoderic invaded Italy in 489, and after being besieged in Ravenna for three years, Odovacar, the barbarian king of Italy, finally surrendered on condition that the two would rule Italy jointly. Soon thereafter, however, he and his family were murdered by Theoderic.

The Ostrogoths developed a kingdom that looked very much like the Roman Empire. King Theoderic, called "the Great," had his capital at the Roman imperial city of Ravenna and issued legislation that looked very much like that of the empire. Many high-ranking officials were wealthy and powerful Roman senators, and the Senate in Rome even regained some of its old authority, such as the right to issue coins. Despite his Arianism, Theoderic also allowed Nicenes full freedom of religion and even became involved in Nicene church controversies, intervening in 502 in a disputed episcopal election at Rome. Even the bishop of Rome had little cause for complaint, for, freed from imperial oversight, he was able to expand his own authority. He began to monopolize the title of **Pope**, which in the past had been applicable to any distinguished bishop.

A gold medallion of Theoderic the Great exemplifies the interaction between Roman and barbarian culture. It bears a Latin legend, "Theodoricus pius princis" ("King Theoderic, pious prince") and depicts Theoderic wearing a Roman uniform and holding a Roman symbol of victory. But it also ostentatiously shows Theoderic with the long hair typical of Germanic royalty.

Theoderic also was well connected in the barbarian world, being related by marriage to the kings of the Vandals, Burgundians, Franks, and Visigoths. In 507, after the defeat of the Visigoths at Vouillé, he occupied Provence in southern Gaul and became the titular king of Visigothic Spain. It appeared that an Ostrogothic Empire was in the making. But toward the end of Theoderic's reign, problems arose. In 522 the influential senators Symmachus and Boethius were accused of treason and executed, resulting in a breakdown in the carefully nurtured partnership with the Roman senators. Theoderic died in 526, and the dream of an Ostrogothic empire died with him.

Theoderic was succeeded by his daughter Amalasuintha, who first served as regent for her young son Athlaric and then ruled as queen in her own right. But making her cousin Theodahad her coruler was a mistake, for in 535 he had her murdered in her bath. A few years later the Ostrogothic kingdom was invaded by the eastern Roman Empire, finally falling in 553.

The Vandals

After their occupation of Roman North Africa between 429 and 439 and their subsequent seizure of Sicily, Sardinia, and Corsica, the Vandals established a powerful kingdom centered at Carthage. Under the leadership of their very able and long-reigning ruler Geiseric (428–477), several Roman attempts to retake Africa were repulsed, and the Vandals became the most oppressive of the barbarian rulers of the western empire, adopting a policy of weakening the Roman senatorial class. Large tracts of Roman land were confiscated, and

In this fifth- or sixth-century mosaic now in the British Museum, a pants-clad and mustachioed Vandal landowner waves farewell while riding away from his fortified villa, which likely had been confiscated from a departed Roman senator.

Romans who held office in the Vandal administration were expected to convert to Arianism. Many Roman senators simply abandoned their property and fled, often to Constantinople. In addition, Christian writers accused the Arian Vandals of savage persecutions of Christians, although it was primarily the Nicene clergy that the Vandals targeted. In an attempt to break the powerful hold of Christian clergy on the people, many Christian bishops were exiled, often to Sardinia. Vandals were prohibited from converting to Nicene Christianity, and persons merely dressed in the Vandal style who were apprehended entering Nicene churches were severely punished by having their hair torn from their scalps. In other regards, however, ordinary Nicenes generally were permitted to worship in peace.

Soon after the sack of Rome in 455 and the kidnapping of the imperial women, Geiseric's son Huneric was married to Eudocia, the daughter of Valentinian, and when Geiseric died in 477, Huneric succeeded him. Under Huneric (477–484), the persecution of Nicenes intensified. Some Nicenes were executed for refusing to convert to Arianism, many bishops were banished to Corsica, and influential Romans were exiled to the Sahara Desert. During his reign, outlying areas of the Vandal kingdom came under attack from the native Moors of North Africa. After Huneric's death, the Vandal kingdom was ruled by Geiseric's descendents. Sporadic persecutions of Nicenes continued, and the Moors made further encroachments onto Vandal territory. The fall of the Roman Empire in the west, however, for the time being prevented any further Roman attempts to reconquer Africa.

In 523, Hilderic (523–530), the son of Huneric and the imperial princess Eudocia, succeeded to the Vandal throne. Because Hilderic was sympathetic to the Nicene views of his mother, he was supported by the Byzantine emperor but disliked by many Vandals, especially the nobles. Hilderic lifted the restrictions on Nicene worship, and when ordinary Vandals began to convert to Nicene Christianity, Vandal nobles became alarmed and formed a conspiracy against him. In 530, Hilderic was imprisoned, and his cousin Gelimer, a staunch Arian, seized the throne. This act gave the Byzantine emperor Justinian just the pretext that he needed for launching an attack on the Vandals in 533.

Within a few months, and after two battles, the Vandal kingdom had been destroyed and North Africa reintegrated into the Roman-cum-Byzantine

Empire. Many surviving Vandal soldiers were recruited into the Byzantine army and sent to the Persian frontier. The Vandals then virtually disappeared from history, and of all the Germans who occupied the Roman Empire, the Vandals probably had the least lasting impact, largely, perhaps, because of the difficulties they had engaging with the Roman population.

The Anglo-Saxons and Irish

In Britain, the Roman population simply retreated in the face of barbarian invasions of **Angles**, **Saxons**, and Jutes that began not long after the Romans abandoned the island in 410. The eastern half of the island was occupied by the invaders, who, at least initially, retained their Germanic culture. Some Britons fled to Armorica in western Gaul, which then became known as Brittany. But other western Britons continued to resist, led first by Aurelius Ambrosius, sometimes called as "the last of the Romans," and then by warlords such as Arthur, the "Duke of Battles," as he was called in the only surviving roughly contemporary reference to him. As "King Arthur," he later became the subject of legends and medieval romances. Circa 500, the Britons inflicted a major defeat on the invaders at the Battle of Mount Badon, the last western Roman victory over the barbarians. Soon after, however, the Britons were overwhelmed, and Britain became partitioned into several independent Anglo-Saxon kingdoms, including Wessex (from West Saxons), Sussex (from South Saxons), Essex (from East Saxons), Mercia (Angles), East Anglia (from East Angles), Kent (Jutes), and Northumbria (Angles). By the ninth century Britain came to be known as England (from "Angle-Land").

At the end of the sixth century, Britain began to be pulled back into the classical sphere. In 597, Augustine, a Roman monk sent by Pope Gregory I, arrived in England for the purpose of "converting" the Anglo-Saxons to Christianity, even though England already had communities of so-called Celtic Christians, the descendents of the previous Roman population. Augustine was appointed bishop of Canterbury, which became the archiepiscopal see of the English church. Within a few years, bishops had been appointed in several English cities, and Roman Catholic Christianity then quickly spread throughout England. At the Council of Whitby in 664, Roman Catholic traditions, such as the date of Easter, were imposed on the surviving Celtic bishops. Meanwhile, Anglo-Saxon kingdoms continued to bicker among themselves. In the 880s King Alfred of Wessex first took the title King of the Anglo-Saxons, but the Anglo-Saxons were not finally united into a single kingdom until 924 by Aethelstan, who also laid claim to Scotland and Wales and took the title King of All Britain.

One of the ironies of history is that even though Ireland never had been occupied by the Romans, after the end of the western Roman Empire, Ireland was to become one of the most important bastions of classical culture. Although Roman culture certainly had penetrated into Ireland during the Roman period and there already were a few Christian communities, formal Roman influence in Ireland did not begin until the 430s, when Patrick, a Briton of curial stock who had been carried off to Ireland as a slave but then escaped, became the self-proclaimed bishop of the Irish. Patrick and other missionaries then converted much of Ireland to the Celtic form of Christianity, which retained its own way of calculating the date of Easter and in which church authority was centered in monasteries. After his death Patrick became the national saint of Ireland. Subsequently, Irish monks took a leading role in the preservation of classical culture after the fall of the western empire.

The Franks

The Franks followed a rather different trajectory. They had originated in the third century CE as a confederation of several different groups living on both sides of the lower Rhine. The most influential Frankish group was the Sicambrians, who already had been mentioned by Tacitus ca. 100 CE. By the fifth century, the Salian Franks were settled in Toxandria (northern Belgium), with their center at Tongres. Subsequently, the Ripuarian Franks crossed the middle Rhine. Other Franks remained across the Rhine in Franconia. Most other barbarian peoples abandoned their original homelands when they occupied the Mediterranean regions of the empire. But the Franks stayed home and simply expanded their original territory into formerly Roman lands. Indeed, the Franks never even really invaded the empire, but they were assigned the responsibility for guarding increasingly large areas of northern Gaul by the imperial government. Even during the barbarian invasion of 406, the Franks remained remarkably loyal to Rome, although they later did sack Trier four times. Thus, with greater justification than any other barbarian people, the Franks could claim that they had simply succeeded to the Roman administration by default.

The different Frankish subgroups were united and the kingdom greatly expanded under **Clovis** (481–511), a member of the **Merovingian dynasty** of Frankish kings, named after Clovis' grandfather Merovech, who in later legend was said to have been the son of the Quinotaur, a five-headed sea monster that had raped Clovis' grandmother. In 486, Clovis defeated the last Roman holdout, Syagrius—another person who sometimes is called "the last of the Romans"—and occupied much of north central Gaul. Twelve years later, during a hard-fought battle with the Alamanni, it was said that Clovis promised to become a Christian. After the Frankish victory, Clovis was baptized as a Nicene Christian by Remigius, the Roman bishop of Reims. His Nicene faith gained Clovis valuable Roman support during his subsequent war with the Visigoths. At the pivotal Battle of Vouillé, Clovis defeated and killed Alaric II, and the Franks occupied most of the Visigothic territories in Gaul, thus becoming the primary barbarian power in Gaul. Immediately afterward, Clovis overthrew other Frankish kings, such as Chloderic, king of the Ripuarians, and Ragnachar, king of Cambrai, and brought all the Franks under his own rule.

THE CONVERSION OF CLOVIS

Constantine was not the only ruler who was confronted by a choice of religions. The king of the Franks, Clovis, who also had been raised as a pagan, faced the same choice. Like Constantine, he opted for Christianity. As a result, both barbarians and Romans shared the same religious beliefs and practices, greatly facilitating the integration of the two populations in the period after the fall of the western Roman Empire. In this passage, the historian Gregory of Tours (*Histories* 2.29–30) describes how, circa 496, Clovis' wife Clotilde influenced him to convert:

> Queen Clotilde continued to pray that her husband might recognize the true God and give up his idol worship. Nothing could

persuade him to accept Christianity. Finally, war broke out against the Alamanni, and in this conflict he was forced by necessity to accept what he had refused of his own free will. It turned out that when the two armies met on the battlefield, there was great slaughter, and the troops of Clovis were rapidly being annihilated. He raised his eyes to heaven when he saw this and was moved to tears. "Jesus Christ," he said, "you who Clotilde maintains to be the Son of the living God, you who see fit to give help to those in distress and victory to those who trust in you, in faith I beg the glory of your help. If you will give me victory over my enemies then I will be baptized in your name." Even as he said this, the Alamanni turned their backs and began to run away. Clovis told the queen how he had won a victory by calling on the name of Christ. This happened in the fifteenth year of his reign. The queen then ordered Saint Remigius, bishop of the city of Reims, to be summoned in secret. She begged him to impart the word of salvation to the king. The bishop asked Clovis to meet him in private and began to urge him to believe in the true God. The king demanded that the bishop baptize him. He proceeded to the baptismal font like a new Constantine. Having confessed omnipotent God in the trinity, he was baptized in the name of the Father, the Son, and the Holy Spirit and was anointed with the sacred chrism with the sign of the cross of Christ.

In a medieval manuscript illumination, the Frankish king Clovis, with Roman clerics on his right and Frankish nobles to his left, is baptized by bishop Remigius at Reims.

During his reign, Clovis shrewdly conciliated the Gallo-Roman aristocracy, and especially the powerful Gallo-Roman bishops, by recognizing their social status and their property rights. And like other barbarian kings, Clovis demonstrated that he was a worthy successor of the Romans by issuing a law code known as the Salic Law. His successors likewise issued laws in the manner of Roman emperors.

After Clovis' death in 511, his kingdom, which was considered to be his personal property, was divided among his four sons: Theoderic I of Metz, Chlodomer of Orléans, Childebert I of Paris, and Chlothar I of Soissons. This policy of partition, which was followed by subsequent Merovingian kings, was to be the bane of the Merovingian dynasty. Not only did it prevent the unification of the kingdom but it also encouraged the intrigues, quarrels, and conflicts for which the Merovingian kings became so well known. At the same time, the Frankish kings could not restrain themselves from interfering in ecclesiastical affairs, bestowing episcopal sees on their favorites, and often appropriating church property.

During the 530s, the Franks occupied Provence, which had been controlled by the Ostrogoths, and absorbed the Burgundian kingdom in the central Rhône River valley, which already had converted from Arianism to Nicene Christianity in 516 under King Sigismund. This gave the Franks control of all of Roman Gaul excepting a coastal strip north of Spain known as Septimania, which continued to be held by the Visigoths.

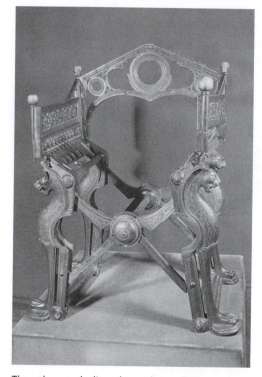

The throne believed to have belonged to Dagobert I was made in the shape of the curule chair of a Roman consul (the sides and back were added centuries later), attesting to barbarian continuity with the Roman past. Subsequent French kings were enthroned using this chair.

Frankish rule in Gaul was never very tight or centralized, and kings had to be circumspect in their dealings not only with their own nobles but also with the powerful old Gallo-Roman landed aristocracy. The central administration consisted primarily only of the king's household. There was a referendary (also called a chancellor) who oversaw legal matters. Local administration was mostly in the hands of local potentates, including Frankish officials such as dukes (military governors) and counts (city administrators), bishops, and landed magnates. Geographically, the Merovingian kingdom came to be divided into several sections that only approximately corresponded to the political divisions of the kingdom. In the northeast was Austrasia, the most heavily Germanic section, consisting of areas on both sides of the Rhine and with its chief city at Metz. To the south and west lay the more Romanized Neustria, consisting primarily of the Loire and Seine River valleys, with its main city at Paris. In the southwest was Aquitania, and in the Rhône Valley Burgundy.

The remainder of the sixth century saw repetitious conflicts among the multiple kings and their various offspring, all of whom were contending to improve their own positions and holdings at the expense of the others. During the second half of the sixth century, an official called the **mayor of the palace**, the rough equivalent of a prime minister, achieved increasing importance in the Frankish administration. In the seventh century, the mayors of the palace began to compete for authority with the king, and the last effective Merovingian king was Dagobert I (623–639), who briefly reunited all of **Francia**, as Gaul now was sometimes called and which gave its name to modern France, under a single rule. Dagobert even entered into a treaty of "perpetual peace" with the Byzantine emperor Heraclius. Dagobert's reign later was looked back on as being the height of Merovingian Frankish civilization, and the image of "good king Dagobert" still survives in France. But, much like the reign of the Roman emperor Valentinian I, it also marked the calm before the storm, and this was the last time that the Merovingian kingdom could be called politically stable.

After the death of Dagobert in 639, the kingdom once again was partitioned. The remaining kings were known as the "do-nothing kings," and the Merovingian decline culminated in 752, when the mayor of the palace, Pippin, deposed Childeric III (743–752), the last Merovingian king, and established the Carolingian Dynasty.

THE BYZANTINE EMPIRE

During the course of the fifth century, the eastern Roman Empire (which in the modern day is called the Byzantine Empire, after the city of Byzantium, where Constantinople had been established) confronted many of the same problems as the west but was able to deal with them more effectively and, as a result, continued to survive. In the sixth century, under the emperor Justinian, the empire again became a Mediterranean-wide empire, and the emperor became the head of both state and church. But afterward, the empire was faced by growing foreign threats. In the early seventh century, after barely winning a long and devastating war with the New Persian Empire, the emperor Heraclius was confronted by an even greater menace.

The Fifth Century

The emperor Theodosius II (402–450) ruled for nearly half a century. For much of this period he was very much under the influence of his elder sister Pulcheria, a consecrated virgin who in 414, at the age of sixteen, was made Augusta. He was much more of a scholar than a soldier and thus was nicknamed "The Calligrapher." His intellectual interests were manifested in several ways. He reorganized the university of Constantinople, giving it thirty-one professors teaching grammar, rhetoric, philosophy, and law. And in 438, he issued the **Theodosian Code**, a compilation of all the significant Roman laws going back to the time of Constantine. It provides a wealth of information about Roman administration and society and the economy and gives us insight into what the emperors thought were some of the most important issues facing them.

During Theodosius' reign there was a continuing lack of Christian unity. After the demise of Arianism, other variant beliefs arose to challenge the

Nicene faith. The third ecumenical church **Council of Ephesus** in 431 condemned **Nestorianism**, which taught that Christ's divine and human natures were completely separate rather than intermingled. Many Nestorians then went into exile in the New Persian Empire, where they survived as the Church of the East; some even settled in China, where their descendents were encountered by Marco Polo.

But the most immediate problem faced by Theodosius was the continuing barbarian threat. Massive new walls were built on the landward side of Constantinople, and, because the government was reluctant to recruit too many barbarians, the empire continued to be plagued by military recruitment problems. The greatest pressure came from the Huns, who had settled in the former Roman province of Dacia (modern Romania) and were dealt with by the simple expedient of buying them off and calling them allies. Their demands became increasingly onerous. Circa 445, Attila, the king of the Huns, adopted a much more adversarial attitude toward the empire, eventually requiring annual subsidies of 2,100 pounds of gold. Numerous embassies, discussed by the Byzantine historian Priscus, one of the ambassadors, went back and forth between the Byzantine and Hunnic courts. In order to enforce his claims to Roman largess, Attila periodically invaded the eastern Roman Empire. After a campaign of 447, the Romans were compelled to evacuate a strip south of the Danube five-days'-march wide. Paradoxically, however, the general freedom from attack resulted in some return of economic prosperity; even much of the subsidy paid to the Huns eventually made its way back to the Roman world in the form of commerce. The Huns also were something of a blessing in disguise: because they also threatened the New Persian Empire, the Romans and Persians found it advantageous to maintain generally peaceful relations.

In 450 Theodosius II died and was succeeded by Marcian (450–457), an elderly senator whose nominal marriage to Pulcheria made him a part of the old dynasty. Marcian decided to call the Huns' bluff and terminated the payment of the subsidy. He was rewarded when, as already seen, the Huns were defeated by the western Roman general Aëtius in 451. Two years later, Attila died of a hemorrhage on his wedding night. He subsequently obtained a reputation as the stereotypical savage barbarian. Christian moralists referred to him as the "scourge of God" for his perceived role in punishing sinful Christians. Meanwhile, Attila's barbarian empire immediately disintegrated; the empire of the Huns was completely destroyed when the subject peoples revolted and defeated them in 454 at the Battle of the Nedao River in Hungary. In this case, however, the cure may have been worse than the disease. During the days of Attila, the Byzantine government had only him to deal with; but after the defeat of the Huns, the subject peoples scattered and caused a multitude of problems for the Byzantines.

An even more serious religious problem now was caused by the **Miaphysites**, also known as Monophysites—both terms from the Greek for "one nature"—who argued that the human and divine natures of Christ were united into a single nature, with the human nature being largely absorbed by the divine. In 448, at the so-called "Robber Council" of Ephesus, the Miaphysites were cleared of heresy. But the accession of Marcian brought a reconsideration of the matter. With the vociferous encouragement of Leo, the powerful and able bishop of Rome, who wrote a "Tome" condemning the Miaphysites, Miaphysite teachings were condemned at the fourth ecumenical **Council of Chalcedon** summoned by Marcian in 451. It validated the teaching that the human and divine natures of Christ were united while at the same time retaining their individual identities. The Chalcedonian definition, which accepted and more closely defined the Nicene Creed, then became the orthodox teaching of the imperial church.

But the Chalcedonian definition continued to be opposed by the Miaphysites of Syria and Egypt, where the Miaphysites—who simply called themselves Christians—eventually developed into the modern-day Jacobites and Copts. The controversy was never resolved, and it created a continuing sense of alienation in the easternmost provinces. The Council of Chalcedon also sowed the seeds of future bickering between east and west by giving the bishop of Constantinople the same status as the bishop of Rome. Leo and his successors found this difficult to swallow, and the offensive clause was expunged from western editions of the council.

Marcian's successor Leo (457–474) largely solved the east's military manpower shortage by locating a new source of Roman recruits in Isauria, in the backwoods of Anatolia. In 474, an Isaurian chieftain named Tarasicodissa, who adopted the more acceptable Greek name **Zeno** (474–491), even became emperor, in much the same way that the Illyrian soldier-emperors had done in the third century. Zeno also attempted to deal with continued religious dissent by issuing in 492 the **Henotikon**, which proposed to satisfy both theological factions by condemning or approving only theologies that both sides already agreed on and by saying nothing at all about Christ's natures. Although this initiative attests to Zeno's good faith, it says little about his sense of political realities, for his compromise in fact satisfied no one, and religious dissent continued to rage.

Under the emperor Anastasius (491–518), economic prosperity returned to the east. He gave tax relief to devastated areas, allowing them get to back on their feet, and relieved the decurions of the responsibility for collecting taxes, which henceforth was done directly by imperial officials. Anastasius also reintroduced a copper coinage that could be exchanged for gold coinage. This restored confidence in the copper currency and meant that the government could issue large numbers of copper coins that circulated as if they were gold coins, resulting in a great expansion of the money supply. It also facilitated exchange at the local level, leading to economic expansion and increased tax revenues. By the end of Anastasius' reign, there were 320,000 pounds of gold in the treasury.

THE COURT OF JUSTINIAN AND THEODORA

[Reference to this page in p. 8 of Color Insert]

Justinian's role as head of both state and church is graphically illustrated in this famous mosaic of 548 from the semicircular apse of the church of San Vitale in Ravenna. Flanked by secular officials and soldiers to his right and clerics on his left, Justinian, with a halo signifying his near divinity, progresses toward the altar carrying the communion bread in a golden paten. The bearded person to his right may be Belisarius; further to his right are soldiers whose shields bear the Christogram. On his left, the bishop of Ravenna, Maximianus, is the only person actually named: as the person who had underwritten the cost of the church and mosaic, he wanted to make sure that no one forgot him. The person between Justinian and Maximianus, who is rather out of place and lacks feet, seems to have been added at a later date. Directly opposite the mosaic of the court of Justinian is a parallel mosaic of the court of the empress Theodora, also depicted with a halo and likewise carrying a communion bowl, who is accompanied by the ladies of her own retinue on her left along with palace eunuchs on her right.

Other problems were not so easily solved. Religious dissent continued to simmer: Anastasius' own religious sympathies were so suspect that he was compelled to subscribe to the Henotikon by those who feared he would support the Miaphysites. The reign of Anastasius also saw an increase in urban violence. The **"Blue"** and **"Green"** chariot-racing fan clubs served as thinly veiled political activist groups that often used violence to support their views on matters such as theological beliefs and imperial appointments. In the course of one riot, Anastasius presented himself bareheaded and offered to resign. The fickle mob declined this magnanimous offer.

The Age of Justinian

By the early sixth century, the Byzantine Empire was back on its feet. The barbarian threat had been subdued, economic prosperity had been restored, and religious dissent had been muffled. At the same time that the western Roman world was coping with the realities of the barbarian settlement, the Byzantine world was on the verge of momentous developments. In 518, after Anastasius died without an heir, a Thracian general, Justin (518–527), was named emperor without any fuss. His reign was generally peaceful and uneventful, and he soon associated his nephew, **Justinian**, in the rule with himself.

When Justinian assumed the throne in 527, he acted in many ways like Augustus and Diocletian before him as he attempted to effect a restoration of past Roman glory. Like them, he was a better administrator than general. He also was greatly influenced by his able wife, Theodora. Early in his reign, Justinian faced political unrest in his own capital. In 532, "Blue" and "Green" rioters, disgusted with misadministration, rampaged throughout the city for

Justinian's basilica of Hagia Sophia served as the cathedral of Constantinople and was the focus of the emperor's connection to the Christian church in the Byzantine Empire. It was here that the emperors were crowned and participated with their families in church services. After the conquest of Constantinople by the Turks in 1453, Hagia Sophia was converted into a mosque and remained such until 1935, when it became a museum.

six days shouting *"Nika!"* ("Conquer"). Justinian was on the point of fleeing when Theodora stiffened his backbone by quoting a saying that exile would be worse than death and that "the purple would make a fine burial shroud." The general **Belisarius** was ordered to suppress the **Nika Rebellion**, as it was called, and some thirty thousands rioters reportedly were massacred.

Justinian's vision for the future was ambitious indeed. In civil affairs, Justinian oversaw the codification all past Roman law, establishing a commission that by the mid-530s had published the *Corpus juris civilis* ("Body of Civil Law"). It consisted of three parts: the *Institutes* (a legal textbook), the *Code of Justinian* (a compilation of imperial statute law from Hadrian until his own day that rendered the Theodosian Code obsolete), and the *Digest* (a synthesis of all past jurists' opinions). At the same time, however, a millennium of tradition came to an end when the philosophical school of Athens was closed in 529.

Along with unifying the law, Justinian also proposed to unify the church, with himself at its head, a form of government known as Caesaropapism, in which the head of state also is the head of the church. At the fifth ecumenical Council of Constantinople in 553, Justinian made his own attempt to unify Chalcedonians and Miaphysites by condemning three Nestorian writers (known as the "Three Chapters"), something both sides could agree on. Once again, however, this conciliatory move had little success.

Hagia Sophia remained the world's largest Christian church until the cathedral of Seville was built in 1402.

Justinian also undertook a massive and expensive building program epitomized by the ostentatious and elaborate reconstruction of the Constantinian church of **Hagia Sophia**, or Holy Wisdom, which had burned during the Nika Rebellion. Justinian collected building material from throughout the Byzantine world, including columns taken from the ancient temple of Artemis (Diana) in Ephesus. Completed in 562 with a dome 182 feet high, Hagia Sophia became the largest church in Christendom. When the church was finished, Justinian reportedly exclaimed, referring to the temple in Jerusalem, "Solomon, I have surpassed you!"

In the realm of foreign policy, Justinian determined to reconquer much of the western Roman Empire. In 533–534, his able general Belisarius, yet another who has been called "the last of the Romans," destroyed the Vandal kingdom in a lightning campaign and began the recovery of North Africa. Then, in 536, Belisarius invaded the Ostrogothic kingdom of Italy and by the end of the year had captured Rome and Naples. In 540, he captured Milan and Ravenna—after the Ostrogoths had offered to make him emperor, an offer he declined—and it looked as though the war was over. But at this point Belisarius was recalled to the east to deal with an attack by the New Persians, and the war in Italy then bogged down. Italy now suffered much the same kind of ruinous warfare as it had during the war against Hannibal. During several sieges of Rome, the aqueducts were cut, the walls broken, and the city

The Byzantine Empire at Its Greatest Extent in 555 under Justinian Justinian recovered much of the western empire and expanded the territory of the empire by over 40 percent.

was often virtually deserted. In 550, Justinian concocted a scheme to marry his cousin Germanus to Matasuintha, the daughter of Amalasuintha, and thus unite the Romans and Ostrogoths, but Germanus' death the next year foiled that plan. The elderly Armenian eunuch Narses then was placed in charge of Byzantine forces. At the Battle of Busta Gallorum in 552 the Ostrogoths were decisively defeated, and by 553 Italy was back in Byzantine hands.

Justinian's plans for reconquest even extended to Spain, and the southeastern part of the peninsula was reoccupied. But at that point the Byzantine offensive ran dry. Justinian's western wars had drained the economy, and, except occasionally for Africa, the newly recovered western territories proved to be a financial and political burden. In addition, Justinian's preoccupation with the west gave the Persians a free hand in the east: in 540 Antioch, the queen city of the Orient, was captured and sacked. Justinian then paid dearly for peace treaties with the Persians. And in the north, the Byzantines faced incursions across the Danube from a whole catalogue of barbarians, including Slavs, Bulgars, Avars, Gepids, Huns, and Catrigurs, who were defeated only with great difficulty.

Justinian's attempts to reform the administration were hindered, however, by his increasing need to squeeze out as much revenue as he could to support his extravagant military and building enterprises. Of great benefit was the development of an imperial silk monopoly. Ultimately, however, Justinian's extravagant spending could no longer be maintained. Military cutbacks led to the failure to maintain frontier defenses and army revolts. Other problems included a great plague in 542 that afflicted even Justinian himself, although he, unlike tens of thousands of others, survived.

Successors of Justinian

After Justinian's death in 565, his successors had to deal with the consequences of his grandiose schemes. Justinian was succeeded by his nephew Justin II (565–578). Justin attempted to deal with religious incompatibilities by persecuting the Miaphysites and was confronted in 568 by an invasion by the **Lombards**, who had lived for centuries on the fringes of the Roman world and who became the last of the barbarian invaders of the old empire. The Lombards occupied much of inland Italy, but they were too weak to dislodge the Byzantines, who controlled the sea, from strongholds near the coast, such as Ravenna and Rome. The Lombards were disunited both politically, with a nominal king attempting to control more than thirty dukes, and religiously, with the population adhering variously to paganism, Arianism, and Nicene Christianity. The last Lombard king surrendered to Charlemagne in 774, but the legacy of the Lombards survives in Lombardy, the name of the northern region of Italy around Milan.

In 573, overwhelmed by the news of defeats by the **Avars** and Persians, Justin apparently became mentally deranged, and his wife, the Augusta Sophia, arranged the promotion of the influential general Tiberius (578–582) to the rank of Caesar, with the surname Constantine. Further attacks by the **Slavs** soon followed, which continued after Justin's death in 578, along with additional attacks on the Balkans by the Avars and by the Persians in the east. In 582, gravely ill, Tiberius crowned the general Maurice (582–602) as Augustus. Maurice did the best he could. In the west, the last Spanish possessions were lost, but Maurice also created the largely autonomous **exarchates** of Ravenna and Carthage, which were intended to maintain themselves independently without great assistance from the east. The Avars were barely kept from Constantinople, and Maurice had a success in the east when his daughter Miriam married the Persian king Chosroes (or Xusru) II (590–628). But his plans to reestablish an emperor in Rome came to naught in 602 when he was killed in a revolt by his general Phocas (602–610). During the reign of Phocas, the last monument in the forum in Rome, a column in his honor, was erected.

Heraclius and the Greek Empire

The reign of the usurper Phocas came to an end in 610, when a fleet commanded by **Heraclius**, the Exarch of Africa, arrived at Constantinople. The senators and army deserted to Heraclius, who executed Phocas with his own hand and then was crowned Byzantine emperor. The reign of Heraclius is looked on by some as the beginning of a truly Byzantine Empire, for it brought a number of great changes. Heraclius was immediately confronted by serious military problems. In 610, the New Persian king Chosroes invaded Syria. In 613, Damascus fell, and in the following year Jerusalem was sacked; the **True Cross** and other Christian treasures were taken back to Persia. In 615, the Persians attacked Chalcedon, just opposite Constantinople, while in 617 the king of the Avars appeared before the land walls of the Byzantine capital. Heraclius almost abandoned the city for North Africa, especially after Egypt, the main source of grain for the empire, was occupied by the Persians in 619, by which time the Persians had occupied nearly all of Anatolia and Egypt. The relative ease of the Persian conquest is explained at least in part by religious differences within the Byzantine Empire: many eastern Nestorians and, in particular, Miaphysites, after years of persecution by the imperial government, preferred a Zoroastrian Persian ruler to what they saw as a Christian heretic.

On this silver plate gilded with gold, the New Persian king Chosroes II engages in the traditionally aristocratic pastime of hunting, shooting a bow from horseback in much the same way that Iranians of over a thousand years earlier had done.

Although Chosroes had succeeded in extending the frontiers of the Sasanian Empire almost to the limits of the old Achaemenid Empire, Heraclius still had a few tricks up his sleeve. Using a shrewd mixture of diplomatic and military moves, and supported by the populace as well as by contributions of the church, Heraclius took the offensive. Because the Byzantines controlled the seas, Heraclius resolved on a bold stroke. Leading the army himself, the first time since Theodosius I that an emperor had done so, in 622 he sailed into the Black Sea with an expeditionary force that penetrated into Armenia. Sasanian forces were defeated, and Heraclius advanced into Persian territory. An attempt of the Persians to induce Heraclius to return by making a joint attack on Constantinople with the Avars in 626 failed when the Avars were bought off and induced to withdraw. Chosroes recalled all the Persian forces, but

On this twelfth-century French plaque, the Byzantine emperor Heraclius overcomes the Persian king Chosroes, whose crown falls to the ground.

after being unable to defeat Heraclius, he was deposed and killed. In 628, the new Persian king, Kavad, whose kingdom had been devastated, made peace with Heraclius, returning all the territory, treasures (including the True Cross), and prisoners that the Persians had captured.

By 628, therefore, Heraclius had been able to defeat, and virtually destroy, the New Persian Empire. The next year, as a consequence not only of this great victory but also of the changing times, Heraclius adopted the ancient Greek title of **Basileus**, or "King," and the Roman emperors finally had an official title. Heraclius acknowledged the Greekness of the Byzantine Empire in other ways as well, by making Greek the official language of the empire. But, after nearly thirty years of warfare in which neither side had gained anything, both empires were totally exhausted. And one consequence of the warfare was that both empires, in their attempts both to prosecute and to recover from the wars, imposed additional taxation on the population that resulted in popular discontent.

THE RISE OF THE ARABS AND ISLAM

Ever since the beginning of Near Eastern civilization ca. 3000 BCE, the centers of cultural, political, and religious innovations had been located either in major river valleys or in the lands bordering on the Mediterranean Sea. Other regions, such as the steppes of central Asia, the Arabian Peninsula, and sub-Saharan Africa, had had little impact on this Near Eastern-Mediterranean core. All this changed in the seventh century CE, when the peoples of the Arabian Peninsula burst dramatically into the Mediterranean world.

Arabia in the Classical World

For centuries, Arabia had existed on the fringes of the classical world. Most of it was extremely arid, punctuated only by occasional oases that permitted the Arab inhabitants to pursue a pastoral way of life based on herding camels, goats, and horses. The population was organized into mobile family groups, much as in the days of the early Hebrews. Agriculture was possible only in a more fertile strip along the Red Sea coast, the **Hejaz**, where a few small urban centers were located. The Arab population was polytheistic, with a multitude of gods, but Arabs generally believed in a remote supreme creator god known as **Allah**, a word that meant simply "god."

In the central Hejaz, the most important city was **Mecca**, a city located just inland from the Red Sea in a barren wilderness with little water. As of the fifth century, Mecca was controlled by an Arab group called the Quraysh, who became merchants and traders in the sixth century when, as a result of conflicts with the Persians, the Byzantines fostered an alternate trade route to the east going from Damascus to Mecca and thence east to obtain spices from India and silks from China. Other urban centers included Yathrib (later **Medina**), a center of agriculture two hundred miles north, but Mecca was the most significant, and eventually became more important than Palmyra as a caravan center. Along with being a trading center, Mecca also was a religious center, with a shrine called the **Ka'aba** that was frequented by the polytheistic Arabs inhabiting most of Arabia.

Once a year, the disunited and often warring peoples of Arabia declared a truce and congregated at Mecca, where disputes were resolved and trade was pursued; this made Mecca into a loose political center as well and gave the Arabs a common sense of identity. The merchants of Mecca entered into agreements with both the Bedouin peoples of the desert and the Byzantines to the north. As the city became more powerful, it became the center of a loose confederation of Arab peoples.

As of the second century CE, northwestern Arabia, populated by Saracens (a Roman name for Arabs), was incorporated into the Roman province of Arabia, but the Roman and Byzantine governments only rarely made any attempt to extend their influence any further into the peninsula. Once Christianity became the state-sponsored religion in the Roman Empire, emperors began to use Christianity for political purposes and to encourage foreign allies to become Christians. Christianity began to penetrate the Arabian Peninsula. For example, a group of Saracens who had migrated from northern Arabia to southern Syria converted to Christianity ca. 374 under their queen, Mavia, on condition that a certain Moses, another Saracen, be made their bishop. And the Himyarites, an Arab people of Yemen in southern Arabia, were provided bishops by the emperors Anastasius and Justin I.

Meanwhile, in the semi-arid regions of northern Arabia and southern Syria, two Arab peoples, the Ghassanids and the Lakhmids, who had migrated all the way from Yemen, became involved in the frontier mix. The Ghassanids became Christians and clients of the Byzantine Empire and guarded the frontier against the attacks of other Arab peoples. But the Lakhmids, who likewise had migrated from Yemen and also converted to Christianity, became Nestorian Christians, were opposed by the Miaphysite Ghassanids, and allied themselves with the Persians after Nestorianism was condemned. In addition, several Arab peoples, especially in southern Arabia, also adopted Judaism. By the sixth century, therefore, monotheism was gaining a strong presence in Arabia.

Muhammad and the Rise of Islam

Around 570, the future prophet **Muhammad** was born into the Quraysh group in Mecca. His father Abdallah (a word meaning "the servant of Allah") died before he was born, and after being orphaned at the age of six he was raised by his uncle. After initially working as a merchant on caravans to Syria, around 610 Muhammad began to have visions in wich he received divine revelations from the angel Gabriel, and three years later he began to preach a monotheistic religion with the messages that "God is one," that it was necessary to surrender to Allah, and that he was Allah's messenger. Whereas pagan Arabs had believed in blind irresistible fate over which man had no control, Muhammad taught that Allah was a merciful God who listened to prayers. Muhammad's religion became known as **Islam**, a word meaning "submission" [to the will of Allah], and the followers of Islam became known as **Muslims** (a word meaning "one who submits"). Muhammad was believed to be Allah's prophet, and the statement of faith of all Muslims became, "There is no God but Allah, and Muhammad is His messenger."

The first converts to Islam were members of Muhammad's own family and unprivileged persons. Muhammad's efforts to spread his teachings more widely, and especially his condemnation of idol worship, met much resistance from the established pagan community, especially from wealthy merchants in Mecca, and brought civil war to Arabia as Arabs attached to the old religion attempted to suppress him and his followers. Some Muslims fled to Ethiopia to escape persecution, and in 622 Muhammad himself took sanctuary in Yathrib, where he already had many supporters. This journey became known as the **Hegira** (or Hijra), and its date became the first year in a new Muslim calendar. Yathrib was renamed Medina ul Nabi, or "city of the prophet," and became the center of operations for several battles with Mecca. Even though neither side was able to achieve a decisive victory, Muhammad's skillful strategies and tactics (such as building an impregnable ditch to defend Yathrib) resulted in his gaining increasing prestige.

Eventually, after a series of mostly peaceful negotiations, Mecca surrendered to Muhammad in 630. Except for a sacred black stone, about seven inches in diameter, which the Muslims believed had fallen from heaven at the time of Adam and Eve, all of the stone idols in the Ka'aba were destroyed. Otherwise, however, Muhammad was very lenient toward his former enemies, pardoning most of them, and this spirit of tolerance toward defeated enemies later became one of the hallmarks of Muslim policy. Mecca, with the Ka'aba, became the holiest site in Islam, which all Muslims faced both during prayer and in death, and which was the destination of the pilgrimage now known as the Hajj that all devout Muslims were expected to make at least once in their lives. Medina, meanwhile, continued as the Muslim capital. Before his death in 632, Muhammad and his followers were able to convert nearly all Arabia to Islam and to bring the Arabs under a single political and religious authority.

CROSS-CULTURAL CONNECTIONS

Throughout this volume, we have seen how different religions have developed in the contexts of different societies. Can you see any common factors in how and why religions develop, in how people relate to their gods, and in how well religions fulfill the promise that they have for their followers?

Islam did not acquire many of its fundamental unifying and organizational characteristics until after the death of Muhammad. In particular, the revelations that Muhammad had received from Allah were collected and codified during and soon after his lifetime in a book of scripture called the **Qu'ran** (or "Recitation"), which became the supreme authority not only for Muslim beliefs but also for Muslim law and life. The Qu'ran, which contains 114 chapters known as "suras," placed great emphasis on morality, preferring moral rather than historical discussions of past events; this can make it difficult to use as a historical source.

The Qu'ran also referred to many events from Jewish and Christian scriptures, thus attesting to the close connections among these three religions. For example, the Muslims, like the Jews and Christians, believed that they were descended from the Hebrew prophet Abraham, thus creating a familial, albeit distant, bond among the adherents of all three religions. And according to Islamic tradition, in one of his miraculous journeys Muhammad was said to have met earlier prophets such as Abraham, Moses, and Jesus. Subsequently, Jews and Christians living under Muslim rule, who came from the same religious traditions as the Muslims, were termed a "**People of the Book**" and were accorded special treatment, such as being allowed to practice their religion if they did not resist and paid a special tax. As in the case of Judaism and Christianity, it was the written scripture that gave Islam its continuity over centuries of time and large geographical spaces. The Qu'ran assumed its standard form almost immediately, and even in the modern day Muslims of different sects use the same Qu'ran.

After the death of Muhammad, controversy arose in the Muslim community over who would succeed him; no arrangements had been made, although it was understood that it should be someone from his family. The choice to be the first **caliph** (successor) ultimately fell on his father-in-law Abu Bakr, although others had supported Ali, Muhammad's cousin and son-in-law (who later became the fourth caliph). This early dispute over leadership later was one of the factors in the Muslim split into the Sunnis (who recognized Abu Bakr) and the Shi'as (who recognized Ali) denominations of Islam. Abu Bakr and later caliphs succeeded to Muhammad's spiritual and temporal authority, but not to his position as prophet, and had no authority to rule in matters of religious doctrine, even though some early caliphs did believe that their authority extended to religious matters not discussed in the Qu'ran. In this regard, Islamic government could be considered to be a **theocracy**, in which the leaders of the church also govern the state, as opposed to the Caesaropapism of the Byzantine Empire.

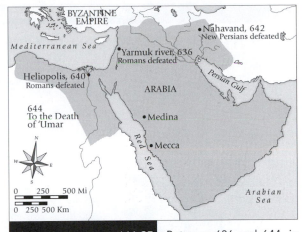

The Confrontation Between Byzantium and the Arabs

Islamic Conquests to 644 CE   Between 636 and 644, in the space of just a few years, Muslims advanced out of Arabia, occupied Byzantine Syria, Palestine, and Egypt, and defeated the New Persians.

Under Abu Bakr, Islam began to expand out of Arabia proper, initially in an attempt to convert the Arabs living under Sasanid and Byzantine rule. During 633, southwestern Mesopotamia (Iraq) was occupied by the Muslim general Khalid, and the Lakhmids were successfully incorporated, even though many of them preferred to remain Christians. Then, in 634, Abu Bakr sent Khalid with an army of nearly ten thousand to invade Byzantine Palestine. After defeating several Byzantine contingents, Khalid captured Damascus in 634, by which time Abu Bakr had been succeeded as caliph by Umar, who replaced Khalid as commander in chief with Abu Ubaida, although Khalid continued as the de facto Muslim commander. Muslim holdings in Palestine continued to expand.

Meanwhile, the Byzantine emperor Heraclius, residing in Antioch, not far from the battlefront, pulled together Byzantine contingents from throughout the empire, including Ghassanid Arabs and even Armenian allies, in an attempt to resist the Arab advances. In August of 636, the Muslim army of about forty thousand met a combination of five Byzantine armies under different commanders totaling about fifty thousand in the **Battle of the Yarmuk River** just east of the Sea of Galilee, on a plain that offered good room to maneuver for the Muslim cavalry. After five days of seesaw battle, the Muslim cavalry worked its way around to attack the Byzantine infantry from the rear. Lack of coordination among the Byzantine commanders forced the Byzantine army into a retreat that became a rout. Many Byzantines escaped, but others were killed in the panic, and those that surrendered were massacred. Heraclius, blaming the defeat on God's wrath, retreated to Constantinople and prepared for the defense of Egypt. Meanwhile, the Muslims consolidated their gains. Antioch fell in 637, and the Muslim conquest of Byzantine territory in western Asia was complete.

Egypt, meanwhile, as often in the past, was a hotbed of religious controversy. The population remained largely Miaphysite. After the Byzantine reoccupation from the Persians in the late 620s, the Miaphysites were persecuted

THE DESTRUCTION OF THE LIBRARY OF ALEXANDRIA

One of the most famous monuments of antiquity was the great library of Alexandria, initially established by the Ptolemaic kings in the third century BCE and said to contain, rather like the modern Library of Congress, copies of works written by virtually every ancient author. Estimates of its holdings ranged in antiquity from four hundred thousand to seven hundred thousand scrolls. And one of the great mysteries of history is what happened to the library. Many accounts circulated in antiquity and continue to be proposed about the library's fate.

In the first century CE, the Roman writer Seneca mentioned "forty thousand books burned at Alexandria" but said nothing about the date or circumstances. Several writers blamed Julius Caesar, including Plutarch, who said in the second century that a fire Caesar set to burn his own ships "spread and destroyed the great library." Other writers, such as Ammianus and the Christian historian Orosius, also blamed Caesar; Aulus Gellius, writing about 180, reports that seven hundred thousand books were accidentally burned. But in the early third century Cassius Dio reported

In this illustration from the fifth-century "Alexandrian World Chronicle," bishop Theophilus of Alexandria, holding the Bible as the proper sort of book to read, stands atop the Serapaeum, which may still have contained the Library of Alexandria, just before its destruction ca. 391.

by the Byzantine government, which was attempting to impose religious unity on the empire. In 639, Egypt was invaded by a Muslim army led by general Amr, a veteran of the Yarmuk campaign. After a Byzantine defeat at the Battle of Heliopolis in 640, Alexandria was surrendered in 641, the same year as the death of Heraclius. The rest of Egypt was occupied relatively easily, and Byzantine efforts to retake the province were unsuccessful.

The Muslim invaders of the Byzantine Empire had succeeded beyond their wildest expectations. They encountered not only a greatly weakened Byzantine army but also a population rendered unhappy not only by the government's that on this occasion only some warehouses of books by the docks were accidentally burned. But this clearly was not the end of the library or libraries at Alexandria, for Plutarch also notes that in the mid-30s BCE, Mark Antony gave Cleopatra two hundred thousand books from the library of Pergamum, perhaps to replace the ones burned by Caesar. And there is evidence not only that during the second century the library established by the Ptolemies was moved to the Serapaeum, the most important temple of Alexandria, but also that works continued to be deposited there as late as the fourth century.

Meanwhile, several other dates for the destruction of the library have been suggested, including (1) 273, when sections of the city were destroyed during Aurelian's suppression of Zenobia's revolt; (2) 365, when a tidal wave destroyed much of the city; and (3) ca. 391, when the Serapaeum was torn down, although because a fourth-century writer attests that the books were stored in a colonnade adjoining the temple proper, the books perhaps escaped destruction.

But perhaps the most famous story about the destruction of the library, which first appears in the work of the thirteenth-century Arab historian Abd-al-Latif, places it in 642, at the time of the Muslim capture of Alexandria. The Muslim general Amr is said to have asked the caliph Umar what to do with the famous library, and the caliph supposedly replied, ""The books will either contradict the Qu'ran, in which case they are heresy, or they will agree with it, so they are superfluous. Burn it!" The books then supposedly provided six months' worth of fuel for the furnaces heating water at Arab bathhouses.

The loss of the collected wisdom stored in the library at Alexandria continues to pique the modern imagination. For example, the thesis of the 1988 Clive Cussler novel *Treasure* is that at the end of the fourth century the library—full of lost knowledge about oil wells and gold mines—was spirited off to a hiding place in the Rio Grande valley, and in the 2004 movie *National Treasure,* a collection of scrolls from the library is discovered. In addition, the modern city of Alexandria now boasts a new "Library of Alexandria" established in 2002 and intended "to recapture the spirit of openness and scholarship of the original Bibliotheca Alexandrina."

financial exactions but also by persecutions of the largely Miaphysite population. In Egypt, in particular, the relatively small Muslim invasion force was assisted by many Miaphysites, who were happy to pay taxes to them instead of to the Byzantine government in the hopes of getting better treatment under Muslim authority.

The Expansion of the Muslim World

Meanwhile, in subsequent decades the Muslim advance continued. In 642, the Sasanids were defeated at the Battle of Nahavand, bringing the New Persian

Empire to an end. In 698 Carthage and Byzantine North Africa were taken, and in 711 the Visigothic kingdom of Spain fell. The Muslim advance was halted only in 732, when the Frankish mayor of the palace, Charles Martel, defeated a Muslim invasion of western Europe at the Battle of Tours. Back in the east, the Muslim advance stalled after the occupation of the Orient. The Byzantines did not experience another major setback until 1071, when at the Battle of Manzikert most of Anatolia was lost to the Seljuk Turks. A shrunken empire then held out until 1453, when, after a desperate defense led by the last Byzantine emperor, Constantine XI Palaeologus (1449–1453), Constantinople was captured by the Turks and renamed Istanbul (from a Greek phrase meaning "in the city").

THE TWILIGHT OF ANTIQUITY

In the Near East and the eastern Mediterranean, there were many breaks with the ancient world in the mid-seventh century, including the destruction of the New Persian Empire, the rise of the Islamic world, and the transformation of the Byzantine world from a Latin-based to a Greek-based administration and culture. One therefore can state with some certainty that in the east, the ancient world ended around 650. In the western Mediterranean, however, the break with classical antiquity might seem to have come much earlier, with the creation of barbarian kingdoms in the fifth century. But, as has been seen, the barbarians largely absorbed Roman culture, so that the ancient world continued to persevere under their auspices: even though there was a political change (and there had been many political changes throughout the course of antiquity), there was no obvious cultural break with the ancient world. So just when can we say that antiquity ended in western Europe?

The Last Latin Classical Writers

One of the great misconceptions about the European post-Roman period is that it was a period when education and literary activity virtually ceased, giving rise to the "**Dark Ages**." This view was largely promulgated by classicists and historians who applied the standards of the classical period to Late Antiquity and who regretted the decline in the composition of secular histories, poetry, and so on and disparaged the quality of the religious literature that they did see fit to acknowledge.

But western Late Antiquity in fact was a vibrant period of literary activity that was, however, different from that of the classical period. The literary works of Late Antiquity were very largely Christian in nature, consisting of sermons, biblical commentaries, and saints' lives. This does not mean, however, that the writing of secular works ceased. Far from it. In the mid-sixth century, Jordanes, an Arian Goth who converted to Nicene Christianity, wrote, probably in Constantinople, one work, *On the Origin and History of the Goths*, covering Gothic history up to his own times, and another, *On the Origin and History of the Roman People*, which did the same for the Romans. His works are interesting in that they discuss relations between Romans and barbarians from the barbarian perspective.

In Gaul, in the later sixth century, bishop Gregory of Tours composed ten books of "Histories" from the Creation to his own time, but concentrating on Gaul in the sixth century. His stories of the antics of Frankish kings, and his personal involvement in many of them, make him one of the most readable historians of all time. Gregory's work was continued up to 641 by a chronicler known as Fredegar, and this work then was extended by others up to the coronation of Charlemagne in 768. Other historical writing, however, consisted of year-by-year chronicles with just a few or no entries per year. And poetry, of both secular and religious nature, was composed by Venantius Fortunatus, an Italian who relocated to Gaul circa 580 and became bishop of Poitiers, for a joint Roman and barbarian audience. So, during the sixth century, the classical tradition was still going strong in western Europe.

Nor did educational institutions vanish. Yes, education often was carried out under the auspices of the church, with much reading of scripture and sacred texts. But this was not always the case. Secular education continued to be just as important for training secular officials as it had been in the Roman period, but there was less of it, so it is less visible in the sources. Grammar, literature, and law (with particular attention to the Theodosian Code) continued to be taught well into the seventh century. In the mid-seventh century, for example, Bonitus, a young man of Clermont in Gaul, "was imbued with the elements of grammar and trained in the Theodosian decrees, and excelling the others of his age, he was examined by the *sophistae* (sophists) and advanced." His legal education then led to his appointment as royal referendary.

At the same time, King Dagobert I assembled at court, in a sort of "palace school," a group of young men who later served as royal advisers, government officials, and bishops. Some of them came from distinguished Roman families. Desiderius of Cahors, for example, belonged to the family of Ruricius, bishop of Limoges ca. 485–510, who in turn was descended from the Anicii, the most aristocratic family of late imperial Rome. After holding the offices of royal treasurer, count of Albi, and patrician of Marseille, in 630 Desiderius was named bishop of Cahors. He and his companions created a literary circle that was the last direct link not only to the classical culture of antiquity but also, and in particular, to the people who had created this culture. Desiderius' surviving letter collection, which maintains the tradition of Roman aristocrats whose letters to each other were the glue that bound the aristocratic elite together, is the last Latin letter collection with a direct connection to classical antiquity. But Desiderius and his fellows had no successors, and in this regard they might truly be called "the last of the Romans."

The Preservation of Classical Culture

Subsequent European writers saw the classical tradition only at a distance and classical literature as a relic of a bygone day rather than as a living tradition with which they had a traceable connection. Thus, in Europe, the end of antiquity was marked in the mid-seventh century by the passing of the last generation with a direct connection to the classical past. In the future, the preservation of the traditions of classical antiquity would be the responsibility of those who looked at it secondhand, as an artifact of great value that certainly deserved preservation and emulation but not one back to which they could trace a personal connection.

The work of preserving classical culture already had begun during the sixth century, when Christian monasteries in Ireland, such as Clonard Abbey, became the focal points of a completely new tradition of Latin literature, known as Hiberno-Latin, which was characterized by obscure classical vocabulary, including Hebrew and Greek, and abstruse, sometimes incomprehensible, allusions. During the sixth and seventh centuries, Irish monks, such as Columbanus (ca. 540–615), pursued missionary work in England, Scotland, and backwoods areas of Europe and established many monasteries, as at Iona, an island on the western coast of England, and Bobbio in northern Italy, where the copying of manuscripts and building of libraries played an important role in the preservation of classical culture.

The break with, and preservation of, classical culture also is attested by many subsequent renaissances in which classical culture was "reborn." The first, the "**Visigothic Renaissance**," brought an explosion of classical culture in seventh-century Spain that helped to preserve classical learning at the same time that it manifested many of the characteristics of the Middle Ages, in particular the compulsion to distill, summarize, and categorize ancient knowledge. Isidore, bishop of Seville from 600 to 636, for example, was a great writer of encyclopedias. Along with the religious works expected of any ecclesiastical writer, such as a compilation of 610 biblical homonyms and synonyms, he also compiled a massive year-by-year chronicle from the Creation to his own day, and a great twenty-book collection of "Etymologies," a catalogue of word derivations drawn from a multitude of classical works that became standard reading in the Middle Ages. Elsewhere, the Goth John of Biclara, who had studied in Constantinople, wrote a chronicle, and even Visigothic kings participated: Sisebut (612–620) wrote biography and poetry, and poetry also survives in the names Chintila (636–640), Reccesvinth (649–672), and Wamba (672–680).

The next renaissance was the **Carolingian Renaissance**, which began in France under the auspices of Charlemagne (768–814) and his successors as rulers of the Carolingian Empire. By this time, barbarian and Roman intellectuals had long since formed a unified group, and in the Carolingian period scholars with barbarian names such as Notker, Theodulf, Einhard, and Alcuin oversaw a revival of education and literary composition and also the preservation of thousands of late antique Latin manuscripts, which by then had moldered to the point of disintegration. By this time, the intellectual worlds of Romans and barbarians had long since been merged.

Another renaissance, in the twelfth century, brought a revival of interest in classical philosophical and scientific ideas and resulted largely from renewed contact with the Byzantine and Islamic worlds as a result of the Crusades, which brought ancient Greek texts and medieval Arabic texts back to western Europe. And finally, of course, there was the Renaissance of the fourteenth century and later, which brought a great revival of learning based on the study of classical sources and in the course of which the **fall of Constantinople** and the Byzantine Empire in 1453 brought many Greek scholars, bearing with them the cultural heritage of the ancient Greek world, to Europe. All of these renaissances attest to the continuing significance that classical culture had for the development of western culture.

> **LEARNING FROM HISTORY**
>
> Every empire that has been discussed in this survey either fell or is going to fall. What does that tell us about the fate of empires throughout history? Do you think that there is any way to prevent this cycle from recurring? Or do you think that all empires, even those of the modern day, are doomed eventually to fall?

The Three Worlds of the Middle Ages

By the year 650, the ancient world had been succeeded by the three worlds of the Middle Ages, composed of (1) western Europe (except for Spain), which followed Roman Catholic Christianity; (2) the old Roman Empire, now known to historians as the Byzantine Empire, concentrated in the Balkans and Anatolia and espousing Eastern Orthodox Christianity; and (3) the Islamic world, comprising the Near East, North Africa, and Spain, controlled by rulers who followed Islam.

The succeeding Middle Ages would last until the beginnings of the modern era in the sixteenth century. But by the end of antiquity, the germs of modern Europe were already there. The divisions of the Frankish kingdom presaged the creation of modern France and Germany; indeed, the Franks gave their name to France, and the Alamanni to the French name for Germany ("Allemagne"). The Anglo-Saxon kingdoms in Britain eventually became **England**. Spain already was a separate entity, ruled first by Visigoths, then by Muslims. Even Italy, increasingly under the authority of the pope in Rome, had its own identity.

As of the seventh century, much of the history of the Mediterranean world would be influenced or even determined by the religious differences among Catholic Christians, Orthodox Christians, and Muslims, which would prevent, and indeed continues to prevent, the kind of cultural unity of the Mediterranean and Near Eastern worlds that had its origin with the Persians, developed during the Hellenistic period, and came to full fruition during the Roman Empire.

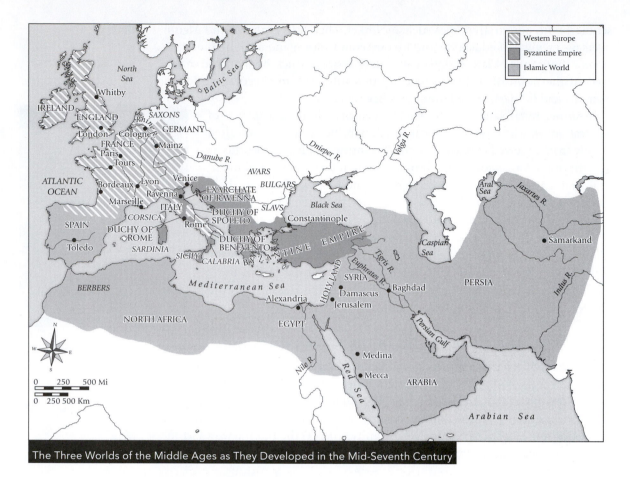

The Three Worlds of the Middle Ages as They Developed in the Mid-Seventh Century

LOOKING AHEAD

It is difficult to say exactly when the ancient world ended. Some scholars see the beginning of the Middle Ages as early as the reign of Marcus Aurelius and the Severan period of the Roman Empire, the same point at which many scholars would place the beginning of Late Antiquity. Others see the break occurring with Diocletian and Constantine just before and after the year 300, or with the beginning of a Christian Empire during the fourth century, or with the transformation of the Roman Empire into the so-called Byzantine Empire anywhere from the fourth to the sixth centuries. For our purposes, several trends suggest that the end of the ancient world came in the seventh century, which was a very different world even from the sixth. Europe saw the culmination of several trends, ranging from the decline of the Roman cultural tradition in Europe to the final merging of the Roman and barbarian populations. In the Byzantine Empire, Greek replaced Latin as the official language. The survival of the Byzantine Empire and the rise of Islam, meanwhile, bring this book back to where it started, in the Near East and eastern Mediterranean, and reminds us that the history of antiquity is not a path that prescriptively leads to western Europe. By the mid-seventh century, the changes that came during Late Antiquity had resulted in the fragmentation of a culturally unified ancient world and the creation of a new tripartite medieval world consisting of Catholic Christian, Orthodox Christian, and Muslim worlds. The ancient world had ended.

FURTHER READING

Bagnall, R. S. *Egypt in Late Antiquity.* Princeton, NJ: Princeton University Press, 1993.

Beckwith, J. *Early Christian and Byzantine Art.* Harmondsworth, UK: Penguin Books, 1970.

Browning, Robert. *Justinian and Theodora* 2nd ed. London: Thames and Hudson, 1987.

Bury, J. R. *History of the Later Roman Empire from the Death of Theodosius I to the Death of Justinian.* 2 vols. London: Macmillan, 1923.

Dagron, G. *Emperor and Priest: The Imperial Office in Byzantium.* Cambridge: Cambridge University Press, 2003.

Donner, F. M. *The Early Islamic Conquests.* Princeton, NJ: Princeton University Press, 1981.

Frend, W. H. C. *The Rise of the Monophysite Movement.* Cambridge: Cambridge University Press, 1972.

Goffart, Walter. *The Narrators of Barbarian History, AD 550–880: Jordanes, Gregory of Tours, Bede and Paul the Deacon.* Princeton, NJ: Princeton University Press, 1988.

Gordon, C. D. *The Age of Attila: Fifth-Century Byzantium and the Barbarians.* Ann Arbor: University of Michigan Press, 1960.

Haldon, John F. *Byzantium in the Seventh Century: The Transformation of a Culture.* 2nd ed. Cambridge: Cambridge University Press, 1997.

Holum, K. G. *Theodosian Empresses: Women and Imperial Dominion in Late Antiquity.* Berkeley: University of California Press, 1982.

Johnson, James-Howard. *East Rome, Sasanian Persia, and the End of Antiquity.* Aldershot, UK: Ashgate, 2006.

Kaegi, Walter E. *Heraclius: Emperor of Byzantium.* Cambridge: Cambridge University Press, 2003.

Moorhead, John. *The Roman Empire Divided, 400–700.* London and New York: Longman, 2001.

Pharr, Clyde, trans. *The Theodosian Code and Novels, and the Sirmondian Constitutions.* Princeton, NJ: Princeton University Press, 1952.

Shahid, Irfan. *Byzantium and the Arabs in the Fifth Century.* Washington, DC: Dumbarton Oaks Press, 1989.

Williams, S., and G. Friell, *The Rome That Did Not Fall: the Survival of the East in the Fifth Century AD.* London and New York: Routledge, 1999.

GLOSSARY

See page xiv for a note on spelling and punctuation. The chapter references indicate the chapter in which the term first appears, not its only occurrence.

ABRAHAM (A'braham) The first Hebrew patriarch, who made a covenant with his god; also the ancestor of the Muslims (Ch 4)

ACHAEAN LEAGUE (Achae'an League) League of Greek cities of the northern Peloponnesus founded in the early third century BCE (Ch 8)

ACHAEMENID DYNASTY (Achae'menid Dynasty) The ruling family of the Old Persians (Ch 5)

ACROPOLIS (Acrop'olis) The high point of the city of Athens and the location of the most important temples (Ch 7)

ADLECTION (adlec'tion) The power of Censors to appoint members of the Senate, later used by the Roman emperors (Ch 10)

AENEID (Aene'id) Vergil's account of the adventures of Aeneas and the most influential of all Roman literary works (Ch 11)

AËTIUS (A ë'tius) Western Roman Master of Soldiers who defeated the Huns in 451 CE (Ch 13)

AETOLIAN LEAGUE (Aeto'lian League) League of Greek cities north of the Gulf of Corinth founded ca. 350/300 BCE (Ch 8)

AGE OF THE PATRIARCHS The first period of Hebrew history, beginning ca. 1800 BCE (Ch 4)

AGE OF TYRANTS A period of Greek history 650–500 BCE during which many tyrants ruled (Ch 6)

AGOGĒ (agoge') The Spartan system for raising male children (Ch 7)

AGRICULTURAL-MILITARY CRISIS Roman inability in the second century BCE to recruit sufficient men for the army (Ch 10)

AHRIMAN (Ahr'iman) The Persian god of darkness and evil (Ch 5)

AHURA MAZDA (Ahura Maz'da) The Persian god of light (Ch 5)

AKHENATON (Akhena'ton) Egyptian pharaoh 1351–1334 BCE (Ch 3)

AKKADIANS (Akka'dians) A Semitic people who lived just upstream from the Sumerians (Ch 2)

ALAMANNI (Alaman'ni) A Germanic people living north of the upper Rhine and Danube Rivers during the third century CE and later (Ch 12)

ALARIC (Alar'ic) Visigothic chieftain who captured Rome in 410 CE (Ch 13)

ALEXANDER III Alexander the Great, king of Macedon 336–323 BCE (Ch 8)

ALEXANDRIA The name given to colonies established by Alexander the Great; the most important was in Egypt (Ch 8)

ALLAH (Al'lah) The creator god of the Arabs (Ch 14)

ALPHABET A simplified writing system in which symbols represent individual sounds (Ch 4)

ALTAR OF VICTORY Altar in the Senate house in Rome that symbolized the senators' pagan beliefs in the Late Roman Empire (Ch 13)

AMBER Fossilized tree resin commonly found near the Baltic Sea (Ch 1)

AMBROSE OF MILAN (Am'brose of Milan') Christian bishop who enforced church authority over the emperor Theodosius I (Ch 13)

AMMIANUS MARCELLINUS (Ammia'nus Marcelli'nus) Historian who wrote of the period 350–378 CE (Ch 13)

AMORITES (A'morites) Semitic peoples who invaded Mesopotamia beginning ca. 2000 BCE (Ch. 2)

AMPHICTYONIC LEAGUE (Amphictyon'ic) An organization of Greek cities intended to protect the Delphic oracle of Apollo (Ch 6)

ANATOLIA (Anato'lia) A geographical territory roughly equivalent to modern Turkey (Ch 1)

ANGLES (An'gles) A barbarian people from far northern Europe who eventually settled in Britain (Ch 14)

ANNONA (anno'na) Income and payments in kind by the late Roman government (Ch 12)

ANTHROPOMORPHIC (anthropomor'phic) In human shape, usually referring to the gods (Ch 2)

ANTIGONID DYNASTY (Anti'gonid) Macedonian dynasty that ruled Macedon 277–168 BCE (Ch 8)

ANTIOCH (An'tioch) City founded on the Orontes River in Syria by Seleucus (Ch 8)

ANTONINE CONSTITUTION (An'tonine) Law issued by the Roman emperor Caracalla in 212 CE granting Roman citizenship to nearly everyone in the empire (Ch 12)

ANTONINE DYNASTY (An'tonine) Dynasty of Roman emperors ruling from 96 to 192 CE (Ch 11)

ANTONY (MARCUS ANTONIUS) (An'tony [Mar'cus Anto'nius]) Roman senator, a member of the Second Triumvirate, defeated by Octavian at Actium in 31 BCE (Ch 10)

APHRODITE (Aphrodi'te) The Greek goddess of love and sex (Ch 6)

APOLOGISTS (apol'ogists) Christians who attempted to rebut accusations made against the Christians (Ch 11)

ARAMAEANS (Aramae'ans) A Semitic people inhabiting the land just to the east of the Phoenicians (Ch 4)

ARCHAIC AGE (Archa'ic) Greek period of history lasting from 776 to 500 BCE (Ch 6)

ARCHIDAMIAN WAR (Archida'mian) The first phase of the Peloponnesian War, 431–421 BCE (Ch 7)

ARCHIMEDES (Archime'des) Hellenistic scientist from Syracuse who invented the field of mathematical physics (Ch 8)

ARCHON (ar'chon) The chief magistrate in most Greek aristocracies and oligarchies (Ch 6)

ARD A wooden scratch plow (Ch 1)

AREOPAGUS (Areo'pagus) Athenian legislative body that initiated legislation in the Archaic Age (Ch 7)

ARĒTĒ (arētē') Excellence manifested is some outward form by the Greeks (Ch 6)

ARGOS (Ar'gos) A Greek city in the northeastern Peloponnesus (Ch 6)

ARIANISM (Ar'ianism) Christian teaching that Christ the son was subordinate to God the father (Ch 12)

ARISTOCRACY (aristo'cracy) A form of government controlled by the aristocrats (Ch 6)

ARISTOCRATS (aris'tocrats) The most privileged members of society who are born into their status (Ch 6)

ARISTOTLE (Ar'istotle) The first Greek practical philosopher, taught in Athens in the late fourth century BCE (Ch 8)

ARMINIUS (Armi'nius) A Romanized German who led the German revolt against Rome in 9 CE (Ch 11)

ARYANS (Ar'y ans) Indo-European people who settled in Iran ca. 2000 BCE (Ch 2)

ASCETICISM (asce'ticism) Practicing a life of physical self-denial (Ch 13)

ASSEMBLY Athenian legislative body consisting of all male citizens (Ch 7)

ASSUR (As'sur) One of the capital cities of the Assyrians (Ch 5)

ASSURBANIPAL (Assurban'ipal) King of Assyria 668–627 BCE (Ch 5)

ASSYRIAN EMPIRE The Assyrian state that developed as the result of Assyrian conquests beginning ca. 745 BCE and lasted until 612 BCE (Ch 5)

ASSYRIANS (Assyr'ians) An Amorite people who settled in the upper Tigris river valley (Ch 2)

ASTROLOGY (astrol'ogy) The science of decoding messages left by the gods in the movements of heavenly bodies (Ch 5)

ASYLUM (asy'lum) Personal security gained by taking refuge in a temple or church (Ch 6)

ATHANASIUS (Athanas'ius) Bishop of Alexandria who defended Nicene theology in the mid-fourth century CE (Ch 13)

ATHENA (Athe'na) The Greek goddess of wisdom (Ch 6)

ATHENIAN CITIZENSHIP LAW Athenian law passed by Pericles in 451 BCE requiring that both parents of citizens be citizens (Ch 7)

ATHENIAN EMPIRE The Athenian domination of the Delian League in the fifth century BCE (Ch 7)

ATHENIAN TRIBUTE LISTS Records of all the Greek cities that paid tribute to Athens (Ch 7)

ATHENS (A'thens) City of eastern Greece dating back to Mycenaean times (Ch 6)

ATON Egyptian god represented by a sun disk with long hands extending from it (Ch 3)

ATTICA (At'tica) The territory in eastern Greece controlled by Athens (Ch 7)

ATTILA (Attil'a) King of the Huns ca. 434–454 (Ch 13)

AUGUSTA (Augus'ta) Title given to women of the Roman imperial family (Ch 12)

AUGUSTINE (Au'gustine) Bishop of Hippo in North Africa and Christian writer in the late fourth and early fifth centuries (Ch 13)

AUGUSTUS (Augus'tus) Honorary title given to Octavian in 27 BCE, later used as a title by all Roman emperors (Ch 10)

AUSPICIUM (auspi'cium) The power that allowed Roman rulers to assess the will of the gods (Ch 9)

AUXILIA (auxil'ia) The auxiliary forces of the army during the Roman Empire, recruited from provincials (Ch 11)

AVARS (A'vars) Barbarian people who threatened the Byzantine Empire as of the late sixth century CE (Ch 14)

BA'AL (Ba'al) The Phoenician storm god (Ch 4)

BABYLONIA (Babylo'nia) Originally the territory in middle Mesopotamia occupied by the Babylonians, later the name collectively of Sumer and Akkad (Ch 2)

BABYLONIAN CAPTIVITY The deportation of many Jews to Babylonia after the fall of Jerusalem in 587 BCE (Ch 5)

BABYLONIANS (Babylo'nians) An Amorite people who settled in middle Mesopotamia (Ch 2)

BACTRIA (Bac'tria) Territory in northwestern Afghanistan (Ch 8)

BAR KOCHBA REVOLT (Koch'ba) Revolt of the Jews against Rome 132–135 CE (Ch 11)

BARBARIAN (barbar'ian) A person who could not speak Greek, hence an uncultured person (Ch 6)

BARBARIZATION (barbariza'tion) The process by which the Roman army included increasing numbers of barbarians (Ch 13)

BASILEUS (basile'us) The Greek word for "King," the title taken by Heraclius and later Byzantine emperors (Ch 14)

BATTLE OF ACTIUM (Ac'tium) Victory in 31 BCE in western Greece of Octavian over Mark Antony (Ch 10)

BATTLE OF ADRIANOPLE (Adriano'ple) Victory of the Visigoths over the Romans northwest of Constantinople in 378 CE (Ch 13)

BATTLE OF GAUGAMELA (Gaugame'la) Battle in Mesopotamia in 331 BCE in which Alexander the Great defeated the Persians (Ch 8)

BATTLE OF ISSUS (Is'sus) Battle in northern Syria in 333 BCE in which Alexander the Great defeated the Persians (Ch 8)

BATTLE OF KADESH (Kadesh') Victory of Ramses II in 1274 BCE over the Hittites (Ch 3)

BATTLE OF LEUCTRA (Leuc'tra) Victory of Thebes over Sparta in 371 BCE (Ch 8)

BATTLE OF MARATHON (Mar'athon) The battle in northeastern Attica in which the Athenians defeated the Persians in 490 BCE (Ch 7)

BATTLE OF SALAMIS (Sal'amis) Naval victory of the Greeks over the Persians off the island of Salamis in 480 BCE (Ch 7)

BATTLE OF THE MILVIAN BRIDGE (Mil'vian) Victory of Constantine over Maxentius outside Rome in 312 CE (Ch 12)

BATTLE OF THE TEUTOBURG FOREST (Teu'toburg) Battle in Germany in which three Roman legions were destroyed by the Germans in 9 CE (Ch 11)

BATTLE OF THE YARMUK RIVER (Yar'muk) Victory of the Arabs over the Byzantines east of the Sea of Galilee in 636 CE (Ch 14)

BATTLE OF THERMOPYLAE (*Thermop'ylae*) Victory of the Persians over three hundred Spartans in northeastern Greece in 480 BCE (Ch 7)

BATTLE OF VOUILLÉ (*Vouillé'*) Victory of the Franks over the Visigoths near Poitiers in 507 CE (Ch 14)

BELISARIUS (*Belisar'ius*) General of Justinian who conquered the Vandals and began the conquest of the Ostrogoths (Ch 14)

BIBLE The sacred text of the Hebrews and, later, the Christians (Ch 4)

BISHOP (*bish'op*) The leader of a Christian community in a city (Ch 11)

BITUMEN (*bitu'men*) Tarlike form of petroleum found near the Dead Sea (Ch 1)

BLUES AND GREENS Chariot racing fan clubs in Constantinople that served as political action groups (Ch 14)

BOEOTIA (*Boeo'tia*) The region of Greece north of the Peloponnesus (Ch 6)

BOEOTIAN LEAGUE (*Boeo'tian*) An alliance of Greek cities in Boeotia led by Thebes (Ch 7)

BOOK OF THE DEAD An Egyptian collection of spells that ensured a happy afterlife. (Ch 3)

BOUDICCA (*Boudic'ca*) British queen who led a revolt against the Romans in 60 CE (Ch 11)

BOULĒ (*bou lē*) The primary legislative body in most Greek cities (Ch 6)

BRONZE Alloy of copper and another metal, usually tin (Ch 2)

BRONZE AGE The period of history from 3000 to 1200 BCE (Ch 2)

CAESAR (*Cae'sar*) Imperial rank intended to show the designated successor of an emperor (Ch 12)

CAESAR (GAIUS JULIUS CAESAR) (*Cae'sar [Gai'us Ju'lius Cae'sar]*) Roman senator and member of the First Triumvirate who used his army to seize Rome (Ch 10)

CAESAROPAPISM (*Caesaropa'pism*) The principle whereby the head of state also is the head of the church (Ch 12)

CALIPH (*caliph'*) Muslim rulers who were the successors of Muhammad (Ch 14)

CAMBYSES (*Camby'ses*) King of Persia 531–522 BCE (Ch 5)

CANAAN (*Ca'naan*) The eastern coast of the Mediterranean Sea (Ch 4)

CANON (*ca'non*) The standard list of books of the Christian Bible (Ch 13)

CAROLINGIAN RENAISSANCE (*Carolin'gian*) Period of literary activity in western Europe during the reign of Charlemagne (768–814 CE) (Ch 14)

CARTHAGE (*Car'thage*) Phoenician colony founded in modern Tunisia in 814 BCE (Ch 9)

CARTOUCHE (*cartouche'*) Rectangle enclosing the name of a pharaoh on monuments and in documents (Ch 3)

ÇATAL HÜYÜK (*Ça'tal Hü'yük*) Village of southern Anatolia, ca. 7400–6000 BCE (Ch 1)

CATILINE (LUCIUS SERGIUS CATILINA) (*Ca'tiline [Lu'cius Ser'gius Catili'na]*) Roman senator killed in 63 BCE attempting to overthrow the state (Ch 10)

CELIBACY (*cel'ibacy*) Sexual abstinence practiced by those leading an ascetic life (Ch 13)

CELTIBERIANS (*Celtiber'ians*) Celtic inhabitants of Spain (Ch 9)

CELTS Indo-European peoples inhabiting inland Europe from Spain to the Balkans, the British Isles, and central Anatolia (Ch 8)

CENTURIATE ASSEMBLY (*Centur'iate*) Roman popular assembly comprised of 193 centuries (Ch 9)

CHALCOLITHIC AGE (*Chalcolith'ic*) "Copper-Stone" Age, ca. 5500–3000 BCE (Ch 1)

CHALDEANS (*Chalde'ans*) A Semitic people who settled in Babylonia (Ch 5)

CHRIST "The anointed one," whom Jews believed was the Messiah; a title applied by Christians to Jesus of Nazareth (Ch 11)

CHRISTOGRAM (*Chris'togram*) The sign of Christ, the Greek letters chi and rho superimposed (Ch 12)

CHRONOLOGY The series of dated events that occurs throughout history (Ch 1)

CHURCH COUNCIL An assembly of Christian bishops that ruled on issues relating to the church (Ch 12)

CHURCH FATHERS Christian writers of Late Antiquity (Ch 13)

CICERO (MARCUS TULLIUS CICERO) (*Ci'cero [Mar'cus Tul'lius Ci'cero]*) Roman consul in 63 BCE, responsible for the execution of Catiline's supporters (Ch 10)

CIMBRI (*Cim'bri*) A Celtic people who invaded Gaul in the late second century BCE (Ch 10)

CITY-STATE A city that functions as an independent state (Ch 4)

CIVILIZATION Form of culture with agriculture, specialization of labor, social differentiation, urbanization, metal technology, and writing. (Ch 1)

CIVITAS (ci'vitas) A city in a Roman province responsible for administering the surrounding local territory (Ch 10)

CLASSICAL AGE The period of Greek history from 500 to 323 BCE (Ch 7)

CLEISTHENES (Cleis'thenes) Archon who established the Athenian democracy in 507 BCE (Ch 7)

CLEOPATRA VII (Cleopa'tra) Queen and pharaoh of Egypt, 51–30 BCE (Ch 10)

CLIENT KING Native king installed by the Romans in a frontier area (Ch 11)

CLIENTELA (cliente'la) Roman social system based on patrons and clients rendering mutual services to each other (Ch 9)

CLOVIS (Clo'vis) King of the Franks 481–511 CE (Ch 14)

CODE OF HAMMURABI (Hammura'bi) Law code issued by Hammurabi, king of Babylon (Ch 2)

CODEX (co'dex) Form of publication in the modern-style book format (Ch 13)

COHORT (co'hort) Six-hundred-man unit of a Roman legion (Ch 10)

COINAGE The issuing of pieces of metal with the same weight and a standardized value (Ch 5)

COLLEGIALITY (collegial'ity) A principle of Roman government in which no office was overseen by a single person (Ch 9)

COLONI (colo'ni) Tenant farmers who worked on the estates of large landowners in the Late Roman Empire (Ch 13)

COLONY (col'ony) A city established in foreign territory to deal with excess population and/or establish trading relations (Ch 6)

COMITATENSES (comitaten'ses) The mobile troops of the late Roman army (Ch 12)

COMITATUS (comita'tus) The court of a late Roman emperor (Ch 12)

COMPULSORY SERVICES Jobs that late Roman emperors believed had to be performed for the empire to survive (Ch 12)

CONCUBINE (con'cubine) Nonspousal sex partner of a ruler (Ch 3)

CONFLICT OF THE ORDERS The struggle of the plebeians to obtain expanded rights and opportunities ca. 500–287 BCE (Ch 9)

CONSTANTINE I (Con'stantine) Roman emperor 306–337 CE (Ch 12)

CONSTANTINOPLE (Constantino'ple) Second capital of the Roman Empire established in the east by Constantine in 330 CE (Ch 12)

CONSTITUTION Generic name for legal enactments in the Roman Empire (Ch 11)

CONSULS (con'suls) The two chief magistrates of the Roman Republic (Ch 9)

CORINTH (Cor'inth) A Greek city on the isthmus between the Peloponnesus and Boeotia (Ch 6)

CORINTHIAN WAR (Corin'thian) War in which Sparta was opposed by Thebes, Corinth, Argos, and Athens, 395–387 BCE (Ch 7)

CORPUS IURIS CIVILIS (Cor'pus iu'ris ci'vilis) "The Body of Civil Law"; a compilation of past Roman law made under Justinian (Ch 14)

COSMOPOLIS (cosmop'olis) The Hellenistic "world city" (Ch 8)

COUNCIL OF CHALCEDON (Chal'cedon) Ecumenical council in 451 that condemned miaphysite teachings (Ch 14)

COUNCIL OF CONSTANTINOPLE (Constantino'ple) Christian ecumenical church council in 381 that definitively condemned Arianism (Ch 13)

COUNCIL OF EPHESUS (Eph'esus) Ecumenical council in 431 that condemned Nestorianism (Ch 14)

COUNCIL OF NICAEA (Nicae'a) Christian ecumenical church council in northeastern Anatolia that defined a statement of Christian belief in 325 CE (Ch 12)

COUNCIL OF THE PEOPLE BY TRIBES Roman popular assembly consisting of all male citizens organized by geographical tribes (Ch 9)

COUNCIL OF THE PLEBS Roman popular assembly consisting of plebeians organized by geographical tribes (Ch 9)

COVENANT A contract between superior and subordinate parties (Ch 4)

CRASSUS (MARCUS LICINIUS CRASSUS DIVES) (*Cras'sus [Mar'cus Lici'nius Cras'sus Di'ves]*) Roman senator, a member of the First Triumvirate (Ch 10)

CRO MAGNON (*Cro Mag'non*) Earliest modern humans of Europe, appeared ca. 45,000 BCE (Ch 1)

CROESUS (*Croe'sus*) King of Lydia 560–547 BCE (Ch 5)

CULT OBJECT An item believed to have religious significance (Ch 1)

CULT OF ROME AND AUGUSTUS The Imperial Cult in the Roman Empire, participation in which demonstrated one's loyalty to Rome and the emperor (Ch 11)

CUNEIFORM (*cune'iform*) A method of writing using characters scratched by a stylus on a clay surface (Ch 2)

CURIATE ASSEMBLY (*Cur'iate*) Roman popular assembly comprised of the thirty *curiae* (Ch 9)

CYBELE (*Cy'bele*) An Anatolian mother goddess (Ch 8)

CYCLOPEAN ARCHITECTURE (*Cyclope'an*) Architectural style using massive stone blocks, named after the mythical Cyclops (Ch 4)

CYNICS (*Cy'nics*) Greek philosophers who advocated "living according to nature." (Ch 8)

CYRUS (*Cy'rus*) King of Persia 550–539 BCE (Ch 5)

DAMNATION OF MEMORY The process by which the Senate condemned a memory of deceased emperor it disliked (Ch 11)

DARIUS I (*Dari'us*) King of Persia 522–486 BCE (Ch 5)

DARK AGES Former view of the period in western Europe after the end of the Roman Empire (Ch 14)

DAVID Hebrew king 1010–970 BCE who captured Jerusalem (Ch 4)

DEBASEMENT (*debase'ment*) Mixing a base metal such as copper with silver or gold coinage to be able to create more coins (Ch 12)

DECELEAN WAR (*Decele'an*) The second phase of the Peloponnesian War, 413–404 BCE (Ch 7)

DECEMVIRS (*De'cemvirs*) Board of ten Roman patricians who created the Twelve Tables in 451 and 450 BCE (Ch 9)

DECIMATION (*decima'tion*) Roman military punishment in which every tenth man in a disgraced army unit was executed (Ch 10)

DECURION (*decur'ion*) A member of the *curia* of a Roman city (Ch 11)

DEFENSE IN DEPTH The Roman military strategy of stationing soldiers at strong points behind the frontiers (Ch 12)

DEFENSIVE AGGRESSION Roman policy of preemptively attacking neighbors who were thought to be too powerful (Ch 9)

DEIFICATION (*deifica'tion*) The process by which a human is made into a god (Ch 10)

DELATOR (*dela'tor*) A Roman informer who received part of the property of anyone convicted on the basis of his report (Ch 11)

DELIAN LEAGUE (*De'lian*) Alliance of Greek cities led by Athens founded in 478 BCE opposed to Persia and headquartered on the island of Delos (Ch 7)

DEME A small territorial district of Athens (Ch 7)

DEMOCRACY A form of government where all male citizens share authority (Ch 7)

DEMOTIC (*demo'tic*) Simplified form of Egyptian hieratic writing (Ch 5)

DENARIUS (*denar'ius*) Standard Roman silver coin, introduced in 212 BCE (Ch 9)

DEPORTATION The practice of relocating defeated peoples far from their homes (Ch 5)

DIADOCHI (*Diadoch'i*) The generals of Alexander the Great who divided up his empire (Ch 8)

DIALECTS (*di'alects*) Different versions of the same basic language (Ch 2)

DIASPORA (*dias'pora*) The spread of the Jews throughout the Near Eastern and Mediterrean world (Ch 5)

DICTATOR A limited-term single chief magistrate of the Roman Republic (Ch 9)

DIOCESE (*di'ocese*) Administrative unit of the Late Roman Empire consisting of several provinces (Ch 12)

DIOCLETIAN (*Diocle'tian*) Roman emperor 284–305 CE who began the Late Roman Empire (Ch 12)

DIONYSUS (*Diony'sus*) The Greek god of wine and madness (Ch 6)

DIVINATION (*divina'tion*) Mystical means of determining the intentions of the gods (Ch 2)

DJOSER (*Djo'ser*) Egyptian pharaoh 2668–2649 BCE (Ch 3)

DOMINATE (*Dom'inate*) One of the terms applied to the Late Roman Empire (Ch 12)

DOMINUS (*Do'minus*) "Lord and Master"; the title of late Roman emperors (Ch 12)

DONATISTS (*Do'natists*) Christian splinter group that taught that clerics who surrendered scriptures lost their spiritual authority (Ch 12)

DONATIVE (*don'ative*) A thanks offering given by newly proclaimed Roman emperors to the army (Ch 11)

DORIANS (*Dor'ians*) Indo-Europeans from northern Greece who settled in the south and ended the Mycenaean civilization. (Ch 4)

DOWRY (*dow'ry*) The property given by a father to a daughter when she married (Ch 2)

DRAMA Theatrical productions consisting of tragedy and comedy (Ch 7)

DUALISM (*du'alism*) A religion that sees the world as a conflict between good and evil (Ch 5)

DYNASTIC SUCCESSION (*dynas'tic*) The principle whereby rulers are succeeded by their children (Ch 12)

DYNASTY (*dy'nasty*) A group of pharaohs, usually connected by family ties (Ch 3)

EARLY DYNASTIC PERIOD (*Dynas'tic*) Period of Sumerian history beginning ca. 2900 BCE (Ch 2)

EBLA (*Eb'la*) Bronze Age trading city in Syria (Ch 2)

ECUMENICAL COUNCIL (*ecumen'ical*) A church council sponsored by the Roman government that legislated for all Christian churches in the world (Ch 12)

EDICT OF MILAN Law issued in 313 by Constantine and Licinius ordering freedom of religion and return of Christian property (Ch 12)

EGYPTIAN EMPIRE Area of Palestine and Syria in the north and Nubia in the south controlled by Egypt (Ch 3)

EKKLĒSIA (*ekklēsi'a*) A Greek assembly of all male citizens (Ch 6)

ELAM (*E'lam*) Bronze and iron-age region east of Mesopotamia in southwestern Iran (Ch 2)

ELECTRUM (*elec'trum*) A naturally occurring alloy of gold and silver (Ch 5)

EMPIRE A state that incorporates several nations and peoples under a single government (Ch 2)

EMPIRE OF THE MEDES An empire of eastern Iran lasting from 612 until 550 BCE (Ch 5)

ENGLAND Modern name of Roman Britain, derived from "Angleland" (Ch 14)

ENLIL (*Enlil'*) The Sumerian sky and storm god (Ch 2)

EPAMINONDAS (*Epaminon'das*) Theban general who developed a new tactic for the phalanx in the 360s BCE (Ch 8)

EPHORS (*e'phors*) The five supervisors of the Spartan kings (Ch 7)

EPICUREANISM (*Epicure'anism*) Hellenistic philosophy based on the teachings of Epicurus of Samos (Ch 8)

EQUESTRIAN CLASS (*eques'trian*) An alternate name for the Roman social class of the Knights (Ch 11)

ETRUSCANS (*Etrus'cans*) A people of northwestern Italy (Ch 9)

EUCLID (*Eu'clid*) Alexandrian mathematician who wrote on geometry ca. 300 BCE (Ch 8)

EUNUCH (*eu'nuch*) A castrated male, often serving in a Near Eastern palace or in some capacity close to women (Ch 4)

EUPHRATES RIVER (*Euphra'tes*) A river running through Mesopotamia (Ch 2)

EXARCHATES (*ex'archates*) Largely autonomous units of the Byzantine Empire in Italy and North Africa (Ch 14)

EXODUS The Hebrew migration from Egypt under the leadership of Moses (Ch 4)

EXTORTION COURT (*Extor'tion*) Roman court established in 149 BCE to try cases of extortion in the provinces (Ch 10)

EYES AND EARS OF THE KING Spies of the Persian king (Ch 5)

FALL OF CONSTANTINOPLE Capture of Constantinople by the Turks in 1453 BCE, the end of the Byzantine Empire (Ch 14)

FERTILE CRESCENT Egypt, the Levant, and Mesopotamia, the region where agriculture and civilization developed in the Near East (Ch 1)

FIRST TRIUMVIRATE (*Trium'virate*) Alliance among Crassus, Pompey, and Caesar begun in 60 BCE to control the Roman government (Ch 10)

FIVE GOOD EMPERORS The first five emperors of the Antonine Dynasty, 96–180 CE (Ch 11)

FLAKED-STONE Type of stone tool created by chipping flakes off a central core (Ch 1)

FLAVIAN DYNASTY (*Fla'vian*) The family of Roman emperors begun by Vespasian, 69–96 CE (Ch 11)

FOEDERATI (*foedera'ti*) Barbarian "allies" of the Roman Empire serving under their own chieftains (Ch 13)

FORUM (*for'um*) The central meeting place of a Roman city (Ch 9)

FRANCIA (*Fran'cia*) Name of the kingdom of the Franks (Ch 14)

FRANKS A Gemanic people living on the lower Rhine River during the third century CE and later (Ch 12)

FREEDMAN/FREEDWOMAN During the Roman Empire, a freed slave who did not yet have all the rights of a Roman citizen (Ch 11)

GAIUS GRACCHUS (*Gai'us Grac'chus*) Roman Tribune of the Plebs assassinated in 121 BCE (Ch 10)

GEOMETRIC STYLE Artistic style of the Greek Dark Ages using simple geometric patterns (Ch 6)

GILGAMESH (*Gil'gamesh*) A legendary Sumerian king who sought eternal life (Ch 2)

GOLDEN AGE OF ATHENS The period of Athenian history between 465 and 431 BCE (Ch 7)

GOLDEN AGE OF ROMAN LITERATURE Period of Roman literary activity from the late Republic through the reign of Augustus (Ch 11)

GOOD RULE The Spartan system of life (Ch 7)

GOTHS A Germanic people initially living north of the Black Sea during the third century CE and later (Ch 12)

GREAT PERSECUTION The last persecution of Christians by the Roman government, 303–311 CE (Ch 12)

GREAT PYRAMID Pyramid built by the pharaoh Khufu of the Fourth Dynasty; one of the Seven Wonders of the World (Ch 3)

GREAT RHETRA (*Great Rhe'tra*) The constitution of Sparta (Ch 7)

GREATER PROCONSULAR IMPERIUM (*Procon'sular Imper'ium*) Power used by Roman emperors of the Principate to command the army (Ch 10)

GREEK DARK AGES Period of Greek history lasting from 1100 to 776 BCE (Ch 6)

GUTIANS (*Gu'tians*) A bronze-age people living in the mountains north of Mesopotamia (Ch 2)

HAGIA SOPHIA (*Ha'gia Sophi'a*) Church of Holy Wisdom built at Constantinople by Justinian (Ch 14)

HAMMURABI (*Hammura'bi*) King of Babylon, ca. 1728–1686 BCE (Ch 2)

HASSUNA CULTURE (*Hassu'na*) Neolithic culture of Mesopotamia, ca. 6000–5250 BCE (Ch 2)

HATSHEPSUT (*Hatshep'sut*) Egyptian female pharaoh 1479–1458 (Ch 3)

HEBREWS (*He'brews*) A Semitic people of Palestine. (Ch 4)

HEGIRA (*Hegir'a*) The journey undertaken by Muhammad from Mecca to Medina in 622 CE (Ch 14)

HEJAZ (*Hejaz'*) A fertile strip of Arabia on the Red Sea coast (Ch 14)

HELENA (*Hel'ena*) Mother of Constantine who built a church on the site of Christ's tomb (Ch 13)

HELIOPOLIS (*Helio'polis*) Egyptian city where Ra was the primary god (Ch 3)

HELLENES (*Hel'lenes*) The Greek name for themselves (Ch 6)

HELLENISTIC AGE (*Hellenis'tic*) Period of Greek history from 323 to 31 BCE (Ch 8)

HELOTS (*hel'ots*) The agricultural slaves of Sparta (Ch 7)

HENOTHEISM (*he'notheism*) Religious belief in which there is a single primary god (Ch 3)

HENOTIKON (*Heno'tikon*) Ruling of the Byzantine emperor Zeno that attempted to end quarrels about religion (Ch 14)

HERACLIUS (*Hera'clius*) Byzantine emperor 610–642 CE who led a crusade against the New Persians (Ch 14)

HERCULES (*Her'cules*) The son of Zeus, a half god (Ch 6)

HERESY (*her'esy*) An illegal Christian belief as determined by church councils and the Roman government (Ch 12)

HEROD (*Her'od*) Roman client king of Judaea (Ch 11)

HERODOTUS (*Hero'dotus*) Athenian writer of the history of the Persian Wars during the 440s BCE (Ch 7)

HETAIRAI (*hetai'rai*) Female "companions" of Greek men at banquets (Ch 6)

HEXAGESIMAL SYSTEM (*hexages'imal*) A Near Eastern number system based on the number sixty (Ch 2)

HIEROGLYPHS (*hier'oglyphs*) Egyptian writing system based on ideograms (Ch 3)

HIPPOCRATES (*Hippoc'rates*) Greek physician who invented scientific medicine in the early fourth century BCE (Ch 8)

HISTORY The recording of the past by means of writing; also, the scientific study of the past (Ch 1)

HITTITES (*Hit'tites*) Indo-European people who settled in Anatolia ca. 2000 BCE (Ch 2)

HOLOCENE EPOCH (*Ho'locene*) The current period of geological history, beginning ca. 10,000 BCE (Ch 1)

HOLY LAND The area of Palestine discussed in the Bible, the destination of many pilgrimages in Late Antiquity (Ch 13)

HOLY MEN/WOMEN Christian ascetics who gained spiritual authority by becoming close to God (Ch 13)

HOMER Greek poet who composed the "Iliad" and "Odyssey" ca. 800–750 BCE (Ch 6)

HOMO ERECTUS (*ho'mo erec'tus*) "Upright human"; ancestors of humans who learned the use of fire (Ch 1)

HOMO HABILIS (*ho'mo ha'bilis*) "Skillful human"; ancestors of humans who created simple choppers and scrapers (Ch 1)

HOMO SAPIENS (*ho'mo sa'piens*) "Thinking human"; ancestor of modern humans who first appeared ca. 400,000 BCE (Ch 1)

HOMO SAPIENS SAPIENS (*ho'mo sa'piens sa'piens*) Fully modern humans, first appeared ca. 100,000 BCE (Ch 1)

HONESTIORES (*honestio'res*) Romans with greater legal privilege in the third century CE and later (Ch 12)

HOPLITE (*hop'lite*) A heavily armed Greek infantryman (Ch 6)

HORTENSIAN LAW (*Horten'sian*) Roman law of 287 BCE by which plebiscites automatically became laws of all the people (Ch 9)

HORUS (*Hor'us*) Egyptian falcon god (Ch 3)

HUMILIORES (*humilio'res*) Romans with lesser legal privilege in the third century CE and later (Ch 12)

HUNS Steppe nomads of Mongolian origin during the Late Roman Empire (Ch 13)

HUNTING AND GATHERING A lifestyle based on hunting animals and gathering plant products (Ch 1)

HYKSOS (*Hyk'sos*) A Semitic people who conquered Egypt around 1730 BCE (Ch 3)

HYPATIA (*Hypa'tia*) Female Neoplatonist philosopher of Alexandria murdered by a mob of Christian monks in 415 CE (Ch 13)

IDES OF MARCH March 15; on this day in 44 BCE Julius Caesar was assassinated (Ch 10)

IMMORTALS The ten thousand man bodyguard of the Persian king (Ch 5)

IMPERIAL CRISIS Period of Roman history from 235 to 284 CE (Ch 12)

IMPERIAL SUCCESSION The process by which one Roman emperor was succeeded by the next (Ch 11)

IMPERIUM (*impe'rium*) The power that allowed Roman rulers to command armies (Ch 9)

INDEMNITY A payment for the costs of the war made by states defeated by Rome (Ch 9)

INDO-EUROPEAN PEOPLES Peoples from the southern Russian steppes who spoke Indo-European dialects (Ch 2)

INITIATION The rituals that allowed one to participate in a mystery cult (Ch 8)

IONIA (*Io'nia*) Western coastal area of Anatolia (Ch 6)

IRON A commonly occuring metal whose extensive use as of ca. 1200 BCE marked the beginning of the Iron Age (Ch 4)

IRON AGE The period of history beginning in the Near East ca. 1200 BCE (Ch 4)

ISHTAR (*Ish'tar*) The Semitic form of the Sumerian goddess Inanna (Ch 2)

ISIS (*I'sis*) Sister and consort of Egyptian god Osiris (Ch 3)

ISLAM (*Is'lam*) A word meaning "submission," the religion established by Muhummad (Ch 14)

ITALIA (*Ital'ia*) The new nation established by the Italian Allies when they revolted against Rome in 90 BCE (Ch 10)

ITALIAN ALLIANCE The system of alliances established by the Romans in Italy during the Roman Republic (Ch 9)

JEROME (*Jerome'*) Christian author who made the definitive translation of the Bible into Latin in the late fourth century CE (Ch 13)

JERUSALEM (*Jeru'salem*) Canaanite city captured by David that became the capital of the Hebrew kingdom (Ch 4)

JESUS OF NAZARETH (*Je'sus of Na'zareth*) The Jewish founder of Christianity during the reigns of Augustus and Tiberius (Ch 11)

JEWS Name given to Hebrews after the creation of the southern Hebrew kingdom of Judah (Ch 4)

JUDAISM (*Ju'daism*) The religion of the Jews (Ch 8)

JUDGES Hebrew leaders after the Exodus (Ch 4)

JULIAN "THE APOSTATE" (*Apos'tate*) Roman emperor 361–363 CE, the last major pagan Roman emperor (Ch 13)

JULIAN CALENDAR (*Ju'lian*) A calendar with 365 days per year and a leap year every fourth year introduced by Julius Caesar (Ch 10)

JULIO-CLAUDIAN DYNASTY (*Ju'lio-Clau'dian*) The family of Roman emperors related to Augustus, 27 BCE - 68 CE (Ch 11)

JULIUS NEPOS (*Ju'lius Ne'pos*) The last western Roman emperor, 474–480 CE (Ch 13)

JURISTS (*jur'ists*) Legal scholars who advised Roman emperors on points of law (Ch 11)

JUSTINIAN (*Justin'ian*) Byzantine emperor 527–565 CE who reconquered much of the western empire (Ch 14)

KA'ABA (*Ka''aba*) A religious shrine in Mecca in Arabia (Ch 14)

KASSITES (*Kas'sites*) Indo-European people who invaded Mesopotamia ca. 1500 BCE (Ch 2)

KING OF KINGS A title of the Persian king (Ch 5)

KING SCORPION A predynastic Egyptian ruler (Ch 3)

KINGDOM OF ISRAEL (*Isra'el*) Northern Hebrew kingdom following the split of the kingdom ca. 930 BCE (Ch 4)

KINGDOM OF JUDAH (*Ju'dah*) Southern Hebrew kingdom following the split of the kingdom ca. 930 BCE (Ch 4)

KNIGHTS Initially, the highest ranking class of the Centuriate Assembly; later, Roman social class ranking beneath Senators (Ch 9)

KRYPTEIA (*kryptei'a*) The annual Spartan investigation of the helots (Ch 7)

LACONIA (*Laco'nia*) The southeastern part of the Peloponnesus in Greece (Ch 6)

LAND LAW A Roman law for distributing public land to landless persons (Ch 10

LAST DECREE OF THE SENATE Command given by the Roman Senate to the consuls to save the state (Ch 10)

LAST JUDGMENT The event that Christians believed would bring the second coming of Jesus Christ and the end of the world (Ch 13)

LATE ANTIQUITY The phase of the ancient world lasting from ca. 200 to ca. 750 CE (Ch 12)

LATE ROMAN EMPIRE The period of the Roman Empire after 284 CE (Ch 12)

LATIFUNDIA (*latifun'dia*) "Wide fields"; the extensive estates of Roman senators (Ch 10)

LATIUM (*La'tium*) Agricultural plain south of the lower Tiber River (Ch 9)

LAWGIVER Greek aristocrat appointed to write down the laws (Ch 6)

LEAGUE OF CORINTH A coalition of Greek cities established by Philip II of Macedon (Ch 8)

LEGATES OF AUGUSTUS (*Le'gates*) Provincial governors who administered the provinces that the emperor was responsible for (Ch 11)

LEGION The largest unit of the Roman army, nominally six thousand men but usually rather less (Ch 9)

LEO THE GREAT Bishop of Rome 440–461 (Ch 13)

LEPIDUS (MARCUS AEMILIUS LEPIDUS) (*Le'pidus (Mar'cus Ae'milius Le'pidus)*) Roman senator, a member of the Second Triumvirate (Ch 10)

LEVANT (*Levant'*) The lands bordering on the eastern Mediterranean coast (Ch 1)

LICINIO-SEXTIAN LAW (*Lici'nio-Sex'tian*) Roman law of 367 BCE requiring that one consul be a plebeian (Ch 9)

LIMETANEI (*limeta'nei*) The troops of the late Roman army stationed on the frontier (Ch 12)

LIMMU LISTS (*Lim'mu*) Chronological list of Assyrian officials and events (Ch 5)

LINEAR A The Minoan writing system (Ch 4)

LINEAR B The Mycenaean writing system (Ch 4)

LINEAR POTTERY CULTURE A Neolithic culture of central Europe, ca. 5500 and 4500 BCE (Ch 1)

LOGOS (lo'gos) The rational force governing the universe proposed by Greek philosophers (Ch 6)

LOMBARDS (Lom'bards) Barbarian people who invaded Italy in 568 CE (Ch 14)

LOWER EGYPT Section of Egypt consisting of the Nile delta (Ch 3)

LYCURGUS (Lycur'gus) Spartan lawgiver ca. 700 BCE (Ch 7)

LYDIA (Ly'dia) A kingdom of western Anatolia lasting from ca. 690 until 547 BCE (Ch 5)

MA'AT (Ma'at') The Egyptian sense of divine order that governed the world. (Ch 3)

MAADI CULTURE (Maa'di) A Neolithic culture of Lower Egypt, ca. 3800–3200 BCE (Ch 3)

MACEDONIA (Macedo'nia) Region of northwestern Greece centered on the Haliacmon River (Ch 8)

MAGI (Ma'gi) The priests of the Medes (Ch 5)

MAGNA GRAECIA (Mag'na Grae'cia) "Great Greece," the region in Sicily and southern Greece where many Greek colonies were founded (Ch 6)

MANICHAEISM (Ma'nichaeism) Near Eastern religion developed in the third century CE that saw the world as a struggle between God and Satan (Ch 13)

MANIPLES (man'iples) 120-man units making up a Roman legion during the Republic (Ch 9)

MANUSCRIPT Hand-made copies of literary works (Ch 13)

MARCUS AURELIUS (Mar'cus Aure'lius) Roman emperor 161–180 CE (Ch 11)

MARDUK (Mar'duk) A Babylonian storm god (Ch 2)

MARIUS (GAIUS MARIUS) (Mar'ius [Gai'us Mar'ius]) Roman general who created the volunteer army ca. 107 BCE (Ch 10)

MARTYRS (mar'tyrs) Christians who were executed for their beliefs (Ch 11)

MASTABA (mas'taba) Rectangular Egyptian chamber tomb (Ch 3)

MATERIAL CULTURE The physical remains left behind by past cultures. (Ch 1)

MATRIARCHAL SOCIETY (matriar'chal) Society in which political power is in the hands of women (Ch 1)

MAYOR OF THE PALACE Frankish officials who competed for authority with the Merovingian kings (Ch 14)

MECCA (Mec'ca) A city of the central Hejaz in Arabia (Ch 14)

MEDINA (Medi'na) An urban center of Arabia (Ch 14)

MEDITERRANEAN SEA (Mediterra'nean) The body of water bordered by Europe on the north, Africa on the south, and the Levant in the east. (Ch 1)

MEGALITHIC CULTURE (Megalith'ic) European culture characterized by the use of megaliths (Ch 1)

MEGALITHS (me'galiths) Large stone monuments comprised of standing stones, ca. 4500–1500 BCE (Ch 1)

MEMPHIS (Mem'phis) Capital of Egypt founded by Menes (Ch 3)

MENES One of the names of the first pharaoh of Egypt (Ch 3)

MERCENARY (mer'cenary) A hired soldier (Ch 4)

MERIMDE CULTURE (Merim'de) A Neolithic culture of Lower Egypt, ca. 4800–4250 BCE (Ch 3)

MEROVINGIAN DYNASTY (Merovin'gian) The family of Frankish kings after the fall of the western Roman empire (Ch 14)

MESOLITHIC AGE (Mesolith'ic) The Middle Stone Age, ca. 10,000–8000 BCE (Ch 1)

MESOPOTAMIA (Mesopota'mia) Modern Iraq, the land watered by the Tigris and Euphrates rivers. (Ch 1)

MESSENIA (Messen'ia) The southwestern part of the Peloponnesus in Greece (Ch 6)

MESSIAH (messi'ah) The person whom Jews believed would bring them victory (Ch 5)

METICS (met'ics) Resident foreigners at Athens (Ch 7)

METROPOLIS (metro'polis) A Greek city that established a Greek colony (Ch 6)

MIAPHYSITES (Mia'physites) Also known as Monophysites, Christians who taught that Christ had only a single divine nature (Ch 14)

MICROLITH (mi'crolith) Tiny flint sliver used for finely crafted tools (Ch 1)

MIDDLE AGES The period of history from the seventh century CE until the beginning of the modern era (Ch 14)

MIDDLE KINGDOM Period of Egyptian history from 2050 to 1786 BCE (Ch 3)

MILITARY ANARCHY Period of Roman history from 235 to 284 CE (Ch 12)

MIME A form of comic drama portraying scenes from domestic life (Ch 8)

MINOAN CIVILIZATION (*Mino'an*) Bronze Age civilization of Crete named after the legendary King Minos (Ch 4)

MINOTAUR (*Mi'notaur*) The legendary bull-headed man of Minoan Crete (Ch 4)

MISHNAH (*Mish'nah*) Jewish oral interpretations of Mosaic law (Ch 8)

MITHRAS (*Mith'ras*) Persian sun god popular in the Roman army during the Roman Empire (Ch 11)

MITHRIDATES VI (*Mithrida'tes*) King of Pontus (119–63 BCE) who engaged in several wars with Rome (Ch 10)

MONARCHY (*mon'archy*) A form of government based on rule by one person (Ch 6)

MONK A person who withdrew from the world either individually or collectively to lead an ascetic life (Ch 13)

MONOTHEISM (*mon'otheism*) The belief that there is only one, single god (Ch 4)

MOS MAIORUM (*mos maio'rum*) "The ways of our ancestors"; the sum total of Roman traditions (Ch 9)

MOSES (*Mo'ses*) The Hebrew leader who led the Hebrews out of Egypt (Ch 4)

MUHAMMAD (*Muham'mad*) Islamic prophet active ca. 610–632 CE (Ch 14)

MUMMIFICATION (*mummifica'tion*) Process used by Egyptians to preserve bodies of the dead (Ch 3)

MUSEUM University established at Alexandria by Ptolemy I and II (Ch 8)

MUSLIMS (*Mus'lims*) The followers of Islam (Ch 14)

MYCENAE (*Myce'nae*) Mycenaean city of central Greece (Ch 4)

MYSTERY CULTS Religions that promised a happy afterlife to initiates (Ch 8)

NARAM-SIN (*Naram-Sin'*) Grandson of Sargon, ca. 2190–2154 BCE (Ch 2)

NARMER (*Nar'mer*) One of the names of the first pharaoh of Egypt (Ch 3)

NATUFIANS (*Natu'fians*) A hunting-gathering people of Syria and Palestine, ca. 10,500 and 8000 BCE. (Ch 1)

NEANDERTHALS (*Nean'derthals*) Human sub-species that appeared ca. 150,000 BCE (Ch 1)

NEOLITHIC AGE (*Neolith'ic*) The New Stone Age, 8000–3000 BCE (Ch 1)

NEOLITHIC REVOLUTION (*Neolith'ic*) Control of the food supply brought by the domestication of plants and animals. (Ch 1)

NEOPLATONISM (*Neopla'tonism*) Philosophical system of the late Roman Empire loosely based on teachings of Plato (Ch 12)

NESTORIANISM (*Nestor'ianism*) Christian teaching that the divine and human natures of Christ are completely separate (Ch 14)

NEW BABYLONIAN EMPIRE Empire in Babylonia lasting from 612 to 539 BCE (Ch 5)

NEW KINGDOM Period of Egyptian history from 1534 to 1070 BCE (Ch 3)

NEW MAN or **NOVUS HOMO** (*no'vus ho'mo*) a Roman Consul who had no ancestors who had been a consul (Ch 9)

NEW PERSIAN EMPIRE Successor to the Parthian Kingdom as of 227 CE (Ch 12)

NEW TESTAMENT Christian scriptures based on the teachings of Jesus of Nazareth (Ch 11)

NICENE CREED (*Ni'cene*) Statement of Christian belief defined at the Council of Nicaea in 325 CE (Ch 12)

NIKA REBELLION (*nika'*) Popular rebellion in Constantinople in 532 CE put down with great slaughter (Ch 14)

NILE RIVER The major river running from south to north through Egypt (Ch 3)

NINEVEH (*Nin'eveh*) Capital city of Assyrian Empire as of the time of Sennacherib (Ch 5)

NOBLES Persons of high status who served as state officials and controlled large tracts of land (Ch 2)

NOBLES Roman Senators who had a consul among their ancestors (Ch 9)

NOMADS Pastoralists who travel on horseback (Ch 5)

NOMARCH (*no'march*) Governor of an Egyptian nome (Ch 3)

NOME An administrative district of Egypt (Ch 3)

NUBIA (*Nu'bia*) The region south of Egypt (Ch 3)

NUBIAN DYNASTY (*Nu'bian*) Dynasty of Egyptian pharaohs from Nubia, 760–656 BCE (Ch 5)

OBSIDIAN (*obsi'dian*) Volcanic glass used to manufacture sharp-edged tools (Ch 1)

OCTAVIAN (*Octa'vian*) Originally Gaius Octavius, then C. Julius Caesar Octavianus after his adoption in Caesar's will; defeated Antony in 31 BCE (Ch 10)

ODOVACAR (*Odova'car*) Barbarian Master of Soldiers who seized Italy in 476 CE and made himself king (Ch 13)

OLD KINGDOM Period of Egyptian history from 2700 to 2200 BCE (Ch 3)

OLIGARCHY (*o'ligarchy*) A form of government controlled by rich and influential people (Ch 6)

OLYMPIAN GODS (*Olym'pian*) The twelve most important Greek gods who met on Mt. Olympus (Ch 6)

THE ONE Neoplatonic transcendent, impersonal, divine principle (Ch 13)

OPTIMATES (*op'timates*) Roman politicians who preferred to work within the Senate (Ch 10)

ORIGINAL SIN The Christian doctrine that the sin of Adam and Eve was inherited by all humans who thus were guilty of sin (Ch 13)

OSIRIS (*Osir'is*) Egyptian god of the underworld, consort of Isis (Ch 3)

OSTRACISM (*os'tracism*) The Athenian practice of voting to determine whether a person should be compelled to go into exile (Ch 7)

OSTROGOTHS (*Os'trogoths*) A barbarian people from north of the Black Sea who eventually settled in Italy (Ch 14)

PAGAN MONOTHEISM (*mon'otheism*) The general trend toward monotheism during the Roman Empire (Ch 11)

PALAEOLITHIC AGE (*Palaeolith'ic*) The "Old Stone Age," 2,000,000–10,000 BCE (Ch 1)

PAN-HELLENIC (*Pan-Hellen'ic*) Relating to all the Greeks collectively (Ch 6)

PAN-HELLENISM (*Pan-Hel'lenism*) A belief in the fourth century BCE that Greeks ought to unite politically as well as culturally (Ch 8)

PANTHEON (*pan'theon*) The sum total of all of the gods of a society (Ch 2)

PAPYRUS (*papy'rus*) Writing material made from the papyrus plant of the Nile (Ch 3)

PARCHMENT Durable writing material made from stretched and cured sheep skins (Ch 8)

PARTHENON (*Par'thenon*) The temple of Athena on the Athenian acropolis (Ch 7)

PARTHIANS (*Par'thians*) Indo-European steppe people who settled in Parthia in northeastern Iran (Ch 8)

PASTORALISM (*pas'toralism*) A lifestyle based on pasturing flocks and herds (Ch 1)

PATERFAMILIAS (*paterfami'lias*) "Father of the family"; the head of a Roman family (Ch 9)

PATRIARCH (*pa'triarch*) An elderly male leader of a family group; also, during Late Antiquity, Christian bishops of Rome, Constantinople, Jerusalem, Antioch, and Alexandria (Ch 4)

PATRICIANS (*patri'cians*) The aristocrats of early Rome (Ch 9)

PAX ROMANA (*Pax Roma'na*) "The Roman Peace"; the Roman Empire during the first and second centuries CE (Ch 11)

PELOPONNESIAN LEAGUE (*Peloponne'sian*) Alliance of Greek cities in the Peloponnesus led by Sparta (Ch 7)

PELOPONNESIAN WAR (*Peloponne'sian*) War between Sparta, Athens, and their allies between 432 and 404 BCE (Ch 7)

PELOPONNESUS (*Peloponne'sus*) the southernmost part of Greece (Ch 6)

PEOPLE OF THE BOOK Jews, Christians, and Muslims, who base their beliefs on written scriptures (Ch 14)

PERGAMUM (*Per'gamum*) Kingdom founded in 281 BCE in western Anatolia by Philetaerus (Ch 8)

PERICLES (*Per'icles*) Athenian politician who oversaw the creation of the Golden Age of Athens in the mid-fifth century BCE (Ch 7)

PERSECUTION (*persecu'tion*) An attempt by the Roman government to punish Christians for their beliefs (Ch 11)

PERSEPOLIS (*Perse'polis*) Capital city of the Persian Empire built by Darius I (Ch 5)

PERSIAN EMPIRE An Iranian empire lasting from 550 to 331 BCE (Ch 5)

PHALANX (*pha'lanx*) A packed mass of Greek hoplites (Ch 6)

PHARAOH (*pha'raoh*) A ruler of Egypt (Ch 3)

PHARISEES (*Phar'isees*) Hellenistic Jews who increased the numbers of prohibitions and regulations in Jewish life (Ch 8)

PHILIP II King of Macedon, 359–338 BCE (Ch 8)

PHILISTINES (*Phil'istines*) An Indo-European people descended from the Peleset living in Palestine (Ch 4)

PHILOSOPHY "Love of wisdom," a form of Greek scientific thought (Ch 6)

PHOENICIANS (*Phoeni'cians*) A Semitic trading people living in the area of modern Lebanon (Ch 4)

PHRATRY (*phra'try*) A Greek social unit composed of families (Ch 6)

PILGRIMAGE (*pil'grimage*) A journey to a sacred site for the purpose of gaining some blessing from a god (Ch 13)

PLATO An Athenian philosopher who taught ca. 390–350 BCE (Ch 7)

PLEBEIANS (*plebei'ans*) The less priviliged citizens of Rome (Ch 9)

PLEBISCITE (*pleb'iscite*) Law passed by the Council of the Plebs (Ch 9)

PLUTARCH (*Plu'tarch*) Greek author of biographies and moral advice in the mid second century CE (Ch 11)

POMPEII (*Pompeii'*) City on the Bay of Naples destroyed by eruption of Mt. Vesuvius in 79 CE (Ch 11)

POMPEY (GNAEUS POMPEIUS) (*Pom'pey [Gnae'us Pom'pei'us]*) Roman senator, a member of the First Triumvirate (Ch 10)

PONTIFEX MAXIMUS (*Pon'tifex Max'imus*) Chief priest of Rome (Ch 9)

PONTIUS PILATE (*Pon'tius Pi'late*) Roman Prefect of Judaea who ordered the execution of Jesus of Nazareth ca. 27 CE (Ch 11)

POPE Title given to a distinguished bishop, during the sixth century CE reserved for the bishop of Rome (Ch 14)

POPULARES (*popular'es*) Roman politicians who preferred to go directly to the popular assemblies (Ch 10)

POTENTIA (*poten'tia*) The "power" of Roman senators and other powerful persons that allowed them to get their way (Ch 13)

PRAETOR (*prae'tor*) Roman magistrate who oversaw law courts or, later, served as a provincial governor (Ch 9)

PRAETORIAN PREFECT (*Praetor'ian Pre'fect*) In the Principate, the commander of the Praetorian Guard; later the administrator of a Prefecture (Ch 11)

PREFECT (*Pre'fect*) A high-ranking equestrian office during the Roman Empire

PREFECTURE (*pre'fecture*) A large-late Roman administrative unit made up of dioceses (Ch 12)

PRESENTISM (*pres'entism*) Assumption that people who lived thousands of years ago behaved in the same way as modern people (Ch 1)

PRIEST-KING Mesopotamian official who combined the duties of king and chief priest (Ch 2)

PRINCEPS SENATUS (*Prin'ceps sena'tus*) The highest ranking member of the Roman Senate (Ch 9)

PRINCIPATE (*Prin'cipate*) The Roman Empire in the form that was established by Augustus, 27 BCE–284 CE (Ch 10)

PROCONSUL (*Pro'consul*) Roman provincial governor who in the past had held the office of consul (Ch 10)

PROCURATOR (*Pro'curator*) An equestrian official during the Roman Empire in charge of tax collection (Ch 11)

PROLETARIATE (*proletar'iate*) The lowest ranking class of the Centuriate Assembly (Ch 9)

PROPHETS Hebrew holy men who spoke on behalf of Yahweh (Ch 4)

PROSCRIPTIONS (*proscrip'tions*) The lists of enemies published by Sulla (Ch 10)

PROSKYNESIS (*proskyne'sis*) Prostration before a near eastern ruler (Ch 5)

PROVINCE A foreign territory annexed by Rome (Ch 9)

PROVINCIALS (*provin'cials*) Inhabitants of a Roman province who did not have Roman citizenship (Ch 10)

PRYTANY (*pry'tany*) The fifty members of an Athenian clan who were part of the Council of 500 (Ch 7)

PTAH City god of Memphis (Ch 3)

PTOLEMAIC DYNASTY (*Ptolema'ic*) Macedonian dynasty that ruled Egypt 323–31 BCE (Ch 8)

PTOLEMAIC SYSTEM (*Ptolema'ic*) Complex astronomical model with the Earth at the center of the universe (Ch 8)

PTOLEMY I (*Ptol'emy*) General of Alexander the Great who gained control of Egypt (Ch 8)

PUBLICANI (*publica'ni*) Local tax collectors in Roman provinces (Ch 10)

PUPPET EMPERORS The western Roman emperors from 455 until 480 CE (Ch 13)

PYRAMID A large monument built in ancient Egypt to serve as a pharaoh's tomb (Ch 3)

PYRAMID TEXTS Magical spells that assured the pharaoh of an afterlife (Ch 3)

PYTHAGORAS (*Pytha'goras*) A Greek philosopher from Samos, ca. 530 BCE (Ch 6)

PYTHIA (*Py'thia*) The priestess of Apollo who acted as the oracle of Apollo at Delphi (Ch 6)

QU'RAN (*Qu'ran'*) The book of Islamic scripture (Ch 14)

RADICAL DEMOCRACY A Greek form of democracy in which all male citizens participated equally in government (Ch 7)

RAMSES II (*Ram'ses*) Egyptian pharaoh 1279–1212 BCE (Ch 3)

RAVENNA (*Raven'na*) City in northeastern Italy that served as a refuge for western Roman emperors in the fifth century (Ch 13)

REPUBLIC The "Public Thing"; the form of Roman government in which sovereign authority lay with the people, lasting from 509 to 27 BCE (Ch 9)

REPUBLICAN EMPIRE Term referring to the Roman acquisition of many foreign provinces during the Roman Republic (Ch 9)

RHODES Island city off the southwestern coast of Anatolia (Ch 8)

RICIMER (*Ri'cimer*) Barbarian Master of Soldiers during the time of the Shadow Emperors who virtually ruled the western Roman Empire (Ch 13)

ROMAN CITIZENSHIP The legal status that conveyed the private and public rights of a Roman citizen (Ch 11)

ROMANCE LANGUAGES Modern languages, such as French and Italian, derived from Latin (Ch 14)

ROMANIZATION The process by which provincials absorbed Roman culture and Romans absorbed provincial culture (Ch 11)

ROME OF THE KINGS The first period of Roman history, 753–509 BCE (Ch 9)

ROMULUS "AUGUSTULUS" (*Rom'ulus "Augus'tulus"*) Child western usurper deposed by Odovacar in 476 CE, often viewed as the last western emperor (Ch 13)

ROSETTA STONE (*Roset'ta*) Tri-lingual Egyptian inscription used to decipher hieroglyphs (Ch 3)

ROYAL ROAD Persian highway going from Susa in Persia to Sardis in Lydia (Ch 5)

RUBICON RIVER (*Ru'bicon*) Shallow river in northern Italy crossed by Caesar in 49 BCE to begin the civil war (Ch 10)

SACK OF ROME IN 410 CE Capture and sack of Rome by the Visigoths in 410 CE (Ch 13)

SADDUCEES (*Sad'ducees*) Hellenistic Jews who relied on written scriptures for the regulation of Jewish life (Ch 8)

SAINTS Christians who were accorded special recognition for steadfastness in their faith (Ch 11)

SAÏTE DYNASTY (*Saï'te*) Egyptian dynasty from the city of Saïs that ruled from 671 until 525 BCE (Ch 5)

SAMARITANS (*Samar'itans*) Followers of the form of Judaism prevalant in the northern Hebrew kingdom of Israel (Ch 4)

SAMARRA CULTURE (*Samar'ra*) Neolithic culture of Mesopotamia, 6000–4800 BCE (Ch 2)

SAMNITES (*Sam'nites*) The most powerful of the Italic peoples (Ch 9)

SAQQARA (*Saq'qara*) Site of earliest Egyptian pyramids just north of Memphis (Ch 3)

SARDIS (*Sar'dis*) Capital city of the kingdom of Lydia (Ch 5)

SARGON (*Sar'gon*) Ruler of the Akkadian Empire, 2270–2215 BCE (Ch 2)

SASANIDS (*Sa'sanids*) Persian dynasty that created the New Persian Empire in 227 CE (Ch 12)

SATRAP (*sa'trap*) The governor of a Persian satrapy (province) (Ch 5)

SAXONS A barbarian people from far northern Europe who eventually settled in Britain (Ch 14)

SCIENTIFIC METHOD System for evaluating evidence introduced by Aristotle (Ch 8)

SCYTHIANS (*Scyth'ians*) A generic ancient name for steppe nomads (Ch 5)

SEA PEOPLES Indo-European invaders who destroyed the Hittite Kingdom, attacked Egypt, and brought the Bronze Age to an end. (Ch 4)

SECOND ATHENIAN LEAGUE Alliance of Athens and its allies, 378–355 BCE (Ch 8)

SECOND TRIUMVIRATE (*Trium'virate*) Alliance among Antony, Lepidus, and Octivian begun in 43 BCE to control the Roman government (Ch 10)

SEDENTARY (*se'dentary*) A lifestyle where humans remained in the same place year round (Ch 1)

SEJANUS (*Seja'nus*) Praetorian Prefect who tried to seize the throne during the reign of Tiberius (Ch 11)

SELEUCID DYNASTY (*Seleu'cid*) Macedonian dynasty that ruled Syria and the east 312–63 BCE (Ch 8)

SELEUCUS (*Seleu'cus*) General of Alexander the Great who gained control of the eastern part of the empire (Ch 8)

SEMIRAMIS (*Semir'amis*) The legendary name of the Assyrian queen Sammuramat (811–808) (Ch 5)

SEMITIC PEOPLES (*Semi'tic*) Peoples of the semi-arid region west and south of Mespotamia who spoke Semitic languages (Ch 2)

SENATE An advisory body that served as the true ruling body of the Roman Republic (Ch 9)

SENATOR A member of the Senate at Rome; in the late empire, also a member of a wider senatorial aristocracy (Ch 9)

SENATORIAL CLASS In the Roman Empire, men who owned enough property to be eligible for membership in the Senate (Ch 11)

SENNACHERIB (*Senna'cherib*) King of Assyria 704–681 BCE (Ch 5)

SEPTUAGINT (*Septu'agint*) Greek translation of the Hebrew Bible begun in the third century BCE (Ch 8)

SERVIAN REFORMS (*Ser'vian*) Roman reforms ca. 500/450 that restructured the army and society (Ch 9)

SESTERTIUS (pl. SESTERCES) (*sester'tius* [*pl. ses'terces*]) A large copper coin of the Roman Empire valued at one-fourth of a denarius (Ch 11)

SEVEN WONDERS OF THE WORLD Monuments considered by ancient writers to have been the greatest of the ancient world (Ch 3)

SEVERAN DYNASTY (*Se'veran*) Dynasty of Roman emperors 193–235 CE founded by Septimius Severus (Ch 12)

SHADOW EMPERORS The western Roman emperors from 455 until 480 CE (Ch 13)

SHAMAN (*sha'man*) A holy man able to communicate with spirits (Ch 1)

SHAME CULTURE Culture in which one's feelings about oneself are determined by how one appears to other people (Ch 6)

SHEBA Queen of an Arabian kingdom on the Red Sea who visited King Solomon (Ch 4)

SHEKEL (*she'kel*) Mesopotamian unit of weight, one sixtieth of a mina (Ch 2)

SHELL DEFENSE SYSTEM The Roman military strategy of stationing nearly all the soldiers on the frontier to prevent invasions (Ch 11)

SIEGE WARFARE The use of engineering techniques to capture walled and fortified places (Ch 5)

SLAVS Barbarian people who threatened the Byzantine Empire as of the late sixth century CE (Ch 14)

SOCIAL WAR Also known as the Revolt of the Italian Allies, 90–88 BCE (Ch 10)

SOCIAL WAR War between Athens and its allies, 377–355 BCE (Ch 8)

SOCRATES (*Soc'rates*) An Athenian teacher active ca. 430–399 BCE (Ch 7)

SOL INVICTUS (*Sol Invic'tus*) "The Unconquered Sun," seen by many in the late Roman Empire as being the only true god (Ch 12)

SOLDIER EMPERORS Roman emperors who had risen through the ranks in the army, beginning in 268 CE (Ch 12)

SOLIDUS (*so'lidus*) The gold coin used by Constantine to put the empire on the gold standard (Ch 12)

SOLOMON (*Sol'omon*) Hebrew king 970–930 BCE who constructed the Hebrew Temple in Jerusalem (Ch 4)

SOPHISTS Greek educators who taught methods of effective argumentation (Ch 7)

SPARTA (*Spar'ta*) The most powerful Greek city in the Peloponessus (Ch 6)

SPARTACUS (*Spar'tacus*) Slave who led a revolt against Rome in 73 BCE (Ch 10)

SPARTAN HEGEMONY Period of Spartan dominance in Greece, 404–371 BCE (Ch 7)

SPARTIATES (*Spar'tiates*) Full Spartan citizens (Ch 7)

SPONDYLUS (*spon'dylus*) Mussel whose shell was used in Neolithic trade (Ch 1)

STASIS (*sta'sis*) The constant competition and conflict characteristic of Greek society (Ch 6)

STOICISM (*Stoi'cism*) Hellenistic philosophy based on the teachings of Zeno of Citium (Ch 8)

STRATĒGOS (*stratēgos'*) "General"; the only high elective office in the Athenian democracy (Ch 7)

STYLUS (*sty'lus*) Small wedge-shaped tool used for writing cuneiform symbols (Ch 2)

SUBSISTENCE ECONOMY A local agricultural economy that produces all of its own needs (Ch 6)

SULLA (LUCIUS CORNELIUS SULLA) (*Sul'la (Lu'cius Corne'lius Sul'la)*) Roman general who used his army to seize Rome in 88 BCE (Ch 10)

SUMER (*Su'mer*) The area of lower Mesopotamia, the location of the earliest Mesopotamian civilization (Ch 2)

SUMERIAN KING LIST (*Sumer'ian*) Sumerian catalogue of both legendary and historical kings (Ch 2)

SUSA (*Su'sa*) Capital city of the Elamites and Persians (Ch 5)

SYNAGOGUE (*syn'agogue*) A Jewish house of worship (Ch 5)

SYRACUSE (*Syr'acuse*) A Greek colony in the eastern coast of Sicily (Ch 6)

TACITUS (*Ta'citus*) Roman historian writing ca. 100 CE who covered the Julio-Claudian and Flavian emperors (Ch 11)

TALENT (*tal'ent*) Mesopotamian unit of weight, about sixty-seven pounds (Ch 2)

TALMUD (*Tal'mud*) Guide to Jewish life written in the fourth and fifth centuries CE (Ch 13)

TELL An artificial mound created by centuries of habitation on the same spot (Ch 4)

TETRARCHY (*Te'trarchy*) The system of rule by four emperors introduced by Diocletian (Ch 12)

TEUTONES (*Teuto'nes*) A Celtic people who invaded Gaul in the late second century BCE (Ch 10)

THALASSOCRACY (*thalasso'cracy*) A sea power. (Ch 4)

THEBAN HEGEMONY Period of Theban dominance in Greece, 371–338 BCE (Ch 8)

THEBES The most powerful Greek city in Boeotia (Ch 7)

THEMISTOCLES (*Themis'tocles*) Athenian archon who led the resistance against the Persians (Ch 7)

THEOCRACY (*theo'cracy*) A society in which the leaders of the church also govern the state (Ch 14)

THEODOSIAN CODE (*Theodo'sian*) Compilation of Roman laws going back to the time of Constantine issued in 437 CE (Ch 14)

THEODOSIUS I "THE GREAT" (*Theodo'sius*) Roman emperor 379–395 who outlawed pagan practices (Ch 13)

THERA (*Ther'a*) Island in the Aegean Sea, site of a Minoan colony (Ch 4)

THESSALY (*Thes'saly*) Large region in northern Greece (Ch 8)

THETES (*thetes*) The landless poor at Athens (Ch 7)

THIRD DYNASTY OF UR Dynasty that gained control of much of Sumer ca. 2100 BCE (Ch 2)

THRACE An ancient region roughly equivalent to modern Bulgaria (Ch 5)

THUCYDIDES (*Thucy'dides*) Athenian writer of the history of the Peloponnesian War in the late fifth century BCE (Ch 7)

TIBERIUS GRACCHUS (*Tiber'ius Grac'chus*) Roman Tribune of the Plebs assassinated in 133 BCE (Ch 10)

TIGLATH-PILEZER III (*Tig'lath-Pile'zer*) King of Assyria, 745–727 BCE (Ch 5)

TIGRIS RIVER (*Ti'gris Ri'ver*) A river running through Mesopotamia (Ch 2)

TITHE A land tax consisting of one-tenth of the crops raised during the year (Ch 10)

TORAH (*Tor'ah*) The first five books of the Hebrew Bible (Ch 4)

TRIBES Divisions of the Roman population based on family membership or residence (Ch 9)

TRIBUNES OF THE PLEBS Ten officials elected by the plebeians to protect their interests (Ch 9)

TRIBUNICIAN POWER (*Tribuni'cian*) Power used by Roman emperors of the Principate to control legislation (Ch 10)

TRIBUTE (*tri'bute*) Tax payments to an empire (Ch 7)

TRIREME (*tri'reme*) A Greek warship with three banks of oars (Ch 7)

TRIUMPH Victory parade granted to a victorious Roman general (Ch 9)

TROY City of northwestern Anatolia that, according to legend, was destroyed by the Mycenaeans. (Ch 4)

TRUE CROSS The cross on which Jesus Christ was crucified (Ch 14)

TUT-ANKH-AMON (*Tut-ankh-a'mon*) Egyptian pharaoh 1333–1324 BCE (Ch 3)

TWELVE TABLES The first written Roman law, created by the Decemvirs 451–450 BCE (Ch 9)

TYRANT An illegal, unconstitutional Greek ruler (Ch 6)

TYRE A Phoenician trading city (Ch 4)

UBAID CULTURE (*Ubaid'*) Neolithic culture of Mesopotamia, 5400–4000 BCE (Ch 2)

UGARIT (*U'garit*) A Canaanite trading city of the Bronze Age (Ch 4)

ULFILAS (*Ulfi'las*) Arian Gothic bishop who brought Arianism to the Visigoths in the 340s CE and later (Ch 13)

UPPER EGYPT Section of Egypt extending from the Nile delta to Nubia (Ch 3)

UR An early Sumerian city (Ch 2)

URARTU (*Urar'tu*) A mountain kingdom north of Assyria (Ch 5)

URUK (*U'ruk*) City representing a Mesopotamian culture dated to ca. 4000 to 2900 BCE (Ch 2)

USHABTI (*ushab'ti*) Clay figurine of a servant who accompanied Egyptians in the afterlife (Ch 3)

VALENTINIAN I (*Valentin'ian*) Western Roman emperor 364–375 during the last Golden Age of the Roman Empire (Ch 13)

VANDALS (*Van'dals*) Germanic people originally from the area of modern Poland (Ch 12)

VASSALS (*vas'sals*) Subject cities and peoples allowed to govern themselves as long as they accepted another ruler's authority (Ch 2)

VENDETTA (*vendet'ta*) A blood feud (Ch 7)

VERCINGETORIX (*Vercinge'torix*) Leader of a Gallic revolt against Julius Caesar in 52 BCE (Ch 10)

VESTAL VIRGINS Six Roman priestesses responsible for keeping the sacred fire of the goddess Vesta burning (Ch 9)

VETO The power of the Roman Tribunes of the Plebs to halt any activity they disapproved of (Ch 9)

VICAR (*vi'car*) The administrator of a late Roman diocese (Ch 12)

VILLA (*vil'la*) A late Roman rural estate that produced most of its own needs (Ch 13)

VINČA CULTURE (*Vin'ča*) Chalcolithic culture of the lower Danube, ca. 6000–3000 BCE (Ch 1)

VISIGOTHIC RENAISSANCE (*Visigo'thic*) Period of literary activity in Visigothic Spain in the seventh century CE (Ch 14)

VISIGOTHS (*Vi'sigoths*) Germanic people from north of the Danube River who entered the Roman Empire in 376 CE (Ch 13)

VIZIER (*vi'zier*) Chief official of the Egyptian pharaoh (Ch 3)

VOLUNTEER ARMY Roman army that accepted men who owned no property (Ch 10)

VULGATE (*Vul'gate*) Latin translation of the Bible made by Jerome in the late fourth century CE (Ch 13)

YAHWEH (*Yah'weh*) The name used for the Hebrew god (Ch 4)

YEAR OF THE FOUR EMPERORS The year 69 CE (Ch 11)

ZENOBIA (*Zeno'bia*) Queen of Palmyra 267–274 CE (Ch 12)

ZEUS The Greek god of lightning and thunder (Ch 6)

ZIGGURAT (*zig'gurat*) A step pyramid used as a temple in bronze-age Mesopotamia. (Ch 2)

ZODIAC (*zo'diac*) The circle of twelve constellations through which the sun, moon, and planets move (Ch 5)

ZOROASTRIANISM (*Zoroas'trianism*) Persian religion founded by Zoroaster ca. 750 BCE (Ch 5)

ILLUSTRATION CREDITS

CHAPTER 1

SSPL via Getty Images, 2; Prehistoric Society, 7; Erich Lessing/Art Resource, NY, 8; Kiss Tamás/Wikimedia Commons, 16; Erich Lessing/Art Resource, NY, 17; Ralph W. Mathisen, 23; Rick Flavin, 23; John Wang, 25; Getty Images, 26; Wolfgang Neeb, 27.

CHAPTER 2

© DeA Picture Library / Art Resource, NY, 34; Bildarchiv Preussischer Kulturbesitz / Art Resource, NY, 37; Ralph W. Mathisen, 41; Trustees of the British Museum, 45; DeA Picture Library / Art Resource, NY, 48; Scala / Art Resource, NY, 54; Erich Lessing / Art Resource, NY, 55; Ralph W. Mathisen, 60.

CHAPTER 3

Werner Forman / Art Resource, NY, 71; Wikimedia Commons, 73; Getty Images, 75; Scala / Art Resource, NY, 76 (R); Werner Forman / Art Resource, NY, 76 (L); Hervé Collart/Sygma/Corbis, 81; The Trustees of The British Museum / Art Resource, NY, 88; Werner Forman / Art Resource, NY, 89; The Metropolitan Museum of Art / Art Resource, NY, 92; The Metropolitan Museum of Art / Art Resource, NY, 93; Keith Schengili-Roberts / Wikimedia Commons, 94; DeA Picture Library / Art Resource, NY.

CHAPTER 4

Erich Lessing / Art Resource, NY, 98; Nimatallah / Art Resource, NY, 101; Erich Lessing / Art Resource, NY, 102; Erich Lessing / Art Resource, NY, 104; The Art Archive / Archaeological Museum Thebes Greece / Gianni Dagli Orti, 106 (T); © National Geographic Society/Corbis, 106 (B); National Archaeological Museum, Athens, 107; Drawn by Boudier, from a photograph by Beato, 111; Werner Forman / Art Resource, NY, 115; DEA / S. VANNINI, 119; Balage Balogh / Art Resource, NY, 121.

CHAPTER 5

The Trustees of The British Museum / Art Resource, NY, 127; Erich Lessing / Art Resource, NY, 128; Ralph W. Mathisen, 129; Ralph W. Mathisen, 130; Erich Lessing / Art Resource, NY, 130; Erich Lessing / Art Resource, NY, 134; The Trustees of the British Museum / Art Resource, NY, 140; Alinari / Art Resource, NY, 145; Erich Lessing / Art Resource, NY, 146; The Trustees of The British Museum / Art Resource, NY, 147.

CHAPTER 6

Ralph W. Mathisen, 157; Ralph W. Mathisen, 160; Ralph W. Mathisen, 161; Bettmann/CORBIS, 163; Ralph W. Mathisen, 164; Ralph W. Mathisen, 166; Marie-Lan Nguyen / Wikimedia Commons, 168; Scala / Art Resource, NY, 172; National Geographic Society/Corbis, 173; Bildarchiv Preussischer Kulturbesitz / Art Resource, NY, 176.

CHAPTER 7

National Gallery, London / Art Resource, NY, 185; Steff / Wikimedia Commons, 187; The Trustees of the British

INDEX

Achaeans, 108
Achaemenes, 141
Achaemenid Dynasty, 141, 145
Achaemenid Empire, 449
Acheulean culture, 2–4, 6
Achilles, 159–60, 230–31
Acropolis, 154, 158, 188, 191, 204, 245
Acte, 205
Actium, 327
Acts of Paul, 420
Acts of Pilate, 420
Adad-Nirari II, 126–27
Adam, 34, 46, 407, 451
Adapa, 34, 42
Adlection, 330
Adobe, 33, 50, 89
Adoption, 374
Adoptive Emperors, 351
Adriatic Sea, 169, 241, 291
Adulescens carnifex, 317
Adultery, 56, 59
Aedile, 280, 282, 292, 319
Aegean Sea, 15, 100–101, 105, 139, 168,
    174, 196, 201, 205, 207, 213–14, 222–23,
    228, 380
Aegina, 165, 169, 195, 203
Aegisthus, 217
Aelius Aristides, 354
Aeneas, 271, 343, 391
Aeneid, 343
Aeolic dialect, 155
Aequi, 283
Aes signatum, 297
Aeschines of Sicyon, 174
Aeschylus, 217
Aethelstan, 437
Aëtius, 423, 442
Aetolian League, 240, 294
Afghanistan, 135, 235–36, 246
Africa, 4, 13, 66, 68, 140, 167, 267, 305, 309,
    335, 360, 385, 447–49
Africanus, 293
Afrocentrism, 167
Afterlife, 8, 41–42, 80, 83, 87, 115, 252–53,
    269, 365–66
Agade, 52, 54
Agaids, 181
Agamemnon, 107, 217
Agariste, 203
Agave, 217
Age of the Patriarchs, 116
Age of Tyrants, 173
Ager Gallicus, 287
Ager pubicus, 288
Ager publicus, 306
Agesilaus, 214
Agglutinative style, 99
Agis II, 210
Agis IV, 240
Agogē, 182
Agora, 158
Agricola, 351, 363
Agricultural-Military crisis, 306, 312
Agriculture, 1, 13–14, 18, 31, 33–35, 38–39,
    39–40, 50–51, 72, 86, 96–97, 100, 103,
    111, 113, 116–17, 136, 154, 157, 165, 180,
    187, 209, 239, 266–67, 269, 271, 305, 331,
    361–62, 399, 401, 410
Agrippa, Marcus, 327, 329, 337, 339,
    346, 353

Agrippina (wife of Claudius), 349
Agrippina the Younger, 347
Agroikoi, 190
Ahab, 122, 128
Ahmose I, 90
Ahriman, 149
Ahura Mazda, 145, 148–49
Aigales, 174
Aigikoreis, 156
Ain Ghaza, 13
Ajax, 159
Akawasha, 108
Akh, 88
Akhenaton, 93, 117, 141
Akkad/Akkadians, 51–55, 98–99,
    115, 133
Akkadian Empire, 52–54
Alamanni, 379, 429, 438–39, 459
Alans, 401, 421
Alaric, 422
Alaric II, 434, 438
Alashiya, 110
Alba Longa, 271
Albi, 457
Albion, 249
Alcaeus, 155, 176
Alcibiades, 209–13
Alcuin, 459
Alesia, 320–21
Aletes, 154
Alexamenos, 367
Alexander Helius, 325
Alexander I, 226
Alexander III the Great, 221, 228–31,
    233–34, 236–37, 241, 244, 247, 254,
    256–57, 293–94, 325, 345, 364
Alexander IV, 237
Alexander Romance, 236
Alexandria, 235, 241, 245, 256, 259, 295,
    328, 360, 394, 405, 418, 420, 454–55
Alexandria Eschata, 247
Alexandria in the Caucasus, 247
Alexandria on the Oxus, 247
Alexandrian World Chronicle, 454
Alfred of Wessex, 437
Ali, 452
Allah, 450, 452
Alphabet, 99, 114, 122, 146, 165, 167,
    269–70, 273
Alps, 269, 334
Altar of Peace, 340, 345
Altar of Victory, 404
Amalasuintha, 435, 447
Amasis II, 140, 143
Amazons, 206, 236
Amber, 15, 100, 360
Ambrose of Milan, 404, 416, 418–19
Amenhotep II, 231
Amenhotep IV, 93
Amici, 291, 354
Ammianus Marcellinus, 417
Amon, 86–87, 91–94, 109, 231, 242
Amon-Ra, 87, 111, 119, 231
Amor, 110
Amorites, 57, 124
Amphictyonic League, 164, 227
Amphipolis, 207, 209, 227
Amr, 454–455
Amratian Culture, 69
Amulius, 271

Amyntas III, 223, 256
An, 37, 41–43, 47, 52–54, 57, 114
Anacreon, 176
Anastasius, 443–44, 450
Anatolia, 10, 13, 16, 37–38, 40, 63, 98,
    100–101, 106–107, 113, 115, 126, 137–39,
    141, 154–55, 190, 196, 198, 201, 214,
    228–31, 237–39, 243–245, 253, 265, 294,
    297, 303, 318, 323, 334, 344, 353, 364,
    379, 381, 385, 391, 407, 418, 448, 459
Anaxagoras, 177
Anaximander, 177
Anaximines, 177
Anchises, 271, 344
Anchorite, 407
Ancus Martius, 273
Ancyra, 342
Angle-Land, 437
Angles, 421, 429–30, 437
Anglo-Saxons, 431, 437, 459
Anicia Juliana, 417
Anicii, 457
Ankh, 328
Annals, 363
Annals of Assurbanipal, 137
Annona, 341, 387, 390, 400
Anthemius, 423
Anthropomorphic gods, 47, 101,
    162, 177
Antichrist, 418
Antigonid Dynasty, 239–40, 243–44, 262
Antigonid Macedonia, 293
Antigonus I Monopthalmus, 237
Antigonus II Gonatas, 238–39
Antigonus III Doson, 241
Antikythera device, 260
Antioch, 244, 342, 360, 394, 447, 453
Antioch in Margiana, 247
Antiochus I, 244, 247
Antiochus III, 243, 246, 294
Antiochus IV Epiphanes, 246, 255, 295
Antiochus VII, 246
Antipater, 237
Antonine Constitution, 376, 383
Antonine Dynasty, 347, 351–52, 355, 358,
    363, 392
Antoninianus, 376–77, 381–82
Antoninus Pius, 347, 354–55, 364
An-Tun, 361
Anu, 52
Anubis, 88
Anxi, 245
Apama, 244
Apeiron, 177
Apella, 181–82
Apennine Mountains, 359
Aphrodite, 114, 162, 271
Apocalypse, 406
Apocrypha, 420
Apollo, 162, 164, 166, 190, 228, 298, 341,
    345, 391
Apollo Lyceus, 256
Apollonia, 326, 342
Apollonius of Rhodes, 261
Apologists, 368
Apostate, 398
Apostles, 367–68, 395
Apparitores, 409
Appian of Alexandria, 364
Appian Way, 298, 316

Appius Claudius Caecus, 286, 289
Apries, 167
Apsu, 43, 57
Apuleius, 252, 363
Aqua Appia, 298
Aqueducts, 190, 360, 362, 377, 446
Aquilius, Manius, 312–313
Aquitania, 422, 432, 440
Arabia/Arabs, 39–40, 49, 114–15, 121, 135, 236, 241, 243, 248, 333, 368, 429, 449–53
Arabic language, 459
Aramaeans, 113, 115, 125–27, 130, 133
Aramaic language, 115, 146
Arata, 251
Aratus, 240–41
Arbogastes, 400, 417
Arcadia, 155, 169, 223–24
Arcadius, 398, 400, 420–21
Arcado-Cypriote dialect, 155
Arcesilaus II, 168
Arch of Augustus, 340
Arch of Constantine, 392, 395
Archaeology, 2, 20, 40, 42, 83, 102, 105, 116, 119, 154–55, 272, 411, 433
Archaic Age, 36, 153, 162, 164–65, 169, 176, 178, 180, 250, 260, 270
Archbishop, 394, 437
Archebios, 246
Archelaoi, 174
Archelaus, 334
Archidamas, 208
Archidamian War, 208
Archilocus, 176
Archimedes, 259
Archon, 157, 188, 190–92, 195, 202
Arctic Circle, 249
Ard, 14, 39, 89, 112
Areobindus, 417
Areopagus, 187–89, 202
Ares, 162
Arĕtĕ, 159, 215
Argades, 156
Argeadae, 224
Argonautica, 261
Argos, 154, 157, 170, 186, 197, 203, 208, 210, 214, 224, 227, 240
Arianism, 394–95, 398, 404, 418, 426, 432, 434–36, 440–41, 447
Arians, 456
Aristagoras, 194
Aristarchus, 258
Aristocracy/Aristocrats, 157–58, 164, 169–74, 181, 186–90, 202, 271, 274, 276–77, 408, 415–16, 439–40
Aristodemus, 154
Aristogeiton, 191
Aristonicus, 296
Aristophanes, 217–18
Aristotle, 190, 228, 230–31, 256–57, 267
Arius, 394
Ark of the Covenant, 120–21
Arles, 323, 394
Armenia/Armenians, 145, 447, 449, 453
Arminius, 334
Armorica, 437
Army recruitment, 127
Arpinum, 318
Arrian of Nicomedia, 247, 364
Arsaces, 245
Arsacid Dyasty, 245
Arsenic, 27, 37–38
Arsinoë, 241
Arsinoë II, 242, 261
Arsinoë III, 243
Art, 7
Artaxerxes II, 214, 228
Artaxerxes III, 234

Artemis, 446
Arthur, Duke of Battles, 437
Aryans, 63, 141
Arzawa, 110
As, 297, 338
Ascanius, 344
Asceticism, 403, 407–8
Ashdod, 115, 130
Ashkelon, 115, 128
Ashtoret, 114
Asia, 4, 23, 115, 129, 136, 149, 228, 232, 235, 244, 296, 304–5, 309, 313, 335, 341, 449
Asiatic Vespers, 313
Askra, 176
Aspasia, 203
Aspondos polemos, 159, 170, 209
Ass men, 174
Assassination, 324–26, 340, 348, 351–52, 378–79, 382, 423
Assembly, 156–58, 181, 187, 192–93, 202, 215, 278–79, 282, 315–16, 347
Assimilation, 271, 274
Assur, 124, 128, 132–33, 135, 137
Assurbanipal, 126, 136–37
Assur-Nadin-Shumi, 129
Assur-Nasir-Pal II, 126–27, 135
Assur-Nirari V, 126, 136
Assur-Ubalit I, 126
Assyria, Assyrians, 46, 57, 98, 109, 111, 115, 124–25, 127, 129–44, 146, 148, 165, 167, 224
Assyrian Empire, 128–29, 136–37, 140, 146
Astarte, 115–16, 128
Astrolabe, 258
Astrology, 139, 251
Astronomy, 24, 57–58, 136, 176, 251, 257–60
Asuras, 149
Asylum, 164
Ataraxia, 254
Athanasius, 418
Athaulf, 432
Atheism, 216
Athena, 162, 165, 188–90, 391
Athena Nike, 206–07
Athena Parthenos, 206
Athena Promachos, 207
Athenagoras of Athens, 368
Athenian Citizenship Law, 203
Athenian Empire, 201, 204, 208, 211, 213, 223
Athenian Tribute Lists, 204–5
Athenians/Athens, 102–3, 109, 154, 157–58, 162, 164–66, 170, 174, 176–80, 186, 188–89, 194–202, 204, 207, 211–15, 217, 221–29, 245, 252, 254, 256, 258, 267, 299, 384, 403, 405, 435, 445
Atlantic Ocean, 114, 248–49
Atlantis, 105
Atoms, 177, 254
Aton, 79, 93–94
Attalid Dynasty, 245
Attalus I, 245
Attalus III, 296
Attic dialect, 225
Attic Nights, 363
Attica, 186, 196, 204, 208–11, 222
Attila, 422–423, 442
Attis, 253
Atum, 87
Augusta, 381, 391, 441, 447
Augustan Age, 361
Augustan History, 379, 417
Augustine of Canterbury, 437
Augustine, Aurelius, of Hippo, 402, 412, 416, 418–19, 425

Augustus (rank), 329, 355, 380, 385–86, 389, 391, 427, 448
Augustus, Gaius Octavianus, 324, 326–29, 331–44, 346–47, 353–54, 358, 369, 375, 383–85, 388, 390, 396, 429, 431, 444
Aulus Gellius, 363, 454
Aurelian, 374, 382, 384, 455
Aurelian's Wall, 382
Aurelius Ambrosius, 437
Aureus, 297, 338, 387
Aurignacian culture, 5–6
Auspices, 269, 276, 342
Auspicium, 272, 277
Austrasia, 440
Auxilia, 338–39, 345
Avaris, 90
Avars, 447–49
Aventine Hill, 279, 310
Azurite, 21

Ba, 88
Ba'al, 98, 114, 122
Ba'al Hammon, 267
Babylon/Babylonians, 57–58, 61, 63, 114, 124, 126–33, 135, 137, 139, 141–42, 145–46, 177, 235–38, 243, 251, 402–3
Babyloniaca, 251
Babylonian Captivity, 135, 138, 142
Bacchae, The, 322
Bacchanalia, 253, 300
Bacchiadae, 157
Bacchus, 162, 253, 299–300
Bacchus worshippers, 342
Bactria, 233, 235, 240–41, 245–47, 249
Badarian Culture, 67–69
Bad-tibiria, 45
Bagadates, 244
Baghdad, 33, 39, 51, 63
Balkans, 14, 21, 23, 63, 103, 113, 381, 401, 421, 448, 459
Balshazzar, 142
Balshazzar's Feast, 142
Baltic Sea, 15, 100, 103, 250, 310, 360
Bandits, 360
Baptism, 252, 365, 402, 418, 439
Bar Kochba Revolt, 353, 366
Barbarian invasions, 381, 397, 438, 447
Barbarian kingdoms, 422, 426–27, 430–31, 456
Barbarians, 160, 194, 218, 228, 250, 257, 267, 306, 345, 355–56, 368, 375, 383, 390, 397, 400, 410, 412, 415–17, 421, 423–27, 429–33, 437–44, 447, 456–60
Barbaricum, 249
Barbarization, 400, 425
Barrows, 24
Barsine, 236
Bartar, 49
Barygaza, 249
Basil the Great, 418
Basileus, 156, 238, 449
Basilica, 406
Basilica Julia, 323
Bastarnae, 295
Bathsheba, 121
Bato, 334
Battles: of Arausio, 311; of Abydos, 212; of Actium, 325, 327; of Adrianople, 400–401, 417, 421, 425; of Aegospotami, 213; of Agen, 311; of Alalia, 269; of Aquae Sextiae, 312; of Arbela, 233; of Asculum, 287; of Beneventum, 287; of Busta Gallorum, 447; of Cannae, 292–293, 334; of Chaeronea, 228; of Chrysopolis, 390; of Cnidus, 214; of Corupedium, 238; of Cynaxa, 222; of Cynoscephalae, 294; of Cynossema, 212; of Cyzicus,

Battles   (continued)
212; of Embata, 224; of Gaugamela,
233; of Heraclea, 287; of Himera, 200;
of Hysiae, 170; of Ipsus, 238; of Issus,
232; of Kadesh, 95; of Lade, 195; of Lake
Regillus, 283; of Lake Trasimene, 292;
of Lake Vadimon, 286–87; of Lautulae,
286; of Leuctra, 223–24; of Lysimicheia,
238–39; of Magnesia, 294; of Mantinea
(371 BCE), 224; of Mantinea (418 BCE),
210; of Manzikert, 456; of Marathon,
196; of Megiddo, 92; of Mount Badon,
437; of Munda, 323; of Mursa, 398; of
Mycale, 200; of Mylae, 289; of Nahavand,
455; of Noreia, 311; of Notium, 212;
of Panium, 243; of Pharsalus, 323; of
Philippi, 326; of Plataea, 226, 391; of
Pydna, 295; of Raphia, 243; of Salamis,
199; of Salassia, 241; of Sentinum, 287;
of Telamon, 291; of Thapsus, 323; of the
Arginusae Islands, 212; of the Caudine
Forks, 286; of the Colline Gate, 315;
of the Eurymedon River, 201; of the
Granicus River, 230–31; of the Graupian
Mountain, 357; of the Great Plains, 293;
of the Hellespont, 390; of the Hydaspes,
231, 235; of the Mauriac Plain, 421,
423; of the Milvian Bridge, 390, 395; of
the Nedao River, 442; of the Teutoburg
Forest, 334–35; of the Trebia River,
292; of the Yarmuk River, 453–54; of
Thermopylae, 199, 234; of Thymbra, 141;
of Thyrea, 186; of Tours, 456; of Vercelli,
312; of Vouille, 434–435, 438; of Zama,
293; of Zela, 323
Battus, 166
Bauto, 400
Bay of Naples, 169, 285, 351, 362
Bedouin peoples, 450
Beehive tombs, 106
Behistun inscription, 145
Belgrade, 360
Belisarius, 444–46
Bent Pyramid, 81
Berenice, 241
Berenice (city), 241, 248
Berenice I, 242
Berenice II, 261
Berossus, 251
Besieger of Cities, 238
Bessus, 233, 235
Bethlehem, 418
Bible, 10, 17, 46, 98, 109, 114–19, 121–22,
128, 130, 134, 142, 243, 256, 258, 406,
418–20
Bimetallic system, 147
Biography, 364, 368
Biology, 257
Bishop, 367, 380, 394–95, 402, 405–6, 413,
416, 418, 423, 431–36, 439–40, 443–44,
454, 457
Bithynia, 244, 313, 363, 368
Bitumen, 17, 19, 47
Black Athena, 167
Black Land, 77–78
Black obelisk, 128, 132
Black Sea, 23, 149, 165–66, 168–69, 190,
205, 212, 222, 228, 313, 345, 379–80,
401, 449
Black stone, 451
Blood feuds, 171, 188, 225
Blood guilt, 271
Blues, 341, 391, 444
Bobbio, 458
Bocchus, 312
Boeotia, 155, 176, 203–4, 208, 213,
222–23, 228

Boeotian League, 204, 223
Boethius, 435
Boioris, 310
Bonitus, 457
Bonn, 360
Book of Judgments, 434
Book of the Dead, 88
Bordeaux, 311
Bosporus, 10
Botany, 257
Boudicca, 349, 357
Boulē, 157–58, 171, 181, 189, 191, 202
Brennus, 284
Breviarium, 434
Britain, 112, 114, 249, 333, 348, 359–60,
374–75, 381, 390, 397, 421, 429, 431,
437, 459
Britannicus, 349
British Isles, 38, 267
Brittany, 437
Bronze, 38–39
Bronze Age, 39–40, 63, 65, 95–99, 101, 103,
107, 109, 111–13, 122, 124–26, 137, 140
Brutus, Marcus, 324, 326
Bucellarii, 414
Bucephala, 235
Bucephalus, 230, 235
Bucolic poetry, 261
Budapest, 360
Buddha, 403
Buddhists, 247
Bulgars, 447
Bull leaping, 101–2
Bulls, 101–103, 105, 129, 166, 365–66, 398
Burgundian Kingdom, 440
Burgundians, 398, 421, 429, 435
Burgundy, 440
Burial practices, 7–8, 17–18, 23–24, 35,
68–70, 81, 83, 86–88, 94, 105–6, 115,
266, 268–69, 272
Burnaburiash, 63
Buto, 70
Byblos, 99, 113–14
Byzantine Empire, 384, 429, 436, 441, 444,
446–55, 459–60
Byzantium, 391, 441

Cadiz, 114, 249
Cadmus, 167
Caepio, 311
Caesar (name), 277–78
Caesar (rank), 374, 380, 385–86, 388–89,
398, 427, 448
Caesar, Gaius Julius, 316, 318, 320–21,
323–26, 328–31, 335, 340, 362–64,
454–55
Caesar, Lucius Julius, 313
Caesarea, 418
Caesarion, 323, 328
Caesaropapism, 394, 445, 453
Cain, 116
Caledonia, 351
Calendar, 53, 66, 323, 451
Calgacus, 357
Caliph, 452–53
Caligula, 347–49, 402
Callimachus, 260–61
Callinicus, 384
Callinus, 176
Calxi, 248
Cambrai, 438
Cambyses, 143–45
Camels, 15, 141, 450
Campania/Campanians, 266, 285, 289
Cana, 248–249
Canaan/Canaanites, 92–93, 100, 113,
116–17, 119–20

Cannae, 311
Canon, 418, 420
Canterbury, 437
Canuleian Law, 281
Canuleius, 281
Cape of Spices, 249
Capitoline Hill, 276, 298
Capitoline temple, 273, 288, 319
Capitoline Triad, 275
Cappadocia, 244
Cappadocian fathers, 418
Capri, 347
Capricorn, 345
Capua, 268, 285
Caracalla, 374–76, 378
Carbo, 311
Carbo, Papirius, 315
Carbon-14, 46
Carchemish, 110, 137
Caria, 205
Carnac, 24
Carolingian Dynasty, 441
Carolingian Empire, 458
Carolingian Renaissance, 458
Carpathian Mountains, 24
Carthage/Carthaginians, 114–15, 200, 236,
257–69, 285, 287, 289–90, 293, 295–97,
307, 309, 323, 348, 360, 411, 423, 435,
448, 456
Cartouche, 73, 76
Cassander, 230, 237–38
Cassian Treaty, 283, 286
Cassiterides, 249
Cassius Dio, 454
Cassius, Gaius, 324, 326
Castor, 283, 345
Castra praetoria, 347
Castration, 253, 415
Çatal Hüyük, 16–18, 20
Catastrophe Model, 426
Catiline, 331
Catiline, Lucius Sergius, 317–18
Cato, Marcus Portius, the Elder, 295, 299,
301, 316
Catrigurs, 447
Catullus, 331
Catulus, 316
Caucasus Mountains, 63, 351
Celibacy, 407–8
Celtiberian Wars, 296
Celtiberians, 291, 296, 307
Celtic Christians, 437–438
Celtic fury, 266
Celts, 224, 238, 266, 269, 284, 291, 295,
304, 310, 321, 331, 345, 433, 437
Cenobite, 407
Censor, 281–282, 329
Census, 281
Centenionalis, 410
Central America, 13
Centuriate Assembly, 278, 280, 289, 294,
298, 356
Centuries, 278–79
Chalcedon, 448
Chalcis, 168–69, 229, 239
Chalcolithic Age, 3, 10, 19–20, 23, 25, 33,
38, 65, 67
Chaldeans, 128–29, 137–39, 141–42
Chandragupta, 244, 248
Chariots, 63, 90–91, 94–95, 105, 108,
110–11, 170, 228, 233, 244, 294, 298,
341, 349, 365, 444
Charlemagne, 427, 447, 457–58
Charles Martel, 456
Chemical warfare, 171
Cherson, 169
Childebert I, 440

Childeric III, 441
Children of Israel, 118
China, 1, 13, 38–39, 244–46, 249, 361, 442, 450
Chintila, 458
Chios, 193
Chiragan, 411
Chi-rho sign, 395
Chlothar I, 440
Chopper, 3
Chosen people, 117
Chosroës II, 448–49
Chrestus, 367
Christ, 366, 394, 402–3, 406, 416–17, 419, 442–43
Christianity/Christians, 10, 118, 142, 177, 343, 349, 363–68, 373, 380, 388–89, 392–97, 399, 401–2, 404–5, 416, 418–20, 425, 431, 436–39, 441, 445, 450–53, 456, 460
Christogram, 395
Chronicles, 417–18, 458
Chronology, 2, 46, 72, 78
Churches, 405–6, 413, 416–17, 436, 445
Church council, 394, 420, 434
Church Fathers, 417
Church of the Apostles, 395
Cicero, Marcus Tullius, 317–18, 320, 326, 331, 419
Cilicia, 110
Cimbri, 310–312
Cimmerians, 129, 137
Cimon, 202–3
Cincinnatus, 283
Cinna, Cornelius, 315, 317, 319
Circumcision, 117
Circus factions, 341, 391, 444
Circus Maximus, 341
Cisalpine Gaul, 269, 292, 320, 322
Citium, 254
Citizenship, 156, 158, 160, 181, 183, 187–189, 192–94, 203, 213, 222, 226, 250, 274–75, 277, 279, 286, 289, 300, 305, 309–10, 312–13, 323, 337–38, 348, 355–56, 359, 368, 376, 380, 383, 402
City of God, 412, 425
City/City-state, 113, 122, 153, 158, 191, 250, 303–4
Civitas, 304, 394
Clan, 154, 174, 189, 191, 277
Clarissimus, 413
Classical Age, 178, 180, 221, 260
Classical culture, 457–58
Claudius, 342, 347–49, 367
Claudius II Gothicus, 374, 381–82, 384
Claudius Lepidus, 412
Claudius Postumus Dardanus, 412
Clay tablets, 43, 98–99, 136
Cleisthenes of Athens, 191–92, 203
Cleisthenes of Sicyon, 174, 191
Cleitus the Black, 230
Clementia, 324
Cleomenes I, 191
Cleomenes III, 240
Cleon, 209
Cleopatra, 167, 241
Cleopatra Selene, 325
Cleopatra VII, 241, 323–25, 327–28, 455
Clermont, 457

Client kings, 334
Client, Clientela, 276–78, 341–415
Climate, 36, 425
Cloaca Maxima, 273
Clodius, 326
Clodius Albinus, 374
Clonard Abbey, 458
Clotilde, 439
Clovis, 434, 438–40
Clytemnestra, 217
Coast, 190–191
Code of Hammurabi, 58–60, 118
Code of Justinian, 445
Code of Ur-Nammu, 58
Code switching, 433
Codex, 419
Coemptio, 275
Cohort, 311
Coinage, 139–40, 148, 165–66, 181, 239, 243, 246–47, 297–298, 327, 337–38, 340, 360, 375–78, 387, 390–91, 396, 410, 420, 443
Collegiality, 277
Coloni, 415
Colonies, 101, 106, 114, 127, 140, 154, 166, 168–69, 207, 225, 235, 244, 267–68, 286, 288, 323, 339
Colophon, 177
Colosseum, 351
Colossus of Rhodes, 238
Columbanus, 458
Columella, 362
Column of Constantine, 391
Column of Marcus Aurelius, 357
Coma Berenices, 261
Comedy, 216–17, 261
Comes, 385
Comitatenses, 386
Comitatus, 385–86
Commagene, 334
Commendatio, 338
Commodus, 347, 358, 373–74, 383
Communion, 402
Competition, 159–60, 190
Composite bow, 90
Compulsory services, 387
Concubine, 78, 116, 121
Confarreatio, 275
Confederation, 224, 240, 283, 438, 450
Confessions, 419
Confessors, 368
Conflict of the Orders, 278–81
Congo River, 267
Conon, 212–14
Consilium, 354, 363, 379
Consistory, 408
Consort, 41, 116
Constans, 397–98
Constantine I, 373, 384, 390–98, 400, 410, 416, 446, 460
Constantine II, 397–398
Constantine XI Palaeologus, 456
Constantinople, 391, 393, 395, 401, 417, 436, 441–43, 445, 448–49, 453, 457–59
Constantius I, 385, 388, 390
Constantius II, 397–98, 418
Constitution, 190–92, 201, 335, 356, 358
Consul, 277, 281–82, 292–94, 310–11, 313–14, 317–18, 320, 322, 326, 330, 348, 362, 374, 421, 440
Consular, 387, 412
Copper, 21, 23, 27, 38, 49, 90, 112, 114, 126
Copper-Stone Age. *See* Chalcolithic Age
Coptic Christians, 73, 420, 443
Corcyra, 168–169, 207
Corfinium, 313

Corinth, 154, 157–58, 164–66, 168–71, 174–75, 186, 189, 197, 207–8, 214, 229, 239, 296, 323
Corinthian style, 163, 260
Corinthian War, 214, 222
Cornelia, 307
Cornwall, 249
Corpus juris civilis, 445
Corrector, 387
Corsica, 269, 290, 305, 435
Cos, 251, 258
Cosmogony, 177
Cosmology, 254–255, 258
Cosmopolis, 250
Council, 157, 181, 187, 192
Councils: of Chalcedon, 443, 445; of Constantinople (381), 404; of Constantinople (553), 445; of Ephesus, 442; of Five Hundred, 192, 202; of Four Hundred, 189, 211; of Nicaea, 394, 404; of the People, 356; of the People by Tribes, 280; of the Plebs, 279–80, 307, 356; of Whitby, 437
Count, 386, 440, 457
Count of the privy purse, 412
Covenant, 117–118, 367
Crassus, Marcus Licinius, Dives, 316–18, 320–21
Cremation, 272
Cresphontes, 154
Crete, 97, 99–100, 102–3, 107, 155, 260
Creusa, 343
Criminal law, 59, 280, 358, 376, 416
Critias, 213
Cro Magnon people, 5, 7
Croesus, 141, 163–64, 189
Croton, 177
Crucifixion, 145, 175, 233, 316
Crusades, 459
Ctesibius, 259
Ctesiphon, 322, 353
Cult objects, 18, 101
Cults : of Dionysus, 253 ; of Isis, 252; of Rome and Augustus, 337
Cult statue, 114
Culture, 5, 42, 80
Cumae, 169
Cuneiform, 42–43, 98, 146
Curia, 277–78, 281, 337, 412
Curia Julia, 323
Curiate Assembly, 278–80
Curio, 326
Curtius, 230
Curule chair, 440
Cyaxares, 137, 139
Cybele, 253, 299, 365
Cyclopean architecture, 105
Cyclops, 105
Cylinder seals, 37
Cylon, 188
Cynics, 254
Cyprian of Carthage, 406
Cyprus, 106, 108, 110, 155, 213, 238, 254
Cypselus, 174–75
Cyre, 166
Cyrene, 166–68, 260
Cyrrha, 170–71
Cyrus, 135, 141–45, 189, 194
Cyrus the Younger, 212, 222
Czar, 427

Dacia, 353, 382, 442
Dacian Wars, 364
Dacians, 383
Daedalus, 102
Dagobert I, 440–41, 457
Dagon, 116, 120

Dalmatia, 345
Damascus, 115, 128, 448, 450, 453
Damirica, 249
Damnation of memory, 342, 352, 374
Danaans, 108
Daniel, 142
Danube River, 9, 23–24, 112, 150, 194, 238, 266, 270, 311, 334–35, 347, 350–51, 353, 356, 375, 380–82, 401, 421, 442
Danuna, 108, 110
Daric, 147–48
Darius I, 144, 149, 191, 194–96, 313
Darius II, 212
Darius III, 231–34, 236
Dark Ages (European), 153, 426, 456
Dark Ages (Greek), 153, 155–56, 158–59, 162–66, 171, 178
David, 98, 120, 366
Day of Blood, 253
Dead reckoning, 114
Dead Sea, 15, 17
Debasement, 376–78
Deborah, 120
Debt slavery, 188–89, 278, 280
Decapitation, 266, 357, 423
Decelea, 212
Decelean War, 211
Decemvirs, 280
Decimation, 316
Decius Mus, 287
Decline and Fall of the Roman Empire, 425
Decree, 358
Decurion, 337, 360, 376–77, 383, 387, 411, 414, 438, 443
Defense in depth, 381
Defensive aggression, 284
Deification, 239, 326, 340, 365, 374
Delator, 348, 351, 358
Delian League, 201, 203–5, 207, 210–11, 223
Delilah, 120
Delos, 204, 245
Delphi, 163–64, 166, 170, 174, 197, 227, 245, 391
Delta, 69, 71, 90, 109, 140
Demagogues, 192, 203, 209
Demaratus, 199
Demes, 191
Demeter, 162
Demetrias, 239
Demetrius of Bactria, 247
Demetrius Poliorcetes, 237–39
Demigods, 162
Demiourgoi, 158, 190
Democracy, 174, 190–91, 193–95, 201, 203, 207–9, 213–14, 217
Democritus, 177
Demons, 42
Demos, 154–55
Demosthenes, 228, 326
Demotic script, 73, 140
Denarius, 297–98, 307, 338–39, 375–77, 388, 390, 410
Dendera, 328
Denmark, 421
Deportation, 126, 128–29, 133, 135, 138, 195
Desert, 40
Deshret, 77
Desiderius of Cahors, 457
Dexippus, 384
Dharma, 246
Diadochi, 237–38
Diakria, 190
Dialects, 51, 155–56
Diana, 345, 446
Diaspora, 142, 256, 366, 402

Dictator, 277, 281–83, 325–26, 329
Dictator for Life, 323
Dictator for Restoring the Republic, 315
Didius Julianus, 374
Dies ater, 284
Digest, 445
Dignitas, 287
Dilmun, 49
Dio Cassius, 374, 383
Diocese, 386–87
Diocletian, 342, 373, 384–86, 388–90, 393, 395–97, 400, 403, 444, 460
Diodorus, 433
Diodotus, 245
Diogenes of Sinope, 254
Diolkos, 173–74
Dionysia, 190
Dionysius of Halicarnassus, 270, 344–45
Dionysius of Syracuse, 174
Dionysus, 162, 190, 253
Dioscorides, 344, 417
Disease, 35
Districts of Alexandria, 241
Divas, 149
Divide and conquer, 321
Divination, 41, 269
Divine Mind, 403
Divine right, 132
Division of empire, 399
Divorce, 50, 59–60, 89, 244, 301, 359
Divus Julius, 340
Djoser, 81
DNA, 5
Dodecapolis, 269
Dokimasia, 202
Dolmen, 24
Domestication of animals, 11, 13
Domestication of plants, 11–12
Dominate, 384–385
Dominus, 385
Domitia, 351
Domitian, 347, 350–52, 362–63
Don River, 249–50
Donatists, 394
Donative, 339, 348, 377, 387
Donatus of Carthage, 394
Do-nothing kings, 441
Dordogne, 8
Dorians, 109, 154–57, 174, 180, 187
Doric dialect, 155, 225
Doric style, 163, 206–7, 260
Dowry, 50, 60–61, 276, 359
Draco, 188–89
Drama, 216, 261
Drusus, 310, 312, 334, 339, 345–47
Drusus (son of Agrippina), 347
Dryland farming, 33
Dualism, 149, 403
Duke, 386, 440
Dur Kurigalzu, 63
Dur-Sharrukin, 135
Dymanes, 156
Dymas, 156
Dynastic succession, 391, 395
Dynasty, 66, 74, 77, 90, 346, 391
Dynasty of Constantine, 398
Dynasty of Valentinian and Theodosius, 398–99
Dynasty Zero of Egypt, 71

Ea, 52
Early Dynastic Period of Egypt, 42, 72
Earth and water, 195, 197
East Anglia, 437
Easter, 394, 438
Eastern Orthodox Christianity, 459–60

Eastern Roman Empire, 420–21, 423, 429, 435, 441–442
Eater of the Dead, 88
Ebla, 54, 98
Ebro River, 291
Ebro Treaty, 291
Ecbatana, 139, 145
Ecclesiazusae, 217
Eclogues, 343
Ecology, 36
Ecumenical council, 394, 442–43
Edict, 358, 388
Edict of Milan, 393
Edict on Maximum Prices, 342
Edin, 42, 116
Education, 361–62, 364, 417, 441, 457, 459
Egypt, Egyptians, 1–2, 19–20, 23, 38–39, 46, 55, 63–67, 70, 72–74, 78–79, 85, 87, 90–91, 93, 96–101, 110, 113, 115–17, 121–22, 124, 131, 133, 137, 140, 146, 162, 165–67, 171, 204, 232–33, 237–38, 240, 243, 246, 258, 284, 293, 323–24, 327–28, 334, 336, 346, 353,361, 379, 394, 407, 420, 443, 458, 453–55
Egyptian Empire, 92, 94, 119
Eighteenth Dynasty of Egypt, 90
Einhard, 459
Eisangelia, 202
Ekklesia, 156, 181, 187
Ekron, 115, 130, 132
El, 114, 117, 268
Elagabal, 379
Elagabalus, 374, 379
Elam, Elamites, 52, 54–56, 60, 109, 125, 129, 137, 145,
Elbe River, 250, 334
Elect, 403
Electrum, 139–40, 147
Elephants, 244, 247, 267, 292
Eleusinian Mysteries, 252
Eleventh Dynasty of Egypt, 86
Emancipation, 275, 280
Emigration, 154
Emperor, 329–30, 338–39, 342, 346–48, 350, 353, 356, 358, 360–61, 364, 373–75, 378–79, 387, 89–391, 395–97, 401, 404–5, 408, 414, 424, 449
Empire of Alexander, 221, 229, 235–36, 238, 241, 246, 255
Empire of Attila, 442
Empire of Palmyra, 381–82
Empire of the Medes, 137–39
Empires, 52–54, 57–58, 62, 91–95, 124, 128, 130, 132, 144, 146, 196, 236, 244, 303, 381, 400–402, 406, 421
Emporion, 168
Empress, 379, 381, 391, 423
En, 48
Encolpius, 362
England, 430, 437, 458
Enheduanna, 52–54
Enki, 41, 43–44, 52, 57
Enkidu, 42
Enlil, 41, 43, 45, 47, 52, 54, 114
Ensi, 48
Enuma Elish, 57
Environment, 35
Epaminondas, 222–24, 233
Ephesus, 176–77, 212, 446
Ephialtes (*strategos*), 202–3
Ephialtes (traitor), 199
Ephors, 181–82, 186, 240
Epic, 261
Epicureanism, 254, 299, 331
Epicurus of Samos, 254–55
Epidaurus, 156
Epipalaeolithic Period, 9

Epirus, 157, 231, 295
Episcopalis audientia, 416
Epistates, 192
Eponymous archon, 187
Equals, 183
Equestrians, 279, 298, 335–36, 339, 343, 350
Eratosthenes, 258
Erech, 37
Erechtheum, 206–7
Ereshkigal, 42
Eretria, 168–70, 194–95
Eridu, 34–35, 42, 44–45
Esarhaddon, 126, 129, 137
Esquiline Hill, 314
Essex, 437
Esther, 142
Etesian winds, 249
Ethiopia, 135, 177, 451
Ethiopian Orthodox Church, 420
Ethnicity, 34, 425, 433
Etruria, 269, 362
Etruscans, 268–70, 272, 274, 276, 278, 283, 298, 341, 348
Etymologies, 458
Euboea, 168–69
Euclid, 258
Eudaemon Arabia, 248–49
Eudocia, 436
Eudoxia, 423
Eumenes I, 245
Eumenes II, 245
Eunuch, 122, 148, 174, 245, 388, 415, 444, 447
Eupatridai, 190
Euphrates River, 10, 33, 35, 39–40, 52, 63, 91, 98, 110, 121, 233, 246, 399
Euric, 434
Euripides, 217, 225, 322
Europe, 4, 25–26, 31, 103, 109, 112, 150, 190, 228, 249, 268, 304, 359, 373, 383, 391, 419, 456, 458–60
Eurypontids, 181
Eusebius of Caesarea, 395, 418
Euthynai, 202
Eve, 407, 451
Evolution, 4
Exarchate, 448
Excommunication, 404
Exile, 173–75, 201, 209, 218, 256, 434, 436
Exodus, 118–19
Extinction, 9
Extortion Court, 306, 309
Eyes and Ears of the King, 146
Ezra, 142

Fabian of Rome, 380
Fabius Maximus, Quintus, 291–92
Fall of the Western Roman Empire, 419, 421, 424
Familia, 277
Fasces, 273, 314
Fasti consulares, 340
Fasti triumphales, 340
Faustina, 354–355
Fayum, 86
Feast of the raw flesh, 253
Female principal, 18
Fertile Crescent, 13
Fertility, 7, 18, 50, 114, 116, 132, 267, 368
Fetters of Greece, 239
Fibulae, 433
Fiduciary coinage, 377
First Celtiberian War, 295
First Dynasty of Egypt, 71–72, 75, 77–78
First Dynasty of Ur, 46
First Illyrian War, 290, 295

First Intermediate Period, 83–84
First Macedonian War, 292, 295
First Punic War, 289, 295, 344
First Sacred War, 170
First Samnite War, 285, 295
First Triumvirate, 320, 322
First Wave of Greek Colonization, 154
Fishing, 9
Five Good Emperors, 351–52
Flaked-stone tools, 4
Flamen Dialis, 275
Flamininus, Titus Quinctius, 294
Flavian Amphitheater, 351
Flavian Dynasty, 346–347, 350–351, 362
Flint, 5, 15, 27
Flooding, 10, 14, 35, 40, 45–46, 48, 65–66, 72, 74, 78, 82–83, 105, 116
Foederati, 400–401, 422, 432, 442
Follis, 387
Foot companions, 225–26
Forms (Platonic), 216, 257
Formulae, 282–83, 358
Fortifications, 16, 18
Forum, 273, 288, 315, 323, 326, 342, 355
Forum of Augustus, 340
Forum of Caesar, 323
Forum of Peace, 351
Fourth Dynasty of Egypt, 81
Fourth Macedonian War, 295–96
Francia, 441
Francisca, 379, 433
Franconia, 438
Frankincense, 114, 121, 249
Frankincense Country, 248
Franks, 379, 381, 390, 400, 421, 423, 427, 429–31, 433–35, 438, 440, 456–57, 459
Fredegar, 457
Freedman/woman, 338, 341, 351, 354, 362, 376
Fregellae, 309
Frontier, 383, 401, 421, 431, 433, 437, 451
Fronto, 354, 364
Frumentarii, 358
Fulvia, 326–327
Fulvius Flaccus, 309
Further Spain, 293, 305
Furthest Alexandria, 235

Gabinian Law, 317
Gabriel, 451
Gaius (son of Agrippina), 348
Gaius Caesar, 337, 346
Gaius Gracchus, 307, 309–10, 312, 326
Galatia, 245
Galatians, 245
Galba, 349–350
Galen, 361
Galileans, 398
Galileo, 258
Galla Placidia, 422, 432
Gallic Empire, 381–82
Gallic War, 321, 331
Gallienus, 374, 380–82
Gallo-Romans, 439
Gandara, 247
Ganges River, 235, 249
Garum, 361
Gath, 115
Gaul/Gauls, 238, 245, 266, 268, 284, 287, 291–92, 309–10, 321, 323, 327, 334–35, 348–49, 360–61, 375, 381, 385, 394, 397–98, 411–12, 423, 429, 434, 438, 440–41, 457
Gaza, 115, 130, 233
Geb, 87
Gedrosian Desert, 235

Geiseric, 423, 435–36
Geleontes, 156
Gelimer, 436
Gelon, 200
Gemma Augustea, 344–45
Gender, 408
Gender roles, 6, 160
Genos, 154
Gens, 277
Gentiles, 367
Geocentric system, 259–260
Geography, 65, 100, 103, 158, 191, 247, 257, 261, 279, 362, 400, 426, 440
Geometric style, 166
Geometry, 258
Georgics, 343
Georgoi, 158
Gepids, 401, 447
Gergovia, 320
Germania/Germany, 334, 362–63, 412
Germanicus, 339, 345, 347–48
Germans, 334, 345, 357–58, 379, 382–83, 433, 435, 437, 440
Germanus, 447
Gerousia, 181–82, 184, 267
Gerzean Culture, 68
Geta, 374–75
Getae, 383
Gezer, 119
Ghassanids, 450–51, 453
Gibraltar, Straits of, 236, 318, 351
Gilgamesh, 10, 42, 47
Giton, 362
Gladiators, 268, 298, 316, 319, 341, 358, 362, 395
Gladius, 311
Glaucia, 312
Gobryas, 145
Gods, 10, 17, 41, 51–52, 63, 68, 72, 78, 80, 86, 93, 101, 105, 116–18, 139, 160, 162–63, 177, 195, 218, 251–52, 254, 258, 365–66, 380, 391, 394–95, 402–403, 405, 407, 418–19, 425, 450–51, 453
God's Wife, 91
Gold, 24, 60, 62, 70, 90, 103, 106, 111, 114, 121, 128, 130–31, 139, 147–48, 168, 181, 227–28, 234, 239, 243, 249, 266, 291, 297, 313, 337, 339, 353, 360–61, 377, 382, 391, 393, 399–400, 410, 435, 442–44
Gold standard, 390, 399
Golden Age, 143, 343, 353, 392: of Athens, 201, 204, 216; of Greece, 201; Age of Latin Literature, 330, 342, 344
Golden Ass, 364
Golden Milestone, 391
Golden section, 162
Goliath, 120
Gomer, 129
Good Rule, 181, 240
Gordian knot, 232
Gorillas, 267
Gospel of Peter, 420
Gospel of Thomas, 420
Gothicus, 382
Goths, 379–81, 384, 398, 401, 433, 456, 458
Governor, 290, 304–6, 309, 335–36, 356, 363, 368, 382, 386, 409
Grace, 418
Grammar, 261, 361, 364, 417, 457
Gratian, 398, 400, 404, 418
Graveyard of the Roman Republic, 296
Great Ennead, 87
Great Ensi of Enlil, 52
Great fire, 367
Great Greece, 168, 287
Great He-She, 87

Great Hymn to Aton, 79
Great King, 145, 148
Great Latin Revolt, 286, 295
Great Mother, 299
Great Persecution, 388, 394–95
Great Pyramid, 82
Great Revolt of the Jews, 349–50
Great Rhetra, 181
Greater proconsular imperium, 330
Greco-Roman culture, 357
Greece/Greeks, 1, 36, 73, 97, 99–101, 103–7,
    109, 114, 140–41, 147, 150, 153–55, 158,
    162–63, 166–67, 170–71, 173, 175, 178,
    193–99, 201, 208, 213, 215, 218–22,
    227, 230, 232, 235–43, 246–51, 265–70,
    273–76, 280–87, 291–98, 315, 318,
    322–23, 326–27, 340, 344–45, 359, 364,
    380, 391, 423, 433
Greek language, 256, 342, 354, 383, 398,
    409, 418–20, 442–43, 448, 456,
    458–60
Greens, 341, 391, 444
Gregory I, 437
Gregory of Nazianzus, 418
Gregory of Nyssa, 418
Gregory of Tours, 439, 457
Gresham's Law, 377
Guardianship of the laws, 189
Gudea, 54, 56
Guilds, 135
Guilt culture, 159
Gulf of Corinth, 170, 174, 240
Gutians, Gutium, 52, 54, 56, 125
Gyges, 137
Gylippus, 211
Gymnasioi, 156
Gymnasium, 160

Ha-bi-ru, 117
Hacilar, 13
Hades, 162
Hadrian, 347, 353–55, 358–59, 363, 445
Hadrian's Wall, 353, 375
Hagia Sophia, 417, 445–46
Hajj, 452
Halaf Culture, 33, 35, 38
Halah, 134–35
Haliacmon River, 224
Hallstatt culture, 266
Hamilcar Barca, 290–91
Hammurabi, 46, 58–62, 126, 188
Hammurabi of Ugarit, 108
Han Dynasty, 245
Hand axe, 2–3
Hanging Gardens of Babylon, 139
Hannibal, 285, 291–93, 297
Hanno, 267
Harappa civilization, 49, 141
Harmodius, 191
Harmost, 214
Harpagus, 141
Harran, 117
Haruspices, 269, 276
Hasan Dag volcano, 16
Hasidim, 255
Hasmonean Dynasty, 255
Hassuna Culture, 33, 38
Hastati, 283
Hathor, 242, 328
Hatshepsut, 91–93
Hatti, 63, 110
Hattusas, 94
Hattusilis III, 95
Hearer, 403, 418
Hebrew, 131
Hebrew kingdom, 119–20, 130, 134, 138
Hebrew language, 256, 418, 420, 458

Hebrews, 90, 113, 115–18, 120, 132,
    366, 450
Hegira, 451
Hejaz, 450
Hektemoroi, 188
Helena, 393, 416–17
Heliaia, 189, 192, 202, 216
Heliocentric system, 259
Heliopolis, 78
Helius, 365
Hellas, Hellenes, 160, 228, 250
Hellebore, 171
Hellenism, 255
Hellenistic Age, 221, 237–39, 247, 250, 254,
    256, 260, 340, 365, 459
Hellenization, 244, 246, 255
Hellespont, 190, 197, 200, 205, 212
Helot revolt, 186, 202, 209
Helots, 184–86, 203, 210, 223
Hemlock, 213, 216
Henotheism, 93
Henotikon, 443–44
Hephaestion, 230
Hephaestus, 37
Hera, 160, 163, 275, 391
Heraclea Pontica, 169
Heracleidae, 154
Heraclitus, 177
Heraclius, 441, 448–49, 453–54
Herakleopolis, 84
Herculaneum, 351
Hercules, 153–54, 156, 162, 226, 358
Heresy, 394, 419, 448
Hermes, 162, 210
Hermit, 407
Herms, 210
Hernici, 283
Hero of Alexandria, 259
Herod, 334
Herodian, 384
Herodotus, 148, 166–67, 175, 198, 218, 270
Heruls, 380, 384, 401
Hesiod, 176
Hetairai, 160
Hetairoi, 225
Hexagesimal system, 41, 57
Hezekiah, 128–31
Hiberno-Latin, 458
Hieratic script, 73, 140
Hiero II, 261
Hieroglyphs, 70, 72–73, 80, 84, 92, 99, 110,
    140, 242, 252
Hilderic, 436
Hill, 190
Hill of Ares, 187
Himalaya Mountains, 248
Himyarites, 450
Hindus, 247
Hippalus, 249
Hipparchus, 259–60
Hipparchus of Athens, 191
Hippeis, 183, 187, 189
Hippias, 191, 198–99
Hippo, 402, 418
Hippocrates, 258
Hippocratic Oath, 258
Hippodrome, 391
Hiram of Tyre, 121
Hispala, 299, 301
Histaeus, 194
Historical Method, 218
Histories, 363
History/historians, 1–2, 26, 46, 72, 105,
    116, 119, 153, 218, 261, 270–72, 289, 299,
    331, 343, 352, 355, 363, 374, 379, 384,
    392, 395, 402, 417–19, 427, 429, 456
Hittite Empire, 94, 109

Hittites, 63, 95, 98, 108, 110, 112, 126
Holocene Epoch, 3, 9
Holocene Extinction Event, 9
Holofernes, 138
Holy Land, 393, 406, 408, 413, 416, 418
Holy men/women, 407
Holy Roman Empire, 427
Holy Spirit, 418, 439
Homer, 107, 155, 175, 260
Homicide court, 188–89
Homo erectus, 3–4, 6
Homo habilis, 3, 6
Homo sapiens, 4
Homo sapiens sapiens, 5–6
Homoioi, 183
Homosexuality, 83, 160, 176, 223, 341, 362
Honestiores, 376, 393, 414–15
Honor, 160, 170–71, 176
Honorius, 398, 420–22
Hopletes, 156
Hoplites, 107, 170–71, 187, 195–96, 200,
    208, 221, 241
Horace, 298, 342, 362
Horatius (Consul), 280
Hor-em-Hab, 94
Horse archers, 322
Hortensian Law, 281
Horus, 70–71, 75, 77–78, 87–88
Horus name, 72, 75–76
Horus of Gold name, 75
Hosea, 134
Hostage, 93, 134, 223
Human sacrifice, 115, 268–69
Humiliores, 376, 414–15
Huneric, 436
Huns, 401, 422–24, 442
Hunting and gathering, 1, 5, 11–12, 14
Hurrians, 90
Huy, 92
Hyksos, 90–91, 93, 117, 119, 129, 284
Hylleis, 156
Hyllus, 156
Hypaspists, 227, 232
Hypatia, 405
Hyphasis River, 235
Hystaspes, 145

Ice Age, 9
Iceni, 357
Identity, 250
Ideograms, 72
Ides of March, 324
Ilai, 182
Iliad, 106–7, 153, 155, 175, 231, 261
Illyria/Illyricum/Illyrians, 224, 230, 290,
    334–35, 381, 384, 418
Imhotep, 81
Immortals, 144, 199, 233
Impalement, 132, 148
Imperial Crisis, 373–74, 379, 385, 395
Imperial cult, 364, 388
Imperial succession, 346, 354, 374,
    385–86, 389, 396
Imperialism, 284
Imperium, 272, 277, 292, 304–5, 330, 335
In manum, 275
Inanna, 37, 41, 44, 47, 50, 52
Incense, 114, 121, 249
Incitatus, 348
Incubation, 251
Indemnity, 290, 294–95
India, 1, 13, 26, 38–39, 49, 63, 114–15, 121,
    128, 135, 141, 143–44, 146, 195, 229,
    235–36, 239, 241, 243–46, 248–50, 258,
    359, 361
Indian Ocean, 235, 247, 249
Indica, 247–48

Indiction, 387
Indo-European peoples, 62–63, 103, 107, 127, 129, 141, 167, 245, 247, 265
Indo-Greeks, 246–47
Indo-Scythia, 248–49
Indus River, 39, 144, 221, 235, 247, 249–50
Inflation, 377, 387
Initiation, 252–53, 365–66
Inlustris, 412–13
Innocent of Rome, 420
Institutes, 445
Interior, 191
Intermediate Periods, 72
Inventions, 424–25
Ionia/Ionians, 154–56, 163, 165, 168, 170, 175, 177, 186, 189, 191, 194, 200–201, 204–5, 208, 211, 213–14, 229, 232, 256, 361, 458
Ionian Revolt, 194, 200
Ionian style, 207
Ionic style, 163, 260
Ionic-Attic dialect, 155
Iran, 37, 109, 127, 135, 139–40, 144, 233, 235, 265
Ireland, 437–38
Irene, 391
Iron, 110–12, 115–16, 122, 126, 154
Iron Age, 96–97, 110, 113, 120–22, 124, 126, 137, 140–41, 265
Irrigation, 35, 259, 267
Isagoras, 191
Isaiah, 131
Isauria, 443
Ishtar, 52, 58, 98, 114, 132, 136, 139
Isidore of Seville, 458
Isin, 42
Isis, 87, 92, 242, 252, 324–25
Islam, 10, 142, 373, 429, 449, 451–53, 456, 459–60
Isocrates, 228
Israel, 20, 117–19, 122, 128, 134–35
Istanbul, 456
Isthmian games, 164, 174
Isthmus of Corinth, 169, 173–74, 199
Italia, 312, 345
Italian Alliance, 289, 291, 293, 308, 310
Italian peoples, 283, 285
Italians/Italy, 100, 169, 177, 236, 262, 268–70, 284, 287, 291, 308–09, 311–13, 316, 322, 326–27, 336, 350–52, 358–59, 361, 375, 381, 385–86, 390, 397, 421, 423, 429, 434, 446, 458
Italic peoples, 266, 272
Iulus, 344
Ius civile, 282

Jacob, 117–18
Jacobite Christians, 443
Jarmo, 13
Jason, 217, 261
Jehu, 128
Jeremiah, 138
Jericho, 12, 16, 18
Jerome, 418, 420
Jerusalem, 98, 120–21, 129–31, 138, 142, 233, 255, 318, 350, 394, 399, 417, 423, 448
Jesus, 403, 452
Jesus Christ, 343, 366, 389, 404, 439
Jewish kingdom, 255
Jews, 135, 138, 140, 142, 241, 243–44, 251, 255–56, 349–50, 353, 366–67, 402, 404, 407, 412, 420, 452
Jezebel, 122
John, 403
John Chrysostom, 418
John of Biclara, 458

Jordan River, 12
Jordanes, 456
Joseph, 117
Joshua, 120
Juba II, 334
Judaea, 142, 243, 334, 366
Judah, 122, 128–31, 135, 138, 142
Judah Maccabee, 255
Judaism, 10, 118, 255, 366, 402, 451
Judex, 283
Judges, 120
Judith, 138
Jugurtha, 311–12, 331
Julia (daughter of Agricola), 363
Julia (daughter of Augustus), 341
Julia (daughter of Caesar), 322
Julia Domna, 374, 376, 379
Julia Maesa, 379
Julian, 398–99
Julian Calendar, 323
Julian Law, 313
Julio-Claudian Dynasty, 346–47
Julio-Claudian family, 346
Julius (villa owner), 411
Julius Nepos, 398, 423
Junius Bassus, 405
Juno, 275
Jupiter, 273, 275, 288, 345, 348
Jupiter Optimus Maximus, 275
Jurist, 358
Jurists, 354
Justin I, 444, 450
Justin II, 447
Justin Martyr, 368
Justinian, 436, 441, 444–45, 447
Jutes, 421, 437
Juvenal, 363

Ka, 87
Ka'aba, 450–52
Kadesh, 134
Kalhu, 126, 135
Kanesh, 126
Karduniash, 63, 132
Karnak, 92
Karosthi script, 246
Kassites, 63, 109, 115
Kavad, 449
Keels, 113
Keeper of the sacred bedchamber, 415
Keftiu, 100
Kemet, 77–78
Kent, 437
Khafre, 82
Khalid, 453
Khorsabad, 129, 135–36
Khufu, 82
King, 156–57, 181–82, 223, 229, 239, 245, 250, 266, 271, 273–277
King archon, 157, 187
King Arthur, 437
King of All Kings, 54
King of Kings, 148, 234, 381
King of Sumer and Akkad, 52, 56, 142, 234
King of the Four Quarters of the Universe, 54, 58, 142, 234
King of the Medes and Persians, 141
King Scorpion, 71, 77
Kingdom of Eleazar, 248
Kingdom of Lydia, 137–38, 140
Kingdom of Toledo, 434
Kingdom of Toulouse, 432
King's Peace, 214, 221–22
Kish, 40, 42, 46, 48, 52
Klēros, 155–56, 158, 171, 183, 185
Knights, 278–79, 298, 305–6, 308–10, 318, 335, 338, 347–48, 351, 376, 378, 381, 413

Knossos, 99, 102, 105–6
Koinē, 261
Komē, 154
Konipedes, 156
Krypteia, 186
Kurgans, 24
Kush, 93, 131
Kushan Empire, 247
Kushite Dynasty, 129

Labda, 174
Labrys, 101–2
Labyrinth, 102
Lachish, 131–32, 134
Laconia, 154, 169, 181, 184
Laelius Sapiens, C., 299, 306
Lagash, 42, 50, 54–55
Lakhmids, 450, 453
Lamasu, 129
Lament for Nippur, 41
Land law, 307, 309, 318, 320
Land of No Return, 42
Languages, 62
Laos, 154
Lapis lazuli, 35, 48, 68, 249
Lapis niger, 273
Larsa, 42
Last Decree of the Senate, 310, 312, 318
Last Judgment, 149, 406, 419
Last of the Romans, 423, 437–38, 446, 457
Late Antiquity, 373, 407–8, 412, 415–17, 419, 427, 456, 460
Late Roman Empire, 373, 384–85, 392, 408–9
Latifundia, 316, 361
Latin language, 256, 266–67, 330–31, 340, 342, 344, 364, 374, 398, 417–20, 427, 431, 456, 460
Latin rights, 286, 300
Latins/Latium, 266, 272, 278, 283, 286, 298, 311, 327
Laurion, 190, 196, 211
Law, 58–59, 79, 118, 133, 136, 146, 158, 189, 192, 215, 251, 256, 275, 280–82, 300, 341, 356, 358, 362, 376, 393, 402, 404–5, 408–10, 413, 416, 420, 431, 434, 439–41, 445, 452, 457
Law code, 56, 58, 79, 146, 171, 188, 431, 434, 441
Law rememberers, 171
Lawgivers, 171, 188, 280
Lead poisoning, 425
Leaf points, 5
League of Corinth, 229, 232, 241
Legate, 304, 313
Legate of Augustus, 335
Legends, 45, 102–3, 106, 122, 141, 143, 153–54, 156, 163, 175, 236, 272–73, 278, 283, 299
Legion, 295, 311, 313, 321, 338–39, 345, 350, 383, 399–400
Lelantine War, 169–70
Lemnos, 195
Lemnos inscription, 270
Leo I, 443
Leo the Great, 405, 423, 443
Leonidas, 199
Lepenski Vir, 9, 23
Lepidus, Marcus Aemilius (consul), 315–16
Lepidus, Marcus Aemilius (triumvir), 325–27
Lesbia, 331
Lesbos, 155, 176, 212
Levallois technique, 4
Levant, 13, 15, 20, 90, 97, 107, 113, 233, 381,
Library, 136, 245, 458

Library of Alexandria, 258, 261, 454
Libya, 109, 166, 168, 373–74
Libyan Palette, 76
Licinia Eudoxia, 423
Licinio-Sextian Law, 281
Licinius, 385, 390, 393
Limitanei, 386
Limmu Lists, 135
Limoges, 457
Linear A, 101, 103–4
Linear B, 103–4
Linear Pottery Culture, 21
Lingua franca, 115
Lion Cave, 15
Lions, 105, 134, 140, 166
Little Sorcerer, 7
Livia, 345–46
Livy, 270, 299, 343, 345
Logos, 177, 255, 403
Loire River, 434, 440
Lombards, 433, 447
Lombardy, 447
Long walls, 203, 213–14
Longinus, 311
Lord and God, 351
Lord and Master, 385
Lot, selection by, 192
Lower Egypt, 66, 69, 77–78, 84, 109, 129,
    242, 328
Lucan, 362
Lucanian cows, 287
Lucanians, 266
Luceres, 274, 277
Lucian of Samosata, 253, 364
Lucilius, 299
Lucius Aelius, 354
Lucius Caesar, 337, 346
Lucius Verus, 347, 356, 364
Lucretia, 276
Lucretius, 331
Lucumo, 269, 274, 277
Lugal, 48
Luki, 109
Lullubi, 54–55, 125
Lupa, 271
Lusitania, 296
Luxor, 231
Lyceum, 256
Lycurgus, 181, 183, 184, 240
Lydia, 137–39, 139–41, 146–147, 163, 165,
    174, 189, 194, 270
Lyneferti, 89
Lyric poetry, 176
Lysander, 212–13
Lysimachus, 236–38, 245
Lysistrata, 217

Maadi Culture, 69
Ma'at, 79, 87–88
Maccabees, 243, 255
Macedon/Macedonia/Macedonians, 157,
    209, 219, 221, 223–240, 244, 247, 256,
    262, 292–95, 305, 324, 326
Macedonian phalanx, 226–28,
    233–44, 295
Macrina, 418
Macrinus, 374, 378, 380
Macro, 348
Maecenas, 342, 345
Magdalenian culture, 5–6
Magi, 139, 141, 145, 149
Magic, 82, 139, 251–52, 266, 280
Magistrate, 189–90, 273, 278, 282, 300,
    308, 330, 338, 356, 363
Magna Graecia, 168
Magnentius, 397–98
Magnus Maximus, 404

Mago, 267
Mainz, 360
Majorian, 398, 423
Malabar coast, 249
Malachite, 21
Malaysia, 249
Mamertines, 289
Mancipatio, 280
Mandane, 141
Mandate, 358
Manetho, 74, 77
Mani, 403
Manichaeans/Manichaeism, 403–4, 418
Manilian Law, 318
Maniples, 283–284
Manus, 275
Manuscript, 342, 417, 419, 458–59
Maracanda, 247
Marathon, 196
Marcellus, 341, 346
Marcia, 358
Marcian, 398, 442–43
Marcomanni, 356
Marcus Aurelius Antoninus, 347, 354,
    356–58, 361, 364, 374–75, 460
Marduk, 52, 57, 60–61, 63, 132, 139, 142
Margiana, 145
Marhabal, 292
Mari, 58, 98, 126
Marius' mules, 311
Marius, Gaius, 310–11, 315, 319, 402
Mark Antony, 324–28, 336, 346, 455
Marriage, 50, 59–61, 89, 121, 129, 138, 160,
    168, 183, 184, 231, 235–36, 240, 274–75,
    281, 301, 341, 359–60, 416–17, 423, 432,
    442, 448
Mars, 271
Mars Ultor, 340
Marseille, 168–69, 248, 268, 457
Martin of Tours, 407, 413
Martyr, 406–7
Masinissa, 293
Mastaba, 69–70, 80–81
Master of horse, 326
Master of offices, 409
Master of soldiers, 391, 400, 408, 420,
    423–24
Materfamilias, 412
Material culture, 2, 433
Mathematics, 57, 136, 176, 257–59
Matriarchal society, 18
Matrona of Constantinople, 407
Mauretania, 312, 334
Maurice, 448
Maurya Empire, 244
Mausoleum of Augustus, 341
Mavia, 450
Maxentius, 385, 390, 392–93, 395
Maximianus, 385, 388–90, 444
Maximinus II, 385, 389–90
Maximinus the Thracian, 374, 380
Maximum Price Edict, 387–89
Mayan civilization, 38
Mayor of the palace, 440–41, 456
Mecca, 450–52
Medea, 217
Medes, 129, 134, 136–39, 141, 148–149
Media, 135, 148
Medicine, 245, 251, 256–58, 362
Medina ul Nabi, 450–51
Medinet Habu, 109
Meditations, 356
Mediterranean Sea, 2, 10, 16–17, 24, 26,
    98–99, 106, 108–10, 114, 121, 128–29,
    138, 140, 165–66, 207, 221, 232, 236,
    239, 241, 248, 256, 261–62, 266, 268,
    270–71, 289, 293, 298–99, 303, 318,

333, 366, 368, 373, 429, 431, 438, 441,
    449,456, 459–60
Medizers Medes, 195
Megacles, 188
Megalithic Culture, 24–25
Megaliths, 24
Megalopolis, 223, 227, 240
Megara, 169, 174, 186, 188, 190, 203–4,
    207–9
Megarian Decree, 207–8
Megaron, 156
Megasthenes, 248
Melania, 408
Melian Dialogue, 210
Melos, 15, 210
Melqart, 114
Memphis, 78, 80, 84, 93, 143
Men of bronze, 137, 171
Menander, 261
Menander (king), 247
Menes, 74–76, 78
Menhirs, 24
Menkaure, 82
Menorah, 350
Mercenaries, 121, 129, 136–137, 140, 171,
    173, 190, 222, 229, 232–33, 237, 241,
    243, 256, 267, 290–91, 332
Mercia, 437
Mercury, 345
Merenra, 85
Merimde Beni-salame, 69
Merneptah stele, 119
Merobaudes, 400
Merovech, 438
Merovingian Dynasty, 438, 440–41
Mesolithic Age, 3, 9–10, 13–14
Mesopotamia, 1, 10, 13, 15, 21–22, 26,
    33–38, 40–43, 46, 54, 56, 58, 62–64,
    66–68, 72, 74, 76–79, 94, 97–98, 101,
    109–10, 113–14, 116–18, 124–25, 129,
    136, 138–39, 141, 144, 148, 162, 233,
    246, 256, 322, 353
Messalina, 349
Messalla, 345
Messana, 289
Messenia, 154, 169, 184, 223
Messiah, 138, 366, 389
Messianic Eclogue, 343
Metal technology, 21, 25, 36, 38–40, 79,
    112, 126
Metal working, 94
Metamorphoses, 345, 364
Metics, 188, 193
Metjen, 79, 83
Metropolis, 166
Metz, 440
Miaphyites, 442–43, 445, 447–48, 451,
    453, 455
Microliths, 5, 9
Midas, 128
Middle Ages, 337, 361, 408, 419, 429,
    458–460
Middle Kingdom of Egypt, 65, 72, 86–87,
    89, 91
Middle Stone Age. *See* Mesolithic Age
Midianites, 117
Mighty Mada, 128
Migration, 13, 120
Milan, 404, 418, 420, 446–47
Miletus, 168–69, 174–75, 177, 194, 207
Military Anarchy, 379, 387
Military tribune, 279, 292, 314
Military tribune with consular powers, 281
Militia, 182, 386, 409, 414
Milliarium, 391
Miltiades, 195–96
Miltiades the Elder, 190

Mina, 49, 56, 62, 243
Minerva, 275
Mining, 15, 21, 23, 187, 190, 196, 201, 207, 211, 360, 390
Minnagara, 249
Minoans, 99, 101, 103, 105–6, 114
Minos, 99, 102
Minotaur, 102
Miriam, 448
Mishnah, 256
Missionaries, 438, 458
Mita, 128
Mitanni, 63, 94, 125–26, 141
Mithraeum, 365
Mithraism, 366
Mithras, 365, 402
Mithridates, 365
Mithridates VI, 313–14, 318, 323
Monarchy, 156, 187, 207, 271, 276
Monastery, 407–8, 438, 458
Mongolia, 247, 401
Monks, 405, 407
Monopyhsites, 442
Monotheism, 117, 122, 366–67, 451
Montu, 110
Montuhotep II, 86
Moors, 436
Moral qualities, 274
Morality, 341, 367, 402, 425, 452
Mortuary temple, 92, 95
Mos maiorum, 274
Mosaic Law, 402
Moses, 117–118, 141, 271, 452
Moses (bishop), 450
Mothakes, 185
Mother goddess, 18, 253
Mounted archers, 127
Mousterian culture, 4, 6
Mt. Ararat, 10
Mt. Athos, 197
Mt. Olympus, 160
Mt. Pentelikos, 206
Mt. Taÿgetus, 182, 184
Mud-brick, 16, 47, 50, 70, 86, 154, 156, 162
Muhammad, 451–52
Mummification, 87–88
Mummius, 296
Muratorian fragment, 420
Murex, 114
Museum, 258
Mushki, 126, 129
Muslims, 132, 429, 434, 451–52, 454–56, 459
Mut, 242, 328
Mutilation, 59
Muwatalli, 95
Mycenae/Mycenaeans, 103–7, 114, 141, 150, 153–55, 187, 217
Myrrh, 114, 121, 249
Mysia, 355
Mystery cults, 252–54, 365, 367
Mythology, 43, 57–58, 87, 153, 160, 162–63, 177, 344
Myths, 299
Mytilene, 174

Nabonidus, 141–42
Nabopolassar, 137
Nabû, 58
Naevia Galla, 412
Names, 277–78, 459
Nanna, 41, 52–53, 136
Naos, 162, 207
Naples, 268, 286, 446
Naqada Culture, 68–70, 72
Naram-Sin, 54–55, 60, 99
Narbonese Gaul, 296, 305, 311, 316, 320

Narmer, 71, 75–76, 76–77
Narmer Palette, 55, 76–77
Narses, 447
Natron, 87
Natufian culture, 12, 18
Natural History, 362
Natural philosophy, 257
Navigation, 114
Navy, 100, 102, 106, 108–9, 114–15, 144, 174, 187, 195–96, 199–201, 203, 205, 208, 210–13, 232–33, 259, 267, 287, 289–90, 362, 390, 423
Naxos, 201
Nazareth, 366
Nazis, 433
Neanderthals, 4, 6–7
Near East, 13, 31, 38, 63, 101, 117, 121–25, 134, 139–40, 144, 148, 150, 162–67, 207, 234, 239, 261, 265, 283, 447, 449, 456, 459–60
Nearchus, 247
Nearer Spain, 293, 305
Nebuchadrezzar, 137–39
Necho II, 129, 137, 140
Nefertiti, 93
Nehemiah, 142
Nekhen, 70–71, 75, 77–78, 84
Neleids, 154
Nemean games, 164
Neodamodais, 210
Neolithic Age, 3, 10–11, 14–26, 32–33, 65, 69
Neolithic Revolution, 11, 14
Neoplatonism, 384, 398, 403, 405
Nephthys, 87
Neptune, 345, 348
Nergal, 42, 58, 136
Nero, 347, 349, 362–63, 367, 373, 383, 402
Nero (son of Agrippina), 347
Nerva, 347, 352, 356
Nestorianism/Nestorians, 442, 445, 448, 451
Neustria, 440
New Babylonian Empire, 137–38, 140
New Kingdom of Egypt, 65, 72, 91–92, 95, 109
New man, 295, 309, 311, 317, 416
New Persian Empire, 379, 441–42, 455–56
New Persians, 380–81, 398–99, 402–3, 437, 446–51, 453
New Stone Age. *See* Neolithic Age
New Testament, 367, 420
Nexum, 280
Nicene Creed, Nicenes, 394, 398, 404, 418, 426, 432, 434–36, 438, 440, 442–43, 447, 456,
Nicias, 210
Nicomedia, 364, 385, 387
Nika, 196
Nika Rebellion, 445–46
Nile River, 19, 36, 39, 64–69, 72, 74, 78, 86, 93, 109, 117, 241, 243, 249, 252, 351, 361, 368
Nîmes, 337
Nimrud, 126–27, 132–33
Nineteenth Dynasty of Egypt, 94
Nineveh, 52, 115, 130, 132, 136–37
Ningirsu, 42, 50
Ninurta, 58
Nippur, 42, 47, 52, 54, 56
Nisibis, 135
Nitocris, 83
Noah's flood, 10
Nobles, 48, 50, 61–62, 78–79, 83–84, 91, 113, 132, 134, 136, 142, 148, 225, 227, 232, 245, 282, 432, 436, 439–40
Nola, 314

Nomads, 127, 129, 245, 401
Nomarch, 78, 83
Nome, 66, 68, 129
Nominatio, 338
Nonviolence, 101
Noricum, 311
North Africa, 2, 25, 31, 114, 166, 289–91, 296, 311, 314, 323, 326–27, 334–61, 363–64, 381, 394, 397, 408, 410–11, 418, 420–21, 423, 426, 429, 435–36, 446, 456, 459
North Sea, 250
Northumbria, 437
Notker, 459
Novus homo, 282
Nubia, 19, 26, 66, 71, 79, 82, 84, 86, 91–93, 129
Nubian Dynasty, 129
Numa Pompilius, 271, 273
Numantia, 296–297
Numantine War, 296
Numen, 271, 275
Numidia, Numidians, 267, 291, 293, 295, 311
Numitor, 271
Nut, 87

Obelisk, 92
Obsidian, 12–17, 23
Ochre, 8, 15
Octavia, 325
Octavian. *See* Augustus, Gaius Octavianus
Odometer, 259
Odovacar, 421, 424, 434
Odysseus, *Odyssey*, 106, 153, 155, 159, 176
Oedipus, 217
Oikistes, 168
Oikos, 154
Oikoumenē, 345
Old Babylonian Empire, 57–58
Old Kingdom of Egypt, 65, 72, 80, 86, 90–91
Old Stone Age, see Paleolithic Age
Old Testament, 389, 420
Oldowan culture, 3, 6
Oligarchy, 164, 171, 174–175, 186, 189, 191, 202, 207–8, 211–14, 267, 281
Olives, 187, 208, 215, 259
Olympia, 164, 391
Olympian gods, 160
Olympias, 229, 231, 237
Olympias (trireme), 198
Olympic games, 164, 174, 226, 349
Olynthus, 227
Oman, 49
Ommana, 248
On the Nature of Things, 331
On Warlike Matters, 424
Opimius, 309–10
Optimates, 308, 310, 315
Optimism, 66, 88
Oracle, 407
Oracle of Apollo, 163–64, 166, 168, 170, 174, 197, 227
Oral tradition, 122, 153, 163
Oratio, 356
Orders of Greek architecture, 162
Oresteia, 217
Orientalizing style, 166–67
Origen, 420
Origin myth, 431
Original sin, 407
Orkney Islands, 249
Orléans, 440
Orontes River, 244, 363
Oscan dialect, 266

Osiris, 85, 87–88, 94, 242, 252
Ostia, 359
Ostracism, 192–93
Ostrogothic Empire, 435
Ostrogothic kingdom, 446
Ostrogoths, 401, 429, 434–35, 447
Otho, 350
Otium, 414
Otzi, 24, 26
Overpopulation, 36, 165–66, 169

P speakers, 265–66
Pactolus River, 139, 147
Paddlewheel ship, 424–25
Paestum, 163
Pagan monotheism, 366
Paganism, 368, 392, 395, 399, 402–7, 419, 425, 447, 451
Pakistan, 1, 249
Palace complex, 99, 106
Palace façade style, 70
Palaeolithic Age, 3–6, 12, 14–15, 18, 31, 66
Palatine Hill, 272–73, 341
Palermo Stone, 74, 82
Palestine, 12, 15, 68, 8–94, 100, 109–10, 142, 238, 246, 256, 379, 402, 407
Palladium, 391
Palmyra, 380–81, 450
Pamphyloi, 156
Pan, 238
Panaetius of Rhodes, 299
Panathenaic festival, 206
Pandataria, 341
Panegyric, 363
Pan-Hellenic Congress, 197
Pan-Hellenism, 164, 227
Pannonia, 349
Pantheon, 41, 116, 267, 353, 365
Papirius, C., 313
Papyrus, 73–74, 114, 242, 342, 419
Paralia, 190
Parallel Lives, 364
Parchment, 245, 342
Paris, 440
Parmenion, 231, 233
Paros, 176
Parthenon, 206, 260, 405
Parthia, 240, 245–46, 248, 353
Parthian Empire, 334, 353
Parthian War, 324, 356
Parthians, 245–46, 249, 320–22, 324, 379
Pasiphaë, 102
Passing under the yoke, 286
Pastoralism, 11, 39–40, 54, 57, 62, 116–17, 120, 450
Pater patriae, 341, 343
Paterfamilias, 274–75, 277, 359
Patriarch, 116, 394, 402
Patrician (rank), 412, 414, 457
Patricians, 274–78, 280–81, 292, 318
Patrick, 438
Patroclus, 230
Patron, 276, 414–15
Patron-Client relationship, 340
Paul, 367–368, 402, 420
Paullus, 292
Paulus, Lucius Aemilius, 295
Pausanias, 200–201, 213
Pax deorum, 365
Pax Romana, 333, 356, 358–60, 399
Peace of Antalcidas, 214
Peace of Callias, 204
Peace of Nicias, 209
Peace of Phoenice, 293
Pecunia, 297
Pediake, 190
Pegasus, 165

Peisistratus, 190–191
Peleset, 109–10, 115
Pelopidas, 222–23
Peloponnesian League, 186, 204, 208–9, 214, 218
Peloponnesian War, 208, 213, 216, 219, 221, 226, 293
Peloponnesus, 154–55, 169, 174, 180, 186, 199, 203, 208, 210, 222–24
Penance, 404, 406
Penelope, 176
Pentakonter, 165–66
Pentakosiomedimnoi, 189
Pentheus, 217
People of the Book, 452
People's Council, 193
Pepi I, 84
Pepi II, 83
Peregrine praetor, 282
Pergamum, 240, 245, 258, 294, 296, 307, 455
Periander, 173–75
Pericles, 202–4, 208–9
Perigordian culture, 5
Perioikoi, 156, 185, 240–41
Periplus, 247, 267
Periplus of the Red Sea, 248
Persecution, 368, 380, 393, 403, 405, 436, 451, 453
Persepolis, 146, 148, 234–235
Perseus, 162
Perseus (Macedonian king), 294
Persia/Persians, 124, 135, 141–47, 160, 163, 175, 177, 189, 191, 195–96, 198, 200–201, 203, 206, 208, 211, 213–14, 221–36, 244, 247, 250, 255, 365, 415, 448, 459
Persian Empire, 140–41, 143, 146–47, 150, 178, 194, 229–35, 365, 379
Persian Gates, 234
Persian Gulf, 248, 353
Persian Invasion, 195–198, 218
Persian Sea, 248
Persis, 244
Persius, 362
Pertinax, 374
Pescennius Niger, 374
Pessimism, 41
Peter, 395, 405
Petitions, 358
Petronius, 362
Peutinger Table, 359
Pezhetairoi, 225
Phaedrus, 362
Phalanx, 170–171, 182, 187, 284
Phallic imagery, 18
Pharaoh, 63, 66, 72–88, 91, 110–11, 117, 119, 121–22, 129, 131, 137, 141, 167, 171, 241–42, 324, 327–28
Pharisees, 256
Pharsalia, 362
Pheidippides, 196
Phidias, 206–7
Philetaerus, 245
Philhellene, 245
Philip II, 221, 223, 226–28, 231–32, 256, 326
Philip III Arrhidaeus, 237
Philip the Arab, 374, 380
Philip V, 241, 243, 292, 294
Philippics, 228, 326
Philistines, 109, 113, 115–16, 120, 128, 130
Philosophers/Philosophy, 176–77, 215–16, 227, 250, 254–55, 257, 261, 298, 318, 349, 356, 362, 364, 366, 384, 398, 403, 441, 445
Philotas, 231

Phocaea, 168
Phocas, 448
Phocians, 227
Phocis, 227
Phoecaea, 269
Phoenicia/Phoenicians, 113–116, 122, 128, 133, 140, 144, 147, 160, 165, 167, 248, 267–68, 289, 360, 373
Phratry, 154, 181, 188
Phrygians, 126
Phrynicus, 195, 217
Phylē, 154
Pictograms, 37, 43
Pietas, 344
Pig men, 174
Pilgrimage, 406, 416
Pilum, 311
Pindar, 155, 229
Pippin, 441
Piracy, 240, 290–91, 317–18
Piraeus, 195, 204, 213
Pisidia, 355
Piso, 362
Pius, 355
Placidia, 423
Plague, 208–9, 356, 380, 382, 423, 447
Plain, 190
Plataea, 196, 209, 223
Plato, 168, 215–16, 254, 256–57, 403
Plautian-Papirian Law, 313
Plautius, M., 313
Plautus, 299
Plebeians, 274, 276–81, 284, 288–289, 298, 309–10, 338, 414–15
Plebiscite, 279–80
Plebs, 274
Pleistocene Epoch, 3, 9
Pliny the Elder, 361–63
Pliny the Younger, 363, 368
Pliocene Epoch, 3
Plotinus, 403
Plutarch, 183, 184–86, 229–230, 232, 259, 314, 324–25, 328, 364, 455
Po River, 269, 284, 288, 291
Poenus, 289
Poitiers, 457
Poland, 382, 433
Polemarch, 157, 187, 193
Polis, 153, 158, 171, 176, 181, 200, 219, 241, 250
Politeia, 158
Politics, 257
Pollux, 283, 345
Polybius, 261, 299
Polychrome pottery, 33
Polycrates, 174
Polygonal blocks, 285
Polytheism, 368, 388, 391–93, 399, 402, 406, 419, 450
Pompeii, 216, 253, 351
Pompey, Gnaeus, "The Great", 316–17, 320, 323–24, 327, 362
Pompey, Sextus, 327
Pompey Strabo, 317–18
Pontifex Maximus, 275, 330
Pontius Pilate, 367, 405
Pontus, 205, 244, 313–14, 363, 368
Pope, 275, 405, 434–35, 437
Populares, 308
Populus, 274, 277–78
Porus, 235–36
Poseidon, 162, 164, 206
Poseidon Erechtheus, 207
Postumus, 381
Potentia, 413–414
Potidaea, 168
Potter's wheel, 37

Pottery, 16–17, 19–23, 25, 31, 33–34, 36, 38, 49–51, 67, 79, 100–101, 103, 106–7, 113, 190, 269, 273
Praeses, 387
Praetextatus, 404
Praetor, 281–82, 290, 304–5, 310, 314–15, 319
Praetorian Guard, 339, 348–50, 374–75, 379
Praetorian prefect, 339, 348, 358, 375, 378, 387, 391, 408, 412
Praetor's Edict, 283, 358
Praise of Ishtar, 53
Praise of Rome, 354
Prasutagus, 357
Predestination, 418
Prefect, 335–336, 339, 367
Prefect of the night watch, 348
Prefecture, 387
Prehistory, 1
Presentism, 2
Pre-Socratic philosophers, 177
Priest-king, 37, 47–48
Priests, 48–50, 79, 83, 93, 101, 109, 134, 139, 143, 149, 162, 245, 255, 271, 275–76, 300, 394, 416
Prince of the Captivity, 402
Princeps, 329–330
Princeps senatus, 282
Principate, 303, 327, 329, 346, 369, 384–85, 394, 396–97, 400, 408, 413–14, 417, 431
Principes, 283
Priscus, 442
Priscus Tarquin, 273
Prism of Sennacherib, 130, 132
Prison, 59
Private rights, 277
Proconsul, 282, 292, 304–5, 330, 387
Proconsular imperium, 347
Procurator, 335
Proletariate, 278–79
Promised Land, 118, 120
Propaganda, 340, 345, 400
Propertius, 345
Prophecy of Neferti, 84
Prophets, 122
Propylaea, 206–7
Proscriptions, 315, 319
Proskynesis, 148, 231, 236, 385
Prostitution, 44, 50, 62, 160, 192, 341, 408
Proto-alphabet, 99, 114
Provence, 434, 440
Province/Provincials, 133, 290, 296, 304–6, 313, 318–19, 333–37, 340, 347, 351–53, 353–58, 375, 380, 382, 386, 394, 414, 421, 442, 450
Provincial council, 337
Proxenos, 226
Prytany, 192
Psammeticus, 174
Psamtik I, 137, 171
Pschent, 77, 242
Ptah, 78
Ptolemaic Dynasty, 238, 240–41, 243–46, 255, 261, 324–25, 454
Ptolemaic Egypt, 293–95, 318, 323
Ptolemaic System, 259
Ptolemaïs, 241
Ptolemy (astronomer), 259
Ptolemy I, 230, 237–38, 241
Ptolemy II, 242, 260–61
Ptolemy III, 243
Ptolemy IV, 243
Ptolemy Keraunos, 238
Ptolemy Philadelphus, 325
Ptolemy V, 73, 243
Ptolemy VII, 307
Ptolemy XII, 323–24

Ptolemy XIV, 328
Ptolemy XV, 328
Public land, 306–7
Public rights, 277
Publicani, 305
Pul, 128, 134
Pulcheria, 441–42
Punic language, 267
Punishment, 118
Punt, 82
Puppet Emperors, 423
Purple dye, 267
Puzur-Assur I, 126
Pylos, 103, 109, 154–55
Pyramid Texts, 82
Pyramids, 80, 82–83, 86, 92
Pyrrhic victory, 287
Pyrrhic War, 287, 295
Pyrrhus of Epirus, 287
Pythagoras, 177
Pytheas, 248–49
Pythia, 163, 391
Pythian games, 164

Q speakers, 265–66
Quadi, 356
Quaestor, 277, 282, 304, 307, 315
Quaestor of the sacred palace, 408
Querns, 12–13
Quinotaur, 438
Quintilian, 362
Quirinal Hill, 331
Qu'ran, 452–53, 455
Quraysh, 450–51

Ra, 78, 86–87, 92, 110, 231, 242
Radagaisus, 421
Radical democracy, 192–193, 202–3
Ragnachar, 438
Ramesseum, 95
Ramnes, 277
Ramses I, 94
Ramses II, 74–75, 95, 117, 119
Ramses III, 109–111
Ransom, 416
Rape of the Sabine Women, 272
Ravenna, 420, 422, 434–35, 444, 446–48
Reccesvinth, 458
Reciprocal duty, 276
Red Pyramid, 82
Red Sea, 118, 121, 241, 249, 450
Red Sea canal, 140, 146, 243, 248, 361
Red slipware, 20, 410
Redemption, 254
Referendary, 440
Reformer of the Constitution, 189
Refugees, 95
Regnum Sullanum, 313, 315
Regulus, Marcus, 290
Reims, 438–439
Reincarnation, 177
Religion, 7, 17–18, 38–39, 47, 78, 87, 101–103, 115–116, 118, 120, 122, 124, 132–33, 138, 142, 159, 162, 182, 189–90, 196, 250, 253, 255, 267, 273, 299, 364–66, 373, 393, 397, 401, 403, 416, 429, 432, 439, 443–44, 449–451, 459
Religion, state, 276
Remigius, 438–39
Remus, 271
Representative democracy, 193
Republican Empire, 297
Res gestae, 417
Res gestae divi Augustae, 342–43
Res publica, 277
Rescript, 358
Restorer of the World, 382

Revelation, 406, 420
Revelation of Peter, 420
Revolt of the Italian Allies, 312–13, 317–18
Revolt of the Jews, 357, 366
Rex, 277
Rhea Sylvia, 271
Rhetoric, 215, 228, 298, 309, 318, 354, 361–62, 405, 417–18, 441
Rhetra, 181
Rhine River, 23, 26, 112, 266, 321, 334–36, 347–50, 375, 379, 381, 421, 429, 438, 440
Rhodes, 238, 240, 294
Rhône River, 168, 440
Richomer, 400
Ricimer, 423
Ripuarian Franks, 438
Rituals, 18, 118, 163, 189, 252, 287, 365
River valleys, 32, 35–38, 40, 51–52, 64–67, 72, 96–97, 100, 103, 107–113, 116, 124, 137, 140–41, 449
Rix, 266
Roads, 259, 286, 288, 337, 339, 359–60, 412
Robber Council of Ephesus, 443
Robigus, 275
Rock paintings, 7
Rock reliefs, 145
Roma, 274, 345, 359
Roman Antiquities, 344
Roman Catholic Christianity, 437, 459–60
Roman Empire, 73, 147, 283, 325, 329–30, 333–34, 336–39, 342, 351–54, 359, 364, 366–68, 373, 379, 384–85, 396, 402, 404, 419, 427, 435, 450, 459–60
Roman peace, 333
Roman Republic, 126, 265, 271, 277, 283, 285, 293, 300, 303–6, 310, 313, 319, 323–35, 339, 342, 346–47, 356, 359, 361–63, 413
Romance languages, 340, 431
Romanization, 340, 357
Romans, 174, 218, 244, 246, 259, 270–71, 278–79, 284, 288, 290–94, 299, 301, 310, 316, 321, 334, 340, 344, 355, 357–58, 364, 373, 397, 417, 425, 429, 431, 433, 437, 447, 457
Rome, 1, 236, 241, 244–45, 261–62, 265, 270–72, 275, 284, 289, 295, 297, 299, 303–4, 309, 311, 313–14, 318, 323–24, 327, 338–40, 343–44, 347, 350–51, 353, 355, 359360, 367–68, 374, 379–82, 385, 366, 390–91, 393–95, 402, 405, 413, 420, 423, 434–35, 438, 443, 446–48, 457
Rome of the Kings, 270–71, 273
Romulus, 271, 273, 277, 424
Romulus "Augustulus", 398, 421, 424
Rosetta Stone, 73, 140
Rostra, 323
Roxanne, 235, 237
Royal Annals, 71, 74
Royal List of Abydos, 74–75
Royal Road, 146
Rubicon River, 322
Rufus, 309
Rugians, 401
Ruricius, 457

Sabbath, 138, 255
Sabellian dialect, 266
Sabines, 272
Sack of Jerusalem, 423
Sack of Rome, 284–85, 295, 334, 421–23, 436
Sacred Band, 228
Sacred War, 164
Sacred Way, 288
Sacrosanctitas, 280, 308
Sadducees, 256

Saguntum, 291
Sahara Desert, 36, 66–67, 69, 267, 334, 360, 436, 449,
Saint, 368, 395, 406, 418, 456
Saïs, 70, 129, 140
Saïte Dynasty, 137–38, 140, 143
Saka, 247, 355
Salamis, 190, 199
Salian Franks, 438
Salic Law, 439
Salinization, 35
Sallust, 331
Salome Alexandra, 256
Salt, 23
Salvation, 365
Salvius, 311
Salvius Julianus, 358
Samaria, 122, 128, 131, 134–35
Samaritans, 122, 135
Samarra Culture, 33–35, 38
Sambaton, 135
Samerina, 135
Sammuramat, 126, 128
Samnite Wars, 287, 306
Samnites, 266, 285–86, 315
Samnium, 286
Samos, 163, 169, 177, 194, 207, 211, 391
Samosata, 364
Samson, 120
Samsu-Iluna, 62–63
Samuel, 120
San Vitale, 409, 444
Sanhedrin, 367
Sanitation, 14
Sappho, 155, 176
Saqqara, 80–81
Saracens, 450
Sardinia, 269, 290, 305, 435–36
Sardis, 139, 141, 146, 194, 199, 341
Sargon of Akkad, 52–54, 98, 141, 271
Sargon II, 126, 128–129, 135–36
Sarissa, 226
Sasanian Empire, 449, 453
Sasanid Dynasty, 379, 455
Satan, 403
Satire, 299, 362, 364
Satrap, Satrapy, 139, 146, 233, 236, 238, 241, 244–45
Saturninus, 312
Satyricon, 362
Saxons, 421, 429–30, 433, 437
Science, 256–257
Scientific method, 139, 257
Scipio Aemilianus, 295, 297, 299
Scipio Nasica, 308
Scipio, Lucius Cornelius, 294, 307
Scipio, Publius Cornelius, 292–93
Scirians, 401
Scotland, 351, 357, 368, 399, 437
Scourge of God, 442
Scramasax, 433
Scraper, 3–4
Scribes, 43, 50, 79, 135, 148, 243
Scripture, 398, 403, 418, 420, 452, 457
Scylax, 144
Scythia, Scythians, 129, 143, 149, 194, 225, 233, 245, 247, 384
Sea of Galilee, 453
Sea Peoples, 107–11, 115, 119
Seax, 433
Secede, 279
Second Athenian League, 223
Second Celtiberian War, 295
Second Dynasty of Egypt, 78, 80
Second Illyrian War, 291, 295
Second Intermediate Period, 90
Second Macedonian War, 294–95

Second Punic War, 291–92, 297, 299
Second Samnite War, 286, 295
Second Sophistic, 354, 364
Second Triumvirate, 326
Second Wave of Greek Colonization, 166, 168, 268
Secret ballot, 307
Secret of empire, 349
Secret Treaty, 294
Secular Games, 343, 380
Sedentary living, 9, 44
Segesta, 210
Seine River, 440
Seisactheia, 189
Sejanus, 347–48
Seleucia, 244
Seleucid Empire, 244–45, 294, 318
Seleucids, 238, 240, 243–46, 255, 262, 293, 311
Seleucus, 237–38, 244, 247–48
Semiramis, 128
Semitic languages, 40, 165
Semitic peoples, 39, 56–57, 62, 90, 98, 115–117, 128
Sempronia, 307
Senate (Carthaginian), 291
Senate house, 343, 346
Senate, Decree of, 300, 342, 356
Senate/Senator, 267, 273–82, 288–89, 292–99, 301, 304–19, 322–26, 329–31, 335, 338–39, 341, 346–56, 360, 363, 374–82, 386, 390, 394, 396, 399, 411–17, 431–32, 435, 448
Senatorial class, 338, 413
Senatus consultum, 282
Seneca, 349, 362, 454
Sennacherib, 126, 129–31, 134, 136
Sennedjem, 89
Senusret III, 86
Septimania, 440
Septimius Severus, 373–34, 378–79
Septuagint, 256, 420
Seranim, 115
Serapaeum, 455
Serapis, 242
Serekh, 70, 72, 77
Serfs, 415
Sertorius, 317
Servian Reforms, 278, 306
Servian Wall, 285, 292
Servius Tullius, 272–73, 278, 285
Sestertius, 297, 335, 338
Set, 70, 87, 90, 111
Seti I, 74–75, 95
Seven Wise Men of Greece, 174, 189
Seven Wonders of the World, 82, 139, 238
Severan Dynasty, 373–74, 460
Severina, 382
Severus Alexander, 374, 379, 383
Severus II, 385, 389–90
Seville, 323
Seviri Augustales, 338
Sextilis, 324
Sextus Tarquin, 276
Sexual relations, 44, 59, 83, 88, 160, 162, 167, 176, 184, 217, 223, 229, 242, 251–52, 276, 403, 407, 438,
Shadow Emperors, 398, 423
Shahanshah, 234
Shalmaneser I, 126
Shalmaneser III, 126–28, 132, 134–35
Shaman, 7
Shamash, 52, 58, 60–61
Shame culture, 159–60
Shamsi-Adad I, 126
Shamsi-Adad V, 126, 128, 136
Shanidar, 12

Shapur, 380–381
Shar-Kalli-Sharri, 54
Sharuppak, 42
Sheba, 121
Shekel, 49, 291
Shekelesh, 110
Shell defense system, 339
Shepherd of Hermas, 420
Shetland Islands, 249
Shi'as, 452
Shiloh, 120
Short chronology, 46
Shoshenq, 122
Shu, 87
Shulgi, 56
Sibylline Oracles, 299
Sicambrians, 438
Sicily, 15, 169, 174, 199, 208, 210, 239, 261, 267–68, 287, 289–90, 292, 305, 311, 313, 316, 335, 423, 433, 435
Sicyon, 174, 186, 240
Sidon, 99, 113, 115
Siege warfare, 127, 130, 208, 290, 292, 446
Sigismund, 440
Siglos, 148
Siliqua, 387
Silk, 244–45, 249, 447, 450
Silk road, 245
Silphium, 167–68
Silvae, 362
Silver Age of Latin Literature, 361–62
Simeon, 407
Simon, 255
Sin, 52, 58, 136, 142
Sinai Desert, 117–18
Sinai Peninsula, 17, 82, 121
Sine manu, 301, 359
Sinope, 168
Sippar, 42
Sisebut, 458
Siwa Oasis, 231
Sixth Dynasty of Egypt, 83–84
Skekelesh, 108
Skulls, 8
Slave revolt, 316–317
Slavery, 50, 56, 62, 79, 82, 117, 148, 154, 156, 159–60, 168, 171, 183–84, 188, 193, 227–28, 232–33, 239, 272, 276, 278, 280, 289, 291, 295, 299, 306, 310–12, 314, 316, 338, 341, 351, 354, 357, 359–60, 388, 408, 414–15, 438
Slavs, 433, 447–48
Snake goddess, 101, 103
Sneferu, 81–82, 84
Sobeknefru, 90
Social structure, 38, 47, 49, 61, 68, 148, 157, 159, 169, 274, 368, 408, 439
Social War (Greek), 224
Socii, 287–89, 300, 308, 312
Socrates, 167, 177, 215–16, 218, 225
Socratic Method, 215
Soil exhaustion, 36
Soissons, 440
Sol Invictus, 382, 395
Soldier Emperors, 374, 381, 385
Solidus, 387, 390, 410
Solomon, 119–20
Solon, 176, 188–91, 193
Solutrean culture, 5–6
Somalia, 248
Son of Ra name, 75–76
Sons of Mars, 289
Sophia, 447
Sophists, 215, 218, 364, 457
Sophocles, 217
Sorcery, 56
South America, 13

Spain, 114, 168, 249, 258, 267, 291–93, 296–97, 303–4, 307, 317, 319, 323, 327, 331, 334–35, 349, 352–53, 361–62, 381, 385, 397, 411, 421, 423, 429, 434, 447–48, 458–59
Sparta/Spartans, 157–58, 162, 164, 169–70, 174, 176, 178, 180–86, 191, 194, 196–4, 207–14, 217, 221–24, 227, 229, 240–41, 251, 274
Spartacus, 316
Spartan Hegemony, 214
Spartiates, 183, 185–186, 193, 209–11, 223, 240–41
Spear land, 225
Specialization of labor, 38
Spectabilis, 413
Spelt, 275
Sphacteria, 209
Sphinx, 166
Sphodrias, 223
Spondylus, 23–24
Spurius Postumius, 299
Star catalogue, 258
Stasis, 159, 188, 200
State religion, 364
Stater, 140, 147, 165
Statira, 236
Statius, 362
Steam engine, 259
Step pyramid, 47, 81
Stilicho, 421
Stipulatio, 280
Stoa Poikile, 255
Stoicism, 254, 298, 356, 362, 366
Stone Age, 3–4, 8, 20
Stone tools, 2–7, 9, 11, 21
Stonehenge, 24–25, 32
Strait of Messina, 289
Strasbourg, 360
Strategos, 191, 193, 195–96, 202–3, 209, 212
Stylus, 43, 101
Subsidy, 442
Subsistence economy, 154, 273
Suetonius, 340, 363, 367
Suevi, 434
Suffets, 267
Sui juris, 275, 301
Sulla, Lucius Cornelius, 312–19, 323, 325, 329–331
Sulpicia, 345
Sulpicius, 314
Sumer, Sumerians, 22, 32, 34, 39–54, 63, 98, 117
Sumeria, 39
Sumerian King List, 44–48, 54, 74
Sumitic peoples, 51
Sun god, 389
Sunday, 393, 405
Sunnis, 452
Suovetaurilia, 365
Supernatural, 7, 251
Superstition, 368
Suppililiuma, 94
Suras, 452
Susa, 55, 60, 137, 146, 234
Sussex, 437
Sussition, 182–83
Swine men, 174
Sword of Damocles, 174
Syagrius, 438
Syllabary, 43
Symmachus, 435
Sympoliteia, 158, 193
Symposium, 160
Synagogue, 138, 251, 256, 404
Syncretism, 86

Syracuse, 169, 174, 197, 200, 208–12, 259, 261, 268, 292
Syria, 12, 17, 54, 92, 94, 106, 110, 128, 132–33, 142, 167, 232, 240, 243, 246, 262, 293, 318, 326, 335, 359, 363, 374, 380, 407, 443, 450–51, 453
Syrian War, 294–95
Syrian Wars, 246
Syrian-Arabian Desert, 40

Tabellarius, 409
Table of Showbread, 350
Tabnit, 115
Tacitus, 347, 349, 357, 363, 367
Tacitus (emperor), 382
Taharqa, 131
Talent, 49, 130–31, 147, 205, 207–8, 232, 245
Talmud, 366, 402
Tamiai, 189, 205
Tanaïs River, 249
Tanis, 242
Tanit, 267, 291, 296
Tarasicodissa, 443
Tarentum, 169, 268, 287
Tarquin the Proud, 273, 276
Tarquinii, 272
Tauroctony, 365
Technology, 19–21, 25, 37–38, 63, 94, 112–13, 259
Tefnut, 87
Tel-el-Amarna, 93
Tell, 98
Tell Halaf, 135
Temenos, 162
Temenus, 154
Temple of the Jews, 119, 121–22, 142, 255, 318, 350, 399
Temple of Venus and Rome, 353
Ten Commandments, 118, 120
Ten Lost Tribes of Israel, 134–35
Tenant farmers, 387, 410, 415
Teos, 176
Terence, 299
Terrorism, 132
Tetrarchy, 384–85, 389–91
Tetricus, 382
Teuta, 290
Teutobod, 310
Teutones, 310–12
Thalassocracy, 102
Thales, 177
Thalestris, 236
Thasos, 168, 201
The Five Thousand, 211
The Four Hundred, 211
The Garden, 254
The March Upcountry, 222
The One, 403
The Republic, 216
The Seven, 146
Theagenes, 188
Theater of Marcellus, 340
Theban Hegemony, 223
Thebes (Egypt), 84, 86, 90–93, 109, 119, 137, 143
Thebes (Greece), 155, 164, 167, 203, 208, 213–14, 217, 222–24, 227–29
Themistocles, 195–96, 199–201
Theocracy, 453
Theocritus, 261
Theodahad, 435
Theoderic I, 440
Theoderic II, 434
Theoderic the Great, 434–35
Theodora, 444–45
Theodosian Code, 441, 445, 457

Theodosian obelisk, 421
Theodosius (son of Galla Placidia), 432
Theodosius I, 397–98, 401, 404, 419, 421, 449
Theodosius II, 398, 441–42
Theodulf, 459
Theogony, 176
Theophilus, 454
Theophrastus, 256
Theopolis, 412
Theories, 177
Thera, 103–4, 166
Theramenes, 212–13
Thermopylae, 199
Theseus, 102, 158
Thesmothetes, 187
Thessalians, 227
Thessaly, 155, 223, 227
Thetes, 187, 189, 192, 196, 202–4
Thigh-flaunters, 183
Third Council of Toledo, 434
Third Dynasty of Egypt, 80–81
Third Dynasty of Ur, 56
Third Intermediate Period, 109
Third Macedonian War, 294–95
Third Punic War, 295
Third Sacred War, 227
Third Samnite War, 286, 295
Third Wave of Greek Colonization, 235
Thirty Years' Truce, 204, 208
Thirty-first Dynasty of Egypt, 72
This, 249
Tholos, 33, 192
Thoth, 88
Thrace, Thracians, 149–150, 176–77, 201, 205, 224, 227, 230, 238, 243, 316, 345, 362, 444
Thracian Chersonese, 190, 195
Thrasybulus, 175, 211–12
Three Chapters, 445
Throne name, 75
Thucydides, 210, 218, 363
Thule, 249
Thutmose, 117
Thutmose I, 91
Thutmose III, 92–93
Tiamat, 57
Tiber River, 265–66, 269, 271, 363, 368
Tiberius, 334–41, 345, 347–48, 383
Tiberius Gracchus, 306, 308–9
Tiberius II Constantine, 448
Tibullus, 345
Tides, 249
Tiglath-Pileser I, 126
Tiglath-Pilezer III, 126, 128, 133–34, 136
Tigris River, 10, 33, 39–40, 57, 63, 124–25, 244, 353
Tigurini, 311–12, 314
Tikulti-Ninurta I, 109, 126
Tikulti-Ninurta II, 126–27
Tin, 38, 49, 112, 114, 267
Tin Islands, 249
Tiryns, 103
Titans, 253
Tithe, 305, 323, 335
Tities, 277
Titus, 347, 350–51, 423
Titus Tatius, 272, 277
Tjeker, 110
Tocharians, 247
Toga, 345, 421
Tomb of Augustus, 354
Tome, 443
Tomis, 345
Tomyris, 143
Tongres, 438
Tool kit, 4

Torah, 118, 138, 142, 255
Torque, 266
Toulouse, 411, 432
Tower of Babel, 116
Towns, 25, 31, 68, 241, 286
Toxandria, 438
Trade, 18, 21, 23, 25, 37, 49, 51, 96–100, 105–107, 109, 112–113, 115, 121–22, 124–25, 127, 130–31, 133, 135, 139–41, 146–47, 153, 162, 165, 167, 169, 171, 173–74, 177, 180, 185, 187, 190, 207–69
Traditores, 394
Tragedy, 216–17
Trajan, 347, 352–53, 361, 363, 368, 383, 392
Trajan Decius, 374, 380, 388
Trajan's Forum, 353
Transalpine Gaul, 291
Transformation Model, 426
Treaty, 95
Treaty of Apamea, 294
Tremissis, 410
Triad, 114
Triakonter, 165
Triarii, 283
Tribe, 274
Tribes, 277, 279
Tribes of Israel, 117, 122, 134
Tribune of the plebs, 279, 281–82, 306, 309–10, 312–14, 326, 330
Tribunician power, 330, 347
Tribute, 128, 132, 134–35, 195, 201, 203, 223, 305, 323, 335, 410
Trier, 385, 438
Trimalchio's Dinner, 362
Trinity, 394, 418–19
Trireme, 196, 198
Trittys, 191
Triumph, 288, 319, 345
Triumvirates, 319, 326
Trojan War, 108, 175, 206
Trojans, Troy, 103, 107–8, 153–54, 159, 163, 175, 271, 343, 391, 431
True Cross, 448–49
Tryphon, 311
Tuff, 285
Tullus Hostilius, 272–73
Turin Papyrus, 74
Turks, 445, 456
Tursha, 270
Tutankhamon, 92
Tut-ankh-amon, 94, 111
Twelfth Dynasty of Egypt, 90
Twelve Tables, 280, 282, 284
Twenty-Fifth Dynasty of Egypt, 129
Twenty-Seventh Dynasty of Egypt, 143
Twenty-Sixth Dynasty of Egypt, 140
Two Ladies name, 75
Tyche, 251
Tyrannicide, 174, 191
Tyranny, Tyrant, 149, 171, 173–75, 186, 188, 191, 194–95, 200, 261, 276
Tyre, 99, 113–14, 121, 233, 267
Tyrian purple, 114
Tyrtaeus, 176, 182

Ubaid Culture, 34–35, 38
Ugarit, 99, 108–9, 114, 267
Ulpian, 358
Umar, 453, 455
Umma, 42
Unconquered Rome, 422

Unification of Egypt, 75
Upper Egypt, 66, 68–71, 77–78, 84–85, 88, 95, 109, 129, 241–242, 328
Ur, 42, 45–46, 48, 52, 117, 126
Ur of the Chaldeans, 117
Uraeus, 77, 242
Urartu, 125–26, 128, 139
Urban praetor, 282, 300
Urbanization, 35, 45, 68, 99, 104, 113, 121, 153, 274
Uriah the Hittite, 121
Ur-Nammu, 56, 59
Uruk, 37, 42, 44, 52
Uruk Culture, 37–38
Urukagina, 50
Usage, 275
Ushabti, 80
Usurper, 391–92, 397, 412
Usus, 275, 301
Utnapishtim, 45
Utu, 41, 52

Valens, 398–401
Valentinian I, 397–401, 441
Valentinian II, 398, 421
Valentinian III, 398, 417, 422–23, 436
Valerian, 374, 380–81
Valerio-Horatian Laws, 280
Valerius, 280
Valley of the Kings, 92
Vandal kingdom, 436, 446
Vandals, 382, 398, 421, 423, 426, 429, 433, 435–37
Varian disaster, 334, 345
Varna, 23–24
Varro, 292, 331
Varus, Quinctilius, 334–35, 339
Vassal, 53, 93, 128–129, 133, 136, 141, 146, 225
Veii, 278, 283
Velites, 283
Venantius Fortunatus, 457
Vendetta, 188
Venus, 271, 318–19, 324, 353, 376
Venus figures, 7
Venus Genetrix, 323
Venus of Laussel, 8
Vercingetorix, 320–21
Vergil, 343
Vespasian, 347, 350–51, 362
Vesta, 275
Vestal Virgins, 271, 275, 327
Vesuvius, 351, 362–63
Veto, 279, 315, 326
Vicar, 387
Victory, 345
Victory stele, 127
Vienna, 360
Viennensis, 412
Villa, 399, 410–12, 414, 417
Villa of the Mysteries, 253
Villages, 14, 16, 23, 31, 33, 68–69, 156, 235, 262, 265, 271–73
Vinča culture, 22–23
Vinča signs, 22
Violence, 106, 308, 432
Virgin, 408, 418, 441
Viriathus, 297
Visigothic kingdom, 456
Visigothic Renaissance, 458
Visigoths, 400–401, 421–23, 429, 432–35, 438, 459

Vitellius, 350
Vitruvius, 362
Vizier, 78, 81, 93
Volcanoes, 103–5
Volsci, 283
Volunteer army, 310–11, 313
Votive statues, 41
Vulgate, 418, 420

Wales, 437
Wamba, 458
Warfare, 18–19
Warka, 37
Warrior vase, 107
Wars of the Diadochi, 237
Weaving, 20–21
Weight standard, 140, 189
Weni, 79, 84–85
Weshesh, 110
Wessex, 437
Western Asia, 2, 25–26, 31, 112, 124, 167
Western Roman Empire, 419–23, 426, 429, 437–39
Whales, 247–48
Wheat, 12–13, 17, 23, 26, 33, 175
White House, 37
Women, status of, 48, 50–51, 55–56, 62, 78, 83, 89, 93, 101, 105, 116, 118, 120, 160, 183–85, 216–17, 239, 241, 275–76, 278, 300–301, 307, 327, 341, 357, 359–60, 415–16, 439
Wooden walls, 198, 200
Works and Days, 176
World Soul, 403
Writing, 1–2, 22, 38–39, 42–44, 52, 72, 80, 99, 104, 142, 155, 175–76

Xanthippus, 290
Xenophanes, 177
Xenophon, 214, 218
Xerxes, 196–201, 229
Xusru II, 448

Yahweh, 117–118, 120, 122, 138, 256, 367
Yarmukian culture, 19
Yathrib, 450–51
Yavanas, 361
Year of the Four Emperors, 349–50
Yellow River, 39
Yemen, 450–51
York, 375
Younger Dryas Period, 12–13, 19

Zagros Mountains, 40, 52, 54–55, 128, 234
Zarathustra, 148–49
Zawi Chemi Shanidar, 12
Zeno, 424, 434, 443
Zeno of Citium, 254–55
Zenobia, 381–82, 384, 455
Zeugitai, 187, 189, 202, 211
Zeus, 10, 160, 162, 164, 190, 231, 242, 246, 253, 255, 275, 364, 391
Zeus-Ammon, 231
Zhang Qian, 245
Ziggurat, 37, 39, 47–48, 56–57, 116, 137, 139
Zodiac, 139, 251, 260
Zoroaster, Zoroastrianism, 145, 149, 365, 403, 448